ETHNOGRAPHIES OF DESERVINGNESS

EASA Series

Published in Association with the European Association of Social Anthropologists (EASA)
Series Editors: Aleksandar Bošković, UFRN Natal / Institute of Archaeology, Belgrade

Social anthropology in Europe is growing, and the variety of work being done is expanding. This series is intended to present the best of the work produced by members of the EASA, both in monographs and in edited collections. The studies in this series describe societies, processes and institutions around the world and are intended for both scholarly and student readership.

Recent volumes:

45. ETHNOGRAPHIES OF DESERVINGNESS
Unpacking Ideologies of Distribution and Inequality
Edited by Jelena Tošić and Andreas Streinzer

44. OTHER ARGONAUTS
Ethnographers Before Malinowski
Edited by Frederico Delgado Rosa and Han F. Vermeulen

43. TRACING SLAVERY
The Politics of Atlantic Memory in The Netherlands
Markus Balkenhol

42. ETHNOGRAPHIES OF POWER
A Political Anthropology of Energy
Edited by Tristan Loloum, Simone Abram, and Nathalie Ortar

41. EMBODYING BORDERS
A Migrant's Right to Health, Universal Rights and Local Policies
Edited by Laura Ferrero, Chiara Quagliariello and Ana Cristina Vargas

40. THE SEA COMMANDS
Community and Perception of the Environment in a Portuguese Fishing Village
Paulo Mendes

39. CAN ACADEMICS CHANGE THE WORLD?
An Israeli Anthropologist's Testimony on the Rise and Fall of a Protest Movement on Campus
Moshe Shokeid

38. INSTITUTIONALISED DREAMS
The Art of Managing Foreign Aid
Elżbieta Drążkiewicz

37. NON-HUMANS IN AMERINDIAN SOUTH AMERICA
Ethnographies of Indigenous Cosmologies, Rituals and Songs
Edited by Juan Javier Rivera Andía

36. ECONOMY, CRIME AND WRONG IN A NEOLIBERAL ERA
Edited by James G. Carrier

For a full volume listing, please see the series page on our website:
https://www.berghahnbooks.com/series/easa

ETHNOGRAPHIES OF DESERVINGNESS

Unpacking Ideologies of Distribution and Inequality

Edited by Jelena Tošić and Andreas Streinzer

berghahn
NEW YORK • OXFORD
www.berghahnbooks.com

First published in 2022 by
Berghahn Books
www.berghahnbooks.com

© 2022, 2025 Jelena Tošić and Andreas Streinzer
First paperback edition published in 2025

All rights reserved. Except for the quotation of short passages for the purposes of criticism and review, no part of this book may be reproduced in any form or by any means, electronic or mechanical, including photocopying, recording, or any information storage and retrieval system now known or to be invented, without written permission of the publisher.

Library of Congress Cataloging-in-Publication Data

A C.I.P. cataloging record is available from the Library of Congress
Library of Congress Cataloging in Publication Control Number: 2022016547

British Library Cataloguing in Publication Data

A catalogue record for this book is available from the British Library

ISBN 978-1-80073-599-6 hardback
ISBN 978-1-80539-754-0 paperback
ISBN 978-1-80539-930-8 epub
ISBN 978-1-80073-600-9 web pdf

https://doi.org/10.3167/9781800735996

Contents

Acknowledgements　　　　　　　　　　　　　　　　　　viii

Introduction. Deservingness: Reassessing the Moral
　　Dimensions of Inequality
　　Andreas Streinzer and Jelena Tošić　　　　　　　　　1

PART I. Deservingness: Genealogies, Struggles and Ideologies

Chapter 1. Caring for the Old and Letting Them Die:
　　A Political Economy of Human Worth
　　Susana Narotzky　　　　　　　　　　　　　　　　31

Chapter 2. Must the Tired and Poor 'Stand on Their Own
　　Two Feet'? Tools for Analysing How Migrants'
　　Deservingness is Reckoned
　　Sarah S. Willen and Jennifer Cook　　　　　　　　68

Chapter 3. Deserving Classes without Class: Explaining the
　　Neonationalist Ascendency
　　Don Kalb　　　　　　　　　　　　　　　　　　　101

Chapter 4. Comparing Deservingness: A Reflexive Approach
　　to Solidarity and Cruelty
　　Erik Bähre　　　　　　　　　　　　　　　　　　126

**PART II. Categories, Policies and Negotiations of
　　Deservingness**

Chapter 5. Hartz IV: Affective and Sensual Registers of
　　Moral Inferiority
　　Stefan Wellgraf　　　　　　　　　　　　　　　　147

Chapter 6. Unemployment, Deservingness and Ideological
    Apparatuses: A Case Study from Turin, Italy
    Carlo Capello   173

Chapter 7. The Politics of Austerity Welfare: Charity,
    Discourses of Deservingness and Human Needs in a
    Portuguese Church Parish
    Patrícia Alves de Matos   199

Chapter 8. 'Here, Morality Is a Sense of Entitlement':
    Citizenship, Deservingness and Inequality in Suburban
    America
    Elisa Lanari   222

PART III. The (Un)Deserving Migrant/Refugee

Chapter 9. Ambivalences of (Un)Deservingness: Tracing
    Vulnerability in the EU Border Regime
    Sabine Strasser   251

Chapter 10. The Politics of Deservingness among Resettled
    Bhutanese Refugees
    Nicole Hoellerer   278

Chapter 11. Suffering and Vulnerability Reconfigured:
    Refugee Images of Hungarian Migrants Working in
    German Refugee Accommodation Institutions
    Ildikó Zakariás and Margit Feischmidt   304

PART IV. Debt Relations: The State, Market Actors and Debtors

Chapter 12. Do Mortgagors in Hardship Deserve Debt
    Relief? Legitimizing and Challenging Inequality during
    the Spanish Home Repossession Crisis
    Irene Sabaté Muriel   333

Chapter 13. Households on Trial: Over-indebtedness,
    State and Moral Struggles in Greece
    Theodora Vetta   359

Chapter 14. Victims, Patriots and the Middle Class: The
    (Un)Deservingness of Debtors in Post-Credit Boom
    Croatia
    Marek Mikuš 385

Afterword. Differentiating Deservingness
    James G. Carrier 413

Index 429

Acknowledgements

This edited volume is the result of collaborative work of several years and involved a number of persons and institutions to whom we would like to express our gratitude. First and foremost, we would like to express our thanks to the contributors of the volume who were ready to enter an inspiring but also long and complex joint conversation about their own and other authors' ethnographic research and theoretical thinking seen through the conceptual lens of deservingness. Our special thanks also go to James C. Carrier, who took over the core task of writing the Afterword. This extended joint process of thinking on how to develop (further) integrative ways of looking at contemporary processes of moralizing inequality and distribution was so inspiring that it kept us all committed throughout a range of challenges, such as changing positions, a range of other research and publication commitments, but also personal hardships and the still ongoing COVID-19 pandemic. This volume is also a result of our continuous exchange with colleagues, who, even though not part of the volume, helped us to develop our thinking about Deservingness, such as Anna Wanka, Annika Lems, Tijo Salverda, Stefan Leins, Hadas Weiss, Dimitra Kofti, Jens Adam, Gisela Welz, Phaedra Douzina-Bakalaki and many others. Our special thanks go to Julene Knox for her always brilliant deep language editing work, which was also much appreciated by the authors of this volume, as well as the excellent editing and formatting work by Ann-Cathérine Pielenhofer.

We would very much like to thank Aleksandar Bošković, who has supported us with the idea for the volume from the start, accompanied us through the publication process and finally generously accepted to act as the EASA Book Series Editor for this volume, even though it appears after he had long given over the Series Editorship. Our thanks also go to Tom Bonnington for guiding us through the core and final publication steps, as well as Marion Berghahn for her interest in the volume. Last but not least, we would like to express our gratitude to the anonymous reviewers and their valuable feedback, as well as the colleagues who took the time to join our discussions and share with us their thoughts.

Discussions upon which this volume is based were supported by the German Anthropological Association (Regional Group Europe), the EASA (Anthropology of Economy Network), the Department of Social and Cultural Anthropology at the University of Vienna. The work on the manuscript has been supported by the University of St Gallen in connection with the SNSF-funded research project 'Europe's Un/Deserving: Moralizations of Inequality in Comparative Perspective'.

Introduction

Deservingness

Reassessing the Moral Dimensions of Inequality

Andreas Streinzer and Jelena Tošić

The work on this volume started from an office conversation in 2016, the editors sharing their outrage about another public controversy sparked by the Austrian conservative right-wing government. Once again, members of the government suggested that asylum allowances were somewhat unjust to 'the population' or 'us taxpayers', or 'hard-working Austrians' and 'Austrian pensioners'. The elements of such messages seemed all too clear: an imagined 'us' threatened by 'undeserving' yet still '(over)assisted' 'Others'. This combination of differentiation and moralized assessment of distribution sparked ever more associations in our ongoing conversations. Over decades, it was claimed that 'lazy immigrants' receive too much welfare or recognition, 'scroungers' abuse welfare systems, and many other similar and contrasting examples. They prompted us to bring together disparate scholarly discussions and analyses of processes of moralized assessments of distribution that seemed to coalesce in specific conjunctures and registers of power.

(Un)deservingness is our attempt at creating a dialogue among these several fields of thematic scholarship and theoretical orientations. In recent years, anthropology in/of Europe has been a thriving scholarly environment for research on those questions. We are very pleased to have in this volume some of the scholars who drive the research that inspired us to think about (un)deservingness as a crucial category of contemporary politics. They come from various ethnographic and theoretical fields. As a comparative discipline, anthropology allows for contrasting cases, contexts and nuances of approaches while analysing the structural features of entangled phenomena.

We hope readers find our approach as useful as we do for the analysis of phenomena that are neither 'small/micro' nor 'large/macro', but rather entangled, distributed and pervasive. The pervasiveness of contemporary moralizations of inequality perhaps makes their consequences even more telling and problematic as they create new ways to reproduce racist, sexist and classist configurations in contemporary capitalisms. By and by, our own moral outrage at frames in public debate about refugees translated into a critical intersectional approach that politicizes how social struggles involve moralization as a way to justify or contest inequality.

(Un)deservingness as Conceptual Heuristic

Our aim in this volume is to provide a comparative and integrative analysis of configurations of distribution. At the most general level, deservingness acts as a moral assessment of processes of distribution. The focus of this volume is on processes where distribution (re)produces unequal societal configurations with particular clarity. This is especially important to us writing during the COVID-19 pandemic and also at a time in which overaccumulation meets increasingly selective redistribution. There has never been more value circulating and yet its distribution has become ever more unequal. In this conjuncture, it seems crucial to us to analyse how inequality is rendered justified or unjustified and to make visible processes by which inequality in outcome or access to resources or legal status is normalized and/or contested.

The question of who deserves what and why raises issues about social struggle and the creation and distribution of value in a range of social configurations in a racist, sexist and capitalist world. Capitalism works through a series of differentiations that order people. We still regard 'class' as the essential concept for analysing social inequality. Anthropologists provide a concept of class that describes social positionality beyond the formal realm of production as most Western Marxisms would (Weiss 2018: 110). Laura Bear and others point to class as generated in gender, race, sexuality and kinship (Bear et al. 2015) and link to a rich literature in Social Reproduction Theory (Bhattacharya 2017; Bhattacharyya 2018). Such a broad conception of class is necessary in order not to lose sight of 'society' while attempting to understand the complexity of categorization within the configurations in which interlocutors are assessed. A formulation of class as 'shifting, interconnected and antagonistic social inequalities' (Kalb 2015: 14) and their reproduction allows us to understand both the historical roots and emergence of deservingness frames and contemporary positional claims. Ethnographic research can observe what Alessandra Mezzadri calls 'fragments' of social order (2021: 1) and reconstruct the specificities of 'how come' certain configurations of class have become crucial in a given situation, at the same time as focusing conceptually and theoretically on how 'actually existing class' can be analysed.

The approach we and the contributors follow in this volume is to look at situations in which (un)deservingness does not smoothly legitimize wealth or poverty, but where it is ambivalently contested and legitimized. The reasons for choosing such entry points are manifold, yet, most importantly, they reveal the always-unfinished emergence of certain configurations, their processuality and the labour that goes into maintaining, creating and undoing them. In economic anthropology and history, such frictions are often discussed under the heading of moral economy (Thompson 1971).

Focusing on frictions among the ideological dimensions of inequality makes visible how moral vocabularies articulate with social struggle (Fraser and Honneth 2003). These could work either as the contestation or legitimization of existing configurations. Contestations often problematize a given configuration of distribution, as is the case when individuals (seen) as members of a group do not have access to resources, but claim that they would deserve to. Legitimization frequently works the other way around, as in arguments that some people, due to their behaviour or moral character, do not deserve access to certain resources. Normalization is the endpoint and outcome of a process in which a certain configuration of inequality appears as 'normal' or even 'natural' so that the very notion of (un)deservingness is sedimented into 'common sense' (Crehan 2016: 136).

In order to explore the emergence of contemporary claims of deservingness, we suggest employing a genealogical approach in terms of tracing ideas of deservingness in different socioeconomic and ideological-political configurations by being especially attentive to implications of them 'not having a history' (Foucault 1977: 139). Our focus thereby lies in tracing the arrangements of resources in which deservingness came to be strongly negotiated in recent decades – the redistributive welfare state in neoliberal capitalism, national citizenship and access to social insurance, contemporary forms of consumer debt and privatized care, and welfare institutions.

Because (un)deservingness is often normalized, moralized assessments of inequality require theoretically informed, reconstructive and comparative ethnography to relate the more open contestations or legitimizations to the hidden or sedimented forms that are key to how societies are organized. To understand how people in specific socioeconomic circumstances conceive of inequality and what they think is right or wrong, just or unjust about it, ethnographic fieldwork can provide substantial insights into the complexities and paradoxes of these conceptions and the social positions of those who attend to them. Such a reconstructive and comparative approach is well equipped to address the actual situations, ideologies and actors, and can be related to various strands of social theory that attempt to explain such configurations of inequality and moralization.

(Un)deservingness is a processual and relational notion rather than a condition. It is situated in structures of power that articulate inequality with specific moral common senses. Structural patterns of racism, sexism, ableism and classism form and cohere the specific patterns of inequality, and also how they are legitimized, normalized or contested. Following Hadas Weiss' writing on values, we are more interested in the work performed by deservingness than understanding it as a mere orientation of people (Weiss 2015: 251). The structural insights into configurations of power need to be combined with a careful and reconstructive analysis of how historical and emerging patterns of contestation and legitimization reconfigure and reinscribe (un)deservingness into the relations between imagined or constructed groups.

While (un)deservingness as an analytical heuristic can be an orientation towards specific questions of inequality, distribution, morality or ideology, it is not in itself an explanation. As the various authors in this volume show, the explanation requires a mutually constitutive relationship between ethnography and theory (Mezzadri 2021).

Arguments and Ideologies of (Un)deservingness

Arguments made about (un)deservingness are often contingent, context-specific and used in morally laden comparative assessments of subjects and their access to unequally distributed resources (Willen and Cook 2016: 96). As such, they indicate access to distribution of resources and recognition as subjects. A concept figuring prominently in arguments about deservingness is the notion of rights or entitlements. If the entitlement of a person or group to certain resources is institutionalized by law or obligation, (un)deservingness can play out as if it were a condition, normalized and/or stabilized in law and social structures. A telling example is property rights when citizens of a state are legally able to own property, whereas noncitizens are not, as is frequently the case in European societies. Whether they can actually afford to buy property or if others think they deserve to own it is an empirical question. The very fact that some people are included in the principal right to own and others are not illustrates the relationships between actual rights and the possibility to enjoy them. Both create a differentiation and both are consequences of the institutionalization of distribution. How they are normalized, legitimized or contested varies across social contexts and times.

It is the aim of this volume to trace such specific contexts and relations in which deservingness is used, what kinds of social imaginaries are mobilized in its use and what is left unaddressed. Because, for instance, public discussions of deservingness often arise along controversies, frequently the assessments of specific subjects are telling in terms of the social imaginary of who deserves what and according to which attributes.

Although these social imaginaries do not necessarily form coherent ideologies, the way in which people conceive of deservingness is seldom accidental. Specific ideologies and how they frame and legitimize inequality play an important role in the patterns we trace and reconstruct through ethnography. Arguably, it is rare that ethnographers encounter coherent ideologies, which is why fragments of (un)deservingness we find in the field are better analysed through a Gramscian lens on common sense.

Common Senses of (Un)deservingness

In conceptualizing and tracing deservingness, we build on Gramsci's seminal insights into the workings of ideology and cultural hegemony. This allows us to further ask about affective and sensing registers of deservingness and how they relate to the broad repertoire of common sense arguments (see e.g. Gramsci 1971; Crehan 2011) regarding social justice that societal actors employ when they claim and contest deservingness in configurations of class as defined above (Hall 2019: 111ff).

On the one hand, this approach makes it possible to grasp claims of deservingness in entangled economic, political-legal and sociocultural societal spheres. On the other hand, a focus on deservingness allows for tracing and 'unpacking' ideologies. It reveals how ideologies work with and rest on accessible common-sense arguments of deservingness, which not only mobilize citizens and arrange group relations, but also potentially 'turn into' law (e.g. cutting social support for asylum seekers). Furthermore, the lens of deservingness shows not only crucial boundaries between different political ideologies, but also the processes and instances where ideologies that are perceived as irreconcilable appear, in surprising ways, as 'strange bedfellows'.

Here, the prism of deservingness allows us to think critically with Gramsci's concept of common sense, which Kate Crehan relates to a specific reading of culture understood as a way of life and hence as a way in which inequalities are lived (Crehan 2011) – that is, the complex and seemingly paradoxical beliefs that people encounter as self-evident truths. An ethnographic exploration of such common-sense-based claims about structural inequalities can examine the play of power and reconstruct why some beliefs at certain times seem to be self-evident, and which actors and groups are involved in that process and in which roles.

After having sketched our approach to (un)deservingness as an ethnographic and reconstructive methodology compatible with critical theories, we go on to revisit disparate discussions in various anthropological fields in which we find inspiring approaches and configurations where moralization legitimizes and 'makes sense of' inequality.

Perspectives in and about Research on Deservingness

Rights, Humanitarian Subjects and Legitimate Suffering

Deservingness represents a highly sensitive barometer of inequality and 'Othering', the analysis of which adds to and complicates existing anthropological explorations of rights and humanitarianism. Rights to specific forms of distribution primarily represent the juridification and institutionalization of entitlement. Deservingness, on the other hand, refers to the moral assessment of whether these entitlements are legitimate and just or contested and unfair. An example is unemployment benefits. Their institutionalization followed negotiations about whether unemployed people deserved to be supported by the imagined community of taxpayers or insurance members. Then, once institutionalized, accessing unemployment benefits became a matter of knowing about them, being eligible according to the formal criteria (such as involuntary job loss and income level) and claiming them. Hence, access to what one is legally entitled to is thought to be rather impersonal, formal and independent of individual assessments of moral character or virtue. Empirically, the distinction is often more gradual than categorical, as the contributors to this volume show. Rights and deservingness can blend into one another when looking at specific histories, sociolegal figures and political aims. Several authors in this volume start from the hypothesis that entitlements have become increasingly conditional upon forms of moral testing – for example, home visits by state actors and other moral assessments of whether a person's behaviour, virtues or character make them morally deserving of support (Fraser and Gordon 1994).

The blending of sociolegal and moral registers into one another is a key field in the ethnographic and theoretical exploration of deservingness. Obvious examples include legal cases about sexual violence that turn into elaborations of the victim's character traits and accusations of signalling immorality as 'invitations' to (predominantly male) sexual violence. The frequent police murders of Black people in the United States often provoke fierce debates about how racism translates into imaginaries of immorality and criminal conduct. (Un)deservingness as an analytical lens productively challenges a clear-cut separation between rights and morality. Instead, it shows how some groups of actors use moralization to legitimize violence or to call impersonal rights into question in relation to others. We caution that debates about deservingness in similar situations act as distractions and attempts to blame victims of direct or structural violence.

The contemporary shift towards conditional forms of social assistance, activation schemes for unemployed people and the increasing selectivity of state redistribution is accompanied by processes of accusation, suspicion and assessment, which makes deservingness such a crucial issue in contemporary economic and political processes. In some cases, individuals/groups might be entitled to forms of social support, but are said not to deserve them. In other cases, they claim to deserve them, but are not entitled to them. Understood in such a way, deservingness is a crucial concept for contemporary struggles for resources and recognition.

A specific understanding of deservingness is to be found on an ontological level in the concept of human rights. The underlying premises of human rights are based on claims of universalism and thus the ultimate claim of equality.[1] The concept of human rights builds on the claim that all humans are entitled to basic rights, regardless of any further assessment of deservingness. Deservingness discourses, on the other hand, often stress conditionality, context-specificity and individual behaviour when used to contest or legitimize entitlements, or make the actual access to what one is entitled to more difficult. As Amartya Sen reminds us, the fact that such discourses are infused with morality should not lead us to think that not having access to, for example, social insurance or the health system is primarily a value judgement (Sen 1981: 17). Rather, we propose carefully separating the mechanics of entitlements, access and outcomes of distribution from the views and values visible in their negotiation. Thus, deservingness is more than, and differs from, discourses about entitlement.

In the specific example of the right to asylum (and thus citizenship), we can see how arguments of deservingness play out regardless of the actual instance of whether asylum is granted or not. Even in European debates about the case of refugees from Syria, who have by and large been considered as asylum-deserving and, as a rule, have been granted asylum (in the course and aftermath of the so-called 'refugee crisis' of 2015), one can often hear arguments of undeservingness as soon as their image as helpless 'bare human' victims (see Malkki 1996) is unsettled. In right-wing arguments and anti-refugee/migrant public discourse, the possession of mobile phones, money or branded clothes is taken up to frame people as 'not-really' refugees or 'merely' economic migrants. For example, in the summer of 2015, a right-wing local politician (a member of the Austrian Freedom Party) posted a sarcastic set of pictures entitled 'find the latest iPhone' on social media showing refugees in Linz, Austria (Schmid 2015).

The issue of forced migration is also a prime social field where the discourse of rights intersects (and forms a disjuncture) with what has been recently explored in the anthropology of humanitarianism. As Liisa Malkki has outlined in her early work on Hutu refugees in Tanzania (Malkki 1996), discourses and policies of humanitarianism imply a specific image of the 'real' refugee, deserving of humanitarian aid and assistance. This image crucially rests on the victimization of individuals and groups, as well as on a strong gendering tendency that frames the ideal human victim as a woman and/or a child, whose 'wounds speak louder than words' (ibid.: 384). Most importantly, humanitarianism 'depoliticize[s] the refugee category and [constructs] in that depoliticized space an ahistorical, universal humanitarian subject' (ibid.: 378).

According to recent work in anthropology, humanitarian reason describes the emergence of thought that considers humanity as moral community, where suffering of fellow humans elicits compassion if the suffering is considered legitimate (Fassin 2012: 252). As a rather recent form of moral sentiment (ibid.: 1) – embedded in, but different from, religious charity – humanitarianism's crucial tension is the one between compassion and repression, rather than the recognition of rights (ibid.: x). In this sense, humanitarianism is a 'politics of precarious lives' (ibid.: 4) resting on inequality, since it is directed 'from above to below, from the more powerful to the weaker, the more fragile, the more vulnerable – those who can generally be constituted as victims of an overwhelming fate' (ibid.). However, compassion is not unconditional, as the idea of humanitarianism implies that there are legitimate sufferers – this idea of legitimacy suggests a boundary-making process between those who suffer legitimately and those whose suffering does not render them deserving. An example is victims of natural disasters – who suffer due to events beyond their control – who are most often understood as deserving of assistance (e.g. Ticktin 2011; Fassin 2012). A more ambiguous example, which shows the selective and historically embedded logic of humanitarianism, is Miriam Ticktin's analysis (2011) of how, even in the context of pronounced anti-immigrant sentiments and restrictive migration policies in France under Sarkozy, having experienced sexual violence rendered immigrant women as 'deserving' of compassion, as well as of the right to be granted legal residence status. Hence, such phenomena as homonationalism can link with imperialist legacies of white saviourism (Puar 2007; Abu-Lughod 2013).

As both examples show, humanitarianism exemplifies how deservingness can play out in different and ambiguous ways. However, the analytical prism of deservingness makes it possible to go beyond the focus on humanitarianism, as claims of deservingness are not bound exclusively to precarious populations (e.g. when the salaries of top managers are discussed in terms of deservingness) and feature other forms of moral politics around distribution.

Furthermore, while humanitarian aid is grounded in the affective-political practice of compassion with certain precarious categories of people in need (those seen as not having contributed to their condition), claims of deservingness are often affectively charged in other ways. Claims of deservingness primarily have the affective quality of deploring injustice, while implying a relational-comparative perspective: one feels entitled to something; concerned about having been unjustly deprived of something; or that someone else has obtained something without having deserved it. Related to, yet distinct from, the affective dimension, we conceptualize deservingness also in terms of *sense/sensing*. We thereby aim to capture the everyday practice dimension of how social difference – and related claims of who deserves what and why – is continuously 'sensed', without necessarily being accountably argued. As noted above, exploring the sense/sensing of deservingness thus lends itself to recapturing Gramsci's notion of common sense.

Deservingness is often 'articulated in a vernacular *moral* register' (Willen and Cook 2016: 96, emphasis in original) that infuses everyday discourse, media reports, political negotiation and legal discourse. As a vernacular moral register, deservingness appears to be much more accessible and employable in everyday use than notions such as rights or humanitarianism, which predispose particular and often expert forms of knowledge. In other words, statements of deservingness are more 'at hand'; they can be easily 'picked up' and employed, and do not necessarily have to rely on accountable argumentation. Related to this point of 'argumentative accessibility', deservingness has a strong and specific affective-emotional dimension. This dimension is not only interesting in terms of its intersections with morality (see, for example, Throop (2012) on 'moral sentiments'), but because it opens an important aspect of differentiation between statements of deservingness and claims referring to rights and humanitarian concepts of legitimate needs.

In such a way, our approach towards deservingness adds to the existing literature: (1) by pointing towards the way in which rights and entitlements are complicated by moral registers that underlie, undermine or attack institutionalized rights through assessments of deservingness; (2) by offering an analytical approach towards inequality that combines power, morality and inequality; and (3) by directing the analytical framework towards all kinds of social arrangements, including those in which humanitarian reason or suffering plays only a minor role. The ethnographic and reconstructive approach that we take furthermore enables the linking of specific settings in which something gets moralized to larger configurations of inequality across time in which actors do the moralizing.

Migration and Migrant (Un)deservingness

Research on mobility has a decades-long history of analysing political and moral questions about migration, asylum and multiculturalism, questions that were exacerbated by the so-called 'refugee crisis' in Europe in 2015. Political parties and groups from across the political spectrum seem to agree on a tacit consensus regarding the European migration regimes at the most basic level. This agreement constitutes categorizing immigrants into those who deserve asylum and others who are undeserving of that status, as well as into those who are welcome as investors or highly skilled professionals and those unwelcome, 'merely' economic migrants, who are often low-skilled and with few resources. Paralleling the electoral successes of right-wing parties in Europe, the boundaries between legal categories, and hence those people who are legally entitled to asylum/citizenship and those to be deported, have been contested among and within political parties and governments, and by social movements and political initiatives all over Europe. This process was accompanied by a remarkable moralization of migration and access to welfare and asylum. A related example is the former Austrian Vice-Chancellor Heinz-Christian Strache's argument (*Krone* 2018) for cutting welfare allowances for asylum seekers (in this case, the minimum monthly allowance), which can be paraphrased as follows: people who have never contributed to the Austrian social system do not deserve to have more monthly allowances than pensioners who worked and paid taxes for years, since this would not be in accordance with social justice. In the aftermath of the so-called 'refugee crisis', this discourse and then policy shift regarding asylum seekers had folded into the overall moralized legitimization of Austrian migration policy marked by increasing deportations and cutting welfare allowances for refugees. According to former Austrian Chancellor and People's Party (ÖVP) leader Sebastian Kurz, such policies would deter others from trying to cross the Mediterranean and risk their lives in search of a better life. Hence, cutting welfare benefits for asylum seekers would contribute to saving lives and would thus, according to Kurz, even represent a moral and humanitarian act (*Welt* 2019). Such moral acrobatics, we argue, form part of the moralization of inequality in general and the argument of deservingness in particular in a racist necropolitical conjuncture.

A focus on immigration and deservingness is of particular interest not only against the background of the rise of anti-immigration rhetoric and policy in the aftermath of the so-called 'refugee crisis', but also because, in hierarchies of deservingness, it is frequently immigrants who occupy the lowest position after the elderly, the ill, people with special needs and the unemployed (e.g. van Oorschot 2006). Assessing hierarchies of deservingness – even if based on simplified heuristic categories – highlights the fact that, for a holistic and integrated analysis of deservingness, as aimed at in this volume, questions of welfare, health, citizenship and migration should not be explored separately. In this sense, the analytical lens of (un)deservingness can also contribute to the 'demigrantization' (Dahinden 2016) of migration research, since it makes how debates and policies on (forced) migration are embedded in and co-produce processes and dynamics of intersectional inequality more accessible.

Furthermore, it is essential to analyse and compare how the category of immigrants is diversified and hierarchized through moral assessments of deservingness. As mentioned above, the common ground of different European (im)migration policies (beyond their ideological differences) is the differentiation between the undeserving 'fake' refugee and economic migrant on the one hand, and the 'real' refugee deserving of humanitarian aid and asylum, as well as the 'desirable' work migrant (e.g. the highly skilled and sought-after professional) on the other. As highlighted by Kristin Yarris and Heide Castaneda, deservingness figures as a 'discursive framing' of displacement, in terms of border crosser's motives for migration (Yarris and Castaneda 2015: 64). It implies a normative binary between the 'voluntary' (economic) undeserving migrant and the 'involuntary migrant' (refugee), whereby political persecution, for example, frequently makes the migrants 'deserving' of refugee status/asylum, whereas climate change or poverty render those fleeing such conditions 'undeserving economic migrants'. The use of policy-driven categories in migration, which typically focus on the dichotomy between forced and voluntary migration, has been shown both to be harmful to migrants and to not reflect migrant experiences (Crawley and Skleparis 2017).

Most recently, the so-called 'refugee crisis' in Europe has fortified this binary and has given the notion of deservingness an acute importance in decisions about asylum or deportation and, in many cases, life and death (Holmes and Castaneda 2016). Both border processes of inclusion and exclusion and the political-public discourses about the so-called 'refugee crisis' focused on 'sorting people into undeserving trespassers versus those who deserve rights and care from the state' (ibid.: 13). An ethnographic approach to migrant deservingness, as highlighted by Holmes and Castaneda (2016) and as pursued in this volume, makes it possible to address the contested nature and mutual impact of political, legal and vernacular moralizing discourses of which (forced) migrants deserve what, and how this relates to the needs and claims of other (domestic) populations defined as vulnerable and in need of or having the right to assistance. Exploring the agents and processes of 'parsing moral deservingness' (ibid.: 18) between (and against) different population categories reveals both the moral dimensions of legal regulations as well as the similarities and differences between legal and (again contested) vernacular claims of deservingness.

To us, deservingness is a fruitful conceptual framework for deepening the analysis of how state actors categorize mobility and thus legitimize migration and welfare policies, as well as the institutional processes and public discourses on migrants. We join Sarah Willen in her observation that there are well-developed approaches for exploring migrants' entitlements and access to social services, while the 'subtler moral positions that undergird them remain conspicuously underinvestigated' (Willen 2012: 805).

Within different assessments of immigration and deservingness focusing on different versions of welfare chauvinism (e.g. Jørgensen and Thomsen 2016), medical anthropology and migration scholars have studied migrants' access to welfare services through the lens of deservingness. Willen has published extensively on migrants' access to health services in Israel (2015). Willen and Jennifer Cook furthermore mapped an analytical approach towards 'health-related deservingness' by carefully separating rights claims from deservingness assessments – the latter being relational, conditional, contextual, syncretic, affect-laden and mutable (Willen and Cook 2016: 97). Willen and Cook propose studying stakeholders, contextual factors and evaluative criteria employed in these assessments, and point to the importance and exploration of how expert knowledge is invoked in what they call 'deservingness debates' (ibid.: 100). Our volume aims to build on this framework and analytically reconnect claims of deservingness to the issue of ideology and go one step further by investigating a range of contemporary fields of social struggle (see below).

In our endeavour to bridge explorations of deservingness in the context of migration with other themes and fields of knowledge, we also draw on approaches to (social) citizenship. As the research by Walter J. Nicholls et al. (2016) shows, focusing on migration and deservingness opens up new avenues of comparative and intersectional perspectives. In their comparative analysis of the culturalization of immigrant youth with precarious legal status in the United States and the Netherlands, the authors show how discourses of deservingness regarding legal status (citizenship) and generation can be interrelated through claims of 'cultural assimilation'.

The notion of social citizenship – originally introduced by T.H. Marshall (1950) and taken up by, for example, Margaret Somers (2008) – represents a promising conceptual pathway to exploring (forced) migration and deservingness in the context of contested processes of distribution in the era of 'market fundamentalism' (ibid.: 2). It is precisely the context of migration that makes profoundly visible the complex dynamic of political citizenship and social citizenship through the ways in which they can become contested both jointly or separately. Apart from arguments of deservingness figuring prominently in the processes of moralizing migrants' access to political citizenship (most prominently through citizenship tests – see van Oers (2014, 2021); Monforte, Bassel and Khan (2019)), they are also in the foreground when arguing against social provisions for (forced) migrants, reflecting neoliberal conditionalities regarding social rights eroding the very social contract upon which citizenship is based. The financial crisis of 2007/ 2008 and its aftermath (see also next section) was the context of increasing conditionality of social citizenship, a development that seriously affects not only 'non-European' (forced) migrants, but also European work migrants. As Lafleur and Mescoli point out, using the example of Italian migrants in Belgium, mobility based on EU citizenship became increasingly conditional upon not claiming social citizenship, as 'the use of welfare by poor EU migrants leads to their depiction as a group that is 'undeserving' of the right to freedom of movement' (Lafleur and Mescoli 2018: 481).

Redistribution, Austerity and Welfare Retrenchment

The financial crisis of 2007/ 2008 was followed by widespread discussions about the systemic failures of capitalism among governments, financial oversight institutions, social movements and populations. A good part of these discussions implicitly or explicitly addressed moral questions. When does the banker's instrumental motivation turn to outright greed and immoral behaviour? How should a state's legal frameworks constrain profit motives to protect its citizens? Such questions, it seems, faded quickly from public discussion, followed by another and uncannily familiar set of moralizations of inequality.

Industrial and financial lobbying groups, alongside political parties, attacked rising government debt as being immoral towards future generations. With Greece as the most prominent example, government debt served as legitimation for an unprecedented restructuring in Southern Europe. Greece received the largest loan in human history, in a programme managed by the European Commission, the European Central Bank and the International Monetary Fund. The political negotiations and public discussions about the questions of international solidarity, about the financing of governments and the design of the eurozone, and even technocratic questions of how to manage a sound refinancing plan, were couched in the moral language of deservingness. Among many other such moralizations, newspapers accused 'the Greeks' of being lazy and wanting to live off others' money (*Bild* 2010), and Eurogroup President Jeroen Dijsselbloem suggested that Greeks had spent too much money on 'booze and prostitutes' (*Reuters* 2017) and were now asking for support. Political and political-economic issues were reframed as a matter of character or immoral habit to question whether 'Greeks' deserved the loans. Northern Europe is not exempt from this process of conditionality of social transfers linked to a moralized discourse about deservingness, with a renegotiation of deservingness criteria of welfare entitlements (van Oorschot 2000) accompanied by an ongoing discourse about welfare scroungers and the long-term unemployed, who are portrayed yet again as simply unwilling to work.

Such recent large-scale reconfiguration of political-economic systems and the role of moral imaginaries in them has frequently drawn on moral grammars of productivism and classism that have been well analysed in the literature. In his examination of the creation of modern labour markets in the early nineteenth century in England, Karl Polanyi describes how the Poor Law Reform of 1834 created categories of the deserving and the undeserving poor among those who had lost their land and were not able to find work in the burgeoning capitalist agriculture or factories (Polanyi 2001: 86). The moralization of selective welfare introduced by this reform meant that those considered undeserving were framed as lazy or unwilling to work, and hence not deserving of benefits or other forms of transfers to substitute labour incomes.

We find very similar processes of welfare restructuration being accompanied by renderings of some beneficiaries as undeserving, commonly analysed under the header of 'the undeserving poor'. Among the scholars following differing notions of how poverty was conceived of as legitimate outcome of character or personal choice is Michael B. Katz. Tracing the genealogies of how poverty was normalized, Katz mentions how the moral categories used to label the poor rendered their poverty not as an outcome of misfortune, but of 'indolence and vice' (Katz 2013: 6) and, hence, as self-inflicted. By extension, judging poverty as deserved was and is not only done in reference to morality, but also by culture or biology (ibid.: 2f).

A frequent theme in (un)deservingness debates is the idea that access to resources makes people dependent on them. Translated into welfare debates, an element of bad moral character is said to be prone to 'dependency', as Nancy Fraser and Linda Gordon state for the US context. Dependency there featured as a keyword of welfare debates and stated that the social figure of the pauper in industrial times was described with a 'moral/psychological register' of dependency (Fraser and Gordon 1994: 316). In the booming industrial capitalism, the heroic subjectivity of the 'upstanding workingman' (ibid.) became the normative ideal of the productive person. Those who could not act as such, like the pauper, were regarded as a morally degraded and corrupted contrast to that sought-after subject position that combined imaginaries of self-sufficiency, freedom and industrial labour.

In twentieth-century Europe and the United States, a distinctly welfare-related form of deservingness emerged. Welfare systems began making a distinction between deserving and undeserving poor early in their development after the Second World War. The United States, despite the expansion of state redistribution, installed a two-track welfare system (see Fraser and Gordon 1994: 321). Deservingness became a political term used to accuse those entitled to welfare of various vices – for instance, using resources in the wrong ways ('welfare cadillacs'), or deliberately relying on assistance instead of seeking to become independent from it ('welfare queens') (see Fraser and Gordon 1994). Revealingly, these accusations were directed mainly against poor Black people, single mothers and others who were socially, spatially and economically marginalized.

These gendered and racialized debates, which became known as the 'culture of poverty debates', started in the 1960s with the work of Oscar Lewis and were followed by debates about the so-called underclasses in the 1970s and 1980s. The literature on poor populations in the United States during these decades points to very selective forms of state redistribution that rely on racialized and gendered forms of discipline (Stack 1974). The rhetoric of deservingness in the United States was reinforced by the attacks on the redistributive welfare systems from the 1970s onwards. The ever more selective forms of assistance and social transfers were legitimized by a series of discourses about the deficient character of those who were in many ways considered as 'Other' to the productive and entrepreneurial ideal types of neoliberal subjectivity.

In the US context in the 1980s and 1990s, anthropologists intervened in these public discourses and policy debates by countering the dominant focus on cultural and moral features of poverty ('culture of dependency'). Examples of such scholarship include Judith Goode's work (e.g. Goode 2018) or the ethnographies of the so-called New Poverty Studies (Goode and Maskovsky 2002).

In Europe, scholarship on the attribution of undeservingness started, to our knowledge, in parallel to the increasing conditionality of social assistance entitlements after the peak of welfare state expansion. One of the exemplary ethnographies of this literature is Leo Howe's *Being Unemployed in Northern Ireland* (1990), in which he explores the production of difference according to moral evaluations of unemployed people. The late 1990s and early 2000s brought about studies on the transformation of redistributive systems after the disintegration of the Soviet Union. One such work is the 'historical ethnography of Hungarian welfare' (Haney 2002: 238), published as the monograph *Inventing the Needy*. In it, Lynne Haney traces the changing categorization of maternal work from 'social responsibility deserving remuneration' (ibid.: 189) to social assistance, which then required an assessment of neediness. Although the literature on socialist and postsocialist welfare rarely mentions deservingness explicitly (with exceptions; see e.g. Dorondel and Popa (2014)), these studies utilize a layered approach towards the state that makes it possible to distinguish between different levels of the administration of access to resources and tracing the transformation of conceptions of deservingness at different scales. An example of such an approach is Chris Hann's analysis of moralizing discourses about workfare (Hann 2016: 9), and, furthermore, Don Kalb's work on worker populism and class (published, for example, in Kalb and Halmai (2011)) and the Kinship and Social Security (KASS) project at the Max Planck Institute for Social Anthropology in Halle, Germany (see e.g. Heady and Schweitzer 2010). Anthropologists research welfare state transformations by pointing towards state austerity – cutting costs for public health or unemployment benefits – and towards the way in which state actors select the beneficiaries who are deserving of assistance. Vincent Dubois' (2015) work especially focuses on these processes of the administration of poverty. Patrícia Alves de Matos and Antonio Pusceddu (2021) link deservingness claims in contemporary Europe to a common sense of austerity in which the moralizing selectivity has already been normalized.

In recent anthropological work, especially on living conditions under tightening austerity after the 2007/2008 financial crisis, it is the precarious themselves who mobilize against elites through moral registers and notions such as 'dignity' (Narotzky 2016). These notions are also taken up by private organizations – such as volunteer, aid, activist or solidarity networks – as a moral vehicle to advance a critique of the neoliberal transformation of welfare states. Andrea Muehlebach (2012), for instance, shows how these moral registers of critique are in themselves ambivalent for the volunteers involved in such networks in Italy, as they reflexively critique that welfare retrenchment, Catholic morality and volunteerism work well together. On the other hand, Giacomo Loperfido and Antonio Pusceddu (2019) show how unevenness and deservingness co-constitute spatial differentiation as a way to study global capitalism through a local lens (Loperfido and Pusceddu 2019).

The literature on social insurance and welfare entitlements from and on Europe and the United States shows how deservingness discourses are tied to increasingly selective forms of social assistance. Through conditionalities, moral assessments and the turn towards 'activation' as a paradigm of redistribution, deservingness has become a key register for calling entitlements into question.

Towards Ethnographies of Deservingness

The literature in which we situate discussions about deservingness in the United States and Europe focuses on processes of state redistribution and welfare provision, as well as migration and citizenship. Debates about redistribution, and especially those about social hierarchies, are crucial fields of contention and transformation in the relationships between populations, states and capital accumulation. Yet, deservingness might bring us to think beyond the social welfare nexus and towards studies on distribution in society at large. Such studies might explore the moral registers of conditionality in private aid organizations (as several chapters in this volume do) or discuss controversies about whether private corporations deserve tax breaks. In other words, while building on the scholarly genealogies of where to locate deservingness, we seek to expand the question of deservingness and ask about its specific role as a powerful tool to (re)produce, institutionalize, justify, negotiate, contest and depoliticize inequality. One way of doing so is to explore the relative class positions of those whose virtues and vices are being discussed.

The breadth of the contributions in this volume shows how fruitful a conversation between subfields of the discipline might be and, furthermore, the variance of research fields in which such questions are raised. Beyond pointing towards the complexity of the phenomenon in scholarship and hence the diversity of approaches to framing and exploring (un)deservingness, we identify several features that we and our contributors by and large share: (1) an ethnographic interest in how deservingness is *done* in a range of contexts; (2) a comparative endeavour of contrasting, juxtaposing and complicating with other cases across scales; (3) a curiosity for reconstructing patterns that connect cases and exploring relations of power and configurations of inequality; and (4) an orientation towards the analysis of 'society' and a critique of its capitalist, racist and sexist structures of inequality.

Such a perspective on inequalities allows for an integrated observation of the several critical junctions (Kalb and Tak 2005) in European and American societies, and how the changing inequalities are produced, legitimized or contested – to us a major way in which class can be reconstructed in its polyvalence and contradictions (Kalb 2015: 14).

In this volume, we foreground three critical junctions: first, the transformation of social welfare systems, specifically variegated austerity accompanied by debates about 'welfare fraudsters' and 'undeserving migrants' exploiting welfare states; second, moral panic about migration that advances a split between a defensive 'we' and general suspicion regarding 'Others', and that led to the blurring (particularly in mainstream public discourse) of legal categories of refugees and migrants; and, third, financial crisis, which led to new ruptures between Northern and Southern European countries and is likely to be rekindled during or after the COVID-19 pandemic.

As the selection of empirical fields and the choice of analytical frameworks suggest, we insist that investigating inequalities from the social sciences requires a critical outlook. As vulnerable people are targeted, socially marginalized groups are scapegoated and migrants are criminalized, anthropology needs to take a closer look and employ tools for critical analysis. In the best-case scenario, such analysis combines rigorous ethnographic work, theoretical determination and an engaged stance that seeks to explore social, political and economic power.

The Chapters in This Volume

This book starts with a topical section of four chapters by scholars working on moral conceptualizations of inequality and discussing central aspects of deservingness. Susana Narotzky takes valuation and valorization as key processes of 'a political economy of human worth' during the COVID-19 pandemic. She proposes an epistemology of ethnographically sensible historical reconstruction in order to understand the consequences of how human worth is assessed, categorized and ordered hierarchically. The consequential classification of 'the elderly' in the Quality Adjusted Life Year (QALY) triage system is her point of departure for exploring the political economy of care and death.

In their chapter, Sarah Willen and Jennifer Cook operationalize the concept of health-related deservingness in the context of migration as a framework for analysing current deservingness debates. This take on deservingness proves to be a timely conceptual lens (and intervention) because it is precisely migrant populations, as well as healthcare systems that migrants often struggle to access, that are marked by extreme vulnerability due to the deregulation of healthcare and ever more restrictive migration regimes. In their theoretical-ethnographic approach to deservingness, Willen and Cook pay special attention to carving out the boundary between rights and deservingness, the latter being understood as 'complex forms of vernacular moral reasoning' embedded in particular and competing forms of common sense.

Don Kalb then links his earlier research on Central and Eastern Europe (Poland and Hungary) and the Netherlands with an analysis of ongoing processes such as Brexit and the COVID-19 pandemic to reconstruct the emergence and current effects of neonationalist mobilization in Europe. In his analysis, deservingness figures as a 'popular call for a just social hierarchy' under conditions of neoliberal dispossession and devaluation of labour, 'particular skills, rights, expectations, spaces, subjectivities and forms of popular culture and social reproduction'. In his chapter, Kalb employs the analytical heuristic of deservingness as a way to add to the analytical work of uncovering and reconstructing 'subtexts of class' in the context of neoliberal transformation.

Finally, Erik Bähre contemplates how the lens of deservingness can enhance reflexive and comparative dimensions of ethnography, and thus its often-downplayed explanatory potential. In his both eclectic and integrative take on deservingness as a 'reflexive and comparative category', he recaptures anthropological engagements with comparison and draws on Rorty's reflexive epistemology of solidarity and cruelty. He arrives at the conclusion that due to its focus on relations (in particular between insiders and outsiders), deservingness enables a novel assessment of the European crisis and, moreover, allows for new forms of comparison.

Part II brings together four ethnographic-theoretical discussions about poverty, exclusion and the transforming arrangements through which those affected are included or excluded from distribution and recognition. The chapters focus on the need to understand structural political and economic aspects, together with processes of subjectivation, bodily experiences, rituals and symbolic frames of reference. In his chapter, Stefan Wellgraf discusses the articulation between social hierarchies, and the affective, bodily and sensual experience of inferiority among his interlocutors, *Hauptschüler*innen* in Berlin. He categorizes corporal reactions such as stomach problems, sleeping disorders and nightmares as sensual and emotional registers at play in the reproduction of social inferiority. Carlo Capello then takes the discussion to municipal centres offering courses that focus on active job seeking for unemployed people in Turin. He asks 'how come' most of the unemployed he worked with accept a discourse and ideology of deservingness according to which they themselves are mainly responsible for their predicament. Such internationalization, according to Capello, happens through hidden rituals and symbolic qualities of these rites of passage of neoliberal ideological apparatuses. Patrícia Alves de Matos then discusses an 'emerging redistributive political regime' in Southern Europe where austerity and the technocratic language of provision to 'those who really need' gave rise to a myriad of religious-based charity organizations as welfare providers. Discussing her work in Portugal, she analyses how the moral topologies of deservingness and welfare provision are a continuation of austerity politics or, rather, a departure from it. In her chapter, Elisa Lanari places her discussion of deservingness in the first large municipality in the United States to fully outsource its welfare services to a private corporation. The historically white, affluent and conservative town of Sandy Springs, Georgia, is the setting for her discussion. In it, deservingness features as a key analytic for understanding the logic of creating and reinforcing hierarchies among the low-income residents by using various types of welfare-providing actors and local ideologies of welfare, entrepreneurship and suburban citizenship. She analyses deservingness as the process through which issues of poverty and structural discrimination are depoliticized and moralized, leading to frames of reference through which low-income residents fashion themselves vis-à-vis welfare providers.

Part III brings together discussions of migration and flight and how people on the move become categorized as legitimate refugees, worthy sufferers or as morally belonging to a community or not. In her chapter, Sabine Strasser analyses the politics of distribution based on the deservingness of refugees as established by the EU–Turkey border regime through the lens of the policy tools of re-admission and resettlement. She traces these policies, associated legal processes of border control and the reaffirmation of a neo-orientalist perspective of the Muslim 'Other' in the everyday lives of young Syrian men on their way to Europe through Turkey. Nicole Hoellerer then challenges the widespread perspective of deservingness as a top-down external process, which is forced upon refugees. In her ethnography of resettled Bhutanese refugees in the United Kingdom, she demonstrates how refugee communities also internally employ notions of deservingness and create inequalities among their own communities through moral categories of belonging. Ildikó Zakariás and Margit Feischmidt discuss the construction of deservingness in the institutional context of philanthropy in the so-called 'refugee crisis' during the summer of 2015 in Hungary. They argue that the commitment to help among those private organizations may be conditional upon constructing and identifying the deserving along sameness and difference. The assessment of legitimate suffering and the distribution of possibilities is, they argue, related to the image of suffering in the imagination of the witness.

Part IV draws on three chapters that discuss the relations of debt as key aspects of the economic crises in Spain, Greece and Croatia. The chapters each take a different ethnographic entry point into analysing the negotiation of deservingness and its relation to wider ideological, political and economic spheres. In her chapter, Irene Sabaté Muriel discusses deservingness using different narratives about debt relief in the Spanish mortgage crisis. She traces how mortgage default, along with the stigma and moral panic associated with it, was reframed by anti-repossession movements after 2009. Their narrative of the crisis as a collective fraud perpetrated by banking elites, with the complicity of public authorities, provided one empirical manifestation of deservingness assessments among others, as defined by the law, welfare institutions, bank employees and the social networks of defaulters. Sabaté argues that it is necessary to relate those different scales of deservingness to the ideological construction, reproduction and naturalization of social inequality. In her chapter, Theodora Vetta uncovers the Greek social cartography of unequally distributed blame, deceit and responsibility through her ethnography of the implementation of the Katseli Law, which protected insolvent households against foreclosure. In the trials, she found that the legal focus was placed on morally charged patterns of evaluating (over)consumption and, hence, whether indebtedness was legitimate in the first place and insolvent households thus deserved to be protected. She argues for understanding indebtedness as a form of rent extraction and class demobilization, and focuses on how the implementation of insolvency protection narrowed possibilities for solidary reaction and collective claim-making in Greece. In his chapter, Marek Mikuš focuses on claims and counterclaims between creditors, debtors and activists in post-credit boom Croatia to analyse the politics of debt. He argues that debt-related activism and parliamentary politics emerged as significant forms of political practice, which draws and reconfigures hegemonic, sub-hegemonic and counterhegemonic concepts of deservingness. He argues that the various registers of deservingness play a crucial role in how various groups claim suffering, rights and economic importance.

The volume concludes with an Afterword by James G. Carrier, which draws together the main ethnographic, analytical and theoretical lines of argumentation, and looks at ways of working out the moral aspects of social, political and economic inequality. Carrier argues for the importance of classification as a general process in which humans engage when forming societies and the specific modes of classifying that – in specific situations – hierarchize social groups.

Andreas Streinzer is a researcher in the project 'Europe's Un/Deserving: Moralizations of Inequality in Comparative Perspective' (2021–24, funded by the Swiss National Science Foundation at the University of St Gallen and researcher at the Institute for Social Research in Frankfurt am Main. He completed his Ph.D. at the University of Vienna, with additional studies in sociology (Lancaster) and critical theory (Frankfurt). He is interested in the reconfiguration of social reproduction, specifically during times of socioeconomic transformation. His dissertation focused on household provisioning in Greece. His current research focuses on wealth taxation and moralizations of distribution and labour. He is co-convenor of the EASA Anthropology of Economy Network, the Working Group Economic Anthropology and the Regional Group Europe at the German Anthropological Association (DGSKA).

Jelena Tošić is Assistant Professor for Transcultural Studies at the University of St Gallen and lecturer at the University of Vienna. Her current writings focus on borderlands in Southeastern Europe, (forced) migration, moralizations of inequality and the anthropology of education. She is currently project leader in the project 'Europe's Un/Deserving: Moralizations of Inequality in Comparative Perspective' (2021–24, funded by the SNSF) at the University of St Gallen. Her recent publications include: 'Populist "Variations" on Migration. Floating Signifiers of Mobility in the Context of the

'Balkan Route' and the COVID-19 Pandemic', *Journal of Balkan and Near Eastern Studies* (2021); and 'African-European Trajectories of (Im)Mobility: Exploring Entanglements of Experiences, Legacies and Regimes of Contemporary Migration' (Special Section), *Migration and Society* (2019), co-edited with Annika Lems.

Notes

1. Notwithstanding the reality of its selective and hypocritical implementation and different local appropriations, as explored by, for example, Goodale (2007) and Cowan et al. (2010).

References

Abu-Lughod, Lila. 2013. *Do Muslim Women Need Saving?* Cambridge, MA: Harvard University Press.

Alves de Matos, Patrícia, and Antonio Maria Pusceddu. 2021. 'Austerity, the State and Common Sense in Europe: A Comparative Perspective on Italy and Portugal', *Anthropological Theory* 21(4): 494–519.

Bear, Laura, Karen Ho, Anna Tsing and Sylvia Yanagisako. 2015. 'Gens: A Feminist Manifesto for the Study of Capitalism – Cultural Anthropology'. Retrieved 29 March 2018 from https://culanth.org/fieldsights/gens-a-feminist-manifesto-for-the-study-of-capitalism.

Bhattacharyya, Gargi. 2018. *Rethinking Racial Capitalism: Questions of Reproduction and Survival*. Lanham, MD: Rowman & Littlefield.

Bhattacharya, Tithi (ed.). 2017. *Social Reproduction Theory: Remapping Class, Recentering Oppression*. London: Pluto Press.

Bild. 2010. 'Pleite-Griechen. Hier feiern sie ihre Finanz-Spritze', 25 April. Retrieved 4 February 2022 from https://www.bild.de/politik/wirtschaft/hier-feiern-sie-ihre-finanzspritze-12316946.bild.html.

Cowan, Jane, Marie-Benedicte Dembour and Richard Wilson. 2010. *Culture and Human Rights: Anthropological Perspectives*. Cambridge: Cambridge University Press.

Crawley, Heaven, and Dimitris Skleparis. 2017. 'Refugees, Migrants, Neither, Both: Categorical Fetishism and the Politics of Bounding in Europe's "Migration Crisis"', *Journal of Ethnic and Migration Studies* 44(1): 48–64.

Crehan, Kate. 2011. 'Gramsci's Concept of Common Sense: A Useful Concept for Anthropologists?', *Journal of Modern Italian Studies* 16(2): 273–87.

——. 2016. *Gramsci's Common Sense: Inequality and Its Narratives*. Durham, NC: Duke University Press.

Dahinden, Janine. 2016. 'A Plea for the "De-migranticization" of Research on Migration and Integration', *Ethnic and Racial Studies* 39(13): 2207–25.
Dorondel, Stefan, and Mihai Popa. 2014. 'Workings of the State. Administrative Lists, European Union Food Aid, and the Local Practices of Distribution in Rural Romania', *Social Analysis* 58(3): 124–40.
Dubois, Vincent. 2015. *La Vie au Guichet. Administrer la Misère*. Paris: Éditions Points.
Fassin, Didier. 2009. 'Moral Economies Revisited', *Annales. Histoire, Sciences Sociales* 64(6): 1237–66.
———. 2012. *Humanitarian Reason: A Moral History of the Present Times*. Berkeley: University of California Press.
Foucault, Michel. 1977. 'Nietzsche, Genealogy, History', in Donald F. Bouchard (ed.), *Language, Counter-memory, Practice: Selected Essays and Interviews*. Ithaca, NY: Cornell University Press, pp. 139–64.
Fraser, Nancy, and Linda Gordon. 1994. 'A Genealogy of Dependency: Tracing a Keyword of the U.S. Welfare State', *Journal of Women in Culture and Society* 19(2): 309–36.
Fraser, Nancy, and Axel Honneth. 2003. *Redistribution or Recognition? A Political-Philosophical Exchange*. London: Verso.
Goodale, Marc. 2007. *The Practice of Human Rights: Tracking Law between the Global and the Local*. Cambridge: Cambridge University Press.
Goode, Judith. 2018. 'How Urban Anthropology Counters Myths against the Poor', in Georg Gmelch and Petra Kuppinger (eds), *Urban Life: Readings in the Anthropology of the City*, 6th edn. Long Grove, IL: Waveland Press, pp. 195–212.
Goode, Judith, and Jeff Maskovsky (eds). 2002. *The New Poverty Studies: The Ethnography of Power, Politics and Impoverished People in the United States*. New York: New York University Press.
Gramsci, Antonio. 1971. *Selections from the Prison Notebooks*, Quentin Hoare and Geoffrey Nowell Smith (eds). London: Lawrence & Wishart.
Hall, Stuart. 2019. *Essential Essays Vol. 1: Foundations of Cultural Studies*, edited by David Morley and Catherine Hall. Durham, NC: Duke University Press.
Hann, Chris. 2016. 'The Moral Dimension of Economy: Work, Workfare, and Fairness in Provincial Hungary', *Working Paper No. 174. Max Planck Institute for Social Anthropology*.
Haney, Lynne. 2002. *Inventing the Needy: Gender and the Politics of Welfare in Hungary*. Berkeley: University of California Press.
Heady, Patrick, and Peter Schweitzer (eds). 2010. *Family, Kinship, and State in Contemporary Europe*. Frankfurt am Main: Campus Verlag.
Holmes, Seth. M., and Heide Castaneda. 2016. 'Representing the "European Refugee Crisis" in Germany and beyond: Deservingness and Difference, Life and Death', *American Ethnologist* 43(1): 12–24.

Howe, Leo. 1990. *Being Unemployed in Northern Ireland: An Ethnographic Study*. Cambridge: Cambridge University Press.
Jørgensen, Martin B., and Trine L. Thomsen. 2016. 'Deservingness in the Danish Context: Welfare Chauvinism in Times of Crisis', *Critical Social Policy* 36(3): 330–51.
Kalb, Don. 2015. 'Introduction: Class and the New Anthropological Holism', in James G. Carrier and Don Kalb (eds), *Anthropologies of Class: Power, Practice and Inequality*, Cambridge: Cambridge University Press, pp. 1–27.
Kalb, Don, and Gabor Halmai (eds). 2011. *Headlines of Nation, Subtexts of Class: Working-Class Populism and the Return of the Repressed in Neoliberal Europe*. Oxford: Berghahn Books.
Kalb, Don, and Herman Tak (eds). 2005. *Critical Junctions: Anthropology and History beyond the Cultural Turn*. Oxford: Berghahn Books.
Katz, Michael B. 2013. *The Undeserving Poor: America's Enduring Confrontation with Poverty*. Oxford: Oxford University Press.
Krone. 2018. 'Pensionisten sollen mehr bekommen als Flüchtlinge', 24 April. Retrieved 4 February 2022 from https://www.krone.at/1697952.
Lafleur, Jean-Michel, and Elisa Mescoli. 2018. 'Creating Undocumented EU Migrants through Welfare: A Conceptualization of Undeserving and Precarious Citizenship', *Sociology* 52(3): 480–96.
Loperfido, Giacomo, and Antonio Maria Pusceddu. 2019. 'Unevenness and Deservingness: Regional Differentiation in Contemporary Italy', *Dialectical Anthropology* 43(4): 417–36.
Malkki, Liisa. 1996. 'Speechless Emissaries: Refugees, Humanitarianism, and Dehistoricization', *Cultural Anthropology* 11(3): 377–404.
Marshall, Thomas H. 1950. *Citizenship and Social Class*. Cambridge: Cambridge University Press.
Mezzadri, Alessandra. 2021. 'Introduction: Marx's Field as Our Global Present', in Alessandra Mezzadri (ed.), *Marx in the Field*. London: Anthem Press, pp. 1–16.
Monforte, Pierre, Leah Bassel and Kamran Khan. 2019. 'Deserving Citizenship? Exploring Migrants' Experiences of the "Citizenship Test" Process in the United Kingdom', *British Journal of Sociology* 70(1): 24–44.
Muehlebach, Andrea. 2012. *The Moral Neoliberal: Welfare and Citizenship in Italy*. Chicago: University of Chicago Press.
Narotzky, Susana. 2016. 'Between Inequality and Injustice: Dignity as a Motive for Mobilisation during the Crisis', *History and Anthropology* 27(1): 74–92.
Nicholls, Walter J., Marcel Maussen and Laura Caldas de Mesquita. 2016. 'The Politics of Deservingness: Comparing Youth-Centered Immigrant Mobilisation in the Netherlands and the United States', *American Behavioural Scientist* 60(13): 1590–612.
Palomera, Jaime, and Theodora Vetta. 2016. 'Moral Economy: Rethinking a Radical Concept', *Anthropological Theory* 16(4): 413–32.

Polanyi, Karl. 2001. *The Great Transformation: The Political and Economic Origins of Our Time*. Boston: Beacon Press.
Puar, Jasbir K. 2007. *Terrorist Assemblages: Homonationalism in Queer Times*. Durham, NC: Duke University Press.
Reuters. 2017. 'Kritik an Dijsselbloem-Äußerungen über "Schnaps und Frauen"', 22 March. Retrieved 4 February 2022 from https://de.reuters.com/article/eu-portugal-dijsselbloem-idDEKBN16T1H2.
Schmid, Fabian. 2015. 'Flüchtlinge und teure Smartphones: Hetze ohne Fakten', *Der Standard*, 9 August. Retrieved 4 February 2022 from https://www.derstandard.at/story/2000020396192/fluechtlinge-und-teure-smartphones-hetze-ohne-fakten.
Sen, Amartya. 1981. *Poverty and Famines: An Essay on Entitlement and Deprivation*. Oxford: Clarendon Press.
Somers, Margaret R. 2008. *Genealogies of Citizenship: Markets, Statelessness, and the Right to Have Rights*. Cambridge: Cambridge University Press.
Stack, Carol B. 1974. *All Our Kin: Strategies for Survival in a Black Community*. New York: Harper & Row.
Thompson, E.P. 1971. 'The Moral Economy of the English Crowd in the Eighteenth Century', *Past & Present* 50: 76–136.
Throop, Jason. 2012. 'Moral Sentiments', in Didier Fassin (ed.), *A Companion to Moral Anthropology*. Oxford: Wiley-Blackwell, pp. 150–68.
Ticktin, Miriam I. 2011. *Casualties of Care: Immigration and the Politics of Humanitarianism in France*. Berkeley: University of California Press.
Van Oers, Ricky. 2014. *Deserving Citizenship: Citizenship Tests in Germany, the Netherlands and the United Kingdom*. Leiden: Brill.
———. 2021. 'Deserving Citizenship in Germany and the Netherlands: Citizenship Tests in Liberal Democracies', *Ethnicities* 21(2): 271–88.
Van Oorschot, Wim. 2000. 'Who Should Get What and Why? On Deservingness Criteria and the Conditionality of Solidarity among the Public', *Policy & Politics* 28(1): 33–48.
———. 2006. 'Making the Difference in Social Europe: Deservingness Perceptions among Citizens of European Welfare States', *Journal of European Social Policy* 16(1): 23–42.
Weiss, Hadas. 2015. 'Capitalist Normativity: Value and Values', *Anthropological Theory* 15(2): 239–53.
———. 2018. 'Reclaiming Meillassoux for the Age of Financialization', *Focaal* 2018(82): 109–17.
Welt. 2019. 'Sebastian Kurz verurteilt Seenotretter im Mittelmeer', 7 July. Retrieved 4 February 2022 from https://www.welt.de/politik/ausland/article196467233/Oesterreich-Ex-Kanzler-Sebastian-Kurz-verurteilt-Seenotretter-im-Mittelmeer.html.
Willen, Sarah. 2012. 'Migration, "Illegality", and Health: Mapping Embodied Vulnerability and Debating Health-Related Deservingness', *Social Science & Medicine* 74(6): 805–11.

———. 2015. 'Lightning Rods in the Local Moral Economy: Debating Unauthorized Migrants' Deservingness in Israel', *International Migration* 53(3): 70–86.

Willen, Sarah, and Jennifer Cook. 2016. 'Health-Related Deservingness', in Felicity Thomas (ed.), *Handbook of Migration and Health*. Cheltenham: Edward Elgar, pp. 95–118.

Yarris, Kristin, and Heide Castaneda. 2015. 'Discourses of Displacement and Deservingness: Interrogating Distinctions between "Economic" and "Forced" Migration (Introduction)', *International Migration* 53(3): 64–69.

Part I

Deservingness: Genealogies, Struggles and Ideologies

1
Caring for the Old and Letting Them Die
A Political Economy of Human Worth

Susana Narotzky

> Plus tu laisseras mourir et plus toi de ce fait même tu vivras.
> Michel Foucault, *Il faut défendre la société*, 227

The 2008 financial crisis brought to the fore the inadequacy of explaining capitalism 'just' in terms of economic inequality. In one protest after the other, unemployed, precarious and dispossessed people spoke in terms of 'dignity', of 'respect', of their 'worth' and of how 'the system' was making them worthless, socially irrelevant, invisible citizens. At the same time, many also vindicated a different framework for measuring values: through cooperation, environmentally sound and local production circuits, mutual care and decommodified transfers. Valuation struggles became visible in this process and highlighted the social discourses and practices creating deservingness in a range of domains, from citizenship entitlements to biological life.

This chapter addresses how older people have been defined and categorized with different kinds of value during the ten years of crisis following 2008 and in the recent practices of dealing with the COVID-19 pandemic, and how the valuation frameworks that defined them are multiple and shifting. I will address these by looking at how different valuation scales (Guyer 2004) of older citizens in Spain are connected to capital valorization processes (Harvey 1999; Melamed 2015; Smith 2017) and austerity policies. To this effect, I will unravel the valuation/valorization articulations in four domains referring to: the public pension system; home as use value and asset; caring practices and infrastructures; and calculations of the value of life during the COVID-19 pandemic. These four domains together help us to understand how the production of different human values enables particular forms of capital accumulation through the construction of a multidimensional grid of unequally deserving subjects. Following insights from political economy, pragmatist valuation, and racial capitalism theories, this chapter addresses the connections between valuation and valorization as they affected elderly people in Spain during austerity and the COVID-19 pandemic.

As the pandemic expanded in March 2020 and the health system was overwhelmed, instructions were given by different institutions stating the triage recommendations that had to be used in the rationing of scarce Intensive Care Unit (ICU) resources. The recommendations were explicitly based on the Quality Adjusted Life Year (QALY) measure that was developed in the 1980s to set priorities in public health expenditures and allegedly maximize benefits to society through the rational allocation of scarce healthcare resources. Deserving scarce health resources was calculated according to the maximization of QALYs. The QALY was defined by its proponent as follows:

> The essence of a QALY is that it takes a year of healthy life expectancy to be worth 1, but regards a year of unhealthy life expectancy as worth less than 1. Its precise value is lower the worse the quality of life of the unhealthy person ... The general idea is that a beneficial health care activity is one that generates a positive amount of QALYs, and an efficient health care activity is one where the cost-per-QALY is as low as it can be. (Williams 2012 [1985]: 423)

The debates on the inequality effects of the QALY quantitative valuation of life are innumerable and I will consider them in the course of the argument; let me just point here to the fact that from the start, the QALY was accused of 'ageism' and of significantly violating the 'equality principle' enshrined in liberal democracies (Harris 1988). The question of who deserved to access ICU resources, which had been made scarce by imposing structural adjustment policies and fiscal restraint, exposed a valuation of people based on the statistical quantitative calculation of life expectancy and measures of 'quality of life'. This caused a furious public debate on the ethics of triage in emergency situations that revisited the different valuation scales giving social value to the elderly, while at the same time their value in the valorization process was made visible.

In what follows, first, I will address the ambivalent valuation of older people as pensioners and their role during the economic crisis after the bailout of the Spanish banking system and the imposition of harsh austerity measures. Second, I will present the infrastructures that have been in place for elderly caretaking since 2006, and how they have affected the value of the elderly and those who cared for them. Here, I will provide two inroads into valorization: one linked to the nursing home business, and the other to the financial and real estate businesses. Third, I will analyse the lethal impact of COVID-19 in nursing homes and the triage recommendations based on QALYs that devalued older and disabled people's lives in a context of austerity-produced scarcity. In the conclusion I will pull together the connections between valuation and valorization that produce the elderly as a particular group of humans who are devalued yet useful for valorization. I wish to argue that deservingness struggles are not exclusively waged in moral terms, but are often tied to forms of valuation that are quantitative, financial and linked to the valorization process.

Although this chapter is written with my long-term fieldwork in mind, it is mostly based on documentary material and addresses the wider situation of Spain in recent years and in the present.

Pensioners and Grandparents

For a while, I have been undertaking a project that centres on the 'valuations of life' as part of working people's struggles for a future in Southern Europe. So far, I have sought to analyse the articulation of human worth, economic value and political power in the context of economic crises and austerity remedies, with a special focus on issues of access to livelihoods, care and the struggle for dignity (Narotzky 2020). My fieldwork in northwestern Spain, in an industrial town of the autonomous region of Galicia, brought to the fore the importance of labour struggles against the Franco dictatorship during the 1960s and early 1970s as constituent elements of a particular idea of personhood based on conquering rights and respect in political and economic terms through organized collective action. Deindustrialization starting in the 1980s resulted in transforming into early retirees the cohorts that had been waging the struggle; in the words of Ramón, a union leader in the 1960s and 1970s, 'the restructuring of the shipyards was a strategy to break down the union movement, they wanted to get rid of organized labour by getting rid of those that had the experience of past struggles, so they forced us into early retirement' (Narotzky 2014, 2015). Thus, early retirees were prevented from transferring their labour-organizing skills to the next generation and their political knowledge was questioned.

These retired workers kept busy as organizers in neighbourhood associations, local politics and cultural/social associations. Their pensions were good, they had been able to buy small apartments and some of their children had gone to university, but the stability that came with industrial jobs had vanished for their children's generation. While many younger cohorts had increasing trouble finding work, retired parents 'invested' in their children's future by giving them money to start small businesses, lending them money to make a down payment on an apartment; they became guarantors of mortgages and also took care of their grandchildren. When the 2008 crisis hit, the importance of pensions grew disproportionately as unemployment, precarity and indebtedness became widespread among the young. All over Spain, but especially in the old industrial regions where pensions were relatively 'good', the pensioners became the bulwark against the absolute destitution of younger adults and children. They distributed money and food, cared for their grandchildren and gave shelter to those whose mortgaged homes were foreclosed – mostly their own children and their families. The value of these old working-class pensioners in the crisis context was hailed in the media and underlined in reports about Spain's resilience in its dire situation (this argument was similar for other Southern European countries).[1] The narrative was that 'thanks to the grandparents', younger families were subsisting. The category of 'grandparent' was taken as a positive identity marker by this older generation, but always as part of a struggle within the larger mobilizations against austerity from 2011 onwards.[2] A more organized movement developed around the defence of the public pension system with the *Marea de pensionistas* (pensioners' tide) as part of this generation's mobilizations (Narotzky 2016). While defending the main income source of the family network, this pensioners' movement also stressed the defence of conquered social rights that needed to be preserved against dispossession for the benefit of future generations.

The pensioners' mobilization reveals an important valuation struggle between the grandparent/pensioner collective and Spanish and European policy-makers, and neoliberal economic experts such as central bank pundits in relation to the public pension system (European Commission 2010, 2012a; Hernández de Cos et al. 2017). While pensioners vindicate their worth as workers, as fighters for social, economic and political rights, as owners of those rights, but also as the grandparents supporting and caring for a network of close kin, they are debased by financial and political experts (with arguments repeated by the media) as 'privileged' and as dispossessing younger generations for their selfish benefit. These experts claim that pensions are responsible for fiscal deficit, future sovereign debt and are unsustainable due to increased longevity, where longevity – an erstwhile marker of 'development' – paradoxically becomes a negative characteristic weighing as an unwarranted cost on public resources.[3]

In the policy/expert discourse on the unsustainability of the public pension system, pensioners are viewed as an impediment to prosperity and to the welfare of younger generations and their future. On the one hand, this narrative presents their longevity as a problem (the 'demographic' argument) because it is a public 'cost' in pensions that the state will not be able to address in the future due to declining contributions – demography, poor wages and unemployment – unless it raises taxes that would penalize mostly younger adults; this assertion holds only insofar as taxes come basically from labour and consumption in the existing regressive fiscal system. Longevity is also viewed as a problem for society as a whole because it detracts from general public health resources and social services by shifting resources to nursing homes and other care infrastructures for the elderly. On the other hand, pensions are presented as a 'privilege' that sets older and younger cohorts against each other, and 'privilege' is unfair in a democracy where the 'principle of equality' of rights among citizens should prevail; defence of the privilege is 'selfish' and hence goes against the public good. The latter arguments are naturalized in terms of demographics and are moralized in economic terms as the 'costs' to society of privileges – from a bygone era – that threaten alleged equal rights in the present.

Pensioners appear only as a demographic problem and a financial cost; they are never recognized as having contributed to the social and economic wealth of the present through their past labours or as having added anything positive to society in the present – be it care work, livelihood income, seed capital, experience or memories.[4] Older people in neoliberal capitalism are useful as consumers – and a growing slice of the service economy is witness to this – or as invisible, unrecognized providers of reproductive assets (income or a home) that enable the devaluation of the active labour force (Narotzky and Pusceddu 2020), or as potential sources of capital through the financial unlocking of the value fixed in their housing assets (Bryan and Rafferty 2014).⁵ But even while they are in fact still valuable for capital accumulation, they are simultaneously devalued in their social and moral worth by powerful social agents and institutions. In what follows, I will try to develop the connection between the two.

Material and Legal Care Infrastructures

During the unemployment, precarization and austerity period following the financial crisis of 2008, the economic situation of the elderly (those aged over sixty-five and seventy-five) in Spain was better than that of younger cohorts. Indeed, rates of relative poverty for them were lower than for those under sixty-five and, generally speaking, the poverty rate decreased for those over sixty-five, mostly due to the fact that this group had the asset of a home, often free of a mortgage, and some savings in the form of deposits, as well as a public pension that varied widely from the noncontributory pension of €366 per month, the minimum pension of around €650 per month to the maximum pension capped at €2,554 per month in 2015. In general, statistical analysis confirms that 'the Spanish pension system not only contributed to the reduction of inequalities, but also became the instrument that buffered poverty risk' (Vidal Domínguez et al. 2017: 144). Their economic worth relative to that of younger age groups increased during the crisis not only in financial terms but also because they were publicly recognized as supporting their younger kin. However, the increased reproductive function of the pension revenue in family networks enabled the devaluation of the labour force because precarious wages did not cover reproduction costs for a majority of employed people, expressing an extractive aspect – beyond exploitation – of wage labour's relationship with capital (Harvey 2003; Lapavitsas 2009; Fraser 2014, 2018; Narotzky and Pusceddu 2020). In addition, the savings and homes of the elderly were targeted by financialization and incorporated into capital valorization circuits. A major expropriation of the elderly was linked to the provision of and access to nursing home services, a case I will develop in the next section.

In 2006, the social democratic government of Rodríguez Zapatero passed the Law of Promotion of Personal Autonomy and Care for Dependent People (BOE 2006). It aimed to provide the material means for addressing the needs of the dependent population – elderly and disabled. The Law was intended to increase the number of publicly funded nursing home places as well as to provide for in-home family or professional carers and other external services, such as adult daycare centres and telecare systems. Although nursing home places and subsidies for in-home care did slowly increase for a few years, the advent of the right-wing government of the Popular Party in December 2011 and the economic crisis reversed the trend, resulting in a transfer of public services to private management or to chartered nursing home arrangements (Tortosa Chuliá et al. 2017).[6] The nursing home coverage ratio[7] – set by the World Health Organization at 5.0 – was reported to be 4.4 in 2015 and 4.1 in 2019 for Spain as a whole, although with huge variations among the Autonomous Communities (ACs)[8] (Envejecimiento en Red 2015; Abellán García et al. 2019).[9]

The criteria for being categorized as deserving within the framework of the Dependency Law refer to physical and mental health as expressed in the greater or lesser autonomy of the elder in relation to everyday tasks. The valuation grids (*baremos de valoración dependencia* (BVD)) are quantitative translations of qualitative valuations of capabilities such as 'recognizing and accessing food', 'washing hands', 'putting on clothes', 'ability to move within the home', 'ability to stand up', etc. (BOE 2007b, 2011a). Social or – occasionally – health services are in charge of applying the valuation grids, a task that is done at the request of the person seeking the in-kind service or subsidy, and must be carried out at home in their everyday environment. As a result, applicants are ranked according to their 'deservingness' of care in three main categories –great, sever, and moderate dependency degrees – and various subcategories (Cervera Macià et al. 2009).

Applying for official recognition as 'dependent' and being granted some form of in-kind or economic aid requires a complex bureaucratic process that takes months or years, and once the applicant has been recognized as deserving, the subsidy can take more than a year to become effective, thus leaving the recipient in what has been defined as 'limbo' (Jiménez and Viola 2019).[10] In any case, elderly people who wanted to access these services had to pay for them. A public nursing home place in 2015 would cost an average of €16,000 a year, of which the client would pay on average €6,000 a year depending on their income, with a similar cost for chartered residences (Vidal Domínguez et al. 2017); a private nursing home place would cost the client anywhere from €1,500 to €2,500 a month, depending on the AC and on the services provided, with an average of around €2,000 a month for Spain as a whole.[11]

The 2006 Law aimed at minimizing direct subsidies, which it defined as 'exceptional', instead providing a wide array of public care services, with co-payment kicking in for people with rent over the IPREM wealth index following the 2012 austerity decree (BOE 2012).[12] When public services are not available – and only then – a substitute subsidy can be obtained to access an equivalent service in the private sector, through a commercial enterprise or a self-employed 'household aid' (*ayuda a domicilio*) carer. These subsidies range from €300 to €715 depending on the dependency ranking and on income as referred to IPREM, with an average of €509 a month (IMSERSO 2017: 75). While subsidies were meant to be exceptional, in practice they continue to account for an important proportion of transfers due to the lack of available public services.[13] In addition, a different kind of subsidy is available that provides monthly payments to family carers who are able and willing to do the job, and who have already been providing care for over a year before applying for the subsidy; here compensation ranges from €150 to €380 in relation to the dependency ranking and rent index, with an average of €320 a month (IMSERSO 2017: 75). But, as noted above, the process of applying for dependency status and claiming for the services or subsidies is complicated, long and arduous, and the decisions of the professionals implementing the valuation grid (BVD) are debatable and can be questioned at different points. In sum, the process places the claimant in limbo.

The waiting list of people wanting to access a public nursing home after being declared 'deserving' of the service is long. This situation depends on the availability of public places in ACs, which varies between a low of 17 per cent in Cantabria to a high of 53 per cent in Extremadura, with an average for Spain of 27 per cent of public places (Envejecimiento en Red 2014). Demand is always higher than supply and dependent people have to settle for an interim waiting period in a private nursing home until there is an opening in a public or chartered home. This requires significant monthly expenditure that cannot be covered by public pension income, especially the lower noncontributory pensions, which are those many women receive.[14]

As a result, in fact, many Dependency Aid applications request the 'family carer' aid category (around 36 per cent in 2016) (IMSERSO 2017: 74). One reason for this is that it enables the maximization of household income by pooling together a meagre pension and a meagre Dependency Aid payment, which means that in a context of precarious labour market opportunities, working-class women may choose to take care of their elder. Another is that someone in the family (generally a woman) is *already* doing the job and has the trust of the 'dependent' person. Finally, another reason is a lack of information on the options granted by the Dependency Law and the complicated bureaucracy (Dizy Menéndez et al. 2010). However, this 'family carer' option is systematically discouraged by the administration, which insists on the need to shift to 'professional' care systems, basically service providers and nursing homes (public, chartered or private). Since 2012, legislation has been passed that reduces income aid and state coverage of social security contributions for family carers, making the carer's opportunity cost higher and her protection lower, a measure that seeks to discourage these applications.[15]

The Dependency Law of 2006 sought to provide a much-needed public service to the elderly and people with disabilities; however, its development and application suffer from various problems. First, applicants and would-be recipients resent the evaluation of everyday capabilities and the grading and ranking of deservingness as a double bind situation: deservingness is tied to physical and mental deterioration, a verdict that many people do not want to undergo; *worthiness is simultaneously an assessment of worthlessness*. Second, the state has not developed a dedicated financial instrument that would support the cost of public provision of services, so it relies on the private sector and on family care as subsidiary providers. Third, after the 2012 'budget stabilization' austerity law, family care has been increasingly discouraged in favour of professional private provision. And, fourth, the bureaucratic complexity and territorial diversity of the Dependency Law implementation process actually discouraged many people from applying, thus voluntarily renouncing their potential entitlements (Cervera Macià et al. 2009; Dizy Menéndez et al. 2010).

Financing the Caring Business: Reverse Mortgage and Nursing Homes

As a result of all of these conditions, most older people who apply for a public nursing home place, even if they receive a substitute dependency subsidy, need some kind of complementary income, at least while they are 'waiting' in the private nursing home. This income comes from liquefying property assets, namely, the house where the retired person lives. As is well known (López and Rodríguez 2011), Spain has a very high proportion of homeowners (over 80 per cent) and many of these, those who have properties free of a mortgage, are reaching retirement age or are already retired. Many are part of the old industrial working class or the white-collar middle classes. There are two options available to people who need to release home equity so as to access the necessary income to pay for a nursing home: one is a lifetime reverse mortgage; the other is to secure a lifelong annuity insurance against the transfer of the property. These systems are suggested to prospective clients by nursing homes, insurance companies, and some banks in website portals and at bricks-and-mortar offices.

With a reverse mortgage, the owner receives a monthly payment against home equity and incurs debt towards the creditor making the payments. The debt only has to be repaid on the death of the owner, although the liquidation value of the home agreed as guarantee might be reached before the retiree dies, at which point money transfers will stop (unless there is an additional annuity insurance contract attached to the reverse mortgage); interest on the debt will continue to accrue until it is repaid by the debtor's estate or the property is repossessed and the remaining debt is paid with the estate of the debtor.[16] Reverse mortgages are considered to have important growth potential linked to the demographic aging trend in Global North countries, but they have been slow to develop securitization instruments as their risks are different from regular mortgages. Models for the calculation of risk in reverse mortgages need to hedge for variations in the housing market and in the longevity of the owner instead of hedging for default (Zhai 2000).[17]

The second financial instrument for providing liquidity against the home asset is an insurance contract where the property is transferred to the insurance company in exchange for a lifelong annuity and the use-right of the property rests with the owner until death (García-Garnica 2013; Banco de España 2017). This product gives the owner a higher monthly revenue, but is hampered by the cultural preference that the home as an asset that expresses past efforts should go to the next generation through inheritance and therefore it is hardly used unless there are no direct heirs.

The 41/2007 Law (BOE 2007a) that regulates these financial devices clearly expresses the intention that this form of financial liquidity of home equity would become a complement to the decreasing purchasing power of public pensions (López Hernández and Rodríguez 2010: 300).[18] At the same time, the reverse mortgage was a clear attempt by financial capital to capture home equity that was free and clear by tapping a specific cohort of older – often relatively poor and middle-income – people into mortgaging it (Timmons and Naujokaite 2011). This process unlocked the value of the home –

which had remained outside of circulation while it was a use value – by transforming it into a financial asset that entered circulation as a form of interest-bearing capital. However, the Law requires the borrower to be properly informed by an independent party of possible risks, so as to avoid the danger of misinformation when these financial products are sold to older people. This is an implicit recognition of the practice of mis-selling to the elderly, which is a variation of the well-known practice of financial exploitation of the elderly (Williamson 2000; Coombs 2014; Fenge and Lee 2018) as well as that of mis-selling financial products to those defined as 'financially illiterate' (Reurink 2018).

The crisis put a momentary halt to this process as the home as an asset became devalued and mortgage repossessions created a glut in many banks' portfolios. But the Governor of the Bank of Spain, followed by the economic media, has been again pushing this financial instrument since 2017 as an interesting complement to a declining public pension system (Banco de España 2017). It is too early to know if the pandemic will accelerate or hinder this process.

As a result, the pensioners who were willing and able to get a place in private or even public nursing homes were not those whose family networks needed their pension income to survive – as these stayed at home and used Dependency Aid for a family carer. Sociologically, elderly people in nursing homes were mostly those able to increase their average pension through recourse to a financial instrument or the selling of property, and whose children were relatively autonomous in terms of income, which freed the pension from kinship claims. Because Spanish reverse mortgage law made it possible to rent the mortgaged house if the owner went into a nursing home, this instrument could provide flexibility and enable the aggregation of different sources of liquid income. At the same time, it would preserve the title to property, something that the next generation would appreciate.

In sum, what transpires in this situation is a complex system of potential expropriation of elderly homeowners' income and assets through a combination of: (1) financial instruments that transform the meaning of the home from an affect-loaded use value into an asset and allow for its liquidity; (2) a social system that provides insufficient support for the elderly in terms of public nursing home access or an inadequate substitute subsidy; and (3) a deficient retirement pension replacement rate. Moreover, the provision of nursing home places has remained largely private even after the few years when the socialist government of Rodríguez Zapatero made an effort to increase places (Envejecimiento en Red 2014, 2015). With the prospective demographic expansion of older cohorts and the privatization of public services expanding after the crisis under the argument of 'professionalizing' care, large private investment funds (mostly French and British capital) have entered the nursing home business in Spain through processes of mergers and acquisitions since 2015.[19] At the same time, tenders to manage public nursing homes have lowered requirements regarding services provided and the number of workers and their qualifications, while simultaneously reducing the threshold price of the tender contract.

Nursing homes were expensive and their services became worse, but they were a good business. With austerity, the quality of provision in nursing homes declined, while the exploitation of the workers and the expropriation of the elderly increased. In some cases, abysmal conditions were reported by kin associations, who pressured the ACs to upgrade their tenders and avoid particular for-profit private providers.[20] The families of nursing home residents repeatedly pointed to these problems and highlighted the lack of care for the elderly that the AC authorities expressed by reducing the requirements for private management of public homes in the tenders. At the same time, the smaller nursing home associations argued that the reduction of threshold prices in tenders was making the provision of services impossible and asked for the prices to be adjusted to real expenses.[21] Indeed, private and chartered nursing homes did not comply with regulations regarding the workforce, medical attention and other general requisites, and were recurrently fined to no avail.[22] A perfect storm was brewing through the conjunction of different actors: the state, which delayed and decreased Dependency Aid and services, reduced pensions and lacked public facilities such as nursing homes; the ACs, which reduced conditions and threshold prices in tenders for elderly care services; and the private nursing homes, which decreased service quality, exploiting workers and charging high prices to clients (Calpena et al. 2020).[23]

And then the pandemic hit, which made many of these issues painfully clear and relevant for understanding the various registers of elderly people's economic and social worth.

COVID-19, Nursing Home Deaths, QALY and Triage

The impact of austerity cuts due to the Memorandum of Understanding that the European Commission drew up with Spain (European Commission 2012b) on healthcare and health conditions resulted in the loss of some 10,000 hospital beds from 2009 to 2017, while many professionals, especially nurses, became unemployed and migrated during these years.[24] However, the distribution of these cuts varies widely in the different ACs, as health is a jurisdiction that has been fully transferred to the regional governments. For example, privatization of healthcare in Catalonia and Madrid outpaced all the other regions in Spain, as did the privatization of social services in general, including Dependency Aid (FADSP 2017).

As the pandemic worsened in March and April 2020, it particularly affected older people, especially those in nursing homes.[25] At the same time, mitigation resources became scarce (especially Personal Protective Equipment, ICU beds and ventilators) and the authorities started to send triage protocols to hospitals, while the media started to inform about the need for triage.[26] It became explicit that older people and people with underlying pathologies that would make their full recovery very difficult would not be admitted to hospital, and would be denied transfer, sent back to the nursing home or to their own home, or would be offered palliative care only.[27] Austerity, privatization of nursing homes and lack of foresight explain the scarcity of resources, but we also need to understand the criteria that underlie the positioning of individuals in particular socially expendable categories of those undeserving of life-saving resources, and what arguments justify them (Li 2009; Skeggs and Loveday 2012).

The authorities repeatedly stressed that there was no discrimination in terms of economic or social positioning involved in triage (even if obvious underlying health conditions often relate to poverty, precarity, etc.), and they added that 'on its own', age was not a criterion either.[28] But they argued that in a situation of scarcity, *justice* requires 'reserving resources that could be very scarce to those who have the greatest chance of survival first, and secondly to those who can have *more years of life saved*, with a view to *maximizing the benefits for the maximum number of people*' (Vergano et al. 2020: 5, translated from Italian, emphasis added).[29] Deservingness to access scarce life-saving resources is justified in terms of the social 'common good' of the preserved life, and measured with a quantitative index: the QALY. The central argument of the QALY is that in relation to the allocation of scarce healthcare resources, the index of deservingness is based on remaining life expectancy and pre-existing health quality.

The implementation of these protocols in some ACs produced a public outcry and in March 2020 the government asked the Spanish Committee on Bioethics to give its advice regarding the triage protocols that had been released by medical associations and some ACs.

Although the Committee asserted that there could be no triage decisions made in terms of age or disability, and insisted on the unique value and dignity of every human life, it also recognized that a first come, first served method was not acceptable in times of scarcity. In its view, an ethical approach demanded that triage give preference to 'the most vulnerable', a criterion apparently opposed to that of maximization of QALYs (de Montalvo Jääskeläinen et al. 2020).

These two contradictory positions – the 'utilitarian'/'productivist' one based on the QALY arguments, and the 'humanist' and 'egalitarian' one based on the unique and equal value of each human life and the protection of the more vulnerable – were simultaneously entangled in economic and moral rationalities assessing 'social value', where the valuation framework was most often left unsaid.[30] In this debate, deservingness was linked to different valuation frameworks: one posited a social calculation of the value of a human being that referred to their relative ability to contribute to society and to the economic cost of preserving that life; the other put forward the universal and equal worth of every individual human being. The productivist vision was based on utilitarian calculations in the allocation of scarce resources, stressing in particular the twin ideas of the opportunity cost of allocating a particular resource to one person instead of another, and the abstract quantitative rationality of utility of a human life for society expressed in the QALY measure and 'years of life saved' in an abstract aggregate form. The QALY valuation framework stresses the potential remaining life years calculated in relation to a life expectancy index and weighted according to quality of life, but whether the maximization of QALYs refers to comparative individual worth or to a social aggregate of worth is particularly ambiguous. In triage situations, it seems to refer to the former only as a means to the latter, without defining what is considered valuable for the common good beyond healthiness. Furthermore, it does not address how to evaluate the 'quality' of life expectancy, for example, or, especially, who is considered more valuable for society and why.[31]

In most nursing homes, corporate management did not particularly care about their residents (as high demand ensured sustained occupancy) and did not care about their workers either, as the crisis had created a seemingly endless cheap and resigned labour pool, always fearing joblessness. Financial extraction that enabled revenues locked in the housing asset to re-enter circulation thus sustaining the realization of capital through exchange, and hyperexploitation in the care services, articulated forms of valorization that were predicated on two categories of expendable people: the carers and the elderly.

Valuation frameworks devalued carers in various ways (e.g. as immigrants, unskilled, female, ethnicized and racialized) and devalued the elderly in quality of life terms. While the QALY value of the elderly residents was debased in triage protocols for their pathologies, disabilities and overall frailty, their potential power as consumers was offset by market conditions: a restricted supply of nursing homes (i.e. lack of choice) on the one hand and high demand for the services on the other.

The fact that in Spain between 50 and 70 per cent of deaths during the first wave of the COVID-19 pandemic were in nursing homes (Secretaría de Estado de Derechos Sociales 2020: 12–14),[32] with high indexes also in most Global North countries, is a sign not only – as has been repeated in the media – of the natural 'vulnerability' of the elderly, but also of the conditions that have produced a social environment that constructed the elderly and those who cared for them as particularly 'undeserving' of care (Fernández-Ballesteros 2020). Elderly people in nursing homes were denied transfer to hospitals, as is evident from protocols that directly discouraged considering transfer.[33] Moreover, statistical information from the official reports of the Red Nacional de Vigilancia Epidemiológica (RENAVE 2020) confirms that while 30 per cent of the over-seventies were not hospitalized, when admitted only 5 per cent of people in this age group received treatment in ICUs. Nevertheless, they were more likely to present serious symptoms and die than the rest of the population (86 per cent lethality).[34] These numbers are still fluctuating, but they are consistent with the triage protocols that proposed avoiding transfer to hospital, thus denying them ventilators and instead referring them to palliative care units.

Another aspect of elderly people's valuation has emerged with the prolongation of confinement and an initial government project (supported by the words of Ursula von der Leyen, the President of the European Commission) that 'vulnerable' people (e.g. the elderly and those with underlying conditions) could be maintained in strict confinement for longer in order to 'protect' them from contagion.[35] This provoked protests from a vocal group of elderly people who pointed out that they had the same rights as any other citizen and could not be discriminated against on the grounds of age. When this project was dropped by the Spanish government, some public voices suggested that in the event of a second wave of COVID-19 infections, the elderly would have to be explicitly discriminated against (being more vulnerable), self-isolate and remain in lockdown instead of forcing 'a massive house arrest', 'sacrificing' everyone equally and causing the destruction of the economy (Carlin 2020). This was not an isolated proposal, but is often repeated by those who are critical of generalized lockdowns. The argument here seems to be that people are responsible for their vulnerability or that it is simply 'natural', a biological fact; the elderly are responsible for their high mortality or they have to accept the law of 'nature'. While undoubtedly the vulnerability of humans to different diseases varies along the life course as well as for genetic reasons, existing pathologies and the characteristics of the virus, in this case the financialized political economic context has produced a particular category of people – the elderly – as expropriable in different ways by different agents, including the state. These practices are both the material expression of how human value is allocated in the Global North and the condition for an extractive valorization process.

Producing Deservingness through Calculation

The QALY triage framework raises a number of contradictions between individual and social valuations of life, between quantitative ways to calibrate qualitative categories of life, and a number of questions as to what criteria are used to assess social value and the common good. It also foregrounds the social production of scarcity and the economic background of optimal allocation. The triage criteria used in the Spanish case are quantitative (maximizing benefits – in life expectancy years – for the greater number of people) and they aggregate an alleged individual benefit into a collective social benefit. However, these triage criteria are in line with the utilitarian argument that has been put forward by public health policy-makers in Europe and elsewhere increasingly since the 1980s to allocate 'scarce' resources (Williams 2012 [1985]). During the pandemic, Spain, followed Italy's lead (Vergano et al. 2020) and started producing written protocols or documents by medical associations that incorporated 'life expectancy' maximization and were based on 'maximizing benefits for the maximum number of people' (Manzano Ramírez 2020: 3, Rubio Sanchíz et al. 2020: 5). In the Spanish case, the QALY measurement instrument was explicitly mentioned as the argument for triage.

Since the mid-1980s, when it was proposed as a public health instrument for the allocation of resources in the UK by the economist Alan Williams in 1985 (Williams 2012 [1985]), the QALY has been fraught with controversy. The Quality Adjusted Life Year

(QALY) measure was critiqued early on for being 'ageist' (discriminating against those with shorter life expectancy) and for putting people in 'double jeopardy' because those who were disabled or had health issues that diminished their quality of life would be further disadvantaged by the QALY accounting (Harris 1987, 1991; Smith et al. 1990; Evans, in Williams and Evans 2012). Those opposed to the QALY pointed to a discriminatory procedure that favoured not only the young but also healthier people, who tended to be wealthier, and that devalued a priori the life of people with disabilities. Two other issues were questioned from a political point of view.

First, the 'scarce resources' premise was critiqued on the grounds that healthcare budgets should be considered relationally to other budget expenditures and valued as a national priority: 'the obligation to save as many lives as possible is *not the obligation to save as many lives as we can cheaply or economically save*' (Harris 1987: 122). Indeed, the production of scarcity in public resources has resulted from the political economy of austerity, regressive taxation and deficit control. Fiscal solvency put forward by austerity policies took precedence over public resources supporting people's wellbeing. Disinvestment targeted health, education and the public pension system, while transferring services to the private sector. As Nancy Pulido has underlined in relation to environmental racism in Flint, Michigan, 'it is *which* lives are subordinated to fiscal solvency that is key' (Pulido 2016: 10), whose lives are devalued and hence can be neglected without major moral or political drawbacks. Second, the 'maximization' premise in which the trade-offs between quantity (of life years) and quality (of life) balance out and can be rendered in a quantitative measure is a fallacy (Crisp 1989). It is no mere coincidence that the QALY notion emerged with the neoliberal turn that Margaret Thatcher imposed on public services, among them the National Health System (NHS).

Moral arguments of distributive justice have been used by both supporters and detractors of the QALY. The former have pointed to the 'inequity' of denying scarce resources to those who could most 'benefit' from them – the young – because 'the objective is to minimize the differences in *lifetime experience of health*' (Williams, in Williams and Evans 2012: 442, emphasis added), and to the QALY's 'objectivity' because it is not based on subjective valuation, but on a predefined algorithm that quantifies the value of life.[36] The latter have insisted that the QALY procedure disregards the equal human rights that should underscore any democratic nation and point to inbuilt discrimination (Evans, in Williams and Evans 2012: 443). The triage dilemma in situations of disaster or pandemic – which is different from triage or allocation of scarce resources to health in normal contexts – highlights the tension between utilitarian perspectives of medical utility and social utility (Hearn 2013) or QALY maximization, and egalitarian perspectives, which state 'that if resources must be allocated unequally, they should be distributed such that the worst off benefit the most' (Greenacre and Fleshner 2017: 36). The latter is generally prevalent in ICUs and Emergency Room triage in normal times, and was the original meaning of triage (in the Napoleonic Wars), but one that by the mid-nineteenth century, in a utilitarian turn, was replaced by giving precedence to those who could return to the battlefield sooner. 'The utilitarian model of triage opts for providing the most good to the most people; the egalitarian model opts for assisting those in greatest need' (Tabery et al. 2008: 116). During a pandemic, the risk of insidious discrimination through the use of utilitarian models has been signalled and hybrid utilitarian-cum-egalitarian models have been proposed as being more just (Tabery et al. 2008).

At the peak of the first wave of the COVID-19 pandemic (March–April 2020) in Spain (and Italy), triage was based on the QALY criterion and was blatantly discriminatory against older people, especially because it was excluding the majority of referrals from nursing homes, giving little or no medical infrastructure or support instead. It was also insidiously discriminatory against the disabled and also against poorer people, who tend to have underlying pathologies resulting in lower recovery potential, a basic triage criterion.

The Valuation of Older People and the Valorization Process

What does this complex situation tell us about the value of a group of people defined by fuzzy and moving boundaries, variously categorized as retired (i.e. nonlabour), pensioners (i.e. state-dependent), grandparents (i.e. morally responsible), family carers (i.e. service providers), asset owners (i.e. having financial potential), nursing home residents (i.e. service consumers), vulnerable (i.e. in need of protection), fragile (i.e. health impaired), deserving of state resources (i.e. the Dependency Law), undeserving of scarce mitigation resources (i.e. QALY-deficient), etc? The aim of this section is to analyse the relations existing between the practices that define these various categories and the valorization process. I wish to show how apparently distant processes such as the housing bubble, the bailing-out of banks and the Memorandum of Understanding of July 2012, as well as the constitutional enshrining of the 3 per cent deficit ceiling and budgetary stability, are entangled with the construction of particular valuation frameworks that configure the social worth of older people and their deservingness of pensions, subsidies or healthcare, and how these processes support the valorization of capital (BOE 2011b).

These processes of valuation are predicated on the articulation of quantitative measures of different kinds, but are mostly tied to an assessment of 'life expectancy' (in demographic terms), of 'costs' (of pensions for the system and of health resources), of 'quality of life' such as the Human Development Index or the various healthcare indexes (Higginson and Carr 2001; Stiglitz et al. 2009; Merry 2011). Valuation processes are linked to 'benefits' accruing in terms of financial market prospects (of the capture of assets) or the realization of profits through exchange (in the growing market for nursing homes), but also to individual revenues and wellbeing (in terms of liquidity and of services). Each of these measures pegs a different value on concrete people, while it simultaneously ascribes them to a collective category, referring them to a general principle for making judgements (Boltanski and Thévenot 1991) and to a particular meaningful field for calculating 'benefits' – a good, a surplus – that shifts valuation from individual to collective parameters (and vice versa) and from a private to a common good. Simultaneously, other more qualitative definitions of value are produced when grandparents are hailed as the bulwarks against the crisis and the providers of care, home and income, or when the retirees themselves claim the heritage of their struggle for democratic and labour rights. Here, too, both the private and the common good are the shifting background against which the value of the elders is justified and appraised. Social value is always morally attached to the common good; what moves and shifts are the grounds on which arguments about value are made, and the instrumental scales used to assess precedence and rank in adjudication of individual positions (Boltanski and Thévenot 1991; Guyer 2004; Fourcade 2016; Fourcade and Healy 2017).

Moreover, these processes appear to be configured by particular legal frameworks and policies implemented at different historical moments. In particular, public investment or disinvestment in concrete services, infrastructures or places contributes to valuing, devaluing or revaluing concrete groups of people, but does this in different ways. Material and discursive forms of adjudicating value to people are entangled along relational processes that take place at various scales and involve diverse, often contradictory 'orders of worth'. Moral and economic aspects are salient both in material and discursive terms, and refer to the life resources being considered. During the financial crisis and austerity years, as the elderly provided income, housing and care to younger adults, they became highly valued – in private and in public – for their material and emotional support to domestic networks. In moral terms, they were valued for their filial responsibility and solidarity; in material terms, they were valued for sharing their livelihood resources. By protecting and providing, they were fulfilling a filial and domestic obligation for the common good and thus accruing worth.

At the same time, policy and public discourses on the unsustainability of the public pension system were presenting an entirely different valuation. Their social status was described as 'privileged', their character as 'selfish' and the system that provided their pension income as 'inequitable'. Three rhetorical devices were used in this process of valuation: first, longevity – a quantitative index that referred to a statistical categorization of the population in demographics, while it also seemed to hold responsible the individual elder, as the sign a couple of pensioners held up in a demonstration indicates: 'forgive us for being alive';[37] second, accounting – the consideration of the pension system in terms of budgetary cost–benefit analysis within a fiscal framework constrained by strong limits to deficit; and, third, individualization – as if the pension was a form of individual savings income owed by the state instead of an intergenerational solidarity system mediated by the state (Le Lann 2010; Le Lann and Lemoine 2012). In addition to re-signifying pensions in terms of capitalization instead of redistribution, individualization presented pensions as benefiting the individual exclusively, which was definitely not the case, as redistribution within the domestic network made clear. In the unsustainability argument, the intergenerational responsibility expressed in the pay-as-you-go scheme was turned into a form the elderly had of extracting 'rent' from the system at the expense of younger generations.[38] In terms of valorization, how did these various valuations play out?

Redistribution of the pension through family networks and the provision of housing and care contributed to the devaluation of younger adults' labour as reproduction costs were partially met outside of the wage and labour market exchange. This aspect has been repeatedly stressed by feminist scholars in relation to household work; here, the pension income adds to the subsidizing of labour reproduction through retired workers' social wage mediated by the state. As a result, valorization in the process of production increases because exploitation is articulated to expropriation and accumulates as profits. The positive valuation of the economic effects of grandparents' sharing of resources supports a precarious labour market of depressed wages and permanent insecurity. But the fact that pensions appear as unjust forms of privileged rent extraction by the elderly obscured the actual valorization process and made it appear as something else in a fetishization of the pension system. In this case, the positive and negative forms of valuation overlap in the valorization process.

In their role as asset holders and consumers, the elderly are captured in other valuation frameworks. Housing, one of the main reproductive elements being shared in the domestic networks that fend off precarity, is discursively transformed from home into asset, an investment to be made profitable. Through a reverse mortgage, the value of the home is realized in the financial circuit of valorization. The grandparents' home as a refuge for those being foreclosed on during the mortgage crisis or for those unable to access housing in the market provided value to the elderly, as we have seen above. As an asset, the home provided a different frame of reference for valuation – one dependent on the housing market. When the housing bubble burst, the value of the home as a security for the loan in the reverse mortgage market decreased, resulting in lower annuities and higher fees. As an asset, the value of the home reflected on the value of its owner and its devaluation during the crisis prevented many elderly people from obtaining the liquidity needed to access a nursing home. Thus, they became devalued in financial terms, which was an obstacle to them receiving professional care in their old age. These valuations enabled different kinds of valorization processes.

As a use value, the home is a barrier to valorization because it keeps value locked away from circulation and realization; it represents tied-up money. In contrast, as an asset in reverse mortgage or home equity loans, it becomes interest-bearing capital and re-enters circulation. Moreover, when the liquid income of the reverse mortgage monthly payment enters the market for care services – via home care professionals or a nursing home – it contributes to the realization of capital through exchange in the service sector and enables the exploitation of low-paid labour – often immigrant women – and hence the accumulation of surplus value. Positive valuation of the home asset, then, provides a path to valorization, while also potentially contributing to the wellbeing of elderly homeowners that can thus access professional care and a complement to the pension when most needed, arguably expressing their worth.

For the elderly, frameworks for valuing care depended on whether they were givers or recipients of care services and on whether the services were paid, unpaid, or provided by public or private institutions or workers. As caregivers, they were generally valued, thus accruing moral recognition and gratitude. As care recipients, the value granted to them – both moral and economic – was extremely diverse and volatile, and often depended on their physical fitness, the caregivers' personal relations to the elderly, the material drudgery of the task, and the social recognition and economic gratification provided by the job (Alber and Drotbohm 2015). With increasing disability, elders tend to be socially considered a 'heavy burden' for those taking care of them, one that only love or money can balance. Thus, in relation to giving or receiving care, the elderly are valued or devalued, taking into account their capacity to provide (services, income or assets), the commodified or decommodified structure for care provision, and the affective bonds involved.

Here, valorization depends on the relation of caring practices to the labour and service markets. Decommodification and filialization of caring practices – as when grandparents take care of their grandchildren – affect valorization through a reduction of reproduction costs of labour, as mentioned above, because retirees' labour is unpaid. When daughters take care of their elderly parents, decommodification hampers valorization, which explains why neoliberal governments are pushing for professionalization and the elimination of family care in the Dependency Law. However, it benefits the fiscal balance of the state because family welfare substitutes for state support via sufficient pensions, dependency subsidies and care facilities, which explains why successive governments have subsidized family care instead of investing in dependency public services. A contradiction that can be observed in the various implementations of the Dependency Law becomes apparent here: on the one hand, the state pushes for the 'professionalization' (meaning commodification) of care and discourages family carers; on the other hand, disinvestment in care infrastructures and labour deregulation present the elderly and their families with the dilemma of either directly providing unpaid care or paying for care in the market. In the latter case, as consumers, the elderly provide effective demand that is necessary for the valorization circuit, one that hinges on their physical devaluation (which paradoxically makes them deserving of dependency public subsidies and services), on the high prices of nursing homes, and on the exploitation and low wages of precarious care labour.

The COVID-19 pandemic has uncovered another valuation framework: the QALY index described above. As a measure seeking to optimize scarce public health resources, the QALY valuation is directly linked to fiscal budgeting, deficit containment and prioritizing life-saving resources so as to maximize the abstract value 'QALY' for the benefit of society as a whole. It relates directly to the application of cost–benefit analysis tools to public budgeting and to the pursuit of efficiency framing public service in a calculative mode of accounting. But efficiency here rests on the negative valuation of people in terms of disabilities and reduced life expectancy, as they will be low priority or 'let die' in triage procedures and adjudication of resources. The QALY creates a rationalized scale for devaluing people, one that clearly affects the elderly as a collective, people with physical and mental disabilities, and those with underlying pathologies. The process of investing in the nursing home business with its potential for expansion, while simultaneously cutting costs, enhances valorization on the back of the devaluation of the elderly consumers and of labour.

The various domains of valuation of the elderly that I have analysed are multifaceted and include different kinds of registers – moral, material, quantitative, qualitative, collective, individual, kinship, economic and political – that signal the existence of diverse value scales where struggles over what is valuable occur. The tensions that become key to the valorization process entail the struggle between quantification and qualification, and between abstract and concrete forms of valuation. In a process akin to what Muniesa et al. (2017) have defined as 'capitalization' – the pragmatic process of valuation by which entities become assets, an investment whose purpose is to accrue money – the elderly see their valuation registers shift into grids of monetary valuation, as a basis providing the grounds to various forms of valorization. Grandparents' filial solidarity shifts into the unsustainable cost of public pensions, forcing a transformation that benefits private pension schemes; the home as a refuge that expresses the biographical lives of its owners shifts into an asset that can be liquefied to access the private nursing homes that will maintain biological life in old age; finally, the inalienable value of concrete life shifts into QALY calculations that allow cost–benefit analysis regarding life-saving resources (Fassin 2018). Fassin has reminded us, following Maurice Halbwachs, that valuations of life are political and defy the 'humanitarian reason' of equal value and 'sacredness' of human lives with blatant inequality (Fassin 2009, 2016; Ginsburg and Rapp 2016).

The QALY valuation of life during the pandemic can be read as an example of biopolitics (Foucault 1997 [1976]: 213–35) in its reference to fostering the life of a population and the focus on the power of 'making live'. But Foucault (ibid.: 226–30) states that in the context of the biopolitical injunction of 'making live', only a conceptual cut (*une coupure*) in the biological continuum of the human species that is itself presented as biological in nature can justify 'letting die' and 'making die' if it is for the good of the species.[39] Speaking about people with disabilities in the United States, Ginsburg and Rapp (2016) point to the eugenics aspect of some discourses and practices aiming at potentially discarding disabled lives, and they signal how old age generalizes the issue of potentially disabled citizens' value. Does the QALY index justify a rupture in the biological continuum of the human species that produces human devaluation? Does it justify discriminatory triage practices that 'let die' on the grounds that they 'make live' the more valued humans? Is the Foucauldian perspective of a political rupture in the biological continuum of humanity useful for understanding how older people's (de)valuation feeds processes of capital valorization?

Following Marx (1999 [1867]), discussions on 'primitive accumulation' or 'accumulation by dispossession' (Harvey 2003), 'pauperization' (Denning 2010), 'surplus population' (Li 2009; Smith 2011) and 'waste lives' (Bauman 2004; Skeggs and Loveday 2012; Gidwani and Maringanti 2016) push the debate further in a useful direction. On the one hand, they underline the violence present in capital accumulation and the constitutive entanglement between exploitation and expropriation in the process. On the other hand, they stress the political production of biological discontinuity as integral to social differentiation and capital accumulation. These processes are jointly addressed in proposals to expand the reach of the racial capitalism concept, in particular Jodi Melamed's (2015) development of Ruth Wilson Gilmore's (2002) perspective where the concept is used to 'name and analyze the production of social separateness – the disjoining or deactivating of relations between human beings (and humans and nature) – needed for capitalist expropriation to work', describing racial capitalism as a technology of anti-relationality and stressing the 'dialectic in which forms of humanity are separated (made "distinct") so that they may be "interconnected" in terms that feed capital' (Melamed 2015: 78).

The Spanish situation shows how the devaluation of older people as privileged 'pensioners' was vocally promoted by experts, policy-makers and the media as early as the 1990s and increasingly after the

Maastricht Treaty. Simultaneously, older people were increasingly valued as a growing market for leisure, wellbeing and health services, but also as targets for financial products other than classical mortgages, as most already owned a home. In this entanglement of valuation practices that refer to different frameworks, the state always seems to facilitate the expansion of particular profitable sectors of the economy, such as private nursing homes that provide basic services to the elderly in exchange for the capture of their assets. Finally, in the context of the COVID-19 pandemic, the biological valuation typical of the efficient allocation of scarce resources to maximizing aggregate life expectancy and 'quality of life' of the population has proved particularly lethal to the elderly residing in nursing homes. They were indeed 'let die' for the 'benefit' of society as a whole in a conjuncture of scarcity that had been politically produced through austerity and on the basis of a biological rupture argument. But they had previously already been set apart, devalued and dispossessed in many ways.

Susana Narotzky is Professor of Social Anthropology at the University of Barcelona. She received the 2020 Prize for Research in the Humanities granted by the Spanish Ministry for Science. She has also been awarded a European Research Council Advanced Grant to study the effects of austerity on Southern European livelihoods (Grassroots Economics (GRECO)). Her work is inspired by theories of critical political economy, moral economies and feminist economics. Her recent writing addresses the themes of making a living in futures without employment, political mobilization and class. Her latest publications are 'The Janus Face of Austerity Politics: Autonomy and Dependence in Contemporary Spain', *Focaal: Journal of Global and Historical Anthropology* (Berghahn Books, 2021) and the edited book *Grassroots Economies: Living with Austerity in Southern Europe* (Pluto Press, 2020).

Notes

1. This representation echoes the academic idea of a Southern European welfare model that rests on the family safety net, although here the main resource in the network is the public pension scheme (Esping-Andersen 1990; Ferrera 1996; Andreotti et al. 2001; Saraceno 2016).
2. The Yay@flauta movement was linked to the 15M-Indignados protests that were initiated in 2011. They have mobilized with the *mareas* (tides)

and the *marchas* (marches) that have taken action since 2012. Their objective is 'to defend the rights of their children and grandchildren'. Retrieved 4 February 2022 from http://yayoflautasmadrid.org/sample-page.
3. Longevity also appears as an increasing risk in financial and actuarial calculations regarding the reverse mortgages being offered to the elderly, as we will see below.
4. Compare this view with French Solidarism (Bourgeois 1896) in the early twentieth century, based on the idea and fairness of social security in the social debt that successive generations had towards their predecessors.
5. This potential is embedded in the 'reverse mortgage' securitization instrument, which is being developed even if its risks are difficult to model (Ortiz et al. 2013).
6. I have used 'chartered' to convey the funding by the state or local authorities of privately owned and managed institutions.
7. This ratio defines the relation between number of beds available and the elderly population potentially requiring them (calculated as total number of beds / total +65 population*100).
8. For example, a 2.2 ratio in Murcia, 3.0 in Andalucía or 3.1 in Galicia as opposed to 6.5 in Aragón, 6.9 in Castilla-La Mancha and 7.6 in Castilla-León, with Madrid at 4.1 and Catalunya at 4.3 around the average.
9. It is interesting to note that the ACs with lower ratios of nursing homes have had lower COVID-19 mortality rates.
10. Retrieved 4 February 2022 from https://www.publico.es/sociedad/dinero-atascos-y-limbo-mortal.html.
11. E.g. https://pensium.es/precios-de-las-residencias-de-tercera-edad-en-espana *(retrieved* 4 February 2022).
12. This index (Indicador Público de Renta de Efectos Múltiples) has remained very stable during the last ten years: €532. 51 from 2010 to 2016; €537.84 from 2017 to 2020 (retrieved 4 February 2022 from http://www.iprem.com.es/#evolucion). This is the index used to calculate subsidies and co-payments.
13. Retrieved 4 February 2022 from https://cincodias.elpais.com/cincodias/2011/05/30/economia/1306734984_850215.html.
14. Public pensions vary from €366 of noncontributory pensions in 2015 to €2,554 of the maximum pensions cap in 2015 (€395 and €2,683 respectively in 2020). Minimum contributive pensions were between €601 and €782 (for 2015). The average contributive retirement pension in 2015 was €1,030. Moreover, pensions are extremely biased along gender lines, with noncontributory, minimum and widow/er pensions (€632 in 2015) concerning women overwhelmingly (Ministerio de Trabajo, Migraciones y Seguridad Social 2018: 206, 209, 224). Private pension plans are minimal in Spain and only concern wealthy people.
15. Real Decreto-ley 20/2012, de 13 de julio, de medidas para garantizar la estabilidad presupuestaria y de fomento de la competitividad (BOE 2012).
16. After an important surge between 2008 to 2010, the housing and bank-

ing crisis resulted in many banks discontinuing the supply of reverse mortgages. As a loan backed by home equity, reverse mortgages were tied to the housing market, which devalued during the crisis, making them risky for lenders and expensive for debtors, as the monthly payments they could negotiate at origin decreased. They have re-emerged as an interesting financial product since 2018. See e.g. https://www.efe.com/efe/espana/economia/la-hipoteca-inversa-una-total-desconocida-que-podria-comenzar-a-emerger/10003-3957474 (retrieved 4 February 2022).
17. There are different kinds of reverse mortgages where the continuity of the payments by the lender is based on a fixed term, or on the tenure by the borrower of the home as primary residence, or on lifetime, etc. (Zhai 2000). In Spain reverse mortgages are generally based on the lifetime of the borrower.
18. 'No cabe duda, pues, de que el desarrollo de un mercado de hipotecas inversas que permita a los mayores utilizar parte de su patrimonio inmobiliario para aumentar su renta ofrece un gran potencial de generación de beneficios económicos y sociales' (Law 41/2007).
19. E.g. https://elpais.com/economia/2018/11/21/actualidad/1542813372_601608.html; https://www.eldiario.es/economia/inversiones-residencias-mayoreslos-envejecimientoante-ofertapublica_0_956454528.html (retrieved 4 February 2022).
20. E.g. https://www.coordinadoraresidencias.com/prensa; https://www.lamarea.com/2020/05/21/denuncia-residencias-catalunya-covid; https://www.elperiodico.com/es/sociedad/20170608/las-familias-denuncian-irregularidades-en-cinco-residencias-publicas-de-ancianos-6093150 (retrieved 4 February 2022).
21. E.g. https://www.elperiodico.com/es/sociedad/20170404/residencias-tercera-edad-colapso-5952199 (retrieved 4 February 2022).
22. E.g. https://www.eldiario.es/sociedad/residencias-coronavirus_0_1030997591.html (retrieved 4 February 2022).
23. E.g. https://ctxt.es/es/20200302/Politica/31527/residencias-de-ancianos-privatizacion-coronavirus-fondos-buitre.htm (retrieved 4 February 2022).
24. E.g. Evolución de la sanidad española en el contexto internacional con especial referencia al impacto de la crisis. Federación de Asociaciones para la Defensa de la Sanidad Pública, Junio 2019, https://www.google.com/url?sa=t&rct=j&q=&esrc=s&source=web&cd=&cad=rja&uact=8&ved=2ahUKEwiDw7Os6LryAhWO3oUKHdojAagQFnoECAIQAQ&url=https%3A%2F%2Fwww.fadsp.org%2Fdocuments%2F2019%2FImpactoSanIntern.doc&usg=AOvVaw39uk7HvgE-L8Ee38y9xWsN (retrieved 4 February 2022).

See also La década perdida. Mapa de austeridad del gasto sanitario en España 2009 al 2018. Amnistía Internacional, Madrid, July 2020, https://www.google.com/url?sa=t&rct=j&q=&esrc=s&source=web&cd=&cad=rja&uact=8&ved=2ahUKEwj84f2Y6bryAhUO4YUKHXPUARIQFnoECAIQAQ&url=https%3A%2F%2Fdoc.es.amnesty.

org%2Fms-opac%2Frecordmedia%2F1%40000032500%2Fobjec t%2F43241%2Fraw&usg=AOvVaw3U5BkqBvJJBUev3PkBG5et (retrieved 4 February 2022); and Informe. Repercusiones de la crisis sobre la atención primaria. Evolución en las CCAA. Federación de Asociaciones para la Defensa de la Sanidad Pública, Abril 2019. https://www.google.com/url?sa=t&rct=j&q=&esrc=s&source=web &cd=&cad=rja&uact=8&ved=2ahUKEwjMzca_6bryAhUGcBQKH fz7D1kQFnoECAIQAQ&url=https%3A%2F%2Fwww.fad sp.org%2Fdocuments%2F2019%2FInformeAPcrisis2019.doc &usg=AOvVaw0PLiQWCR42JtgyT9AHBKHF (retrieved 4 February 2022).

25. In May 2020, the official reported data estimated the death toll of the elderly in nursing homes to be 66 per cent, most of them in the ACs of Madrid, Catalunya, Castilla y León and Castilla-La Mancha. Retrieved 4 February 2022 from https://www.rtve.es/noticias/20200514/radiografia-del-coronavirus-residencias-ancianos-espana/2011609.shtml.

26. This is explicitly stated in documents drawn up by medical associations and institutions (Esquerdo et al. 2020; García-Llana et al. 2020; Manzano Ramírez et al. 2020; Mur de Víu 2020; Organización Médica Colegial de España 2020; Rubio et al. 2020). But see the defence of equal human dignity and against exclusion of older and disabled people by de Montalvo et al. (2020). Newspapers strongly debated these protocols: see https://www.lavanguardia.com/vida/20200320/474273746104/uci-triaje-coronavirus-valor-social-esperanza-vida-pacientes-colapsar.html; https://www.lavanguardia.com/vida/20200426/48714890909/residen cias-mayores-coronavirus.html (retrieved 4 February 2022).

27. E.g, https://www.federacionfed.org/20-000-personas-han-podido-mor ir-de-coronavirus-en-las-residencia; https://www.lavanguardia.com/vida/ 20200402/48266668820/salut-recomienda-no-poner-respirador-paci entes-mas-80-anos.html; https://www.lavanguardia.com/vida/20200406/ 48329557057/dilemas-eticos-epidemia.html; https://www.eldiario.es/ma drid/documento-hospital-Madrid-residencias-coronavirus_0_10285 47274.html (retrieved 4 February 2022).

28. 'No ingresar a personas en las que se prevé un beneficio mínimo, como, por ejemplo … situaciones funcionales muy limitadas, condiciones de fragilidad, etc.' and 'Ante pacientes críticos con otras patologías críticas … se debe valorar ingresar prioritariamente a quien más se beneficie o tenga mayor expectativa de vida, en el momento del ingreso' (Rubio Sanchíz et al. 2020: 11).

29. This document was produced on 6 March 2020 by the Società Italiana di Anestesia Analgesia Rianimazione e Terapia Intensiva (SIAARTI) and was the basis for the first triage documents produced in Spain.

30. Documents vaguely stated the need to take into account the 'social value' of the sick person, i.e., 'Tener en cuenta el valor social de la persona enferma' (Rubio Sanchíz et al. 2020: 12). 'Social value' has been defined in pandemic triage models as the value of first responders (e.g. health

staff and other 'essential' workers) and those most necessary for the reproduction of society (Hearn 2013). But the Spanish protocols do not define 'social value'.
31. This is particularly problematic for anti-discriminatory criteria that are generally subscribed to by many nation-states. It raises important issues surrounding how people with disabilities are valuated and how the value of people who live in low-quality life conditions such as the jobless, the poor, the homeless, the incarcerated, or those in refugee camps is socially assessed.
32. Methodologies for calculating the number of deaths of elderly nursing home residents are inconsistent, as some sources consider only people who have died in the nursing home, while others also consider those who have died in the hospital, but were residents of a nursing home. See https://envejecimientoenred.es/una-explicacion-de-los-datos-de-fallecidos-por-coronavirus-en-centros-residenciales (retrieved 4 February 2022).
33. For Catalonia, see https://cadenaser00.epimg.net/descargables/2020/04/01/dbb972d767c4a3b28e2c866cc3e0cb65.pdf?int=masinfo (retrieved 4 February 2022).
34. E.g. https://www.isciii.es/QueHacemos/Servicios/VigilanciaSaludPublicaRENAVE/EnfermedadesTransmisibles/Paginas/InformesCOVID-19.aspx(retrieved 4 February 2022).
35. E.g. https://www.lavanguardia.com/internacional/20200412/48449391944/leyen-comision-europea-confinamiento-mayores-ancianos-coronavirus-covid-19.html; https://www.elperiodico.com/es/sanidad/20200417/sanidad-baraja-alargar-confinamiento-ancianos-verano-7931585 (retrieved 4 February 2022).
36. Inspired on the Valuation of Statistical Life procedure (Aldy and Viscusi 2007) and its actuarial cost–benefit analysis in which money (willingness to pay (WTP)) is traded for reduced mortality risk (see Fourcade (2009) for a critique) and on its implementation in public policy design and efficient resource allocation (EPA), QALY produces an abstract quantification of characteristics that are socially produced in order to justify a particular process of resource allocation.
37. https://www.eldiadevalladolid.com/Noticia/ZE05EBCED-9C0B-AE0F-BD597B67E9D21403/201902/Los-jubilados-vuelven-a-reclamar-unas-pensiones-dignas; https://paradigmamedia.org/otro-lunes-al-sol-en-valdeolleros-ecos-de-la-marea (retrieved 4 February 2022).
38. A recent calculation states that for every euro invested by the pensioner into the system, they get €1.74. The report by the Bank of Spain defines the distributive pension system as one where the participants invest during their working life through social contributions in order to get back a rent when they retire (Moraga and Ramos 2020: 1).
39. 'En effet, qu'est-ce que le racisme ? C'est, d'abord, le moyen d'introduire enfin, dans ce domaine de la vie que le pouvoir a pris en charge, une coupure : la coupure entre ce qui doit vivre et ce qui doit mourir. Dans

le continuum biologique de l'espèce humaine, l'apparition des races, la distinction des races, la hiérarchie des races, la qualification de certaines races comme bonnes et d'autres, au contraire, comme inférieures, tout ceci va être une manière de fragmenter ce champ du biologique que le pouvoir a pris en charge ; une manière de décaler, à l'intérieur de la population, des groupes les uns par rapport aux autres' (Foucault 1997 [1976]: 227). And Foucault adds: 'Autrement dit, la mise à mort, l'impératif de mort, n'est pas recevable, dans le système de bio-pouvoir, que s'il tend non pas à la victoire sur les adversaires politiques, mais à l'élimination du danger biologique et au renforcement, directement lié à cette élimination, de l'espèce elle-même, ou de la race' (ibid.: 228).

References

Abellán García, Antonio, Aceituno Nieto, María del Pilar and Diego Ramiro Fariñas. 2018. 'Estadísticas sobre residencias: distribución de centros y plazas residenciales por provincia. Datos de julio de 2017'. *Informes Envejecimiento en red*, nº 18. Retrieved 4 February 2022 from http://envejecimiento.csic.es/documentos/documentos/enred-estadisticasresidencias2017.pdf.
———. 2019. 'Estadísticas sobre residencias: distribución de centros y plazas residenciales por provincia. Datos de abril de 2019'. *Informes Envejecimiento en red*, nº 24. Retrieved 4 February 2022 from http://envejecimiento.csic.es/documentos/documentos/enred-estadisticasresidencias2019.pdf.
Alber, Erdmute, and Heike Drotbohm (eds). 2015. *Anthropological Perspectives on Care: Work, Kinship, and the Life-Course*. New York: Palgrave Macmillan.
Aldy, Joseph E. and W. Kip Viscusi. 2007. 'Age Differences in the Value of Statistical Life: Revealed Preference Evidence', *Review of Environmental Economics and Policy* 1(2): 241–60.
Andreotti, Alberta, Marisol García, Aitor Gómez, Pedro Hespanha, Yuri Kazepov and Enzo Mingione. 2001. 'Does a Southern European Model Exist?', *Journal of European Area Studies* 9(1): 43–62.
Banco de España. 2017. *Guía de acceso a la hipoteca inversa. Segunda Edición*. Madrid: Banco de España.
Bauman, Zygmunt. 2004. *Wasted Lives: Modernity and Its Outcasts*. Cambridge: Polity Press.
BOE (Boletín Oficial del Estado). 2006. Ley 39/2006, de 14 de diciembre, de Promoción de la Autonomía Personal y Atención a las personas en situación de dependencia. BOE núm. 299, de 15 de diciembre de 2006, Referencia: BOE-A-2006-21990.
———. 2007a. Ley 41/2007, de 7 de diciembre, por la que se modifica la Ley 2/1981, de 25 de marzo, de Regulación del Mercado Hipotecario y otras normas del sistema hipotecario y financiero, de regulación de las

hipotecas inversas y el seguro de dependencia y por la que se establece determinada norma tributaria. BOE núm. 294, de 8 de diciembre de 2007, Referencia: BOE-A-2007-21086.

———. 2007b. Real Decreto 504/2007, de 20 de abril, por el que se aprueba el baremo de valoración de la situación de dependencia establecido por la Ley 39/2006, de 14 de diciembre, de promoción de la autonomía personal y atención a las personas en situación de dependencia. BOE núm. 96, de 21 de abril de 2007, Referencia: BOE-A-2007-8350.

———. 2011a. Real Decreto 174/2011, de 11 de febrero, por el que se aprueba el baremo de valoración de la situación de dependencia establecido por la Ley 39/2006, de 14 de diciembre, de Promoción de la Autonomía Personal y Atención a las personas en situación de dependencia. BOE núm. 42, de 18 de febrero de 2011, Referencia: BOE-A-2011-3174.

———. 2011b. Reforma del artículo 135 de la Constitución Española, de 27 de septiembre de 2011. BOE núm. 233, de 27 de septiembre de 2011, Referencia: BOE-A-2011-15210.

———. 2012. Real Decreto-ley 20/2012, de 13 de julio, de medidas para garantizar la estabilidad presupuestaria y de fomento de la competitividad. BOE núm. 168, de 14 de julio de 2012, Referencia: BOE-A-2012-9364.

Boltanski, Luc, and Laurent Thévenot. 1991. *De la justification : les économies de la grandeur*. Paris: Gallimard.

Bourgeois, Léon. 1896. *Solidarité*. Paris: Armand Colin. Retrieved 4 February 2022 from http://classiques.uqac.ca/classiques/bourgeois_leon/solidarite/solidarite.html.

Bryan, Dick, and Mike Rafferty. 2014. 'Political Economy and Housing in the Twenty-First Century: From Mobile Homes to Liquid Housing?', *Housing, Theory and Society* 31(4): 404–12.

Calpena, Mar, Ana Sharife, José Luis Marín, Xosé Manuel Pereiro, Gorka Castillo and Alberto García Moyano. 2020. 'Aparcamientos de ancianos S.A.', *Ctxt*, 29 March. Retrieved 4 February 2022 from https://ctxt.es/es/20200302/Politica/31527/residencias-de-ancianos-privatizacion-coronavirus-fondos-buitre.htm.

Carlin, John. 2020. '¿Toca un referendum?', *La Vanguardia*, 24 May. Retrieved 4 February 2022 from https://www.lavanguardia.com/opinion/20200524/481361702765/coronavirus-covid-esescalada-espana-espana.html.

Cervera Macià, Montserrat, José A. Herce San Miguel, Guillem López Casanovas, Gregorio Rodríguez Cabrero and Simón Sosvilla Rivero. 2009. 'Informe final del grupo de expertos para la evaluación del desarrollo y efectiva aplicación de la Ley 39/2006 14 de diciembre de promoción de la autonomía personal y atención a las personas en situación de dependencia', *IMSERSO*, September. Retrieved 4 February 2022 from https://www.serviciossocialescantabria.org/uploads/documentos%20e%20informes/informe_SAAD_GrupoExpertos.pdf.

Coombs, Jessica. 2014. 'Scamming the Elderly: An Increased Susceptibility to Financial Exploitation within and outside of the Family', *Albany Government Law Review* 7(1): 243–66.
Crisp, Roger. 1989. 'Deciding Who Will Die: QALYS and Political Theory', *Politics* 9(1): 31–35.
De Montalvo Jääskeläinen, Federico, et al. 2020. 'Informe del comité de bioética de España sobre los aspectos bioéticos de la priorización de recursos sanitarios en el contexto de la crisis del coronavirus', Comité de Bioética de España. 25 March. Retrieved 4 February 2022 from http://assets.comitedebioetica.es/files/documentacion/Informe%20CBE-%20Priorizacion%20de%20recursos%20sanitarios-coronavirus%20CBE.pdf.
Denning, Michael. 2010. 'Wageless Life', *New Left Review* 66: 79–97.
Dizy Menéndez, Dolores, Isabel de la Torre Prados, Olga Ruiz Cañete, Marta Fernández Moreno, Luis Ayuso Sánchez, Luciano Miguel García and Jesús Rogero García. 2010. *Dependencia y familia: una perspectiva socio-económica.* Madrid: IMSERSO.
Envejecimiento en Red. 2014. 'Estadísticas sobre residencias: distribución de centros y plazas residenciales por provincia. Datos de diciembre de 2013'. *Informes en Red*, nº 7. Retrieved 4 February 2022 from http://envejecimiento.csic.es/documentos/documentos/enred-estadisticasresidencias2013.pdf.
———. 2015. 'Estadísticas sobre residencias: distribución de centros y plazas residenciales por provincia. Datos de junio de 2015'. *Informes en Red*, nº 13. Retrieved 4 February 2022 from http://envejecimiento.csic.es/documentos/documentos/enred-estadisticasresidencias2015.pdf.
Esping-Andersen, Gosta. 1990. *The Three Worlds of Welfare Capitalism.* Princeton: Princeton University Press.
Esquerdo, Maribel, et al. 2020. 'Recomanacions per suport a les decisions de limitació d'esforç terapèutic (LET) per pacients amb sospita de covid-19 i insuficiència respiratòria aguda (IRA) hipoxèmica'. Salut / Emergències Mèdiques, Generalitat de Catalunya, 23 March.
European Commission. 2010. 'Green Paper: Towards Adequate, Sustainable and Safe European Pension Systems', 7 July. Retrieved 4 February 2022 from http://ec.europa.eu/social/main.jsp?langId=en&catId=89&newsId=839&furtherNews=yes>.
———. 2012a. 'White Paper: An Agenda for Adequate, Safe and Sustainable Pensions', 16 February. Retrieved 4 February 2022 from http://eur-lex.europa.eu/LexUriServ/LexUriServ.do?uri=COM:2012:0055:FIN:EN:PDF.
———. 2012b. 'Spain: Memorandum of Understanding of Financial Sector Policy Conditionality'. Retrieved 4 February 2022 from https://ec.europa.eu/economy_finance/eu_borrower/mou/2012-07-20-spain-mou_en.pdf.
FADSP (Federación de Asociaciones para la Defensa de la Sanidad Pública). 2017. 'La privatización sanitaria de las comunidades autónomas 2017'. *FADSP 4º Informe*, nº 151, June.

Fassin, Didier. 2009. 'Another Politics of Life Is Possible', *Theory, Culture & Society* 26(5): 44–60.
———. 2016. 'The Value of Life and the Worth of Lives', in Veena Das and Clara Han (eds), *Living and Dying in the Contemporary World*. Berkeley: University of California Press, pp. 770–83.
———. 2018. *Life: A Critical User's Manual*. Cambridge: Polity Press.
Fenge, Lee-Ann, and Sally Lee. 2018. 'Understanding the Risks of Financial Scams as Part of Elder Abuse Prevention', *British Journal of Social Work* 48(4): 906–23.
Fernández-Ballesteros, Rocío. 2020. 'Covid-19: ¿Ha habido discriminación en función de la edad?', *The Conversation*, 21 June. Retrieved 4 February 2022 from https://theconversation.com/covid-19-ha-habido-discriminacion-en-funcion-de-la-edad-140982.
Ferrera, Maurizio. 1996. 'The "Southern Model" of Welfare in Social Europe', *Journal of European Social Policy* 6(1): 17–37.
Foucault, Michel. 1997 [1976]. *Il faut defender la société. Cours au Collège de France, 1976*. Paris: Gallimard/Seuil.
Fourcade, Marion. 2009. 'The Political Valuation of Life', *Regulation & Governance* 3: 291–97.
———. 2016. 'Ordinalization', *Sociological Theory* 34(3): 175–95.
Fourcade, Marion, and Kieran Healy. 2017. 'Categories All the Way Down', *Historical Social Research* 42(1): 286–96.
Fraser, Nancy. 2014. 'Behind Marx's Hidden Abode: For an Expanded Conception of Capitalism', *New Left Review* 86: 55–72.
———. 2018. 'Roepke Lecture in Economic Geography – From Exploitation to Expropriation: Historic Geographies of Racialized Capitalism', *Economic Geography* 94(1): 1–17.
García-Garnica, María del Carmen. 2013. 'The Regulation of Reverse Mortgages in Spain as a Financial Instrument to Contribute to the Support of Dependent Persons', *Journal of International Aging Law & Policy* 6(1): 50–76.
García-Llana, Helena, et al. 2020. 'Recomendaciones del comité de ética para la asistencia sanitaria (CEAS) para la toma de decisiones en unidades de cuidados intensivos (UCI) durante la pandemia del Covid-19', Salud Madrid – Hospital Universitario La Paz – Centro de Ética Asistencial, 22 March.
Gidwani, Vinay, and Anant Maringanti. 2016. 'The Waste-Value Dialectic: Lumpen Urbanization in Contemporary India', *Comparative Studies of South Asia, Africa and the Middle East* 36(1): 112–33.
Gilmore, Ruth Wilson. 2002. 'Race and Globalization', in Ron Johnston, Peter J. Taylor and Michael J. Watts (eds), *Geographies of Global Change: Remapping the World*. Oxford: Blackwell, pp. 261–73.
Ginsburg, Faye, and Rayna Rapp. 2016. '"Not Dead Yet": Changing Disability Imaginaries in the Twenty-First Century', in Veena Das and Clara Han (eds), *Living and Dying in the Contemporary World*. Berkeley: University of California Press, pp. 525–41.

Greenacre, Mathew, and Katherine Fleshner. 2017. 'Distributive Justice in Disaster Triage', *University of Western Ontario Medical Journal (UWOMJ)* 86(1): 35–37.
Guyer, Jane I. 2004. *Marginal Gains: Monetary Transactions in Atlantic Africa*. Chicago: University of Chicago Press.
Harris, John. 1987. 'QALYfying the Value of Life', *Journal of Medical Ethics* 13: 117–23.
———. 1988. 'More and Better Justice', *Royal Institute of Philosophy* 23: 75–96.
———. 1991. 'Unprincipled QALYs: A Response to Cubbon', *Journal of Medical Ethics* 17: 185–88.
Harvey, David. 1999. *The Limits to Capital*. London: Verso.
———. 2003. *The New Imperialism*. Oxford: Oxford University Press.
Hearn, James D. 2013. 'Social Utility and Pandemic Influenza Triage', *Medicine and Law* 32(2): 177–90.
Hernández de Cos, Pablo, Juan Francisco Jimeno, and Roberto Ramos. 2017. *El sistema público de pensiones en España: situación actual, retos y alternativas de reforma. Documentos Ocasionales*, N.º 1701. Madrid: Banco de España.
Higginson, Irene J., and Alison J. Carr. 2001. 'Measuring Quality of Life: Using Quality of Life Measures in the Clinical Setting', *British Medical Journal* 322: 1297–300.
IMSERSO. 2017. 'Informe de la comisión para el análisis de la situación actual del sistema de la dependencia, de su sostenibilidad y de los actuales mecanismos de financiación, para evaluar su adecuación a las necesidades asociadas a la dependencia', 6 October. Retrieved 4 February 2022 from https://dependencia.info/imagenes/informe-comision-analisis-dependencia.pdf.
Jiménez, Sergi, and Analia Viola. 2019. 'Observatorio de la dependencia. Tercer Informe, Noviembre 2019', *Estudios sobre la economía Española 2019/42*, FEDEA, Madrid.
Lapavitsas, Costas. 2009. 'Financialised Capitalism: Crisis and Financial Expropriation', *Historical Materialism* 17: 114–48.
Le Lann, Yann. 2010. 'La retraite, un patrimoine?', *Genèses* 80: 70–89.
Le Lann, Yann, and Benjamin Lemoine. 2012. 'Les comptes des générations. Les valeurs du futur et la transformation de l'État social', *Actes de la Recherche en Sciences Sociales* 194(4): 62–77.
Li, Tania M. 2009. 'To Make Live or Let Die? Rural Dispossession and the Protection of Surplus Populations', *Antipode* 41(1): 66–93.
López, Isidro, and Emmanuel Rodríguez. 2011. 'The Spanish Model', *New Left Review* 69(3): 5–29.
López Hernández, Isidro, and Emmanuel Rodríguez López. 2010. *Fin de Ciclo Financiarización, Territorio y Sociedad de Propietarios en la Onda Larga del Capitalismo Hispano (1959–2010)*. Madrid: Traficantes de Sueños.

Manzano Ramírez, Alberto, et al. 2020. 'Recomendaciones éticas para la toma de decisiones en la situación excepcional de crisis por pandemia Covid-19 en las Unidades de Cuidados intensivos – Cuidados Críticos', Osakidetzia-Servicio Vasco de Salud, 23 March. Retrieved 4 February 2022 from https://www.cmb.eus/posicionamiento-del-colegio/apoyo-colegio-medicos-bizkaia-al-documento-consenso-grupo-referentes-uci-cuidados-criticos-osakidetza-3.

Marx, Karl. 1999 [1867]. *Capital: A Critique of Political Economy. Volume I.* Online Version: Marx/Engels Internet Archive. Retrieved 4 February 2022 from https://www.marxists.org/archive/marx/works/1867-c1/.

Melamed, Jodi. 2015. 'Racial Capitalism', *Critical Ethnic Studies* 1(1): 76–85.

Merry, Sally Engel. 2011. 'Measuring the World: Indicators, Human Rights, and Global Governance', *Current Anthropology* 52(3): 83–95.

Ministerio de Trabajo, Migraciones y Seguridad Social. 2018. *Seguridad Social. Presupuestos. Ejercicio 2018. Informe Económico-Financiero.*

Moraga, María, and Roberto Ramos. 2020. 'Una estimación del rendimiento financiero del Sistema de Pensiones', *Boletín Económico* 3/2020: 1–12.

Muniesa, Fabian, et al. 2017. *Capitalization: A Cultural Guide.* Paris: Presse des Mines.

Mur de Víu, Carlos. 2020. Protocolo de coordinación a pacientes institucionalizados en centros residenciales de la Comunidad de Madrid durante el periodo epidémico ocasionado por el Covid-19', DG Coordinación Sociosanitaria, Comunidad de Madrid, 18 March. Retrieved 4 February 2022 from https://www.losgenoveses.net/Personajes%20Populares/Diaz%20Ayuso,%20Isabel/diazayuso%20y%20el%20coronavirus/ayusoresidencias/protocolos/03.%20Protocolo-de-Mur-Version-3.24.03.20.pdf.

Narotzky, Susana. 2014. 'Structures without Soul and Immediate Struggles: Rethinking Militant Particularism in Contemporary Spain', in Sharryn Kasmir and August Carbonella (eds), *Blood and Fire: Toward a New Anthropology of Labour.* New York: Berghahn Books, pp. 167–202.

———. 2015. 'The Organic Intellectual and the Production of Class in Spain', in James G. Carrier and Don Kalb (eds), *Anthropologies of Class: Power, Practice and Inequality.* Cambridge: Cambridge University Press, pp. 125–64.

———. 2016. 'Between Inequality and Injustice: Dignity as a Motive for Mobilization during the Crisis', *History and Anthropology* 27(1): 74–92.

———. (ed.). 2020. *Grassroots Economies: Living with Austerity in Southern Europe.* London: Pluto Press.

Narotzky, Susana, and Antonio Maria Pusceddu. 2020. 'Social Reproduction in Times of Crisis: Inter-generational Tensions in Southern Europe', in Susana Narotzky (ed.), *Grassroots Economies: Living with Austerity in Southern Europe.* London: Pluto Press, pp. 143–73.

Organización Médica Colegial de España. 2020. 'Informe de la Comisión Central de Deontología en relación a la priorización de las decisiones sobre los enfermos en estado crítico en una catástrofe sanitaria', 23 March. Retrieved 4 February 2022 from https://www.cgcom.es/sites/default/files/u183/coronavirus-_n.p._comision_central_de_deontologia_en_relacion_a_la_priorizacion_de_las_decisiones_sobre_los_enfermos_23_03_20.pdf.

Ortiz, Carlos E., Charles A. Stone and Anne Zissu. 2013. 'When Do Securitized Reverse Mortgages Become Liabilities', *Journal of Structured Finance* 19(1): 57–64.

Pulido, Laura. 2016. 'Flint, Environmental Racism, and Racial Capitalism', *Capitalism Nature Socialism* 27(3): 1–16.

RENAVE (Red Nacional de Vigilancia Epidemiológica, Instituto de Salud Carlos III). 2020. 'Informe 31', 14 May. Retrieved 4 February 2022 from https://www.isciii.es/QueHacemos/Servicios/VigilanciaSaludPublicaRENAVE/EnfermedadesTransmisibles/Documents/INFORMES/Informes%20COVID-19/Informe%20n%c2%ba%2031.%20Situaci%c3%b3n%20de%20COVID-19%20en%20Espa%c3%b1a%20a%2014%20de%20mayo%20de%202020.pdf.

Reurink, Arjan. 2018. 'Financial Fraud: A Literature Review', *Journal of Economic Surveys* 32(5): 1292–325.

Rubio Sanchíz, Olga, et al. 2020. 'Recomendaciones éticas para la toma de decisiones en la situación excepcional de crisis por pandemia covid-19 en las unidades de cuidados intensivos', Sociedad Española de Medicina Intensiva, Crítica y Unidades Coronarias (SEMICyUC), 19 March. Retrieved 4 February 2022 from https://semicyuc.org/wp-content/uploads/2020/03/%C3%89tica_SEMICYUC-COVID-19.pdf.

Saraceno, Chiara. 2016. 'Varieties of Familialism: Comparing Four Southern European and East Asian Welfare Regimes', *Journal of European Social Policy* 26(4): 314–26.

Secretaría de Estado de Derechos Sociales. 2020. 'Informe del grupo de trabajo COVID 19 y residencias', Versión final 24/11/2020, Ministerio de Derechos Sociales y Agenda 2030

Skeggs, Beverly, and Vik Loveday. 2012. 'Struggles for Value: Value Practices, Injustice, Judgment, Affect and the Idea of Class', *British Journal of Sociology* 63(3): 472–90.

Smith, Alwyn, Alan Maynard, Grimley J. Evans and John Harris. 1990. 'The Ethics of Resource Allocation', *Journal of Epidemiology and Community Health* 44: 187–90.

Smith, Gavin A. 2011. 'Selective Hegemony and Beyond – Populations with "No Productive Function": A Framework for Enquiry', *Identities* 18: 2–38.

Smith, Neil. 2017. 'The Concepts of Devaluation, Valorization and Depreciation in Marx: Toward a Clarification', *Human Geography* 10(1): 4–19.

Stiglitz, Joseph, Amartya Sen and Jean-Paul Fitoussi. 2009. 'The Measurement of Economic Performance and Social Progress Revisited', Document de travail de l'OFCE, *OFCE* n° 2009-33.

Tabery, James, Charles W. Mackett and the University of Pittsburgh Medical Center Pandemic Influenza Task Force's Triage Review Board. 2008. 'Ethics of Triage in the Event of an Influenza Pandemic', *Disaster Med Public Health Preparedness* 2(2): 114–18.

Timmons, J. Douglas, and Ausra Naujokaite. 2011. 'Reverse Mortgages: Should the Elderly and US Taxpayers Beware?', *Real Estate Issues* 36(1): 46–55.

Tortosa Chuliá, Mª Ángeles, Amadeo Fuenmayor Fernández, and Rafael Granell Pérez. 2017. 'Instrumentos de financiación y gestión en residencias de personas mayores'. *Informes Envejecimiento en red*, n° 16. Retrieved 4 February 2022 from http://envejecimiento.csic.es/documentos/documentos/enred-finanresi-16.pdf.

Vergano, Marco, et al. 2020. 'Raccomandazioni di etica clinica per l'ammissione a trattamenti intensivi e per la loro sospensione, in condizioni eccezionali di squilibrio tra necessità e risorse disponibili. SIAARTI, Pubblicato il 06.03.2020'. Retrieved 4 February 2022 from https://www.google.com/url?sa=t&rct=j&q=&esrc=s&source=web&cd=&cad=rja&uact=8&ved=2ahUKEwiJl4qT8rryAhVKyYUKHeJOBmwQFnoECAIQAQ&url=https%3A%2F%2Fwww.quotidianosanita.it%2Fallegati%2Fallegato2675063.pdf&usg=AOvVaw3hI8jItKdTiMBMrQ9vdw1l.

Vidal Domínguez, MªJesús, et al. 2017. *Informe 2016. Las personas mayores en España. Datos estadísticos estatales y por Comunidades Autónomas*. Madrid: Ministerio de Sanidad, Servicios Sociales e Igualdad, IMSERSO.

Williams, Alan. 2012 [1985]. 'The Value of QALYS', in Stephen Holland (ed.), *Arguing about Bioethics*. London: Routledge, pp. 423–27.

Williams, Alan, and J. Grimley Evans. 2012. 'The Rationing Debate: Rationing Health Care by Age', in Stephen Holland (ed.), *Arguing about Bioethics*. Abingdon: Routledge, pp. 439–46.

Williamson, Odette. 2000. 'Protecting Elderly Homeowners from Predatory Mortgage Lenders', *Clearinghouse Review* 34(5–6): 297–310.

Zhai, David H. 2000. 'Reverse Mortgage Securitizations: Understanding and Gauging the Risks. Special Report', *Moody's Investors Service*, 23 June.

2

Must the Tired and Poor 'Stand on Their Own Two Feet'?

Tools for Analysing How Migrants' Deservingness Is Reckoned

Sarah S. Willen and Jennifer Cook

> MARTIN: Would you also agree that Emma Lazarus' words etched on the Statue of Liberty – give me your tired, your poor – are also part of the American ethos?
> CUCCINELLI: They certainly are – give me your tired and your poor who can stand on their own two feet and who will not become a public charge. That plaque was put on the Statue of Liberty at almost the same time as the first public charge law was passed – very interesting timing.
> MARTIN: Although you mention – the American dream is built on this idea that this is a place where you can come and build –
> CUCCINELLI: It's part of it.
> MARTIN: – a life.
> CUCCINELLI: Yeah, it's part of it.

In the late summer of 2019, Ken Cuccinelli, acting director of the United States Citizenship and Immigration Service in the Trump administration, decided on the fly to rewrite the iconic words of Emma Lazarus, etched onto the base of the Statue of Liberty, during an interview with National Public Radio host Rachel Martin.[1] Lazarus' poem, 'The New Colossus', was written in 1883 as part of a campaign to raise funds for the statue's pedestal. The poem was moving, and the campaign was successful. Cuccinelli's comments, offered in defence of the administration's proposal to deny a path to citizenship for legal immigrants who drew on public benefits, pervert the sonnet's fundamental thrust:

> Not like the brazen giant of Greek fame,
> With conquering limbs astride from land to land;
> Here at our sea-washed, sunset gates shall stand
> A mighty woman with a torch, whose flame
> Is the imprisoned lightning, and her name
> Mother of Exiles. From her beacon-hand
> Glows world-wide welcome; her mild eyes command
> The air-bridged harbor that twin cities frame.
> 'Keep, ancient lands, your storied pomp!' cries she
> With silent lips. 'Give me your tired, your poor,
> Your huddled masses yearning to breathe free,
> The wretched refuse of your teeming shore.
> Send these, the homeless, tempest-tost to me,
> I lift my lamp beside the golden door!'

For Lazarus and those who helped fund the 'beacon-hand' of 'imprisoned lightning' that 'glows world-wide welcome', migrants' yearning required little explanation. For this 'Mother of Exiles', all seeking refuge deserve entry through the United States' 'golden door'. Yet Cuccinelli, along with the administration he served and the voters who put Trump in the White House, saw things otherwise. From their standpoint, only immigrants who can support themselves financially are deserving of American beneficence. He viewed this not as a reinterpretation, let alone a gross misconstrual, of the historic symbolism of the Statue of Liberty and 'The New Colossus'; rather, he claimed that his interpretation – and not the more capacious interpretation circulating globally in art, media and politics for well over a century – reflected the genuine 'American ethos'.

Cuccinelli is of course wrong, but that is not our point in this chapter. Rather, our aim is to show that social scientists' capacity to understand – and intervene in – debates about migration and, in particular, about migrants' health will depend on our ability to identify, uncover and analyse the values and presumptions they entail – in other words, our ability to understand how 'deservingness' is reckoned by local actors with their own particular values, commitments and agendas. To this end, we aim to operationalize the concept of 'health-related deservingness' (Willen 2012a, 2012b) and illuminate its significance in debates about migration and health in diverse settings and at multiple levels of analysis (Bourgois et al. 2017; Snell-Rood and Carpenter-Song 2018; Viladrich 2019).[2]

The significance of this task could not be starker or clearer than it is now, as this volume goes to press with a global pandemic still raging around us. Think, for instance, of those migrants to the United States, many of whom Cuccinelli would no doubt have spurned, who were quickly remoralized as 'essential workers'. In the US economy, some high-paid, high-status roles have long been viewed as more or less unquestionably 'essential' to society's functioning – doctors, for instance. But in pandemic times, the calculus shifted and a vast new cadre of 'essential workers' found their social roles reappraised, among them hospital custodians and nursing home staff, delivery workers, farm workers and food production workers – many of them low-paid, low-status, often racialized and frequently migrants. Neither the nature of their work nor its intrinsic importance changed when the COVID-19 pandemic struck the United States in early 2020. And yet, at a moment's notice, these newly 'essential' workers were suddenly recast as valued and deserving – but deserving of what? Of brief spates of Friday evening pot-banging praise – or safe working conditions, adequate personal protective equipment included? Of laudatory media coverage – or of a living wage, including health insurance and retirement benefits?

In this chapter, as in this volume more broadly, we explore how shifting 'moral grammars and vocabularies' (see Streinzer and Tošić, Introduction to this volume) such as these are deployed to situate people – or resituate them – within sociomoral space. How do such grammars and vocabularies emerge and become settled as hegemonic forms of common sense? How, after becoming stabilized in ideological and discursive regimes, might such grammars and vocabularies become unsettled, transformed, perhaps even inverted? Furthermore, how are such moral regimes experienced, sensed and embodied? These are among the vital questions at the centre of this collection, and they inform our project in this chapter.

We begin by considering how the notion of deservingness has been conceptualized in recent social science scholarship, where migrants form but one among many groups whose deservingness regularly comes into question. We then offer a framework for analysing deservingness debates, with a particular focus on those related to migrants' health. The framework comprises three core elements: the *stakeholders* involved, the *contexts* in which such debates take place and the *evaluative criteria* employed. In the final section, we put this framework into action by analysing health-related deservingness debates in three migration settings: one in North America, another in Western Europe and a third in the Middle East. Overall, we aim to provide strong scaffolding for a wide-ranging, interdisciplinary enquiry into both how health-related deservingness is reckoned and how local deservingness assessments can affect the health of individuals and the communities in which they live.

Conceptualizing Deservingness

In an important sense, deservingness can be understood as the flip side of rights. Whereas rights claims are expressed in a formal juridical discourse that presumes fundamental equality before the law, deservingness claims are articulated in a vernacular moral register that is situationally specific and context dependent. In other words, deservingness debates often have less to do with empirical evidence than with competing everyday responses to normative questions.

These vernacular responses generally mix subjective attitudes and presumptions with taken-for-granted truths regarded as collective 'common sense'. For instance, a debate might revolve around the question of 'Who should have access to this particular healthcare service?' or 'Should this person receive financial support in accessing this form of healthcare?' During the COVID-19 pandemic, debates have raged around precisely such questions of resource allocation. Now that effective vaccines exist, new debates have emerged, especially around gaping disparities in access between the Global South and the Global North. In many instances, the vernacular reasoning deployed in such debates is but loosely tethered to empirical realities. Often it carries a powerful emotional charge.

In a moment of public health crisis, normative and policy questions demand carefully reasoned answers. Yet in this chapter, as in this volume, our aim is not normative but ethnographic. Our common project is an exercise in historically grounded critical scholarship – but it is also, at least in part, an attempt to nuance and complicate precisely those debates that will become heightened as state, civil society and individual stakeholders the world over grapple with the ethico-moral struggles that define this historical moment, among them the erosion of the post-Second World War order, the imposition of austerity regimes, the arrival of large refugee populations from the Global South (and, as this chapter goes to press, from war-torn Ukraine) in Global North destinations, and increasing pressure to confront the violent lives and afterlives of colonial conquest and racist domination.

How do rights claims and deservingness assessments differ? Both are social constructions (Schneider and Ingram 2005), but they diverge in key respects. First, unlike rights discourses, which presume blindness to individual particularities, deservingness assessments are relational. One assesses others' relative deservingness on the basis of two key factors: an implicit sense of one's own deservingness and a sense of social connection to those whose deservingness is in question.

Second, deservingness assessments are conditional on presumed or actual features of those whose deservingness is in question – intrinsic or extrinsic, mutable or immutable – regardless of their salience. In short, rights ostensibly have universal significance, even when they are not universally enjoyed in practice, whereas deservingness is always reckoned in conditional, and relational, terms.

Third, conceptions of deservingness are always grounded in a particular social and political context. Fourth, deservingness assessments are syncretic; they are simultaneously grounded in multiple sources of moral insight and experience. For instance, they may reflect an amalgamation of professional expertise, 'common sense' and personal beliefs and experiences. Fifth, they are infused with affect, or emotion. Sixth, they are mutable; they are liable to shift and change in response to new knowledge and evolving circumstances. Finally – and perhaps self-evidently – deservingness assessments are implicit, unspoken and invisible.

In short, vernacular ways of reckoning deservingness in general, and health-related deservingness in particular, involve complex forms of moral reasoning. The impact of such assessments is neither arcane nor trivial. At the local and national levels, questions of 'who deserves what' are pivotal, if implicit, throughout the political process. They shape the discourse and practice of legislators and policy-makers (Chock 1991; Heyman 1998; Guetzkow 2010), bureaucrats and social workers responsible for the distribution of social welfare benefits (Blomberg et al. 2017; de Wilde 2017; van Oorschot et al. 2017; Fassin 2012), healthcare institutions (Horton 2004; Wailoo et al. 2006), clinicians (Marrow 2011; Holmes 2012; Vanthuyne et al. 2013; Huschke 2014), the media (Yoo 2002, 2008) and ordinary citizens (Gilens 1999; Katz 1989; Will 1993). At an international level, such questions challenge us to confront the profound health implications of contemporary patterns of global inequality.

Deservingness and Welfare

Although the impact and salience of vernacular deservingness assessments have garnered attention in multiple fields, the most robust body of research on deservingness to date continues to take welfare as its focus. Some social scientists have sought to operationalize deservingness in terms of measurable variables or normative criteria (de Swaan 1988; Feather 1999; van Oorschot 2000, 2006; Appelbaum 2001; Appelbaum et al. 2003). Others have explored the impact on deservingness assessments of recipient characteristics like racial or ethnic background (Gilens 1999; Morgen and Maskovsky 2003; Horton 2004; Yoo 2008; Guetzkow 2010; Kootstra 2016); the social positioning, demographic characteristics or emotional state of deservingness 'evaluators' (Olsen et al. 2003; Verkuyten 2004); level of responsibility for, or degree of control over, the circumstances producing a need for support (de Swaan 1988; Will 1993; van Oorschot 2000; Appelbaum 2001; Appelbaum et al. 2003; Scott 2008); and real or presumed associations with criminality (Morgen and Maskovsky 2003; Olsen et al. 2003). Other scholars have examined the impact of context, including economic factors such as unemployment levels (Blekesaune and Quadagno 2003), as well as national and personal ideological frameworks (van Oorschot 2000). Additional avenues of enquiry include the impact of neoliberal influences on welfare and healthcare policy and practice (Rylko-Bauer and Farmer 2002; Horton 2004; Bambra and Smith 2010; Guetzkow 2010) and the impact of the media on public perception (Gollust et al. 2010; Lepianka 2017; van Doorn and Bos 2017; van Oorschot et al. 2017; Viladrich 2019). Still other influential studies examine how constructions of 'undeservingness' ignore structural inequalities and reproduce negative, often racialized stereotypes (Katz 1989; Gilens 1999; Yoo 2008). In general, deservingness assessments vary based on perceptions of social proximity between the subjects of debate and those rendering their evaluations (Newton 2005; Grove and Zwi 2006).

More recent areas of enquiry include the role of implicit attitudes (de Vries 2017) and incorrect beliefs on deservingness perceptions (Geiger 2017) and deservingness assessments of the rich (Ragusa 2017; Sadin 2017). Finally, an important new area of enquiry among both quantitative and qualitative social scientists involves the impact of sociopolitical changes – including mass migration, the spread of neoliberal ideas of responsible subjecthood, and the imposition of austerity policies in the wake of economic crisis (Roosma and Jeene 2017; Streinzer and Tošić, Introduction to this volume).

While these new empirical developments are noteworthy, what remains absent from much of the current work on deservingness is precisely the sort of nuanced, textured ethnographic insight advanced by the present collection.

Health-Related Deservingness

In contrast to this robust welfare literature, the question of how deservingness is reckoned in the health domain is a relatively new area of enquiry (see e.g. Scott 2008; Gollust and Lynch 2010; Gollust et al. 2010; Lynch and Gollust 2010). This is a complex matter of great significance, especially in an era of neoliberal pressures towards healthcare privatization and commoditization, soaring healthcare costs, growing health disparities both within countries and between rich and poor regions, and massive waves of unregulated migration over land and sea. In countries with historically strong commitments to universal healthcare and social service protections, existing rights and entitlements are increasingly imperilled (Larchanché 2012).

Important research questions abound: how do divergent stakeholders – the privileged and the disadvantaged, policy-makers and voters, clinicians and patients – reckon health-related deservingness? What criteria influence deservingness assessments and what role does ideology play? Who is responsible for providing healthcare and how should costs be covered? How do moral questions of deservingness intersect with juridical questions of rights? How do they relate to questions of 'fairness' (Daniels 2008; Lynch and Gollust 2010)? When are inclusive deservingness assessments purely aspirational and when are they grounded in precedent, policy or law?

In pursuing these questions, it is important to remember that health involves far more than just the presence or absence of disease or injury – and, moreover, more than just access to curative care. Equally important, if not more so, are the social determinants of good health: the upstream factors and structural conditions that predispose certain individuals and communities to be healthy in the first place (WHO Commission on Social Determinants of Health 2008). For example, given the 'structural vulnerability' (Quesada et al. 2011) many migrants endure, their access to social determinants may be as limited as their access to curative care (Castañeda et al. 2015). Even under the best of circumstances, structural vulnerability renders many migrants more vulnerable, and less capable of addressing their health needs, than their citizen counterparts. This is especially true during the COVID-19 pandemic, when mobile and migrant populations – and especially those racialized to their discursive and ideological detriment – face heightened rates not only of exposure to the novel coronavirus, but also of dying as a result (Bowleg 2020; Devakumar et al. 2020; Gee et al. 2020; Hardeman et al. 2020; Maness et al. 2020; Orcutt et al. 2020). Failure to recognize these interlocking forms of disadvantage can perpetuate the tacit politics of blame that lead many stakeholders to deem migrants undeserving.

Not surprisingly, migrant health has become a central theme in the emerging literature on health-related deservingness. Scholars have asked, for instance: how do local and national policies, especially in the domains of immigration and health, affect local conceptions of deservingness (Marrow 2011; Haas 2012; Oliverio-Lauderdale 2014; Marrow and Joseph 2015)? How do healthcare professionals' unspoken moral assumptions about their migrant patients influence clinical interactions (Marrow 2011; Holmes 2012; Larchanché 2012; Vanthuyne et al. 2013; Holmes et al. 2020)? How do migrant health advocates deploy notions of human rights, humanitarianism and other 'idioms of social justice mobilization' (Willen 2011; Willen et al. 2017) in claiming migrants' deservingness, and with what effect (Gottlieb et al. 2012; Tiedje and Plevak 2014)? How is migrants' deservingness framed, and contested, in the public health literature (Viladrich 2012)? And what about migrants' perspectives? Do different migrant groups regard themselves as deserving of access to healthcare or of the social determinants of good health? How do others' negative assessments affect their lived experience (Chavez 2012; Larchanché 2012)? These are all crucial questions that demand further enquiry.

Health-Related Deservingness: A Framework for Analysis

'Deservingness debates' involve conversations, either in public or behind closed doors, in which divergent stakeholders express or enact competing views about whether a particular person or social group deserves a certain kind of attention, investment or care. Although professional considerations and empirical evidence may play a role, such debates frequently hinge on vernacular assumptions that rely less on empirical evidence than 'common-sense' knowledge and subjective moral commitments. Despite the pivotal role such assumptions play and their tangible effects, they tend to remain unspoken and implicit.

Elsewhere we have proposed that these vernacular forms of moral reasoning urgently require investigation – from multiple stakeholder and disciplinary perspectives, in different contexts and professional settings, and using a range of research methods (Willen 2012a). We develop this argument below. Our project is framed not by normative philosophical questions – for instance, about health and distributive justice – but rather by empirical social scientific questions: how are moral assessments and ethical decisions made in everyday social contexts? How do they find expression in particular forms of discourse and social practice? What sort of consequences do they effect?

Below we offer a model for investigating how different forms of vernacular moral reasoning inform local conversations about the kinds of health-related attention, investment and care migrants do or do not deserve, and on what grounds. To parse the assumptions implicated in such debates, three key considerations demand attention: the range of relevant stakeholders, the multiple layers of context in which debates unfold and the evaluative criteria stakeholders employ.

Stakeholders

The array of stakeholders engaged in local deservingness debates varies depending on the migrant group involved, the health resource in question, the domain in which a point of tension or contention arises, and the personal stakes for individual stakeholders. These may include policy-makers (elected and appointed), politicians, the media (journalists, pundits, etc.), advocacy groups, and members of the broader public in their capacities as citizens, voters and media consumers. In the health domain, other key stakeholders include not only healthcare providers (physicians, nurses, allied health professionals, etc.), but also public health professionals, clinical office staff, insurance administrators and other 'street-level bureaucrats' (Lipsky 1980) who serve important gatekeeping functions. Ethicists, including bioethicists and public health ethicists, may be stakeholders as well. Migrants are, of course, key stakeholders in all such debates. Yet their voices are often muted – or, more egregiously, ignored.

Although professional considerations influence many stakeholders' views, subjective commitments also play a crucial role. Politicians, for instance, are elected to represent their constituents, but their own moral values – and concern for their political futures – also play a role. Public health workers hold core professional commitments (for example, to make wise use of public resources or to follow scientific best practices), but also face political considerations and personal interests, some moral and some tactical (for example, to protect one's professional credibility or job security). In healthcare settings, administrative staff must juggle professional expectations, institutional mandates and personal views. For example, if a hospital's chief financial officer insists on upfront payment from undocumented patients, administrators may take it upon themselves to subject all patients they suspect to be undocumented – for instance, all patients with names that suggest Latinx heritage – to heightened scrutiny.

Clinicians, like administrators, are also beholden to professional, personal and political commitments, but they are bound by ethical codes that impose additional obligations as well (e.g. the Hippocratic Oath). Advocates, activists and private citizens are also important stakeholders in deservingness debates. They may be more open and explicit about their political and moral commitments than those acting in a professional role.

To date, scholarship on deservingness has tended to focus primarily on the views of relatively advantaged stakeholders – those with power, influence or, at the very least, a public voice. This, we contend, is insufficient. Instead, researchers need to investigate how deservingness is reckoned both in relation to and, furthermore, from the perspectives of those most directly affected: individuals and groups commonly represented as undeserving. Research on migrants' perspectives may reveal appreciable differences between their own ethical calculus and modes of moral reasoning, on the one hand, and those of other, nonmigrant stakeholders, on the other hand. Moreover, their views of their own and others' relative deservingness are likely to influence their care-seeking behaviour as well as their overall health and wellbeing (see e.g. Larchanché 2012).

Context

Context is another key element in deservingness debates. Four contextual domains are especially significant: history, law, politics and economics. Below we highlight a few considerations that arise in each, recognizing that these domains themselves overlap and entwine.

From a historical perspective, one might ask: how have past experiences – either negative (e.g. drought, famine, political turmoil and war) or positive (e.g. France's legacy as home of the droits de l'homme) – influenced current views of migrants and migration? Does a particular locale have its own history as a 'receiving' community, a 'sending' community – or perhaps both at different times? Has it historically been welcoming or restrictive towards migrants? How do views of current migrant populations compare with attitudes towards earlier arrivals and why?

The legal realm is extraordinarily complex in its own right. At the international level, to what relevant international treaties and conventions is a given country signatory, and how do those international commitments influence policy-making, advocacy efforts and public opinion? At the national level, who is and is not permitted either to enter the country or to immigrate, and under what conditions? How does national migration law influence public opinion regarding newcomers' opportunities, or lack of opportunities, for membership and social inclusion? How have migration laws changed over time?

The impact of political and economic context on local deservingness debates cannot be underestimated. In the political realm, to what degree is migration a local concern and in what respects? What role do political ideologies and other value systems (e.g. religion) play in framing local debate? How do such commitments inform the views of influential political parties? Vocal minorities? The courts? Advocacy and activist groups? Do migrants themselves play an active role in local political conversation? If not, what impedes their participation?

In economic terms, how is the local economy performing, and what economic role do migrants play? Are they regarded as a boon or a threat to the local economy? Are they viewed as a valued source of labour or unwelcome competitors for citizen-workers? Local public health and clinical care systems also demand consideration. What health services can migrants access, and who foots the bill? Are these systems overburdened – or perceived to be – and, if so, how are migrants' health needs conceptualized and discussed?

Evaluative Criteria

Finally, what evaluative criteria inform local debates about migrants' health-related deservingness? In reckoning migrants' relative deservingness, stakeholders often make presumptions about migrants' lives and life circumstances that mix collective 'common sense', personal attitudes and politicized forms of emotion. The connections between such presumptions and empirical realities may be tenuous at best. Van Oorschot (2000) suggests that five evaluative criteria, summarized using the acronym CARIN, inform deservingness assessments: control, attitude, reciprocity, identity and need (see also Williamson et al. 2021). Drawing inspiration from van Oorschot but taking migration as our specific focus, below we highlight five more specific considerations that shape local debates about who migrants are and what they do – or do not – deserve: migration motives, legal status, moral character, vulnerability and social proximity to members of the broader society. Although these characteristics figure in general assessments of migrants' deservingness, they are especially salient in reckoning their deservingness of health-related attention, investment or care.

Migration Motives

Migrants' presumed motives feature prominently in local deservingness debates. An especially bright line is assumed to distinguish 'economic migrants' (who ostensibly left their country to pursue economic opportunity) from 'forced migrants' (presumed to have fled violent conflict, political persecution or natural disaster). Although this distinction is typically presented as clear-cut and self-evident, realities are considerably more complex (see e.g. Yarris and Castañeda 2015). For instance, asylum seekers who have fled violence or oppression but fail to translate their experiences into bureaucratically legible categories will likely find their claims denied. Other migrants leave home fleeing poverty, including impoverishment resulting from climate change, only to find that their migration circumstances are not deemed worthy of recognition or status in their new countries of residence.

People tend to be viewed and treated in very different ways depending on their classification as either 'economic' or 'forced' migrants – categories that (often mistakenly) are presumed to be distinct. 'Forced' migrants generally are represented as unfortunate, faultless victims of circumstance who deserve society's attention and material support. This logic is often invoked to mobilize humanitarian and human rights commitments at the national and international levels. 'Economic' migrants, in contrast, are often assumed to have chosen freely to migrate and, on these grounds, are deemed responsible for their own fates.

This pattern of moral valuation can vary – for instance, when national policies themselves influence how particular groups' deservingness is reckoned. Policies that prohibit asylum seekers from working while their petitions are pending, for example, force them to rely on interim government support. As a result, migrants who would otherwise be regarded as faultless and hence deserving victims may be reimagined as a burden to society (Sales 2002; Watters 2007).

Legal Status

Presumptions about migrants' legal status also figure centrally in local deservingness debates. Although the very notion of legal status would seem to hinge on a straightforward distinction, such matters are often far from clear-cut. Deservingness debates rarely account for this complex fluidity.

There is, of course, nothing natural or self-evident about legal statuses; they are human creations designed to meet political demands. They are also varied, amenable to change and differentially enforced. A wide range of possible statuses exists both across migration settings and even within a single country. For instance, some residence visas permit study but forbid work, and some time-delimited work permits forbid permanent residence or family reunification. Migrants seeking asylum or refugee status may hold a temporary status valid only while their petitions are pending. And in countries that grant citizenship on the basis of *jus soli* (birthright citizenship), statuses may vary within a single household or family. Often, violating the terms of one's authorization can automatically trigger a loss of legal status and consequent slip into 'illegality'.

Yet legal status is more than just a juridical category; it is also morally charged, and different forms of status are imbued with different moral valences. Unauthorized border crossing, for instance, may be interpreted as evidence of immorality – or, worse still, of criminality. In either case, presumptions about legal status powerfully influence stakeholder assessments.

Moral Character

Debates about health-related deservingness often hinge on impressionistic judgements about multiple aspects of migrants' moral character. For instance, stakeholders may make assumptions about a migrant's or migrant community's economic productivity, personal responsibility, fulfilment of family obligations and associations with criminality. Are migrants seen as contributing to the economy, or to society, through their labour, whether skilled or unskilled? To pay taxes? To depend on welfare, social support or government programmes? Are they seen as willing to integrate into the broader society? Are their initial migration motives regarded as legitimate? On all of these counts, vernacular presumptions influence deservingness debates, even when they are contradicted by empirical evidence (Chauvin et al. 2013; Chauvin and Garcés-Mascareñas 2014).

The same holds true for family status. How are migrants' family configurations imagined in comparison to idealized notions of a 'normal' family? Are parents viewed as more morally upstanding, and hence more deserving, than single adults? Are mothers more deserving than fathers? Are parents who live with their children more deserving than those who have entrusted their children to the care of extended family members?

The element of 'criminality' is a complicated one, especially given the recent convergence of immigration enforcement efforts and criminal justice in what has been described as 'crimmigration law' (Stumpf 2006). When migrants with precarious legal status engage in informal or illicit activities as a survival strategy (for example, working or selling goods without a permit, or using other people's identification documents), their actions may be interpreted as signs of immorality and hence undeservingness. Associations between migrants and criminality, even when spurious, are often bandied about with the explicit goal of inflaming xenophobic sentiment.

Vulnerability

Presumptions of vulnerability also figure prominently in deservingness debates. Migrants considered especially vulnerable may be more likely to draw sympathy and, as a result, may be regarded as more deserving than those viewed as less vulnerable.

Various criteria are used to gauge migrants' vulnerability, including gender, sexual orientation or sexual identity, physical or mental disability, past experiences of victimization (e.g. status as a survivor of violent crime, domestic violence or sex trafficking), life stage and health status. Certain individuals – for instance, women, children, the elderly, the severely ill, people with disabilities and individuals with nonconforming gender or sexual identities – may be regarded as more vulnerable than other migrants and, on that basis, more deserving. However, depending on local context and relevant stakeholders' views, certain migrants' claims of vulnerability may be deemed suspect – for instance, because they fail to conform to social norms, are perceived as attempts to 'cheat the system' or bear some form of social stigma. In some cases, for instance, migrants living with HIV/AIDS have not been seen as deserving due to unfounded fears of disease transmission, or because of stereotypical associations with morally fraught issues of sexuality. The example of HIV reveals how evaluations of migrant morality and discussions of vulnerability can intersect in ways that affect deservingness assessments more broadly.

The relative visibility of one's source of vulnerability or affliction can also play a role in how deservingness is assessed. Sometimes a visible ailment (for example, a missing limb resulting from a landmine accident) is more likely to garner a sympathetic evaluation than a condition that is less visible (for example, mental illness). As a result, migrants who have suffered often feel pressure, whether implicit or explicit, to bare their afflictions and 'perform' vulnerability, even when doing so is embarrassing, humiliating and/or contrary to their own sense of agency.

Social Proximity

Perceived social proximity between migrant populations and citizens is another key criterion in local deservingness debates. Proximity may be reckoned in terms of ostensibly intrinsic features (e.g. race/ethnicity, language or religion) or extrinsic features (e.g. willingness to learn the local language, follow local gender norms or otherwise endeavour to integrate into the broader society). Presumptions of social proximity generally lead migrants regarded as more 'like us' to be deemed more deserving than others. On the other hand, in some contexts, stakeholders may invoke societal values like diversity or multiculturalism in an attempt to advocate for inclusiveness.

Assessments of social proximity are deeply influenced by local context. In relatively homogeneous societies, for instance, racial, ethnic, religious or cultural difference may be regarded as a threat to the collective. In countries with a long history of immigration, new migrants may be discursively aligned with older migrant groups with whom they share, or are presumed to share, key features. Aspects of local ideological, political and historical context can influence perceptions of social proximity and heighten concern about particular groups (for example, about migrants of colour in majority white societies or about Muslim migrants in societies that are predominantly Christian).

Health-Related Deservingness: Three Debates

How do these forms of vernacular moral reasoning figure in localized debates about migrants' health-related deservingness? To address this question, we turn now to three cases: one from North America, one from Western Europe and one from the Middle East. In discussing each case, we engage all elements of the framework introduced above (stakeholders, context and evaluative criteria) while foregrounding one of the three. Each case provides a vivid illustration of how vernacular conceptions of health-related deservingness can be implicated in the domains of migrant health research, policy or practice.

Organs for the Undocumented?
A 'Bungled Transplant' in the United States

In 2003, seventeen-year-old Jesica Santillan underwent a heart and lung transplant at Duke University Medical Center in Durham, North Carolina. Just after the surgery, routine post-operative blood tests revealed a terrible mistake: Santillan had received organs of an incompatible blood type. In a frantic effort to correct the error, her doctors procured another set of organs and performed a second transplant. Yet the damage was too great for her already weakened system and she died several days later.

The story of the 'bungled transplant' (Wailoo et al. 2006) made local and national headlines. How could such a mistake occur in one of the nation's premier medical institutions, the American public wanted to know. Who was to blame? As the media dug deeper into the details of the case, the tone of the conversation shifted, and spectators began asking a decidedly more contentious question: did Santillan even deserve a transplant in the first place?

From a clinical standpoint, physicians establish eligibility for organ transplantation using complex biomedical algorithms. In Santillan's case, postmortem eligibility debates revolved not around biology, but around biography – especially the fact that Santillan and her mother had entered the United States without legal authorization when she was thirteen. Commentators labelled Santillan an 'illegal immigrant' and debated whether or not she deserved the medical care she had received. Some contended that only citizens should have access to 'citizen organs' (Chavez 2006: 292) and declared Santillan and other 'illegals' inherently undeserving. Others pointed to Santillan's youthful innocence and life-threatening illness as evidence of her deservingness. The tragedy of Santillan's death and ensuing controversy highlighted an important but underexamined issue: the impact of vernacular deservingness assessments on broader debates about migration and health.

The tragedy of Santillan's death also spurred high-profile debate among an impassioned array of stakeholders. Should Santillan have received a heart and lung transplant in the first place? After the botched transplant that led those organs to fail, should she have received a second? Pundits and the general public seized on her story as an opportunity to debate a broader set of questions. Should undocumented immigrants receive healthcare in the United States at all? If so, what kind of care ought they to receive, under what conditions and with what limitations, if any? Finally, who should pay?

In Santillan's case, as in any deservingness debate, context matters. Despite the country's 'melting pot' origin myth, the history of restrictive immigration policy and anti-immigrant sentiment in the United States runs deep (Ngai 2004). Especially in times of economic vulnerability, US public opinion has tended to portray migrants and immigrants, and unauthorized migrants in particular, as a drain on resources and a threat to national sovereignty (Chavez 2012; Portes et al. 2012). When Santillan and her family moved to the largely agricultural southern state of North Carolina in 2003, a new wave of Latinx migrants seeking agricultural work had just begun to arrive (Kochhar et al. 2005). Although US citizens generally have been loath to take up jobs in the agricultural sector, fears of economic competition and cultural and demographic change have at times fuelled xenophobic sentiment, especially in places like North Carolina, where Latinx immigrants are a relatively new population (Marrow 2011).

A wide range of stakeholders participated in the stormy debates that erupted around Santillan's treatment and subsequent death, among them the two medical institutions involved in her care, the media, right-wing political pundits and a white, middle-aged, local businessman named Mack Mahoney, who first learned of Santillan's illness from the local newspaper. Compelled by her plight, Mahoney founded a charity to support her medical care and became the family's informal, if self-appointed, spokesman. In his public statements, Mahoney cited Santillan's youthful innocence as well as her frail, deteriorating body as evidence that she was a deserving candidate for transplant surgery. At times, he even infantilized her by describing her as a dying 'baby', even though at seventeen she was nearly a legal adult (Wailoo et al. 2006: 304).

Following Santillan's death, a heated media debate focused on her unauthorized migration status. Conservative commentators leveraged her story to intervene politically in national conversations about immigration. Right-wing pundit Michelle Malkin, for instance, contended that Santillan symbolized a larger problem in the United States where '[t]he costs of illegal alien health care are crippling hospitals across the country' (Malkin 2003). In Malkin's narrative, Santillan was one of millions of 'illegal aliens' flooding the country seeking access to already-scarce resources.

Yet Malkin's account ignored several key facts. First, unlike most unauthorized migrants in the United States, Santillan's mother was covered by an employment-based private health insurance policy. Given the United States' employment-based insurance system, Santillan therefore was covered as her dependant. Additional costs were covered by private donations generated through Mahoney's charity.

Another conservative columnist, Joe Kovacs, compared Santillan to a different young woman awaiting a lung transplant, Lauren Averitt. According to Kovacs, Averitt – a desperately ill, law-abiding citizen – clearly was more deserving than Santillan; 'illegal aliens like Jesica, he wrote, 'are able to leapfrog ahead of the many thousands of U.S. citizens patiently waiting and praying for their own personal miracle' (Kovacs 2003). From his standpoint, citizenship is more than a legal status; it is imbued with moral meaning – with life-or-death implications. In his account, Santillan's unauthorized border crossing is portrayed as both criminal and immoral, as is her supposed desire and ability to jump ahead of US citizens on the transplant waiting list. Here, Santillan herself is assigned culpability despite her youth and vulnerability, and even though her mother (and not she herself) initiated their migration.

The institutional stakeholders, Duke Medical Center and the United Network for Organ Sharing (UNOS), adopted a markedly different tactic. In their official responses, neither addressed Santillan's legal status. Each issued a carefully worded public statement in a cool, professional tone that contrasted sharply with the heated media fervour. Duke's response was particularly measured, likely due to concerns about legal liability for Santillan's death.

Much can be learned from this case about how migrants' health-related deservingness is reckoned. Above all, the contentious conversation following Santillan's death reveals just how low the threshold can be for involvement as a stakeholder – and, moreover, how quickly a relatively distant set of stakeholders can turn a localized discussion about a particular individual's health needs into a lightning rod for much broader public debate.

Not Sick Enough: Illness, Vulnerability and Deservingness in Western Europe

In 2008, a very different deservingness debate unfolded in the United Kingdom concerning Ama Sumani, a 39-year-old woman of Ghanaian origin and mother of two who was forcibly removed from her hospital bed in Cardiff, Wales, where she was being treated for malignant myeloma, a form of cancer (Lawrance 2012).[3] Five British Home Office agents moved her into a wheelchair, drove her to Heathrow Airport and put her on a plane to Ghana against her will. Before her 'removal' from the United Kingdom, Sumani had appealed the decision and petitioned to remain on compassionate grounds due to the life-threatening nature of her illness and lack of accessible treatment in her home country.[4] Her appeal was denied. Unable to access treatment in her country of origin, she died two months later.

Sumani's case highlights the critical impact of context on local deservingness debates and their outcomes. How did historical, political and legal circumstances influence her treatment by the British authorities? How might her fate have been different had her case been adjudicated in France? We explore these questions below.

In the heated public debate about Sumani's case, some British physicians and other sympathetic observers argued that her forcible removal would constitute a gross human rights violation. An editorial in *The Lancet* labelled it an act of 'atrocious barbarism' and rightly anticipated that her deportation would precipitate her death (*The Lancet* 2008). Yet several Members of Parliament vocally supported the actions of the Home Office. Without denying the likelihood of her imminent death, they claimed that her case failed to meet the necessary threshold of 'very exceptional' suffering required to activate the country's humanitarian relief mechanism.

In the United Kingdom, historically, healthcare provision to migrant populations has been uncontroversial and, until relatively recently, access to care was virtually the same for all. However, after an increase in asylum applications in the 1970s and 1980s, anxieties about growing migrant populations spurred the passage of laws distinguishing between 'ordinary residents' eligible for free healthcare through the National Health Service and 'non-ordinary residents' who can access only certain health services and only for a fee (*The Lancet* 2008). Seriously ill migrants ordered to leave the United Kingdom may seek relief from removal through appeal under Article 3 of the European Convention on Human Rights, which prohibits any action that would constitute 'inhuman treatment' (Council of Europe 1950). Decisions regarding humanitarian relief are made by an immigration judge on a case-by-case basis. Sumani's case was deemed unexceptional and her appeal was denied (Lawrance 2012).

How might Sumani's fate have been different in France? In both countries, unauthorized migrants are often viewed with suspicion. Yet French policies regarding sick migrants have tended to be more favourable than their British analogues. In 1998, following an intensive campaign by a coalition of advocacy organizations, an informal, discretionary practice of granting temporary residency permits to seriously ill migrants became institutionalized (Ticktin 2011; Fassin

2012). The resulting new arrangement, an 'illness residency permit', was created precisely to prevent the deportation of people with serious illnesses who would lack access to appropriate care following repatriation – people like Ama Sumani.

On the surface, the contours of the French and UK policies are similar. Both revolve around the same questions: does the migrant's illness meet the threshold of 'life-threatening' severity? Would appropriate treatment be accessible in his or her home country? What differs is the deservingness threshold, which would appear to be lower in France. Importantly, medical experts play an integral role in the French context, whereas immigration officers are the primary adjudicators in the United Kingdom (Fassin 2011; Ticktin 2011; Larchanché 2012). In Ama Sumani's case, context made all the difference.

'Pirate' Daycares and Infant Deaths in Israel

During a six-week period in early 2015, five infants died in Tel Aviv, Israel, in what migrant advocates and the media described as 'pirate' daycares, or 'child warehouses', in the city's neglected southern neighbourhoods.[5] Among them were two four-month-old babies who died within a 48-hour period. The local media were quick to publicize these deaths (see e.g. David 2015; Kashti 2015; Vilnai 2015a, 2015b, 2015c), both involving infants born in Israel to Eritrean parents who had arrived, without authorization, seeking asylum.

In the first of these cases, a baby girl was left alone in a crib with a bottle of formula (Vilnai 2015b), possibly tied to her head (David 2015), and choked to death. The next day, in an adjacent neighbourhood, a baby boy died of suffocation; his death went unnoticed until his mother came to pick him up after work and found him lying on his stomach, unresponsive. Immediately after this pair of deaths, migrant advocacy organizations and human rights groups demanded swift government action and the media reported on 'marathon meetings' in the subsequent days 'among the relevant government ministries, in collaboration with the municipality' (Vilnai 2015c). If the deceased infants had been born to Jewish-Israeli citizen parents rather than non-Jewish asylum seekers from Africa, how might their fates have been different?

For nearly two decades, 'pirate' daycares like these were the only viable option for most infants and toddlers (age 0–3) born in Israel to unauthorized migrant parents, including both migrants who arrived explicitly in search of work and those, like the Eritrean parents of these unfortunate children, who arrived seeking asylum. Although asylum seekers in Israel are officially forbidden from working, they receive no benefits from the government and therefore must find employment in order to sustain themselves and their families. Their employment options are thus sharply limited, pay is low, work conditions are often harsh and parents have little flexibility in determining their work schedules. As a result, some children are in daycare for fifteen hours per day or more – or even overnight, in some cases for multiple nights in succession.

Significantly, no public daycare frameworks are provided for any children in this age bracket, including Israeli citizens' children. Yet the private daycares that serve Israeli parents face tighter scrutiny – not only from the authorities, but also from parents, who, as citizens, risk little in voicing their concerns.

As of 2015, an estimated seventy to eighty 'pirate' daycares were operating in the Tel Aviv area, serving approximately 2,500 children and charging as little as 500 Israeli shekels (approximately US$132) per month for care that often exceeds what counts as 'full-time' by Israeli standards (Vilnai 2015b; Mesila staff, personal interview). For Israeli politicians, the media and the broader public, this spate of deaths came as no surprise; in the preceding two years, at least ten others had been recorded in similar settings (Vilnai 2015c). Indeed, the risks and dangers of these unregulated daycares had been detailed, and roundly condemned, in the State Comptroller's 2013 annual report (Office of the State Comptroller 2013).

Thousands of children do survive these settings, but the short-term and long-term risks are legion – and well known. In many such daycares, a single adult, usually a woman with a migrant background, is responsible for as many as twenty or even thirty children (Office of the State Comptroller 2013) whereas the national average ratio in Israel is one to six (David 2015). As a result, children tend to spend as much as twelve to fifteen hours each day isolated in a crib with no daily routine and with minimal attention, physical contact or direct interaction with others, whether children or adults. Neither do they receive much stimulation (e.g. stories, toys, music, art activities or outdoor playtime), although televisions are sometimes present. Most facilities are located in crumbling residential buildings, often in private apartments where rents are cheap. Among other hazards, many lack fire escapes and adequate ventilation, and some have unauthorized electrical connections, unsecured doors or gates and unsafe balconies.

From a health standpoint, the long-term impact of spending one's critical first years in settings like these is almost universally devastating. According to Mesila, a municipally run social welfare organization in South Tel Aviv that had been responding to these unregulated care settings and their effects for more than a decade: 'By the time they enter formal educational settings, every one of these children suffers at least one if not more forms of developmental delay' (Mesila Aid and Information Center 2006). The report continues: 'we are convinced that the overwhelming majority of infants and young children in these frameworks meet the criteria for children at risk as a result of spending most hours of the day in an atmosphere of physical and emotional deprivation that severely delays their development' (Mesila Aid and Information Center 2006). These conclusions were echoed in the State Comptroller's 2013 report.

What 'common-sense' assumptions and moral commitments made it possible for key stakeholders in the political and policy realms to ignore these well-known risks for years, even decades? The infants who died certainly could not be suspected of poor 'moral character'. In terms of 'migration motive', they were neither 'economic' nor 'forced' migrants; although their parents fled countries in tumult, they were born in Israel. Since Israel has no *jus soli* provision, however, they are not eligible for Israeli citizenship.

One might expect that the young age and associated 'vulnerability' of these children would garner concern for their health and development, and, in some respects, this has been the case. Since the 2000s, children of migrant parents have been among the few members of migrant communities for whom national and municipal stakeholders have expressed concern. For example, a network of supervised private daycares (Unitaf) was established under the supervision of Mesila in 2005, with major philanthropic (as opposed to government) support. Unitaf daycares are roughly comparable to those serving Jewish-Israeli children, but they are more expensive for parents than the informal arrangements described above – and they are unable to meet existing demand.

Changes benefiting these children have been driven both by pressure from local migrant and child advocacy groups and, not insignificantly, by a cultural emphasis on children and reproduction that has long found expression in the country's robust and institutionalized tradition of (selective) pronatalism (Kahn 2000; Kanaaneh 2002). Yet the overriding factor shaping Israeli attitudes towards children of migrant parents is social proximity. The clearest illustration of how proximity is reckoned in Israel is the country's Law of Return. Established to invert the genocidal logic of the Nazi regime, this legal provision offers full citizenship benefits to anyone with a bureaucratically legible tie to the Jewish people. For those who lack such a tie, however, citizenship (and even permanent resident status) is almost completely unattainable regardless of country of origin or current legal status.

On the basis of this ethnonational logic, virtually everyone residing in Israel falls into one of three groups: ratified citizens (Jewish-Israelis, including the native-born and immigrants arriving under the Law of Return); Palestinians (who are represented as the country's 'real' 'Others'); and 'other' 'Others' – global migrants who have arrived in Israel for a variety of economic and/or political reasons and cannot readily be slotted into either of the first two groups (Willen 2019). For the vast majority of politicians, policy-makers and citizens, societal attention, investment and care ought to focus primarily – some would say exclusively – on the country's Jewish-Israeli citizens. Other groups are constructed not simply as undeserving, but as a threat to the country's economy, identity and even, in some instances, its existential security.

Immediately after this wave of infant deaths, the Prime Minister's Office announced that it would begin working with Mesila to scale up the small network of Unitaf daycares (which would continue to rely heavily on support from private philanthropy) (Mesila Aid and Information Center 2015). It is impossible to know precisely how key stakeholders' responses might have differed had the deceased infants been born to Jewish-Israeli citizen parents rather than African asylum seekers. Given the contours of Israel's local moral economy (Willen 2019), however, it seems likely that state, local and nongovernmental actors, under pressure from citizens and the media, would have responded much sooner – and with considerably greater decisiveness.

Conclusion

In this chapter, we have argued that social scientists' capacity to understand – and intervene in – debates about migration, and especially about migrants' health, depends on our ability to understand how deservingness is reckoned by local actors espousing divergent values, commitments and agendas. To this end, we presented an analytical framework that highlights the key role of stakeholders, contextual factors and evaluative criteria in debates about health-related deservingness. As the deservingness debates analysed here make clear, conceptions of deservingness are fundamentally expressed in a moral register; they are vernacular expressions of value as opposed to juridical notions of right. As such, deservingness inevitably is reckoned in ways that are relational, conditional, context-dependent, syncretic, affect-laden and mutable. Put simply, deservingness assessments are rooted in moral, ideological and political assumptions that reflect different – and competing – forms of 'common sense'.

Of course, common sense reflects hegemonic narratives and understandings of past and present; of inclusion and exclusion; and, above all, of what (and who) matters. In the present era, we are seeing the emergence – or, perhaps more accurately, the resurgence – of divergent modes of 'common sense' and deeply conflicting systems of cultural hegemony (Gramsci 1971). Factors contributing to these cleavages, many of them driven by technological 'advances', include intensive media polarization, the erosion of confidence in once broadly credible institutions and sources of authority (e.g. journalists, scientists and political leaders), and the diminishing role of empirical evidence in public and policy debates – itself a matter of grave and urgent concern. The possibility of lightning-fast digital communication and widespread reliance on social media also play central roles. These are the circumstances that make it possible, for example, for a Trump administration official to radically reinterpret Emma Lazarus' poem on the fly, during a nationally broadcast radio interview, and insist that migrants are welcome in the United States only if they 'can stand on their own two feet and … will not become a public charge'.

In closing, we highlight two areas of enquiry that demand further attention. First, we know too little about how different groups of migrants – and members of other vulnerable groups – conceptualize their own deservingness. What sort of social contracts do they perceive, envision or hope for? How do they participate in, or respond to, the frequently contentious deservingness debates transpiring in their communities of residence (and, at times, swirling around them)? What barriers impede their ability to speak out and participate in these debates on their own behalf? These questions all demand closer scrutiny.

Second, it is increasingly evident that racism, discrimination and other forms of oppression and exclusion impair health and shorten lives (see e.g. Holmes 2013; Castañeda et al. 2015; Horton 2016; Bailey et al. 2017; Castañeda 2019). The violent effects of racism have emerged with chilling clarity as racialized individuals and communities have faced dramatically heightened rates of COVID-19 infection (and mortality) relative to those racialized as white (Bowleg 2020; Devakumar et al. 2020; Gee et al. 2020; Hardeman et al. 2020). What are the health effects for migrants and their families of being made to feel unwelcome and undeserving of society's attention, investment or care? We need to engage such questions with robust epidemiological methods and evidence (Orcutt et al. 2020), but that is but one vital step. By listening to migrants, foregrounding their experiences and supporting their efforts to speak publicly on their own behalf, anthropologists can make vital contributions to conversations – in academia and beyond – about the specific ways in which exclusion and sociopolitical abjection harm health.

Only with strong tools and robust conceptual frameworks can we begin to parse our messy and confusing twenty-first century reality – an era in which notions of the collective 'we' are proving more fragile than many of us would have hoped, and in which some would exile even Lady Liberty, that silent-lipped 'Mother of Exiles', from the American body politic.

Acknowledgements

An earlier version of this chapter was published in Felicia Thomas (ed.), *The Handbook of Migration and Health* (Cheltenham: Edward Elgar, 2016). Portions of the chapter draw on two of the first author's earlier publications (Willen 2012a, 2012b).

Sarah S. Willen is Associate Professor of Anthropology at the University of Connecticut, where she also directs the Research Program on Global Health & Human Rights at the Human Rights Institute. A medical and sociocultural anthropologist, she is author or editor of four books and many articles. Her first book, *Fighting for Dignity: Migrant Lives at Israel's Margins* (Philadelphia: University of Pennsylvania Press, 2019), has received multiple awards, including the Edie Turner First-Book Prize in Ethnographic Writing, the Yonathan Shapiro Prize for Best Book in Israel Studies and the Stirling Prize in Psychological Anthropology. She is Principal Investigator of 'ARCHES | the AmeRicans' Conceptions of Health Equity Study' and co-founder of the 'Pandemic Journaling Project'.

Jennifer Cook is currently a postdoctoral fellow at the John Goodwin Tower Center for Public Policy and International Affairs, Southern Methodist University. In her work she uses multi-sited ethnography to examine the intersection of legality, morality and wellbeing in transnational migration. Her recent publications include: 'Navigating Legality: Transnational Mixed-Status Families and the U.S. Family-Based Immigration System' (*Journal of Ethnic and Migration Studies*, 2020) and 'Transnational Migration and the Lived Experience of Class Across Borders', (in *Handbook of Culture and Migration*, edited by Jeffrey Cohen and Ibrahim Sirkeci, Cheltenham: Edward Elgar, 2021).

Notes

1. 'Morning Edition', 13 August 2019. Retrieved 5 February 2022 from https://www.npr.org/2019/08/13/750727515/rule-would-penalize-immi grants-to-u-s-for-needing-benefits.
2. Although the terms 'migrant' and 'immigrant' are often used interchangeably, they are not synonymous. Frequently these terms are employed as ostensibly neutral, empirically grounded descriptors of particular individuals or groups, yet different terms convey different ideological messages about who is expected to keep moving and who deserves to stay. Since individuals on the move often do not – and perhaps cannot – know whether their residence in a given location is temporary or permanent, or what sort of status will ultimately be available to them, the open-ended terms 'migrants' and 'migration' hew closest to the variability, as well as the uncertainty, associated with many contemporary patterns of human mobility.
3. Sumani arrived in the United Kingdom in 2003 on a tourist visa. She later obtained a student visa and enrolled in finance classes, but her poor English skills and insufficient educational preparation prevented her from completing her course of study. Her myeloma was diagnosed in 2006 and she was placed on dialysis after the cancer spread to her kidneys. The Home Office ordered her 'removal' to Ghana, arguing that her employment violated the terms of her student visa (Lawrance 2012).
4. In the United Kingdom, the response to visa violations is 'removal', which does not affect a migrant's opportunity to apply for future visas, rather than 'deportation', which does. Migrants may be deported if they have committed crimes or entered illegally (Blinder 2016).
5. Data for this section draw on ethnographic research conducted by the first author in Tel Aviv in 2014, supplemented by official reports and media coverage. This research phase, part of a larger study initiated in 2000, included interviews with staff at Mesila, visits to three 'pirate' daycares and an interview with the head of a Unitaf daycare.

References

Appelbaum, Lauren D. 2001. 'The Influence of Perceived Deservingness on Policy Decisions Regarding Aid to the Poor', *Political Psychology* 22(3): 419–42.
Appelbaum, Lauren D., Mary Clare Lennon and John Lawrence Aber. 2003. 'How Belief in a Just World Influences Views of Public Policy', National Center for Children in Poverty, Columbia University. Retrieved 5 February 2022 from https://doi.org/10.7916/D8765Q2R.
Bailey, Zinzi D., Nancy Krieger, Madina Agénor et al. 2017. 'Structural Racism and Health Inequities in the USA: Evidence and Interventions', *The Lancet* 389(10077): 1453–63.
Bambra, Claire, and Katherine E. Smith. 2010. 'No Longer Deserving? Sickness Benefit Reform and the Politics of (Ill) Health', *Critical Public Health* 20(1): 71–84.
Blekesaune, Morten, and Jill Quadagno. 2003. 'Public Attitudes toward Welfare State Policies', *European Sociological Review* 19(5): 415–27.
Blinder, Scott 2016. 'Briefing: Deportations, Removals, and Voluntary Departures from the UK', 3rd revision, Oxford, Migration Observatory at the University of Oxford. Retrieved 5 February 2022 from http://migrationobservatory.ox.ac.uk/wp-content/uploads/2016/04/Briefing-Deportations.pdf.
Blomberg, Helena, et al. 2017. 'Social Assistance Deservingness and Policy Measures: Attitudes of Finnish Politicians, Administrators and Citizens', in Wim van Oorschot, Femke Roosma, Bart Meuleman and Tim Reeskens (eds), *The Social Legitimacy of Targeted Welfare: Attitudes to Welfare Deservingness*. Cheltenham: Edward Elgar, pp. 209–24.
Bourgois, Philippe, et al. 2017. 'Structural Vulnerability: Operationalizing the Concept to Address Health Disparities in Clinical Care', *Academic Medicine* 92(3): 299–307.
Bowleg, Lisa. 2020. 'We're Not All in This Together: On COVID-19, Intersectionality, and Structural Inequality', *American Journal of Public Health* 110(7): 917.
Castañeda, Heide. 2019. *Borders of Belonging: Struggle and Solidarity in Mixed-Status Immigrant Families*. Stanford: Stanford University Press.
Castañeda, Heide, et al. 2015. 'Immigration as a Social Determinant of Health', *Annual Review of Public Health* 36: 375–92.
Chauvin, Sébastien, and Blanca Garcés-Mascareñas. 2014. 'Becoming Less Illegal: Deservingness Frames and Undocumented Migrant Incorporation', *Sociology Compass* 8(4): 422–32.
Chauvin, Sébastien, Blanca Garcés-Mascareñas and Albert Kraler. 2013. 'Employment and Migrant Deservingness', *International Migration* 51(6): 80–85.
Chavez, Leo R. 2006. 'Imagining the Nation, Imagining Donor Recipients', in Keith Wailoo, Julie Livingston and Peter Guarnaccia (eds), *A Death Retold*. Chapel Hill, NC: University of North Carolina Press, pp. 276–91.

———. 2012. 'Undocumented Immigrants and Their Use of Medical Services in Orange County, California', *Social Science & Medicine* 74(6): 887–93.

Chock, P.P. 1991. '"Illegal Aliens" and "Opportunity": Myth-Making in Congressional Testimony', *American Ethnologist* 18(2): 279–94.

Council of Europe. 1950. 'European Convention for the Protection of Human Rights and Fundamental Freedoms, as amended by Protocols Nos. 11 and 14', *ETS 5*. Retrieved 5 February 2022 from www.refworld.org/docid/3ae6b3b04.html.

Daniels, Norman. 2008. *Just Health*. Cambridge: Cambridge University Press.

David, Ariel. 2015. 'Who Will Save the Refugee Children of Tel Aviv?', *Ha'aretz*, 5 April. Retrieved 5 February 2022 from www.haaretz.com/news/israel/.premium-1.650425.

De Swaan, Abram. 1988. *In Care of the State*. New York: Oxford University Press.

De Vries, Robert. 2017. 'Negative Attitudes towards Welfare Claimants: The Importance of Unconscious Bias. Claimants', in Wim van Oorschot, Femke Roosma, Bart Meuleman and Tim Reeskens (eds), *The Social Legitimacy of Targeted Welfare: Attitudes to Welfare Deservingness*. Cheltenham: Edward Elgar, pp. 93–112.

De Wilde, Marjolijn. 2017. 'Deservingness in Social Assistance Administrative Practice: A Factorial Survey Approach', in Wim van Oorschot, Femke Roosma, Bart Meuleman and Tim Reeskens (eds), *The Social Legitimacy of Targeted Welfare: Attitudes to Welfare Deservingness*. Cheltenham: Edward Elgar, pp. 225–40.

Devakumar, Delan, et al. 2020. 'Racism, the Public Health Crisis We Can No Longer Ignore', *The Lancet* 395(10242): e112–e113.

Fassin, Didier. 2012. *Humanitarian Reason*. Berkeley: University of California Press.

Feather, Norman T. 1999. *Values, Achievement, and Justice*. New York: Kluwer Academic/Plenum.

Gee, Gilbert C., Marguerite J. Ro and Anne W. Rimoin. 2020. 'Seven Reasons to Care about Racism and COVID-19 and Seven Things to Do to Stop It', *American Journal of Public Health* 110(7): 954–55.

Geiger, Ben Baumberg. 2017. 'False Beliefs and the Perceived Deservingness of Social Security Benefit Claimants', in Wim van Oorschot, Femke Roosma, Bart Meuleman and Tim Reeskens (eds), *The Social Legitimacy of Targeted Welfare: Attitudes to Welfare Deservingness*. Cheltenham: Edward Elgar, pp. 73–92.

Gilens, Martin. 1999. *Why Americans Hate Welfare*. Chicago: University of Chicago Press.

Gollust, Sarah E., Paula M. Lantz and Peter A. Ubel. 2010. 'The Polarizing Effect of News Media Messages about the Social Determinants of Health', *American Journal of Public Health* 99(12): 2160–67.

Gollust, Sarah E., and Julia Lynch. 2010. 'Who Deserves Health Care?', *Robert Wood Johnson Foundation Working Paper Series* WP-48.

Gottlieb, Nora, Dani Filc and Nadav Davidovitch. 2012. 'Medical Humanitarianism, Human Rights, and Political Advocacy', *Social Science & Medicine* 74(6): 839–45.

Gramsci, Antonio. 1971. *Selections from the Prison Notebooks*, eds and trans. Q. Hoare and G. Nowell Smith. London: Lawrence & Wishart.

Grove, Natalie J., and Anthony B. Zwi. 2006. 'Our Health and Theirs: Forced Migration, Othering, and Public Health', *Social Science & Medicine* 62: 1931–42.

Guetzkow, Joshua. 2010. 'Beyond Deservingness: Congressional Discourse on Poverty, 1964–1996', *Annals of the American Academy of Political and Social Science* 629: 173–97.

Haas, Bridget M. 2012. 'Suffering and the Struggle for Recognition: Lived Experiences of the US Political Asylum Process', Ph.D. dissertation. San Diego: University of California.

Hardeman, Rachel R., Eduardo M. Medina and Rhea W. Boyd. 2020. 'Stolen Breaths', *New England Journal of Medicine* 383(3): 197–99.

Heyman, Josiah. 1998. *Finding a Moral Heart for US Immigration Policy*. Washington, DC: American Anthropological Association.

Holmes, Seth M. 2012. 'The Clinical Gaze in the Practice of Migrant Health', *Social Science & Medicine* 74(6): 873–81.

Holmes, Seth M. et al. 2020. 'Deservingness: Migration and Health in Social Context', *BMJ Global Health* 6(S1): e005107.

———. 2013. *Fresh Fruit, Broken Bodies*. Oakland: University of California Press.Holmes, Seth M. et al 2020. 'Deservingness: Migration and Health in Social Context', *BMJ Global Health* 6(S1): e005107.

Horton, Sarah. 2004. 'Different Subjects', *Medical Anthropology Quarterly* 18: 472–89.

———. 2016. *They Leave Their Kidneys in the Field*. Oakland: University of California Press.

Huschke, Susann. 2014. 'Performing Deservingness: Humanitarian Health Care Provision for Migrants in Germany', *Social Science & Medicine* 120: 352–59.

Kahn, Susan. 2000. *Reproducing Jews*. Durham, NC: Duke University Press.

Kanaaneh, Rhoda A. 2002. *Birthing the Nation*. Berkeley: University of California Press.

Kashti, Or. 2015. 'Israeli Government's Apathy Is Killing Foreign Workers' Children', *Ha'aretz*, 31 March. Retrieved 5 February 2022 from www.haaretz.com/opinion/.premium-1.649736.

Katz, Michael B. 1989. *The Undeserving Poor*. New York: Pantheon Books.

Kochhar, Rakesh, Roberto Ruro and Sonya Tafoya. 2005. *The New Latino South*. Washington DC: Pew Hispanic Center.

Kootstra, Anouk. 2016. 'Deserving and Undeserving Welfare Claimants in Britain and the Netherlands: Examining the Role of Ethnicity and

Migration Status Using a Vignette Experiment', *European Sociological Review* 32(3): 325–38.

Kovacs, Joe. 2003. 'Transplants for Illegals Igniting US Firestorm', *World Net Daily*, 6 March. Retrieved 5 February 2022 from www.wnd.com/2003/03/17606.

The Lancet. 2008. 'Migrant Health: What Are Doctors' Leaders Doing?', *The Lancet* 371: 178.

Larchanché, Stéphanie. 2012. 'Intangible Obstacles: Health Implications of Stigmatization, Structural Violence, and Fear among Undocumented Immigrants in France', *Social Science & Medicine* 74(6): 858–63.

Lawrance, Benjamin N. 2012. 'Humanitarian Claims and Expert Testimonies', *Ghana Studies* 15/16: 251–86.

Lepianka, Dorota. 2017. 'The Varying Faces of Poverty and Deservingness in Dutch Print Media', in Wim van Oorschot, Femke Roosma, Bart Meuleman and Tim Reeskens (eds), *The Social Legitimacy of Targeted Welfare: Attitudes to Welfare Deservingness*. Cheltenham: Edward Elgar, pp. 127–48.

Lipsky, Michael. 1980. *Street-Level Bureaucracy*. New York: Russell Sage Foundation.

Lynch, Julia, and Sarah E. Gollust. 2010. 'Playing Fair: Fairness Beliefs and Health Policy Preferences in the United States', *Journal of Health Politics, Policy and Law* 35(6): 849–87.

Malkin, Michelle. 2003. 'America: Medical Welcome Mat to the World', *vdare.com*, 20 February. Retrieved 5 February 2022 from www.vdare.com/articles/america-medical-welcome-mat-to-the-world.

Maness, Sarah B., et al. 2020. 'Social Determinants of Health and Health Disparities: COVID-19 Exposures and Mortality among African American People in the United States', *Public Health Reports* 136(1): 18–22. Retrieved 5 February 2022 from https://journals.sagepub.com/doi/pdf/10.1177/0033354920969169.

Marrow, Helen. 2011. 'Deserving to a Point: Undocumented Immigrants in San Francisco's Universal Access Healthcare Model', *Social Science & Medicine* 74(6): 846–54.

Marrow, Helen, and Tiffany Joseph. 2015. 'Excluded and Frozen Out: Unauthorised Immigrants' (Non)Access to Care after US Health Care Reform', *Journal of Ethnic and Migration Studies* 41(14): 2253–73.

Mesila Aid and Information Center. 2006. *Annual Activity Report*. Tel Aviv: Mesila Aid and Information Center.

———. 2015. *Summer 2015 at Mesila*. Tel Aviv: Mesila Aid and Information Center.

Morgen, Sandra, and Jeff Maskovsky. 2003. 'The Anthropology of Welfare "Reform"', *Annual Review of Anthropology* 32: 315–38.

Newton, Lina 2005. 'It Is Not a Question of Being Anti-immigration', in Anne Schneider and Helen Ingram (eds), *Deserving and Entitled*. Albany, NY: SUNY Press, pp. 139–73.

Ngai, Mae M. 2004. *Impossible Subjects*. Princeton: Princeton University Press.

Office of the State Comptroller. 2013. 'Annual Report'. Retrieved 5 February 2022 from http://old.mevaker.gov.il/serve/contentTree.asp?bookid=644&id=196&contentid=&parentcid=undefined&sw=1920&hw=1010.

Oliverio-Lauderdale, Daniela. 2014. 'Contradictions and Exclusions: An Ethnographic Study of African Im/migrants' Right to Health in Italy', MA dissertation. Vancouver: University of British Columbia.

Olsen, Jan Abel, Jeff Richardson, Paul Dolan and Paul Menzel. 2003. 'The Moral Relevance of Personal Characteristics in Setting Health Care Priorities', *Social Science & Medicine* 57: 1163–72.

Orcutt, Miriam, et al. 2020. 'Global Call to Action for Inclusion of Migrants and Refugees in the COVID-19 Response', *The Lancet* 395: 1482–83.

Portes, Alejandro, Patricia Fernández-Kelly and Donald W. Light. 2012. 'Life on the Edge: Immigrants Confront the American Health System', *Ethnic and Racial Studies* 35(1): 3–22.

Quesada, James, Laurie Kain Hart and Philippe Bourgois. 2011. 'Structural Vulnerability and Health', *Medical Anthropology* 30(4): 339–62.

Ragusa, Jordan. 2017. "Do the Rich Deserve a Tax Cut? Public Images, Deservingness Criteria and Americans' Tax Policy Preferences", in Wim van Oorschot, Femke Roosma, Bart Meuleman and Tim Reeskens (eds), *The Social Legitimacy of Targeted Welfare: Attitudes to Welfare Deservingness*. Cheltenham: Edward Elgar, pp. 316–34.

Roosma, Femke and Marjolein Jeene. 2017. 'The Deservingness Logic Applied to Public Opinions Concerning Work Obligations for Benefits Claimants', in Wim van Oorschot, Femke Roosma, Bart Meuleman and Tim Reeskens (eds), *The Social Legitimacy of Targeted Welfare: Attitudes to Welfare Deservingness*. Cheltenham: Edward Elgar, pp. 189–208.

Rylko-Bauer, Barbara, and Paul Farmer. 2002. 'Managed Care or Managed Inequality? A Call for Critiques of Market-Based Medicine', *Medical Anthropology Quarterly* 16(4): 476–502.

Sadin, Meredith. 2017. 'They're Not Worthy: The Perceived Deservingness of the Rich and Its Connection to Policy Preferences', in Wim van Oorschot, Femke Roosma, Bart Meuleman and Tim Reeskens (eds), *The Social Legitimacy of Targeted Welfare: Attitudes to Welfare Deservingness*. Cheltenham: Edward Elgar, pp. 299–315.

Sales, Rosemary. 2002. 'The Deserving and the Undeserving? Refugees, Asylum Seekers and Welfare in Britain', *Critical Social Policy* 22(3): 456–78.

Schneider, Anne L., and Helen M. Ingram. 2005. *Deserving and Entitled: Social Constructions and Public Policy*. Albany, NY: SUNY Press.

Scott, Charity. 2008. 'Belief in a Just World', *Hastings Center Report* 38(1): 16–19.

Snell-Rood, Claire, and Elizabeth Carpenter-Song. 2018. 'Depression in a Depressed Area: Deservingness, Mental Illness, and Treatment in the Contemporary Rural US', *Social Science & Medicine* 219: 78–86.

Stumpf, Juliet P. 2006. 'The Crimmigration Crisis', *American University Law Review* 56: 367–419.

Ticktin, Miriam. 2011. *Casualties of Care*. Berkeley: University of California Press.

Tiedje, Kristina, and David J. Plevak. 2014. 'Medical Humanitarianism in the United States', *Social Science & Medicine* 120: 360–67.

Van Oorschot, Wim. 2000. 'Who Should Get What, and Why? On Deservingness Criteria and the Conditionality of Solidarity among the Public', *Policy & Politics* 28(1): 33–48.

———. 2006. 'Making the Difference in Social Europe', *Journal of European Social Policy* 16(1): 23–42.

Van Doorn, Bas, and Angela Bos. 2017. 'Are Visual Depictions of Poverty in the US Gendered and Racialized?', in Wim van Oorschot, Femke Roosma, Bart Meuleman and Tim Reeskens (eds), *The Social Legitimacy of Targeted Welfare: Attitudes to Welfare Deservingness*. Cheltenham: Edward Elgar, pp. 113–26.

Van Oorschot, Wim, Femke Roosma, Bart Meuleman and Tim Reeskens (eds). 2017. *The Social Legitimacy of Targeted Welfare: Attitudes to Welfare Deservingness. Globalization and Welfare*. Cheltenham: Edward Elgar.

Vanthuyne, Karine, Francesca Meloni, Monica Ruiz-Casares, Cécile Rousseau and Alexandra Ricard-Guay. 2013. 'Health Workers' Perceptions of Access to Care for Children and Pregnant Women with Precarious Immigration Status', *Social Science & Medicine* 93: 78–85.

Verkuyten, Maykel. 2004. 'Emotional Reactions to and Support for Immigrant Policies', *Social Justice Research* 17(3): 293–314.

Viladrich, Anahí. 2012. 'Beyond Welfare Reform: Reframing Undocumented Immigrants' Entitlement to Health Care in the United States', *Social Science & Medicine* 74(6): 822–29.

———. 2019. '"We Cannot Let Them Die": Undocumented Immigrants and Media Framing of Health Deservingness in the United States', *Qualitative Health Research* 29(10): 1447–60.

Vilnai, Orly. 2015a. 'Three Infants Died This Month Because of Harsh Conditions in Daycares for Children of Asylum Seekers', *Ha'aretz*, 25 February. Retrieved 5 February 2022 from www.haaretz.co.il/news/orly/.premium-1.2573759.

———. 2015b. 'Four-Month-Old Infant Dies in Daycare for Children of Asylum Seekers in South Tel Aviv', *Ha'aretz*, 29 March. Retrieved 5 February 2022 from www.haaretz.co.il/news/education/.premium-1.2601973.

———. 2015c. 'Another Infant Dies in the "Child Warehouses" in South Tel Aviv, the Fifth in Two Months', *Ha'aretz*, 30 March. Retrieved 5 February 2022 from www.haaretz.co.il/news/education/1.2602929.

Wailoo, Keith, Julie Livingston and Peter Guarnaccia (eds). 2006. *A Death Retold: Jesica Santillan, the Bungled Transplant, and Paradoxes of Medical Citizenship*. Chapel Hill, NC: University of North Carolina Press.

Watters, Charles. 2007. 'Refugees at Europe's Borders: The Moral Economy of Care', *Transcultural Psychiatry* 44: 394–417.

Will, J.A. 1993. 'The Dimensions of Poverty: Public Perceptions of the Deserving Poor', *Social Science Research* 22: 312–32.

WHO Commission on Social Determinants of Health. 2008. *Closing the Gap in a Generation: Health Equity through Action on the Social Determinants of Health*. Geneva: World Health Organization.

Willen, Sarah S. 2011. 'Do "Illegal" Migrants Have a "Right to Health"? Engaging Ethical Theory as Social Practice at a Tel Aviv Open Clinic', *Medical Anthropology Quarterly* 45(3): 303–30.

———. 2012a. 'How Is Health-Related "Deservingness" Reckoned?', *Social Science & Medicine* 74(6): 812–21.

———. (ed.). 2012b. 'Special Issue – Migration, "Illegality", and Health: Mapping Embodied Vulnerability and Debating Health-Related Deservingness', *Social Science & Medicine* 74(6): 805–11.

———. 2019. *Fighting for Dignity: Migrant Lives at Israel's Margins*. Philadelphia: University of Pennsylvania Press.

Willen, Sarah S., Michael Knipper, César E. Abadía-Barrero, Nadav Davidovitch. 2017. 'Syndemic Vulnerability and the Right to Health', *The Lancet* 389: 964–77.

Williamson, Abigail F., Sarah S. Willen, Kristin K. Lunz Trujillo, Colleen C. Walsh. 2021. 'Whose Health Deserves Investment? A Crowdfunding Conjoint Experiment,' American Political Science Association Annual Meeting. Zoom/Seattle, WA. October 3.

Yarris, Kristin, and Heide Castañeda (eds). 2015. 'Special Issue – Discourses of Displacement and Deservingness: Interrogating Distinctions between "Economic" and "Forced' Migration", *International Migration* 53(3): 64–69.

Yoo, Grace J. 2002. 'Constructing Deservingness', *Journal of Aging and Social Policy* 13: 17–34.

———. 2008. 'Immigrants and Welfare: Policy Constructions of Deservingness', *Journal of Immigrant & Refugee Studies* 6(4): 490–507.

3

'Deserving Classes without Class'
Explaining the Neonationalist Ascendancy

Don Kalb

March 2020. On the borders of the European Union (EU), with the COVID-19 pandemic threatening human lives, sociality and welfare everywhere, Syrian refugees on the 'Balkan Route', bombed out of Idlib, are being beaten in the forests with wooden clubs by Romanian border guards before they are thrown back on to Serbian territory for further humiliations.[1] Romanian return migrants, fleeing the Italian and Spanish COVID-19 lockdowns *en masse*, are being told over the social networks that they should never have come back, contagious as they are imagined to be and a danger for a woefully underfunded public health system for which they have not paid. Further south, the Mediterranean is once again a heavily policed cemetery for migrants and refugees from the civil wars in the Middle East and North Africa – collateral damage of Western imperial delirium and hubris – as Greece is being hailed by the President of the European Commission for being the 'shield' behind which Europe can feel safe from the associated criminality. Meanwhile, Viktor Orbán has secured his corrupt autocracy in Hungary for another indefinite stretch of years after the Parliament gave him powers to single-handedly fight the COVID-19 pandemic and its long-term economic after-effects in the name of the Magyars and in the face of never-subsiding threats from the outside to the nation. Orbán will also continue, even more powerfully so now, to fight immigrants, gypsies, gays, feminists, cultural Marxists, nongovernmental organizations (NGOs), George Soros, population decline, the EU and everyone else who might be in his way. In Budapest, critique from the EU is rejected as being 'motivated by politics'. Vladimir Putin, too, has just been asked by the Russian Parliament to stay on indefinitely in his regal position so as to safeguard Russia's uncertain national future. Recep Tayyip Erdogan of Turkey is sure to be inspired and will not renege from his ongoing and unprecedentedly brutal crackdown on domestic dissent and 'traitors to the nation' while his armies are in Syria and Libya. Turkish prisons will continue to overflow.

All these, and manifold other events not mentioned here, are part of processes in the European East that have been continuous for at least a decade, all with a surprisingly steadfast direction. They appear to be diverse, occasioned by ethnographically unique and therefore apparently contingent events. Anthropologists, professionally spellbound by local fieldwork, are often easily swayed into describing them in their singularities. But that singular appearance is misleading. A more global anthropological strategy claims that these and kindred events are systemically rooted, interlinked and produced by an uneven bundle of global, scaled, social and historical forces (as in 'field of forces'). That field of global forces steadily cascades into, and then becomes dynamically incorporated within, a variegated terrain of national political theatres that produce this paradoxical simultaneity of shockingly singular events that on closer scrutiny reveal uncanny deeper family resemblances with each other. It is therefore instilling an unsettling sense of general systemic change, of a new historical era's arriving, of a liberal *Endzeit* ('the end of US hegemony', etc.).

These forces can summarily – and by now quite consensually – be described as the gradually accelerating implosion of a global regime of embedded and multiscalar solidarity arrangements ostensibly meant to share common prosperity via 'development', 'redistribution' and 'reform', however partial and skewed, arrangements that supported a popular and institutionalized belief that in the end 'all boats would be lifted'. These arrangements were anchored in national Fordism, liberal internationalism, welfare states, Keynesianism and restrictions on cross-border finance – Keynes' 'death of the rentier'. In their turn, these arrangements were fundamentally anchored in the Cold War with the Soviet Union and its promise of doing all those things even better. When that promise imploded from within (in 1989 and earlier), a universal planetary-wide and neoliberalized Darwinian competition emerged, with freely flowing capital in search of cheap but disciplined labour, deregulation and liberalization, rising domestic inequality and precarity, and domestic and international rivalry on all scales under the hubristic orchestration of the self-declared 'winners of the Cold War' – with a rising China gradually but powerfully emerging in the background as the new 'workshop of the world' and the new centre of accumulation.

Neonationalism appears from within this unfolding field of fragmenting forces as a contradictory bind driven, first of all, by class processes. When I say this, I do not mean class as a static condition or an 'economistic reduction', or as a sort of billiard ball-type of social group that comprises masses of people in exactly similar conditions with similar consciousness. I mean 'anthropological class' and 'relational class' (Kalb 2015): a set of basic relations of social reproduction; a set of power balances that shape the direction of social interactions and the overall 'arrow of time'; a bundle of relations of value in the broadest sense, of labour, of property, of distribution, of social worth and of recognition; and a determined set of relations of valorization of and by capital, and, vice versa, of devaluation and abandonment. This chapter thus links up with Mikuš' and Vetta's chapters in this collection, which both bring back dynamic and conflictive social relations into the study of 'moral deservingness'. However, class in the current chapter has even less to do with a well-delineated empirical group than in their work. This here is class in macrohistorical anthropology, focused on the shifting relational properties and directions that drive a whole process of capital accumulation and an epoch in world history, including, roughly, the shifting direction of its cultural and political antagonisms. But it is part of the same agenda as those of Mikuš and Vetta: to return key social relations back to the core of anthropological research interests and explanations.

Within this field of forces, neonationalism expresses itself as a tortuous desire for popular sovereignty (including sometimes a claim for the sovereignty of domestic capital) at the very moment of its dwindling. But it is not a sovereignty demanded effectively vis-à-vis globalized capital. Rather, it is a sovereignty that seeks to enact and/or re-enact an imagined 'rightful' social hierarchy that is seen as threatened or effectively stolen, a hierarchy expressed in claims towards deservingness domestically as well as internationally. These claims inevitably include their punitive flipside: humiliation of the undeserving and their ejection from the elevated community of the worthy.[2] This vision of sovereignty for the majority national people, including the humiliation that it requires domestically and internationally, is variably steeped in the well-known registers of racism, xenophobia, chauvinism and patriarchy, and it hits out revengefully at the perceived 'classes dangereuses' and selected subaltern populations, which are seen as being of 'low or no value', 'a cost', a 'threat' to any type of security and a 'moral corruption'. But, importantly, it also lashes out at the 'cosmopolitan classes' of elites and the higher-educated urbanites who are said to have embraced universal human rights over and above the civil or social rights of their compatriots within the national state, and have allegedly been willing to sell out those national 'classes of labour' whom they deem to be of less merit to international capitalist predators or have just abandoned them. That is one way of framing the argument that I have been trying to make, in various fashions, since the end of the 1990s (see e.g. Kalb 2000, 2002, 2005) when such forces began to stir in the sites that I was working on and living in (but it was and is not at all limited to those sites): the Netherlands, Belgium, Austria, Hungary and Poland – small European nations, both Eastern and Western, very different in an empirical and historical sense, but nevertheless together pointing the way.

This universalizing argument is amply corroborated by ongoing events in the West of the continent, which paint a similarly cohesive-cum-variegated picture as those in the East. Marine Le Pen, Matteo Salvini and the 'Fratelli di Italia' still pose a credible threat in terms of democratically overthrowing liberal globalist governments in France and Italy on behalf of the 'people' and 'the nation', and against the elites, the EU, immigrants, Muslims, the Left, communism (sic!) and finance capital. Dutch politicians, with a three-decade-long neoliberal right-wing anti-immigrant mobilization behind them and in the face of the global COVID-19 calamity, still believe one cannot send any money to Italy and the European South as it may well be spent on 'alcohol and women'. In the Dutch press, anonymous reactions to less brutal views often echo the tone of the claim that Southern countries were nothing more than 'dilapidated sheds ... even with our money they will never do the necessary repair works'.[3] Until its impressive policy turnaround in April/May 2020 in the face of the COVID-19 pandemic and fast-escalating EU fragmentation amid a world of hostile and nationalist great powers, the German government did not disagree. It was Angela Merkel herself who, in the wake of Brexit, had set up the Dutch as the leaders of a newly conceived right-wing 'frugal' flank in the EU under the historical banner of the Hanseatic League with the mission of facing down the federalist and redistributionist South now that the British were no longer involved. That Hanseatic banner suggested that penny-counting, competitive mercantilism, and its inevitable corollary – austerity and downward social pressure for 'the losers' – was ingrained in the competitive

North and would persist in order to sustain a just and natural hierarchy based on proven 'merit', both domestically and internationally. Britain, meanwhile, has valiantly elected to leave the EU in order to 'take back control' from international bureaucratic elites on behalf of what Boris Johnson imagines as the 'brilliant British nation'.[4] That nation will refuse labour migrants from the mainland and seek a future in the global Anglosphere, beefed up by a revitalized British Commonwealth where, presumably, when it comes to ceremony, not juridical equality between nations but global nostalgia for Empire and deference for the Queen and her brilliant Britain will rule (see Campanella and Dassu 2019).

Jonathan Friedman has called the driving relational mechanism behind this process 'double polarization', a mechanism that in his theoretical framework of 'global systemic anthropology' is associated with the globalization and financialization of capital (Friedman 2003, 2015; Friedman and Friedman 2008). The notion referred to the mutually reinforcing structural trends of social (vertical) as well as cultural (horizontal) polarization within globalizing nation-states. I still think this is a useful way of capturing the deeper dynamic, one that is certainly more analytically effective than all the condemnatory talk about populism coming from liberal pundits in political science and the media, who seem to have forgotten about the extremely effective populism of their own Reagans and Thatchers. However, I propose that we might even better think in terms of 'double devaluations'. This refers to the underlying classes, population categories and spaces. Neonationalist 'deservingness' discourses are often a populist response to systematic material as well as discursive processes of devaluation. The liberal distinctions between economic, political and cultural make only limited sense here. Double devaluation processes, like double polarization processes, are a comprehensive anthropological package.

Nevertheless, there is an urgent need to shift the analytic vocabulary concertedly away from the emic idioms of the neonationalists and the alt-right itself ('the people against the corrupted globalist and financial elites and the immigrants they bring in and protect'), which continue to echo through in the Friedmannian vision, and indeed have historically informed it.[5] At the same time, and confirming Friedman, it remains essential to keep grounding our vocabulary in systematic visions of the underlying capitalist transformation(s) on all levels and, other than Friedman, focus on how such transformations exactly impinge on our varied livelihoods and subjectivities – something that was often lacking in the liberal narratives, except for recent ritual regrets about rising macro-inequalities and now well-known brutal injustices such as the mass early dying of dispossessed workers in the Appalachians from official prescribed drugs (see e.g. Müller 2017); that lack of genuine interest has been less notable among the more genuinely conservative ones (see e.g. Vance 2016). We should also refuse a facile compartmentalization of 'economics' here and 'culture' there, as liberal authors and some Marxists are wont to do. Therefore Mouffe and Laclau, too, are clearly too slippery, too culturalist after their abandonment of class approaches.[6]

Marxism and Marxist anthropology offer tools that are potentially more precise than Friedman's macrotendencies, less culturalist than Mouffe's approach, and less provincial in their notion of 'the political' than liberal political science. The core notion of such a Marxist anthropology is class, relationally and anthropologically conceived. This includes an idea of polarization between and within classes, such as alluded to (though ultimately evaded) in Friedman's double polarization account, for which my double devaluation tries to make up. But before we get into something as aggregate and seemingly well-defined as classes in the sense of 'mass collectivities', we need something much more basic and in a sense more micro-anthropological: 'classness', in its fundamental meaning of compulsory dependent social reproduction (Kalb 2015; G. Smith 2015), a social reproduction that for the vast majority of people can only happen within historically circumscribed relational transactions with capitalist governing and ruling classes, classes that own and regulate, and that exploit, extract and dominate. For 'anthropological class', it is those daily relational transactions within fields of forces that develop in ways over which few have any control that we need to focus on (see also Tilly 1998, 2001).

In order to do so, I propose we bring the notions of value (including the value of labour, but also property, skills, education, habitats and commons), merit and deservingness (the latter two more Weberian than Marxist, though theoretically rather underarticulated) into play. I believe that we can help explain the neonationalist ascendancy by looking at the dialectic between the valorization of capital on the one hand, and the devaluation of labour, place, sunk capital, and inherited commons and habits on the other; the (neoliberal) tyranny of market-based individual and competitive 'merit' and its order of meritocracy and ranking; and the emergent counterclaim of the sheer collective social and cultural deservingness, the worth and dignity, of the 'national-popular' beyond individual 'pecuniary' merit as paid out by markets – including the evocation and manipulation of deservingness by political entrepreneurs – all in connection with such an anthropological idea of class, social reproduction and a vision of polarizing and variegating capitalist transformation.

Concretely, and with a focus on deservingness, we should see the neonationalist ascendancy as an expression of a rising countermovement, in the Polanyian sense (see also Szombati 2018; Kalb 2019), against the 'law of value' and its imposed social and spatial devaluations, in the Marxian sense. The latter inflicts systematic bouts of devaluation on particular skills, rights, expectations, spaces, subjectivities, and forms of popular culture and social reproduction. This devaluation includes dispossession and disenfranchisement, but is not limited to that. In this context, Michael Sandel speaks usefully of the 'tyranny of merit' (Sandel 2020). Merit is defined as a property of the individual, and is expressed in terms of talent and personal educational and professional success amid the flux of markets. However, deservingness, in the present context, is a collective political claim on the state and on state elites, with implications also for capital. It is a claim for recognition of worthiness, for rightful subsidiarity, for reciprocal loyalty of states and citizens as well as elites and subjects, and for the protection of rights that are seen as being under threat. In sum, it is a plea and an argument for an honoured place within a hierarchy of respectability, a popular call for repair and the return of a just social hierarchy. And it is a way of talking about 'class without class', not unlike E.P. Thompson's eighteenth-century rebellious English crowds (Thompson 1978), and, as such plebeian, tortuous and angry. Also, it is anchored in the contemporary demise of the Left in the Global North and the consequent ideological obsoleteness of the heritage of the 'working class century' (Therborn 2020a), for which the neoliberals who are now condemning the populists have worked so hard. It expresses the aspiration for 'the people' to be respected as 'middle class', as 'Staatstragende Klasse' at the precise moment of its evaporation, as in similar historical episodes of 'double devaluation' in capitalism such as the period from the 1890s to the 1930s (Volkov 1978; Kracauer 1998; Neumann 2009 [1942]).

The European Continent as Laboratory for the Anthropology of Neonationalism

Anthropologists working on the European continent have in retrospect done profoundly anticipatory, indeed uncommonly predictive work on the rise of neonationalism long before it broke the global liberal hold (Holmes 2000, 2019; Gingrich and Banks 2005; Gingrich 2006; Kalb 2009; Kalb and Halmai 2011), and a younger generation continues to build on that.[7] I single out neonationalism over and above currently competing terms such as 'populism' or 'illiberalism' because it produces less conceptual confusion and covers more cases. Neonationalism also partially overlaps with Stuart Hall's 'authoritarian populism', which has become increasingly popular. However, Hall's concept is rooted in a very different epoch and arguably lacks the important element of anger against cosmopolitan and globalized elites. It therefore fails to fully grasp the Left/Right fuzziness of the present conjuncture as well as the problems the Left is in. Neonationalism, it is essential to emphasize, is not seen here primarily as the aggregate sum of individual opinions. This is the baked-in misconception of much political science and sociology research anchored in methodological individualism, survey methodologies and poll outcomes.[8] It is the other way round: neonationalism is a public social and cultural context, a conjuncture if you like, generated within a structured and knowable field of social and historical forces that undergirds it. While Holmes, Gingrich, Banks, myself and others may have evinced an appropriate theoretical instinct twenty years ago, this is not because we were struck by clairvoyance. Anthropologists working in the centre of the continent were exposed early and in profound ways to this conjuncture (this is also true for those working on India; see Blom Hansen (1999)). The Italian Veneto, Austria, the Netherlands, Poland and Hungary were all avant-garde continental cases for the neonationalist ascendancy. It was from within these sites that we could already see the potentially general properties, amid the obvious differences, of what was going on.

The processes leading to such conjunctures were sped up by the imposed austerity and policy failures during the financial crises. But it was only in 2016, with the rise of Donald Trump and the referendum that led to Brexit, that our continental insights attained an aura of global or Northern universality and began to be noted among non-Europeanists. Anglo-Saxon media in the preceding years had regularly shrugged off the rise of neonationalist populisms in the EU with a reference to historical fascism and communism on the continent: not such good liberal democrats, historically, those continentals, was the often explicit suggestion, and they would point at obvious problems with cultural and social memory in the old world. The truth was that the representative electoral systems on the continent made popular organic processes visible long before they could strike at the heart of the state. In contrast, the British and US systems, majoritarian winner-takes-all two-party systems, with stark plutocratic tendencies in the latter case, did not permit similar subterranean trends to crystallize before they would become overwhelming. In Britain it was only with the political *Fremdkörper* of a referendum that the hold of the party elites would be broken. In the United States, it required, not surprisingly, a maverick billionaire in real estate, gambling and showbusiness – not finance, not technology, not the oil and defence-industrial complexes – coming from outside the political establishment to wrestle down the globalist hegemony within the Republican Party.

In both cases, the switch of allegiance of 'socially conservative working classes' in the provinces (the Midwest, the North, the 'red wall', etc.), as Michael Lind (2020) and others have simplifyingly called them, towards a populist Right was decisive, as it had been in Europe. This includes the refusal of white, black and Latino working classes to vote for Hillary Clinton. Electoral abstentions are an important part of the process of hegemonic change we are talking about: there was an active refusal on the part of their former beneficiaries to defend the Left liberal elites because there seemed little left to be defended anymore. This was not unlike what had happened in 1989 with the communists in Eastern Europe. In fact, we were now witnessing the second 'decommunization', this time as a slow-motion process hitting the social democrats and left liberals in the West. In the United Kingdom, anthropologists such as Gillian Evans and Jeannette Edwards (Edwards, Evans and Smith 2012; Evans 2012, 2017a, 2017b) have described how working classes in Britain had already been turning towards identifications as 'white' and ethnic in the early 2000s, and thus abandoning the political orbit of labour. This was long before the Brexit breakthrough. There was nothing exceptional here. Everywhere in the Global North, working classes, in particular the lowly educated, had over the last few decades increasingly stopped voting (Mair 2013). Illusions of inherent Anglo-liberal exceptionalism as compared to the continent, produced by the political time bubble in the United States and the United Kingdom for as long as that bubble lasted, evaporated at once in 2016. The West as a whole now appeared illiberal and populist, and with a loud bang, a world historical epoch seemed to have come to a close.

Anglophone anthropologists now realized that they had long preferred to study people that they overtly liked and that they favoured politically, and that they had shown little interest in the illiberal Right, let alone fascism. They also became aware that they had generally ignored questions of class, and indeed of 'the white working class'. This was the summary feeling, put too cryptically perhaps here, coming out of the *American Ethnologist* special issue dedicated to the rise of the populist Right in 2017 (see in particular Gusterson (2017); Walley (2017); see also, for a next stage of the debate, Maskovsky and Bjork-James (2020)). These two issues, the question of the populist Right and the question of class, are intimately connected: the Northern working class had been 'out' among anthropologists as it had been 'out' among policy-makers, media pundits and capitalists. A neoliberal complicity that may seem surprising to many.

I speak of neonationalism as what connects our cases. What we have seen emerging in the last three decades is obviously not the classic liberal civic nationalism of nineteenth-century liberal nation-state-making that an earlier wave of writing on nationalism in anthropology and history was oriented upon (Gellner 1983; Anderson 1991; Hobsbawm 1992; Hobsbawm and Ranger 1992; Eriksen 1993; Smith 1995). The present nationalisms are ethnic (or ethnoreligious), breathe anger and nostalgia, and instead of liberal congregate as illiberal. They are pervaded by dreams of imagined national golden times and greatness unjustly ended by conspiring dark internationalist forces. But they are also believed to be capable of being brought back by the sheer force of national will and excellence. Such visions are often fed by a combination of historically objective as well as imaginary (self-)victimization at the hand of alliances between imperial actors, EU bureaucrats, transnational capital, culturally liberal and cosmopolitan state elites betraying the nation, and immigrants or minorities protected by human rights regimes and open borders. Some of them, including the East European ones and Trumpism, indulge in painting 'cultural marxism', 'sexo-marxism' and anti-fascist anarcho-communism as the deeper enemy (see Seymour 2020).

These nostalgias are a complex politicocultural product of the popular stagnation, public decline and rising inequalities amid fast neoliberal and technological change. Brexit Britain replays its memories of victory in the Second World War and its glorious forlorn empire in both cinematic, literary and political theatre. In its new constitution and the new historical museums in Budapest, Orbán's Hungary celebrates the hierarchy of 'estates', the sociocultural order of property and propriety, of the Habsburg Empire, of which it imagines itself to be the prodigious son and brilliant historical co-owner. The mercantilist Dutch celebrate their golden age of the seventeenth century in museums and research, and continue to believe that debt is *Schuld*, while being one of the most privately indebted societies in Europe. They are also back to fetishizing a mercantilist 'gold standard' of which they were once the standard-bearer, a gold standard imagined to be embodied in the current neoliberal architecture of the euro (Kalb 2020) and their own carefully curated triple-A rating. They have forgotten about the unnecessary popular misery inflicted on the Dutch by sticking to the gold standard as one of the last nations in the 1930s (see Kalb 1997) and they do not like to hear about the free gift for the actual pricing of their competitive exports derived from sharing their euro with less creditworthy, more import-addicted and therefore obviously less deserving countries.[9] Nostalgias are painfully distortive, but in the current context in the Global North, they seemingly have to be lived and acted out everywhere (see also Campanella and Dassu 2019).

The Class Conundrum: Absent Presence and Present Absence

Importantly, many, but not all, of these neonationalisms are, at least rhetorically, *Left-Right national socialisms strictu sensu* (see Kalb (2011); a crucial difference with Hall's authoritarian populism, hinting at its limitations for grasping the present context adequately), hence the confusion on the Left. Neonationalist political claims often demand social protection and recognition for 'majority national working classes' and support for domestic entrepreneurs, who steadily combine in the coalition of the deserving. Quite a few of them have an anti-neoliberal feel (with the partial exceptions of the 'Hanseatic' cases, at least before the COVID-19 pandemic, on which I have no space to elaborate here). The historical context within and against which they act sums up what they are about: they are driven by the contradictions of the neoliberal globalizations of the last forty years. But they are not the resolution of these contradictions, and keep embodying and prolonging them in twisted ways. Contradictions here not just in the abstract – although in a Marxian sense that too – but as concretely operating in, and transformative of, the daily lives of situated subjects; contradictions that have often worked in dispossessive, devaluing and disenfranchising ways for many, sometimes violently so, producing pervasive feelings of popular abandonment. Such abandonment was routinely denied, obscured and misrecognized by existing liberal political vocabularies, technocratic knowledges and governance paradigms. Fake news, now a favourite object of scorn for liberals, is absolutely nothing new and was almost 'expertly' scripted into neoliberal governance through abstract and biased forms of accounting singularly centred on GDP growth, national accounts and abstract quantitative averages of everything as if these were reliable and sufficient descriptions of what was happening in people's lives. This basic historical context in large measure defines the nature of the neonationalisms we are presently confronted with, and this figured prominently in the anthropological political economy approach that I and my collaborators were promoting in 'Headlines of Nation, Subtexts of Class' (Kalb and Halmai 2011; Kalb 2011; see also Kalb 2015, 2019). Nowadays, of course, parts of the same insight are being repeated over and over again in simplified ways by journalists, commentators and liberal theorists who before 2010 had little or no eye for all this (recently, for example, Lind 2020; Goodhart 2017; Krastev 2017), and who often imagine, significantly, that it was only with the financial crises of 2008–12 that illiberal populism began to gain momentum. However, these are systematic relational properties of long-term class-driven processes that already began in the late 1970s, both in Eastern and Western Europe. This was surely a fresh and exciting discovery to make in the early 2000s and my point is that it was not accidental that anthropologists of continental Europe were among the first to articulate it.

There were two further reasons for this anthropological vanguard role (a role hardly acknowledged elsewhere) – one empirical, the other theoretical. There was a network of mostly junior researchers converging on Budapest and the Central European University (CEU), discussing political and economic dynamics in Central/Eastern European urban settings. Budapest was obviously a rich intellectual and geographical-political focal point for the contradictions of neoliberal globalization in Europe – so much so, in fact, that the CEU would subsequently be expelled from a transformed Hungary gripped by a violently assertive neonationalist politics.[10] We shared a critical attitude towards the neoliberal transformations that were working themselves out, piecemeal, incrementally, over a longer period, in the sites in Eastern and Western Europe that we were studying. Those urban sites, from postsocialist Györ (Bartha 2011), Cluj (Faje 2011; Petrovici 2011), Wroclaw (Kalb 2009) and Kikinda (Vetta 2011) to the Marche industrial district (Blim 2011) and the Ticino region in central and northern Italy (Stacul 2011), were generating right-wing popular sensibilities before our very eyes. These were often articulated by emerging neonationalist movements, right-wing labour unions and proto-party formations.

The second reason for continental anthropology's vanguard role lay in the enabling theoretical framework offered by Jonathan Friedman's anthropology of global systems, which was hardly read by anthropologists in the United Kingdom and the United States. Friedman's work from the late 1970s to the early 2000s had creatively assembled a notion of 'double polarizations' driven by the denationalization of capital as a consequence of overaccumulation in the old core, including the consequent demise of national welfare statism and the collapse of the class compromises behind it. Friedman, it is also worth noting, had developed this vision earlier than Giovanni Arrighi (1994), and with a keener sense of the potential right-wing rather than left-wing political consequences (Friedman 2003, 2015; Friedman and Friedman 2008). To focus on situated class trajectories and related relational dynamics in both everyday lives and within political fields, as we were doing, was a way to bring Friedman's anthropology of global systems – an avowedly abstract undertaking in search mainly of historical 'tendencies' rather than lived realities – back on the ground and make it run (see also Kalb 2013, 2015). As individual hopes for middle classness and the expected proofs of individual merit were being denied amid the celebratory public bonfire of 'the middle classes', 'democracy' and 'civil society' that neoliberalism was, the devalued groups of workers we were researching responded by embracing collectivist ethnonational calls for deservingness.

Class is the absent presence and the present absence behind the ascendancy of the neonationalist (and often populist and illiberal) Right, and deservingness is its agonistic rhetorical claim.[11] Let me clarify that claim, because this is logically not a mere empirical statement, either for the absences or for the presences. In 'Headlines of Nation, Subtexts of Class', we did write that the people being mobilized behind neonationalist banners were 'broadly working class people'. While this was somehow empirically correct for the cases that we were studying in the book, this was not meant to be a covering empirical law or an exclusivist claim. Also, the prefix 'broadly' was supposed to do some serious but perhaps understated empirical work, while also *sotto voce* invoking a theoretical twist. We were clearly not just talking about that classic twentieth-century icon, the blue-collar industrial working classes, even though we were referring to them too (such as in Kalb (2009), Bartha (2011) and Vetta (2011)). Our definition allowed for the likelihood that many were in fact precariats, entre-precariats, small entrepreneurs, direct producers, technical managers, lower clerical personnel, shopkeepers, even higher-educated persons such as teachers, accountants and of course retired workers (but not mainly 'lumpen proletarians', as Clyde Barrow (2020) claims for the United States, problematically in my eyes). We also assumed that their actual class 'positions' may often have been less than well defined, temporary and shifting, fuzzy rather than fixed or well demarcated (on class and fuzziness more generally, see Kalb (2015)). Nor was class just about 'work' or income. Biographies and whole lives, Marx's 'living labour', including their whole habitats, were what we were aiming at. We were referring in a good Marxian sense to the whole sphere of reproduction of people and households who lacked access to substantial capital or high-value property, or highly marketable and therefore meritocratic 'human capital', in spatial contexts of devaluation that were also part of the polarizing logic of capital: The 'common people' in common places who could reasonably be pitched as the people against the elites (see also Kalb 2011, 2015). The *sotto voce* theoretical twist was that while some or many of these people might have preferred to see themselves as middle classes, a powerful and broadly shared aspiration as well as a social myth deeply inscribed into the capitalist machine, the point was that those imagined middle classes, too, were feeling the inescapable and often degrading force of the law of value in many aspects of their lives (Kalb and Mollona 2018; Therborn 2020a; see more generally on the anthropology of the middle class Weiss (2019)). The point is that deservingness tends to be claimed by those who feel the sharp forces of devaluation, but not by those who have long learnt to live with being devalued. As electoral statistics almost everywhere show (Therborn 2020b), the 20 per cent poorest in societies of the Global North never figure highly among those now claiming collective deservingness and voting for the neonationalists. It is those for whom double devaluation is a new and unexpected painful experience, just like in the 1890s and the 1930s (Volkov 1978; Kracauer 1998; Neumann 2009 [1942]). And because they are claiming 'class without class', they tend to indulge in marking the social and cultural boundaries with those who have always already been devalued and who are the pet object of elite compassion, exactly those governing classes who have allegedly abandoned the deserving popular-national.

Recent research does offer lots of evidence for this 'broadly working class' account, even though in the United States and the United Kingdom, the Trump and Brexit electoral mobilizations did rely heavily on classical right-wing older suburban middle classes with property and financial outlays, the classical electorates for the Tories and the Republicans. Among those earning more than $50,000 a year, Trump scored majorities everywhere. Trumpian politics was also fed by billionaires' money (the Koch brothers, etc.). Importantly, we were talking about coalitions and alliances in which 'broadly working-class people' were being mobilized, both electorally and in actual movements, alliances that could not become politically dominant without broad working-class support. Such alliances were never ideologically 'classist', even though they might be a symbolic feast for 'American workers', 'working-class families', 'Magyar workers', 'the common people', 'la France profonde', etc. There was no impulse towards solidarity as a class in relation to capital and the state. This was 'class without class' (see Kalb 2019), and in the context of multiple globalizations, above all of capital and finance, globalizations often enabled and celebrated by social democrats and left liberals in power, the 'elite'. And so it became the nation versus the elite exactly at the point that capital had escaped the cage of the nation-state.

Further, we had already a keen feeling that metropolitan working classes in dynamic labour markets, who were younger and higher educated, often on a precarious track towards merit as 'creative classes', might be less susceptible to the neonationalist mobilizations than those in the provinces, the secondary cities, the suburbs and exurbs, which *we* were studying. Recent events have shown this to be a good hunch. The spatial divides of neoliberal capitalism, mostly reflected too in state policies of investment, redistribution and planned abandonment, are an essential part of the class story that is playing itself out. The Left-Right call for the ethnonation poses the devalued provinces and the outer boroughs, their inhabitants and 'their ways of life', against the disloyal capitals and the metropoles.

Our argument was straightforward: without substantial ('white') working-class support for the new neonationalisms and their claims for majoritarian popular deservingness, the latter would not break the liberal cosmopolitan hold over the political centre. Workers, broadly conceived, would have to abandon the social democratic parties in sufficient numbers in order for the new Right to shift the scales, a process that had started in the late 1970s. That abandonment had been going on in many places for a long while, whether in postsocialist Europe, neoliberal Britain, the Netherlands, the United States or Italy. The new Right often had something for them that the by now 'third way' Left no longer offered: recognition of their inherent cultural worth as part of the national people, and a promise, however elusive, of social or economic redistribution and protection of inherited rights, life modes and communities.[12] The neonationalist Right – not just the 'extreme right' or 'radical right' of the political scientists and journalists, though they too. The point is that some of their claims were becoming hegemonic and adopted by the centre; even the centre Left – as in the Netherlands and Denmark – was sometimes making an offer to the abandoned majority in the provinces for a new potential belonging, a belonging to an ethnonationally defined world of recognition of their collective deservingness, possibly protection and even renewed valorization and productivity, the latter being of great relevance for one's enduring sense of worth and security in a capitalist world and the ultimate form of redistributed recognition. And the offer was made in a style that spoke to their senses,[13] a style that could at the very least help to elicit a protest vote. By 2010, big minorities of national electorates everywhere (>25–30 per cent) had long stopped voting – let alone actively belonging to established political parties – and this quarter of the electorate was heavily biased towards lower-educated working people of all ages and sexes, mainly in the provinces, whose skills and habitats had been devalued by capital as well as the state. Ethnonationalist political entrepreneurs with the right gusto could aim at pushing the electoral scales over in one good go. The abandonment of a solidary politics of class from the 1980s to the 2010s by governing and ruling classes, and the reciprocal abandonment by provincial working classes of a complicit social democracy, produced new and twisted presences as well as absences of class within a counterpolitics of the ethnonation. As Žižek (2008: 267) poignantly pointed out, this was the return of the repressed in characteristically tortuous and traumatic ways.

Coda

In the early 2000s, Charles Tilly called upon anthropologists to join a new mode of what he called relational studies of class and inequality that he was hoping would develop new insights in sociology, illustrated by his own 'Durable Inequality' (1998). Class analysis is still in need of a more anthropological approach, working against the reifications and reductions of mainstream sociology, economics and political science that tend to monopolize our gaze. We need 'expanded class', as I wrote a good time ago (Kalb 1997): to describe and analyse a contradictory and shifting vital field of forces, creating pressures and setting limits for social life, while generating determinate tendencies of development and thus rendering directionality to social processes in space and time.[14] Class should have been a verb rather than a substantive, as E.P. Thompson insisted long ago. That anthropological agenda requires us to understand that the valorization of capital spans politics, society, economics, culture and space, all of that, in uneven, contradictory and contentious ways: capitalism is a living, structured and contradictory social totality, and not just 'an economy'. It is that whole that we should try to aim at. As Mikuš and Vetta argue brilliantly in this volume, claims about collective deservingness are not only moral stories. Rather, they help to configure a collective politics that is rooted in the contradictions and antagonisms of capitalist social relations as they shift and unfold. Our entry into this clockwork as anthropologists, as I have argued, lies within the dialectics of economic value, social and cultural worth ('values', 'individual merit', 'collective deservingness' and 'status'), power, place and livelihood. Terry Turner (2005) once wrote that we need a value theory of labour rather than a labour theory of value. That remains overwhelmingly true. Such a value theory of labour is often expressed emically in liberal ideas of individual merit and collectivist ideas of deservingness and undeservingness. Turner also inspires the notion of 'double devaluation', a devaluation both material and discursive, with a connotation of public abandonment. In an age when the whole of social life seems to be subjected to a 'real subsumption' under capital (as Harvey (2018) and Hardt and Negri (2018, 2019) concur), there is a political need for a value theory of current social life as a whole, one that, unlike theories of liberal individual merit and collective national-popular deservingness, refuses to celebrate intraclass divisions and cultural boundaries that steadily require humiliation and punishment of the undeserving. For that, we arguably need a politics of 'class with class' that can include all classes of labour, and an end to the politics of 'deserving classes without class' that drives the neonationalist ascendancy.

Don Kalb is Professor of Social Anthropology at the University of Bergen, where he leads the 'Frontiers of Value' project. He recently co-led the 'Financialization' project at the Max Planck Institute for Social Anthropology in Halle. His work focuses on relational anthropologies of capitalism, class, financialization and the illiberal. His latest books are *Anthropologies of Class* (Cambridge University Press, 2015, with James Carrier), *Worldwide Mobilizations: Class Struggles and Urban Commoning* (Berghahn, 2018, with Mao Mollona) and *Financialization: Relational Approaches* (Berghahn, 2020, with Chris Hann). He is Founding Editor of *Focaal – Journal of Global and Historical Anthropology* and of *FocaalBlog* (Berghahn Books).

Notes

1. This episode and the other ones related in the next three paragraphs are a selection from reports in the *Financial Times*, *The Guardian* and *NRC Handelsblad* (the Netherlands) in the last week of March and the first days of April 2020. Thanks to Oana Mateescu for pointing out discussions on Romanian social networks. This text is written well before the Ukrainian war. Obviously, the Russian attack on Ukraine is relevant for the topic at hand in multiple ways.
2. I am not claiming that this is the only way in which deservingness is discursively deployed in the current epoch. In addition, one can use the language of deservingness to make a case for the respect and care that migrants deserve, or even differentiate among migrants between the deserving and the nondeserving. The point I am making is that: (1) deservingness is a public claim that attaches to a group or a category and is made towards the state; (2) the 'majority people' is now a category to whom such claims attach and by whom such claims are being made; (3) in particular, such claims are also made by and for, broadly, the capitalistically 'devalued' working classes.
3. NRC, 30 March 2020, comments on 'Europese solidariteit is juist ook in het Nederlandse belang'.
4. *The Economist*, 30 January 2020.
5. With *PC Worlds* (2019), Jonathan Friedman has arguably descended into the neonationalist Right himself, an embarrassing slide from his earlier structural Marxism that was probably intellectually enabled by his abstract structuralism, his conceptual focus on global/local and on national 'elites' instead of capital, and his neglect of class, conceptually as well as 'on the ground'.
6. For a good discussion, see Laclau and Mouffe (1985); Laclau (2004); Anderson (2017): 93–99; Mouffe (2018).
7. For example (without a claim to completeness – excuses to those left out): Buzalka 2008, 2018, 2020; Makovicky 2013; Stacul 2014, 2018; Keskula 2015; Koch 2016, 2017; Pasieka 2016, 2017; Shoshan 2016; Cammeli 2017; Szombati 2018; Teitelbaum 2017; Thorleifsson 2017, 2019; Scheiring 2020. See also Bangstad et al. 2019. As in all similar work in other disciplines, there is an alternating and overlapping use of terms and focus from 'far Right' to 'populism' to 'illiberalism' and to 'neonationalism'.
8. Hence also the tendency among political scientists to attribute the rise of the Right to immigration, xenophobia and 'white shift' rather than broader political economic transformations; see Kaufman (2018); Mudde (2019). Their surveys simply repeat what people think they know about themselves at this moment in time, but what they know and don't know is an effect of hegemonic push and pull.
9. See Kalb (2018) for a more detailed discussion of Hungary and the Netherlands.
10. This is a good moment to recall the energizing intellectual and profes-

sional atmosphere that the young (2003) Department of Sociology and Social Anthropology at CEU in the heart of Budapest, from which it has now been expelled, had been enabling all through these years. We should all hope that it can be re-created in the new Vienna campus.
11. Edelman, Scoones and others place the crisis not among workers, but among peasantries, farmers and people in the disinvested countryside (Scoones et al. 2018; Edelman 2019). I should note that I have no quarrel with this, as those sites are explicitly included in my definitions. However, I do have a problem with 'peasants'. Their numerical weight in the Global North is simply too small, strictly speaking. I taste a bit of Chayanov's populism here and I must admit I lean towards Lenin in that historical debate on the fate of the peasantry, certainly in the present context; see Brass (2015). 'Broadly working class' seems to represent their actual relationships of social reproduction minimally as well as 'peasantry'.
12. Thomas Frank (2004) has presciently pointed at the substitution of economic redistribution by cultural recognition as key to the advance of the Right as the US Democrats and European Social Democrats were cancelling redistribution. This turned out to be a general insight.
13. See the set of studies offered in Kapferer and Theodossopoulos (2019). Moffit (2016) is among those inspired by Laclau and Mouffe, who tend to reduce populism to style and miss out on the crucial issue of the class and value substance.
14. Note that Nancy Fraser and Rahel Jaeggi have been calling for an 'expanded notion of capitalism'. I cannot agree more (Fraser and Jaeggi 2018).

References

Anderson, Benedict. 1991. *Imagined Communities: Reflections on the Origin and Spread of Nationalism*. London: Verso.

Anderson, Perry. 2017. *The H-Word: The Peripeteia of Hegemony*. London: Verso.

Arrighi, Giovanni. 1994. *The Long Twentieth Century: Money, Power and the Origins of Our Time*. London: Verso.

Bangstad, Sindre, et al. 2019. 'The Politics of Affect: Perspectives on the Rise of the Far-Right and Right-Wing Populism in the West', *Focaal: Journal of Global and Historical Anthropology* 83: 98–113.

Barrow, Clyde. 2020. *The Dangerous Class: The Concept of the Lumpenproletariat*. Ann Arbor: University of Michigan Press.

Bartha, Eszter. 2011. '"It Can't Make Me Happy That Audi Is Prospering": Working-Class Nationalism in Hungary after 1989', in Don Kalbe and Gabor Halmai (eds), *Headlines of Nation, Subtexts of Class: Working Class Populism and the Return of the Repressed in Neoliberal Europe*. Oxford: Berghahn Books, pp. 92–112.

Blim, Michael. 2011. 'A Long March to Oblivion? The Decline of the Italian Left on Its Home Ground and the Rise of the New Right in Their Midst', in Don Kalb and Gabor Halmai (eds), *Headlines of Nation, Subtexts of Class: Working Class Populism and the Return of the Repressed in Neoliberal Europe*. Oxford: Berghahn Books, pp. 142–55.

Blom Hansen, Thomas. 1999. *The Saffron Wave: Democracy and Hindu Nationalism in Modern India*. Princeton: Princeton University Press.

Brass, Tom. 2015. 'Peasants, Academics, Populists: Forward to the Past?', *Critique of Anthropology* 35(2): 187–204.

Buzalka, Juraj. 2008. 'Europeanisation and Post-peasant Populism in Eastern Europe', *Europe-Asia Studies* 60(5): 757–71.

———. 2018. 'Post-peasant Memories: Populist or Communist Nostalgia?', *Eastern European Politics and Society* 32(4): 988–1006.

———. 2020. *The Cultural Economy of Protest in the Post-Socialist European Union: Village Fascists and Their Rivals*. Abingdon: Routledge.

Cammeli, Maddalena Gretel. 2017. 'Fascism as a Style of Life: Community Life and Violence in a Neofascist Movement in Italy', *Focaal: Journal of Global and Historical Anthropology* 79: 89–101.

Campanella, Edoardo, and Marta Dassu. 2019. *Anglo Nostalgia: The Politics of Emotions in a Fractured West*. London: Hurst.

Edelman, Marc. 2019. 'Hollowed Out Heartland, USA: How Capital Sacrificed Communities and Paved the Way for Authoritarian Populism', *Journal of Rural Studies*, https://doi.org/10.1016/j.jrurstud.2019.10.045.

Edwards, Jeannette, Gillian Evans and Katie Smith. 2012. 'Introduction: The Middle-Class-ification of Britain', *Focaal: Journal of Global and Historical Anthropology* 62: 3–16.

Eriksen, Thomas Hylland. 1993. *Ethnicity and Nationalism: Anthropological Perspectives*. Chicago: University of Chicago Press.

Evans, Gillian. 2012. '"The Aboriginal People of England": The Culture of Class Politics in Contemporary Britain', *Focaal: Journal of Global and Historical Anthropology* 62: 17–29.

———. 2017a. 'Social Class and the Cultural Turn: Anthropology, Sociology and the Postindustrial Politics of 21st Century Britain', *Sociological Review* 65(1): 88–104.

———. 2017b. 'Brexit Britain: Why We Are All Postindustrial Now', *American Ethnologist* 44(2): 2015–19.

Faje, Florin. 2011. 'Football Fandom in Cluj: Class, Ethno-nationalism and Cosmopolitanism', in Don Kalb and Gabor Halmai (eds), *Headlines of Nation, Subtexts of Class: Working Class Populism and the Return of the Repressed in Neoliberal Europe*. Oxford: Berghahn Books, pp. 78–91.

Frank, Thomas. 2004. *What's the Matter with Kansas? How Conservatives Won the Heart of America*. New York: Owl Books.

Fraser, Nancy, and Rahel Jaeggi. 2018. *Capitalism: A Conversation in Critical Theory*. Cambridge: Polity Press.

Friedman, Jonathan. (ed.). 2003. *Globalization, the State and Violence*. Walnut Creek, CA: AltaMira Press.
———. 2015. 'Global Systemic Crisis, Class and Its Representations', in James Carrier and Don Kalb (eds), *Anthropologies of Class: Power, Practice and Inequality*. Cambridge: Cambridge University Press, pp. 183–99.
———. 2019. *PC Worlds: Political Correctness and Rising Elites at the End of Hegemony*. Oxford: Berghahn Books.
Friedman, Kajsa Ekholm, and Jonathan Friedman. 2008. *Modernities, Class, and the Contradictions of Globalization: The Anthropology of Global Systems*. Lanham, MD: AltMmira Press.
Gellner, Ernest. 1983. *Nations and Nationalism*. Ithaca, NY: Cornell University Press.
Gingrich, Andre. 2006. 'Neo-nationalism and the Reconfiguration of Europe', *Social Anthropology* 14(2): 196–217.
Gingrich, Andre, and Marcus Banks (eds). 2005. *Neo-nationalism in Europe and beyond: Perspectives from Social Anthropology*. Oxford: Berghahn Books.
Goodhart, David. 2017. *The Road to Somewhere: The New Tribes Shaping British Politics*. London: Penguin.
Gusterson, Hugh. 2017. 'From Brexit to Trump: Anthropology and the Rise of Nationalist Populism', *American Ethnologist* 44(2): 209–14.
Halmai, Gabor. 2011. '(Dis)Possessed by the Spectre of Socialism: Nationalist Mobilization in "Transitional Hungary"', in Don Kalb and Gabor Halmai (eds), *Headlines of Nation, Subtexts of Class: Working Class Populism and the Return of the Repressed in Neoliberal Europe*. Oxford: Berghahn Books, pp. 113–41.
Hardt, Michael, and Toni Negri. 2018. 'The Multiplicities within Capitalist Rule and the Articulation of Struggles', *tripleC* 16(2): 440–48.
———. 2019. 'Empire: Twenty Years on', *New Left Review* 120: 67–93.
Harvey, David. 2018. 'Universal Alienation and the Real Subsumption of Daily Life under Capital: A Response to Hardt and Negri', *tripleC* 16(2): 449–53.
Hobsbawm, Eric. 1992. *Nations and Nationalism since 1780: Programme, Myth, and Reality*. Cambridge: Cambridge University Press.
Hobsbawm, Eric, and Terence Ranger (eds). 1992. *The Invention of Tradition*. Cambridge: Cambridge University Press.
Holmes, Douglas. 2000. *Integral Europe: Fast Capitalism, Multiculturalism, Neo-fascism*. Princeton: Princeton University Press.
———. 2019. 'Fascism at Eye Level', *Focaal: Journal of Global and Historical Anthropology* 84: 62–90.
Kalb, Don. 1997. *Expanding Class: Power and Everyday Politics in Industrial Communities, The Netherlands 1850–1950*. Durham, NC: Duke University Press.
———. 2000. 'Localizing Flows: Power, Paths, Institutions, and Networks', in Don Kalb et al. (eds), *The Ends of Globalization: Bringing Society Back in*. Lanham, MD: Rowman & Littlefield, pp. 1–32.

———. 2002. 'Afterword: Globalism and Post-socialist Prospects', in Chris Hann (ed.), *Postsocialism: Ideals, Ideologies and Local Practice*. London: Routledge, pp. 317–35.

———. 2005. 'From Flows to Violence. Politics and Knowledge in the Debates on Globalization and Empire', *Anthropological Theory* 5(2): 176–204.

———. 2009. 'Conversations with a Polish Populist: Tracing Hidden Histories of Globalization, Class, and Dispossession in Postsocialism (and beyond)', *American Ethnologist* 36(2): 207–23.

———. 2011. 'Introduction: Headlines of Nation, Subtexts of Class: Working Class Populism and the Return of the Repressed in Neoliberal Europe', in Don Kalb and Gabor Halmai (eds), *Headlines of Nation, Subtexts of Class: Working Class Populism and the Return of the Repressed in Neoliberal Europe*. Oxford: Berghahn Books, pp. 1–36.

———. 2013. 'Financialization and the Capitalist Moment: Marx versus Weber in the Anthropology of Global Systems', *American Ethnologist* 40(2): 258–66.

———. 2015. 'Introduction: Class and the New Anthropological Holism', in James Carrier and Don Kalb (eds), *Anthropologies of Class*. Cambridge: Cambridge University Press, pp. 1–27.

———. 2018. 'Deep Play: Finance, Demos and Ethnos in the New Old Europe', in Bruce Kapferer (ed.), *The Margins of the State*. London: Sean Kingston Publishing, pp. 23–66.

———. 2019. 'Post-Socialist Contradictions: The Social Question in Central and Eastern Europe and the Making of the Illiberal Right', in Jan Breman et al. (eds), *The Social Question in the Twenty-First Century: A Global View*. Berkeley: University of California Press, pp. 208–27.

———. 2020. 'Introduction: Transitions to What? On the Social Relations of Financialization in Anthropology and History', in Chris Hann and Don Kalb (eds), *Financialization: Relational Approaches*. Oxford: Berghahn Books, pp. 1–41.

Kalb, Don, and Gabor Halmai (eds). 2011. *Headlines of Nation, Subtexts of Class: Working Class Populism and the Return of the Repressed in Neoliberal Europe*. Oxford: Berghahn Books.

Kalb, Don, and Mao Mollona (eds). 2018. *Worldwide Mobilizations: Class Struggles and Urban Commoning*. Oxford: Berghahn Books.

Kapferer, Bruce, and Dimitrios Theodossopoulos (eds). 2019. *Democracy's Paradox: Populism and Its Contemporary Crisis*. Oxford: Berghahn Books.

Kaufman, Eric. 2018. *Whiteshift: Populism, Immigration and the Future of White Majorities*. London: Penguin.

Keskula, Eeva. 2015. 'Reverse, Restore, Repeat! Class, Ethnicity, and the Russian Speaking Miners of Estonia', *Focaal: Journal of Global and Historical Anthropology* 72: 95–110.

Koch, Insa. 2016. 'Bread and Butter Politics: Democratic Disenchantment and Everyday Politics on an English Council Estate', *American Ethnologist* 43(2): 282–94.
———. 2017. 'What's in a Vote? Brexit beyond Culture Wars', *American Ethnologist* 44(2): 225–30.
Kracauer, Siegfried. 1998. *The Salaried Masses: Disorientation and Distraction in Weimar Germany*. London: Verso.
Krastev, Ivan. 2017. *After Europe*. Philadelphia: University of Pennsylvania Press.
Laclau, Ernesto. 2004. *On Populist Reason*. London: Verso.
Laclau, Ernesto, and Chantal Mouffe (eds). 1985. *Hegemony and Socialist Strategy*. London: Verso.
Lind, Michael. 2020. *The New Class War: Saving Democracy from the Metropolitan Elite*. New York: Atlantic Books.
Mair, Peter. 2013. *Ruling the Void: The Hollowing of Western Democracy*. London: Verso.
Makovicky, Nicolette. 2013. '"Work Pays": Slovak Neoliberalism as Authoritarian Populism', *Focaal: Journal of Global and Historical Anthropology* 67: 77–90.
Maskovsky, Jeff, and Sophie Bjork-James (eds). 2020. *Beyond Populism*. Morgantown, WV: West Virginia University Press.
Moffit, Benjamin. 2016. *The Global Rise of Populism: Performance, Political Style, and Representation*. Stanford: Stanford University Press.
Mollona, Massimiliano, and Don Kalb. 2018. 'Notes for a Contemporary Urban Class Analysis', in Don Kalb and Mao Mollona (eds), *Worldwide Mobilizations: Class Struggles and Urban Commoning*. Oxford: Berghahn Books (Dislocations), pp. 1–30.
Mouffe, Chantal. 2018. *For a Left Populism*. London: Verso.
Mudde, Cas. 2019. *The Far Right Today*. London: Polity.
Müller, Jan-Werner. 2017. *What Is Populism?* London: Penguin.
Neumann, Franz. 2009 [1942]. *Behemoth: The Structure and Practice of National Socialism, 1933–1944*. Chicago: Ivan R. Dee.
Pasieka, Agnieszka. 2016. 'Reenacting Ethnic Cleansing: People's History and Elitist Nationalism in Contemporary Poland', *Nations and Nationalism* 22(1): 63–83.
———. 2017. "Taking Far-Right Claims Seriously and Literally: Anthropology and the Study of Right-Wing Radicalism', *Slavic Review* 76(1): 519–29.
Petrovici, Norbert. 2011. 'Articulating the Right to the City: Working-Class Neo-nationalism in Postsocialist Cluj, Romania', in Don Kalb and Gabor Halmai (eds), *Headlines of Nation, Subtexts of Class: Working Class Populism and the Return of the Repressed in Neoliberal Europe*. Oxford: Berghahn Books, pp. 57–78.
Sandel, Michael. 2020. *The Tyranny of Merit: What's Become of the Common Good?* London: Allen Lane.

Scheiring, Gabor. 2020. *The Retreat of Liberal Democracy: Authoritarian Capitalism and the Accumulative State in Hungary*. London: Palgrave Macmillan.

Scoones, Ian et.al. 2018. 'Emancipatory Rural Politics: Confronting Authoritarian Populism', *Journal of Peasant Studies* 45(1): 1–20, https://doi.org/10.1080/03066150.2017.1339693.

Seymour, Richard. 2020. 'Why Is the Nationalist Right Hallucinating a "Communist Enemy"?', *The Guardian*, 26 September.

Shoshan, Nitzan. 2016. *The Management of Hate: Nation, Affect, and the Governance of Right Wing Extremism in Germany*. Princeton: Princeton University Press.

Smith, Anthony. 1995. *Nations and Nationalism in a Global Era*. Cambridge: Polity Press.

Smith, Gavin. 2015. 'Through a Class Darkly, But Then Face to Face: Praxis through the Lens of Class', in James Carrier and Don Kalb (eds), *Anthropologies of Class: Power, Practice and Inequality*. Cambridge: Cambridge University Press, pp. 72–89.

Stacul, Jaro. 2011. 'Class without Consciousness: Regional Identity in the Italian Alps after 1989', in Don Kalb and Gabor Halmai (eds), *Headlines of Nation, Subtexts of Class: Working Class Populism and the Return of the Repressed in Neoliberal Europe*. Oxford: Berghahn Books, pp. 156–72.

———. 2014. 'The Production of "Local Culture" in Post-Socialist Poland', *Anthropological Journal of European Cultures* 23(1): 21–39.

———. 2018. 'Redeveloping History in Postsocialist Poland', *Focaal: Journal of Global and Historical Anthropology* 81: 72–85.

Szombati, Krisztof. 2018. *The Revolt of the Provinces: Anti-gypsyism and Right-Wing Politics in Hungary*. Oxford: Berghahn Books.

Teitelbaum, Benjamin. 2017. *Lions of the North: Sounds of the New Nordic Radical Nationalism*. Oxford: Oxford University Press.

Therborn, Göran. 2020a. 'Dreams and Nightmares of the World's Middle Classes', *New Left Review* 124(July/August): 63–88.

———. 2020b. *Inequality and the Labyrinths of Democracy*. London: Verso.

Thompson, E.P. 1978. 'Eighteenth-Century English Society: Class Struggle without Class?', *Social History* 3(2): 133–65.

Thorleifsson, Cathrine. 2017. 'Disposable Strangers: Far-Right Securitization of Forced Migration in Hungary', *Social Anthropology* 25(3): 318–34.

———. 2019. *Nationalist Responses to the Crises in Europe: Old and New Hatreds*. Abingdon: Routledge.

Tilly, Charles. 1998. *Durable Inequality*. Berkeley: University of California Press.

———. 2001. 'Relational Origins of Inequality', *Anthropological Theory* 1(3): 355–72.

Turner, Terence. 2005. Marxian Value Theory: An Anthropological Perspective. *Anthropological Theory* 8(1): 43–56.

Vance, J.D. 2016. *Hillbilly Elegy: A Memoir of a Family and Culture in Crisis*. London: HarperCollins.

Vetta, Theodora. 2011. '"Nationalism Is Back!" *Radikali* and Privatization in Serbia', in Don Kalb and Gabor Halmai (eds), *Headlines of Nation, Subtexts of Class: Working Class Populism and the Return of the Repressed in Neoliberal Europe*. Oxford: Berghahn Books, pp. 37–57.

Volkov, Shulamit. 1978. *The Rise of Popular Antimodernism in Germany: The Urban Master Artisans, 1873–1896*. Princeton: Princeton University Press.

Walley, Christine. 2017. 'Trump's Election and the "White Working Class": What We Missed', *American Ethnologist* 44(2): 231–36.

Weiss, Hadas. 2019. *We Have Never Been Middle Class: How Social Mobility Misleads Us*. London: Verso.

Žižek, Slavoj. 2008. *In Defense of Lost Causes*. London: Verso.

4

Comparing Deservingness
A Reflexive Approach to Solidarity and Cruelty

Erik Bähre

As pointed out in the Introduction and other chapters in this volume, deservingness is a central mechanism in contemporary European politics. It is at the core of various forms of redistribution: whether of money, after the 2007/2008 global financial crisis; of migrants coming from Africa and the Middle East; and, more recently, of healthcare and other forms of support related to the COVID-19 pandemic. Deservingness draws our attention to the morality and relationality of these very different crises involving people, finance and health.

In this chapter, I would like to follow up on the approach to deservingness taken by Streinzer and Tošić in the Introduction by focusing particularly on the complex relationship between ethnography and comparative approaches. By putting deservingness at the centre of ethnography, the contributors to this volume have successfully upended presumed categories that are typically – often unreflexively – used for comparing distributional regimes in contemporary Europe. How does deservingness shed light on people's experiences, languages and moralities as contingent upon social and political circumstances in contemporary Europe, especially regarding distribution? How can such a contextual and reflexive approach to deservingness be the foundation for a comparative approach that enables ethnographers to explain differences? Answering these questions requires a historical understanding of how Western categories for comparison are part of global power relations (Fox and Gingrich 2002). This chapter takes a deeper look at how deservingness contributes to an ethnographic approach that is both reflexive and comparative.

An ethnographic approach to deservingness is important in that it focuses on what takes place 'behind the model'. It is particularly capable of revealing the tensions between how things should be and how they actually work out and are experienced in everyday life. It examines how states, nongovernmental organizations (NGOs) and companies formulate redistribution in policies, laws and regulations as well as in managerial protocols and procedures. Such models and procedures stipulate entitlements and forms of inclusion in discourses that are often neutral and technical. The ethical dimensions of such an impersonal approach to redistribution become much clearer when ethnographically studying how laws, policies and solutions work out in everyday life. Ethnography provides insight into how people undergo classifications and bureaucratic procedures that are inherently part of distributional policies and institutions. An ethnographic approach to deservingness reveals these experiences most clearly by focusing on people who are situated on the border of inclusion and exclusion; people who can, to some extent, claim to be included but simultaneously experience being undeserving. Of particular interest are situations where society sees 'these' people as simultaneously deserving and undeserving. Such situations reveal the ambiguous social processes that underlie deservingness, which revolve around the boundaries of empathy towards people who can be seen as insiders just as easily as outsiders, and around the mobilization of moralities that are contingent upon social and political circumstances.

An ethnographic approach to deservingness offers an empirical and conceptual space for the diversity of experiences and practices; it shows how ethics and morality are imbued in policies, laws and languages that are presented as technical and practical solutions. It also offers insights into the tensions and conflicts that are part of redistribution policies, and shows when and how such tensions are mobilized into specific forms of protest.

However, ethnographic research also has its shortcomings in that it contributes less to *explaining* phenomena. The ethnographic approach to interpretation, experience, language and translating lived worlds into others occurs at the expense of the ability to explain differences. Thus, taking a more reflexive approach has been very helpful in deconstructing comparative categories by showing that they are not as universal or neutral as has often been assumed. Reflexivity has revealed that many comparisons used to formulate explanations can be ideological and Eurocentric. Nevertheless, reflexivity has also made comparisons and explaining differences increasingly marginal.

Deservingness, as a new conceptual framework, offers a way out of this dilemma by enabling an ethnographic approach that is both reflexive and comparative. It offers a conceptual space to reflect on the positionality of the researcher and to incorporate research contexts into the analysis – contexts that always destabilize universal claims, while simultaneously enabling new forms of comparison that significantly diverge from more established categories such as 'the state'.

Here I will explore deservingness as a reflexive and comparative category in two ways. First, I look at how reflexivity caused explanatory approaches, which hinged on comparative approaches, to become less common in anthropology from the 1970s onwards, a methodological and epistemological shift that was connected to the process of decolonization. Second, I explore more recent debates that steer anthropology and ethnography in a direction that is both reflexive and comparative. The development of this new epistemology again seems to be related to a shifting balance of global power, specifically the end of the Cold War, which had a major impact on Europe and anthropological scholarship. I suggest that deservingness meets the epistemological 'requirements' set within this debate, especially because it places a reflexive relational perspective on social realities that departs from the more established categories often used for comparisons within Europe. To further explore deservingness as an analytical category, I turn towards the reflexive epistemology developed by Rorty (1995) that explores how one can simultaneously be aware of the fact that concepts and languages are historically contingent, and at the same time formulate a politically viable agenda for justice and solidarity.

I use Rorty's reflexive epistemology as the starting point of a comparative approach to deservingness. Particularly valuable is how Rorty sees solidarity as inherently cruel. A reflexive approach to solidarity reveals these cruelties, which I argue are also a central feature in deservingness. With the help of this epistemology, I explore how deservingness is a reflexive and comparative concept that allows us to analyse the more painful and cruel social developments in contemporary Europe.

Explaining Deservingness through Serendipitous Comparison

When objectivist epistemology left ethnography, so did comparison. This becomes particularly poignant in Geertz's 'Deep Play' (1973), a seminal contribution to this cultural shift in anthropology. Geertz argued that money is not characteristic of utilitarian calculations, but rather establishes relations between people and the groups they belong to. For example, bets men placed at cockfights had to be interpreted symbolically, given that money played an important role in the articulation of masculinity and the creation of hierarchies between men and the groups to which they belong.[1]

Geertz famously developed 'thick description' as the key characteristic of an interpretative approach to ethnography. He argued that knowledge is produced within specific networks of interactions in which the ethnographer participates. In this study, Geertz carefully reflected on his role as a researcher and the position he had vis-à-vis the people he engaged with during fieldwork and the situations that undergirded interpretations. Instead of comparing 'his' society with 'their' society, Geertz argued that people construct meaning together. Instead of presenting himself and his society as superior, he described how he was seen as a funny guest that became part of a web of interpretations: he was a visitor interpreting what the Balinese interpreted.

Equally important, but not addressed quite as explicitly as reflexivity, is the ability of the researcher to be in control of the research process. One of the characteristics of ethnographic research is that the anthropologist has little control over the research situation, the language used, the social encounters and the conversations with people. This lack of control makes ethnography a method that allows unexpected and serendipitous encounters, conversations and ideas to emerge.

Geertz starts his study by demonstrating that he is not in control of the research process. He describes how he tries, without much success, to establish relationships with the Balinese. He feels he and his wife are ignored: 'For them, and to a degree for ourselves, we were nonpersons, specters, invisible men' (Geertz 1973: 56). The serendipitous character of his ethnographic research becomes poignant when he describes how his relationship with and, therefore, his understanding of the Balinese change drastically after the police raided a cockfight, forcing him and his wife to flee along with the other Balinese spectators. The Balinese interpreted this as an act of solidarity and henceforth the couple were no longer treated as invisible outsiders. When Geertz interprets the cockfight, it is not his intention to show it as a representative case that characterized Balinese society. Instead, he illustrates how the cockfight, especially the betting between the men, offered important insights into the sociality of money and the establishment of social hierarchies and boundaries.

Geertz later explains how his contribution to a reflexive epistemology was part of a global shift in power relations:

> The end of colonialism altered radically the nature of the social relationship between those who ask and those who are asked and looked at. The decline of faith in brute fact, set procedures, and unsituated knowledge in the human sciences, and indeed in scholarship generally, altered no less radically the askers' and lookers' conception of what it was they were trying to do. Imperialism in its classical form, metropoles and possession, and Scientism in its, [sic] impulsions and billiard balls, fell at more or less the same time. (Geertz 1988: 131–32)

This 'double fall of scientism and imperialism' (Conquergood 1991: 179) impacted ethnographic comparison, which had been embedded in an objectivist epistemology. As Kuper writes: 'The new cultural anthropology did not aspire to compare and explain' (1994: 541). The cultural turn instead examined positionality, reflexivity and the power and politics of representation in ethnographic writing.[2] Interpretative epistemology made comparison more problematic because it challenged the understanding that cultures, societies and meanings could be clearly distinguished from one another and placed in a hierarchical relationship (Fox and Gingrich 2002).[3] While controlled comparison suggested controlling the research process and the relationship between what is studied and society at large, it was also carried out within the politics of colonialism intended to control the people ethnographers were studying.[4]

Fox and Gingrich formulated a new orientation towards comparison in anthropology: 'The monopolistic, universalist and objectivist claims made in the name of comparison in anthropology today are not necessary' (2002: 5–6). The relatively new debate on ethnographic comparison also takes place against a backdrop of political change. European politics particularly influenced the comparative approach in ethnography, leading anthropologists to try and establish a new vocabulary that allows for new ways of comparing societies, events and experiences.

During the Cold War, ethnographers usually met nationally or in the United States at international conferences. However, the end of the Cold War in 1989 changed this and had major consequences for the networks and debates among ethnographers, which has shaped what ethnography is or should be. The European Association of Social Anthropologists (EASA) was established in 1989. Two years later, the Africa-Europe Group for Interdisciplinary Studies

(AEGIS), where many anthropologists also meet, was established. The foundation of the Central European University in Budapest (Hungary) in 1991 with an international department of anthropology and sociology, and the establishment of the prestigious Max-Planck-Institut für Ethnologische Forschung in 1999 in Halle (in the former East Germany) were also important developments.

These new European associations and institutions strengthened anthropology networks in Europe and encouraged anthropologists to reflect on how national traditions influenced ethnography. This brought about an increased awareness of anthropology's diversity in Europe as well as in the Global South (Bošković and Erikson 2008). New European associations and research institutes, as well as publications such as the one by Bošković and Erikson (ibid.), meant that national differences in doing anthropology were discussed reflexively, thus avoiding the creation of hierarchies between North versus South, East versus West, and French/Anglo-American versus the rest. Ethnographic comparison began by comparing diverse national ethnographic traditions (see also Fox and Gingrich 2002).

Another reason for the return of comparison to ethnography was the advancement of a European research agenda intended to strengthen scientific developments and stimulate cooperation across national and disciplinary boundaries. The European Research Council (ERC), founded in 2007, typically requires researchers to set up and lead a research team in order to receive funding. Unlike individual research projects, teams have to work collaboratively, and the added value of such collaboration has to be specified. What is the added value of conducting a project that involves, for example, four ethnographies as opposed to conducting four individually funded smaller ethnographic projects? This inevitably raises the question of comparing ethnographic findings.[5]

The comparative question also became more prominent as a result of the selection process for large research grants. Proposals are typically reviewed and selected by interdisciplinary panels (see Lazar 2012; van der Veer 2014: 11; Meyer 2017). The scholars conducting these processes are not always familiar with the epistemology on which ethnography had been based since the 1970s, or are sometimes even hostile towards an epistemology that is not rooted in an objectivist tradition. In order to successfully acquire funding and ensure that ethnography remains a legitimate method, anthropologists have had to respond to questions like: how do you compare ethnographic evidence? It is a challenge to reintroduce the comparative approach that explains difference without returning to an unreflexive, and sometimes naïve, objectivist epistemology.

Lazar (2012) looks at how to compare fieldwork on trade unions in Bolivia and Argentina. She proposes distinguishing two kinds of comparison: representative and disjunctive. She points out that both types have value, but produce different insights that need to be evaluated using different criteria. Representative comparison is defined as the more traditional way of comparing representative cases, people and events, which means that findings can be analysed side by side. Disjunctive comparison is reflexive about the role of the researcher who does the comparative work, and thus acknowledges that understanding is inevitably a human process. The criterion for disjunctive comparison is not primarily whether cases or research participants are representative of society at large; instead, the focus is more on the opportunity to encounter unexpected differences that urge us to ask new kinds of questions and establish a new vocabulary for analysing these differences. Lazar shows how disjunctive comparison opens up new avenues for theoretically exploring the construction of political selfhood (ibid.: 361).

Candea (2016) also places the ethnographer as the starting point for making comparisons. He distinguishes between what he calls frontal and lateral comparisons: frontal being comparisons between 'us' and 'them', and lateral between 'them' and 'them'. Both types of comparison are understood as playing important roles and as able to reinforce one another and strengthen ethnographic theory. Both can also be reflexive, Candea argues, but the reflexivity differs, since the researcher is positioned differently in each one: 'In frontal comparison we put ourselves to the test. In lateral comparison we put each other to the test. The two moves are mutually constitutive' (ibid.: 218).

Contributions to the special issue of *Social Analysis* entitled 'Cutting and Connecting: "Afrinesian" Perspectives on Networks, Relationality and Exchange' examine how Melanesian ethnography and African anthropology influenced one another (Myrhe 2013). Englund and Yarrow (2013) propose a comparative ethnography that recounts what they define as 'relational knowledge production'. This means that ethnographers have to reflect on how their theories and concepts are established within specific contexts, which implies including themselves in the comparison. Ethnographic comparisons, they argue, are valuable because 'they destabilize and complicate the terms [used for comparison] themselves, which in turn provides the basis for a descriptive language more finely attuned to the specificities of particular contexts' (ibid.: 144). This kind of comparison primarily serves to deconstruct categories.

Van der Veer's book *The Value of Comparison* (2016) criticizes the predominant epistemology found in most social sciences (economics, sociology and political science). He argues against the universal claims often made by social scientists, and states that they are based on specific Western models of cognition, structure and rationality that are believed to be universal. Thus, they ignore global differences and assume that Western societies and people are representative of the entire world. He points out that 'one of the greatest flaws in the development of a comparative perspective seems to be the almost universal comparison of any existing society with an ideal-typical and totally self-sufficient Euro-American modernity' (ibid.: 28). This does not mean that concepts developed in the West cannot be used in a comparative method, and van der Veer himself engages critically with Weberian and Maussian concepts. However, this does mean that these ideas and models need to be treated reflexively by recognizing that they are produced within a specific context. Comparison can only work when one realizes that a universal claim is problematic and always involves a historical understanding of how Western ideas and models are part of a globalization process, which are hence charged with global power relations.

Van der Veer's book presents a detailed agenda for reflexive comparison by formulating four advantages of an anthropological approach to comparison: a thorough understanding of the problem of cultural translations of difference; an ability to study a fragment that is not a model of, but sheds light on, a larger whole; a generalism that acknowledges how nations and civilizations are historically integrated; and an understanding of the body and its disciplining that goes beyond a limited cognitive notion (van der Veer 2016: 10). He argues that ethnography can make specific contributions because it is well suited to examining and understanding the dynamic relationship between the fragment and the whole. The fragment, the everyday, or 'micro' in ethnography is not studied because it is believed to represent the whole. But while it may not represent the whole, the fact that the fragment can only be understood in relation to global historical changes is precisely what makes the fragment important for understand the whole. The opposite is also true, where large-scale historical change can only be understood through detailed ethnographic evidence of particular situations (ibid.: 25).[6] At the same time, van der Veer focuses less exclusively on reflexivity during ethnographic fieldwork, stating that a comparative approach is not as concerned with the positionality of the ethnographer as it is with the positionality of the ideas and concepts that academics develop.

It is by no means a coincidence that these epistemological questions are discussed in contemporary Europe. Just like the decolonization process unsettled a hierarchical comparison between countries and set the scene for Geertz's interpretative approach, so have political developments in post-Cold War Europe confronted anthropologists with 'new' kinds of differences that call for reflexive and comparative analyses. They have contributed to a serendipitous comparison that reflects on the positionality of the researcher.

Comparisons can be and often are made by using 'old' established categories – for example, welfare programmes in European nation-states, or EU legislation and policies regarding migration in different countries. A serendipitous comparison requires new concepts, and I understand deservingness as a new, unsettling category that enables a reflexive comparison. Certainly, the theoretical challenges that the study of deservingness in this volume brings to the fore are rooted within a specific European context. But deservingness is an important heuristic concept that defines crises in new ways that make it possible to explore redistributional regimes from a relational point of view around the world. Thus, a focus on deservingness allows for a reflexive and comparative approach that leads to new explanations for how redistributional regimes take shape and become part of people's lived world.

In the Introduction to this volume, Streinzer and Tošić argue that the conceptual value of deservingness lies in its moral evaluation of relations. Drawing on the work of Fassin and Ticktin, among others, regarding suffering and humanitarianism, they propose deservingness as a theoretical and methodological lens for examining how the recognition of suffering is based on whether suffering is seen as legitimate. Deservingness, as a new concept for comparing the morality of distribution processes, thus takes the (mis)recognition of a fellow human being as the starting point for analysis. As an analytical category, it begins by questioning how the legitimacy of human suffering is inherently tied to political developments in Europe; how these developments relate to people living outside of Europe; and how markets and states make up forms of redistribution that stipulate whether certain people are in or out. This reflexive treatment of deservingness, based on the recognition of fellow human beings in Europe, raises fascinating opportunities for comparing distributional regimes.

Reflexivity, Comparison and Cruelty

Deservingness draws our attention to the cruelty of redistributional regimes and the solidarity on which they are based. It draws our attention to people who are excluded because they are seen as undeserving, and to situations where people feel it is not necessary to empathize with others because of what they supposedly personify – for example, 'their' behaviour is regarded as detrimental to the common good. This volume shows how a critical analysis of deservingness sheds light on the less benevolent, even cruel dimensions of redistribution in Europe.

Rorty's ironic approach to solidarity is helpful for unpacking deservingness as both a reflexive and comparative concept. Rorty is concerned with epistemological questions regarding objectivity and morality. He argues that the distinction between objectivity and morality is temporal and contingent, and he rejects the claim that morality is universal and extraneous to people, their languages and their ways of understanding the world. He writes: 'The fundamental premise of the book is that a belief can still regulate action, can still be thought worth dying for, among people who are quite aware that this belief is caused by nothing deeper than contingent historical circumstance' (Rorty 1995: 189).

In addition to recognizing morality as contingent, Rorty also contends that we should not resort to a kind of relativism that makes morality meaningless and impossible to uphold or express. The irony that morality is contingent and yet crucial to our understanding of the world leads Rorty to explore the private–public divide. Publicly, one needs to uphold a certain morality that is expressed through ever-expanding forms of solidarity. Privately, one needs to be aware of the contingency of morality, and that the vocabulary used to conceptualize the world is never final and needs to be open to change. This requires a degree of reflexivity about one's own role in shaping morality and understanding. In other words, in order for moralities to be important in public life, one must be reflexive in private. In this way, Rorty acknowledges that moralities are shaped by specific communities and societies, and recognizes the contingency of those important to us. He outlines a liberal utopia where people have debates guided by deep-seated moralities and convictions, while still being aware of the contingency of the language that shapes these debates and the thoughts, metaphors and ideas they produce. Reflexivity here means that when people debate their moralities and state their convictions, they are aware that they do so as members of a particular community with contingent convictions (see also Bähre 2020).

Rorty identifies three key mechanisms that shape solidarity, which can be summarized as: the boundaries of solidarity, the hierarchies within it and the moralities that support it (Rorty 1995; see also Bähre (2020) on solidarity and financialization in South Africa). These three mechanisms lead to three sets of questions that help develop deservingness as both a reflexive and comparative concept, similar to what Streinzer and Tošić did in the Introduction:

1. How can we compare the boundaries of solidarity and to whom solidarity is extended? Why are people excluded and what is the role of deservingness in this process of exclusion from solidarity?
2. Why do particular hierarchies emerge *within* solidarity? Does deservingness challenge or reflect hierarchies among those who are included? How can we explain these inequalities in terms of degrees of deservingness or notions of being responsible for the wellbeing of others?
3. When and how are notions of deservingness mobilized in order to achieve the ideological conformity on which solidarity is built?

All three sets of questions draw attention to the idea that solidarity is *also* a manifestation of cruelty (Rorty 1995). It becomes clear when people are excluded, when hierarchies emerge within solidarity and when solidarity requires people to comply with certain moralities. Deservingness offers an important perspective on the complexity of solidarity, specifically that it can be both supportive and oppressive, and that while it extends humanity to others, it can also be dehumanizing. Deservingness is a helpful methodological perspective for achieving a thorough understanding of the connections between the benevolent and cruel dimensions of solidarity.

Rorty's ironic approach to solidarity might not seem to be the most likely starting point for this contribution, given that it is part of his analysis of the epistemology of knowledge. Moreover, although Rorty acknowledges that solidarity can be cruel, he presents it as a way to counter the success of universalizing totalitarian political ideologies, which is quite different from what I aim to do here. Nevertheless, there are several reasons why I find his approach to solidarity useful for developing a methodology of deservingness.

I find Rorty's way of connecting private and public realms, and of using literature as an avenue where these realms can relate to one another disharmoniously, particularly useful to ethnography. Ethnographic approaches to deservingness and solidarity explore and elucidate incongruences, helping us make sense of why people say one thing but do something else, or say one thing at one moment and say something contradictory later on. Rorty's ironic approach is valuable in perceiving how people strive towards individualism, autonomy and freedom, while simultaneously acting as social beings that have a fundamental need to belong. But such belonging is not without its complications. Studying deservingness places our focus on the cruelty of how solidarity is extended, and thus helps us understand the ambivalent processes on which solidarities are based.

Boundaries, Hierarchies and Conformity

Rorty's focus on language leads him to emphasize the role of literature. In the final part of *Contingency, Irony, and Solidarity*, he uses literature to understand solidarity and cruelty as not necessarily opposed to each other, but rather that solidarity is a form of cruelty. He is particularly interested in fictional literature:

> That is about the ways in which particular sorts of people are cruel to other particular sorts of people. Sometimes works on psychology serve this function, but the most useful books of this sort are works of fiction which exhibit the blindness of a certain kind of person to the pain of another kind of person ... They are the books which dramatize the conflict between duties to self and duties to others. (Rorty 1995: 141)

According to Rorty, this conflict is inherent to solidarity and is where deservingness plays a central role. Solidarity always means that distinctions are made between 'us' and 'them', and discourses about deservingness mark these duties to self and to others, as well as the distinctions that legitimize or challenge these duties. Rorty believes literature is important because it offers a new vocabulary, which in turn presents a new way of seeing the world and of identifying with people. Therefore, books that confront us with what is *not* familiar are of particular interest. The vocabulary in these books relates to the following question: 'what sorts of things about what sorts of people do I need to notice?' These are books that stimulate doubt and confront us with the temptations of cruelty. Rorty discusses writings by Vladimir Nabokov and George Orwell to show how both authors use cruelty as a central trope in their work. For Nabokov, these were everyday cruelties produced by private pursuits, especially the cruelty of not noticing the suffering of others (Rorty 1995: 157). For Orwell, these cruelties were perpetrated by particular groups and were justified by the rhetoric of equality. Orwell also points out that the perpetrators fail to see their cruelty (ibid.: 171–73).[7]

Authors like Nabokov and Orwell are not the only ones who produce new vocabularies and new ways of seeing the world. People who are confronted with such cruelties in their everyday lives do so too, and it is the task of ethnography to examine these vocabularies and explore how they are contingent upon people's experiences. By formulating this examination as 'the task of ethnography' and not 'merely' as a possible contribution of ethnographic research or an option, it becomes more explicit that methodologies are not only scientific 'tools' for gathering knowledge; they are also moralizing devices that call for empathy and the recognition of fellow human beings. The questions then become: what kinds of languages do people use to express their ideas about deservingness? What do stories, autobiographical accounts, art, poetry, pop music, Instagram and WhatsApp messages say about the Nabokovian cruelty of not noticing the suffering of others and the Orwellian cruelty that is justified by a rhetoric of equality? A methodological approach to deservingness examines these cruelties by carefully investigating the languages – to which I might add imageries – that express them.

However, ethnography is not only about languages and images, but also about what people do, how they engage with one another and how they are involved in actions. Languages are contingent upon events and histories, and in order to understand this, it is important to show how solidarity is shaped, how people are involved in it and how it might produce cruelty. Focusing on solidarity allows us to closely examine the material or economic dynamics of deservingness.

The cruelty of solidarity manifests itself in three distinct social processes that contribute to the suppression of individual liberties by forcing people to conform to the 'we'.

The first social process of this 'we' formation is the cruelty of exclusion. Because solidarity is based on the identification of a 'we', it automatically requires a 'them'. How is the line between 'we' and 'them' defined and legitimized? When some people are more entitled than others, when some deserve while others do not, to what extent is this related to the image that people have of others? In order to understand how these boundaries change over time, it is important to ascertain which identities play a role in shaping them, and if these boundaries are more rigid in some situations than in others, it is crucial to look at both sides of the relationship. In other words, what I mean is that in order to understand how deservingness shapes solidarity, the 'we' and the 'they' perspectives must be included.

This regards not only what people say, but also what they do. In terms of deservingness, actions often revolve around technicalities and procedures that are part of entitlements, none of which are morally neutral. They depend on classifications and categories, and thus on morally charged contingent languages. Furthermore, 'them' is not a unit of study. Being excluded does not necessarily bring people together into another 'we', although at times some might believe or experience this differently when confronted with deservingness.

When exploring boundaries, it is methodologically most fruitful to examine situations in which there are simultaneously grounds for inclusion and exclusion, since this is where the boundaries of solidarity are affirmed, shaped or negotiated.

The second social process that produces cruelty takes place *within* solidarity. An appeal to solidarity can be a manifestation of inequality, even cruelty. When solidarity is highlighted and when people or institutions put forward claims that are the outcome of solidarity, one should ask the following questions: with whom is one expected to show solidarity, and does solidarity go both ways? Are there inequalities within solidarity that result in, to paraphrase Orwell, some being more equal than others?

Shifting attention away from the boundaries of solidarity that define insiders and outsiders, and focusing on what takes place within solidarity offers insight into other kinds of cruelty. While still connected to deservingness, these new cruelties revolve around two other issues. The first concerns who is called upon to help the deserving. Unequal demands to help can be placed on people within solidarity groups or institutions built on solidarity (e.g. welfare programmes). Such unequal demands can alleviate or exacerbate certain inequalities – for example, progressive taxation that requires wealthier citizens to contribute more, or flat tax rates that require relatively high contributions from poorer citizens. Inequalities within solidarity can be highly gendered, for example, when unpaid work performed by women is less valued and less visible. Inequality can also be a result of free-riders, or, in other words, apparently deserving people who do not have to contribute when others are in need. Unless one believes that resources are made out of nothing, research into deservingness should always also show who is expected to contribute and help those who are defined as deserving. By doing so, deservingness provides a lens that can identify inequalities within solidarity; it shows that appeals to deservingness not only means that some people are entitled to receive something, but also that it puts claims on specific groups or social categories to help the deserving.

The second issue of cruelty within solidarity is that deservingness can be a mechanism that promotes inequality. Solidarity can be used to camouflage personal interests as collective interests and thus actually reinforce inequalities. When personal interests are hidden behind a rhetoric of solidarity, solidarity becomes oppressive and illiberal. Some might not have the opportunity, power or legitimacy to put forward their own personal interests or define solidarity in a different way. Similarly, when someone says that 'we' are entitled to solidarity or that 'we' are deserving, one must question on which authority, and if such authority possibly denies the diversity of needs or desires within solidarity.

The third social process in which deservingness plays a crucial role in solidarity is possibly the cruellest mechanism. It concerns how deservingness requires ideological conformity. What do people have to do or say in order to become or remain deserving of solidarity? How and when are particular ideologies mobilized in ways that affect deservingness? Rorty points out that such ideologies are important for understanding when people sense a moral duty to extend solidarity towards other human beings. People can be identified as one of 'us' as well as one of 'them', and certain differences can be irrelevant, while others can draw sharp, dehumanizing boundaries. As an example, he points to antisemitism, where identities that connect people become relevant, where Christian ideologies of caring for fellow human beings offer insufficient solace and where being a Jew is the line that separates 'us' from 'them'. He expresses his liberal utopia in his plea for an ever-expanding 'we' where 'traditional differences' no longer matter. Yet he does not argue for progressively including more people or for differences to become increasingly irrelevant; instead, he calls for a reflexive approach to the ideologies that create boundaries between 'us' and 'them'. This is possible when we cast doubt on our own ways of seeing the world, of realizing that one's own moralities and ideologies are not superior and are historically contingent. Thus, self-doubt is what makes it possible to identify with others. In short, Rorty argues that identification with other people is based on a deep-seated distrust of ethnocentrism. Focusing on the contingency of these ideologies and moralities, including one's own, is crucial to understanding the ideological dimension that underpins deservingness, which resonates closely with ethnographic approaches to morality. When and how do certain historically contingent ideologies emerge, creating divisions between 'us' and 'them'? What are the ideological grounds for some defining others as undeserving? And when and how are these ideologies contested and then replaced with other ideologies that can be either more divisive or more empathetic? Methodologically, this would lead to an analysis of how ethnocentrism and doubting one's own ideologies and moralities play a role in defining people as deserving or not. Rorty writes:

> The self-doubt seems to me the characteristic mark of the first epoch in human history in which large numbers of people have become able to separate the question 'Do you believe and desire what we believe and desire?' from the question 'Are you suffering?' In my jargon, this is the ability to distinguish the question of whether you and I share the same final vocabulary from the question of whether you are in pain. (1995: 198)

Deservingness as a Reflexive and Comparative Concept

Unlike the 'old categories' of comparison often used in Europe to compare units and models (e.g. government or population groups), deservingness is a perspective that uses relationships as the analytical starting point. It is a concept that offers an assessment of the European crisis that begins with the relations between insiders and outsiders.

In this manner, deservingness allows for new kinds of comparison. This becomes particularly clear in Rorty's reflexive epistemology, where he calls for increased social justice and solidarity. He sees increased solidarity not as an ever-widening circle that includes more and more people, but as based on empathy and the recognition of fellow human beings. This means that the 'litmus test' of solidarity is not measured against the amount of people being included, but by the ability to see people as fellow human beings. This, I find, is what deservingness is about. And, just like solidarity has cruel dimensions, so does deservingness have its less benevolent dynamics. Just like solidarity produces specific types of harshness, so does deservingness have its dark side that needs investigating and explaining. Light must be shed on these negative aspects of deservingness that revolve around those who are excluded from, for example, redistributional regimes; the hierarchies produced among people who are included; and the suppression of people's freedoms when requiring some level of ideological conformity. These questions offer fertile ground for reflexive and comparative analysis.

Acknowledgements

I thank Andreas Streinzer and Jelena Tošić for their encouraging feedback on an earlier version of this chapter, Jill Haring and Julene Knox for carefully editing my English, and Marilena Poulopoulou for assisting with the style and bibliography. This project has received funding from the European Research Council (ERC) under the Horizon 2020 Research and Innovation Programme (Grant Agreement No. 682467).

Erik Bähre is Associate Professor at the Institute of Cultural Anthropology and Development Sociology at Leiden University. He carries out research on money and finance in everyday life in South Africa and Brazil and is the Principal Investigator of the ERC Consolidator Project 'Moralising Misfortune: A Comparative Anthropology of Commercial Insurance'. He is the author of *Money and Violence: Financial Self-Help Groups in a South African Township* (Brill, 2007) and *Ironies of Solidarity: Insurance and Financialization of Kinship in South Africa* (Zed Books, 2020).

Notes

1. See Ortner (1984) on how this symbolic approach differs from that of Turner. Generally, Geertz is regarded as the founding father of reflexivity in ethnography, but the issue of the positionality of the researcher has also been developed by Gluckman (1940) and the Manchester school that Turner was part (see Fox and Gingrich 2002).
2. On the cultural turn, see, among others, and Ortner (1984); and Clifford and Marcus (1986).
3. See also Fox and Gingrich (2002: 4) on the holocultural approach to comparison that in the 1950s was presented as a '"truly scientific" methodology' in anthropology. See also Holy (1987); Kuper (1994); and Herzfeld (2001).
4. Said (1978), Spivak (1988) and Bhabha (1990) have shown how crucial it is to critically examine knowledge production within colonial power relations. See also Fox and Gingrich (2002) on their influence on comparison.
5. At the same time, it would be too deterministic to suggest that European or national political changes were the only reason why more attention was given to comparative ethnography. Individual interests, contributions, as well as research traditions and networks also mattered a great deal.
6. See also Kapferer (2015) on studying events. Kapferer critically engages with the work of Gluckman, and Deleuze and Guattari to examine how ethnography can help us understand rupture, conflict and fragmentation

in everyday life, which are therefore sources of social change that transcend that specific event.
7. Although Rorty acknowledges that solidarity is cruel, he is optimistic about solidarity as a political project.

References

Bähre, Erik. 2020. *Ironies of Solidarity: Insurance and Financialization of Kinship in South Africa*. London: Zed Books.
Bhabha, Homi K. 1990. *Nation and Narration*. London: Routledge.
Bošković, Aleksandar, and Thomas Hylland Eriksen. 2008. 'Introduction: Other People's Anthropologies', in Aleksandar Bošković (ed.), *Other People's Anthropologies: Ethnographic Practice on the Margins*. Oxford: Berghahn Books, pp. 1–19.
Candea, Matei. 2016. 'On Two Modalities of Comparison in Social Anthropology', *L'Homme* 218: 183–218.
Clifford, James, and George Marcus (eds). 1986. *Writing Culture: The Poetics and Politics of Ethnography*. Berkeley: University of California Press.
Conquergood, Dwight. 1991. 'Rethinking Ethnography: Towards a Critical Cultural Politics', *Communication Monographs* 58(2): 179–94.
Englund, Harri, and Thomas Yarrow. 2013. 'The Place of Theory: Rights, Networks, and Ethnographic Comparison', *Social Analysis* 57(3): 132–49.
Fox, Richard G., and Andre Gingrich. 2002. 'Introduction', in Andre Gingrich and Richard G. Fox (eds), *Anthropology, by Comparison*. London: Routledge, pp. 1–24.
Geertz, Clifford. 1973. *The Interpretation of Cultures: Selected Essays*. New York: Basic Books.
——. 1988. *Works and Lives: The Anthropologist as Author*. New York: Basic Books.
Gluckman, Max. 1940. 'The Kingdom of the Zulu of South Africa', in Meyer Fortes and E.E. Evans-Pritchard (eds), *African Political Systems*. Oxford: Oxford University Press, pp. 25–55.
Herzfeld, Michael. 2001. 'Performing Comparisons: Ethnography, Globetrotting, and the Spaces of Social Knowledge', *Journal of Anthropological Research* 57(3): 259–76.
Holy, Ladislav (ed.). 1987. *Comparative Anthropology*, Oxford: Blackwell.
Kapferer, Bruce. 2015. 'Introduction: In the Event: Toward an Anthropology of Generic Moments', in Lotte Meinert and Bruce Kapferer (eds), *In the Event: Toward an Anthropology of Generic Moments*. New York: Berghahn Books, pp. 2–28.
Kuper, Adam. 1994. 'Culture, Identity and the Project of a Cosmopolitan Anthropology', *Royal Anthropological Institute of Great Britain and Ireland* 29(3): 537–54.

Lazar, Sian. 2012. 'Disjunctive Comparison: Citizenship and Trade Unionism in Bolivia and Argentina', *Journal of the Royal Anthropological Institute* 18(2): 349–68.

Meyer, Birgit. 2017. 'Comparison as Critique', *HAU: Journal of Ethnographic Theory* 7(1): 509–15.

Myrhe, Knut Christian. 2013. 'Introduction', *Social Analysis: The International Journal of Social and Cultural Practice* 62(4): 1–24.

Ortner, Sherry. 1984. 'Theory in Anthropology since the Sixties', *Comparative Studies in Society and History* 26: 126–66.

Rorty, Richard. 1995 [1989]. *Contingency, Irony, and Solidarity.* Cambridge: Cambridge University Press.

Said, Edward. 1978. *Orientalism.* New York: Pantheon.

Spivak, Gayatri Chakravorty. 1988. *Can the Subaltern Speak?* Basingstoke: Macmillan.

Van der Veer, Peter. 2014. 'The Value of Comparison: Transcript of the Lewis Henry Morgan Lecture Given on November 13, 2013', *HAU: Journal of Ethnographic Theory* (1–13).

———. 2016. *The Value of Comparison.* Durham, NC: Duke University Press.

Part II

Categories, Policies and Negotiations of Deservingness

5

Hartz IV

Affective and Sensual Registers of Moral Inferiority

Stefan Wellgraf

How can affective and sensual registers of deservingness be depicted without falling into an individualistic trap? How can the complexity of situational dynamics and the immediacy of sensual experiences be grasped without becoming ahistorical? How can the moral and affective dimensions of inequality be thought of as interrelated? To answer these questions, I examine Hartz IV, the official name for some forms of German unemployment benefits, as a contemporary mode of undeservingness in Germany, which builds upon older notions of moral inferiority. In particular, I focus on how pupils graduating from Berlin *Hauptschulen* react to such ascriptions of moral blame in affective and sensual ways.

The *Hauptschule*, typically attended by pupils of lower socioeconomic and/or immigrant status, is located at the bottom of the federal German school system, often noted by international education surveys such as PISA for its lack of opportunities for social mobility. Many of its pupils face unemployment and thus enrol in the Hartz IV system after leaving school. Even though the *Hauptschule* has been abolished or is now known by new names in some regions of Germany as a result of recent educational reforms, the underlying structures of institutional discrimination, based primarily on class and ethnicity (Gomolla and Radtke 2003), as well as the tendency to morally charge the outcomes of educational hierarchies, remain intact. This chapter addresses the moral significance of hierarchies of deservingness, as well as the affective and sensual registers these hierarchies activate among the pupils. It is based on ethnographic research among *Hauptschüler* (*Hauptschule* pupils) during their last year in school in the Berlin districts of Lichtenberg and Wedding in 2008/2009 and in Neukölln in 2012/2013. My publications on the results of this research focus on 'the social production of contempt' (Wellgraf 2012) and 'the emotional experience of inferiority in neoliberal times' (Wellgraf 2018), thus highlighting the devaluing moral ascriptions and the affective dimensions of current forms of inequality.

The term 'Hartz IV' originates from a 2005 law 'on modern services in the job market', which regulated cuts in social expenditure. The new regulations included, among other things, a combination of unemployment and social assistance below the level of previous social assistance, a reduction in the duration of unemployment benefits and a change in the criteria for job placement. But more than this, the term has come to signify a general shift from welfare capitalism to neoliberalism. Hartz IV loads structurally produced unemployment with the moral suspicion of laziness and enacts a meritocratic ideology of continuous activation. It relies upon both traditional figurations and naturalizations of undeservingness, dating back to the nineteenth century, as well as on new modes of 'governmentality', introduced in Germany beginning in the 1990s. It is based on the distinction between a morally degenerate 'underclass', on the one hand, and those working-oriented poor, who are deemed worthy of help and support, on the other hand (Katz 1993; Gans 1996; Lindner and Musner 2008). The Hartz IV label can be understood as the contemporary German version of the 'undeserving poor'; it rearticulates a division of the unemployed into moral categories of worth. It intensifies the moralization of social inequality, emphasizing individual responsibility to a much stronger degree than existed previously and demanding constant movement and activity as signs of social worthiness (Sayer 2005; Lessenich 2008).

The fear of unemployment indicates social valorizations of labour work (Kocka 2000; Bierwisch 2003). In Europe, wage labour only became a commodity and a central vehicle for the distribution of status and recognition during the course of modernization. During industrialization, society became a working one, in which social participation was mediated through integration into the capitalist labour market, and social success was geared to the model of gendered wage labour. In earlier European epochs, when work was more strongly associated with physical dangers, work itself was seen as a source of fear, and liberation from the need for heavy physical labour was longed for as a privilege. This relationship has by now been reversed: currently, fear is directed towards the loss or absence of work. As a social category and sociopolitical problem, unemployment only established itself after 1900, when a distinction between poverty and unemployment began to be made (Jahoda et al. 1975; Zimmermann 2006; Bohlender 2012). Since then, being unemployed has entailed a perceptible social flaw and a noticeable loss of status. From the *Hauptschule* pupils' point of view, the threat of unemployment represents the danger of not successfully negotiating the imminent step into adulthood. This step threatens to perpetuate and possibly exacerbate problems resulting from a school career dominated by failures and humiliations. The term 'precarity' acquires a double connotation in this context, drawing our attention towards current social transformations, to the accompanying rise of unstable labour positions and new categories of social worth. But it also hints at the heightened sense of insecurity, the transversal character of and the affective ways in which the current crisis is both perceived and experienced.

Facing youth unemployment, *Hauptschüler* react to Hartz IV mainly via an affective and sensual register. Hartz IV signals the future they most wish to avoid and yet already sense coming. The most prominent emotional response in such situations is fear, often combined with shame, envy and anger. My approach to examining their reactions does not treat emotions and affects as ontologically different categories, but rather views them on a continuum with gradual differences in regard to form and appearance. The empirical challenge is to not treat them as 'natural' expressions or merely individual sensations, but to relate them to cultural norms and social structures, thus highlighting their moral and political dimensions, as well as their contingency and situatedness. It will be shown that state institutions like the *Hauptschule*, which (re)produce marginalized populations, are highly affectively charged and deeply implicated in moral questions, with norms and values crystallizing around questions of social deservingness, though often in rather hidden and contested ways (Fassin 2015).

In this chapter, I sketch different, though closely related, forms of managing ascriptions of moral inferiority: (1) (Dis-)Identification: borrowing Freud's (1999) notion of the uncanny, I distinguish three forms of the uncanny relating to social, personal and existential fears of the future. (2) Embodiment: on a bodily level, the fear of unemployment produces uneasiness, stress and multiple psychosomatic reactions, like stomach problems and sleeping disorders. (3) Blame Games: because of the heavy moral load of Hartz IV regulations, everyday communication about them is marked by a mix of sarcasm and irony, as well as associations of guilt and subsequent accusations. (4) Fear Deferral: different morally loaded forms of fear and defence paradoxically lead to an amplification and intensification of the fear of unemployment. An example of this is the constant demand for employment applications from school authorities, which are seen as a sign of deservingness and provide a sense of being active, but also build upon and constantly reimpose the threat of Hartz IV.

(Dis)Identification: Three Forms of the Uncanny

Moralization often works through processes of personalized moral exemplarity – the (dis)identification with certain social types or subject figures that are deemed (un)deserving. In the evolution of the figure of the undeserving poor, there has been a long history of mythical personifications, especially in times of moral panic and economic crisis. These include the 'scrounger', which emerged in 1970s Britain, and the 'welfare queen', a highly racialized, gendered rhetorical figure that became prominent in the United States in the 1980s (Morano 2019: 61–74). Recently, much of this moral scapegoating has targeted migrants. In Germany, *Hauptschüler* – mostly of low socioeconomic and immigrant status – are emblematic of both the poor and the stranger.

With regard to pupils' self-perceptions, the blame game accompanying recent German welfare reforms is highly ambivalent. In their self-perceptions, they struggle with the common moral delegitimization of certain personalized images of moral unworthiness and undeservingness, with the former highlighting ascriptions of negative personal characteristics and the latter emphasizing a lack of dedication. At the same time, the stereotyped images that have become associated with Hartz IV in Germany since the early 2000s hit quite close to home, uncannily resembling the life paths of their relatives and their own projected futures.

In their efforts to find internships that could provide employment qualifications, the pupils gradually became aware of their miserable situation in the labour market during tenth grade, at around sixteen years old, which was mainly due to structural conditions and not their individual failings. The fear of unemployment grew during this period into a clearly perceptible collective feeling, which became an enormous emotional burden for many of them in the months leading up to graduation. Almost all the secondary school pupils I met during my research periods were afraid of living on unemployment and being dependent on state social benefits. These fears often intensified in imagined visual scenarios, as well as in frightening images of Hartz IV, the Jobcenter, which administers Hartz IV, and the Arbeitsamt, a colloquial term, officially changed several years ago to Agentur für Arbeit (Agency for Work).

ERIC: 'One of those old drunks in the street – I do not want to be that at all. Everybody wants to find work later. And I don't want to live at home and get Hartz IV. That would be bad.' Eric comes from a family with a history of financial debts, severe accidents and repeated suicide attempts. He struggled for years to find work after leaving school. For him, a life financed by social benefits is associated with unemployment and images of an older alcoholic sitting on the street. Eric has absorbed morally charged negative images of a life of social dependence, which resemble traditional moral divides that separate the respectable working class from the *Lumpen*. 'Hartz IV addicts' thus personify a contemporary version of the undeserving poor of the nineteenth century. Eric's depiction indicates processes of cultural figuration, combining typified social models of (un)worthiness and (negative) media representations into palpable cultural figures, from which he actively tries to distance himself, but to which he nevertheless bears a relation in stereotyped depictions of the 'underclass' (Hartigan 2005; Ege 2013). A life dependent on state social benefits is seen as a horror scenario to be avoided, as not living in line with the desired future of having a secure job, one's own home and a family.

Eric's East Berlin classmate Justine shares a similar outlook on life: 'I'm really afraid that one day I'll be sitting on the street, that I'll have to beg for money, that I won't have a job, no family, nothing at all.' In this passage, too, the iconic motif of the unemployed sitting on the street begging for money appears as a nightmarish imagined personal future. To have a job and to be able to feed a family are at the centre of one's self-image of a good and fulfilled life, without both of which future life would seem worthless – as simply 'nothing'. The fear of unemployment and dependence on state social benefits is particularly virulent precisely because it seems particularly likely. Many *Hauptschüler* are therefore afraid of the very path that many of them are unintentionally heading towards in the future. This also affects pupils like Angelika, who stood out by having achieved a middle school diploma in the *Hauptschule* and who had already submitted dozens of job applications:

ANGELIKA: I definitely don't want to go to the Jobcenter. That I will get a letter some time [asking] 'What's going on? You have to go to the Jobcenter. You don't have a job': that's what I'm most afraid of.

S.W.: Have you been there before?

ANGELIKA: No, but I have an appointment on the 13th. They just want to know what I'll do after school. But I don't like it; I've never been to the Jobcenter before, and I don't want to be there either. I don't want anything to do with it at all. Or with the Arbeitsamt [employment office].

Angelika articulates panic-stricken fear at receiving a letter informing her that she has to go to the state employment agency because she has not found training or a job. It turned out that she had already received one of these letters and had an appointment in about a week. In her rejection, she is indifferent concerning the Jobcenter and the Arbeitsamt, and in general she mistrusts state authorities of this kind. This morally inflected distinction among the jobless usually becomes increasingly relevant in the years after leaving school, with the Arbeitsamt being reserved for those who already were employed in previous years. Angelika's rigorous rejection is closely related to family experiences: her older sister was also unable to find a job after finishing school, and finally had to accept a 'one-euro job', working as a cleaner before later finding a job as a chambermaid in a hotel. These extremely low-paid 'one-euro jobs' are a particularly controversial activation measure adopted as part of the Hartz IV regulations. They can include any legal activity that is not deemed immoral for up to thirty hours a week. Refusal to accept a 'one-euro job' is usually interpreted as undeservingness, resulting in a reduction in social benefits. Angelika, whose professional goal is to become a 'very good hotel manager', is afraid, as she reported during our interview, of being 'simply obliged to do any kind of work', just like her sister, and thus no longer being able to realize her own professional dreams: 'I don't want to end up like her. Absolutely not.'

The fear of Hartz IV, the Jobcenter and 'one-euro jobs' has an uncanny component. Sigmund Freud (1999) uses the dual meaning of the word in his text 'Das Unheimliche' ('The Uncanny'), playing with the ambiguous semantics of (*un*)*heimlich* consisting of *heim* (home) and *heimlich* (secretly), which indicates something repressed or hidden. The uncanny is thus not new or foreign, but something all too familiar, which has, however, been suppressed for a period of time. It often appears in the figure of a doppelganger, which seems to be identical or at least very similar to the person who fears the uncanny. Angelika's sister, with whom she otherwise feels closely connected, apparently fulfils this doppelganger function; in her fate as a 'one-euro jobber', she represents both the familiar and the temporarily suppressed fear of a failed professional life. Angelika distances herself from this fate and thus implicitly also from her sister, while at the same time recognizing that they are both motivated and especially hardworking. This brings the underlying tension of the current regimes of deservingness to the fore, resulting in a moralization of what are, in fact, structural forms of inequality. This means that in practice, the distinction between deserving and undeserving remains precarious, constantly falling short of its own standards of judgement.

The uncanny has another closely related component. Some pupils are not only afraid of professional failure, but also of themselves – that they may not be able to uphold their own moral standards of self-worth, dedication and motivation for much longer. This leads to a personalization of questions of (un)deservingness and to real moral conflicts. For example, Ali, a pupil in Wedding from a migrant family, had received a conviction for a theft a few years earlier. It has since been expunged from his record, but he is afraid that he will be drawn into the shadow economy if he does not succeed in the official job market. He also mentioned that this could result in further convictions, which would prohibit him from accessing the training he aspires to in the security industry. At the time, Palestinian refugees in particular were faced with a situation in which their temporary residence permit status did not allow them to work. This systematically drew them into illegal forms of labour, which was in turn culturalized and scandalized as being a primary feature of 'Arab clans'.

The list of fear-examples is long. Niklas, a high school pupil from Lichtenberg who has lived in a children's home since the death of his mother from untreated cirrhosis of the liver, longs to finally be allowed to move out when he turns eighteen. Yet, at the same time, he is very afraid of 'not getting to grips with' the responsibility of having to take care of himself, also having had the experience of debt in his family. Safa, a pupil from Neukölln, above all feared succumbing to the fate of joblessness and losing sight of her dreams for the future: 'I am afraid that I will stop learning. I actually want to continue, but at the moment I have become a bit lazy. Somehow I don't want to learn anymore and I don't feel like it.' Towards the end of her time at school, Safa was still articulating ambitious goals. She dreamed of graduating from secondary school with a vocational baccalaureate degree and then studying either interior design or fashion design.

But at that time, she already knew that it would be 'hard to achieve' her goal. In the end, she just missed out on receiving a middle school diploma due to a poor grade in mathematics. After school, she immediately married, gave birth to two children and moved to Lebanon with her husband. After having trouble with her in-laws there, she returned to Berlin, where she eventually found an apprenticeship in a dental office despite wearing a headscarf.

However, fear of the future expressed itself not only with regard to possible professional, educational or personal failure, but also in a more existential way as a fear of fate, of unforeseeable incidents that threaten one's existence. The number of dramatic, sad and potentially traumatic events in the life stories of the pupils I accompanied was striking: divorces, deaths of close family and friends, stories of flight and expulsion, serious illnesses, accidents and crimes were not the exception, but rather seemed to be the rule. Several more life stories will briefly illustrate this. Mohamad grew up in a Palestinian refugee family; his parents split up after the family arrived in Germany and he was often beaten by his father. Anna lived apart from her parents, who immigrated from Kazakhstan and now worked in southern Germany. Ibo recounted the escape of his Kurdish family from Syria after persecution and Imad's criminal career with the 'Bandidos' – a notorious criminal gang – took off after his father's death. It is not surprising that these negative experiences re-appear in the form of fears for the future. Eric, for example, was afraid that 'something might go wrong' or that he 'won't be able to manage money later on'. His own fears for the future were closely related to the fate of his father, who was paraplegic as a result of a motorcycle accident and had tried to commit suicide several times, as well as that of his heavily indebted brother, who had also become unable to work due to several accidents.

Many secondary school pupils were thrown off-track by such personal catastrophes during the decisive years of their education. The effects of the selection mechanisms in the hierarchical German school system, with *Gymnasium* at the top and *Hauptschulen* at the bottom, are notoriously difficult to reverse. They solidify and transform early negative experiences into lasting exclusion, which, in turn, gives rise to far-reaching problems later in life, often marked by precarity and prolonged cycles of crisis. Through ideologies of meritocracy (Solga 2009), systemic disadvantages that manifest in education are interpreted as personal failures and character deficiencies, as signs of being 'stupid' or 'lazy'; thus, they become a lasting mark or stigma on the pupil's social identity – a devalued identity against which they struggle, but with which they are nevertheless afflicted. Processes of identity formation, which usually demand a certain consolidation of social role models and sustaining self-ascriptions, are made significantly more difficult by the negative attributions to *Hauptschüler* as prospective Hartz IV recipients.

Following Freud (1999), the psychological effect of (dis)identifying with negative moral exemplars can be interpreted here as three interconnected forms of the 'uncanny': social fear of professional failure, personal fear of giving up on oneself and submitting to a seemingly hopeless situation, and, finally, existential fear of fate – notably frequent in the biographies of the pupils and their families. Social fears concerning a future of unemployment articulated themselves in terrifying scenarios of social slippage and were symbolically personified by doppelgangers from their immediate families or circles of friends. Fears of unemployment were uncanny because the pupils were afraid of something unpleasantly familiar to them. Unemployment stood for a way of life deemed unworthy, which they therefore wanted to avoid, but that they often ended up experiencing unintentionally due to structural discrimination.

Embodiment: Incarnated Hierarchies of Worth

These fears also had palpable physical effects. The somatic character of stigmatization has to date been conveyed primarily in artistic, cinematic and literary representations of precarious conditions, particularly impressively in the Dardenne brothers' cinematic work. Their 1999 film *Rosetta* portrays a teenager living on a housing estate who is desperately searching for a job and a 'normal life'. She suffers from stomach cramps, outbursts of anger and moral dilemmas arising from her social situation. In anthropology and cultural theory, the corporeal dimension of social exclusion has been addressed more recently in studies of embodiment, which argue that the body is a medium of expression that is deeply implicated in social norms and power structures (van Wolputte 2004; Mascia-Lees 2011). This turn towards the body is accompanied by and connected to a growing interest in emotions, affects and the senses. From this perspective, questions of deservingness render themselves apparent corporeally, with the following example hinting at unexpected physical manifestations, as well as some rather typical incarnations:

FIELD DIARY: English class, last lesson for today. Most of the pupils are a bit tired. Martin suddenly has acute shortness of breath. He gasps for air and can hardly stand up. The teacher says he should get some 'fresh air'. Jamil and I accompany him outside, where we sit in the sun. Martin reports pain in his lungs and stomach area and he repeatedly bends over as if he has severe cramp. 'When things get bad, I have disturbances in my heart rhythm and a kind of epileptic seizure', he warns us in advance. We recommend that he relax. But he definitely wants to get back to class as soon as possible. 'I need every minute of class, just in English. Even if the grades don't matter now anyway. I still want to leave school with a good report card.'

Then, he asks me if I have my mobile phone with me. He feels calmer knowing I can always call an emergency doctor if he 'breaks down after all'. I don't think that's very calming. 'My hand is numb', Martin suddenly shouts. He now also has pain in his back. His doctor thinks it's an 'anxiety disorder', a kind of panic state that overcomes him when he feels breathlessness. He calls it a 'state of shock'. The attending doctors have not yet found anything: some believe it is asthma, others suspect a virus, but so far nobody has a proper explanation. Martin seems pale, tired and gaunt. His hair is hanging so far over his face that it is almost impossible to recognize him. He performs the breathing exercises that the doctor recommended. 'Dude, let's call a doctor', Jamil says. I recommend waiting and seeing: 'The few minutes of English are not so important now either. You better get some rest first.' But Martin absolutely wants to go back to class. On the way back, he needs a break on the stairs. He asks me to open the window for him once we have arrived in the room on the top floor. Martin immediately continues his English exercise. The teacher smiles contentedly; the problem seems to have been solved.

This was a depressing scene, especially since it was not an isolated case. I could not determine the causes of his physical complaints, but the social situation seemed to me to play an essential role in Martin's discomfort. When I met him again the next day, he was still complaining of nausea. When I asked him if he had been to the doctor, he replied evasively. When I enquired what his mother had to say, he said: 'What should she think about it?' Later, I learned of his family circumstances. His single, unemployed mother had been assigned an individual social worker, but refused this form of state assistance. What is striking in this situation is both his frightening degree of panic and his extraordinary level of identification with the moral call to work hard in school.

Different *Hauptschüler* embodied their social conditions in different ways. There was a powerful group of pupils, mostly from migrant backgrounds, who performed excessive masculinity and corporealized a counterculture to school, similar to what Paul Willis (1977) describes in *Learning to Labour*, with the notable exception that they did not end up in manual labour, but in unemployment. There were also calm pupils, like Martin, who tried to improve their slim chances by dutifully following the rules and demands of schooling. The bodies of both groups were a product of society, upon which structures and values inscribed themselves, and also producers of society in that they influenced their surroundings and created social arrangements. In this context, the sociologist Robert Gugutzer, following Anthony Giddens, speaks of a 'duality of structure and embodiment', thus pointing out that social structures and embodied actions mutually influence and produce each other (Gugutzer 2015: 149). Martin's health complaints indicate how family relationships and social fears can inscribe themselves within the body. The physicality of his anxiety was clear in the typical physiological symptoms of nausea, dizziness, shortness of breath and abdominal pain. However, emphasis on the physical experiences of social exclusion should not lead to the conclusion that pupils were unable to reflect upon their situations. Rather, fear of the future also demonstrated itself physically, and physical anxiety symptoms were partly the result of rational considerations – in Martin's case, of the relevance of English in the professional world and the importance of school grades for one's self-esteem.

Martin was afraid of being left behind in a subject that was considered particularly relevant to his desired profession. In a figurative sense, he was afraid of falling further into social isolation. This can be related to recent changes in social self-assessment that sociologists such as Neckel (2008) recognize. According to this, consensual identification with the middle class, which characterizes the old Federal Republic of Germany, is being reduced in contemporary society in favour of antagonistic self-attributions. One should add that this trend towards polarization can also be observed among the already-marginalized secondary school pupils in Neukölln. Alongside the widespread fear among the middle class of slipping into precarity, the pupils clung from below to the hope of achieving middle-class status, with which they associated at least a certain degree of security and respectability. This situation was marked by changed conditions among what was once called 'the working class'. On the one hand, 'old' proletarian worker pride was no longer available as a point of positive identification because of the almost ubiquitous precarious professional situations of the pupils' parents. On the other hand, *Hauptschüler* were hit particularly hard by the cultural devaluation of the 'new lower class' and the growth of precarious work, resulting in mainly poorly paid and unstable jobs. With cultural ascriptions of worth relating to manual labour no longer salient and new regimes of (un)deservingness institutionalized through welfare and labour market reforms, the borders of status and respectability among people in the lower levels of Germany's social hierarchy became hard-won. Martin's desperate behaviour seemed to reflect some of these societal tensions.

When I asked directly about classification in Germany's social hierarchy in my first study of Berlin *Hauptschule* pupils in 2008 and 2009, almost all of them located themselves somewhat below the middle, at level three or four on a scale of one to ten. They justified this self-classification in the lower middle class by saying that there was still a disrespectful group that consisted of 'gypsies', 'the handicapped' and 'school dropouts' below them, while the distance between them and those secondary school pupils, with whom they symbolically associated the social 'middle class', was only regarded as insignificant, since a middle-school leaving certificate could – at least in theory – also be obtained at the *Hauptschule*. With this self-assessment, the moral coding of social hierarchization was upheld, with the pupils assigning themselves as flattering a position as possible within it. The precarious longing for middle-class status was articulated likewise in a demonstrative orientation towards consumerism, which often aimed to show that one had 'made it'. But the pupils' inclination towards ostentatious consumer products was, in turn, often read by their peers as a sign of rather desperate social aspirations, exposing them as mere 'wannabes'.

The pupils mostly lacked bourgeois images of moral self-worth and the material resources of the middle class. The reasons why these factors are so decisive is revealed in two ethnographic studies of young people in precarious circumstances from Austria. Gerlinde Malli (2010) presents struggling adolescents affected by drug addiction, unemployment and homelessness in institutional youth-care settings, some of whose families have been living in poverty for two or three generations. Gilles Reckinger (2010) studied lower-middle-class young people who stumbled at school due to biographical difficulties or family break-ups, but who could partly compensate for their lack of school qualifications by resorting to a middle-class habitus and could thus better adapt to the precarious conditions of the neoliberal labour market. At the end of their school careers, pupils like Martin came to a fork in the road, where they tended towards one of these two options. Martin's commitment to English lessons showed how seriously he took this upcoming choice of action. His unstable body indicated how strained he was by the moral load of this looming bifurcation.

Blame Games: Hartz IV Dialogues

Berlin high school pupils 'spoke' not only with their bodies. Due to their palpable social insecurity, there was a real need to exchange information about their social positions. The threat of unemployment was addressed in various ways in the tenth grade, both in class discussions and informal conversations. Talking about unemployment was influenced by culture, with fears articulated using pre-existing slogans. Metaphors and discursive nodal points such as *Brennpunktschule* (literally 'hotspot school', meaning schools associated with 'social problems', often used to designate 'Hauptschulen' in poor areas like the ones described here) or Hartz IV played an important role in these exchanges, in which moral assessments were bundled and processed linguistically. Talk about these issues was loaded with accusations of guilt or responsibility and characterized by tension and contradictions. In some cases, a sense of irony with regard to familiar stigmatizing attributions surfaced, in which the negative behaviour of fellow pupils was commented upon with jokes aimed at relieving some of the stress of the situation. At the same time, constant confrontation with negative attributions reproduced itself symbolically in rather hostile forms of communication and (self-)accusation:

> ROBERTO: Schools with more than 75 per cent Hartz IV [families] will get 100,000 euros more next year. Only those *Brennpunktschulen* will get that.
>
> TEACHER: Why is it that there are hotspot schools?
>
> MUSTAFA: Depends on where the schools are located. Here 98 per cent of the pupils come from Neukölln. Almost all of them are foreigners, people who are poor or have problems. They then let their anger out at school, against teachers or classmates.
>
> BURAK: Some are just smarter and others more stupid.
>
> ROBERTO: But for that we also get new computers!
>
> BURAK: And then someone cuts the cables again.

TEACHER: Who cuts the cables?

BURAK: The hotspot pupils!

MUSTAFA: School here is actually easy. Everybody lives his life and you don't get beaten up.

TEACHER: What makes a hotspot school so different?

PUPILS: Bullying. Absenteeism. Pupils against teachers.

TEACHER: Poor attitude to learning and a very low graduation rate.

BURAK: Pupils who sit around being lazy and doing nothing.

MUSTAFA: I also swear to myself every Saturday in bed that I will finally do my schoolwork. That's laziness! I usually do my own things, but I'm lazy at school.

YUSSUF: There are lots of opportunities to do something here.

THEO: Nonsense, our school is the poorest in the world.

DUC: Right!

MUSTAFA: You should go to your home country and not eat so much rice.

ROBERTO: In some schools here there are holes in the walls everywhere.

TEACHER: How many of you pupils have an apprenticeship position?

ROBERTO: I am the only one who has one coming up.

THOMAS: And I am going into the army.

THEO: I will earn more money than all of you put together.

TEACHER: Two have an apprenticeship. Later on, two or three might make it through the OSZ [highly controversial and stigmatizing 'training centres']. That's a maximum of five out of forty-five. Well, congratulations! And how many permanent truants do we have? [Takes the class register and starts counting out loud in a sarcastic tone.]

THEO: Almost the whole school ends up on Hartz IV [i.e. the pupils' parents are on Hartz IV themselves]. Nobody pays for books. That's why the school is poor.

BURAK: I don't think it's the Hartz IV children.

MUSTAFA: My mother works, but she still gets Hartz IV.

THEO: Undeclared work!

MUSTAFA: You are annoying! But many foreigners, who perhaps don't speak German, think that they'll have more money for their family if they moonlight and get Hartz IV.

THOMAS: But then you don't get a pension.

TEACHER: Where does Hartz IV come from?

MUSTAFA: From those who work. But many foreigners think they will get more this way. Some of the Arabs here in Sonnenallee, they are really rich. The shisha bars and casinos are all full of Arabs. I know some of them. They live in Rudow. They all drive big cars and have a lot of girlfriends.

ROBERTO: Why do pupils go to hotspot schools?

TEACHER: Because the education authority sends them here. We get the pupils who don't complain or who get kicked out of other schools.

ROBERTO: But we might also get new smartboards.

TEACHER: What do I do with smartboards under such conditions? I like chalkboards so much more anyway.

Based on the pupils' reference to the prospect of state subsidies for particularly problematic schools, a discussion about the assessment of the school's own situation enfolded during an ethics class. The discussion first focused on questions of social exclusion associated with the label *Brennpunktschule*, which are provided with special aid due to their remarkable failure to provide an education, but are simultaneously denied regular increases in funding for the same reason. Using the keyword 'Hartz IV', the discussion then shifted to everyday forms of securing a livelihood under precarious conditions. In the course of the conversation, the differences of opinion among the pupils and the assumption of hegemonic patterns of interpreting social hierarchy stand out. Mustafa and Roberto assessed the situation positively and referred to even worse schools and opportunities. Theo and Duc disagreed by pointing to the catastrophic lack of funding for their school. Burak emphasized the pupils' collective shortcomings and faults. The teacher also presented a negative assessment of the situation in school. Surprisingly, in the course of the pupils' discussion, they tagged themselves as one of the biggest problems in the school. They accused themselves of having low intelligence and admitted a lack of commitment to their studies. They repeated stigmatizing stereotypes of *Hauptschüler* as stupid and lazy and thus as responsible for their own situation. The common accusation that migrant families abuse the German welfare system was also confirmed but relativized with regard to the pupils' own families. In addition, various racist insults and individual hopes for extraordinary wealth were expressed.

Although the class discussion offered a seemingly welcome opportunity for exchange among those affected, it did not lead to mutual support in the face of precarious conditions. Rather, it illustrated the common tendency towards solidarity reduction and patterns of blame-apportioning under neoliberalism. Ascriptions of (un)deservingness are both contested and confirmed on an individual basis, but they have already become part of general beliefs about society. Such common-sense constructions play a crucial role in legitimizing class structures – especially as institutional architectures tend to mask class differences – by reproducing negative stereotypes and causing unequal social positions to seem logical (Gramsci 1971; Crehan 2016). Heterogeneous judgements and everyday experiences are articulated that reveal overarching patterns indicating strong moralization of the 'social question'. However, the example above also shows that 'common sense' is an uneven and contested narrative territory.

Through language, fears may be generated and mobilized, named and communicated, intensified and mitigated. The prevailing negative appraisal of their social situation during the course of the conversation will not have eased pupils' existing fears about the future. Those who were still relatively positive prior to the discussion were confronted with a devastating assessment by the teacher. In addition, all the pupils were able to determine whether they would be among the few who would receive an apprenticeship – the common way to obtain work qualifications among those who do not attend university – or among the majority without one once they had completed school. This also applies to those pupils who did not take part in the discussion, like the young women present and shy young men like Martin. The pupils' self-positioning of themselves as attending a problem school and the somewhat negative tone of the conversation indicate that it created negative feelings of disappointment, forlornness and frustration.

The terms 'Brennpunktschule' and 'Hartz IV' provided the framework within which the discussion unfolded. Originally, Hartz IV served as an abbreviation for the 'Fourth Law for Modern Services on the Labour Market' conceived by Social Democrat and Volkswagen manager Peter Hartz. It was the last of a batch of laws that transformed the German welfare regime into an activating welfare state in the early 2000s. Germany was a laggard in the neoliberal restructuring of the welfare state. In the 1980s, the United States and the United Kingdom were pioneers in neoliberal development under the Reagan and Thatcher regimes. In Eastern European transition countries, a neoliberal reform agenda had already been implemented in the 1990s (Ther 2014). The Hartz reforms stipulated that unemployment benefits would not be paid out until individuals' savings are used up, and thus unemployment began to be accompanied to a greater extent than previously by impoverishment. At the same time, a new form of low-wage sector emerged: Hartz IV recipients became dependent upon either additional offers in the official low-wage sector or the unofficial black market in order to secure an adequate material livelihood. The example Mustafa mentioned was probably a form of 'stocking up'.

Soon after the welfare reforms were introduced, the term 'Hartz IV' started to be used colloquially to describe, above all, a new kind of basic monetary provision linked to obligations and restrictions. In addition, Hartz IV came to refer in a typifying way to negative character traits, such as those classically associated with 'pauperism' and more recently the 'new lower class'. It became a stigmatizing ascription, a discrediting label for and a sign of moral failure of persons or groups of people who had achieved low levels of education or were unemployed (Goffman 1963). This also meant a return to the language of undeservingness, to a remoralizing of poverty linked to neoliberal visions of society (Muehlebach 2012; Morano 2019). Devaluing attitudes towards the unemployed in need of care, which became the state model in the course of the Agenda 2010 reform programme, was symbolically condensed in the cipher of Hartz IV, which was now regarded as a shorthand for precarious situations or failed labour market biographies. The Neukölln *Hauptschule* pupils used the term not only for descriptive but also for defamatory purposes. Since the pupils' parents were to a great extent dependent upon Hartz IV, negative self-images and their own fears for the future were indirectly articulated in their use of the term.

In young people's linguistic practices, derogatory, individualizing attributions were reproduced and social development tendencies thus translated into everyday school life. The conversation in the passage quoted above was injurious, a precarious form of dialogue in which social and moral accusations of guilt and ideological resentments stand out. This version of 'narrated precariousness' does not focus on attempts to subsequently establish coherence and biographical continuity, a mode of processing that Ove Sutter (2013) attends to in interviews with precariously employed people in Austria. In the dialogues about Hartz IV that occurred at the Berlin school, negative attributions and attempts at individual profiling at the expense of classmates dominated. A blame game emerged; dialogues of accusations and negative ascriptions unfolded, marked by individualizing and dividing tendencies.

Fear Deferral: Applications as Signs of Deservingness

The more relentlessly the door to the labour market closes, the more obsessively attention is focused on the remaining narrow gap. During regular lessons, elective courses and in individual efforts, the pupils repeatedly expressed hope of securing an apprenticeship despite adverse circumstances that made this an unlikely outcome. They were invited to feel like agents with the opportunity to make choices and take action. Nevertheless, their efforts were not totally voluntary: Not only were applications for apprenticeships part of the school curriculum, but they were also interpreted as a sign of deservingness. Refusing to apply for an apprenticeship could result in punishments, ranging from disciplinary measures in school to later cuts in social assistance.

Intense preoccupation with questions of where and how to apply was a channel for the fear of unemployment. In vocational orientation class, in which tenth-graders were primarily concerned with opportunities for placements in the labour market, this defensive fear was particularly palpable. In the first half of the school year, lessons revolved again and again around internships, which were discussed over months with regard to portfolios and oral interviews. This resulted in a striking discrepancy between the number of applications submitted and the rather low success rate. At the same time and increasingly in the second half of the year, the teacher repeatedly checked on the status of submitted applications. This also resulted in a problem of persuasion, as the pupils were exhorted to try harder, but without any real promise of success:

> FIELD DIARY: The teacher desperately admonishes the pupils to accept the counselling offers from Jobcenters and independent providers. According to her, the pupils miss their appointments too often, and then usually have a guilty conscience. A pupil who has completed an internship in the social sector proudly recounts that she is allowed to continue her work there voluntarily. She is very happy about this, as she hopes

that it will give her a chance to get an apprenticeship. 'Normally only high school graduates are allowed to work there.' The teacher encourages her to take up the offer 'absolutely, you should take it' and not to 'screw it up'. Next, she asks the pupils to talk about their career aspirations. Theo wants to work as a salesman or as a businessman in the retail trade. 'I don't know. I don't know', replies another pupil, who was recently kicked out of the network counselling programme because, like many others, he no longer attended his sessions. The teacher points out that this was noted at the job centre and communicated to the school. 'If you want to seek help later on, it can cause you difficulties if you have not taken advantage of past offers of help.' 'How are they supposed to know what I want if I don't know myself?', the pupil reacts, annoyed. Martin wants to work in IT, Susanne wants to become a geriatric nurse and Jasha wants to study at university, but already knows that it will be 'difficult'. The pupils ask how much you earn from an apprenticeship and how you can find out. 'Seven hundred euros', says someone who seems to know his way around. Subsequently, the teacher again asks about the status of the pupils' applications. Many already have completed seven, eight or ten applications; others do not know where to apply. 'You must write at least one hundred', scolds the teacher and encourages the pupils again to accept the offers of counselling.

The pupils had numerous assistance programmes at their disposal when looking for an apprenticeship. The school, the Federal Employment Agency and various external institutions offered counselling and help with applications. As a result, the pupils had access to multiple application counsellors, some of whom were in competition with each other. However, this enormous social effort did not result in a noticeable improvement in their chances in the labour market. Existing training places remained vacant rather than accept *Hauptschüler*. The continued exclusion of parts of the population, despite a shortage of skilled workers, was justified by the fact that many pupils were labelled in official jargon as 'nicht ausbildungsfähig' (incapable of work training), and thus embodied the opposite of the 'employability' demanded by the neoliberal work regime. This contemporary semantic label re-actualizes the distinction between deserving and undeserving and exacerbates it, since even if work is available, the pupils are not seen as fit due to a generalized negative moral assessment. In this context, one unpleasant task the various vocational counsellors had was to indirectly 'cool down' pupils' expectations and to give them a 'realistic' self-image, thus preparing them for a life of precariousness (Walther 2015).

At the same time, 'offers of assistance' were accompanied by welfare state monitoring. The teacher's threats indicate that a failure to consider such offers could be noted by the state and have a negative impact on the job centre's later assessments of deservingness. The Berlin Network for Training mentioned here was run by the Federal Employment Agency, which was also responsible for subsequent assessments of Hartz IV payment rates. This led to a paradoxical situation: on the one hand, applications from secondary school pupils had little prospect of success; on the other hand, there was a threat of penalties if pupils refused to prepare applications or if, given the limited possibilities available, they did not know which positions to apply for. The fact that the pupils were not lacking in motivation when they actually seemed to have an opportunity is demonstrated by the example of the young woman who sought to recommend herself for an apprenticeship by working for free. Managing unemployment in this way produced desperate teachers and frightened pupils.

This application system, based on fear and intimidation, affected not only the pupils, but also the social workers who looked after them. They likewise often found themselves with one foot in unemployment, as an interview with the application assistant at the school shows:

MRS FÖRSTER: In principle, it is my job to help people. We are looking for opportunities for pupils who have a particularly difficult time finding an apprenticeship, perhaps even finding anything. Actually, I like my work. The hardest part is not the pupils: it's all the admin. Because we also have to make reports and write assessments.

S.W.: How many of the supervised pupils find a training place?

MRS FÖRSTER: If it's one out of the twenty pupils we supervise we are happy. But we also have cases that are really difficult to mediate, mostly because of high absenteeism rates. We are also working on this with the young people. We look after the pupils after they have left school.

S.W.: How did you come to be employed here at the school?

MRS FÖRSTER: I come from an independent business, a private education service. Originally, I was trained in the natural sciences and then came here through a vocational preparation course. We all only have temporary employment contracts. I can't afford a burnout like the teachers here: I lack the professional security. We usually work from one semester to the next, sometimes longer, but for a maximum of two years. I have already changed institutions several times, as the programmes are always limited in time. In between, I have been unemployed from time to time. Since you have to register as unemployed three months in advance, you are always confronted with this issue yourself. This is of course an enormous burden, in addition to the emotional strain of the work, but you learn to live with it. Unfortunately, this creates a lot of competition among colleagues. Some social workers work only for the employment office. Fortunately, I am used to dealing with this stress. So far, I have always managed somehow. It's not nice; I wish it were different. Especially because of the pupils, who need consistency. How are they supposed to learn constancy themselves if their mentors are always dropping out?

S.W.: What feelings do the pupils come to you with?

MRS FÖRSTER: The pupils here in the tenth grade are very afraid of the new road that awaits them beginning in the summer. Even finishing school is a big step, and then the professional insecurity, that makes the pupils afraid. They try to repress it, but it's still noticeable. But that's normal. I think everyone has that. Some insist on applying to an enormous number of apprenticeships. Others don't apply at all because they think they'll be rejected anyway. With some, we go along to the interviews, when they panic too much.

The social worker's insecure employment situation is a result of the privatization of what was once called the welfare state. At the time of my research, the Federal Employment Agency usually only offered short-term 'career entry support' programmes to commercially oriented companies and then, according to Mrs Förster's assessment, generally chose less expensive rather than more convincing offers. Application assistants had to be flexible in precarious employment relationships. They too were driven by the constant fear of unemployment. At the time of the interview in February, Mrs Förster assumed that her position would not be extended beyond the end of the school year in June, as the scope of the local programme for career-entry assistants was set to be reduced from nine to five positions and, in addition, another training company had already been awarded the contract.

A further, complementary form of dealing with uncertain futures was revealed in additional offers from the school, about which the pupils were supposed to be motivated and optimistic. These included the Teach First Fellow Programme, the School Turnaround development programme and numerous workshops. These were based on a demonstrably positive approach that was expressed, inter alia, with showy, quizlike elements and a pronounced culture of praise. In an explicit rejection of the 'ideological trench warfare' of earlier generations of social workers, which was understood to be old-fashioned, a form of social commitment understood as 'contemporary' was represented. This appealed to the idea that pupils and teachers were responsible for their own outcomes, instead of criticizing structures of social inequality. However, in the process of implementing such programmes, contradictions emerged. There was a striking gap between their high-sounding promises and the rather meagre effects on day-to-day school life. And in the course of their everyday work with the pupils, some of those carrying out the programmes expressed doubt regarding the appropriateness of this approach. During a training workshop at one of these educational institutions, the pupils had to write on a poster that featured a large yellow 'smile' and the sentence: 'I firmly believe that I can find a job that I like.' They were supposed to enter their names and mark 'Yes', 'Maybe' or 'No'. With the exception of one pupil who was negative and one who was undecided, all the others followed the unspoken request to place themselves in the 'Yes' field, thus also claiming deservingness. The poster then hung in the classroom for weeks, sending the implicit moral message that it is the pupil's will and commitment that is the key to success.

Even such penetrating optimism cannot eliminate the fear of unemployment if it is not accompanied by real improvements in secondary school pupils' structural situation in the labour market. The evocative character of these measures and the constant urging to make applications were accompanied by a strong moral impetus that aligned compliance with deservingness. But these measures could only deceive pupils for a certain period of time. Sooner or later, they developed a quite realistic sense of their chances of finding a job and even their teachers had problems justifying the constant demand for applications. The school's application madness, as expressed in the frequent request to prepare over a hundred of them, only drew attention to the threatening negative scenario. The application system, which was accompanied by warnings and hopes, intimidation and surveillance, produced the very fears it claimed to banish.

Conclusion

Recent transformations in Germany's labour market policy, such as the Hartz IV reforms based on the principles of 'demanding and promoting', contribute significantly to the intensification of moral ascriptions of undeservingness among the working class. According to sociologist Stephan Lessenich, the currently observable 'reinvention of the social' is based, above all, on activating individual responsibility:

> At the centre of the new mode of government is a trend towards transitioning from public to private security, from collective to individual risk management, from social insurance to personal responsibility, from state provision to self-care. The goal of this changed programme is the sociopolitical construction of double responsibility, and that means to oneself, as well as to society, as a responsible subject. (Lessenich 2008: 82; translation mine)

Unemployment, even in times of crisis, is regarded less as a largely involuntary collective fate and more as a sign of individual misconduct, which results in moral devaluations and welfare state sanctions. The school system plays a decisive role in this process that attributes responsibility for their employment outcomes to the strata of those with a low-level education (Solga 2006). The insecurity society produces is also reflected among the segments of the labour market that are particularly threatened by unemployment, where it contributes to alienation and a loss of solidarity. This creates a social background for the fear of many secondary school pupils of unemployment and the associated dangers of personal 'failure'.

This chapter demonstrates how a moral discourse on deservingness around education and work is linked to affective and sensual registers. Institutional architectures produce affective dynamics like stress and aggression, and affect bodies in a way that increases the likelihood of pupils falling into affective and sensual states such as boredom or hopelessness. Attending to such affective and sensual registers ethnographically can offer insights into both adaptations to and subversions of the institutionalized moral order (Slaby and Bens 2019). This moral order is always one that is simultaneously affective and sensual. Ideologies of social inferiority are conveyed by placing sensitive bodies in hostile environments. They are internalized and incarnated in unsettling ways, experienced in affective rather than discursive modes and explained largely through common-sense narratives of social (un)worth.

Moral evaluations of self and other are central to reproducing class structures. The figure of the undeserving proves persistent because it serves a variety of functions in legitimating the social order, ranging from economic arguments for cutting welfare to providing social scripts for acceptable behaviour and apportioning moral blame to those who are seen as not fitting the competitive norms of market society (Gans 1996; Morano 2019). This attests to neoliberal forms of inequality, resulting in the claim that those at the bottom of educational hierarchies are themselves responsible for their social situation, and thus disallowed from making inclusionary claims in terms of deservingness. That such forms of injustice do not result in open revolt and political mobilization on the part of the precariat has much to do with their moral framing, which is partly accepted even by those whom it deems undeserving. However, the lay normativity examined here does not simply mirror the moral assumptions that underwrite Germany's hierarchical education system, but also engages with it in deeply ambivalent and conflictual ways (Sayer 2005). Vernacular moral registers and common-sense scripts often reproduce dominant ideologies of worth and deservingness, thus leading to (self-)accusations and blame games. These are also intrinsically linked with a set of negative emotions, such as shame and fear, and to bodily states of insecurity. The moral dimension of inequality registered here is one deeply implicated in the workings of power. Social change requires not only a better material outlook for the pupils entering the labour market, but it would also require changing the underlying moral grammar of the current regimes of work, welfare and education.

Stefan Wellgraf holds a Heisenberg scholarship at the Institute for European Ethnology of Humboldt University in Berlin. He has published on migration, class and popular culture, most recently in a monograph on the affective dimensions of exclusion in educational settings (*Schule der Gefühle. Zur emotionalen Erfahrung von Minderwertigkeit in neoliberalen Zeiten*, Wellgraf 2018). His current ethnographic research deals with right-wing movements, particularly in the context on (post)hooliganism.

References

Bierwisch, Manfred (ed.). 2003. *Die Rolle der Arbeit in verschiedenen Epochen und Kulturen*. Berlin: Akademie Verlag.
Bohlender, Matthias. 2012. 'Von "Marienthal" zu "Hartz IV". Zur Geschichte und Gegenwart des Regierens von Langzeitarbeitslosen', in Mathias Lindenau and Marcel Kressig (eds), *Zwischen Sicherheitserwartung und Risikoerfahrung*, Bielefeld: Transcript, pp. 141–66.
Crehan, Kate. 2016. *Gramsci's Common Sense: Inequality and Its Narratives*. Durham, NC: Duke University Press.

Ege, Moritz. 2013. *'Ein Proll mit Klasse'*: *Mode, Popkultur und soziale Ungleichheiten unter jungen Männern in Berlin*. Frankfurt am Main: Campus.
Fassin, Didier. 2015. *At the Heart of the State: The Moral World of Institutions*. London: Pluto Press.
Freud, Sigmund. 1999. 'Das Unheimliche', in *Gesammelte Werke 12*, Frankfurt am Main: Fischer, pp. 228–68.
Gans, Herbert. 1996. *The War against the Poor*. New York: Basic Books.
Goffman, Erving. 1963. *Stigma: Notes on the Management of Spoiled Identity*. Englewood Cliffs, NJ: Spectrum Books.
Gomolla, Mechtild, and Frank-Olaf Radtke. 2003. *Institutionelle Diskriminierung. Die Herstellung ethnischer Differenz in der Schule*. Wiesbaden: VS.
Gramsci, Antonio. 1971. *Selections from the Prison Notebooks*. New York: International Publishers.
Gugutzer, Robert. 2015. *Soziologie des Körpers*. Bielefeld: Transcript.
Hartigan, John. 2005. *Odd Tribes: Toward a Cultural Analysis of White People*. Durham, NC: Duke University Press.
Jahoda, Marie, Paul Lazarsfeld and Hans Zeisel. 1975. *Die Arbeitslosen von Marienthal*. Frankfurt am Main: Suhrkamp.
Katz, Michael (ed.). 1993. *The 'Underclass' Debate: Views from History*. Princeton: Princeton University Press.
Kocka, Jürgen (ed.). 2000. *Geschichte und Zukunft der Arbeit*. Frankfurt am Main: Campus.
Lessenich, Stephan. 2008. *Die Neuerfindung des Sozialen. Der Sozialstaat im flexiblen Kapitalismus*. Bielefeld: Transcript.
Lindner, Rolf, and Lutz Musner (eds). 2008. *Unterschicht. Kulturwissenschaftliche Erkundungen der 'Armen' in Geschichte und Gegenwart*. Freiburg: Rombach.
Malli, Gerlinde. 2010. *'Sie müssen nur wollen'. Gefährdete Jugendliche im institutionellen Setting*. Konstanz: UVK.
Mascia-Lees, Frances (ed.). 2011. *A Companion to the Anthropology of the Body and Embodiment*. Malden, MA: Blackwell.
Morano, Serena. 2019. *Moralising Poverty: The 'Undeserving' Poor in the Public Gaze*. London: Routledge.
Muehlebach, Andrea. 2012. *The Moral Neoliberal: Welfare and Citizenship in Italy*. Chicago: University of Chicago Press.
Neckel, Sighard. 2008. 'Die gefühlte Unterschicht. Vom Wandel der sozialen Selbsteinschätzung', in Rolf Lindner and Lutz Musner (eds), *Unterschicht. Kulturwissenschaftliche Erkundungen der 'Armen' in Geschichte und Gegenwart*. Freiburg: Rombach, pp. 19–40.
Reckinger, Gilles. 2010. *Perspektive Prekarität. Wege benachteiligter Jugendlicher in den transformierten Arbeitsmarkt*. Konstanz: UVK.
Sayer, Andrew. 2005. *The Moral Significance of Class*. Cambridge: Cambridge University Press.

Slaby, Jan, and Jonas Bens. 2019. 'Political Affect', in Jan Slaby and Christian von Scheve (eds), *Affective Societies: Key Concepts*. Abingdon: Routledge, pp. 340–51.
Solga, Heike. 2006. 'Ausbildungslose und die Radikalisierung ihrer sozialen Ausgrenzung', in Heinz Bude and Andreas Willichs (eds), *Das Problem der Exklusion. Ausgegrenzte, Entbehrliche, Überflüssige*. Hamburg: Hamburger Edition, pp. 121–46.
———. 2009. 'Meritokratie – die moderne Legitimation ungleicher Bildungschancen', in Heike Solga, Justin Powell and Peter Berger (eds), *Soziale Ungleichheit. Klassische Texte zur Sozialstrukturanalyse*. Frankfurt am Main: Campus, pp. 63–72.
Sutter, Ove. 2013. *Erzählte Prekarität. Autobiografische Verhandlungen von Arbeit und Leben im Postfordismus*. Frankfurt am Main: Campus.
Ther, Philipp. 2014. *Die neue Ordnung auf dem alten Kontinent. Eine Geschichte des neoliberalen Europa*. Berlin: Suhrkamp.
Van Wolputte, Steven. 2004. 'Hang on to Your Self: Of Bodies, Embodiment, and Selves', *Annual Review of Anthropology* 33: 251–69.
Walther, Andreas. 2015. 'The Struggle for Realistic Career Perspectives: Cooling-out versus Recognition of Aspirations in School-to-Work-Transitions', *Italian Journal of Sociology of Education* 7(2): 18–42.
Wellgraf, Stefan. 2012. *Hauptschüler. Zur gesellschaftlichen Produktion von Verachtung*. Bielefeld: Transcript.
———. 2018. *Schule der Gefühle. Zur emotionalen Erfahrung von Minderwertigkeit in neoliberalen Zeiten*. Bielefeld: Transcript.
Willis, Paul. 1977. *Learning to Labor*. New York: Columbia University Press.
Zimmermann, Bénédicte. 2006. *Arbeitslosigkeit in Deutschland. Zur Entstehung einer sozialen Kategorie*. Frankfurt am Main: Campus.

6

Unemployment, Deservingness and Ideological Apparatuses
A Case Study from Turin, Italy

Carlo Capello

From my fieldwork diary, Turin, 6 March 2015:

> In the afternoon I went to Centro Lavoro Torino to attend another open orientation lesson ... As before, there were more or less twenty in attendance listening to the tutor, the young being in the minority.
>
> The lesson focused on the matter of the job interview as our tutor offered advice on presentation and the best way to answer questions and fill out tests. The teacher – who proved pleasant and rather efficient – informed us that she herself worked as a recruiter for a number of firms.
>
> The lesson mainly consisted in advice that to my mind was rather trivial: you should dress appropriately for the interview, be self-confident without being arrogant, you must be honest, pleasant and friendly and you must not speak badly of your previous employers.
>
> Towards the end of the lesson there was an interesting verbal exchange. G., a factory worker, said that during his last interview he had been asked why his previous job contract had lasted only a month. A question he found particularly frustrating considering that they were offering him a contract for just a week. The tutor, however, said his reaction was wrong, as even such a brief contract was in any case an opportunity. Then she reproached him, saying he was too critical, adding that for that reason, had she been on the board, she would never have recruited him.

The participants also included Simone, the husband of Sara, the former secretary I met and interviewed some months ago. When the lesson was over, I asked him what he thought of it. He told me he found it very useful, adding that he intended to bring his wife to the next one.

Outside Centro Lavoro's seminar room, I ran into Giuliano, who I had met there some months ago, and I asked him how his job search was going: 'The search isn't going anywhere [pause]; it is shit! The system has bombed, it has collapsed, there is nothing to be found!', he replied.

This ethnographic vignette illustrates rather effectively some of the issues arising from my enquiries on unemployment and unemployment policies in Turin, which are explored further in the following pages. The anthropological description of the courses on 'active job search' offered at the Centro Lavoro Torino – a job centre funded by the municipality – provides us with insights into the wider public management and control of unemployment, eliciting its ideological and symbolic dimensions. This local service is part and an expression of a neoliberal approach to unemployment that offers partial, ideologically connoted and moralistic responses to this structural problem. These policies are, in fact, founded on a moral assessment of joblessness, referring to an ideological model of the 'deserving unemployed', to which every jobless person is expected to conform (Howe 1990, 1994).

The enquiry into Centro Lavoro Torino is just one part of wider research I conducted between 2014 and 2017 on the experience and meaning of unemployment in the peripheries of Turin (Capello 2020). The contradictions of the contemporary Italian economy manifest themselves quite clearly here in these neighbourhoods that used to be working-class communities built up around factory work in the car industry and above all around the Fiat company (Capello 2018). In Italy today, the search for employment is an arduous task due to a post-Fordist and neoliberal economy prone to structural crisis and cyclical recessions (Gallino 2013): the official rate of unemployment has remained at around 10 per cent solidly for years. This quandary is particularly evident in Turin, where the global economic crisis exacerbated a social reality already impaired by deindustrialization (Vanolo 2015), leading to the growth of unemployment. There are a number of jobs – especially manual work and factory jobs – that are becoming increasingly scarce within the local productive horizon; this is what Giuliano was talking about when he said that 'the system has bombed, it has collapsed, there is nothing to be found'.

The larger job market is surely more complex and fluid, but this is my interlocutors' experience of it – made up of mostly unemployed people over the age of forty, who spent considerable time searching for new employment after losing their previous jobs. Furthermore – notwithstanding some exceptions – the unemployed I knew were so-called low-skilled, low-tier workers. Simone, for example, had held the position of warehouseman in many small local firms, while his wife was previously employed as a secretary. Giuliano was a bricklayer and a low-skilled factory worker, although at the time he had been out of work for many years. I focused my research on unemployed low-skilled blue-collar and white-collar workers, because their plight descends directly from the transition of Turin's economic structure from a Fordist industrial economy to a postindustrial one – and also because they are therefore the metonymic symbol of contemporary Turin (Capello 2018).

Centro Lavoro Torino is a prime site for observing the neoliberal governmentalities and ideological practices through which the crisis and great productive transformation are locally managed, on the basis of national and European guidelines (Gallie 2004). These policies are part of the wider transformation of the welfare state through which 'individualization and responsibility have nowadays become the key-words of contemporary social policies' (Dubois 2009: 167; see also Dubois 2008). The problem, in the case of unemployment policies, is that the individualistic logics behind these reforms generate the paradox – especially in Italy – of stimulating activation and autonomy in the search for employment at the very moment in which the labour market is almost totally stuck (Paugam 2013).

The ethnographic analysis shows how these policies are linked to a moralizing discourse, centred on the distinction between the deserving and undeserving unemployed, with a profound ideological meaning. The appeal to deservingness works as an ideological tool to moralize and legitimize inequalities (Streinzer and Tošić, Introduction to this volume), preserving the economic system from critique through a 'reversal of responsibility' that blames the victims for their own predicament. Centro Lavoro Torino is part of a larger apparatus that aims to sustain and transmit this ideological and moralistic view of unemployment as its courses convey the idea that the possibility of finding a job depends purely on the efforts and ability of the jobseeker.

However, why and to what extent did my interlocutors accept the individualistic and moralizing view of unemployment? The people I met were attending the classes on active job search not only because they believed these would be useful in terms of finding work, but also because the lessons allowed them to present themselves as active and deserving jobseekers. From this point of view, the courses are, for them, a sort of rite of passage to a new, more 'positive' status – a rite gifted with a magical meaning, in the sense of de Martino's theory (2015): a symbolic tool that gives the useful illusion of still being able to act in the world. To fully grasp the ritual dimensions of the course on active job searching, we need to consider the particular condition of unemployed people: their liminal state (Newman 1999). However, before diving into these more symbolic aspects of our discourse, it is necessary to briefly investigate the economic and social context of postindustrial Turin.

Turin: A Blocked Transition

Centro Lavoro Torino is located in a part of the city that has strong symbolic value. It can be found in a neighbourhood on the outskirts of the city, near the Mirafiori plant – the Fiat factory par excellence – the concrete symbol of the industrial and Fordist history of Turin. This is no coincidence, as the Centro Lavoro is part and expression of the policies elaborated by the municipality to cope with the social and economic problems of the peripheries, which have borne the brunt of the global recession.

The global crisis has been particularly severe in Turin, having a big impact on every productive sector – in particular, medium-scale industry and the building sector, which has helped to sustain the local economy since the turn of the century. During the worst period of the recession – from which the city has not yet really emerged – between 2010 and 2014, some 15,000 jobs in the industrial sector and 5,000 in the construction industry were lost (Vanolo 2015). This is one of the reasons why the official rate of unemployment has rocketed since the turn of the century, reaching 12 per cent of the workforce at the time of my fieldwork. Most of the people I met in the field had indeed lost their jobs because of the global crisis, following company failures, closures and mass dismissals caused by the crisis. Furthermore, due to the economic recession, it proved very difficult for them to find new employment and most of them had been waiting for new opportunities for years – yet another reason why we can say that the unemployed are currently the living symbol of contemporary Turin, just as the factory workers were in the 1970s. The plight of my interlocutors is a metonym for the wider city's predicament. If, as we will see, the unemployed are blocked in a liminal state – because lack of employment implies a loss of social identity (Newman 1999) – Turin is a liminal city: it has left behind its industrial past, only to find itself caught in limbo, in a long and indefinite phase of transition (or liminality) (Capello 2018, 2020). Today the city – like its unemployed – finds itself in a state of suspension, gifted with some degree of resilience (Vanolo 2015), but doubtless full of problems and stuck in a state of pending.

However, if the recession has had such a negative effect on Turin (Revelli 2016), it is because of the many contradictions already rife in the local economic model; it is mainly because of the economic and political decisions that were taken in the late 1980s, associated with the detachment from the previous industrial and Fordist economy. The global crisis has brought simmering tensions to the surface and accelerated processes already at work, further strengthening the dynamics of deindustrialization and the expulsion of the excess workforce.

Turin's current problems are deeply rooted in the past, in the difficult and strained economic transition from an industrial to a postindustrial economy. From the 1960s to the 1990s, Turin was an archetype of the 'Fordist city' (Tranfaglia 1999; Giaccaria 2010; Berta 2011): it was founded on an economic base made up of metal mechanics factories and the automobile complex centred around the Fiat company; the entire social and political life of the city was influenced by the Taylorist factory system, with a sort of functional interaction between the Fordist organization of work and Keynesian political dispositives. Even though Turin was never really a 'one-company town', it developed a symbiotic relation of domination and dependence with Fiat.

However, although the Fordist system deeply influenced the local community, its tenure was rather short-lived. Fordism still haunts the city like a spectral presence (Molé 2012; Muehlebach 2012), but the long economic conversion started as far back as the 1980s. What followed was an indefinite period of uncertainty, with alternate phases of crisis and recovery. An economic and social uncertainty grew throughout the 1990s when the Fiat company started its programmes of productive restructuration and delocalization, clearly signalling the end of the car industry era. It was at this time that Turin truly passed from a Fordist economy to post-Fordism, a passage that the local power elites – following wider hegemonic national and international political lines – no longer tried to control by means of the loosely Keynesian policies of the 1970s, but through neoliberal policies (Belligni and Ravazzi 2012). Since then, local authorities have invested in the remaking of mobility infrastructure and have tried to promote the development of new sectors of the economy, such as tourism and the leisure industry (Capello and Semi 2018). Moreover, following a hegemonic model that now seems to be the norm worldwide (Semi 2015), Turin was governed as a company, dedicated to the diktat of the market. This neoliberal management, which implied huge public investments in the new economic sectors at the same time as budget cuts for the municipal social welfare sector, reached its apex with the hosting of the Winter Olympic Games in 2006. But, besides the rhetorical celebration of the city 'on the move', the policies merely resulted in a gentrification of the city centre and the abandonment of the peripheries – places that had been strongly hit by the deindustrialization process and subsequently by the global recession. Consequently, the sense of neglect and abandonment felt by a large part of the inhabitants led to the electoral loss of the political coalition that had governed Turin for the previous twenty years, ushering in the victory of the new 'populist' Movimento 5 Stelle during the municipal elections in 2016.

So, as noted above, the great crisis in Turin began well before 2008. It started with a constant decline in local industrial production, epitomized by the fate of the Fiat Mirafiori plant, where the number of employees has shrunk from a high of 60,000 in the 1970s to its current level of fewer than 5,000. This long and difficult industrial decline is the main cause behind the massive drop in employment, the high level of redundancy of factory workers and the negative job market situation in general. The transition to a 'tertiary economy' – centred around services and tourism, and managed through neoliberal pro-market policies – has not brought the city the new resources promised by the hegemonic discourses; on the contrary, for most working-class people, the transition has ushered in a further decline in job opportunities and the end of their social world, which for years had revolved around production work and the factory.[1]

Many of my informants expressed their sense of discomfort with regard to these transformations, stressing that, from their point of view, the partial closing of the Fiat factories was the beginning of the end. Franca, a former domestic worker who had been unemployed for many years, told me 'as Turin is only an industrial town, based on Fiat, if you take Fiat away, what else is there in Turin? Nothing else. There are new jobs, now, but it is difficult to get these new jobs'.

While Franca noticed the effects of a badly managed productive transition, Guido, another unemployed man who used to work as an accountant, stressed the fact that the productive transformation had a negative effect on many ordinary workers: 'Today', he said, 'there are some opportunities, but not in work that can be done by everybody. They don't need that stuff anymore.'

The economic transition has drastically reduced the number of jobs in the factory sector without offering enough opportunities in the service economy. From the standpoint of the workers expelled from the shrinking factory system, this process is perceived as a sort of 'unequal exchange', because their age along with their lack of skills and experience make it practically impossible for them to get into these kinds of jobs.[2]

For all these reasons, it could be said that Turin is stuck in a liminal state, waiting, like the unemployed themselves, for economic opportunities that are late in coming. The policies elaborated over the past twenty years by the local and national governments to manage the transition were designed to convert the deindustrialization process into an opportunity for general economic revival, but they have had a limited effect (Vanolo 2015; Revelli 2016). Above all, these policies – which were aimed at stimulating the third sector of the economy – have failed to provide a solution to the needs of the many people made redundant or marginalized by the productive conversion. The working class – the orphan of the factory – has been neglected or, at best, offered services merging the individualistic logic of neoliberalism with some kind of paternalistic help (Fassin 2004; Muehlebach 2012). It is within this context of economic crisis and neoliberal policies that the Centro Lavoro and its classes on active job searching must be analysed.

Liminality, Undeservingness and Ideological Apparatuses

As we have seen, the experiences of unemployment I encountered during my fieldwork are linked to neoliberal expulsive dynamics (Sassen 2014), through which many workers, and blue-collar workers in particular, are expelled from the active workforce. Some of them have been able to find new jobs and new possibilities, but only after considerable time and effort. But for most of my informants, the wait for new employment seemed endless.

Therefore, we find that Siegfried Kracauer's description of job centres in Berlin during the German recession – despite being written a century ago – remains more than apt in describing the predicament of jobseekers in Turin today: 'The typical space of the unemployed – the job centre – is not a vital space. It is a passage through which the unemployed should reach a new working existence. Unfortunately, the passage is now very obstructed' (Kracauer 1982 [1930]: 135).

By summoning the insights of the German cultural critic, I primarily mean to point out some structural dimensions of joblessness. Lack of work implies an ambiguous situation – besides the obvious economic problems – that can easily be identified as a 'marginal' or 'liminal' condition (Van Gennep 1909; Turner 1982). The unemployed are liminal subjects, because they find themselves awaiting, in transition from their previous occupation to the potential new one and, above all, because as nonworkers they have an uncertain, indeterminate subjectivity (Newman 1999; Spyridakis 2013).[3] Indeterminacy, as an absence of structuration, contaminates the nonworker's entire social existence: the lack of a job affects income, but also the other, "latent" functions of employment (Jahoda 1982; Pappas 1989), conditioning social roles and statuses, social relations and the temporal organization of daily life. In a social reality like Turin, a former industrial and working-class community, employment is in fact one of the main criteria for social recognition. Without income, without status, deprived of their usual routines and of many of their relationships, unemployed people are living a liminal existence.

Kracauer highlights that this marginal condition should be temporary. Still, for many unemployed, this is not the case due to the contradictions and inequality of the job market. For most of my interlocutors, the wait for new employment, and the status associated thereto, could continue indefinitely. Franca, Simone and Giuliano were stuck in the liminal phase of their involuntary rite of passage through nonwork (Spyridakis 2013), not knowing when or whether they would be able to celebrate the postliminal rituals of reaggregation again.

Suspended in liminality, they were living that strained experience of existential immobility that Ghassan Hage (2009) called 'stuckedness' – a stuckedness associated with a process of 'social disqualification' (Paugam 2013). Alongside the loss in status guaranteed by work and a decrease in material resources, the unemployed experience a moral assessment that easily slips into negative prejudice, as Franca noticed in her interview:

> Because unemployment is something you can't understand or trust unless you experience it firsthand. There are people who stare at you wonder-

ing, how it is possible that you don't get a job? ... People think you don't want to work ... When they ask why you haven't found a job yet, they're thinking that you're not doing your best. That you aren't searching well enough, or that you are waiting for a permanent place as a council employee. That's not true! In my opinion, it's because they see the unemployed as lazy, someone who is not willing to lift a finger.

In Turin, the general tendency is to judge the unemployed in negative terms, to consider them lazy, too choosy or incapable to find a job – a tendency similar to that described by Leo Howe (1990) in his pioneering research on unemployment in Belfast. Common sense affirms that the unemployed deserve their plight because they do not spend enough time or effort searching for a job or because they do not accept the offers they receive, so they deserve neither respect nor assistance.[4] Consequently, the only way the unemployed could possibly counter this negative assumption is to be constantly on the lookout for work. For my informants, this meant that regular attendance at the lessons on active job search and frequent visits to the Centro Lavoro also became a way to demonstrate that they deserved help or respect. However, by doing so, the unemployed, instead of questioning the stigmatizing representations of their condition, seem to accept it, strengthening the ideological rhetoric of deservingness (Howe 1994).

Although the rhetoric of deservingness – and the moral condemnation of jobless people that it conveys – is older than the current neoliberal hegemony, it is quite clear that contemporary policies are strictly linked thereto (Dubois 2009; Paugam 2013; Streinzer and Tošić, Introduction to this volume). In fact, the connection is quite clear if we consider the current Italian system of unemployment benefits. At the time of my research, there were three kinds of benefits: 'mobility' benefits, 'Naspi' and 'mini-Naspi', granting a share of any previous salary only to ex-workers and only for a limited time. The motivation behind these limited benefits is evidently that only those who have already worked for a certain period in the past deserve to be assisted by the state, and that in any case said assistance must be brief, as the unemployed must find a new job as soon as they can.

The recent introduction in Italy of the so-called 'citizenship income' in 2018 has led to no concrete change. On the contrary, far from being a truly guaranteed basic income, the new benefit is merely the implementation – quite late in comparison to other European countries (Paugam 2013) – of those workfare policies that offer support only in exchange for the 'activation' of nonworking people.[5]

Nevertheless, the reform provoked huge public debate. While critics of the 'citizenship income' maintain that it discourages people from looking for work, its supporters describe it as a means to push people to enter the job market, pointing to the contract stipulated between the subject receiving the benefit and the municipal job centres – in a way that is not dissimilar from the analogous benefit systems in Germany and the United Kingdom. However, from both perspectives, active job search – instead of citizens' needs or their right to a good life – is the yardstick to use when measuring and evaluating whether or not a person deserves to be assisted by the public welfare system.

Therefore, the courses on active job search analysed here are an expression of the ideology of deservingness, operating as neoliberal governmentality dispositives and ideological apparatuses. While simply presented as practical tools that aspire to better one's chances of finding a new job, the lessons themselves are anthropotechniques aimed at transforming an unemployed person into a deserving jobseeker, following the neoliberal model of 'entrepreneur of him/herself': ready to invest their 'human capital' to obtain new job opportunities. Herein we find one of the main distinctive traits of neoliberalism that distinguishes this ideology from classic liberalism (Foucault 2008): the idea that the cherished model of the 'rational actor' has to be taught to and imposed on subjects by means of a panoply of technologies of the self and a thorough 'conduction of the conductions' (Dardot and Laval 2013).

In fact, what is most striking concerning the lessons on active job searching was their explicit ideological dimension, the open valorization of the model of the entrepreneur and the naturalization of the labour market. An explicit neoliberal representation was taught and prescribed during the lessons. I argue, then, that the Centro Lavoro corresponds to an 'Ideological State Apparatus' in Althusser's terms (1971). Indeed, for the Marxist philosopher, what characterizes this kind of dispositives, distinguishing them from the repressive apparatus, is that they do not work by the use of force or by means of disciplinary techniques, but rather through and for ideology, by means of rituals and practices of subjectivation that are, at the same time, practices of subjection.

Subjectivation processes – which are at the core of both Foucault's approach to technologies of power and Althusser's theory of ideology (Butler 1997; Macherey 2014), and above all the latter's insistence on the ritual dimension – are crucial in fully understanding active job search classes and activation policies at large. The unemployed are drawn to the classes not only because they are looking for a job, but also because – as liminal subjects – they long for a more deserving status than that of jobless people. In this sense, as we will see, the courses also become a sort of ritual: a rite of passage to become deserving jobseekers as well as a magical rite promising to quickly win back the job and identity they lost.

Centro Lavoro Torino: What It Is and How It Works

How does Centro Lavoro Torino, this small but meaningful apparatus, work?[6] Centro Lavoro is a public facility that hosts free services to help people in finding a job; it is clearly distinct, in its organization as well in its agenda, from local job centres. The latter are founded and managed by the metropolitan district government, while the Centro is founded by the city council and managed by independent social cooperatives whose staff are composed of educators and human resources experts. Centro Lavoro offers computers, faxes and phones for the use of people looking for work, as well as a number of other services, such as individual courses in career change and reorientation, a help desk for assistance in writing CVs, a help desk for psychological issues and, above all, open lessons on active job searching that people can attend, or leave, at will.

The staff members I spoke to assigned considerable value to their work and took great pride in offering a free service that seemed to receive such a positive public response. In particular, they stressed that they were there to respond to a real need. One person in charge of the service, for example, told me:

> Actually, we are the only service open to everybody, so we have become a general place for people's needs, desires and problems. I'm aware that people coming here for the interview process – that's exactly what I do here, the first interview – do so because they need to talk about their lives, and they need someone to listen to them. What they say is: 'I'm searching for a job, but nobody wants to listen to me.' In my opinion, this is the only place left where people can say: 'I can go there and find someone who really listens to me.'

The importance of listening to people's grievances reported by the operators and some of the users themselves, and of the help offered to people in need, is an example of a more general phenomenon already noted by Didier Fassin (2004) in France and by Andrea Muehlebach (2012) in Italy. Both scholars show how the market ideology is often interlinked with a politics of compassion, a 'moral neoliberal' that responds to the social problems generated by neoliberalism with personal sympathy, piety and charity.

However, Centro Lavoro's first mission is to help people find a job or, better, teach them how to be autonomous in their search. Therefore, training courses on job seeking and open lessons are at the core of the service.

The staff declared that the individual training courses were the service they valued the most. Following a preliminary interview on previous work experience and personal 'proactivity', proving the concrete desire to follow the courses and find work, users can access the course free of charge. Subsequently, users are offered some proposals for professional requalification and a certain number of one-on-one active job search lessons, followed by collective training sessions on job hunting attended by small groups of users.

As shown by individual training courses, the service's aim is to stimulate the 'activation' of unemployed people. The founding assumption of the aforementioned practices is that most of the difficulties in finding a new job derive from the passivity of the subjects themselves or, at least, from wrong or inefficient methods. Anna, one of the operators, was quite clear about that:

> CARLO: So, in your opinion, these active job search activities are useful, aren't they?
>
> ANNA: They are if the person has the will to carry them out. If the person is really motivated.
>
> CARLO: What do you mean?
>
> ANNA: I mean that we can do all that is deemed necessary, but if the person is not really looking for a job, and is not active and autonomous, it's hard to achieve results. In fact, there are some people here who are simply 'parked', because their idea of looking for work is like, every fifteen days I take a look at the ads you gave me, I wait for you to send an application concerning the two offers I'm interested in, then I wait for the next meeting.

Francesca, another staff member, was even more explicit in drawing the line between active and passive search, and thus in tracing a moral distinction between the deserving unemployed and the undeserving ones:

> There's a passive form of job searching and an active one, the one that leads you to success [pause]; the passive search [pause], imagine all the

discouraged people who stay at home and wait, they don't move, don't actually do anything concrete to find a job. Consider that out of six million unemployed people, only three million are actively in search, while the remaining three million are not.

Besides the more structured and personalized training courses, Centro Lavoro organized open lessons on active job search. During the time of my fieldwork, five lessons were offered regularly: one focused on the bases of the active search, one on writing CVs, one on the use of the internet in looking for employment, one on LinkedIn and the last one on job interviews. The open lessons were mainly a mix of ideological assertions and more or less original advice. The lesson on how to use LinkedIn and other social media for job hunting was quite emblematic in this regard. The teacher began affirming how useful LinkedIn is for the contemporary job market, then simply opened up her account and projected it onto a widescreen. Then she went on to explain how to create an account and how to write an apt résumé. Finally, she explained that you have to look for the profiles of entrepreneurs, managers and human resources employees at the firms and companies you are interested in working with and ask them to be in contact. After having attended some of the lessons, Paolo, a former high-tech worker, raised many doubts about their usefulness:

> Personally, some of the things proposed at Centro Lavoro made me smile. I mean, at the beginning it's like they are talking about something exceptional, then you go to the European Community's online page about CVs and you read word for word what they are saying. They're not saying anything new. They're simply stating the directives received from above. As I said, it's good that they provide this service, but everything depends on who is on the other side.

Indeed, the main point of the classes is less about giving practical advice than about stimulating autonomy and entrepreneurial spirit among the participants. That is the reason why I see them as a ritual, aiming to mould the subject to conform to the neoliberal model of the active and deserving jobseeker. Every lesson started by stressing that the aim of the courses is to render the unemployed autonomous and active, as Francesca told me:

> We help them and support them towards this aim, because the goal of the educator – of the person working in a service like ours – is to teach people how to become autonomous. We give them the tools so they can go off and do what they please; when I teach them what to do, I give them tools, I teach techniques – this is already a great response, although not so concrete.

Among the lessons observed, the one on CVs was the most explicit in this regard. In a class of around twenty people, the teacher started by presenting the seminar: 'It's a lesson in which I explain the best ways to write a CV [pause], so that you may have the tools to do so on your own. Here [at Centro Lavoro] we give you all the useful things we can. Of course, not an actual job, but we help you search for it and be autonomous in it.'

In these propositions, we can detect the influence of the typical liberal notion according to which the ideal subjectivity is an autonomous and independent agent – even in a predicament like unemployment. At the same time, the propositions can be more precisely labelled as 'neoliberal', since what distinguishes neoliberal ideology from classic liberalism is the idea that the subject is not spontaneously autonomous and rational, so that autonomy and instrumental rationality have to be taught and imposed (Dardot and Laval 2013). Francesca went on to say that 'this refers to what I said before on autonomy: that not every active person is autonomous. Autonomy is a matter of a person's indoctrination, the acquisition of a method'.

The construction of this 'ideal, deserving subject' through indoctrination is strictly connected to a naturalization of the labour market and the valorization of work flexibility, as highlighted in these examples heard during the lesson on CVs: 'When thinking about your CV, you should think of a commercial. It's a metaphor. I say so because once a man was annoyed by the term. When we're looking for a job, we are a product. So, what is the employer? The consumer! And what is the CV? It's nothing other than the advertisement of ourselves! Or basically our brand!'[7]

The commodification of the workers is not only taken for granted; it is also presented as something positive. More than that, commodification, it is said, should be emphasized through self-branding as the best means of finding a job. As many scholars have noted (Dunk 2002; van Oort 2015; Boland 2016; Gershon 2016), the purpose of every course on job searching is to teach people how to sell themselves better, passively accepting their subaltern position with reference to the market and employers.

During the first lesson on the fundamentals of active searching, the educator stressed the necessity for workers to adapt: 'You need to be flexible, yes. [Pause] Some years ago, frequent change in employment was seen as negative; nowadays, everybody knows it's common. Actually, it's even predicted that over our working life we will change between at least five sectors. We must be conscious of this and be flexible.' Furthermore, being in search of employment is presented as an opportunity: 'He who seeks, shall find. And if you find a job you enjoy, you add five days to your week!'

The valorization of autonomy and the pro-market ideology carry with them a moral evaluation of the unemployed that distinguishes between the active jobseekers – deserving help and respect notwithstanding their misfortune – and the passive one, who deserves their own state of joblessness. This moral assessment depends in part on the fact that, according to the logics of the lessons, searching for a job is a job in itself – one that must be carried out with diligence and constancy. Therefore, from the staff members' point of view, or rather from the perspective of the ideological position that they fill, passive and inefficient searching is a symptom of undeservingness:

> ANNA: Because the passive search category includes the voluntary unemployed as well as the nonvoluntary one who suffers from psychological problems, discouragement, little proactivity or a proclivity towards withdrawal. And then there is the voluntary unemployed, the one who stays at home, at ease, claiming to be unemployed while not actually looking for a job.
>
> CARLO: But why? Because they're disappointed or because they're naïve?
>
> ANNA: Well, it depends. Also because they don't actually need it, because there are some people who if they don't need to work, they don't work! In this country [pause], this country is very generous with jobseekers' benefits. There are some who need subsidies to get to the end of the month and it is right, of course, but there are others that happily live on the dole.

All the neoliberal doctrine's traits are presented in the lessons as axioms and tools to find a job. It is possible to note here a fundamental assumption, common to all the active job search policies, which states that if you accept the neoliberal rules, if you assimilate the neoliberal subjectivity, you will find a job. 'He who seeks, shall find', as the teacher said. Accordingly, this assumption is linked to the idea that if people cannot find a job, it is because they are not motivated enough or are unable to sell themselves on the market. Joblessness is constructed, within this apparatus, as an individual trouble (Mills 1959) that depends on the unemployed person. The individualization process leads to a more or less explicit blaming of the unemployed, who are depicted as lazy and idle, because they lack proactivity or because they are dependent on social welfare benefits. The sentence quoted above, 'he who seeks, shall find', is the meaningful expression of the perspective that belies the national and European transformations of the public welfare system, meant to render jobless people less dependent on subsidies and public help (Gallie 2004; Dubois 2009; Brodkin and Marston 2013; Paugam 2013).

Also regarding unemployment, behind these neoliberal policies and reforms we can find 'a radical individualization according to which all social crises are perceived as individual crises, and all inequalities are put in relation with individual responsibility' (Dardot and Laval 2013: 440–41). There are basically two kinds of explanation for the phenomenon of unemployment, which are present both in public culture and in the political arena (Sharone 2013): structural explanations that stress economic factors and the systemic flaws, on the one hand, and individualistic ones, which instead reduce the problem of finding a job to personal qualities and individual flaws, on the other hand. At the risk of simplifying a complex matter, we can say that while Keynesian and social-democratic policies were premised on the structural vision, contemporary hegemonic approaches refer more and more to the individualistic interpretation. Courses on active job search are a part of the dispositives transmitting the latter, the ideological function of which is quite clear. With their emphasis on activation, autonomy and personal efforts, these courses lead jobless people to believe that it is somehow their fault if they are unable to find a job. The rhetoric of deservingness operates as an ideological tool that 'reverses the responsibility' from the 'flawed system' to the 'flawed self' (Sharone 2013), blaming the unemployed themselves while concealing the structural contradictions of the job market in a late-industrial economy.

But how do the unemployed respond to the message conveyed by the courses? Generally, the participants in my research referred to the structural explanation of unemployment, always ready to point to the effects of the global financial crisis or to the worsening local economy. Indeed, they experienced the inequity of the job market on a daily basis. Moreover, the structural interpretation allows a reduction in the stigma and guilt associated with their liminal situation (Newman 1999; Sharone 2013). However, as we will see in the next section, I detected a different trend among the unemployed who attended Centro Lavoro. In their anxious search for work and respect, they seemed to end up accepting the individualistic vision of unemployment and the moral judgement it implies.

A Symbolic Efficacy?

Since Centro Lavoro Torino sees a fair number of users every day, it is not easy to depict a typical user. However, during my fieldwork, I noted that most of them were people over the age of forty. On the basis of my observations, I can say that they were men and women who had lost their jobs due to the economic depression and had been looking for a new one for a long time. On the other hand, the open lessons were also attended by young men and women. However, only a fraction of the regular users attended the individual job-seeking training course or the open lessons, since many of them went to Centro Lavoro to access the computers, the internet and the job ads board in the main hall. Finally, a few seemed to use the site simply as a stable and secure place to wait until they found a new job. If we put aside the latter aspect, most of the users can be seen as searching for a job in an active way, without any obvious success. At the Centro Lavoro, for example, I often met and talked with Pietro, a fifty-year-old bartender who, in 2013, had been laid off from the company where he had worked for twenty years. He used to go to Centro Lavoro every other day to look for job ads and to print his CVs or to send them via the internet. Once he told me that, since becoming unemployed, he had sent more than seven hundred CVs and requests, without response. Although he tried to follow the advice provided by the Centro Lavoro, and notwithstanding his strenuous efforts, he had been looking for a new job for over two years.

To understand the relationship between jobseekers like Pietro, Paolo and Simone on the one side, and Centro Lavoro as a dispositive on the other, it is necessary to take a number of factors into account. It must be stressed, in the first place, that many of the services are quite useful for the unemployed, because at Centro Lavoro they can use the internet, consult job offers and ads, and use a public phone and a fax to respond to job offers. Furthermore, it is important not to underestimate the value of the listening service, of the psychological support desk and of the reorientation courses. As noted by Fassin (2004) in his research on the Centres d'écoutes in France, identifying the ideological and disciplinary nature of these kinds of services does not automatically mean declaring them to be useless. Indeed, for example, many users are not able to write an efficient CV. More significantly, many of them are no longer accustomed to navigating the labour market and need to find someone to simply listen to their problems, fears and anxieties. Fabio, a forty-year-old unemployed man who lost his job when the firm he worked for as a salesman went bankrupt in 2013, told me that the centre was very important for him for the following reason:

> FABIO: By a stroke of luck, I found Centro Lavoro, where the staff sort of indoctrinates you to search for a different job. On Tuesday I'll be meeting this [pause] doctor, this professional who will give me some advice on how to start a new career. He'll have a look at my experience, my work skills and he'll help me apply to some firms and businesses.[8]
>
> CARLO: And is it useful, in your opinion?
>
> FABIO: In my opinion it's very useful. I've described Centro Lavoro to some friends as the heaven of the unemployed. It doesn't seem true that there is a centre where you can find educators and lessons on job seeking. For example, on Monday there is a very interesting seminar on LinkedIn. On Tuesday, as mentioned, I will be meeting the educator to talk about how to start a new career. All this is very useful because there are many services at your disposal, including the internet, as I no longer have it at home.

Fabio and the other users have many different needs. As mentioned above, they suffer not only from lack of income, but also because they miss the latent functions of work, such as the organization of their daily routine and the formation of social relationships outside the family. Going to Centro Lavoro partially responds to these needs, since it gives them the opportunity to meet other people and provides structure and meaning to their day.

All this explains, in part, why people like Fabio seem to agree to being 'indoctrinated'. We have to consider that, from his point of view, accepting the proposed model of the active and deserving jobseeker is part of his 'job to find a job' – an expression he himself used to describe his situation. Moreover, as we have seen, the liminal condition of the unemployed – their lack of status and recognition – leaves them prone to the subjectivization process. However, this does not mean that the jobseeker model as self-entrepreneur is accepted unquestioningly. On the contrary, there was always some ambivalence towards this ideological discourse. During the classes, the participants' comments and questions wavered between enthusiasm deriving from finally being assisted and doubts regarding what seemed to be an abstract and unreal representation of the unemployment experience. During one lesson in March 2015, the teacher was talking about the importance of looking for and choosing the ideal job, when a woman interrupted her, saying: 'But we aren't single beings, are we? We're always linked to someone else, husband or children, so what can we do? We don't live alone, and we can't choose on our own, can we?' Listening to such an abstract and ideological assertion about free choice, the woman could not help but react by pointing out some of the burdens and constrictions any jobseeker has to deal with.

To give just one further example, the presentation of the psychological support service was interrupted many times by Mauro, a former warehouseman aged about fifty. Mauro insisted – against the opinion of the in-house psychologist – that although it was true that most of them were depressed, the cause of their illness was patently the lack of work; in fact, he continued, they were there to try to solve this practical problem, not their personal psychological condition. When I interviewed him, Mauro referred to a structural explanation for his prolonged lack of employment: 'What the newspapers say is not true, the crisis is not over. You can't find anything. In a year, I have only had two job interviews.' Like most of the people I talked to, he linked his personal difficulties to the stuck condition of the labour market after the global recession.

On the contrary, as seen above, the neoliberal discourse that supports the active job search courses tries to minimize the importance of the economic structure for understanding unemployment. This ideology simply affirms that where job opportunities are scarce, people are required to compete more and more in order to seize the few remaining resources. Indeed, the practical purpose of the courses is to teach workers the best strategies to use when competing in a weak market (van Oort 2015; Boland 2016; Gershon 2016). The doctrinal core of neoliberalism is, in fact, the valorization of competition, which is always presented as a positive factor from both an economic and a personal viewpoint (Harvey 2005). Since neoliberal doctrine is not interested in solving the social issue of unemployment, which is considered normal and natural, its only proposal consists in boosting competition among jobless people (Kwon and Lane 2016).

How did the individualistic and meritocratic discourse – emphasizing competition and personal effort – affect my interlocutors? Among them, one of the most enthusiastic was Francesco, a factory worker aged about forty who had been out of work for over two years. He told me that he liked the services offered at Centro Lavoro: 'Because I can see that they are very active … they oversee me, I mean, thanks to them now I know how to behave during a job interview.' Then he said he agreed with the logic of the courses because 'the effort must come from me'.

Above all, Francesco appreciated the practical suggestions concerning CVs and job interviews, but he also appreciated the ideological discourse of Centro Lavoro. Talking about another long-term unemployed friend of his, he told me: 'but you know, he isn't really looking for ... [pause] He's got a brother who is helping him [pause] so he's not active; he is not like me.' At least in part, by accepting the individualistic logic of the active job search, unemployed people implicitly also accept the assumption that it is their fault that they find themselves in this predicament.

Paolo, the ex-white-collar worker we met earlier in the chapter, expressed a similar view on Centro Lavoro's courses:

> Their purpose is to push a little because they know that most of the people don't have the ability to actively search for a job. In fact, I have also seen this; unfortunately, there are many people who say: eh, there's no work. But you have to search for it through the right connections and you have to move around; you can't just wait for a job to fall into your lap.

In order to understand why Francesco and Fabio accept – at least partially – this individualistic discourse, we must first reflect on dispositives and ideological apparatuses, which follow the logic of interpellation (Althusser 1971). In other words, ideology works through processes of subjectivation that are, at the same time, dynamics of subjection (Butler 1997). Ideology and its apparatuses offer individuals a role, an identity, a subjectivity. In our case, the ideological apparatus offers liminal, statusless subjects a more positive perception of themselves, since they seem to move from the negative, undeserving role of jobless people to the more positive one of jobseekers. Although it in no way guarantees that they will find a new job and then a new real status, the active search dispositive offers at least a more positive subject position. Following the courses and the advice taught there, people like Fabio and Francesco were given the impression of being real jobseekers, active in their search for work and therefore deserving of help, recognition and, moreover, employment.

From an anthropological perspective, one of the most noteworthy of Althusser's (1971) insights can be found in his assertion that ideological apparatuses mould subjectivities by means of rituals that generate practices. In this sense, the active job search courses can be seen as 'rites of passage': becoming an active, deserving jobseeker was, for my interlocutors, the first step towards completing the transition. Clearly, the users' ultimate purpose is to leave the liminal state of unemployment by finding a job, not just to remain jobseekers.

However, the dispositive is useful and effective in offering them the illusion – a typical neoliberal one – that the result depends only on their will and dedication to look for a job. After all, ideology has always to do with deception, since it is founded on an imaginary relationship between the subject and their real world (Althusser 1971) – in this case, the delusion consists in underestimating the structural nature of mass unemployment to overemphasize individual action.

Furthermore, the illusory dimension points to the other ritual side of the lessons on active job search: their magical meaning. Sophie Divay (2001), in an article on services for the unemployed in France, suggests that educators can be compared to 'witch doctors', since they give hope to jobseekers thanks to their charisma and by means of the collective faith in the efficacy of the dispositive itself. However, more than charisma, I think that in our case, the intermingling between illusion and hope is the crucial point. The structural interpretation of unemployment, although more realistic and closer to the lived experience of my interlocutors, can lead to a fatalistic position (Sharone 2013; Strauss 2016) that intensifies the 'unemployment trap', comprising depression and self-retreat (Reyneri 2011). On the contrary, although illusory, the individualistic view seems to give the unemployed more hope and motivation.

In anthropological terms, we can say that unemployment can imply a 'crisis of the presence', what Ernesto de Martino (2015) defined as the feeling of being acted upon by larger and uncontrollable forces, such as – in this case – the strictures and contradictions of a job market no unemployed can control. Instead, by giving the unemployed an active and deserving subjectivity as real jobseekers, the courses offer them – just as magic-religious rites do in de Martino's theory – the illusory but perhaps necessary feeling of still acting in the world. As Paolo said, 'yes, I believe, however, that it is a matter of personal illusion … These job centres, I don't believe in them 100 per cent, but if you look at the situation [pause], it is not such a bad thing'.

Conclusion

The main question behind this chapter reflects what Leo Howe (1994) wondered about in his ethnographic essay on the ideology of deservingness: why do many unemployed people accept an individualistic and moralizing view of unemployment that then blames them as bearing full responsibility for not having a job?

As we have seen, Centro Lavoro and the classes taught there are a small local instance of larger neoliberal policies, which are founded on a simplistic view of unemployment while resorting to the rhetoric of personal effort and deservingness to receive legitimization. All the services offered at Centro Lavoro imply the assumption that looking for a job is a job in itself that requires constant effort. This leads to a moralistic distinction between active jobseekers – deserving respect and help – and the passive unemployed, who, in one way or another, are seen as deserving of their predicament because they are judged to be lazy or unwilling to work.

Centro Lavoro and its classes are then part of the ideological state apparatus that sustains and transmits this moralistic view of unemployment, whose function is to deflect critique from the system by blaming the victims for its contradictions. As an ideological apparatus, it works through rituals and practices to mould subjectivities. As I have argued, my interlocutors accepted the logic of deservingness that lies behind the active job search classes because of the ritual dimension of these courses, which seemed to offer them the more positive status of active jobseeker as well as the illusion of easily finding a job through personal effort.

It is not easy to understand how and why an ideological discourse, like that of deservingness, which is currently so pervasive, spreads out and takes hold in public culture. But, as I hope I have shown, following Althusser's suggestion to have a closer look at ideological apparatuses is a good starting point for an ethnographic answer.

Carlo Capello is Associate Professor of Cultural Anthropology at the University of Turin. He has researched such topics as Moroccan transnational migration, family ties in Southern Italy and the cultural construction of the person, all investigated within a framework of critique of contemporary capitalist ideology. Further developing this critical line of enquiry, his current interests focus on the anthropology of work and unemployment, to which he dedicated his latest book *Ai margini del lavoro. Un'antropologia della disoccupazione a Torino* (2020).

Notes

1. For a comparison, see – among many other cases – the volume edited by Narotzky and Goddard (2017), as well as the ethnographic research by Mollona (2009) on the fate of the steel industry in Sheffield.

2. See Walley (2013) for a similar interpretation of the consequences of deindustrialization in Chicago and the United States at large.
3. But see Lane (2016) for a critical stance on the use of the trope of liminality with regard to unemployment.
4. It must be underlined that the unemployed are not always and necessarily condemned from a moral point of view, as Serge Paugam demonstrated in his comparative work (2013). While a social disqualification of joblessness and poverty prevails within European societies, there are also many instances of 'integrated poverty' – typical of countries and regions where lack of work is common and widespread – in which unemployment is not stigmatized.
5. For an anthropological analysis of the various forms of basic income and their social consequences, see Ferguson (2015).
6. It must be stressed that, despite the fact that I am using a sort of 'ethnographic present' to describe it, some aspects of the service have changed since the time of the research.
7. On the teaching of self-branding techniques aimed at unemployed people in the United States, see the noteworthy research by Ilana Gershon (2016).
8. It must be noted that the Italian verb *indottrinare* used by Fabio – as well as by Francesca (see above) – carries the same negative connotations as in English.

References

Althusser, Louis. 1971. 'Ideology and Ideological State Apparatuses. Notes towards an Investigation', in *Lenin and Philosophy and Other Essays*, trans. B. Brewster. New York: Monthly Review Press, pp. 85–126.
Belligni, Silvano, and Stefania Ravazzi. 2012. *La politica e la città. Regime urbano e classe dirigente a Torino*. Bologna: Il Mulino.
Berta, Giuseppe. 2011. *Fiat-Chrysler e la deriva dell'Italia industriale*. Bologna: Il Mulino.
Boland, Tom. 2016. 'Seeking a Role: Disciplining Jobseekers as Actors in the Labour Market', *Work, Employment and Society* 30(2): 334–51.
Brodkin, Evelyn Z., and Gregory Marston (eds). 2013. *Work and the Welfare State: Street-Level Organizations and Workfare Politics*. Washington DC: Georgetown University Press.
Butler, Judith. 1997. *The Psychic Life of Power: Theories in Subjection*. Stanford, CA: Stanford University Press.
Capello, Carlo. 2018. 'Torino liminale. Riflessioni antropologiche su postfordismo e disoccupazione', in Carlo Capello and Giovanni Semi (eds), *Torino. Un profilo etnografico*. Milan: Meltemi, pp. 27–48.
———. 2020. *Ai margini del lavoro. Un'antropologia della disoccupazione a Torino*. Verona: Ombre Corte.
Capello, Carlo, and Giovanni Semi (eds). 2018. *Torino. Un profilo etnografico*. Milan: Meltemi.

Dardot, Pierre, and Christian Laval. 2013. *La nuova ragione del mondo*, trans. R. Antoniucci and M. Lapenna. Rome: DeriveApprodi.
De Martino, Ernesto. 2015. *Magic: A Theory from the South*, trans. D.L. Zinn. Chicago: Hau Books.
Divay, Sophie. 2001. 'Chômage, malchance et traitement social', *Ethnologie française* 31(1): 153–59.
Dubois, Vincent. 2008. *La vie au guichet. Relation administrative et traitment de la misère*, 3rd edn. Paris: Economica.
———. 2009. 'La trasformazione dello stato sociale alla lente dell'etnografia. Inchiesta sul controllo degli assistiti sociali', *Etnografia e ricerca qualitativa* 2: 163–87.
Dunk, Thomas. 2002. 'Remaking the Working Class: Experience, Class Consciousness, and the Industrial Adjustment Process', *American Ethnologist* 29(4): 878–900.
Fassin, Didier. 2004. *Des maux indicibles. Sociologie des lieux d'écoute*. Paris: La Découverte.
Ferguson, James. 2015. *Give a Man a Fish: Reflections on the New Politics of Distribution*. Durham, NC: Duke University Press.
Foucault, Michel. 2008. *The Birth of Biopolitics*, trans. G. Burchell. Basingstoke: Palgrave Macmillan.
Gallie, Duncan (ed.). 2004. *Resisting Marginalization: Unemployment Experience and Social Policy in the European Union*. Oxford: Oxford University Press.
Gallino, Luciano. 2013. *Il colpo di stato di banche e governi*. Turin: Einaudi.
Gershon, Ilana. 2016. '"I'm Not a Businessman, I'm a Business, Man!": Typing the Neoliberal Self into a Branded Existence', *HAU* 6(3): 223–46.
Giaccaria, Paolo. 2010. 'La FIAT e Torino: lavoro, relazioni industriali e immagini della città operaia', in Marco Santangelo and Alberto Vanolo (eds), *Di capitale importanza. Immagini e trasformazioni urbane di Torino*. Rome: Carocci, pp. 57–73.
Hage, Ghassan. 2009. 'Waiting Out the Crisis: On Stuckedness and Governmentality', in Ghassan Hage (ed.), *Waiting*. Carlton: Melbourne University Press, pp. 97–106.
Harvey, David. 2005. *A Brief History of Neoliberalism*. Oxford: Oxford University Press.
Howe, Leo. 1990. *Being Unemployed in Northern Ireland: An Ethnographic Study*. Cambridge: Cambridge University Press.
———. 1994. 'Ideology, Domination and Unemployment', *Sociological Review* 42(2): 315–40.
Jahoda, Marie. 1982. *Employment and Unemployment: A Social-Psychological Analysis*. Cambridge: Cambridge University Press.
Kracauer, Siegfried. 1982 [1930]. *La massa come ornamento*, trans. M.G. Amirante Pappalardo and F. Maione. Napoli: Prismi.
Kwon, Jong B., and Carrie M. Lane. 2016. 'Introduction', in Jong B. Kwon and Carrie M. Lane (eds), *Anthropologies of Unemployment:*

The Changing Study of Work and Its Absence. Ithaca, NY: Cornell University Press, pp. 1–17.
Lane, Carrie M. 2016. 'The Limits of Liminality: Anthropological Approaches to Unemployment in the United States', in Jong B. Kwon and Carrie M. Lane (eds), *Anthropologies of Unemployment: The Changing Study of Work and Its Absence*. Ithaca, NY: Cornell University Press, pp. 18–33.
Macherey, Pierre. 2014. *Le sujet des normes*. Paris: Éditions Amsterdam.
Mills, Charles Wright. 1959. *The Sociological Imagination*. Oxford: Oxford University Press.
Molé, Noelle. 2012. 'Hauntings of Solidarity in Post-Fordist Italy', *Anthropological Quarterly* 85(2): 376–96.
Mollona, Massimiliano. 2009. *Made in Sheffield: An Ethnography of Industrial Work and Politics*. New York: Berghahn Books.
Muehlebach, Andrea. 2012. *The Moral Neoliberal: Welfare and Citizenship in Italy*. Chicago: University of Chicago Press.
Narotzky, Susana, and Victoria Goddard (eds). 2017. *Work and Livelihoods*. Abingdon: Routledge.
Newman, Katherine. 1999. *Falling from Grace*, 2nd edn. Berkeley: University of California Press.
Pappas, Gregory. 1989. *The Magic City: Unemployment in a Working-Class Community*. Ithaca, NY: Cornell University Press.
Paugam, Serge. 2013. *Les formes élémentaires de la pauvreté*. Paris: Presses Universitaires de France.
Revelli, Marco. 2016. *Non ti riconosco. Un viaggio eretico nell'Italia che cambia*. Turin: Einaudi.
Reyneri, Emilio. 2011. *Sociologia del mercato del lavoro*. Bologna: Il Mulino.
Sassen, Saskia. 2014. *Expulsions: Brutality and Complexity in the Global Economy*. Cambridge, MA: Harvard University Press.
Semi, Giovanni. 2015. *Gentrification. Tutte le città come Disneyland?* Bologna: Il Mulino.
Sharone, Ofer. 2013. *Flawed System/Flawed Self: Job Searching and Unemployment Experience*. Chicago: University of Chicago Press.
Spyridakis, Manos. 2013. *The Liminal Worker: An Ethnography of Work, Unemployment and Precariousness in Contemporary Greece*. Farnham: Ashgate.
Strauss, Claudia. 2016. 'Positive Thinking about Being out of Work in Southern California after the Great Recession', in Jong B. Kwon and Carrie M. Lane (eds), *Anthropologies of Unemployment: The Changing Study of Work and Its Absence*. Ithaca, NY: Cornell University Press, pp. 171–90.
Tranfaglia, Nicola. 1999. 'L'incerto destino della capitale del miracolo', in Nicola Tranfaglia (ed.), *Storia di Torino. Vol. 9. Gli anni della Repubblica*. Turin: Einaudi, pp. 7-47.

Turner, Victor. 1982. *From Ritual to Theatre*. New York: Paj Publications.
Van Gennep, Arnold. 1909. *Les rites de passage*. Paris: Émile Nourry.
Vanolo, Alberto. 2015. 'The Fordist City and the Creative City: Evolution and Resilience in Turin, Italy', *City, Culture and Society* 6: 69–74.
Van Oort, Madison. 2015. 'Making the Neoliberal Precariat: Two Faces of Job Searching in Minneapolis', *Ethnography* 16(1): 74–94.
Walley, Christine. 2013. *Exit Zero: Family and Class in Postindustrial Chicago*. Chicago: University of Chicago Press.

7

The Politics of Austerity Welfare

Charity, Discourses of Deservingness and
Human Needs in a Portuguese Church Parish

Patrícia Alves de Matos

In June 2015, I met Cristina at the Catholic church in the most densely populated and impoverished parish of Setúbal, a postindustrial city located 50 km south of Portugal's capital city. Cristina was thirty-five, very thin and angry, with fearless eyes and deep dark circles underneath. She asked to speak directly with the priest; she wanted to be seen as soon as possible by the church volunteers. For more than an hour, the volunteers reconstructed her trajectory, asking various questions about her birthplace, where she had lived, with whom and how. They did so in order to evaluate Cristina's household financial situation and living conditions, and to decide on granting her access to the Social Refectory (SR) – a food charity scheme (see below). Cristina delivered the few official documents she had while narrating her past, present and future needs.

Cristina had been married for ten years to the father of her two daughters. She was the victim of systematic domestic violence and abuse. In 2014, her shame at an unwanted pregnancy forced her to have a clandestine abortion, which led to medical complications and hospitalization for more than a month. While she was at the hospital, her daughters' godfather helped her by taking care of them at the abandoned flat where he lived. Her mother paid to move the few things Cristina had in her old house. When we met in 2015, Cristina was unemployed and was receiving some financial help from two family members and a close friend. She had no gas at home and got her water and electricity informally through a direct connection to her neighbours' water and energy cables.

Cristina recounted how she had tried to access the RSI, but was denied.[1] When applying, she gave the address of her daughter's godfather as her own, but because his income was above the state threshold, the request was denied. She blamed the state for delegating responsibility for welfare support to her family and friends, a form of enforced dependency that she could not easily accept: 'If the state doesn't help me, who will?' 'Help' for Cristina meant fulfilling her basic needs: access to food resources, shelter, a job and nurturing her capabilities to protect herself and her daughters from physical harm. For her, this should be the responsibility of the state because her present needs and claims on resources were legitimated by her past trajectory of work and societal contribution: 'I worked all my life to support myself; I don't want to live off the RSI. I want to work, have a job and support myself and my daughters!' In Cristina's narrative, implicit or explicit reference to her growing livelihood needs and eroding social rights was a way of criticizing the state's responsibility in the breakdown of a social contract linking wage labour and welfare entitlements – a universal agreement that ensured her the right of 'deserving to be helped' (*merecer ser ajudada*) without moral judgements or accusations of welfare-dependency:

> If you want, you can come to my house to see how I'm living. I don't have a proper bed, I don't have a fridge and I don't have an oven. Even if I want to cook more at home, I can't. Also, if I had a gas oven I wouldn't have money to buy the gas. The other day I gave my only pair of trainers to one of my daughters so that she could go to school; you will see, I'm not lying, I have no furniture, I have nothing.[2]

I offer Cristina's story as an illustration of a recent historical conjuncture in Portugal, shaped by severe austerity-led processes of dispossession that have accelerated the neoliberal reconfiguration of the nature and forms of state welfare distribution.[3] In various European countries, including Portugal, such reconfiguration magnified the role of the third sector (e.g. nongovernmental organizations (NGOs), civil society and religious organizations) as a critical source of distribution, advice and provisioning for those confronting a severe crisis of social reproduction as a consequence of cuts in central welfare spending, withdrawal of state services, increasing conditionality and rising unemployment.[4] A limited yet significant anthropological literature has investigated how third-sector organizations as both moral endeavours and political and economic projects sustain neoliberal austerity regimes; the relations between poverty alleviation policies and the cultural and institutional embeddedness shaping diversity in the organizational forms of charities; as well as the links between volunteering discourses and practices, emergent ethical relationships and the meanings of economic crisis (e.g. Caplan 2016; Douzina-Bakalaki 2017; Venezuela-Garcia et al. 2019; Koch and James 2020; Pusceddu 2020).

Building upon this literature, in this chapter, I explore the relations between charity, discourses of deservingness and human needs with the broader aim of problematizing the politics of austerity-led transformations of welfare distribution in Portugal. I draw from ethnographic fieldwork carried out in Setúbal between 2015 and 2016 that focused on households' livelihood provisioning strategies to confront the austerity crisis and their interactions with religious regulatory welfare institutions.[5] By examining the administrative and relational dimensions of food charity provisioning in a Catholic church parish, I interrogate a set of related questions: to what extent do the rationality and pragmatics of religious food charity constitute a departure from or continuation of distributive politics of austerity? How is the political and social legitimacy of needs negotiated and challenged between volunteers, claimants and recipients? How do charity claimants articulate and mobilize needs as a way of making distributional and recognition claims? In depicting the practices, interactions and contested discourses of deservingness mediating the charitable allocation and reception of material and recognition resources, this chapter offers a window into the tensions and contradictions underpinning the emergence of distributive austerity regimes.

The chapter begins by exploring how the emergence and implementation of austerity welfare distribution in Portugal were firmly grounded in a governmental rhetoric focused on the moral valuation of needs to the detriment of rights. I show that the inevitability of austerity measures was framed by government agents as guided by the imperative of attending to the needs of fiscal consolidation and the requirements of 'those in greater need' (*os que mais precisam*). The former was justified in light of the 'national social emergency', and the latter enabled restricting welfare state support to a set of morally deserving 'ideal types' of citizens. I argue that the moral valuation of a language of needs, in lieu of a language of rights, played a crucial role in legitimating intervention in the underlying logics and rationales of welfare state distribution, while simultaneously contributing to depoliticizing the unequal and devastating social and human effects of austerity policies. The chapter then turns to examining how the government's favouring of a language of needs over a language of rights, in political rhetoric and welfare policy, is expressed in the bureaucratic and relational dimensions of a food charity scheme run at a Catholic church. I focus mainly on how church volunteers and claimants mobilize discourses of deservingness to sustain distinct conceptions of human need. Drawing inspiration from Nancy Fraser's (2013) proposal for a politics of needs interpretation, I analyse how volunteers' quest to assert 'real need' (*verdadeira necessidade*) is mediated by bureaucratic procedures of data gathering and moral typologies of deservingness. The latter expresses a long-standing tendency to causally link poverty to individual failures of behaviour and perceived deficiencies in moral character (Katz 2013), which enables volunteers to classify, rank and enact a 'hierarchy of deservingness' (Little 1994; van Oorschot 2006; Willen 2012; Holmes and Castañeda 2016; Otazu and Sabaté Muriel 2020) that defines the value and legitimacy of needs and their carriers. Moral typologies of deservingness are integral to how volunteers distinguish between 'real' and 'false' needs, expanding their discretionary power in the allocation and distribution of food resources. As a counterpoint to volunteers' notion of 'real need', claimants mobilize the notion of need as a 'vernacular morality', mainly used as a language of contention with which to criticize and challenge the dominant logics of austerity welfare distribution, which they experience as a breakdown in the social contract of mutual obligations between the state and citizens.[6] I argue that the dominant logics of austerity welfare are both reproduced and challenged by how volunteers and claimants deploy moral discourses of deservingness to negotiate the legitimacy of competing visions of human need. In the concluding and final section, I discuss how the politics of austerity welfare in Portugal is primarily shaped by a struggle over the moral valuation of needs that expresses a clash between antagonistic value and ethical frameworks emerging out of distinct ways of imagining and acting upon livelihood projects and forms of citizenry belonging.

Distribution Shifts: From a Language of Rights to a Language of Needs

The anthropological literature emphasizes specific shifts and discontinuities arising from austerity policies that suggest a broader reconfiguration in the articulation of the needs of states, capital and the people: in particular, the deepening of the neoliberal reconfiguration of the welfare state, the growing financialization of capital extraction, and the dismantlement of the aspirations and models of livelihood improvement and upward mobility across generations. The austerity policies of spending cuts, privatizing healthcare and welfare reform contributed to redefining moral obligations between citizens and the state, entailing retrenchment of people's sense of citizenship entitlements and expectations of livelihoods improving over generations. This was facilitated by the fetishization of sovereign debt as *the* determining national, collective obligation – a process through which financial capital has historically captured the national state's fiscal policies. Bear (2015: 178) argues that this capture led to the submission of people's needs, moralities and socialities to a 'universe of calculi' permeated by violence, destitution and abstraction. Indeed, in Portugal as well as in the other so-called 'PIGS'[7] countries in the years immediately following the sovereign debt crisis, politicians' embrace of technical terms such as 'public debt', 'deficit', the 'spread of public bonds' and 'fiscal adjustment' served to depoliticize and naturalize growing social inequality and class polarization directly linked to the fiscal policies of austerity. It has been well documented by now that the fiscal policies of austerity have fuelled a violent crisis of social reproduction, affecting people's ability to ensure even their physical reproduction, as illustrated in the pronounced rise of food banks, the growing number of homeless people and widespread indebtedness (Garthwaite 2016; Cooper and Whyte 2017). Austerity policies have ushered in a 'dynamics of reversal' (Knight and Stewart 2016: 2; see also Knight 2015), undermining people's hopes and expectations of a 'life worth living' for themselves and the next generation (Narotzky and Besnier 2014). The above shifts suggest a reconfiguration of the articulation of the needs of states, capital and people, primarily shaped by the devaluation and subordination of the latter to the former.[8]

In this section, I explore how the right-wing coalition government implementing the austerity adjustment programme in Portugal sought to gather popular legitimation regarding austerity policies by promoting a political rhetoric and welfare policy broadly grounded in a moral valuation of 'needs' to the detriment of rights. This was instrumental in achieving two aims: legitimizing intervention in the logics and rationales of welfare distribution, giving rise to a new 'architecture of need'; and depoliticizing the unequal effects of austerity measures upon the most impoverished populations.[9]

In 2011, the Social Democratic Party won the national elections and formed a parliamentary majority in coalition with the Christian

Democrats. Since the beginning of the implementation of the austerity adjustment programme (between 2011 and 2014), the right-wing coalition government announced its wish to go 'beyond the Troika' (*ir para além da Troika*). In contrast with other European settings, in Portugal, the government's quest to legitimize harsh tax increases and wage and welfare cuts was not mainly framed by a tactic of external blaming (Moury and Standring 2017). The government took it upon itself to save the country from the errors of past governments in light of the 'national social emergency'. The austerity demands tying the government to the Troika provided the institutional and political conditions to accelerate the neoliberal redefinition of rights and the welfare logics of redistribution, challenging to accomplish with a democratic mandate (Rodrigues and Adão e Silva 2015). The willingness to go 'beyond the Troika' was progressively underpinned by a dramatization of 'patriotic duty' and 'historical mission'. The 'need' to overcome the 'dramatic' national social emergency demanded going 'beyond the Troika' as a means of fulfilling the patriotic aim of economic recovery. The government's political and moral valuation of the national need for fiscal sustainability and the necessity of managing scarce resources – thereby restricting state welfare support to 'those in greater need' – illustrates how the deepening of the neoliberal restructuring of welfare state provisioning was underpinned by a shift of emphasis from a language of rights towards a language of needs.

The notions of sustainability and scarcity acted as the central antipolitics metaphors with which popular consent was pursued. Such pursuit was expressed in the simultaneous prioritization of 'reforming the state and its welfare functions' – through the necessary technocratic spending cuts choices for which there was no alternative – *and* attending to 'those in greater need' (that is, restricting welfare support to the morally deserving).[10] In other words, 'reforming the state' through increasing the number of eligibility criteria to access welfare benefits, expenditure cuts and tax increases was necessary due to the state's bankruptcy (i.e. lack of resources), and attending only to those 'in greater need' was justified as a way of making better use of the scarce available resources (i.e. 'make the social security system sustainable', a phrase often used by government politicians).[11]

The government's austerity quest for fiscal sustainability, because of the 'need' to confront a 'national social emergency', reversed an incomplete process of income inequality reduction set in motion in the late 1990s through public investment and an increase in noncontributory social transfers. From the late 1990s up to 2009, the official poverty rate in Portugal decreased from 22.5 per cent to 17.9 per cent, while from 2009 to 2014, it increased to 19.5 per cent. If the poverty rate were to be calculated according to the Consumer Price Index rather than the annual average national income, the poverty rate would have risen from 17.9 per cent to 24.2 per cent, which corresponds to 2.5 million people (Rodrigues 2016). Impoverishment and destitution during the austerity programme were the result of mass unemployment and a regressive policy of noncontributory social transfers shaped by severe cuts and growing conditionality, targeting in particular those benefiting from such forms of poverty reduction as Cristina mentioned at the beginning of this chapter. Those most affected by the austerity cuts were not the 'middle classes', as disseminated through the mainstream media, but the poorest of the poor. The level of income inequality between the wealthiest 10 per cent and the poorest 10 per cent rose from 9.2 per cent in 2009 to 10.6 per cent in 2014; when comparing the wealthiest 5 per cent and the poorest 5 per cent in the same period, income inequality increased from 14.7 to 18.7 per cent (Rodrigues 2016).

The masking of the unequal effects of austerity policies through the rhetorical deployment of the anti-politics metaphors of sustainability and scarcity entailed the enactment of a policy response aimed at those 'in greater need'. In 2011, the Social Emergency Programme was launched by the Ministry of Solidarity and Social Security with the aims of 'fighting the lack of efficiency' (in state redistributive practices) and 'changing the paradigm of social response to severe material deprivation'. The programme targeted specific population segments (e.g. impoverished households, long-term unemployed, and elderly and disabled persons), with a budget of €630 million for 2012. The programme laid out several policy projects to be carried out in partnership with third-sector institutions and civil society organizations, including the 'Food Emergency Programme' to expand the network of soup kitchens (the food charity scheme analysed in the next section is part of this programme). As a consequence, the number of soup kitchens in Portugal skyrocketed from 62 in 2011 to 843 in 2015.[12] During the austerity adjustment programme, while state expenditure was dramatically reduced, particularly noncontributory social transfers, state funding to the third sector grew (Joaquim 2015). The Social Emergency Programme mainly benefitted third-sector institutions through increased state budget funding, the speeding-up of the simplification of legal procedures associated with equipment acquisition, state-funded training for third-sector managing directors and an exclusive line of micro-credit devoted specifically to third-sector institutions. As Joaquim (2015) notes, the Social Emergency Programme not only entailed decreased social spending and increased state funding to the third sector. It also implied a shift in the model and logic of welfare redistribution, with the state delegating its responsibilities to the third sector while reinforcing a broader philosophy of charity and poor relief in welfare provisioning.

Such a shift would not have been possible without a political rhetoric centred on the imperative of attending to the national need for fiscal sustainability, together with the necessity of managing scarce state resources by redefining welfare state protection as last-resort assistance to 'those in greater need'. The anti-politics metaphors of sustainability and scarcity were useful in securing widespread traction for the welfare reforms being undertaken and concealing its unequal and divisive effects due to their technocratic *and* moral underpinnings. These two dimensions facilitated a shift in the discursive political framing of the allocation and distribution of welfare resources from a language of rights to a language of needs. In the next section, I explore further how this shift is expressed in a Catholic food charity scheme by focusing on the deployment of discourses of deservingness to sustain different conceptions of human need.

Charity Encounters, Deservingness and Visions of Human Need

Until 2011, the church in the most impoverished parish of Setúbal, in which more than 40 per cent of the local population were concentrated, offered only one type of food charity: the delivery of monthly food baskets.[13] These were prepared by volunteers, after receiving donations from private entities and the Banco Alimentar Contra a Fome (the major national food bank). In the context of the expansion of the state-sponsored Programme of Food Emergency, the church priest designed what I will call the 'Social Refectory' (SR), a food charity aid scheme in which each person pays according to their means. The priest envisioned the SR as an instrument of poverty relief and social intervention, to increase feelings of self-esteem among the poor population, and to stimulate self-responsibility and participation in the local community.

The SR is situated within the church, close to the main entrance. The restaurant space is approximately 40 square metres, and has a few tables and chairs and a self-service desk where recipients go to pick up their food. They can eat in or take food away – which most people do. The SR is open every day of the year between 7 PM and 8.30 PM. The meals are not made in the church, but are prepared by a subcontracted private company, and more than thirty volunteers organize and distribute the food and provide cleaning services.

To gain access to the SR, claimants first have to attend the Atendimento Social (AS; Social Counselling) at the church. The AS consists of a scheduled encounter between church volunteers and claimants, in which the former evaluate the claimant's financial situation and decide whether to grant access to the SR. This takes place every week, on Wednesdays and Fridays from 9 AM to 12.30 PM, excluding July and August, with four female volunteers in their midsixties and seventies. The volunteers complete a one-year training course with social workers from Caritas Portugal,[14] in which they learn about the applicable legal frameworks and state welfare procedures, and gain knowledge on the collection and analysis of the claimants' data.

An appointment is scheduled with Deolinda (a volunteer, aged fifty-one), the person responsible for the preparation of the monthly food baskets and the cleaning of the communal spaces in the church. Claimants are informed about the documents they should bring, which include identity cards, receipts for valid household expenses (e.g. utility bills, including rent or mortgage, gas, water and electricity) and medical expenses, and evidence of household members' earned income. The threshold for access to the SR is a maximum household monthly income of €750 after deductions for valid expenses. Volunteers have a grid, designed by the priest, divided by income bracket, with corresponding meal prices ranging from €0.10 to €4.

The AS takes place in a small room next to the priest's office, which used to be an archive of books, brochures and religious material. Files for each claimant fill the folders on the shelves. At the AS appointment, volunteers fill out a form with the claimant's personal data, make copies of the relevant documents and put everything together in a plastic folder, which is later archived in alphabetical order. This information has evaluative, regulatory and institutional purposes, and church volunteers are obliged to send it to the state social security services and to Caritas in order to validate information and detect potential fraud.

At the AS sessions, the volunteers' main aim is to identify the 'real needs' (*as necessidades reais*) of claimants. Volunteers would often explain to claimants at the beginning of each session that before 'providing help', they had to understand the claimant's 'situation' because 'we try to help everyone, but we need to know the person's situation'. Getting to know the claimant's 'situation' – and thus their 'real needs' – was mediated by how volunteers deployed the bureaucratic procedures of information gathering together with moral typologies of deservingness. The deployment of these instruments facilitated the discretionary and arbitrary intervention of the volunteers in the distribution and allocation of food resources. Volunteers' discretionary capabilities could either restrict or expand the support given to claimants, which was only possible in the first place because of how claimants' 'needs' were made and remade as 'real' by volunteers through material and moral instruments.

In one of the AS sessions, I came to know Antonio, a fragile, unemployed man in his late sixties. Teresa, one of the volunteers, had been told by a friend that Antonio had been an immigrant in Switzerland for many years and benefited from a Swiss state pension, which he did not declare to the Portuguese tax authorities. Teresa started the session without mentioning this information, proceeding with the usual questions:

TERESA: How much do you pay in rent?

ANTONIO: Around €200.

TERESA: Do you have any income?

ANTONIO: No, none.

TERESA: Then how do you pay the rent?

ANTONIO: I don't pay it.

TERESA: Do you live alone?

ANTONIO: Yes.

TERESA: What was your work before?

ANTONIO: I was a truck driver, for twenty years; I worked in Switzerland. I had 65,000 francs in savings, but my wife and son rob[bed] me, and I came back to Portugal with 20 francs in my pocket.

TERESA: For how long have you not paid rent?

ANTONIO: Three months.

TERESA: Is it rent or a bank loan instalment?

ANTONIO: It's a bank loan, but I have to eat.

Antonio brought with him all the necessary documentation in a folder, including a medical document stating that he had suffered from severe depression and suicidal tendencies. Teresa proceeded with her questioning, hoping for some sort of revelation regarding the rumour her friend had told her. Antonio had six children: two girls and four boys. Two of the boys had emigrated to England and Brazil, and Antonio had no contact with the others. Antonio added that one of his sons, knowing about his clinical condition, attempted to become his legal guardian: 'His goal was to take away the Swiss pension I'll receive in the future. My sons don't care about me.' Finally, Teresa asked: 'So, you'd like to access the SR?', 'Yes, I have friends who go there; they tell me the food is good and you pay according to your means', 'Yes, but right now we don't have any vacancies; it is very complicated – let me call the refectory'.' Teresa made the call and told Antonio that no vacancies were available. Antonio insisted that being able to get food through the SR was very important to him, given the economic hardship he was facing. Suddenly, Teresa's husband – who is also a volunteer at the refectory, distributing tickets and organizing food packages – came into the room: 'Look, Mr Antonio, we know that you have a Swiss state pension, that you were the owner of a restaurant and that you can make ends meet quite well by yourself. The SR is only for those who really need it, so you will need to prove to us that you don't have any income before we can grant you access to the SR!' Visibly upset, verging on tears and with his hands shaking, Antonio insisted he did not have a Swiss state pension, though in the past he had a small local restaurant for a brief period:

ANTONIO: But how do I prove to you that I don't have an income?

TERESA: You should go to the social security bureau and ask for a declaration stating that you have no income.

ANTONIO: But today is Friday – I will not be able to go there before Monday, meanwhile what do I eat?

Antonio had been denied access to the SR because he fitted the volunteers' moral-typological profile of the 'poor who lie, manipulate and try to cheat the system for their benefit'. Volunteers' moral typologies of deservingness classify and differentiate the poor and their needs, along a continuum ranging from the 'professional' to the 'newly poor' – expressions that form part of an emic repertoire volunteers use among themselves when speaking about the claimants. The 'professional poor' are described as manipulative or fake; they know how to cheat the system and combine different sources of distributive resources for their benefit. The 'newly poor' broadly denotes middle-class individuals who have 'fallen from grace'; they are poor for reasons outside their control and even if they knew how and where to ask for help, they are too ashamed to do so. In between these two broader categories, volunteers would often refer to those dependent on charity – 'they prefer to live on charity rather than teach their sons and daughters to fight and change their lives; they get accustomed to being poor'; those who abused the various charitable institutions in the city; those who tricked the system, lied and accepted help from multiple places; those who did not need any help, often Roma people, either because volunteers considered them to have other businesses (informal illegal activities such as drug trafficking or tobacco smuggling), or because they exhibited consumption habits deemed to be irresponsible (e.g. smoking or drinking); those whose possessions seemed to indicate that they had money (e.g. good clothes, a car or expensive smartphones); those who did not fulfil their parental obligations and preferred to spend their money on nights out entertaining friends; those who 'really needed' help, often living alone with few resources (e.g. single mothers with a solid work ethic who had been abused by family, partners and state institutions); elderly people, particularly women; young people who showed a commitment to study, self-discipline and responsibility; and, finally, those categorized as the 'newly poor'. Not all 'newly poor' were deemed to be deserving of help, but only those who showed humility and willingness to reinvent themselves as deserving poor.

The moralization of food charity denies support to those who, like Antonio, do not conform to the volunteers' typologies of deservingness. Antonio's need was denied by the volunteers' perception of his unworthiness. Antonio's case is representative of how volunteers' discretionary morally grounded power to define 'real need' may converge with the government's aim of restricting welfare support to 'those who really need it'. At the same time, volunteers' moral typologies of deservingness may also be mobilized and acted upon by claimants in ways that enable expanding people's capabilities to shift entitlements, particularly vis-à-vis the state. Maria's case is illustrative in this regard.

Maria (who was aged fifty-one in 2016) was a single mother of three underage boys, working as a subcontracted technical assistant in the refectory of a secondary school, earning the national minimum wage.[15] As subcontractors, Maria, and many other women I came to know, had an employment contract that ran only from the beginning until the end of the academic year (from September until June). Being entitled to neither holiday nor Christmas pay, Maria was paid only ten times a year. She was also not entitled to unemployment benefits because in order to be eligible, one has to have registered social security contributions in the twelve months prior to the request. Her meagre income was the only one coming into the household, which is why she decided to request access to the SR: 'I can come here after work, take the meals with me and make them stretch for more than one day.' Nonetheless, when Teresa was doing the accounting of income minus expenses to determine if Maria's household income was above €750, and thus determine the price she would pay for each meal, she realized that it was still very high (€350 after expenses). This was because Maria lived in social housing, paying a symbolic rent and also due to a lack of medical expenses. At one point, Maria said: 'Now I even regret having bought a new freezer, which I am still paying for by instalments. But I only bought it because friends and relatives sometimes helped me with food, which we don't eat immediately but I didn't want to throw it away. And I also started to make salty pastries to sell; it's not much money but helps to pay for my kids' education.' Confronted with this, Teresa replied: 'Well, in that case I think we should consider the freezer loan instalment as an expense.' By doing so, Teresa actually reduced Maria's household income and in turn the amount to be paid for each meal.

The volunteers always responded with a deep sense of compassion and empathy to Cristina, whom we met at the beginning of this chapter. A single mother, who had worked all her life to support herself, she displayed self-sacrifice for the benefit of her daughters and had been abandoned by the state in a moment of severe economic hardship. Teresa went to great lengths to help Cristina, including visiting her house and arranging to gather donations from the church followers (e.g. furniture, kitchen appliances and clothing for her daughters). Teresa commented that she could not bear the idea of seeing such 'a hardworking young woman' living in those conditions, by herself, with two daughters. After being granted access to the SR, Cristina was further helped by Sara, another volunteer, whose cousin worked as a municipal social worker. Sara's cousin intervened on behalf of Cristina so she could secure social housing and explained to her the best form to fill out to ensure she would get the RSI. In 2016, Cristina was living with her two daughters in social housing, paying a symbolic monthly amount of €5; she had been able to access the RSI and received €320 a month, and was finishing high school through a specific training programme at the local jobcentre. Following Teresa's advice, she planned to look for a job after increasing her educational credentials. Her partner, who worked informally as a car mechanic, was living with her. In one brief meeting at the church, while talking about how her life was going, Cristina made sure to specify with regard to her partner that 'if you see me in a car with him it's only because he works with cars'.

Most of the charity claimants I met at the church were undoubtedly aware of how typological deservingness criteria drove volunteers' discretionary and arbitrary decisions regarding food aid allocation. Some claimants would make an effort to conform to the volunteers' expectations of moral deservingness through modesty in terms of their physical appearance, clothing and possession of expensive goods (e.g. a car or a smartphone), frugal consumption habits, display of a solid work ethic, or gratitude and deference (rather than confrontation) in their verbal interactions with the volunteers. Doing so enabled claimants to secure access to the SR while also enhancing access to resources of various kinds – including getting privileged information about a job opening or a personal favour that could facilitate navigating the paperwork and bureaucratic procedures to access municipal housing.

However, claimants' instrumental adherence to volunteers' expectations of moral deservingness co-existed with the deployment of needs as a vernacular morality with which to challenge the distributive politics of austerity. How Cristina narrated her needs – 'If the state doesn't help me who will?', 'I worked all my life to support myself; I don't want to live off the RSI. I want to work, have a job and support myself and my daughters!' – was predicated not only on material lack, but also, more importantly, on a valuation of legitimate claims to resources and provisioning responsibilities. Needs were mobilized as a vernacular morality of social distribution grounded in relational obligations, as chains of 'in-order-to' practices located in a present and future time, as well as a tool to make claims and shift entitlements to resources – particularly vis-à-vis the state.

The charity encounters I observed and followed in Setúbal reflect how austerity welfare in Portugal has intensified the morally based discretionary and arbitrary powers of volunteers in the allocation and distribution of food resources to severely impoverished populations. Charity volunteers' mobilization of moral discourses of deservingness to classify and differentiate the behaviours and perceived character attributes of claimants in their quest to identify 'real need' determines who is entitled to what resources, how and why. Hence, the power to define 'real need' represents the power to establish access to resources, the legitimacy of claims to resources and provisioning responsibilities. As depicted in the cases of Antonio and Cristina, volunteers' quest to define 'real need' can both restrict or expand people's capabilities to assess fundamental livelihood resources and instruments to negotiate their claims to entitlements regarding the state. The notion of 'real need' driving the volunteers' charitable work co-exists with claimants' articulation and definition of needs as a vernacular morality of critique and contention vis-à-vis the loss of entitlement to resources, rights and aspirations. By mobilizing need as a vernacular morality, claimants emphasized two dimensions of human need: need as the lack of material resources *and* needs whose fulfilment enables relational capabilities to sustain life across generations, claim worth and respect, and articulate aspirations for the future (e.g. paying for and supporting children's education, as in the case of Maria).

Conclusion: The Politics of Austerity Welfare and the Struggle over the Valuation of Needs

During the implementation of the austerity adjustment programme (between 2011 and 2014), the Portuguese government mobilized specific categories and meanings of needs to gather popular support for the inevitability of austerity, and also to depoliticize and neutralize the unequal effects of the policies being implemented. The national needs for fiscal sustainability and the needs of 'those in greater need' were instrumental in asserting the legitimacy of deepening the neoliberal reconfiguration of welfare state distribution through growing conditionality, the delegation of state responsibilities to the third sector and the reinforcement of a broader logic of charitable relief for the poor. Austerity in Portugal has constituted a privileged framework with which to reinforce a profound shift towards a moral valuation of a language of needs to the detriment of a language of rights framing the access, allocation and distribution of welfare resources.

Charity encounters reveal how volunteers and claimants mobilize moral discourses of deservingness to sustain distinct visions of human need. The emic typologies of moral deservingness deployed by volunteers to define 'real needs' – ranging from the 'professional' to the 'newly poor' – classify and differentiate the worth and value of each need and its carrier. Typologies of moral deservingness intensify the discretionary interventions by volunteers in the allocation and distribution of food resources. In her ethnography of volunteerism in Northern Italy, Muehlebach explores how neoliberalism is predicated on the production of a 'highly moralized kind of citizenship', which is integral to a broader movement of transformation and retrenchment of welfare state provisioning (2012: 6). In the case examined in this chapter, volunteers' moral pursuit of 'real need' contributes to the dual purpose of reinforcing the government's austerity quest to shift the mutual obligations between citizens and the state and also to challenge it. In some circumstances, volunteers' discretionary power grounded in moral typologies of deservingness can enhance people's capabilities to shift entitlements to resources, particularly vis-à-vis the state.

While charity claimants instrumentally adhere to volunteers' registers of deservingness as a way of accessing fundamental livelihood resources, they simultaneously struggle to redefine and conceptualize their needs as a 'vernacular morality'. They do so by articulating needs as grounded in the normative relations of dependency, responsibility and obligation underpinning their livelihood pursuits, projects and aspirations, and also as an idiom to criticize the failure of the state in ensuring people's inalienable right to food security, social protection and conditions for the development of relational capabilities. In doing so, charity recipients, while never losing sight of the imperative of survival, stress an 'embedded' (Polanyi 1944) notion of human needs, linking the experience of human need with scarce resources *and* with the moral weight (Gough 2017) that needs express with regard to popular values concerning conceptions of dignity, worth and aspirations.

As recently noted by James and Koch (2020), welfare bureaucracies cutting across the state, the market and civil society have often been addressed in the literature through a Foucauldian and governmentality-oriented lens. This has favoured a dominant representation of organizations of welfare provisioning as top-down structures for the reproduction of neoliberal ideology and the reinforcement of technologies of control and surveillance. In the context of the charity encounters I followed, it was not merely the enactment of bureaucratic practices that led to the dehumanization of claimants and their needs, but also the moral register of deservingness and worthiness through which volunteers pursued the definition of 'real need'. Moral deservingness was enacted as an instrument with which to deny or expand people's capabilities to access material and immaterial resources of various kinds to fulfil their needs.

Anthropological investigations have stressed how austerity is not only a political and economic project, but also a moral one that aims to redefine ethical and caring relationships. Building upon this insight, I want to suggest that the struggle over the moral valuation of needs is at the core of the politics of austerity welfare. Different agents (e.g. government representatives, charity volunteers and claimants) mobilize the idiom of needs to express various livelihood projects and models that frame the modalities of engagement between the state and its citizens – that is, the role of the state as an agent of distribution and its responsibilities for the wellbeing of citizens. In Portugal, specific needs are mobilized and morally valued to sustain the inevitability of the predicament of austerity and the restriction of welfare support (e.g. by the government), the quest to assert 'real need' (e.g. by charity volunteers) or the mobilization of need as a vernacular morality with which to challenge the state betrayal of its moral duties (Koch 2018), and to reinstate entitlement to resources on the grounds of the normative dependencies and relations driving people's pursuit of survival and worth against the imperatives of austerity welfare (e.g. by charity claimants).

Narotzky (2016) has suggested that in the post-2008 financial crisis among the disenfranchised Spanish working classes, a political-economic framework for directing collective grievances is increasingly being superseded by a moral economy approach. People's experiences of citizenship destitution, welfare dispossession and inability to project a life into the future were increasingly articulated in moral terms – instead of the traditional idioms of exploitation and domination that shaped older generations of the Fordist working classes. According to Narotzky, people's 'systematic humiliation has produced a struggle to change the moral frameworks in which making a life acquires value and meaning, while also creating conditions of possibility for obtaining basic resources while regaining dignity' (2016: 75).

Narotzky's insight into the growing deployment of moral arguments to struggle against the destructive logics of austerity pushes us to ask the following question with regard to the material investigated in this chapter: can a struggle over the moral value of needs be effective in terms of superseding the austerity-led dispossession of rights? On the one hand, in the immediacy of daily life, doing so may reinforce the structural drivers of power and destitution, make the satisfaction of basic human needs increasingly dependent on the discretionary benevolence of third-sector agents, while also increasing people's dependency on personalized networks through which vital livelihood resources circulate. On the other hand, within the context of the church parish, it was apparent that claimants' mobilization of needs as a vernacular morality was effective in enabling shifting entitlement to resources and secure access to resources essential to sustain the reproduction of the household and the agency of dependent others.

While it is impossible to provide a conclusive answer to the question raised above, the ambivalence of acting upon destructive dynamics through moral arguments contains a hidden political tension that shows that austerity is not an all-encompassing reality and totalizing frame for those subject to its imperatives. Instead, how the moral value of needs became a sphere and language of contention in austerity Portugal seems to reflect what Karl Polanyi designated as a 'double movement' to characterize the parallel and contradictory movements of the intense marketization of people's livelihood practices, meanings and projects, and also the strategies of the latter to resist being colonized by the market's disembedding logics and advances.

Patrícia Matos is an economic anthropologist trained in Lisbon and London. She is currently a postdoctoral researcher in the project 'Negotiating Livelihoods under Transformative Politics: Crisis, Policies and Practices in Portugal 2010–2020', based at CRIA/ISCTE at the University Institute of Lisbon. Her writings address the themes of neoliberalism, precarity and labour; gender, body politics and social reproduction, and austerity welfare, needs and moralities of distribution. Her book *Disciplined Agency: Neoliberal Precarity, Generational Dispossession and Call Centre Labour in Portugal* was published by Manchester University Press in July 2020.

Notes

1. RSI stands for Rendimento Social de Inserção, or Social Insertion Income. Introduced in 1996, it is a guaranteed minimum income scheme comprising a monetary component (the cash benefit) that is a universal right, though means-tested, transitory and a labour-market insertion programme. It is aimed at individuals and families who are in a situation of severe economic deprivation.
2. Importantly, Cristina expresses how rights and deservingness, rather than being two opposed and mutually exclusive frames, can blend into each other in particular circumstances and rationales. She experiences the lack of support from the state as the breakdown of a social contract in which she was institutionally entitled and morally deserving of 'help' in accessing material livelihood and recognition resources. For more on the relationship between rights and deservingness in the anthropologi-

cal, rights and humanitarianism literatures, see the Introduction to this volume by Streinzer and Tošić.
3. In 2011, Portugal signed a 'Memorandum of Understanding' with the 'Troika' (the European Commission, the European Central Bank and the International Monetary Fund (IMF)) binding the country to a four-year plan of austerity measures in exchange for a €78 billion bailout. Between 2011 and 2014, the government implemented severe cuts to state spending, harsh tax increases and a reduction of welfare benefits. As in other countries on the indebted periphery of the eurozone, Portuguese policies of austerity entailed measures of 'internal devaluation' (Blyth 2013) – wage repression, precarious employment and mass unemployment – that contributed to the most violent and rapid transfer of income from labour to capital in democratic Portugal (Reis et al. 2013).
4. The current rise of the third sector in Europe replicates 'the rise of NGOs' in Africa following the imposition of structural adjustment packages from the 1980s onwards. NGOs were instrumental in the advancement of the neoliberalization of the state's redistributive functions through privatization, neoliberal welfare reforms and the dissemination of the entrepreneurial ethos (Pfeiffer and Chapman 2010).
5. Ethnographic research was conducted within the context of the European Research Council-funded project 'Grassroots Economics: Practice, Meaning and Project in the Pursuit of Livelihood', coordinated by Susana Narotzky and based at the University of Barcelona. See: http://www.ub.edu/grassrootseconomics (retrieved 14 February 2022).
6. Theorizations of human need are underpinned by a recurrent ambivalence, in that the notion of need can simultaneously designate exigencies of physical survival as well as the aspirations and hopes conducive to a 'good' life (e.g. Soper 1981; Springborg 1981; Doyal and Gough 1991) – or between thin and thick approaches to human need, and objectivist and relativist conceptions. The aforementioned ambivalence thus encompasses the commensurable and incommensurable dimensions of human needs as expressed in factually driven needs whose fulfilment determines people's capabilities for material survival, and value-laden needs whose satisfaction determines people's capabilities for defining a worthy livelihood. By mobilizing needs as a vernacular morality, I am referring in particular to how charity claimants articulate and identify their needs according to normative livelihood moralities of responsibilities, obligations and dependencies that designate valued conceptions of citizenship and entitlement to resources.
7. The PIGS acronym, often used in a derogatory manner, originally refers to the peripheral economies of the Southern European countries of Portugal, Italy, Greece and Spain, and dates back to the 1990s. The acronym was again popularized during the European sovereign debt crisis.
8. To a great extent, the austerity policies implemented in Europe and beyond following the 2008 Great Recession follow a similar rationale to the IMF-sponsored structural adjustment programmes that have been

applied since the 1980s in Latin America or Africa: to create conditions conducive to the expansion of market fundamentalism through a focus on the repayment of debt to stimulate economic growth. These programmes have often implied a trade-off between economic growth and the satisfaction of basic human needs (e.g. Max-Neef et al. 1991).
9. Haney's study of changing Hungarian welfare regimes in the latter part of the twentieth century highlights how 'states not only create provisions to redistribute benefits but also articulate historically specific conceptions of need. By constructing "architectures of need", states define who is in need and how to satisfy those needs' (2003: 7).
10. Here I draw inspiration from Ferguson's notion of 'anti-politics' (1994), a term used to account for the paradoxical outcomes of failed developmental projects that address poverty in Lesotho, where the re-articulation of debt as a 'technical problem' contributed to concealing its political causes and expanding bureaucratic state power. Similarly, following the Great Recession of 2008, the implementation of austerity adjustment programmes in various European countries was very much shaped by how technocratic bodies of governance envisioned sovereign debt management as a purely technical problem to be approached through spending cuts and/or tax increases. However, the technocratic dimension of austerity did not prevent its grounding in a language of 'hyper-moralisation' (Muehlebach 2016: 5) expressed, for instance, in how the metaphor of the 'Broken Society' used by David Cameron in the United Kingdom during the campaign for the 2010 general election was later instrumental in the moral legitimation of the highest cut in public spending in the post-Second World War period (i.e. the Welfare Reform Act of 2012) (Clarke and Newman 2012). As noted by Powers and Rakopoulos (2019), it is possible to trace a general continuum linking neoliberal, structural adjustment and austerity policies in the Global South and the Global North in terms of how the notion of scarcity is used as an instrument of moral normativity and societal control.
11. Similarly to the British context (Clarke and Newman 2012), the Portuguese government sometimes characterized the restrictive welfare policies being undertaken as conducive to a higher degree of fairness in the allocation and distribution of resources. In Portugal, the political uses of the idiom of fairness to legitimize divisive policies were not focused on the dichotomy between 'skivers and strivers'; instead, the government characterized austerity policies as a sort of justice repair conducive to greater fairness between generations. Parents and children were called upon to become agents of austerity, as illustrated in the reasoning that cuts in present pension beneficiaries were imperative in order to ensure the sustainability of the system in the future. Parents were called upon to sacrifice themselves in the present for the wellbeing of their children in the future. Or, conversely, children should accept the burden of fewer rights, social protection and stable employment as a way of mitigating the irresponsible and unsustainable excesses of their parents.

12. See: https://www.dn.pt/portugal/interior/cantinas-sociais-serviram-quase-48-mil-refeicoes-por-dia-no-primeiro-semestre-4723210.html (retrieved 14 February 2022).
13. Forty per cent corresponds to roughly 50,000 inhabitants.
14. Caritas Portugal, founded in 1945, is the official Catholic Church organization in Portugal for charity and social relief.
15. The national minimum wage was €505 in 2015 and €530 in 2016.

References

Bear, Laura. 2015. *Navigating Austerity: Currents of Debt along a South Asian River*. Stanford: Stanford University Press.
Blyth, Mark. 2013. *Austerity: The History of a Dangerous Idea*. Oxford: Oxford University Press.
Caplan, Pat. 2016. 'Big Society or Broken Society? Food Banks in the UK', *Anthropology Today* 32(1): 5–9.
Clarke, John, and Janet Newman. 2012. 'The Alchemy of Austerity', *Critical Social Policy* 32(3): 299–319.
Cooper, Vickie, and David Whyte (eds). 2017. *The Violence of Austerity*. London: Pluto Press.
Douzina-Bakalaki, Phaedra. 2017. 'Volunteering Mothers: Engaging the Crisis in a Soup Kitchen of Northern Greece', *Anthropology Matters* 17(1): 1–24.
Doyal, Len and Ian Gough. 1991. *A Theory of Human Need*. London: Macmillan.
Ferguson, James. 1994. *The Anti-politics Machine*. Minneapolis: Minnesota University Press.
Fraser, Nancy. 2013. *Fortunes of Feminism: From State-Managed Capitalism to Neoliberal Crisis*. London: Verso.
Garthwaite, Kayleigh. 2016. *Hunger Pains: Life inside Foodbank Britain*. London: Policy Press.
Gough, Ian. 2017. *Heat, Greed and Human Need: Climate Change, Capitalism and Sustainable Well-Being*. Cheltenham: Edward Elgar.
Haney, Lynne. 2003. *Inventing the Needy: Gender and the Politics of Welfare in Hungary*. Berkeley: University of California Press.
Holmes, Seth M., and Heide Castañeda. 2016. 'Representing the "European Refugee Crisis" in Germany and beyond: Deservingness and Difference, Life and Death', *American Ethnologist* 43(1): 12–24.
James, Deborah, and Insa Koch. 2020. 'Economies of Advice', in *Oxford Research Encyclopedia of Anthropology*. Oxford: Oxford University Press. Retrieved 14 February 2022 from https://oxfordre.com/anthropology/view/10.1093/acrefore/9780190854584.001.0001/acrefore-9780190854584-e-20.
Joaquim, Claúdia. 2015. *Proteção social, terceiro setor e equipamentos sociais: que modelos para Portugal*. Retrieved 14 February 2022 from

https://www.ces.uc.pt/observatorios/crisalt/documentos/cadernos/CadernoObserv_III_fevereiro2015.pdf.

Katz, Michael. 2013. *The Undeserving Poor: From the War on Poverty to the War on Welfare*. New York: Pantheon Books.

Knight, David. 2015. *History, Time, and Economic Crisis in Central Greece*. London: Palgrave Macmillan.

Knight, David, and Charles Stewart. 2016. 'Ethnographies of Austerity: Temporality, Crisis, and Affect in Southern Europe', *History and Anthropology* 27(1): 1–18.

Koch, Insa. 2018. *Personalising the State: An Anthropology of Law, Politics, and Welfare in Austerity Britain*. Oxford: Oxford University Press.

Koch, Insa, and Deborah James. 2020. 'The State of the Welfare State: Advice, Governance and Care in Settings of Austerity', *Ethnos*. DOI:10.1080/00141844.2019.1688371.

Little, Margaret H. 1994. '"Manhunts and Bingo Blabs": The Moral Regulation of Ontario Single Mothers', *Canadian Journal of Sociology* 19: 233–47.

Max-Neef, Manfred, Antonio Elizalde and Martin Hopenhayn. *1991. Human Scale Development: Conception, Application and Further Reflections, Volume 1*. New York: Apex Press.

Moury, Catherine, and Adam Standring. 2017. 'Going beyond the Troika: Power and Discourse in Portuguese Austerity Politics', *European Journal of Political Research* 56(3): 660–97.

Muehlebach, Andrea. 2012. *The Moral Neoliberal: Welfare and Citizenship in Italy*. Chicago: University of Chicago Press.

———. 2016. 'Anthropologies of Austerity', *History and Anthropology* 27(3): 1–14.

Narotzky, Susana. 2016. 'Between Inequality and Injustice: Dignity as a Motive for Mobilisation during the Crisis', *History and Anthropology* 27(1): 74–92.

Narotzky, Susana, and Niko Besnier. 2014. 'Crisis, Value, and Hope: Rethinking the Economy', *Current Anthropology* 55(9): 4–16.

Otazu, Mikel A., and Irene Sabaté Muriel. 2020. 'Merecimiento y lenguages de la injusticia', *Etnográfica* 24(1): 157–64.

Pfeiffer, James, and Rachel Chapman. 2010. 'Anthropological Perspectives on Structural Adjustment and Public Health', *Annual Review of Anthropology* 39: 149–65.

Polanyi, Karl. 1944. *The Great Transformation: The Political and Economic Origins of Our Time*. Boston: Beacon Press.

Powers, Theodore, and Theodoros Rakopoulos. 2019. 'The Anthropology of Austerity: An Introduction', *Focaal* 83: 1–12.

Pusceddu, Antonio Maria. 2020. 'The Moral Economy of Charity: Advice and Redistribution in Italian Caritas Welfare Bureaucracy', *Ethnos*. DOI:10.1080/00141844.2019.1687538.

Reis, José, et al. 2013. *A Anatomia da Crise: identificar os problemas para construir alternativas*', *Observatório da Crise e Alternativas*. Coimbra:

CES. Retrieved 14 February 2022 from https://www.ces.uc.pt/ficheiros2/files/Relatorio_Anatomia_Crise_final__.pdf.
Rodrigues, Carlos. 2016. *Desigualdade do Rendimento e Pobreza em Portugal*. Lisbon: Fundação Manuel dos Santos.
Rodrigues, Maria de Lurdes, and Pedro Adão e Silva. 2015. *Governar com a Troika: políticas públicas em tempos de austeridade*. Coimbra: Almedina.
Soper, Kate. 1981. *On Human Needs*. Brighton: Harvester Press.
Springborg, Patricia. 1981. *The Problem of Human Needs and the Critique of Civilisation*. London: George Allen & Unwin.
Van Oorschot, Wim. 2006. 'Making the Difference in Social Europe: Deservingness Perceptions among Citizens of European Welfare States', *Journal of European Social Policy* 16: 23–45.
Venezuela-Garcia, Hugo, Miranda J. Lubbers and James G. Rice. 2019. 'Charities under Austerity: Ethnographies of Poverty and Marginality in Western Non-profit and Charity Associations', *Journal of Organizational Ethnography* 8(1): 2–10.
Willen, Sarah S. 2012. 'Migration, "Illegality", and Health: Mapping Embodied Vulnerability and Debating Health-Related Deservingness', *Social Science & Medicine* 75(6): 805–11.

8

'Here, Morality Is a Sense of Entitlement'

Citizenship, Deservingness and
Inequality in Suburban Atlanta

Elisa Lanari

It was a slow day at the Compassionate Action Network (CAN), Sandy Springs' largest social service organization. Marie, a cheerful, easygoing woman in her fifties, had just finished teaching me the ropes of client interviewing and we were a little bored. Looking out from our tiny office, we saw that three other volunteers – all upper-middle-class white women like Marie – had gathered in the deserted waiting room to chat. Roberta, a seasoned volunteer always privy to the organization's news and gossip, was telling the others about a client who had 'broken her heart' earlier that morning. The client, a middle-aged Black man, had made an appointment with her to discuss his need for financial assistance. 'He was so humble', Roberta insisted, 'that he didn't even *want* to ask for help. To us, to his relatives, the government, or whoever.' She paused, a murmur of compassion spreading among the group. Then she reflected out loud: 'See, that's what's great about what we do. Some days you see people who try to take advantage of the system. But then, there are all these people who really get to your heart.'

During their downtime, CAN volunteers (most of them women) would often gather in the photocopy room, or in another space that granted them some degree of privacy, exchanging similar details about their service interactions. That morning, upon hearing Roberta's account, Marie noted that she had met that 'sweet man' too: she had given him vouchers to obtain food and clothing. 'He was so embarrassed to ask if he could get a pair of shoes from the thrift store', she recalled, with a hint of sadness in her voice, 'that he wanted to pay for them. He said he needed slacks to go to church.' Roberta reflected out loud: 'See, it's things like these, that you wouldn't even think of in your life! Two weeks ago I threw away boxes of clothes that I had accumulated in my basement for twenty years. Stuff and stuff. I had never opened those boxes in years.' 'Oh yeah, I've got so much stuff in my house', interjected Miss Laurel, an elderly volunteer. 'These are the things we take for granted.'

During the months I spent as a volunteer and ethnographer inside CAN's offices and waiting rooms, I often saw volunteers note how different their clients' lives were from their own, even though they lived less than a mile apart.[1] Their comments and assessments of 'deservingness' fixated on one aspect of the clients' personality or on a seemingly trivial detail of their service interactions: a door slammed, a 'well-behaved' child, a worn-out pair of shoes or a 'positive' attitude displayed in the face of economic hardship. Some volunteers linked those traits to clients' progress on their path to achieving self-sufficiency. Others refrained from making these assessments and saw their job as fundamentally concerned with bringing some 'hope' and 'joy' to less fortunate neighbours. Above all, they noted how different their clients' lives were from their own, seeing this gap as emblematic of their privileged class status and of the polarized nature of Sandy Springs as a 'city of two extremes'.

In this chapter, I focus on similar power-laden interactions among women volunteers, clients and service providers in places like CAN in order to understand how framings of deservingness emerged and were negotiated in Sandy Springs, Georgia in the United States. In 2005, this majority-white and affluent suburban area managed to obtain fiscal and political independence from the nearby city of Atlanta and majority-minority Fulton County by creating an autonomous municipality.[2] Shortly thereafter, the newly established city of Sandy Springs became nationally and internationally well known for pioneering the 'twenty-first century model of local government', having outsourced most of its services first to a private corporation and then to multiple private contractors (Porter 2006; Segal 2012).

Today, Sandy Springs is characterized by a rapidly urbanizing landscape and an increasingly diverse population, with working-poor Black, Latinx and other immigrant groups constituting ca. 42 per cent of its over 100,000 residents (US Census Bureau n.d.).[3] How does a largely white municipality built on secessionist anti-welfare stances tackle the growth of poverty and diversity within its boundaries? How were its neoliberal governing strategies and 'colorblind' racist discourses (Bonilla-Silva 2009) adapted to deal with this changing context? In what follows, I uncover the racially and morally inflected framings of deservingness that have shaped immigrants' and poor people's *conditional* incorporation into this newly formed political community. Following Streinzer and Tošić (see the Introduction to this volume), I argue that deservingness can be used as a heuristic to reveal the tensions and power differentials that inform local responses to inequality. From this perspective, we can begin to understand how differently positioned individuals come to support (or, inadvertently, reproduce) private sector-driven approaches that, while purportedly addressing social problems, ultimately exacerbate longstanding racial, class and gender divides.

A large body of scholarship has demonstrated how, in the public imagination, notions of deservingness are closely linked to race and other markers of difference (Watkins-Hayes and Kovalsky 2016: 196). Here, I use ethnography to trace how these moral framings emerged and evolved in one particular community. As a municipality created to allow white homeowners to flee from the unwanted influence of a minority-led government and of 'undesired' Black and brown populations, Sandy Springs offers a unique viewpoint to observe how racial ideologies have historically become enmeshed with practices and discourses surrounding welfare and taxation. At the same time, by focusing on Sandy Springs, I foreground the role played by nonstate actors in shaping contemporary processes of social redistribution and defining their underlying moral grammars. I thus shift the focus of analyses of deservingness from the national to the urban scale as 'the central institutional, political and geographical interface upon, within and through which the contradictory politics of capitalist restructuring are currently being fought out' (Brenner 2000: 374).

In the United States, the 1996 welfare reform (passed under Bill Clinton) marked a shift towards the progressive neoliberalization and privatization of the welfare state. Since then, US anti-poverty discourse and ideology have increasingly centred on the goal of promoting 'work attachment' and reshaping poor people's behaviours, transforming them from passive welfare recipients into entrepreneurial and self-governing citizen-subjects (Goode and Maskovsky 2001; Collins and Mayer 2010).[4] On the one hand, the reform curtailed cash assistance for single-parent households; on the other hand, it expanded social service programmes 'designed to enhance personal well-being and addressing barriers to employment', such as 'job training, adult education, mental health treatment, substance abuse treatment and other programs promoting economic self-sufficiency' (Allard 2009: 3, 5). Parallel to these shifts was the 'reterritorialization' of the welfare state through the devolution of services to states, and thence to a diffuse network of private and public agencies (Morgen and Maskovsky 2003). Inside these agencies, workers and volunteers were given the responsibility (and the power) 'to counsel, encourage, and discipline clients' by regulating their access to local resources and social programmes (Watkins-Hayes 2009a: 287). This situation has opened up new possibilities for nonprofit actors of different class, racial and gender backgrounds to interject their own views and assessment of deservingness into everyday service interactions (ibid.; see also Morgen 2001).

As a consequence of these shifts and of the diversifying landscape of American poverty (with suburban poor populations doubling in number over the past two decades), place and geography have become key factors in shaping people's experiences and access to social services. Scholars have thus begun to investigate how anti-poverty policy is differentially implemented at the 'street level', stressing, for instance, how local political culture and 'institutional characteristics shape social program administration in … subtle but profound ways' (Allard 2009: 148; see also Morgen 2001; Watkins-Hayes 2009b). However, more qualitative research is needed in order to understand how suburban communities that 'appear very "middle class" on the outside' (Allard 2017: 2) deal with the unexpected growth of poverty from both a practical and an ideological standpoint.

In their seminal volume entitled *The New Poverty Studies*, Judith Goode and Jeff Maskovsky called on anthropologists to investigate the 'regimes of disappearance' surrounding issues of poverty and inequality by focusing not so much 'on poor people's invisibility but on the terms in which they are permitted to be visible in public discourse' (2001: 2). I hereby extend this call to suburbs, specifically to a majority-white, resource-rich, privatized suburban community where the nature of poverty as 'a political, economic, and ideological effect of capitalist processes and state activity' (ibid.: 3) is especially hidden from view. In this context, nonprofit workers, volunteers and philanthropists acted as especially powerful mediators in the delivery of social programmes.

I begin by providing an overview of the demographic shifts that led Sandy Springs to embark on private sector-driven efforts to create assistance programmes for its newcomer poor and immigrant residents. We will thus see how government officials, philanthropists, corporations, religious institutions, welfare agencies and women's charities all became part of the networks constituting Sandy Springs' 'civic infrastructure' of aid (Schuller 2012). They all contributed to the allocation of money and resources to worthy causes and 'deserving' subjects; to the recruitment of middle-class retirees and stay-at-home wives into the ranks of caring, resourceful citizen-volunteers; and to the implementation of new policies and programmes targeting 'needy' residents of colour. If, on the one hand, I parse out the 'vernacular moral grammars' (Willen and Cook 2016: 96) employed by these different actors, on the other hand, I show how low-income residents appropriated these hegemonic notions of deservingness, using them to access particular services and/or forge claims of belonging to the city and its institutions.

My ethnographic examples focus on Latina women, most of whom hailed from Mexico, had no immigration papers and were employed in the low-wage service industry. As newcomers to the Atlanta region with a precarious legal and economic status, Latinx residents experienced both subtle and overt forms of discrimination, including racializing discourses that construed them simultaneously as 'invisible/visible Others' – invisible as 'ghost workers, yet highly visible as families needing education and healthcare' (Villenas 2001: 5).[5] Moreover, at the time of my fieldwork in 2016, the national public sphere was saturated with the anti-immigrant rhetoric of US presidential candidate Donald Trump, who resorted to dehumanizing racist language to portray 'illegal' Mexicans as rapists and criminals (Moreno 2015; Davis 2018). Trump's hateful rhetoric appealed to sentiments that had been boiling under the surface during the years of the Barack Obama presidency, when mounting opposition to national healthcare expansion and immigration reform helped consolidate stereotypes of undocumented migrants as the 'new undeserving' (Watkins-Hayes and Kovalsky 2016: 211).

Here, I seek to account for these different scales of (in)visibility, showing how Latina participants grappled with national and local politics of disappearance, negotiating underlying narratives of immigrant (un)deservingness. I especially foreground the everyday tactics and 'micropractices of citizenship' (Flores 2015: 399) through which Latina women 'ma[d]e a space for themselves in their new city', coming to understand themselves as members of the Sandy Springs' community who were entitled to particular rights and privileges (Galvez 2009: 16–17).

A City of Two Extremes

'To me, Sandy Springs is a city of two extremes, where you go from the really, really rich to the really, really poor. And it sucks.' Sitting across from me in one of the client rooms at CAN, Rhonda sighed as she uttered these words, a sigh that appeared to be a mixture of exhaustion and realism. As the organization's recordkeeper and a young Black woman working two jobs, Rhonda's life was defined by other people's needs and demands: those of clients asking for services, of volunteers complaining about slow computers and of her disabled mother in need of full-time care. That day she looked especially tired: instead of sporting her usual sophisticated business casual attire, she was wearing a simple red sweater with skinny jeans. Our interview seemed to provide an unexpected break in her routine, which she used to reflect on the difficulties she had to overcome in her life and on how those changed her perspective on Sandy Springs. 'I was born and raised just a few blocks from here', she explained, noting that the city was much less diverse during her childhood. 'I didn't grow up around Black people; in elementary school I was one of the few Black kids around. And even though I was low income, I didn't know I was low income. I was hanging out with rich people and acting like poverty was not my problem.'

Rhonda's life took a sudden turn in high school, when her mother became disabled, lost her job, exhausted her savings and defaulted on her mortgage payments. As they waited for her disability pension to be disbursed, Rhonda and her mother became homeless, leaving to stay with friends and then moving into transitional housing in South Atlanta. It was during these times of economic hardship that her mother turned to CAN for help and that Rhonda realized that Sandy Springs had become home to many working-poor residents who depended on the organization to make ends meet. Years later, after graduating from college, she decided to interview for a job with CAN, as she wanted to 'give back and get out of her Sandy Springs' little bubble'. At the time of our interview in 2013, she had been at CAN for five years, but was still supplementing her income by working at a local fast food chain, where she had been employed since high school. As much as she liked being part of CAN, she was contemplating a career move – something she eventually did in 2017, quitting her job to work in the fashion industry.

Rhonda's narrative contains some of the moral grammars of deservingness common to other 'success stories' published on the

CAN website: a catastrophic event pushing people into poverty; a local nonprofit able to supplement the shortages of the local welfare system; the decision to 'give back' to the organization after recovering from economic hardship; and the importance of hard work and personal initiative to achieve upward mobility. In her role as a nonprofit worker, Rhonda resorted to these moral grammars to assess help-seekers' behaviours. At the same time, as a working-class woman of colour, she was deeply aware of the invisibility of racialized poverty in Sandy Springs, a place traditionally associated with white economic privilege and secessionist cityhood.[6]

Since the early 2000s, Sandy Springs has witnessed major demographic shifts, reflecting broader trends of suburbanization of poverty (Sweeney 2016; Allard 2017) and the rise of Atlanta as a 'new' destination for Latinxs and other foreign-born immigrants (Kochhar et al. 2005; Odem 2008). In particular, Sandy Springs saw a growing influx of working-poor Latinx and Black residents, who were drawn to the area by the demand for cheap labour in the local service economy and by the availability of affordable apartment complexes accessible via public transportation.

As a result of these shifts and of the parallel decline of the white population (largely due to white flight to outer suburbs), Sandy Springs demographics have become significantly more diverse. Based on the last census, 58 per cent of the residents are white, non-Hispanic, while 19 per cent identify as Black, 12 per cent as Latinx, 7 per cent as Asian and 4 per cent with two or more races (US Census Bureau n.d.). Poverty rates, at 11 per cent according to the most recent data, have also grown exponentially in the 2010s, spurred by a widening gap in income and homeownership between white-headed households and Black- and Latinx-headed ones (City of Sandy Springs 2020 and 2017: 37).

These contrasts also shaped the sensorial experience of conducting fieldwork in Sandy Springs, such as when, during my daily rides across neighbourhoods lined with plantation-style houses and country clubs, I would turn the corner and suddenly reach one of the segregated, underfunded public schools attended by Latinx children, or the parking lot of CAN's food bank, crowded with Black and brown families, seniors and refugees carrying their heavy bags and shopping carts to the nearest bus station. In the early stages of my research, white upper-middle-class female participants would often take me on similar rides through low-income neighbourhoods so that I could 'see' the challenges that Sandy Springs faced with regard to housing, schools and social services. These women felt entrusted with raising awareness about these issues and used the emotions elicited by witnessing the spectacle of a 'ruined built environment', as a 'medium for socializing citizens into the attention necessary to develop new stances on poverty' (Fennell 2015: 211–12).

Many saw these experiences as a call for action. This was the case for Karen, local nonprofit leader and long-time community volunteer. Looking out from her car window as we were driving through one of Sandy Springs' 'problem' neighbourhoods, she reflected: 'As the city grows, and the school system and the community grow, it's becoming a real challenge for the city to become *one* city. You know, to deal with the diversity of the needs and the wants and the lifestyles. We have to merge the needs of those *two* communities and make them into equal pieces of [pause] citizenship.'[7] Because of its diversifying population, Sandy Springs no longer approximated suburban ideals of social and racial homogeneity. To tackle the polarizing effects of these transformations, Karen argued, Sandy Springs would not only have to create new social programmes, but would also have to *redefine the moral grammars of belonging* underlying its cityhood project.

Nonprofit organizations – with their armies of caring, resourceful volunteers – played a crucial role in this process.

From Private City to 'Caring' Community

Throughout the last two decades, as the suburbanization of poverty and the growth of immigrant residents settling outside of the urban core proceeded rapidly, in parallel with the rollback and privatization of the US welfare state, churches and community-based organizations in metropolitan Atlanta began offering services and assistance to needy residents. In the 1980s, eight Christian congregations in Sandy Springs joined forces to create a centralized organization, the Compassionate Action Network, offering assistance to disadvantaged families. Diversification trends continued in the following decades, leading various Catholic and Protestant churches to expand their community outreach efforts, asking Latinx ministers and activists from nearby communities to help create various initiatives for immigrant youth and families.

Most of the nonprofit activists with whom I talked in Sandy Springs were proud to be running, funding and recruiting volunteers for their organizations *locally*, rather than affiliating themselves with larger metropolitan organizations, and cited the city's uniquely supportive environment as the reason for this choice. Here is how Felipe, an Afro-Dominican pastor working with Latinx youth, described this environment: 'I could not find a better city to do what I am doing. I don't think any other city would respond like Sandy Springs responds to need-based organizations: people donating, people volunteering, they come around at any cost to help the underprivileged kids and families in the area.' Echoing Karen's statements about creating 'one' inclusive city, Felipe noted that this eagerness to help had become even more pronounced since the establishment of the municipality in 2005: 'When our organization started, there was Fulton County. Now *we* are the community, so *we* have to take care of our community, we have to take care of our own. That's a big difference.'

The efforts that Sandy Springs has recently put into channelling some of its resources to create a local social safety net may, at first, appear to be a departure from the anti-welfare stances that have historically characterized its cityhood movement. But the two projects actually rest on similar material and ideological grounds. For decades, Sandy Springs' cityhood movement and its emergent nonprofit sector fed on and supported each other through a shared pool of people and resources, harnessed by Eva Galambos – Sandy Springs' 'founding mother' and leader of the incorporation battle. Around Galambos had gathered a group of white upper-middle-class women who, beginning in the 1980s, took the lead in establishing new charities and nonprofits focusing on issues as various as zoning, social services, the arts and environmental preservation.

For decades, these women-led activist networks acted as quasi-governmental entities, filling the gap between Fulton County's absent administration and the needs of the local population. After Sandy Springs became a municipality (with Galambos as its mayor) in 2005, these networks did not lose their importance. As a matter of fact, it was the parallel increase in low-income and immigrant populations that fuelled their continued expansion. As welfare state retrenchment and widening inequalities resulted in a strained suburban safety net (Allard and Roth 2010), women identified a growing need for channelling local resources into the creation of programmes benefiting their disadvantaged neighbours.

While women-led charities and religious institutions have been crucial in supporting this emerging civic infrastructure of aid, over the past few decades, collaborations with the corporate sector have also multiplied, extending to Fortune 500 companies headquartered in Sandy Springs (Mercedes Benz, UPS, Comcast and Cox Enterprises, among others). Once lured to the city by huge tax breaks and controversial land deals (Ruch 2015), these companies have showed their commitment to the community by making gifts and donations to local nonprofits and supporting workforce training programmes. These 'cross-pollinations' between for-profit and nonprofit sectors were facilitated by the fact that many of the women who sat on the boards of organizations like CAN were also active members of the Chamber of Commerce, as well as of local chapters of the Rotary, Lions and Optimist Clubs – organizations often described to me as key sites for informal 'business deals'. Similar 'elite networking' practices (Holland et al. 2007: 173) connected nonprofit leaders with the moneyed members of local churches and synagogues, which acted as key supporters, and at times even as initiators, of programmes for immigrant youth and their families.

Sustained by this 'tight-knit private sector philanthropic economic growth machine' (Jones-Correa 2016: 164), social and immigrant service organizations have thus grown into key avenues for the cultivation of those very values that were foundational to Sandy Springs' cityhood project: volunteerism, entrepreneurialism and care for the 'local'. In their various roles as volunteers, activists and philanthropists, upper middle-class white women were seen as perfectly embodying these local standards of deservingness. Participants would often resort to politically conservative gendered narratives to express these views, stressing how women's 'natural nurturing capacities' (along with the privilege of being able to quit their jobs to devote themselves to full-time motherhood) made them perfect not only for childrearing but also for community work.

Despite being couched in highly moralized and feminized languages and framed as a byproduct of a comfortable suburban life, the labour performed by women volunteers and philanthropists formed a key element of Sandy Springs' political economy. Marxist feminist scholars have shown how the labour of social reproduction has always been integral to the dynamics of capitalist accumulation (di Leonardo 1987; Federici 2012). Rather than being incompatible with moral ideologies and social obligations, neoliberal capitalism in fact functions through the 'the creation of zones of nonremuneration seemingly untouched by the polluting logics of market exchange', such as charity or volunteer labour (Muehlebach 2012: 6).

In the United States, the ideology of volunteerism gained wider significance during the years of Clinton's presidency, precisely at a time marked by neoliberal economic restructuring and increasing restrictions to welfare programmes. With the passage of the

Personal Responsibility and Work Opportunity Reconciliation Act (PRWORA) in 1996, in fact, President Clinton terminated programmes that provided cash assistance to poor mothers with children, tying those benefits to work. The reform posited self-sufficiency, full employment and acculturation to market rules as solutions to the vexing problem of welfare 'dependency' (Fraser and Gordon 1994). While 'ending welfare as we know it', Clinton also made a strong call for volunteerism and community service as a 'corollary of responsible citizenship for *all* Americans' (Hyatt 2001: 203–4). Since then, the volunteer has emerged as the new model citizen, who operates outside of formal state structures, supplying the labour that is essential to their functioning, especially in an era of increasing budget cuts and stretched resources.

Sandy Springs has taken this reconfiguration of the relations between state and nonstate actors to the extreme, weaving neoliberal ideals of volunteerism into local framings of the 'deserving' poor. As one of my participants aptly noted, the city's approach to social issues, just like its formula of local government, is based upon the 'perfect three-legged stool': public needs, private partners and volunteers who can 'make anything happen'. Ever since its first day of operations, Sandy Springs has been partnering with private corporations to provide all of its municipal services with the exception of the Fire and Police Departments, schools, and human services—the latter still under Fulton County's purview.[8] This model of 'minimal' government, with its limited bureaucracy and social expenditure, *depends* on a large body of high-skilled, resourceful, mostly women volunteers to fulfil residents' needs. Karen perfectly summarized this reality when she explained to me, back in 2010, that 'the mayor and all the people who got elected are very, very, very fiscally conservative; they don't think that the government should do anything more than they absolutely have to. They don't want to pay for anything, and they think that the nonprofits should do a whole lot on their own'.

In the past two decades, philanthropists and nonprofit leaders like Karen have been crucially involved in reconfiguring the relations among the three pillars (or 'legs') of Sandy Springs' government model as new needs have arisen. As these women took up new roles inside organizations like CAN, the values they embodied came to constitute the unmarked standard in assessing clients' (un)deserving behaviours. As a matter of fact, nonprofit programmes worked to transform help-seekers into similar kinds of entrepreneurial citizen-volunteers.

Acts of Heroism on a Small Scale

The labour that upper middle-class white women put into raising awareness and resources to tackle suburban poverty was routinely recognized in civic and organizational venues, such as through special prizes and 'humanitarian awards' that celebrated Sandy Springs 'unique' spirit of volunteerism. Inside social service agencies like CAN, small details of the built environment served as reminders of the contribution made by 'kind' and 'compassionate' volunteers to the organization's workings. In one of the break rooms, a cork board above the refrigerator was filled with thankyou cards and letters from clients. In the middle of the board, someone had hung a quote from President Clinton: 'Volunteering is an act of heroism on a grand scale. And it matters profoundly. It does more than help people beat the odds; it changes the odds.'

These public celebrations of the qualities of volunteers need to be analysed in relation to the logics underlying CAN programmes. From the perspective of the organization, tying cash assistance to attendance at financial literacy classes, encouraging clients to enrol in career readiness workshops and implementing a 'food choice' model that made clients responsible for picking food items from the pantry's shelves were all steps that would help clients achieve long-term self-sufficiency. These programmes encouraged neoliberal modes of subject-making, seeking to transform clients into productive and responsible individuals able to care for themselves and their families (Rose 1993; Cruikshank 1999).

As someone who combined proper affect with autonomous action, who cared about oneself by caring for others (Muehlebach 2012: 8), the (white female) volunteer embodied precisely the values that the organization sought to cultivate in its clients.[9] Help-seekers were constantly exposed to these ideologies in the form of 'success stories' profiling the traits of the 'deserving' client: someone 'who doesn't just want to receive, but also to give'. This ideal paradigm of self-guided recovery from poverty was illustrated in the promotional video that the organization released in 2016, where a Black woman with a college degree in accounting explained how much CAN had helped her when, after being laid off from work, she faced dire financial need. She then recounted how, a few months after taking a mandatory accounting class, she went back to the organization and volunteered to *teach* that same class, while also helping clients fill out their tax returns.

This pressure to conform to the ideal of a 'model client' was often revealed when, over the course of a service interaction, clients would thank volunteers for their service. In this instance, many would add things like 'Sometime when I am no longer in need of assistance, I would like to come back and donate my time here' or 'You know, I used to volunteer at a food bank and charity downtown'. While these statements could be interpreted as a way to negotiate the stigma attached to receiving aid, volunteers often saw them in a different light. Some regarded these phrases as nothing more than a script that clients had learned to perform and would warn me: 'they all say that. Maybe some of them actually did volunteer, but you will hear these stories a lot'. Seeing such 'stories' as an indication that the clients in question knew all too well how to navigate the system, senior volunteers would instruct me to process their requests for help perfunctorily, deeming them less worthy of the organization's time and resources. Others resorted to narratives about former aid recipients who had joined the CAN volunteer and staff body to sketch a portrait of the 'deserving' client as she who had freed herself from charity's 'toxic' influence and was now able to contribute her labour to a privatized system of social service provision.

As anthropologist Susan Hyatt has noted, the celebration of volunteerism and self-governance as 'prerequisites for good citizenship in the postwelfare state' is particularly dangerous when applied indiscriminately to working-poor and middle-class communities as it 'promulgates a false egalitarianism that renders both the poor and the nonpoor commensurate in terms of their access to the material resources necessary to carry out effectively those tasks' (2001: 208). This 'false egalitarianism' obscures multiple social hierarchies with regard to class, race and gender. First, white volunteers and corporate donors in Sandy Springs enjoy the power to decide who should have access to community resources and social programmes, and on what terms. Second, neoliberal ideologies of volunteerism rest upon the 'masculinist romance of the free, unencumbered, self-fashioning individual' (Fraser 2016), ignoring the fact that women of all classes have to shoulder most of the labour of social reproduction. The latter includes not only family and household labour but also volunteer labour in neighbourhoods, schools and local communities.

And yet while the volunteer labour of Sandy Springs' upper-middle-class women was publicly recognized, the unremunerated or poorly remunerated work that *other women* (most of them of colour) performed in the low-wage service sector, as well as in local churches, family networks and resource-poor neighbourhoods, remained largely invisible. This fact is even more paradoxical when one considers that it was largely through outsourcing some of the tasks of social reproduction to low-wage service workers (e.g. domestic workers, restaurant workers and nannies) that middle-class and upper middle-class women were able to build a career and devote time to charity work (Collins and Mayer 2010: 111). When pressured to take up volunteering positions, working-class mothers in turn cannot rely on the same strategies of privilege to solve the conflict between paid labour and the labour of social reproduction. In the next section, we will see how Latina women countered these processes of invisibilization by appropriating dominant framings of deservingness.

Giving back, Rising above

Moral assessments of Latinx residents' (un)deserving behaviours were not limited to the CAN offices and food pantry. Inside Sandy Springs' public schools, a series of initiatives aimed to help and 'educate' Latinx families. Some of these initiatives – led by white parents and philanthropists – adopted a 'deficit framing' of Latinx parents (Valencia 1997), seeing them as *lacking* education, language skills, adequate housing and, most of all, knowledge on how to properly educate their children. While seemingly more 'welcoming' than other community responses to the arrival of Latinx populations (especially in nearby suburban towns that embraced harsh anti-immigrant policing practices), these attitudes reflect a subtler, often unacknowledged form of benevolent racism (Villenas 2001). These approaches in fact deny agency to Latinx parents and reproduce colonial relations of cultural and ideological domination through the 'normalization of white/Western middle-class cultural ways', including mothering practices and formal community volunteering, 'and the pathologizing of Latino cultures' (ibid.: 9).

All of the Latina mothers with whom I worked were extremely aware of the 'controlling images' (Collins 2000; Dyrness 2011) that schools, nonprofits and government officials projected onto them. In response, they insisted that they were not passive recipients of help, but rather contributed to schools' activities however they could: 'I try to overcome whatever obstacle', Guadalupe, a single mother of two children, told me. 'If there is an event at the school, or a trip – like if they're taking the kids to a museum – I donate money, and, if I can, I try to donate a little more.' This relationship of mutual help among peers could help strengthen community ties: 'That's what it is about; if the school helps you, or the teacher helps your daughter, you try to help them too. This way, we all help each other and create a little chain [*una cadenita*].'

If, on the one hand, Latina mothers sought to refashion their subjectivities according to middle-class standards of volunteerism and 'parental involvement', on the other hand, they never failed to acknowledge the constraints they faced when trying to conform with these normative ideals. Some narrated the experiences of racism and institutional discrimination that they had faced upon discovering that their children had been unfairly placed in remedial classes. Others reflected on barriers and power dynamics shaping their relationship with the schools, such as language or documentation status.[10] While 'naming and recognizing the … enormous risks and fiercely difficult circumstances' that they had to overcome in order to give their children a good education (Alexander 2018: 424), immigrant mothers also acknowledged how *other* Black and Latina women – nonprofit leaders, school employees, etc. – had worked to pave the way for their civic and political engagement.

Among them was Yolanda, a Venezuelan woman employed as a bilingual community liaison at Mill Creek elementary school, where she had helped establish the first parent–teacher association (PTA) entirely staffed by Latinx parents.[11] In spite of being located in a largely white, upper middle-class residential neighbourhood, Mill Creek had a student body comprising 98 per cent students of colour, the majority of them Latinxs, all of them economically disadvantaged. Drawing on her background as a Venezuelan immigrant, mother and resident of one of the neighbourhoods that fed into the school, Yolanda gained the trust of Mill Creek's parents, whom she helped learn the ropes of PTA management and eventually take ownership of the organization. She believed that it behoved school educators to remove some of the obstacles that prevented Latinx parents from participating in school activities, such as limited financial resources, erratic job schedules, language barriers and fears of being arrested or deported by Immigration and Custom Enforcement (ICE) on their way to the school. Rather than adopting a deficit framing like other school educators, Yolanda started by recognizing parents' own pedagogies and cultural resources so as to 'instil in them the certainty that there is no one with more influence to inspire and motivate their children than themselves' and that 'they were the ones who had to take charge, and make decisions [about the PTA]. They had the right to do it'.

Helena, a strong-willed Mexican woman in her thirties, was one of the first mothers to join the PTA back in 2014. She recounted her first meeting with Mill Creek's bilingual school employees as a turning point, which changed her perception of the school and of Latinx parents' place in it:

> At first I felt shy, because, you know, I am from Mexico and it's not the same school system as in Mexico. But when I first went to the school, I was surprised to find many people who spoke Spanish ... There was one school employee, Nancy, she was Puerto Rican; she helped us a lot. She gave me opportunities. Since then, every year I've tried to help, by going to parent workshops on how we can help our children with homework, or with reading ... There's a lot we can do as parents, but sometimes we Latinos don't know; it's hard to start.

At first, Helena was performing small tasks, like making photocopies and preparing games for the children, until one day 'the principal told me I had very good opinions, and asked me if I wanted to become part of the school governance council. That made me feel like an important person, and that the school took my opinions into account'. This experience filled her with a sense of pride and strength, which she strove to pass down to her children:

> After I first sat in a meeting of the school governance council, I felt like the people at the front office started treating me differently, and I also started looking at them in the eyes. Now I tell my children, 'you always have to keep your gaze high', because we are all equal and you are not a lesser human than others. Never look down, or else people will think that you are just wasting their time. Or worse, that you are not confident enough.

For Montserrat, the PTA treasurer, this self-confidence was shaken every time she looked at the total amount of donations that the association collected every year. 'That's nothing compared to the other school', she observed, referring to the school that Latinx children used to attend before Mill Creek was built and that is now 77 per cent white. 'The parents there are rich, so they can donate twice or three times as much as we do. And they write checks; they don't have to pay in cash like us.' While admitting feelings of inadequacy, Montserrat traced them to deeper forms of exclusion: 'Mill Creek was built to remove Latinos from the other public schools in the city', she told me, alluding to the controversial redistricting decision that had led to the construction of the school back in 2008. 'I know that they built a nice, new building for us, but it's still racism. It was like a rejection for Latino families; we felt rejected.'

Having endured multiple forms of discrimination, Latinx parents were proud to see their efforts finally recognized by administrators –

including a special prize from the national PTA organization. Yet they remained hesitant at the prospect of taking on too many responsibilities with regard to the school's management. Helena and Montserrat believed in the importance of 'giving', but thought that this labour would be best spent 'helping and educating their own Latinx community'. They were determined to use the skills and resources they had derived from this experience to tackle larger structural issues, such as affordable housing and anti-immigrant policing. The two women, just like school employee Yolanda, thus redrew the boundaries of Sandy Springs' 'caring' community, decentring middle-class ideals of parental involvement. Instead, they drew attention to the 'motherwork' that Latina women performed through their waged employment and volunteer engagements, to the benefit of their own and other Latinx children and community members (Collins 1994; Caballero et al. 2019). This "motherwork" served as the basis for asserting their moral worthiness and staking membership claims to the local community (Lanari 2022).

Latinxs Negotiating Citizenship and Deservingness in Polarizing Times

As Streinzer and Tošić suggest in the Introduction to this volume, deservingness framings are always relational, contingent and context-specific. We must therefore see Latina mothers' portrayals of themselves as competent parents, engaged citizens and caring volunteers as embedded within a broader historical and political context that shaped the terms of their visibility in local public discourse.

While framings of the 'good' immigrant and 'model minority' stereotypes pitting minority groups against each other have long characterized US immigration discourse (e.g. di Leonardo 1994; Kim 1999; Coutin 2003; Fernandes 2019), in the past decade, media and policy discourse have become increasingly dominated by a 'dichotomous framing that cast migrants', especially Latinxs, 'as either sinners or saints' (Dingeman-Cerda et al. 2016: 63; see also Patler and Gonzales 2015). Under Obama's presidency, undocumented immigrant youth were 'placed front and centre of progressive efforts to bring about comprehensive immigration reform at the federal and state levels', while deportations and criminalization of noncitizens increased both at the national and state levels (Dingeman-Cerda et al. 2016: 70). Debates surrounding the Affordable Care Act, passed by President

Obama in 2010, also triggered national anxieties about the possibility for undocumented migrants to access public healthcare ('Opinion: Immigrants' 2009). These distinctions between 'good' and 'bad' migrants, citizens and noncitizens were exacerbated under Trump, who routinely used nativist discourses to support restrictive immigration policies such as border walls and travel bans.

As the 2016 presidential campaign (and my own fieldwork) progressed, the local reverberations of these national discourses became increasingly palpable. I thus observed Latinx participants increasingly caught between two poles when negotiating the terms of their inclusion in the Sandy Springs community – having to contain the negative media exposure created by Trump's rhetoric, while proving to be 'needy' and worthy recipients of aid. In a situation where federal and state governments were seen as absent or, worse, as perpetrators of 'legal violence' (Menjívar and Abrego 2012) and enforcers of 'deportation regimes' (de Genova and Peutz 2010), the city – with its privatized infrastructure – became a key site to forge claims towards civic and political inclusion (Isin 2000; Lanari 2022; Varsanyi 2006).

Thus, by taking charge and growing the school's PTA, undocumented Latinx parents showed that they were as invested in the city of Sandy Springs as white homeowners, cultivating similar values: volunteerism, parental involvement, hard work, education and neighbourhood safety. They also framed their labour as critical to maintaining white middle-class standards of suburban living: as Yolanda, speaking to an imaginary audience of white homeowners, once told me, 'this is your workforce, you know, the people who clean your million-dollar houses, who take care of your children, who mow your lawns, who work at all the nice restaurants you want to have'.

For over thirty years, white homeowners had claimed to be fighting to protect these values and to create a separate municipality so that they could enjoy the level of services and 'quality of life' that they felt they 'deserved' (Committee for Sandy Springs n.d.b). Unsettling these extractive and exclusionary logics, immigrants are now claiming that they, too, are entitled to protect their neighbourhoods from gentrification and unwanted development (Lanari 2019a), and that they do not simply *need*, but rather *deserve* good schools and services, especially in light of the multiple forms of legal exclusion and economic dispossession that they have endured. In so doing, women like Helena and Montserrat also challenge affective dispositions of shame, shyness and 'humbleness' projected onto them by their 'benevolent' white neighbours.

Conclusion

In the past two decades, Sandy Springs has engaged in the 'social fantasy' (Wilson 2014) of creating a community whose extreme racial and socioeconomic divides could be bridged thanks to the heroic actions of (white) women philanthropists and volunteers. I have argued that the strong emphasis placed on charitable giving must be seen as part of the city's own social contract – a necessary complement to the scaling-back and privatization of government services that it has so eagerly embraced. In this context, building a social safety net almost becomes an 'affective choice' and even an opportunity for profit, rather than a right to be guaranteed through public policy and juridical protections (Adams 2013: 11).

Therefore, private sector-driven initiatives to help disadvantaged residents ultimately reinforce the racial and economic hierarchies that underlie Sandy Springs' cityhood project. Much like at the time of incorporation, today white homeowners and corporate donors are granted the power to decide how to redistribute the community's surplus resources, thereby defining the moral and behavioural traits that make poor residents of colour 'deserving' of such aid. Moreover, as Sandy Springs' 'philanthrocapitalist' economy continues to grow (Wilson 2014), these privileged groups can resort to the moral grammars of volunteerism to 'fuel a reserve army of labor willing to work for low wages', or for no wages at all, only 'to avoid the "undeserving" designation' (Watkins-Hayes and Kovalsky 2016: 198).

Through their efforts to join the PTA, Latina mothers did not simply reproduce dominant standards of deservingness; they also unsettled middle-class-centric discourses about parental involvement to foreground their own and other women's 'motherwork', naming the obstacles and forms of discrimination that they had to overcome in order to perform these tasks. Mirroring widespread narratives that described Sandy Springs as a 'city created by volunteers' (Porter 2006: 42), Latina women saw *their own* attempts at caring for the local community as laying the foundations for making broader claims of cultural and political belonging to the city and its institutions. Insofar as they are shaped by private actors and partially feeding into classed, gendered and racialized notions of moral worth, these paths of civic inclusion cannot substitute for the legal and political citizenship rights granted by the state (Flores 2016). Nevertheless, by unearthing the tensions inherent in these narratives of deservingness, we can begin to render visible and repoliticize poverty, inequality and immigrant claim-making in white suburbia.

Acknowledgements

The author would like to thank her participants in Sandy Springs, as well as Micaela di Leonardo, Nazlı Özkan, Elizabeth Derderian and Vanessa Watters, who read and commented on earlier versions of this chapter. Thank you to Jelena Tošić and Andreas Streinzer for their guidance and feedback on this chapter. The research was supported by the Wenner-Gren Foundation Dissertation Fieldwork Grant, the National Science Foundation Doctoral Dissertation Research Improvement Grant N. 1528569 and the Graduate School at Northwestern University.

Elisa Lanari is a cultural anthropologist and research fellow at Max Planck Institute for the Study of Religious and Ethnic Diversity in Göttingen, where she has undertaken a research project focusing on migration and 'superdiversity' in small northern Italian towns. She is also preparing her first book manuscript, which combines history and ethnography to explore the capitalist racial projects and emerging political possibilities of Atlanta's diversifying suburbs.

Notes

1. This chapter is based on a total of eighteen months of ethnographic research carried out between 2010 and 2016, but more intensively between 2015 and 2016. Research methods included: participant observation, semi-structured interviews, archival research, media and document analysis, and volunteering experiences with local nonprofit organizations. Throughout the chapter, I use pseudonyms to ensure participants' confidentiality.
2. In the United States, voting districts, states or jurisdictions are designated as 'majority-minority' when less than 50 per cent of its total population identifies as white, non-Hispanic. Municipal incorporation is the process through which the majority of residents of a formerly 'unincorporated' area ask the Georgia General Assembly to legally recognize the area as an autonomous municipality, provided with its own charter and local government.
3. I hereby adopt the gender-inclusive, nonbinary term 'Latinx' when referring more broadly to the experiences of US Latino/a populations. In some instances, I use the term 'Latina' to reflect my interlocutors' own self-identification and recognize the gendered nature of their experiences.
4. The ideologies of self-sufficiency and 'work attachment', which became widespread in anti-poverty policy and discourse in the 1990s, can be seen as the last iteration in a long series of victim-blaming explana-

tions that see poverty as rooted in the cultural and moral behaviours of low-income (especially Black) families. For an analysis of how these explanatory frameworks have historically been deployed to draw distinctions between deserving and undeserving poor, see Watkins-Hayes and Kovalsky (2016).
5. Following other scholars (de Genova and Ramos-Zayas 2003; Browne and Odem 2012), I see the racialization of Latinx in the United States as fundamentally related to histories of colonialism and imperialism in the Americas, current immigration-control policies, the changing structures of the local and global markets, and the stratification of labour.
6. Sandy Springs' cityhood movement took shape between the 1970s and 1990s, when homeowners grew increasingly frustrated with Fulton County's majority-Black, Atlanta-based administration, demanding more control over zoning and real estate development. In addition, local residents vehemently opposed the county's tax policy, claiming that they were carrying a disproportionate fiscal burden when it came to financing services such as welfare, public transit, hospitals and facilities in the denser, majority-Black areas of South Fulton (Galambos 2011: 92, 143; Connor 2015a). For many, the desire to 'stop subsidizing the city of Atlanta' was a key reason to support the movement for municipal incorporation (Committee for Sandy Springs n.d.a). For an analysis of the racist and secessionist implications of the cityhood movement, see Connor 2015b; Rosen 2017; Lanari 2019b.
7. I hereby follow anthropologists and other scholars who conceive of citizenship not only as a formal institution defining individual rights and duties, but also as 'a modality of belonging that must be achieved through everyday practice' and that can be contingent, depending on public recognition (Isin and Nielsen 2008; Muehlebach 2012: 18; Lazar 2013). This is especially evident in the case of migrants, who, even when they do not have legal rights, can still be ascribed membership in a political community and 'made' into certain kinds of gendered, classed and racialized subjects (Ong 1996). In my analyses of citizenship and city-making in Sandy Springs (Lanari 2022), I attend in particular to the role of nonstate actors such as corporations, NGOs and civil society organizations in mediating relations between states and subjects (Gordon and Stack 2007). I document how notions of national citizenship often 'become entangled with other forms of political belonging, at different levels including the urban and the transnational' (Koning et al. 2016: 123).
8. In addition to supporting private sector-driven solutions to social issues, 34 per cent of families in Sandy Springs opt to send their children to private schools – more than twice the regional percentage (City of Sandy Springs 2017: 37).
9. Elsewhere in my work (Lanari 2019b), I demonstrate how CAN directors and staff members did not seamlessly implement neoliberal poverty agendas. Rather, they sometimes reworked notions of 'self-sufficiency' into broader structural critiques of poverty and inequality.

10. Georgia has one of the highest percentages of unauthorized migrant population of all US states (Pew Research Center n.d.). In the last decade, the state has passed a series of measures limiting the rights of undocumented immigrants with regard to housing, transportation, healthcare and access to higher education. Most notably, Georgia responded to the Department of Homeland Security's 287(g) Secure Communities Program by passing state laws that invested local police with the power to demand immigration 'papers' during routine policing, detain and report individuals to ICE. Suburban counties around Atlanta were among the first to cooperate with ICE, leading to increasing numbers of arrests, detentions and deportations of undocumented migrants, including many with noncriminal backgrounds (Shahshahani 2009). In this context, living as an undocumented person means grappling with a condition of 'forced immobilization' (Stuesse and Coleman 2014) that prevents one from carrying out even the simplest daily tasks, such as attending a school event.
11. In the United States, most elementary schools have a parent–teacher organization (affiliated with state and national PTAs), whose goal is to foster family engagement and partnerships between the school and the local community.

References

Adams, Vincanne. 2013. *Markets of Sorrow, Labors of Faith: New Orleans in the Wake of Katrina*. Durham, NC: Duke University Press.

Alexander, Rebecca. 2018. 'A mamá no la vas a llevar en la maleta: Undocumented Mothers Crossing and Contesting Borders for Their Children's Education', *Anthropology & Education Quarterly* 49: 413–27.

Allard, Scott. 2009. *Out of Reach: Place, Poverty, and the New American Welfare State*. New Haven: Yale University Press.

———. 2017. *Places in Need: The Changing Geography of Poverty*. New York: Russell Sage Foundation.

Allard, Scott, and Benjamin Roth. 2010. *Strained Suburbs: The Social Service Challenges of Rising Suburban Poverty*. Washington DC: Brookings Institution.

Bonilla-Silva, Eduardo. 2009. *Racism without Racists: Color-Blind Racism and the Persistence of Racial Inequality in America*, 3rd edn. Lanham, MD: Rowman & Littlefield.

Brenner, Neil. 2000. 'The Urban Question: Reflections on Henri Lefebvre, Urban Theory and the Politics of Scale', *International Journal of Urban and Regional Research* 24: 361–78.

Browne, Irene, and Mary Odem. 2012. '"Juan Crow" in the Nuevo South? Racialization of Guatemalan and Dominican Immigrants in the Atlanta Metro Area', *Du Bois Review* 9: 321–37.

Caballero, Cecilia, et al. (ed.). 2019. *The Chicana Motherwork Anthology*. Tucson: University of Arizona Press.

City of Sandy Springs. 2017. 'Comprehensive Plan'. Retrieved 11 March 2022 from https://www.sandyspringsga.gov/comprehensive-plan
———. 2020. 'Analysis of Impediments to Fair Housing 2020'. Retrieved 21 March 2022 from https://www.sandyspringsga.gov/community-development-block-grant
Collins, Jane L., and Victoria Mayer. 2010. *Both Hands Tied: Welfare Reform and the Race to the Bottom in the Low-Wage Labor Market*. Chicago: University of Chicago Press.
Collins, Patricia Hill. 1994. 'Shifting the Center: Race, Class and Feminist Theorizing about Motherhood', in Evelyn Nakano Glenn, Grace Chang and Linda Rennie Forcey (eds), *Mothering. Ideology, Experience and Agency*. New York: Routledge, pp. 371–89.
———.2000. 'Mammies, Matriarchs, and Other Controlling Images', in Patricia Hill Collins (ed.), *Black Feminist Thought: Knowledge, Consciousness, and the Politics of Empowerment*. New York: Routledge, pp. 69–96.
Committee for Sandy Springs. n.d.a. *Why Do the People of Sandy Springs Want Their Own Government?* [pamphlet]. Galambos Files, Russell Library. Athens, GA: University of Georgia.
———. n.d.b. *Survey of Sandy Springs Registered Voters. September 9–10, 1998. Open End Responses* [survey]. Galambos Files, Russell Library. Athens, GA: University of Georgia.
Connor, Michan Andrew. 2015a. 'Race, Republicans, and Real Estate: The 1991 Fulton County Tax Revolt', *Journal of Urban History* 44: 985–1006.
———. 2015b. 'Metropolitan Secession and the Space of Color-Blind Racism in Atlanta', *Journal of Urban Affairs* 37(4): 436–61.
Coutin, Susan Bibler. 2003. 'Suspension of Deportation Hearings and Measures of "Americanness"'. *Journal of Latin American Anthropology* 8: 58–94.
Cruikshank, Barbara. 1999. *The Will to Empower: Democratic Citizens and Other Subjects*. Ithaca, NY: Cornell University Press.
Davis, Julie Hirschfeld. 2018. 'Trump Calls Some Unauthorized Immigrants "Animals" in Rant', *New York Times*, 16 May. Retrieved 14 February 2022 from https://www.nytimes.com/2018/05/16/us/politics/trump-undocumented-immigrants-animals.html.
De Genova, Nicholas, and Ana Y. Ramos-Zayas. 2003. 'Latino Racial Formations in the United States: An Introduction', *Journal of Latin American Anthropology* 8: 2–16.
De Genova, Nicholas, and Nathalie Peutz (eds). 2010. *The Deportation Regime: Sovereignty, Space, and the Freedom of Movement*. Durham, DC: Duke University Press.
Di Leonardo, Micaela. 1987. 'The Female World of Cards and Holidays: Women, Families, and the Work of Kinship', *Signs* 12: 440.
———. 1994. 'White Ethnicities, Identity Politics, and Baby Bear's Chair', *Social Text* 41: 165–91.

Dingeman-Cerda, Katie, Edelina Muñoz Burciaga and Lisa M. Martinez. 2016. 'Neither Sinners nor Saints: Complicating the Discourse of Noncitizen Deservingness', *Association of Mexican American Educators Journal* 9(3): 62–73.
Dyrness, Andrea. 2011. *Mothers United: An Immigrant Struggle for Socially Just Education*. Minneapolis: University of Minnesota Press.
Federici, Silvia. 2012. *Revolution at Point Zero: Housework, Reproduction, and Feminist Struggle*. Oakland, CA: PM Press.
Fennell, Catherine. 2015. *Last Project Standing: Civics and Sympathy in Post-welfare Chicago*. Minneapolis: University of Minnesota Press.
Fernandes, Sujatha. 2019. 'The Right Kind of Immigrant: The Narrative of Deserving and Undeserving Immigrants', *BESE*. Retrieved 14 February 2022 from https://www.bese.com/the-right-kind-of-immigrant-the-narrative-of-deserving-and-undeserving-immigrants.
Flores, Andrea. 2015. 'Empowerment and Civic Surrogacy: Community Workers' Perceptions of Their Own and Their Latino/a Students' Civic Potential', *Anthropology & Education Quarterly* 46: 397–413.
———. 2016. 'Forms of Exclusion: Undocumented Students Navigating Financial Aid and Inclusion in the United States', *American Ethnologist* 43: 540–54.
Fraser, Nancy. 2016. 'Second-Wave Feminism and the "New Spirit of Capitalism"'. Retrieved 14 February 2022 from https://www.versobooks.com/blogs/2525-second-wave-feminism-and-the-new-spirit-of-capitalism-by-nancy-fraser.
Fraser, Nancy, and Linda Gordon. 1994. 'A Genealogy of Dependency: Tracing a Keyword of the US Welfare State', *Signs* 19: 309–36.
Galambos, Eva. 2011. *A Dream Come True: My Very Good Life*. Bloomington, IN: AuthorHouse.
Galvez, Alyshia. 2009. *Guadalupe in New York: Devotion and the Struggle for Citizenship Rights among Mexican Immigrants*. New York: New York University Press.
Goode, Judith, and Jeff Maskovsky (eds). 2001. *The New Poverty Studies: The Ethnography of Power, Politics and Impoverished People in the United States*. New York: New York University Press.
Gordon, Andrew, and Trevor Stack. 2007. 'Citizenship beyond the State: Thinking with Early Modern Citizenship in the Contemporary World', *Citizenship Studies* 11(2): 117–33.
Holland, Dorothy, et al. (eds). 2007. *Local Democracy under Siege: Activism, Public Interests, and Private Politics*. New York: New York University Press.
Hyatt, Susan. 2001. 'From Citizen to Volunteer: Neoliberal Governance and the Erasure of Poverty', in Judith Goode and Jeff Maskovsky (eds), *The New Poverty Studies: The Ethnography of Power, Politics, and Impoverished People in the United States*. New York: New York University Press, pp. 201–35.

Isin, Engin F. (ed.). 2000. *Democracy, Citizenship and the Global City*. London: Routledge.
Jones-Correa, Michael. 2016. '"The Kindness of Strangers": Ambivalent Reception in Charlotte, North Carolina', in John Mollenkopf and Manuel Pastor (eds), *Unsettled Americans: Metropolitan Context and Civic Leadership for Immigrant Integration*. Ithaca, NY: Cornell University Press, pp. 163–88.
Kim, Claire Jean. 1999. 'The Racial Triangulation of Asian Americans', *Politics & Society* 27: 103–36.
Kochhar, Rakesh, Roberto Suro and Sonya Tafoya. 2005. 'The New Latino South: The Context and Consequences of Rapid Population Growth', Pew Research Center. Retrieved 14 February 2022 from http://www.pewhispanic.org/2005/07/26/the-new-latino-south.
Koning, Anouk, Rivke Jaffe and Martijn Koster. 2015. 'Citizenship Agendas in and beyond the Nation-State: (En)Countering Framings of the Good Citizen', *Citizenship Studies* 19(2): 121–27.
Lanari, Elisa. 2022. "Speaking up, Rising above: Latina Lived Citizenship in the Metropolitan US South." *Citizenship Studies* 26 (1): 38–54.
———. 2019a. 'Envisioning a New City Center: Time, Displacement, and Atlanta's Suburban Futures', *City & Society* 31: 365–91.
———. 2019b. '"Peaceful Little Revolutions" in the New South: Race, Inequality, and City-Making in Suburban Atlanta', Northwestern University, ProQuest Dissertations Publishing.
Lazar, Sian. 2013. 'Introduction', in Sian Lazar (ed.), *The Anthropology of Citizenship: A Reader*. Malden, MA: Wiley-Blackwell, pp. 1–22.
Menjìvar, Cecilia, and Leslie J. Abrego. 2012. 'Legal Violence: Immigration Law and the Lives of Central American Immigrants', *American Journal of Sociology* 117: 1380–421.
Moreno, Carolina. 2015. '9 Outrageous Things Donald Trump Has Said about Latinos', *HuffPost*. Retrieved 14 February 2022 from https://www.huffpost.com/entry/9-outrageous-things-donald-trump-has-said-about-latinos_n_55e483a1e4b0c818f618904b.
Morgen, Sandra. 2001. 'The Agency of Welfare Workers: Negotiating Devolution, Privatization, and the Meaning of Self-Sufficiency', *American Anthropologist* 103: 747–61.
Morgen, Sandra, and Jeff Maskovsky. 2003. 'The Anthropology of Welfare "Reform": New Perspectives on US Urban Poverty in the Post-welfare Era', *Annual Review of Anthropology* 32: 315–38.
Muehlebach, Andrea. 2011. 'On Affective Labor in Post-Fordist Italy', *Cultural Anthropology* 26: 59–82.
———. 2012. *The Moral Neoliberal: Welfare and Citizenship in Italy*. Chicago: University of Chicago Press.
Odem, Mary. 2008. 'Unsettled in the Suburbs: Latino Immigration and Ethnic Diversity in Metro Atlanta', in Audrey Singer, Susan W.

Hardwick and Caroline Brettell (eds), *Twenty-First Century Gateways: Immigrant Incorporation in Suburban America*. Washington DC: Brookings Institution, pp. 105–36.

Ong, Aihwa. 1996. 'Cultural Citizenship as Subject-Making: Immigrants Negotiate Racial and Cultural Boundaries in the United States', *Current Anthropology* 37(5): 737–62.

'Opinion: Immigrants, Health Care and Lies'. 2009. *New York Times*, 10 September. Retrieved 14 February 2022 from https://www.nytimes.com/2009/09/11/opinion/11fri2.html.

Patler, Caitlin, and Roberto Gonzales. 2015. 'Framing Citizenship: Media Coverage of Anti-deportation Cases Led by Undocumented Immigrant Youth Organisations', *Journal of Ethnic and Migration Studies* 41: 1–22.

Pew Research Center. n.d. 'US Unauthorized Immigrant Population Estimates by State, 2016'. Retrieved 14 February 2022 from https://www.pewhispanic.org/interactives/u-s-unauthorized-immigrants-by-state.

Porter, Oliver. 2006. *Creating the New City of Sandy Springs: The 21st Century Paradigm: Private Industry*. Bloomington, IN: AuthorHouse.

Rose, Nikolas. 1993. 'Government, Authority and Expertise in Advanced Liberalism', *Economy and Society* 22: 283–99.

Rosen, Sam. 2017. 'Atlanta's Controversial "Cityhood" Movement', *The Atlantic*, 26 April. Retrieved 14 February 2022 from https://www.theatlantic.com/business/archive/2017/04/the-border-battles-of-atlanta/523884.

Ruch, John. 2015. 'Neighbors May Sue City over Approved Ashton Woods Housing Plan', *Reporter Newspapers*, 21 August. Retrieved 14 February 2022 from https://www.reporternewspapers.net/2015/08/21/neighbors-may-sue-city-over-approved-ashton-woods-housing-plan.

Schuller, Mark. 2012. *Killing with Kindness: Haiti, International Aid, and NGOs*. New Brunswick, NJ: Rutgers University Press.

Segal, David. 2012. 'A Georgia Town Takes the People's Business Private', *New York Times*, 23 June. Retrieved 14 February 2022 from http://www.nytimes.com/2012/06/24/business/a-georgia-town-takes-the-peoples-business-private.html.

Shahshahani, Azadeh. 2009. 'Terror and Isolation in Cobb: How Unchecked Police Power under 287(g) Has Torn Families Apart and Threatened Public Safety', American Civil Liberties Union, Atlanta. Retrieved 21 March 2022 from https://www.aclu.org/other/terror-and-isolation-cobb-how-unchecked-police-power-under-287g-has-torn-families-apart-and.

Stuesse, Angela, and Matthew Coleman. 2014. 'Automobility, Immobility, Altermobility: Surviving and Resisting the Intensification of Immigrant Policing', *City & Society* 26: 51–72.

Sweeney, Kate. 2016. 'Suburban Poverty: Atlanta's Hidden Epidemic', *90.1 FM WABE*. Retrieved 14 February 2022 from http://news.wabe.org/post/suburban-poverty-atlantas-hidden-epidemic.

US Census Bureau. n.d. 'QuickFacts: Sandy Springs City, Georgia.' Retrieved March 10 2022 from https://www.census.gov/quickfacts/fact/table/sandyspringscitygeorgia/LND110210.

Valencia, Richard R. (ed.). 1997. *The Evolution of Deficit Thinking: Educational Thought and Practice*. Abingdon: RoutledgeFalmer.

Varsanyi, Monica W. 2006. 'Interrogating "Urban Citizenship" vis-à-vis Undocumented Migration', *Citizenship Studies* 10: 229–49.

Villenas, Sofia. 2001. 'Latina Mothers and Small-Town Racisms: Creating Narratives of Dignity and Moral Education in North Carolina', *Anthropology & Education Quarterly* 32: 3–28.

Watkins-Hayes, Celeste. 2009a. 'Race-ing the Bootstrap Climb: Black and Latino Bureaucrats in Post-reform Welfare Offices', *Social Problems* 56(2): 285–310.

———. 2009b. *The New Welfare Bureaucrats: Entanglements of Race, Class, and Policy Reform*. Chicago: University Of Chicago Press.

Watkins-Hayes, Celeste, and Elyse Kovalsky. 2016. 'The Discourse of Deservingness', in David Brady and Linda M. Burton (eds), *The Oxford Handbook of the Social Science of Poverty*. New York: Oxford University Press, pp. 193–220.

Willen, Sarah, and Jennifer Cook. 2016. 'Health-Related Deservingness', in Felicity Thomas (ed.), *Handbook of Migration and Health*. Cheltenham: Edward Elgar, pp. 95–118.

Wilson, Japhy. 2014. 'Fantasy Machine: Philanthrocapitalism as an Ideological Formation', *Third World Quarterly* 35: 1144–61.

Part III

The (Un)Deserving Migrant/Refugee

9

Ambivalences of (Un)Deservingness
Tracing Vulnerability in the EU Border Regime

Sabine Strasser

During the long summer of migration in 2015, when Europe proclaimed a 'refugee crisis', the demarcation between deserving and undeserving refugees became prevalent in the attempts by the European Union (EU) to take control of border crossings into Europe. While EU Member States engaged in extensive and controversial debates about the (re)distribution of refugees between EU countries, negotiations between the EU and Turkey intensified the management of external border control and led to the release of the EU-Turkey Statement on 18 March 2016. The Deal's mastermind, Gerald Knaus, the Austrian policy advisor and head of the think tank European Stability Initiative (ESI), proposed this enhanced control of the EU's external borders to reduce irregular migration while simultaneously protecting the EU's high moral standards.[1] This strategy became paradigmatic of the externalization of the EU Mediterranean border, which was established to prevent migrants from drowning during passages across the Aegean Sea, but also to deter them from entering the EU irregularly (Rygiel et al. 2016: 317). Since the agreement depends on Turkish collaboration in rigorous border control, the EU had to offer strong incentives to an increasingly authoritarian Turkish government. A closely monitored €6 billion programme, the EU Facility for Refugees in Turkey, was established to provide humanitarian assistance and education for refugees alongside equipment for migration control. In exchange,

Turkey was required to prevent refugees from crossing to Europe and to accept the re-admission of asylum seekers identified as not in need of international protection by the Greek asylum administration. Furthermore, 'resettlement' of one Syrian refugee from Turkey to Europe for each Syrian sent back from Greece was agreed upon and a Humanitarian Admission Plan (HAP) was activated to establish resettlement as a key tool of the new border regime.[2] The acceleration of Turkey's EU accession negotiations, including visa liberalization for Turkish citizens – objectives that were also initially set out in the Statement – were never put into practice.

Although the number of people informally crossing to Greece dropped from over one million in 2015 and 2016 to approximately 40,000 in 2018, the agreement was a failure, even according to Knaus.[3] Thousands of refugees got stuck on the Greek islands in unbearable conditions and the number of people crossing irregularly has been increasing again since 2019, stopped only temporarily by the COVID-19 pandemic in March 2020.[4] Knaus has seen the slow decision-making process in asylum procedures and the lack of support for the Greek administration from the EU as the main problems. Because the Turkish government approved the re-admission of legally rejected and thus 'nondeserving' asylum seekers from the EU in addition to offering temporary accommodation to some four million refugees, Knaus does not consider the deal a moral problem or an indication of a lack of EU responsibility. Hence, as long as the EU Member States develop such resettlement schemes and thus provide safe passage and redistribution, Knaus sees no reason to call the suggested agreement itself into question. Instead, he identifies a severe political crisis that can only be solved by an accelerated administration, able to send rejected asylum seekers from the Greek islands to Turkey quickly, and by the redistribution of people deserving international protection throughout the EU Member States.[5] Yet, understanding deservingness as compliance with the EU border regime's legal and moral principles means that only countries that accept re-admission agreements, such as Turkey, and only travellers who did not enter the EU irregularly are seen as eligible for EU support.[6]

Despite this rise in the politics of deservingness, the EU Member States have in fact been rather unsuccessful in two respects. First, they have failed to support Greece, Malta and Italy cope with the high number of arrivals. Second, they have not implemented the Commission's suggestion for the EU Resettlement Framework, which aims at creating safe and legal pathways at least for the most vulnerable people.[7] Instead of the envisioned distribution, years after the refugee crisis proclaimed in 2015, the EU Commission is still operating with only small voluntary pledges from some Member States, but only the most vulnerable travellers are eligible for resettlement.[8]

Vulnerability is decisive for refugees' in determining refugees' (un)deservingness and thus whether they will be rescued and resettled or left behind for re-admission, temporary protection or even deportation. Until recently, vulnerability, now identified as a key term in the distribution of refugee resettlement, has attracted surprisingly little attention in the theoretical debates on humanitarianism and sexual democracy. Yet, in my reading of the ethnographic material, there is a gendered, sexualized and neo-orientalizing potential in 'vulnerability', which is still widely unchallenged as a yardstick of resettlement and thus as a moralized assessment tool of (un)deservingness.

In my analysis of this politics of (un)deservingness, I address the entanglement of the EU–Turkey border regime and its voluntary resettlement scheme for the most vulnerable (and thus most deserving), and explore how EU Member States select refugees according to a vaguely defined notion of vulnerability within the EU's Resettlement Framework.[9] I argue that this initiative for resettlement is crucial in order to first identify and then separate 'vulnerable' and 'deserving' from 'undeserving' refugees. Further, I employ Jasbir Puar's (2007) concept of homonationalism to carve out racialized and sexualized variations of claims to European supremacy. Whenever conservative powers line up with LGBTIQ+ and gender equality claims in order to justify their racist positions against 'migrants' and 'Muslims', they discursively present the 'Other' as homophobic and misogynous in contrast to European countries and themselves, who are considered as gay-friendly and gender egalitarian. Similarly, overemphasizing gender and representing minoritized men mainly as perpetrators and 'women of the Other' as victims of their 'culture' are versions of this neo-orientalist discourse (Ticktin 2011; Abu-Lughod 2013; Strasser 2014) and essential to the idea of vulnerability of travellers on their way to Europe. Needless to say, these same nationalist forces often simultaneously contribute to sexual and gender-based discrimination in the same social and political environment.

Drawing on my long-term ethnographic field experience in Turkey and several fieldtrips exploring the EU–Turkey as well as Syrian borderlands, I will zoom in on the journey of two friends and show how their future was shaped by the EU-Turkey Statement and its politics of (un)deservingness. I will examine if resettlement based on vulnerability can ensure 'safe and legal alternatives' (UNHCR

2019) for those in need of international protection and how far the EU Resettlement Framework reaffirms or can avoid the epistemic violence of neo-orientalism premised on gender inequality and a lack of sexual democracy among refugees, particularly Muslims. My aim is to contribute to the current debate on (un)deservingness in the fields of humanitarianism and border studies (as suggested by Streinzer and Tošić in the Introduction to this volume) with a twofold analysis: first, of how the distribution of asylum rights is moralized and framed within the discourse of gender equality and sexual democracy in Europe; and, second, of how the humanitarian language in the border regime, expressed through the politics of deservingness in the selection of vulnerable migrants along lines of gender and sexuality, curtails individual asylum rights and transforms them into ambiguous compassion for the most 'vulnerable'/'deserving'.

Flight to Turkey: Deserving to Be a Registered Refugee

I met Isaak and Ghalip in March 2016 at the spring party organized by a local humanitarian association in Bodrum.[10] I got to know them there as Jake and Connor, and due to their language skills and the diversity of the guests, I actually believed that they were Canadians who – just like two young Germans and me – volunteered in that same association. Syrian refugees had not been allowed to stay and register in Bodrum (situated in the Turkish Aegean province of Muğla) since the autumn of 2015, when the flow of refugees was at its peak and preparations for the EU-Turkey Statement had begun. The Bodrum Peninsula was a hotspot during the summer of 2015 and sadly gained fame in the global refugee discourse due to Alan Kurdi, the toddler who was washed ashore in September 2015 (Perl and Strasser 2018). This event and the protection of the tourism industries were considered as the main causes for the regional governor's decision to prohibit registration in Bodrum in 2015, which aimed at clearing the peninsula of refugees to stop departures from its shores in spring 2016. Only 10 km away from the island of Kos, Bodrum saw thousands of exhausted people passing through, who would hide for a day or two before moving on to Europe in the grey of dawn. Some locals organized themselves into humanitarian associations and provided breakfast, sanitary products and healthcare; some brought children's toys; others sold equipment such as life jackets and water bottles to the travellers; and some even joined the smugglers.

However, the majority watched, baffled and compassionate, as every day people headed off towards Europe in rubber boats.

Yet, almost all of the travellers had left when I arrived in Bodrum at the beginning of March 2016. I soon learned that my new friends, Jake and Connor, were in fact Syrian citizens, called Isaak and Ghalip, who had left their hometown together and got stuck in Turkey after ten failed attempts to cross to one of the Greek islands. Luckily, they had arrived in Turkey by plane before all Syrians had to apply for visas for flights from January 2016 onwards and the Syrian–Turkish border was sealed off by a wall. They had planned to enter the EU and then move on to Canada. However, with the upcoming deal between the EU and Turkey, they stopped trying to cross to Greece in December 2015, when the gendarmerie was no longer turning a blind eye to refugees and the area had been militarized by NATO as well as the Greek and Turkish coastguards.

'Everything happens for a reason!', Isaak explained with a smile, when he and Ghalip showed me around their house. After a couple of weeks in a rather cheap seaside hotel, they ran out of money and one of their new British friends invited them to stay in their fancy but remote summerhouse, which was empty during the winter months. Standing on the terrace, with a view over the Aegean coastline, they pointed out landmarks of meeting places for their failed attempts at crossing to Greece, overwriting the beautiful landscape with their uncanny memories. Left behind in Turkey with no money or jobs during the quiet winter of a summer resort, they looked for work to cover their daily needs. They tried to avoid public transport, particularly at night, because they were not registered as refugees and there were unsettling rumours that Turkey was not only sealing its border with Syria but was also sending back nonregistered Syrian refugees to southeastern Turkey or even to Syria. Soon after our visit to the house, people from the local humanitarian association found small jobs for Isaak and Ghalip, such as gardening, babysitting, cleaning and interpreting for the association from Arabic to English during the many visits by international humanitarian missions to the small number of stranded Syrians. These diverse teams comprising Doctors without Borders and MediCare International, or organizations like the United Nations High Commissioner for Refugees, regularly visited Bodrum and, like myself, tried to assess the impact of the 'Deal' in the area. None of these representatives actually believed this deal had been a success and all expected a new wave of refugees to arrive soon. However, Isaak and Ghalip were determined not to try again and to stay in Bodrum and find alternatives to moving on. Again, people from the local association, who described themselves as having been at the frontline of rescuing refugees during the summer of 2015 (many of them citizens of different European countries or recently naturalized), recruited wealthy Turkish friends who finally managed to organize official registration for Isaak and Ghalip in the province of Muğla. This registration provided temporary protection according to the recently adopted Turkish Law on Foreigners and International Protection (LFIP) including the temporary protection regime, which had been in effect since 2014. This ambiguous legal status entitled Syrians (in contrast to all other non-European nationalities) to access healthcare, education, the labour market, restricted mobility within the country, and, only for a select few, a shortcut to Turkish citizenship.[11]

When I returned a year later, in June 2017, both Isaak and Ghalip had found jobs that, though they worked irregularly, allowed them to earn a modest income and to think about their future. The experience of ambiguity in the face of a permanent temporariness (Biner 2016) due to Turkish legislation was a source of anxiety for the young men, as was the everyday interrelation of mobility and stuckedness in the EU–Turkey borderland that allows some, like me, to move about freely and visit the Greek islands on a daytrip while forcing others to stay put (Tošić and Lems 2019). Despite their rather privileged situation on the peninsula and their middle-class and above-average educational background it became quite obvious that Isaak and Ghalip would have access neither to a proper job nor to a university education in this holiday resort. They were successful in getting registered and thus categorized as refugees with limited protection in Turkey but felt stuck in Bodrum since mobility had become existential in their lives (Hage 2005). How Isaak and Ghalip, who had been close long-term friends and had travelled together for almost two years, departed from Bodrum in different directions sheds light on how EU (ir)responsibility in its border regime shapes people's lives and is legitimized by the politics of (un)deservingness.

Framing Deservingness: Figures of the Crisis

'On the most general level, deservingness is a moral assessment of processes of distribution' (Streinzer and Tošić, Introduction to this volume). Hence, applying deservingness as an analytical lens enables observers to explore how these processes of distribution provide access to social goods, countries or health unequally. Recent contributions to the debate on deservingness in the field of humanitarianism that deals with migration and border management have introduced such oxymorons as compassionate repression (Fassin 2005), armed love (Ticktin 2011), repressive autonomy (Strasser 2014) or the humanitarian border (Walters 2011; Topak 2014; Ticktin 2016) to bring together humanitarianism and surveillance or care and control (Dijstelbloem and van der Veer 2021). These concepts thus allow anthropologists to deal with the inevitable contradictions and complexities of deservingness in the field of moral anthropology. Yet, humanitarianism not only intersects with materiality and bureaucracies of migration control and border management: it also produces, transforms and represents hierarchical relations, and thus regulates access to, for example, goods, healthcare or legal status based on the moral language of the politics of (un)deservingness.

Numerous anthropological studies on the EU border regime (e.g. Anderson 2014; Içduygu and Aksel 2014; Hage 2016; Soykan 2016; Hess et al. 2017; de Genova 2017; Şimşek 2017), on moralities, affects and the deadly effects of EU borders (e.g. Albahari 2016; Stierl 2017; Perl 2019) and the vivid debate on the entanglement of care and control at humanitarian borders (Walters 2011; Ticktin 2016; Dijstelbloem and van der Veer 2021) discuss rights and restrictions as questions of EU (ir-)responsibility (Perl and Strasser 2018). Holmes and Castañeda (2016) pointed out how the proclaimed 'refugee crisis' in Germany contributed to the sorting of 'undeserving trespassers' from those deserving rights and access to goods. Later, when hegemonic public opinion and politics shifted away from compassion, the distinction between deserving, 'real' refugees and undeserving migrants morally prepared the ground for and organized exclusion and deportation. Until the early 2000s, surprisingly little attention was paid to gender and sexuality in migration studies (the core elements of the public and political discourse on immigration in the Global North). Since then, gendered performance and credibility have been examined (e.g. Luibhéid 2008; McKinnon 2009) and the focus on the premise of heteronormativity in migration research has been dismantled (Akin 2017). With these approaches, the complexity of gender and sexualities at the intersection with humanitarianism, border management and ways of politics of deservingness have gained significance (Koçak 2020).

The shift in public perception and the lack of scholarly insight into gendered and racialized discourses during the so-called refugee crises were highlighted by Johanna Neuhauser, Sabine Hess and Helen Schwenken (2016) as the simultaneous underexposure and overexposure of gender.¹² They explored gendered and racialized knowledge production to analyse the astonishing interest in the protection of women of the 'Other' and in gender equality in the course of the proclaimed crisis. However, the analysis of this strange interest in protecting, saving or rescuing women from the 'Other' is not new because it represents a variation of Gayatri C. Spivak's argument in her seminal essay 'Can the Subaltern Speak?' (1988), in which she coined the expression 'white men saving brown women from brown men' for the postcolonial Indian context. Abu-Lughod (2013) reiterates this problem as a question for the post-9/11 context when she asks: 'Do Muslim women need saving?' In the context of the EU refugee crisis, gendered figures were carved out and juxtaposed as perpetrators and victims, pure and contaminated, deserving and undeserving in the public arena. Similar to the controversial debate on the 'end of multiculturalism' and the question of whether 'multiculturalism is bad for women' in the early 2000s (Okin 1999), gendered oppositions of victims and perpetrators were entangled with racialized ideas of modernity and backwardness, secularism and Islam, all equally problematic (Strasser and Holzleithner 2010; Strasser 2014). Well-known gendered figures, constructed and reconstructed in the public arena, became crucial for the distinction between deserving and undeserving refugees during the proclaimed crisis and the EU-Turkey Deal: (1) *Muslim men* run away from Syria, Afghanistan and Pakistan, leaving behind their families instead of protecting them from ISIS or the Taliban. Strangely, these men are simultaneously perceived as cowardly and dangerous, deportable in this discourse because they are contaminated with the violence and chaos of wars in their countries and dangerously incapable of living gender equality. (2) *Muslim women* are considered as victims of patriarchal kinship structures and are thus condemned to passivity; yet, when they come to Europe, they seem to represent a strong threat to the hard-won success of gender equality in European countries with their headscarves and their lived subordination. They cannot be sent back. Since in racist or right-wing (and, often enough, also in left-wing and liberal feminist) thinking, Muslim women do still need saving (as Abu-Lughod (2013) showed), they must be educated and liberated. (3) Similarly, underaged men and women are constructed as *unaccompanied minors* in need of protection (Lems et al. 2020) in highly gendered ways. At first, they were shielded by the UN Convention on the Rights of the Child and were perceived as highly vulnerable and needy. Later, when their number had risen in 2015, they were also perceived as suspicious and as cheating regarding their age, origin and routes in order to demand protection as unaccompanied minors. When they turned eighteen, public opinion transformed the men in particular into threatening perpetrators who might sexually harass European women, as experienced in Cologne and other cities on New Year's Eve 2016. The figure of the unaccompanied minor shifted from a deserving victim-child to the perilous perpetrator-man most evidently expressed in a rather unsettling *Charlie Hebdo* caricature representing the drowned child Alan Kurdi as a groper if he had had a future (Perl and Strasser 2018).

Similar to the overexposure and underexposure of women in the context of gendered and racialized violence, LGBTIQ+ people are now considered – after a long period of struggle by activists (see ILGA-Europe)[13] – as vulnerable and deserving of international protection (Directive 2011/95/EU).[14] This assumption of an urgent need for resettlement to a 'Western' country that guarantees gender equality and sexual democracy frames the sexual and moral suppression of gay subjects in Muslim countries as undisputed problems of the 'Other', irrespective of the colonial history and present diversity of queer identity formation in the Muslim world (e.g. Shakhsari 2012; Han and O'Mahoney 2014; Shah 2018) as well as of anti-Muslim racism within the EU (Fekete 2005). Furthermore, LGBTIQ+ subjects, similar to women in the gender discourses already described, are exposed to epistemic violence and constructed as vulnerable subjects finding their 'safe haven' only in 'the West', protected by its liberal and thus superior European values. According to Jasbir Puar (2007), homonationalism represents the claim of white supremacy among certain right-wing political, racist and/or xenophobic orientations by lining up with gay communities in Western societies. In this perception, sexual minorities owe their rights to liberal and democratic states in contrast to 'Others' (particularly in the 'Muslim world') who do not guarantee the safety of these minorities. Therefore, the comparison of lived experiences of gay Muslims 'give[s] us a clearer picture of the contours of globalisation in relation to sexuality' (ibid.: 88) and enables us to grasp the entanglement of resettlement, and its homonationalist potential, with the politics of (un)deservingness.

Turkish Law and EU Resettlement

Regarding international protection in Turkey, there are two relevant categorization issues based on the vocabulary of (un)deservingness that create immense insecurity among refugees. First, access to asylum is restricted to refugees from Europe due to the perpetuation of the geographical limitation in the new Turkish migration legislation, which has been in effect since 2014. The clause was a hangover from the early days of the 1951 UN Refugee Convention, which was focused on displaced people in Europe. Despite EU pressure to eliminate the clause, Turkey considers all non-Europeans as ineligible for refugee status. Instead, it provides only temporary protection in times of crisis and mass influx (such as for Syrians) or, if travellers are not Syrian, conditional protection that provides even less access and protection (Paçacı Elitok 2018).[15] Furthermore, by differentiating between Syrians (under temporary protection) and other, non-European nationalities (under conditional protection) who are expected to wait in satellite cities for resettlement by the UNHCR, this Turkish migration law introduced a distinction between refugees of different nationalities that is, according to international standards, illegal.

Resettlement of Syrians is a second means of differentiating between refugees, this time based entirely on moral grounds, which is not only tolerated but was actually introduced by the EU-Turkey Deal. While before the Deal it was mainly people from minority groups in Afghanistan who were resettled (although in tiny numbers), Syrians became the currency of the one-to-one exchange across the EU border after the implementation of the Deal in March 2016. Refugees of other nationalities who had for a long time been waiting for a UNHCR decision on their case were forced to find alternative solutions and move on; their prospects of resettlement have in fact worsened since 2011, when the numbers of refugees from Syria increased and their resettlement became the highest priority in the global resettlement agenda. The UNHCR nonetheless backed this Deal as an appropriate management solution to control chaos, and the EU hailed it as a success.[16]

The main dynamic of this Deal was an exchange programme that aimed at the *removal* from the Greek islands of any undeserving migrants from 20 March 2016 onwards, independent of their nationality. Similarly, *re-admission* of all returned migrants by Turkey, which is recognized as a 'safe third country' (Paçacı Elitok 2018), is expected, and so-called Geri Gönderme Merkezi (Return Detention Centres) are provided or at least supported by the EU for their detention.[17] Finally, for each Syrian among the returned migrants (protected in Turkey according to the Deal), one Syrian is eligible for resettlement to the EU. Refugees can be selected for resettlement by the UNHCR when registered in Turkey and identified as vulnerable according to the newly established EU criteria, provided that they have not been caught crossing to Europe illegally. In its Resettlement Framework, the EU emphasized that help with refugees would be provided particularly to those countries who are committed and reliably adhere to the terms of the re-admission agreements.[18]

In October 2019, the EU Commission's Progress Report on the Implementation of the European Agenda on Migration published current developments in relation to the EU-Turkey Deal and the €6 billion distributed in the Facility for Refugees in Turkey programme.[19] The numbers of migrants from Greece re-admitted into Turkey has not even reached 2,000 people since 2016, with the majority of them being non-Syrians. Around 25,000 have been resettled in eighteen different Member States. The Deal not only affects refugees within Turkey, but has assisted the return of 15,000 migrants from Turkey to Afghanistan, as well as to Pakistan, Iraq and Iran.[20] There are no reliable studies on how (voluntary) return with EU support is organized in Turkey. Yet, all in all, only 'good' refugees obeying the border regime are considered to deserve resettlement and only 'good' countries that comply with this regime deserve support with their high numbers of refugees and are eligible for resettlement programmes to EU Member States.

Deserving Resettlement and Assessing Vulnerability

Considering the EU border regime, one key question in the analyses of the EU-Turkey Statement is the issue of who deserves to be resettled according to which criteria. Of course, resettlement is meant to safeguard people who have greater need of protection than others and to provide them at least with an opportunity for a safe future. In recent decades, Western European countries have made mainly ad hoc contributions to resettlement programmes, responding to special calls from the UNHCR and the European Commission, as the recent HAP for Syrians confirms. In 2016, more than 22.5 million people were forced to leave their countries of origin and more than one million were classified as in need of protection and of being resettled to a safe country by the UNHCR. Since 2000, the EU has aimed to develop its own resettlement programme, not least in order to justify its restrictive border management. These efforts were channelled into the Joint Resettlement Programme in 2012 and finally into the EU Resettlement Framework in late 2018.[21] Although this Framework was established within the Common European Asylum System (CEAS), resettlement is, while recommended by the Commission, still not unified law. Furthermore, the resettlement of 25,000 people to the EU in five years across eighteen Member States can hardly be called a success. Nonetheless, the EU celebrated its key role in the global resettlement arena at the Geneva Global Refugee Forum in December 2019 and has pledged 30,000 resettlement places in 2020. The former Commissioner for Home Affairs, Ylva Johansson, said in this context: 'Resettlement is a key tool in ensuring that people in need of protection do not put their lives at risk and reach the EU via safe and legal pathways. It is a key component of the comprehensive approach to migration we need to continue developing, including strong partnerships with third countries.'[22]

Katharina Bamberg (2018) from the European Policy Centre problematizes the EU Resettlement Framework when she refers to the lack of a mandatory number of resettlements, the conflation of family reunification and resettlement, and the confusion of resettlement with Humanitarian Admission Programmes, all of which cause lower standards of protection and fewer places for resettlement candidates in need. Furthermore, eligibility is restricted in Article 6 of the Framework and refers to 'persons who have irregularly stayed, irregularly entered, or attempted to irregularly enter the territory of the Member States during the five years prior to resettlement' (ibid.: 9). The EU thus established resettlement as an exclusive and safe pathway to Europe, and aims to discourage alternative initiatives to get to Europe informally. Bamberger concludes convincingly that the EU resettlement strategy reveals that rather than providing protection, the migration management approach of this Framework and its eligibility criteria are deterring possible candidates from making resettlement applications. In the aftermath of the EU-Turkey Deal, it has become clear that Member States did not fulfil their pledges, deterred refugees from applying and, finally, aimed to keep them in Turkey in the long run (ibid.: 9). In the entangled approaches of aid and control at humanitarian borders, the EU Resettlement Framework gives priority to control and reduces care to management strategies.

The UNHCR has framed resettlement as an issue of deservingness shaped by categories of vulnerability. The UNHCR Vulnerability Screening Tool describes vulnerability as holistic and circumstantial.[23] The Tool is meant to be more a guide than a rigid or exhaustive means of measurement and, using highly delicate language, it lists vulnerability factors that are expected to be assessed by trained and sensitive experts. However, the employment of vulnerability to tailor the protection of people on the move has hidden exclusionary effects.

It highlights children, women and LGBTIQ+ people as categories at risk in certain circumstances (forced migration, statelessness, trafficking, etc.), but does not consider the fact that (all) refugees might be vulnerable under certain conditions. In the selection process for EU resettlement, a deserving refugee has to be selected by the UNHCR experts too, but due to Member States' expectations, they should be not only 'vulnerable' but also 'compliant', 'healthy' and 'harmless' – because in order to be considered deserving of rescue, an individual should not have tried to cross borders illegally and must be proven to be no threat to the future host society. Only such vulnerable refugees were seen as eligible (see Bamberg 2018) and eventually accepted by a particular EU Member State. Vulnerability has not disappeared from the politics of deservingness, but has to be considered as an additional yardstick used for the moral assessment of eligibility for 'good' or suitable refugees. These preconditions further shift asylum from an entitlement approach towards a moralized and humanitarian approach shaped by deservingness; they give priority to control and also expand the distribution of access to protection to those in need according the UNHCR and EU guidelines, yet unequally by default. Thus, vulnerability is not only a tool for assessing the need for protection, but also divides people into good victims deserving of rescue and undeserving refugees (straight men, terrorists left behind for re-admission, detention or even deportation).

Flying into Europe: Deserving to Be a Vulnerable Refugee

Isaak and Ghalip were both born and grew up in the city of Homs, where the first Syrian protests against the government ignited in 2011. Isaak was born into a liberal Sunni family and although his father was a political supporter of the opposition to the Asad regime, the family did not support Islamist movements and were not even practising Islam. Isaak has always felt solidarity with Jews, who, according to his school education, were supposed to be his enemies. Ghalip's family was slightly more observant and, at least initially, more reluctant and critical about the mainly Sunni Muslim resistance movement. Both grew up in a protected middle-class environment, as far as was possible for Sunnis at that time in Syria. However, after Isaak's father was kidnapped by sectarian militias in the fourth year of the civil war and Ghalip had finished his BA, the families accepted that their sons would leave Syria together in November 2015. Syria offered hardly any future prospects, except military service for the Asad regime, which they both wholeheartedly rejected.

Ghalip grew up in a middle-class district of Homs as a member of the Circassian minority. Yet, being part of the Sunni majority, Circassians also suffer discrimination and subordination at the hands of the Alawite regime. Well-educated, fluent in English, open-minded and curious, politically interested but not an activist in his home country, of Muslim background but barely practising, ambitious and hardworking in relation to his education, he passed the entrance exams for foreign Master's students to the Turkish university system on his first attempt. 'Life is very difficult for us', he often said, 'you always have to ask yourself if you are doing the right thing.' In this context, he was referring to such issues as whether to leave your country of origin or fight in an obscure war, remain a practising Muslim or become an atheist, risk your life in a dinghy or stay put, start an education in Turkey or apply for resettlement, fall in love or remain independent during this turbulent period of life.

Isaak always wanted to leave Syria because he 'felt so lonely and unaccepted'. He had been 'trying to fit in for so long', but no one appreciated what he was into. 'I was so different, probably because I was overprotected! That's why I am a bit soft and not tough; it's because of my parents – not my sexuality!' He missed a year of schooling, staying at home because he 'felt so low' after his first love affair with a young man ended and left him deeply hurt. For this reason, he started university a year later than his friends and then was unable to attend courses for another year because of the war. Questioning his sexual identity and on his way to becoming gay, he did not feel at home in 'this homophobic country'. What he, as well as Ghalip, complained about more than the regime was social control in their neighbourhoods, and their lifestyle and longing for self-determination not being accepted. Isaak knew from a young age that he was different, preferring long and well-groomed hair, fancy and fashionable design, and being interested in the English lyrics of such global celebrities as Britney Spears, Justin Bieber and Adam Lambert. He fought his battles with conservative elements in his own family and in society in his very own way, convinced, he said, that he could 'smile them off' instead of 'telling them off'. 'But, I didn't want to hide away any longer; I wanted to be accepted just the way I am.' The opening of the Balkan Route gave him the opportunity to finally leave a country that has always rejected, neglected and persecuted people like him.

In Bodrum, Isaak and Ghalip enjoyed the social and cultural diversity of the humanitarian association and quickly adapted to their new environment, enjoying shopping malls and coffee and cake at famous chains. Yet, fear was lurking around the corner because time was passing quickly and they worried about their future. During my first stay, I joined Ghalip when he decided to apply to be a student and wanted nothing more than to get rid of his refugee status. 'Back to life' for him meant becoming a student, finding work and having another citizenship. During the application process for various Turkish universities, he felt insecure and doubtful. Nevertheless, he was successful and won a place at one of the best universities in the country. Still in Bodrum, he fell in love with a young woman from Istanbul, who had been volunteering in the local humanitarian association. With the financial and emotional support of her parents, they decided to find a flat for him close to her family in Istanbul. Shortly after he had moved there and had begun his Master's in structural engineering, he was informed that, due to the suitability of his education and future profession, he (just like doctors, teachers, nurses, etc.) had been selected as one of the Syrian refugees who could apply for Turkish citizenship. In 2020 he completed his Master's. He now hopes to be able to find work or to soon begin a Ph.D. in the Netherlands, where his girlfriend is studying – one of the many young people who want to escape the increasingly authoritarian Turkish government.

Isaak knew from the beginning that he had to move on – despite the good friends he had in Bodrum and the dance company he belonged to with the Ukrainian trainer he adored. During my first stay in 2016, we had discussed resettlement options and I had started to inform some local and national refugee and migrant associations, as well as the LGBTIQ+ association KaosGL, about Isaak – a young man stuck in Bodrum who aimed to be resettled to the United States or Canada.[24] Fluent in English and very familiar with US popular culture, he dreamed of living in an English-speaking country, preferably Canada, where one of his best friends was already living. But when the UNHCR officer finally showed up in Bodrum one day and mentioned Austria's HAP as a fast way to move on (which meant waiting six to twelve months instead of two years or more), he decided to follow his 'destiny'. Since he had been hoping to reach Vienna via the Greek islands and the Balkan Route in the autumn of 2015 anyway, it seemed to be a good temporary solution. 'Everything happens for a reason', he repeated, and shrugged when he reminded me of a dream he had: 'You remember? I dreamed that I would fly into Vienna and literally everyone was laughing at me.'

Before Isaak was resettled to Europe, he was interviewed three times and had two cultural training sessions conducted by the

International Organization of Migration (IOM) in a fancy hotel in Istanbul as well as a health examination. In the first interview, the UNHCR checked Isaak's eligibility for the programme in a 'highly professional way', he said. 'You definitely have to be gay to pass this test', he told me – 'you have to know expressions like bottom and top, etc. and you have to be experienced'. Then he was examined by a Turkish commission of the Directorate General of Migration Management (DGMM). He was furious after this interview, because more than ten people with fierce expressions were in the room and forced him to talk about his sexuality in Arabic – 'I had never talked about sexuality in Arabic before'. Some members of this commission, in his opinion, aimed to prove that he was not gay, but instead was trying to bypass the migration legislation; others assumed that he only wanted to go to Europe to enjoy a gay sex life, which he found extremely offensive: 'I had to tell them that I did not want to go to Europe for sex but to be accepted the way I am.' He was taught that in Europe, the United States and Canada, he would be treated equally since same-sex orientation and other identity formations were 'legally allowed and socially accepted', he said, referring to the terminology of the IOM training.

Austria, in cooperation with the UNHCR, has implemented three HAPs since 2013. All three were designed for particularly vulnerable Syrian nationals (who are officially registered as refugees and are residing in Jordan or Turkey) and altogether they accepted 1,900 people. The most recent was conducted between 2016 and 2017 (before the Austrian People's Party (ÖVP)/Freedom Party (FPÖ) anti-immigration coalition government came into power in Austria in December 2017 and stopped this programme).[25]

After twenty months of travelling, Isaak finally flew into Vienna on 12 July 2017 on a regular ticket and with a visa. The plan was for him to begin a new life on the HAP III resettlement programme. In Vienna, due to his English-language skills, he was often invited by activists and NGO representatives to take part in film projects and interviews, and also to speak at conferences, like the one in Vienna City Hall where he was expected to proudly represent a group of refugees from his new hometown. However, he felt insulted at being labelled as a 'refugee' and left the conference in protest. He sent me an Instagram picture with an alternative designation on his conference badge – 'free bitch'. Later he explained to me in an email that this expression was inspired by Britney Spears' 'bitchology'.[26] Since he is now living 'in a free country where I can express myself without being scared', as he put it, 'bitch' is meant to convey that he is no longer the 'obedient shy boy', but is proud to be a bitch who speaks his mind and stands up for his beliefs, and refuses to tolerate insults or any labels given to him. Yet, he claimed, his new rights as a resettled refugee in a safe country have exchanged his exclusion due to his sexual orientation in Syria for marginalization because of the Syrian and Muslim identity imposed on him in Vienna, which is encapsulated by the notion 'refugee': 'I am sexually free, but I am incarcerated culturally and a Muslim ID has been imposed on me against my will.' Simultaneously, he is aware of being free to travel within Europe without a visa, of his right to study on a monthly student's grant and his decent life with new friends – in short, he is free to be a 'bitch' and also speak up against the label 'refugee', which he aims to overwrite and get rid of. And after his first year in Vienna, he said, with a twinkle in his eye: 'Sabine, I have never seen a gay couple kissing or holding hands in the street. Didn't they say "legally allowed and socially acceptable"?'

While Isaak did become the deserving traveller able to enter Europe on a plane, Ghalip, his best friend for years in Syria, was not considered deserving of resettlement. Although he, as a Circassian Sunni Muslim, also wanted to leave Syria due to social control, lifestyle and numerous other restrictions, he was not categorized as gay and thus did not fit the concept of vulnerability. Both have managed to start a new life, become students in public universities and form steady relationships; both are haunted by frightening memories from 2015 and both have worked hard to get rid of the label 'refugee', which they experience as degrading and subordinating. While Ghalip became a Turkish citizen planning his future (despite the political turmoil in the country), Isaak, the 'deserving' and protected one, is still struggling to liberate himself from the gratitude expected of him and, he assumes, all 'refugees'. Eventually, he even said he wanted to reject his stipend in order to break free from state dependency and debt.

The Ambivalence of Deservingness: Concluding Remarks

In this chapter, I have drawn on the experiences of two young men affected by the politics of (un)deservingness that is entangled in the EU-Turkey Statement. I have illustrated how resettlement has contributed to legitimizing the EU border regime: a small number of selected refugees considered vulnerable (mainly women, children and LGBTIQ+ people) and in need of international protection are transferred to a safe country. Meanwhile, the majority, who obviously do not belong to a group considered vulnerable enough to deserve protection, are left behind – under temporary protection or, worse, in order to be detained and deported. In tracing eligibility to resettlement schemes, the concept of vulnerability appeared as the key social and moral assessment tool for identifying deservingness. In this context, the politics of (un)deservingness assists in differentiating between 'good' and 'bad'; it separates deserving from undeserving travellers, and those who are allowed to access the EU from those who are denied entry. In short, it assists the irresponsible EU border regime (Perl and Strasser 2018) to organize and legitimate exclusion while insisting on EU moral superiority. The ambiguous tool of vulnerability is shaping individuals' mobilities, rights and futures. I have shown that a self-identification as LGBTIQ+ has become a core dimension of vulnerability for the UNHCR, a category later echoed by the EU border regime and included in its politics of deservingness, yet expanded with such qualifications as legal and moral compliance and social adaptability. Entangled with discourses of sexual democracy and gender equality, vulnerability has been transformed by the EU border regime into a marker of deservingness and has reaffirmed the epistemic violence of neo-orientalism in its border regime, implying that a lack of sexual democracy and gender equality is inherent to Muslim societies.

Rather than calling into question resettlement schemes that transfer people at risk from potentially dangerous environments on the grounds of sexual practices or orientation, I am interested in the ambivalences of vulnerability as a tool for 'rescuing' women and LGBTIQ+ people. Gender equality as much as sexual democracy in racist and exclusionary discourses have been identified as repressive tools of the resettlement regime similar to the accusation of 'tradition-based violence' in the postmulticulturalism and 'homonationalism' discourse. Vulnerability has been identified as the prime analytical instrument for studying the ambivalent politics of deservingness. Vulnerability could be understood as a vaguely defined yet sensitive barometer for measuring a potential threat to refugees in their host countries, but simultaneously for measuring the lack of women's rights and gay-friendliness in 'other (Muslim) cultures'. In this sense, the 'vulnerabilization' of refugees based on gender and/or sexual orientation figures as a precondition of deservingness and thus discloses the ambivalences of the deservingness of the vulnerable in the EU border regime. Despite Europe's indignation about increasing authoritarianism in Turkey, the 'Deal' was not discussed as a moral issue of EU irresponsibility. Instead, experts and policymakers alike presented it as an opportunity to end the smugglers' business, to prevent death in the Mediterranean and to protect the EU's high moral standards.[27]

The EU-Turkey Statement facilitated the rise of resettlement as a major tool of border management, which was debated heatedly among EU Member States throughout the so-called refugee crisis. Resettlement once offered hope to travellers stuck in Iran, Turkey, Libya or other countries on their (more or less) dangerous journey to Europe. However, later, based on a vague concept of vulnerability, resettlement was turned into a decisive tool for separating deserving from undeserving refugees and has been useful in protecting claims of superiority rather than promoting moral sentiments, humanitarian practices and responsibility. Vulnerability as a tool of the EU migration regime was implemented as an ambivalent control-oriented yardstick instead of to improve access to the EU via safe pathways.

The analysis of resettlement as a tool of the EU politics of (un)deservingness gives insight less into the persecution and violence experienced in a conflict zone than into the epistemic and exclusionary violence of homonationalism that makes claims to white supremacy and EU superiority to the constructed 'Other' in the Muslim world.

When Isaak arrived in Austria, Chancellor Sebastian Kurz from the ÖVP had just won the national elections and established a coalition government with the far-right FPÖ. Kurz was well known for his anti-Muslim politics and declared the strict control of EU external borders and the protection of Austria as his main aims. Furthermore, he repeatedly emphasized the need to teach gender equality and sexual democracy to those immigrants already living in Austria. Yet, Kurz obviously did not mean LGBTIQ+ or women's rights, because, in the following year, he tried hard to delay the right to same-sex marriage despite the Constitutional Court's declaration that the ban on marriage for gay and lesbian couples was unconstitutional. And instead of rescuing third-country Muslim LGBTIQ+ people and women from their allegedly sexually illiberal countries and social environments, he repeatedly rejected any cases of resettlement to Austria, even the resettlement of unaccompanied children. The inconsistency of this politics of (un)deservingness can best be exemplified by the case of a teenager from Afghanistan who had arrived in Austria as an unaccompanied minor at about the same time as Isaak. In an interview, he said that he feared being persecuted in his home country for being gay. An Austrian court rejected his asylum application in August 2018, and in the official reports it was maintained that he did not *walk, act or dress* like a gay man.[28] Hence, 'saving' Muslim gay men from their Muslim countries simply reiterates the myth of European superiority rather than actually meeting the promise of 'legally allowed and socially accepted' sexual democracy or gender equality.

Acknowledgements

I thank Jelena Tošić and Andreas Streinzer for their invitation to participate in the workshop and this book, their excellent guidance through the project and their valuable remarks on the chapter; Theodora Vetta and Julia Pauli for the discussion of earlier versions of this chapter; Veronika Siegl and Janine Dahinden for their productive critique; and the participants of the BeNeFri seminar (with Janine Dahinden) and the Interdisciplinary Centre for Gender Studies seminar (Veronika Siegl and Tina Büchler) at the University of Bern in the autumn of 2020 for their fruitful comments. My special gratitude goes to Isaak and Ghalib, who have become close friends and critical discussants of my chapter since we met in Bodrum in 2016. As they both aim to escape the harmful label 'refugee', I do not disclose their names here. Many thanks to Julene Knox for her careful reading and editing of the text.

Sabine Strasser is Professor of Social Anthropology at the University of Bern. She has been the director of several research projects funded by the Swiss National Science Foundation (SNSF) focusing on moral economies across European borders ('Intimate Uncertainties'), tourism and infrastructures in uncertain times ('Trapped in Paradise'), and unaccompanied refugee youth in Turkey and Switzerland ('Transnational Biographies of Education'). Her work is situated at the intersection of feminist, postcolonial and border studies. Her recent work addresses effects of borders in everyday lives and the globalization of deportation as an arbitrary response to mobility. Her paper on 'Transnational Moralities' (Perl and Strasser 2018) and the special issue with Annika Lems and Kathrin Oester on 'Children of the Crisis' (Lems et al. 2020) are among her most recent publications.

Notes

1. European Stability Initiative (ESI): https://www.esiweb.org (retrieved 15 February 2022).
2. The EU provides funding for humanitarian assistance, education, migration management, health, municipal infrastructure and socioeconomic support, as presented in the Fact Sheet: https://ec.europa.eu/neighbourhood-enlargement/sites/near/files/frit_factsheet.pdf (retrieved 15 February 2022). For details of the HAP for Syrians suggested by the EU Commission, see https://ec.europa.eu/commission/presscorner/detail/en/IP_15_6330 (retrieved 15 February 2022).
3. See the numbers of sea and land arrivals as provided by the UNHCR: https://data2.unhcr.org/en/situations/mediterranean/location/5179 (retrieved 15 February 2022). Links to Knaus' public statements and ESI newsletters can be found at https://www.esiweb.org/proposals/evacuate-islands-eu-turkey-20 (retrieved 15 February 2022).
4. According to the UNHCR data, the number of arrivals in Greece doubled between 2017 and 2019 and increased to more than 74,000 in 2019. June, July and August 2019 saw the highest numbers of arrivals in Greece since the EU–Turkey Statement: https://data2.unhcr.org/en/situations/mediterranean/location/5179 (retrieved 15 February 2022). Thousands of refugees arrived at the Greek–Turkish border in February 2020 after the Turkish President announced that Turkey would no longer prevent migrants from crossing into Europe (https://www.nytimes.com/2020/02/29/world/europe/turkey-migrants-eu.html, retrieved 15 February 2022). On the impact of the COVID-19 pandemic at the EU–Turkey border in March 2020, see also Ayata (2020) and Ayata and Fyssa (2020).
5. Gerald Knaus has repeated this argument on different occasions: see e.g. the interview with the *NZZ*, 13 January 2020: https://www.nzz.ch/international/gerald-knaus-in-der-migrationsfrage-hat-europas-politik-versagt-ld.1532491 (retrieved 15 February 2022) or in *Der Tagesspiegel*: https://www.tagesspiegel.de/politik/erfinder-des-eu-tuerkei-deals-fuer-fluechtlinge-in-vier-monaten-haben-wir-die-naechste-grosse-krise/25498616.html (retrieved 15 February 2022).
6. I borrow the notion of 'travellers' from Khosravi (2010) to avoid the distinction between refugees and migrants that is also employed to identify deserving and undeserving individuals (see Holmes and Castañeda 2016).
7. EU Resettlement Framework: https://www.europarl.europa.eu/legislative-train/theme-towards-a-new-policy-on-migration/file-jd-eu-resettlement-framework (retrieved 20 March 2022). Resettlement is the process of selection and transfer of a refugee from a country in which they are registered as a refugee in need of international protection to a third country that has granted them permission to stay on the basis of long-term or permanent residence status.

8. Austria's Chancellor Kurz strictly rejects receiving further refugees, even during the COVID-19 crises in March 2020 (*Der Standard*, 4 March 2020): https://de.reuters.com/article/sterreich-fl-chtlinge-idDEKBN 20R1XD (retrieved 15 February 2022).
9. This lack of precision, which makes addressing 'vulnerabilities' so complex, has recently been studied by an international team headed by Luc Leboeuf (https://www.eth.mpg.de/5419436/news-2020-04-08-01, retrieved 15 February 2022) and discussed in a policy brief published by Population Europe in January 2019 (https://population-europe.eu/policy-brief/vulnerability, retrieved 15 February 2022).
10. Isaak and Ghalip are pseudonyms.
11. Later, in 2016, Turkey shifted from 'hospitality' towards 'integration', offering basic humanitarian services and the right to access education, health services and (albeit still to a limited extent) the labour market (Şimşek 2017: 161).
12. See Strasser (2016) on the 'crisis-effect' and the shift of power relations when a crisis is proclaimed.
13. ILGA-Europe on Asylum in Europe: https://www.ilga-europe.org/what-we-do/our-advocacy-work/asylum-europe (retrieved 15 February 2022).
14. Directive 2011/95/EU of the European Parliament and of the Council of 13 December 2011 on standards for the qualification of third-country nationals or stateless persons as beneficiaries of international protection, for a uniform status for refugees or for persons eligible for subsidiary protection, and for the content of the protection granted (https://eur-lex.europa.eu/legal-content/EN/TXT/PDF/?uri=CELEX:32011L0095&from=EN, retrieved 15 February 2022).
15. 'The 2014 Temporary Protection regulation, the 2016 Work Permit regulation for the beneficiaries of the Temporary Protection and the 2017 Citizenship regulation have all been introduced in response to the Syrian refugee crisis' (Paçacı Elitok 2018: 8).
16. UNHCR on EU-Turkey Deal: http://www.unhcr.org/news/press/2016/3/56ec533e9/unhcr-eu-turkey-deal-asylum-safeguards-must-prevail-implementation.html (retrieved 15 February 2022).
17. 'Categorization of Turkey by the European Commission as a "safe third country" has triggered a debate both because of the post-return human rights violations and because of concerns about Turkey's eligibility to be considered as a safe country' (Paçacı Elitok 2018: 8).
18. Seventh Report from the European Commission on the progress of the EU-Turkey Statement: https://ec.europa.eu/neighbourhood-enlargement/system/files/2017-09/20170906_seventh_report_on_the_progress_in_the_implementation_of_the_eu-turkey_statement_en.pdf (retrieved 20 March 2022).
19. Progress Report on the Implementation of the European Agenda on Migration: https://ec.europa.eu/migrant-integration/library-document/progress-report-implementation-european-agenda-migration_en (retrieved 20 March 2022). According to this report, the EU has made

re-admission agreements with twenty-three countries and an effort to push for effective return.
20. The number of 15,000 migrants from Turkey to Afghanistan is relevant since the number of deported refugees from Europe is small and rather symbolic, but the collaboration in the Deal allows the number of returned Afghan and Pakistani nationals from Turkey to increase.
21. EU Resettlement Framework: https://www.europarl.europa.eu/legislative-train/theme-towards-a-new-policy-on-migration/file-jd-eu-resettlement-framework (retrieved 20 March 2022).
22. European Commission: https://ec.europa.eu/commission/presscorner/detail/en/IP_15_6330 (retrieved 15 February 2022).
23. UNHCR Vulnerability Screening Tool: https://www.unhcr.org/protection/detention/57fe30b14/unhcr-idc-vulnerability-screening-tool-identifying-addressing-vulnerability.html (retrieved 15 February 2022). For an analysis of the UNHCR's role in queer refugees' resettlement and the practices of performing and proving one's deservingness, see Koçak (2020).
24. KaosGL, a Turkish LGBTIQ+ association: https://www.kaosgl.org (retrieved 15 February 2022).
25. *Flucht und Asyl in Österreich. Fragen und Antworten* (*Flight and Asylum in Austria. Questions and Answers*): https://www.unhcr.org/dach/wp-content/uploads/sites/27/2018/01/AT_UNHCR_Fragen-und-Antworten_2017.pdf (retrieved 15 February 2022).
26. In order to explain his idea clearly, he sent me Britney Spears' post under #*bitchology* or #*ItsBritneyBitch*. The post states:
    'Bitchology
    Being a Bitch means…
    I stand up for myself and my beliefs
    I stand up for those I love
    I speak my mind, think my own thoughts
    or do things my way
    I won't compromise whats [sic] in my heart
    I live my life MY way
    I won't allow anyone to step on me
    I refuse to tolerate injustice
    It means I have the courage &
    strength to allow myself to be me
    So try to stomp on me, douse my inner flame,
    Squash every ounce of beauty I hold within
    You won't succeed
    And if that makes me a Bitch, so be it
    I embrace the title and i'm [sic] proud to be a Bitch!'
    https://www.instagram.com/p/0WCecrG8IX/?utm_medium=copy_link (retrieved 15 February 2022).
27. According to the EU report on the implementation of the EU-Turkey Statement in September 2016, daily crossings were reduced from 1,700

to under 100 after March 2016: http://europa.eu/rapid/press-release_ MEMO-16-3204_en.htm (retrieved 15 February 2022).
28. In *Der Falter*, 15 August 2018 and *Süddeutsche Zeitung*, where this case is described as driven by prejudices (*Vorurteilen*) followed by stupidity (*Dämlichkeit*): https://www.sueddeutsche.de/politik/negativer-bescheid-fuer-fluechtling-nicht-schwul-genug-fuer-oesterreich-1.4093297 (retrieved 15 February 2022).

References

Abu-Lughod, Lila. 2013. *Do Muslim Women Need Saving?* Cambridge, MA: Harvard University Press.
Albahari, Maurizio. 2016. *Crimes of Peace: Mediterranean Migrations at the World's Deadliest Border*. Philadelphia: University of Pennsylvania Press.
Akin, Deniz. 2017. 'Queer Asylum Seekers: Translating Sexuality in Norway', *Journal of Ethnic and Migration Studies* 43(3): 458–74.
Anderson, Ruben. 2014. *Illegality Inc.: Clandestine Migration and the Business of Bordering Europe*. Berkeley: University of California Press.
Ayata, Bilgin. 2020. 'The Limits of Protection, Prevention and Care: A Miniseries on Refugees in the COVID-19 Pandemic', *Eurozine*, 31 March. Retrieved 15 February 2022 from https://www.eurozine.com/the-limits-of-protection-prevention-and-care.
Ayata, Bilgin, and Artemis Fyssa. 2020. 'Politics of Abandonment: Refugees on Greek Islands during the Coronavirus Crisis', *Eurozine*, 14 April. Retrieved 15 February 2022 from https://www.eurozine.com/politics-of-abandonment.
Baban, Feyzi, Suzan Ilcan and Kim Rygiel. 2017. 'Syrian Refugees in Turkey: Pathways to Precarity, Differential Inclusion, and Negotiated Citizenship Rights', *Journal of Ethnic and Migration Studies* 43(1): 41–57.
Bamberg, Katharina. 2018. 'The EU Resettlement Framework: From a Humanitarian Pathway to a Migration Management Tool', *European Migration and Diversity Programme at the European Policy Centre Discussion Paper*. Retrieved 15 February 2022 from http://aei.pitt.edu/94238/1/pub_8632_euresettlement.pdf.
Biner, Özge. 2016. *Türkiye'de Mültecilik. İtica,, Geçicilik ve Yasallık, "Van Uydu Şehir Örneği"*. Istanbul: Istanbul Bilgi Üniversitesi Yayınları.
De Genova, Nicholas (ed.). 2017. *The Border of 'Europe': Autonomy of Migration, Tactics of Bordering*. Durham, NC: Duke University Press.
Dijstelbloem, Huub, and Lieke van der Veer. 2021. 'The Multiple Movements of the Humanitarian Border: The Portable Provision of Care and Control at the Aegean Islands', *Journal of Borderlands Studies* 36(3): 425–42.

Fassin, Didier. 2005. 'Compassion and Repression', *Cultural Anthropology* 20(3): 362–87.
Fekete, Liz. 2005. 'Anti-Muslim Racism and European Security State', *Race & Class* 46(1): 3–29.
Hage, Ghassan. 2005. 'A Not So Multi-sited Ethnography of a Not So Imagined Community', *Anthropological Theory* 5(4): 463–75.
———. 2016. '*État de siège*: A Dying Domesticating Colonialism?', *American Ethnologist* 43(1): 38–49.
Han, Enze, and Joseph O'Mahoney. 2014. 'British Colonialism and the Criminalization of Homosexuality', *Cambridge Review of International Affairs* 27(2): 268–88.
Hess, Sabine, et al. (eds). 2016. *Der Lange Sommer der Migration. Grenzregime III*. Berlin: Assoziation A.
Holmes, Seth M., and Heide Castañeda. 2016. 'Representing the "European Refugee Crisis" in Germany and beyond: Deservingness and Difference, Life and Death', *American Ethnologist* 43(1): 1–13.
Içduygu, Ahmed, and Damla B. Aksel. 2014. 'Two-to-Tango in Migration Diplomacy: Negotiating Readmission Agreement between the EU and Turkey', *European Journal of Migration and Law* 16(3): 336–62.
Khosravi, Shahram. 2010. *'Illegal' Traveller: An Auto-Ethnography of Borders*. Basingstoke: Palgrave Macmillan.
Koçak, Mert. 2020. 'Who is "Queerer" and Deserves Resettlement?: Queer Asylum Seekers and Their Deservingness of Refugee Status in Turkey', *Middle East Critique* 29(1): 29–46.
Lems, Annika, Kathrin Oester and Sabine Strasser. 2020. 'Children of the Crisis: Ethnographic Perspectives on Unaccompanied Refugee Youth in and en Route to Europe', *Journal of Ethnic and Migration Studies* 46(2): 315–35.
Luibhéid, Eithne. 2008. 'Queer/Migration: An Unruly Body of Scholarship', *GLQ: A Journal of Lesbian and Gay Studies* 14(2–3): 169–90.
McKinnon, Sara L. 2009. 'Citizenship and the Performance of Credibility: Audiencing Gender-Based Asylum Seekers in U.S. Immigration Courts', *Text and Performance Quarterly* 29(3): 205–21.
Neuhauser, Johanna, Sabine Hess and Helen Schwenken. 2016. 'Unter- oder überbelichtet: Die Kategorie Geschlecht in medialen und wissenschaftlichen Diskursen zu Flucht', in Sabine Hess et al. (eds), *Der Lange Sommer der Migration. Grenzregime III*. Berlin: Assoziation A, pp. 176–95.
Okin, Susan. 1999. 'Is Multiculturalism Bad for Women?', in Joshua Cohen and Matthew Howard (eds), *Is Multiculturalism Bad for Women?*. Princeton: Princeton University Press.
Paçacı Elitok, Seçil. 2018. 'Turkey's Migration Policy Revisited: (Dis) Continuities and Peculiarities', *Instituto Affari Internazonali (IAI) Papers* 18/16.

Perl, Gerhild. 2019. '*Migration as Survival: Withheld Stories and the Limits of Ethnographic Knowability*', *Migration and Society: Advances in Research* 2(1): 12–25.
Perl, Gerhild, and Sabine Strasser. 2018. 'Transnational Morality: The Politics of Death and Responsibility across the Mediterranean', *Identities: Global Studies in Culture and Power* 25(5): 507–23.
Puar, Jasbir. 2007. *Terrorist Assemblages: Homonationalism in Queer Times.* Durham, NC: Duke University Press.
Rygiel, Kim, Feyzi Baban and Suzan Ilcan. 2016. 'The Syrian Refugee Crisis: The EU–Turkey "Deal" and Temporary Protection', *Global Social Policy* 16(3): 310–20.
Shah, Shanon. 2018. *The Making of a Gay Muslim: Religion, Sexuality and Identity in Malaysia and Britain.* Cham: Springer International Publishing.
Shakhsari, Sima. 2012. 'From Homoerotics of Exile to Homopolitics of Diaspora: Cyberspace, the War on Terror, and the Hypervisible Iranian Queer', *Journal of Middle East Women's Studies* 8(3): 14–40.
Şimşek Doğuş. 2017. 'Turkey as a "Safe Third Country"? The Impacts of the EU–Turkey Statement on Syrian Refugees in Turkey', *Perceptions* XXII(4): 161–82.
Soykan, Cavidan. 2016. 'Turkey as Europe's Gatekeeper: Recent Developments in the Field of Migration and Asylum and the EU–Turkey Deal of 2016', in Sabine Hess et al. (eds), *Der Lange Sommer der Migration. Grenzregime III*. Berlin: Assoziation A, pp. 52–60.
Spivak, Gayatry C. 1988. 'Can the Subaltern Speak?', in Cary Nelson and Lawrence Grossberg (eds), *Marxism and the Interpretation of Culture*. London: Macmillan, pp. 271–313.
Stierl, Maurice. 2017. 'A Fleet of Mediterranean Border Humanitarians', *Antipode* 50(3): 704–24.
Strasser, Sabine. 2014. 'Post-Multikulturalismus und "repressive Autonomie": sozialanthropologische Perspektiven zur Integrationsdebatte', in Boris Nieswand and Heike Drotbohm (eds), *Kultur, Gesellschaft, Migration. Die reflexive Wende in der Migrationsforschung. Studien zur Migrations- und Integrationspolitik*. Wiesbaden: Springer-Verlag, pp. 41–67.
———. 2016. 'The Crises Effect: Global Moral Obligations, National Interventions and the Figure of the Pitiful/Abusive Migrant', *Ethnologia Balkanica* 18: 47–66.
Strasser, Sabine, and Elisabeth Holzleithner (eds). 2010. *Multikulturalismus queer gelesen. Zwangsheirat und gleichgeschlechtliche Ehe in pluralen Gesellschaften*. Frankfurt am Main: Campus.
Strasser, Sabine, and Elif Eda Tibet. 2020. 'The Border Event in the Everyday: Hope and Constraints in the Lives of Young Unaccompanied Asylum Seekers in Turkey', *Journal of Ethnic and Migration Studies* 46(2): 354–71.

Ticktin, Miriam. 2011. *Casualties of Care: Immigration and the Politics of Humanitarianism in France*. Berkeley: University of California Press.
——. 2016. 'Thinking beyond Humanitarian Borders', *Social Research* 38(2): 255–71.
Topak, Özgün E. 2014. 'The Biopolitical Border in Practice: Surveillance and Death at the Greece–Turkey Borderzones', *Environment and Planning D: Society and Space* 32: 815–33.
Tošić, Jelena, and Annika Lems. 2019. 'African-European Trajectories of (Im)Mobility: Exploring Entanglements of Experiences, Legacies and Regimes of Contemporary Migration', *Migration and Society* 2(1): 1–11.
UNHCR (United Nations High Commissioner for Refugees). 2019. 'Turkey – Fact Sheet October 2019. Situation Report'. Retrieved 15 February 2022 from https://reliefweb.int/report/turkey/unhcr-turkey-fact-sheet-october-2019.
Walters, William. 2011. 'Foucault and Frontiers: Notes on the Birth of the Humanitarian Border', in Ulrich Bröckling, Susanne Krasmann and Thomas Lemke (eds), *Governmentality: Current Issues and Future Challenges*. New York: Routledge, pp. 138–64.

10

The Politics of Deservingness among Resettled Bhutanese Refugees

Nicole Hoellerer

In response to the 'refugee crisis' in Europe, some scholars have proposed 'refugee nations', such as 'Refugia' (van Hear and Cohen 2015), 'an autonomous region in which refugees would live and work, separated from the communities for whom their presence has become so politically problematic' (Crawley 2018). Proponents of this idea envision a community of refugees from various countries of origin, who share a 'mobile commons across ethnic divides' (van Hear 2016), which emerges 'organically and cumulatively' by bringing together 'disparate solidarities and transnational practices' (van Hear 2018). The idea is not new: in the past, other scholars (e.g. Mortland 1987) argued that refugees in exile create some sort of *communitas* that 'transcends distinctions of rank, age, kinship position' (Turner 1967: 100). From this viewpoint, the experience of becoming and being a refugee removes hierarchies and differentiations in favour of an egalitarian community, which learns to share (or at least accommodate) different, intercultural values, norms and practices. In the United Kingdom, service providers actively foster the creation of refugee community organizations (RCOs), based on shared traits and a common country of origin, to which support can be outsourced once governmental aid ends (Hoellerer 2018). The idea is that if refugees learn to support themselves, it will ultimately lead to empowerment (Mitchell and Correa-Velez 2010: 104), which is reminiscent of the old proverb 'give a man a fish and you feed him for a day, teach a man to fish and you feed him for a lifetime' (see also Ferguson 2015). As discussed elsewhere (Hoellerer 2018), UK policy-makers assume that refugees 'naturally' come together in order to serve the 'greater good' of all community members, leaving aside ethnic, religious, social and economic differences, making everyone equally deserving of support – similar to the proposed 'refugee nations' mentioned above.

Migration may engender new ideas, values and lifestyles, and requires a negotiation and transformation of relationships and hierarchical structures (Colson 2003: 8). However, my research demonstrates that although refugees may share a common experience of displacement and – in this ethnography – even a shared country of origin and language, refugee communities are diverse and heterogeneous, and often experience internal conflicts (see also Mitchell and Correa-Velez 2010). Thus, I address deservingness at the microlevel of small, social networks – a refugee community itself. By looking at resettled Bhutanese refugees in the United Kingdom, I aim to unpack the politics of deservingness – that is, the active process of creating and maintaining in- and exclusion ('Othering') by means of attributing or contesting deservingness – in order to shed light on the challenges of community development in refugee resettlement. I argue that the politics of deservingness occurs on various levels: within *and* between social groups, as well as in political, public and media discourses (Hall 1996; Zetter 2007). As Streinzer and Tošić argue in the Introduction to this volume, deservingness is a moral assessment of processes of distribution – this chapter explores these processes from within a community. Migration and community development encompass complex, continuous processes of labelling, negotiations of multiple identities and boundaries, as well as social power and control (Colson 2003: 1–2). The chapter explores how deservingness is subject to both external and internal representations and classifications, and how my refugee informants determine who is a 'deserving' insider and an 'undeserving' outsider.

I outline how, on the one hand, Bhutanese refugees sense a mutuality with each other, acknowledging a similarity in experience, practices and histories – a 'refugee-ness', which they partially share with other refugees. Through their 'refugee' label, they consciously politicize themselves vis-à-vis other identities (such as voluntary migrants) and 'reproduce a politicized version of an institutional category' (Zetter 2007: 187; see also Hall 1996: 15). On the other hand, Bhutanese refugees operate through 'Othering' within their *own* community. They may share a common country of origin and certain values and norms that unite them, but this does not automatically lead to egalitarian relationships. It is particularly relevant – as my informants often remarked – that they did not know one another in Bhutan, or even in Nepalese refugee camps, and may have nothing in common other than a shared history of forced displacement, camp life and resettlement. Rather, they (re)produce hierarchies and (re)imagine internal differences. Ultimately, Bhutanese refugees create boundaries not only to demarcate themselves from those outside of their community, but also from those *within* their community. Therefore, I argue that internal and external boundary-making operates along ascribed deservingness.

In this chapter, I outline how a refugee community may be internally divided through the establishment, negotiation and contestation of imagined differences, creating potentially antagonistic assertions of 'us' versus 'them' (Baumann 1996: 172; Voicu 2013: 169) and determine who is, and who is not, deserving of group membership and support. Thus, this chapter attempts to shed further light on Bhabha's query: 'How do strategies of representation or empowerment come to be formulated in the competing claims of communities where, despite shared histories of deprivation and discrimination, the exchange of values, meanings and priorities may not always be collaborative and dialogical, but may be profoundly antagonistic, conflictual and even incommensurable?' (2004: 32).

This chapter can therefore be read as a caution against the positivist assumption that refugee communities – or, indeed, 'refugee nations' – are the solution for 'refugee crises' and can overcome inequalities and structural violence, and consequently 'absolve' the Global North of its obligation to assist forced migrants across the world (Crawley 2018). It echoes Streinzer and Tošić's argument in the Introduction to this volume that '[t]he underlying premises of human rights are based on claims of universalism and thus the ultimate claim of equality' and that ethnographies of complex negotiations of claims of (un)deservingness within and across communities can offer an insight into how rights discourses are intersected and unsettled through the ascriptions of unequal distributions of belonging.

A Cautionary Note

The most significant concern with 'making claims' on refugee community divisions, 'Othering' and internal notions of deservingness is the danger of fostering the right-wing narrative of 'ungrateful refugees undermining refugee service provision'. My research builds upon the works of, among others, Malkki (1997), Zetter and Pearl

(2000), Kelly (2003), Muggah (2005) and Zetter (2007), who have examined these topics for decades. The claim that refugee communities are divided internally – partly by notions of deservingness – is not intended as a moral judgement on refugees. It should instead be understood as a critical examination of the notion of homogeneity among refugees, who 'naturally' come together for the 'greater good'. Thus, it is not a criticism of the refugee community, but of notions of deservingness permeating the everyday lives of a group of people.

On a final note, it is not my intention to generalize my qualitative data to be applicable to all Bhutanese refugees in the United Kingdom or, indeed, globally. In addition, I do not argue that such issues are prevalent in all refugee communities across the world. However, the study of such a small group and the everyday debates on deservingness allows us to critically examine the notion of homogeneous refugee communities in various discourses.

Who Are Bhutanese Refugees?

In order to understand the refugees' perspectives on deservingness, it is essential to briefly outline the circumstances leading to their forced displacement.

Bhutanese refugees originate from Bhutan, a small landlocked nation between the 'Asian giants' India and China. Ethnic Nepalese people (sharing a language, Nepali, and a religion, Hinduism) have been settled in Bhutan for more than two hundred years and mostly engaged in agricultural practices as cash-crop farmers. Due to various geopolitical and sociopolitical events and circumstances in the 1970s and early 1980s (see Joseph 1999; Hutt 2007), Bhutan's Buddhist ruling elite adopted the so-called 'One Nation, One People' agenda in the 1980s, attempting to homogenize the population under one language (Dzongkha) and religion (Mahayana Buddhism). The elite portrayed this as 'authentic Bhutanese culture', which was to be 'preserved' at all costs (Hutt 1996: 398). Fearing the political mobilization of Nepali Bhutanese, the ruling elite created laws and acts to systematically remove citizenship from the Nepali-speaking minority, resulting in the (often forceful) expulsion of more than 100,000 people in the late 1980s and early 1990s.

Therefore, the clash between the Bhutanese Buddhist elite and Nepali Bhutanese can be defined as an 'ethnic conflict' (Joseph 1999; Hutt 2007). The issue originated in the perceived differences (e.g. in language, religion and sociocultural practices) between several social and ethnic groups living in Bhutan, which were used as a justification to expel the 'Other' – that is, what the ruling elite perceived as non-Bhutanese or non-native – in order to maintain power. More importantly, in the Bhutanese context, only one (ethnic) culture has been deemed 'authentic' and 'native' by the Bhutanese ruling elite, and therefore deserving of citizenship.

Bhutanese Refugee Resettlement

Nepali Bhutanese fled to East Nepal, where the United Nations High Commissioner for Refugees (UNHCR) established seven refugee camps in 1992. After twenty years of bilateral talks between Nepal and Bhutan (mediated by the UNHCR), no durable solution (such as repatriation to Bhutan or integration in the first country of asylum, i.e. Nepal) could be found and, in 2006, the United States proposed third-country resettlement, offering more than 60,000 places. By 2015, 100,000 Bhutanese refugees had been resettled in the United States, Canada, Australia, New Zealand, Norway, Denmark, the Netherlands and the United Kingdom, making it the most 'comprehensive' and 'successful' refugee resettlement programme in the history of the UNHCR (*Himalayan Times* 2015).

The first Bhutanese refugees arrived in the United Kingdom in 2010 and by 2014 (the end of this programme in the United Kingdom), about 350 refugees had resettled in Greater Manchester, Leeds, Sheffield and Bradford. These areas were chosen by the government due to the availability of housing and public services. In line with the United Kingdom's Gateway Protection Programme, Bhutanese refugees received Indefinite Leave to Remain in the United Kingdom, which gives them the same rights to live, work and study in the United Kingdom like any other resident, as well as claim benefits and welfare payments. Moreover, they are able to apply for citizenship after five years of permanent residence in the United Kingdom (UNHCR 2001: 8–9; Wright et al. 2004: 15).

Refugee resettlement entails the organized migration of recognized refugees, which is of particular importance for the public discourse, in which there is an ongoing debate about 'genuine' and 'fake' refugees.[1] Bhutanese refugees are *not* asylum seekers or so-called 'voluntary' migrants.[2] The distinction entails very different rights and duties. Refugees have several rights, while asylum seekers often do not, until they receive refugee status. In the United Kingdom, recognized refugees – such as Bhutanese refugees – have the right to be unified with their families (in their country of refuge) and a right to housing. On the other hand, asylum seekers are often housed in detention centres, have no right to live and work in the United Kingdom until their status is approved, and face the risk of deportation (Sales 2002: 464–66).³ As I will explore further below, this categorization – or labelling – as a refugee and the correlating notions of deservingness are significant not only for state bodies and the host community, but also for refugees themselves.

To date, there is no possibility to return to Bhutan and therefore Bhutanese refugees have to learn to exist in and interact with their new environment in resettlement. Service provision in resettlement influences my informants' lives; and these negotiations, adaptations and transformations to this new environment are a lifelong process (Mortland 1987: 378).

Although a small community in comparison to larger refugee groups (e.g. the approximately 12,000 Palestinian refugees in the United Kingdom), the focus on one specific refugee community allows for an in-depth analysis of internal notions of deservingness, and how refugees themselves employ narratives to create boundaries between insiders and outsiders within their own community.

The Fieldsite

The research on which this chapter is based was conducted in Greater Manchester and other cities in northern England (e.g. Leeds, Sheffield and Bradford) between 2013 and 2014.⁴ Manchester is a diverse city, with more than 15 per cent nonwhite residents – 9 per cent of whom are South Asian migrants or self-identify as British South Asian (Office for National Statistics 2011). As Bromley (2000: 2–3) argues, instead of 'passive' migrants who fully assimilate into the British host culture, immigrants have 'actively transformed' the United Kingdom by creating new and diverse 'cityscapes' – Manchester is one example of these transformed urban centres. There are small South Asian markets and shops dotted across the city, allowing my informants to purchase familiar products. Several Hindu temples (*mandir*) in Manchester are well-attended by my Hindu interlocutors. Most refugees lived scattered throughout the city, rather than in 'enclaves', and therefore had to travel across the city to access schools, jobs and governmental and nongovernmental facilities. All my informants expressed their happiness to live in Manchester, which they regarded as 'green' (with many parks), 'friendly' and 'multicultural'.

My informants – like most refugee populations – come from a wide range of social, cultural, educational and economic backgrounds, showing that they are not one, homogeneous community. For example, some of my older informants over the age of forty never went to school and are illiterate, while others have university degrees and professional work experience. Some come from a family of farmers and labourers in Bhutan, while others descend from high-status government officials or religious leaders. Older informants were born in Bhutan, while almost all under the age of twenty were born in Nepalese refugee camps. Almost all of them lived in refugee camps in Nepal for nearly twenty years and arrived in the United Kingdom between 2010 and 2013. As they resided in various refugee camps, many of my informants did not know each other before arriving in the United Kingdom. During my fieldwork, most of my informants were unemployed and fully reliant on benefit and welfare payments.

The *Lhotshampa* Issue

The issue of labels, categorizations and deservingness was a theme throughout my fieldwork. For example, during my second fieldwork day, one of my informants complained about academic works and international media referring to Nepali Bhutanese as *Lhotshampas* (literally 'southern border dweller'; see Evans [2009]).[5] He explained: '*Lhotshampa* can be everybody living in the South of Bhutan, even Chinese, Indian, Tibetan, Bhutanese, Nepali. I'm annoyed that people call us *Lhotshampa*. Please don't call us that.'[6]

The term *Lhotshampa* is not a 'native', common word in Bhutanese language and thus does not originate from the categorized people themselves. It was invented and imposed from above (by the Bhutanese state) – similar to the creation and adoption of the category 'refugee' in political and public discourses in the Global North – to denote 'acceptance of the [Nepalese] as a distinct cultural and linguistic unit' (Joseph 1999: 139; see also Hutt 1996: 400). This category was later used to declare *all* Nepali Bhutanese in the South of Bhutan as *ngolops* (DZ: anti-nationals) and illegal immigrants, thus rendering them 'undeserving' of Bhutanese citizenship.

My informants never refer to themselves as *Lhotshampas* and, similar to Hutt's observations (2007: 6–7, 400) of Nepalese refugee camps, they use the term 'Nepali Bhutanese' (Nepali: *bhuṭani nepaliharu*). But categorizations such as *Lhotshampa* (or 'refugee') are important tools for the creation of similarity and difference. By inventing the term *Lhotshampa*, the rulers of Bhutan amplified 'ethnic' distinctions between Nepali Bhutanese and the Bhutanese Buddhist elite, and made it into a bureaucratic category that can be used to classify, manage and control the 'Other', who has become undeserving of living in Bhutan (Joseph 1999: 139).[7]

More importantly, it fostered the idea that all Nepali Bhutanese are part of one all-encompassing group that can be easily identified. However, as my informants confirmed, Nepali Bhutanese in Bhutan did not perceive themselves as a coherent, homogeneous group that is significantly distinct from other Bhutanese residents.[8] One older informant recalled that in Bhutan 'we were all different, but we were all Bhutanese. Suddenly, they call us *Lhotshampa*, and say we are not the people of Bhutan'. Even in resettlement, the term *Lhotshampa* continues to be a debated issue among my informants.

During a speech to a predominantly academic audience at an international workshop on Bhutanese refugee resettlement, Bhutanese refugee representatives emphasized that researchers, journalists, governments and service providers should refrain from using the term *Lhotshampa* and instead adopt other, more accepted terms to refer to Bhutanese refugees. One researcher in the audience dismissed the refugees' demand as a 'petty issue' and argued that the rejection of the word is 'impractical', as it offers a 'useful' and 'simple' categorization, allowing easy identification. This comment highlights the importance of simple classifications in political, public and academic discourses. If we compare the word *Lhotshampa* with terms such as 'refugee', 'asylum seeker' and 'migrant', we can see similar processes of categorization – or labelling – of individuals, which consequently bestow different levels and rights of access (to, for example, support, funds, and civil and legal rights). Similar to the distinction between deserving refugee and undeserving economic migrants in discourses in the Global North (see e.g. Holmes and Castañeda 2016), Nepali Bhutanese sensed that the term *Lhotshampa* signified the notion of 'undeservingness' and therefore rejected it.

When Bhutanese refugees arrived in Britain, they were grouped together by British service providers as one refugee community, deserving of protection. But in comparison with the term *Lhotshampa* – which implied being undeserving of Bhutanese citizenship – my informants do not resist the classification as refugees. Rather, they stress their mutuality and distinctiveness as Bhutanese refugees in order to adapt and respond to state politics and immigration law (Amit and Rapport 2002: 939; see also Baumann 1996). They are, in

Kelly's (2003: 41) words, a 'contingent community' that adopts labels imposed from 'above', emphasizing the 'refugee-ness' as a unique aspect of its 'imagined' identity, and therefore becomes a 'deserving' social group.

The 'Refugee' Label

In late 2010, the Sinha family arrived in the United Kingdom and were settled in Greater Manchester.[9] A few weeks after their arrival, someone graffitied 'Pakis go home' on the Sinha's fence.[10] A charitable organization working with resettled refugees intervened and held an 'awareness event' in the neighbourhood, explaining to the predominantly white British residents who Bhutanese refugees are and why they are in the United Kingdom. The organization attempted to replace the neighbours' assumption of ethnic identification – 'Pakis' or South Asians – with a more convenient label: 'refugee-ness', which carries with it the supposition of 'victimhood' and 'involuntary migration'. The Sinhas had the feeling that the British community in their area began to support them after the event, offering assistance (e.g. car rides to supermarkets or other facilities) and goods (e.g. toys and clothes for children).

The label 'refugee' – a powerful legal category in UK public discourses at the time[11] – was adopted by my informants, by which they emphasize their 'right to be here', because they were 'victims of the Bhutanese government'. Bhutanese refugees make conscious use of the notion of 'refugee-ness' to gain access to resources from the state, nongovernmental organizations (NGOs) and the host community that are exclusively reserved for recognized refugee communities, whereby they portray themselves as one cohesive community, which shares the experience of 'victimhood' (Hoellerer 2018).

Labels do not operate in a vacuum, but are created, shaped and utilized by institutional and bureaucratic bodies (Zetter 2007: 180, 184). Refugees – as labelled individuals – have become subject to the authority of international in addition to national laws, as well as being 'targets' of humanitarian intervention and funding regimes (Turton 2002). This 'refugee' label has to be distinguished from ethnic, cultural and personal identity, although all are shaped 'within institutionalized regulatory practices' (Zetter 2007: 173). But while cultural identity is based on the negotiation of shared sociocultural values and practices within a community, the 'refugee' label is based on negotiations of classifications between Euro-American governmental and nongovernmental institutions (Malkki 2002: 356) and applied selectively only to those who are perceived to fit within the 1951 Refugee Convention. The 'refugee' label and the subsequent legal differentiations between the 'deserving' refugee and the 'undeserving' asylum seeker and migrant serve the interests of nation-states to assign privileges or punitive measures to individuals depending on whether they fall within or outside these criteria (Malkki 2002: 356; Sales 2002: 473; Baba 2013: 2–4). Here, I compare the 'refugee' label to the term *Lhotshampa*, which served the interest of the Bhutanese elite in order to define the 'Other' and (similar to the 'refugee' label) ascribed or removed 'deservingness'. Thus, such labels are not neutral classifications of people, but create powerful, convenient images. National and international institutions, such as the United Nations (UN) or the British government, create 'new kinds of persons' through these bureaucratic labels (Hacking 2006: 2).

These classifications portray the refugee as a 'helpless victim' of nationalist governments (e.g. Bhutan), war and conflict, or natural and environmental disasters (Malkki 2002: 356; Zetter 2007: 173, 176; see also the Introduction to this volume). They are 'victims in need of humanitarian aid', as they have been forcibly removed from their homelands, cultures and communities (Chatty 2010: 56–58), which perpetuates the humanitarian paradigm of aid intervention as a response to 'deserving people in need' (Colson 2003: 10). However, scholars (e.g. Malkki 1997: 224) caution against this victimization, as it denies refugees their agency and ability to challenge as well as utilize national and international systems of power. Rather than portraying 'refugee-ness' as a 'spoiled identity', the label can be a highly valued status and commodity, which serves *both* those who created the label and those who claim it (Zetter 2007: 186, 188). For aid agencies and charitable organizations in the United Kingdom, the 'victim narrative' serves to attract funding and donations from governmental and private (philanthropic) bodies.

However, ownership and the use of labels is not a one-way, top-down process: labelled individuals interact with, refashion, adopt and use classifications for their own purposes (Hacking 2006: 5; Zetter 2007: 186; Gemie 2010: 31). Bhutanese refugees may not have an impact on the bureaucratic classification 'refugee' itself, but nevertheless make conscious use of it within certain contexts. For Bhutanese refugees, the 'refugee' label allows them to claim a status of the 'deserving' refugee, who has to be protected and has the right to stay in the United Kingdom. The narrative of victimhood and deservingness can be understood as a 'weapon of the weak' (Williams 2006: 867; see also Scott 2008) and my informants actively use the 'refugee' label in discourses with public institutions and nonrefugees in order to highlight their protected status. As one Bhutanese refugee once explained, 'I am a refugee; I deserve help from the government and people'.

Thus, Bhutanese refugees have learned to adopt the label in conversation with institutions and nonrefugees and – depending on the context and the 'audience' – adapt it to their own needs in a 'masterful manipulation of their marginal status' (Gemie 2010: 31; see also Malkki 1997). These labels have consequences in everyday life, especially in the context of refugee resettlement (Colson 2003: 2; Zetter 2007: 179). As outlined in the ethnographic example in Greater Manchester above, my informants believed that the British neighbours began to support Bhutanese refugees, perceiving them as 'deserving of help'. Throughout my fieldsite, my informants used the 'refugee' narrative to obtain support from their local communities and charities. For example, Bhutanese RCO chairpersons approached charities with an information package about Bhutanese refugees and their 'story of plight and misery', perpetuating the victim narrative. They were also able to successfully receive government and NGO funding for community events and projects by specifically highlighting their needs as refugees (see Hoellerer 2016). This demonstrates the active adoption of the 'refugee' label and the appropriation of humanitarian discourses on deservingness by the labelled individuals themselves in order to gain access to resources (see also Zetter 2007).

There was also some solidarity with other refugees. For example, Bhutanese refugees in Greater Manchester fostered relationships with Somali and Palestinian refugees. This was driven especially by young men, who played football with refugees from other countries in 'refugee football teams' (see Hoellerer 2016). During the time of my fieldwork, the Syrian refugee crisis emerged. Some informants sensed parallels between their own history and that of the Syrian people. One day, when watching the news on TV over lunch, one of them angrily exclaimed: 'Why doesn't anyone help the people in Syria? [President Assad] kills people, like the [Bhutanese elite] killed us, and nobody helps – like in Bhutan! People don't care! We should help them … because we understand.' In fact, some Bhutanese refugees collected small donations for Syrian refugee camps in Lebanon and Jordan, and displayed solidarity on social media.

Solidarity, however, is not bestowed universally and has its limits. In the Introduction to this volume, Streinzer and Tošić draw on Fassin's (2012: 4) critique of humanitarianism as a 'politics of precarious lives' – a vertical, top-down process of moral categorization. There are also horizontal processes taking place – both within and across refugee and migrant communities – which imply an allocation of assistance and (anti-)solidarity by utilizing claims of (un)deservingness. For example, there was much talk and consternation between Bhutanese refugees about 'African migrants', many of whom they perceived to be undeserving of calling themselves refugees, as they were seen as 'economic migrants', who had 'nothing to fear' in their countries of origin, 'unlike us'. Therefore, my informants consciously perpetuated the narrative of 'deserving' refugee versus 'undeserving' economic migrants prevalent in the Global North, mostly in order to gain advantages. This demonstrates that refugees do not necessarily perceive refugees and migrants other than themselves as equally deserving of support. This signifies an additional layer within the politics of deservingness, whereby hegemonic categorizations are adapted and adopted by those who are affected by them and used to their advantage.

Furthermore, there is a gap between how institutions and policies fashion and use labels (for example, as a means to control 'migrants' and foster 'integration') and how refugees themselves perceive, assess and even try to become the label (Zetter 2007: 189). Bhutanese refugees use the 'refugee' label exactly *because* of the inherent victim narrative, which they use to legitimize their residence in the United Kingdom to nonrefugees. They do so because refugees are certain 'types' of victim and my informants perceived themselves as 'passive' victims of political persecution and forced exile.

Internally – among Bhutanese refugees – their own definition of the 'refugee' label is a powerful tool to create similarity and difference *between* them. Here, the emphasis is not on the 1951 Refugee Convention definition. Rather, most of my informants define their Bhutanese 'refugee-ness' through their biography; that is, their shared experience of forced migration from Bhutan, their lives in the refugee camps in Nepal and their experience with organized resettlement. These interpretations of Bhutanese 'refugee-ness' are contested among my informants and create substantial fissures within the community. Therefore, labels (such as 'refugee-ness') and related notions of deservingness are not only imposed vertically (top-down), but are also employed horizontally and can become tools for internal differentiations.

Politics of Deservingness in Bhutanese Refugee Communities

Community and social networking are essential elements of everyday life for Bhutanese refugees (see also Hoellerer 2018). As one of my informants stated:

> It is said that we are social animals, we have to socialize in our community … Community is like an organ in our body. Lack of community is similar to a lack of an organ in our body … So it is not possible to live alone without the community.

Community support is also a vital part of refugee resettlement in the United Kingdom: through the so-called Community Development Approach (CDA), refugees are encouraged to found grassroots RCOs to which governmental support can be outsourced, once state and charitable bodies stop their assistance (six months after arrival). These RCOs serve one main purpose: to obtain benefits from governmental and nongovernmental bodies only available to formalized associations, in order to provide essential services, such as language and 'integration' courses, assistance with interaction with state authorities and financial support for cultural events and community projects (see also Kelly 2003).

Bhutanese refugees may stress their mutuality *outwards* in order to demonstrate a strong, unified community, adapting and responding to state politics (Baumann 1996). After all, communities are reliant on commonality between their members. These shared traits, beliefs and histories may not be actual (sociocultural, physical, historical, etc.) realities, but are located in the imagination of community members (Anderson 2006), who give meanings to these shared symbols or vocabularies. These interpretations are not fixed, static or homogeneous, but allow diverse, heterogeneous and even contradictory communities to emerge (Rapport and Overing 2000: 62–63), complicating their notions and senses of deservingness. In other words, who deserves support is dependent on the biographies, contexts, discourses, practices and audiences in which it is evoked. Thus, notions of deservingness are assessed individually and heterogeneously by processes of negotiation within internal social hierarchies and are highly contextual in nature.

However, individuals belong to many social groups simultaneously and thus adopt several different 'cultures', practices and loyalties, which change over time (Baumann 1996: 23, 172; Eidson et al. 2017). Migrants affiliate not only with their 'native' social networks, cultures and practices, but also with those of the receiving society (Zetter 2007: 187). In turn, this allows for the tolerance of multiple, hybrid notions of boundaries by recognizing that who lies beyond the boundaries of a community in one instance may be included within its confines on other occasions (Shaw 2006: 29). For example, they may stress their Nepali identity, by means of shared values and norms, language (Nepali) and social practices (e.g. dietary habits and celebration of Nepali New Year, rather than *Losar*, the Bhutanese New Year). When interacting with Nepali migrants in the United Kingdom, my informants place emphasis on their Nepali-ness. The affiliation goes both ways, as one of the Nepali friends of a Bhutanese refugee family remarked: 'We are only friends, but actually, we are family – we are the same people.' In addition, due to the limited number of Bhutanese refugees, Nepali migrants are appropriate and 'deserving' marriage partners. Some of my young (male) informants even travelled to Nepal after receiving (refugee) travel documents in order to marry Nepali women. However, their Nepali Bhutanese-ness is distinct from Nepali and Bhutanese *national* identity and *ethnicity* because of their shared history of 'refugee-ness'.[12]

This territorial affiliation is expanded when they fashion social networks with the South Asian community resident in Britain, accentuating a wider 'South Asian identity', sharing practices such as religion, values or commensality of food, as well as South Asian popular culture (e.g. 'Bollywood') and fashion. As one of my informants confirmed: 'We are the same – Indian people and us – we all come from the same place, we look the same, pray the same, eat the same food.' Bhutanese refugees have reliable social networks and close friendships in the British Asian community, and often work in Asian businesses. Therefore, Bhutanese refugees' sense that they are deserving members of the British Asian community – a sentiment that is largely reciprocated by that community.

But Bhutanese refugees perceive themselves as not quite the same as (British) Nepalis or (British) South Asians. What binds my informants together is their specific definition of 'refugee-ness', which is not only determined by the characteristics they share with Nepali people – and which distinguish them from the Bhutanese – but more importantly by the particular circumstances in which they have found themselves since the 1980s and their unique 'collective biography'.

Thus, their Bhutanese 'refugee-ness' is based on a shared history of exile from Bhutan in the 1980s and the 1990s, life in refugee camps in Nepal *and* the collective experience of resettlement within an organized programme. As a highly diverse group of people from all social, economic and educational backgrounds, who suddenly found themselves gathered together against their will in refugee camps in Nepal, they required this (imagined) commonality in order to foster solidarity and therefore ensure a relatively peaceful life in the refugee camps. Refugee resettlement disrupted social relations established in the camps and my informants in the United Kingdom had to create new social networks in resettlement, based on their shared experience of this organized migration.

Bhutanese refugee identity and related notions of deservingness are, in Hall's words, 'multiply constructed across different, often intersecting and antagonistic discourses, practices and positions' (1996: 4). Because it is influenced by internal dynamics of change, as well as by the experience of migration, policy and bureaucratic intervention, Bhutanese 'refugee-ness' is 'hybridized' and adapted to the context in which refugees find themselves. For example, by the time I began my fieldwork in 2012, those who arrived in the United Kingdom in 2010 were already conceiving of themselves as 'British Bhutanese refugees' (as distinct from, for example, American Bhutanese refugees – i.e. those who resettled to the United States), who created social networks within and outside of the Bhutanese refugee community that shaped their perceptions and representations of cultural identity, distinct from Bhutanese refugees who resettled in other nation-states.[13]

Yet, this solidarity and mutuality have their limits, and deservingness is not universally bestowed on all Bhutanese refugees within their community. As Streinzer and Tošić point out in the Introduction to this volume, assessments of deservingness are conditional: they require the creation of boundaries and a process of 'Othering', in which (real and imagined) individual behaviours, identities and biographies are evaluated. But rather than focusing on top-down assessments, my ethnography illustrates that these deservingness assessments are also taking place horizontally. As discussed elsewhere (Hoellerer 2018), my fieldwork revealed that, at the time, Bhutanese refugees were unable to form a single, united RCO, as their perception of 'refugee-ness' (and thus of who deserves support from formalized associations) is a highly contested category, leading to animosities between individuals and social groups, and internal arguments about who may speak for the community as a whole – an important role for a small community of about four hundred people. Community in this context is not only a tangible and bounded social group of people sharing common traits and interests, but also a concept that is created and maintained by community members by utilizing notions of deservingness and the creation of 'us' and 'them'.

Othering

Community is often defined not only by what it *is*, but also by what it *is not* (Amit and Rapport 2002: 985). Cohen (1985) highlights that unity is created through exclusion and the imagination and consciousness of others 'beyond their boundaries' – a process of 'Othering' that distinguishes between 'us' and 'them' (Barth 1998; Hall 1996); between insiders who are deserving of support and outsiders who do not deserve assistance from the community. Similar to the term *Lhotshampa*, the categories determining 'us' versus 'them' within the Bhutanese refugee community are embedded in historical, political and institutionalized discourses and contexts (Hall 1996: 3–4). More importantly for my informants, individual actions, decisions, affiliations and autobiographies impact on who *is* and who *is not* considered a Bhutanese refugee internally, and thus a member of the community who deserves support. Outsiders are often excluded from everyday social life, meetings, events or excursions, and do not benefit from the exchange of information and resources. This mirrors Streinzer and Tošić's comment in the Introduction that rather than understanding deservingness as a condition, it is a 'processual and relational notion' that is highly contextual.

Bhutanese refugees often refer to individual biographies to determine similarity and difference. For example, although Nepali Bhutanese may share a common history of life in Bhutan, those who left Bhutan before Bhutan's nationalist policies were established in the 1980s, as well as those who stayed in Bhutan (rather than fleeing to Nepal), are said to lack the experience of forced migration and are therefore undeserving of membership in the community. Some go so far as to refer to them as 'traitors', who are said to have made 'arrangements' with the Bhutanese government in order to be allowed to stay in Bhutan. In absence of 'any other explanation', those who stayed 'cannot be trusted'. The few individuals in the United Kingdom who are Nepali Bhutanese but did not experience forced migration are often ostracized from social networks and are not 'deserving' of becoming full members of the various Bhutanese RCOs, and are therefore not entitled to official community support.

Similarly, those (mostly highly educated) Bhutanese refugees who did experience exile from Bhutan, but fled to other countries (e.g. India) and arrived in the United Kingdom as asylum seekers before resettlement began – and thus did not live in the refugee camps in Nepal – might not be considered Bhutanese refugees within my informants' social groups.[14] As several of my informants explained, these individuals may have experienced the conflict in Bhutan, but they did not 'have to endure the miserable camp life and struggle'. Bhutanese refugees in Nepal (unsuccessfully) fought to be allowed to return to Bhutan or receive compensation;[15] Bhutanese refugee asylum seekers in nations in the Global North are thus accused of being 'deserters of the cause', who 'left the community for a better life abroad'. In addition, they are said to lack the shared experience of organized resettlement and therefore – according to some Bhutanese refugees – do not deserve to be members of the community.

This demonstrates that individual actions, decisions, affiliations and biographies impact on who is and who is not considered a Bhutanese refugee *internally*, and thus deserving of membership, support and status in the overall community as well as in RCOs. Thus, deservingness is not based on factual hardship or solidarity, but on individual merits, which are assessed by key power players within the community (see Hoellerer 2018). However, these distinctions are not mutually agreed upon within the community in the United Kingdom, engendering further division between Bhutanese refugees, leading to the split of 350 Bhutanese refugees into several smaller RCOs (comprising between thirty and fifty members), which are unable to compete with larger RCOs (e.g. for funding).[16] They are therefore powerless to provide much-needed assistance to Bhutanese refugees, such as translation services, support with bureaucratic processes, assistance with access to the labour market, education and health services, and 'integration' tools (see Hoellerer 2018). These processes are a good example of how the politics of deservingness is an active part of community development.

In addition, issues arose due to religious divisions. A group of about fifty resettled Bhutanese refugees converted from Hinduism and Buddhism to Christianity either in the refugee camps or (more commonly) on arrival in the United Kingdom. Conversion to Christianity in refugee resettlement nations is not unusual (see 'Bhutan's Forgotten People' 2014), as Christian churches are able to 'provide economic and social support and act as a central organizing point for community life' (ibid.), especially in countries in which government support is limited (e.g. the United States). In my fieldsite, conversion was not debated as a spiritual matter among my informants and little importance was given to the supposed renunciation from the 'traditional religion'. Nevertheless, conversion and religious divisions became an important factor in community divisions. In one instance, Hindu refugees were incensed with a few Christian Bhutanese refugees, who were accused of visiting newly arrived refugees to convince them to convert to Christianity because 'Britain is a Christian country' and non-Christians were said to be perceived as undeserving of government support by the British government.[17] The rumours of these 'missionary visits' furthered mistrust and thus divisions in the community, which cannot be easily bridged, even after several 'intervention' attempts by local NGOs. This also demonstrates that Bhutanese refugees arrive in the United Kingdom to an already-existing structure of community organizations, and who 'deserves' membership to any of these organizations is a highly debated and contentious issue.

Bhutanese RCO divisions peaked in 2013 when Bhutanese refugees were the only community who had two RCO football teams in the Manchester Refugee Football Cup (a charity event), while all other refugee communities only had one (per country of origin). Because of the community divisions, they were unable to form one team – or, more accurately, the young football players were prevented from forming one team under the direction of RCO leaders. On another occasion, a 'rival' RCO coerced their members into refusing to collaborate with me on a film project I initiated with one Bhutanese RCO, because funding was provided through one particular RCO they had disagreements with (see Hoellerer 2018). Overall, during my fieldwork, my research – and I – have become subject to these RCO divisions, leading to me losing important contacts with informants, who believed that I provided more support to one rather than the other RCO. My attempts to mend this distrust were not always successful and demonstrate that these divisions go beyond their own refugee community.

Furthermore, service providers – both in refugee camps and in resettlement in the Global North – often attempt to 'obscure' internal social differences, such as age and gender, by targeted aid and policy intervention, rendering all refugees in a camp (or in resettlement) as 'equals' vis-à-vis nonrefugee service providers and agencies (Mortland 1987: 389–90; Hoellerer 2016). But although traditional social stratifications such as age, the caste system or ownership of property may have lost importance through intervention by international agencies in Bhutanese refugee camps in Nepal (Muggah 2005; Evans 2010), other traits become emphasized and elevate some individuals above others. For instance, education, gender and religion (Hinduism and Christianity) have an impact on hierarchical structures and one's position within the community.

For example, although traditional gender roles were changing in the United Kingdom, leadership positions were still predominantly held by men. All Bhutanese RCOs were led by men and the running of RCOs was still in the hand of predominantly male board members.

During my fieldwork, women hardly participated in formal RCO meetings (such as Annual General Meetings) and rarely provided input on the direction of RCOs. Women were not actively excluded from these meetings or organizational matters, but it was taken for granted that 'decisions should be made by the men', as one woman told me while waiting in the kitchen for an RCO meeting to end. The liberal notion of women deserving an equal say in the running of their community did not feature, raising the question of whether issues concerning women (e.g. access to childcare) were perceived as being as important as other matters. Similarly, those who benefited from higher education before, during or after the displacement occurred were often in charge of deciding how RCO funds should be spent, and organized RCO events and support projects (e.g. language and literacy classes). Their leadership in RCOs translated into a higher status within the refugee community as a whole and produced new hierarchies that played an important part in everyday social interaction.

Bhutanese refugees invested significant amounts of their time and resources to support each other within the confines of their chosen RCOs. Those in charge often played a part in coercing members into not engaging with members of 'rival' communities. Due to these antagonisms, extended family members would stop social interactions in everyday life, would refuse to attend important life events (e.g. marriages or births) or overall would halt any form of engagement with one another. As I have outlined elsewhere (Hoellerer 2018), the small sizes of the various Bhutanese RCOs – often containing only thirty to fifty members – led to Bhutanese RCOs being unable to compete with larger RCOs in the United Kingdom, and therefore they failed to provide vital services to the community, contrary to the vision of United Kingdom service providers. Therefore, these divisions have real consequences in everyday life, as well as for support provision for refugees.

These disputes and power struggles also demonstrate that the experience of forced migration does not 'magically' erase boundaries within and between communities or create an egalitarian *communitas* as envisioned by proponents of 'refugee nations' and the CDA in the United Kingdom. The creation of refugee communities in host countries is still dependent on the groups' perspective on who *is* and who is *not* deserving of membership and leadership in these communities. The ethnographic examples demonstrate that the politics of deservingness is not only employed within political and public discourses on migration in the Global North, but is also a powerful tool within a refugee community, impacting on the everyday life of refugees.

Concluding Comments

In the Introduction to this volume, Streinzer and Tošić argue that assessments of deservingness depend on contexts and 'situated genealogies', and are subject to power struggles and disputes 'between unequally positioned actors'. They highlight the importance of academics, researchers and practitioners revealing the arbitrariness and hypocrisies in these politics of deservingness. But the politics of deservingness is not only employed from the outside: it is also a powerful tool *within* a community. By drawing on ethnographic fieldwork with resettled Bhutanese refugees in the United Kingdom, I demonstrated that categories determining 'us' versus 'them' are embedded in historical, political and institutionalized discourses, and that individual biographies, affiliations and relationships are carefully assessed not only by top-down institutions, but also within refugee communities themselves. I showed that Bhutanese 'refugee-ness' is a contested category and the politics of deservingness has become a tool for internal differentiations, limiting the ability of formalized RCOs to assist resettled refugees in the United Kingdom. The development of community and its inherent 'Othering' have the potential to produce and accentuate internal differences, leading to conflicts and factionalism rather than unity (Shaw 2006: 29), and therefore call into question the effectiveness of the CDA in refugee resettlement, as well as global discussions on the creation of autonomous 'refugee nations'.

I also highlighted that communities can expand or limit their boundaries depending on economic, political and social advantages (Shaw 2006: 29), demonstrating both the agency of refugee groups *and* the adaptability of deservingness. Notions of deservingness may be key features of community development and maintenance, but boundaries are adaptable, temporal, imagined (Anderson 2006) and symbolic (Cohen 1985). Therefore, Bhutanese refugee communities in the United Kingdom and their notions of deservingness are symbolic constructs within the specific context of refugee resettlement and migration policy.

Thus, claims that refugees universally bestow deservingness on each other and are able and willing to create a global refugee community based on an imagined mutuality may be too optimistic. Echoing the critique of the inadequacy of the 'refugee' label, which reduces the complexity of forced migration and displacement into a single, all-encompassing category (Zetter 2007: 176, 188), it is equally problematic to deny that refugees from different countries of origin and religious, social and economic backgrounds may (re-)create and reinforce internal antagonisms, social polarization and differentiation (Shaw 2006: 29) by employing similar mechanisms to the top-down politics of deservingness. All human communities and societies operate by employing imagined and symbolic boundaries, and refugees are no exception. In order to understand and resolve such issues (e.g. in refugee camps), it is essential to engage refugee communities themselves, and analyse and reflect on the underlying causes for such differentiations, which I have attempted to do in this chapter.

Acknowledgements

I want to thank the editors of this volume for their consideration and comments on drafts of this chapter, as well as Dr Nick Gill (University of Exeter) for his helpful feedback. I also want to thank my former Ph.D. supervisors Dr Froerer and Dr Staples (Brunel University) for their continued support.

Nicole Hoellerer has completed a Ph.D. in anthropology at Brunel University London and was a postdoctoral research fellow for the ASYFAIR research project at the University of Exeter. Her Ph.D. ethnography on refugee resettlement in the United Kingdom laid bare the practice–policy gap in the United Kingdom's migration service provision. She was the lead researcher for ASYFAIR, and conducted court ethnographies in Germany and Austria, exploring legal procedures in refugee status determination within the Common European Asylum System (CEAS). Her recent publications provide sociolegal analyses of asylum and immigration law and practice in Europe.

Notes

1. During my Ph.D. (until 2015/16), the debate in Europe regarding whether people crossing the Mediterranean to reach Europe were refugees or migrants had just been ignited. See the Introduction to this volume, as well as Strasser in Chapter 9. See also Baba's (2013: 2–4) discussion on 'public angst' towards immigrants.
2. Reactive (refugee) migrants have to flee due to political circumstances beyond their control, while proactive (voluntary) migrants actively decide to migrate due to economic, educational or social mobility (Chatty 2010: 30–33).

3. Research (e.g. Zetter and Pearl 2000: 696; Sigona et al. 2004: 8; Spicer 2008: 493) suggests that asylum seekers are more prone to social exclusion both from society *and* services, due to restricted rights and entitlements (in comparison to refugees), as well as discriminatory media coverage.
 4. I conducted fourteen months of ethnographic fieldwork, which combined participant observation with interviews (including research with children and young people, who are 'competent social actors' and provide insight into the refugees' lives – see e.g. Spicer [2008: 494]). The relatively small number of Bhutanese refugees in the United Kingdom – around 350 to 400 – allowed me to study the impact of both resettlement programmes and national policies (such as the Community Development Approach) on a single community.
 5. Dzongkha: from *lho* (South); *tsham* (border); *pa* (adjective).
 6. I refer to my informants as Bhutanese refugees, Nepali Bhutanese or Bhutanese Nepali.
 7. The terms *Lhotshampa* or Nepali Bhutanese should not be understood as an ethnicity – that is, a biological fact or 'primordial attachment' into which someone is born – but rather as an 'imagined' (Anderson 2006) and 'situational' identity, used to 'mark out a differentiated identity to create social and physical boundaries' (Barth 1998).
 8. With the exception of language: Nepali Bhutanese retained their Nepali language, although it became mixed with Dzongkha, Hindi and English.
 9. All names in this work have been changed to preserve anonymity.
10. 'Paki' is an abbreviation of 'Pakistani' and is often used derogatorily in the United Kingdom to describe individuals with brown skin or dark complexion, based on the assumption that individuals with these physiological traits are from a Pakistani or South Asian migratory background.
11. This has changed after fieldwork in course of the 'refugee crisis' – see Strasser, Chapter 9 in this volume.
12. They do not necessarily evoke a *national* identity, which signifies belonging to a specific national territory (e.g. Bhutan or Nepal) and a common *national* history and culture (Voicu 2013: 171). Rather, my informants' experience of (forced) migration created a 'hyphenated' and 'deterritorialised' identity, which is not tied to any nation-state (Bromley 2000: 14).
13. 'Bhutanese refugee-ness' is not the identity of a singular ego, but one that is constructed through relations and discourses with others and their 'culture', and is therefore a cultural identity (Voicu 2013: 162–68).
14. About five to ten of my informants arrived in the UK as asylum seekers before 2010, mostly doctors, nurses and teachers.
15. For example, during the 'Long March Home' in May 2007 (see Evans 2010: 178, 304).
16. For example, there are about 12,000 Palestinian refugees in the United Kingdom, compared to about 350 Bhutanese refugees. Even if only a fraction of Palestinian refugees were to organize themselves as RCOs, they still vastly outnumber my informants; therefore, Bhutanese RCOs may not be 'attractive' to all funding bodies and thus might not obtain the

necessary financial means to provide effective assistance to their members (see also Zetter and Pearl 2000; Sigona et al. 2004; Hoellerer 2018).
17. It is very common for established refugees to assist refugees who have just arrived in the resettlement country via the resettlement programme. New arrivals rely heavily on established refugees to become part of an already-existing social network and thus to gain access to information, facilities and support in order to navigate the unfamiliar social, economic, political and cultural environment.

References

Amit, Vered, and Nigel Rapport. 2002. *The Trouble with Community: Anthropological Reflections on Movement, Identity and Collectivity*. London: Pluto Press.

Anderson, Benedict. 2006. *Imagined Communities*. London: Verso.

Baba, Marietta L. 2013. 'Anthropology and Transnational Migration: A Focus on Policy', *International Migration* 51(2): 1–9.

Barth, Fredrik. 1998. *Ethnic Groups and Boundaries: The Social Organization of Culture*. Long Grove, IL: Waveland Press.

Baumann, Gerd. 1996. *Contesting Culture: Discourses of Identity in Multiethnic London*. Cambridge: Cambridge University Press.

Bhabha, Homi. 2004. *The Location of Culture*. New York: Routledge.

'Bhutan's Forgotten People'. 2014. *101 East*, 2014 Season, Episode 15. *Al Jazeera*, 22 April.

Bromley, Roger. 2000. *Narratives for a New Belonging: Diasporic Cultural Fictions*. Edinburgh: Edinburgh University Press.

Chatty, Dawn. 2010. *Dispossession and Forced Migration in the Middle East*. Cambridge: Cambridge University Press.

Cohen, Anthony. 1985. *The Symbolic Construction of Community*. London: Routledge.

Colson, Elizabeth. 2003. 'Forced Migration and the Anthropological Response', *Journal of Refugee Studies* 16(1): 1–18.

Crawley, Heaven. 2018. 'Why We Need to Protect Refugees from the Big Ideas Designed to Save Them', *The Independent*, 28 July. Retrieved 16 February 2022 from https://www.independent.co.uk/voices/refugee-immigration-europe-migrants-refugia-self-governance-a8467891.html.

Eidson, John, et al. 2017. 'From Identification to Framing and Alignment: A New Approach to the Comparative Analysis of Collective Identities', *Current Anthropology* 58(3): 340–59.

Evans, Rachel. 2009. 'Inheriting the Past and Envisioning the Future: Young Bhutanese Refugees' Political Learning and Action', Ph.D. dissertation. Oxford: St Antony's College, Oxford University.

———. 2010. 'The Perils of Being a Borderland People: On the Lhotshampas of Bhutan', *Contemporary South Asia* 18(1): 25–42.

Fassin, Didier. 2012. *Humanitarian Reason: A Moral History of the Present Times*. Berkeley: University of California Press.
Ferguson, James. 2015. *Give a Man a Fish: Reflections on the New Politics of Distribution*. Durham, NC: Duke University Press.
Gemie, Sharif. 2010. 'Re-defining Refugees: Nations, Borders and Globalization', *Eurolimes* 9: 28–37.
Hacking, Ian. 2006. 'Kinds of People: Moving Targets', Tenth British Academy Lecture, 11 April. London: The British Academy.
Hall, Stuart. 1996. 'Introduction: Who Needs "Identity"?', in Stuart Hall and Paul du Gay (eds), *Questions of Cultural Identity*. London: Sage Publications, pp. 1–17.
Himalayan Times. 2015. 'One Lakh Bhutanese Refugees Resettled Outside Nepal', 20 November.
Hoellerer, Nicole. 2016. 'Community in Refugee Resettlement: An Ethnographic Exploration of Bhutanese Refugees in Manchester (UK)', Ph.D. dissertation. London: Brunel University.
———. 2018. 'The Pitfalls of the Community Development Approach in Refugee Resettlement in the UK: An Ethnographic Analysis of Community Divisions amongst Bhutanese Refugees in Manchester, UK', in Andrew Nelson, Alexander Rödlach and Roos Williams (eds), *The Crux of Refugee Resettlement: Rebuilding Social Networks*. New York: Lexington Books, pp. 125-143.
Holmes, Seth M., and Heide Castañeda. 2016. 'Representing the "European Refugee Crisis" in Germany and beyond: Deservingness and Difference, Life and Death', *American Ethnologist* 43(1): 12–24.
Hutt, Michael. 1996. 'Ethnic Nationalism, Refugees and Bhutan', *Journal of Refugee Studies* 9(4): 397–420.
———. 2007. *Unbecoming Citizens: Culture, Nationhood and the Flight of Refugees from Bhutan*. New Delhi: Oxford University Press.
Joseph, Mathew. 1999. *Ethnic Conflict in Bhutan*. New Delhi: Nirala Publications.
Kelly, Lynnette. 2003. 'Bosnian Refugees in Britain: Questioning Community', *Sociology* 37(1): 35–49.
Malkki, Liisa. 1997. 'Speechless Emissaries: Refugees, Humanitarianism and Dehistoricization', in Karen Fog Olwig and Kirsten Hastrup (eds), *Sitting Culture: The Shifting Anthropological Perspective*. London: Routledge, pp. 223–54.
———. 2002. 'News from Nowhere: Mass Displacement and Globalized Problems of Organization', *Ethnography* 3(3): 351–60.
Mitchell, Jenny, and Ignacio Correa-Velez. 2010. 'Community Development with Survivors of Torture and Trauma: An Evaluation Framework', *Community Development Journal* 45(1): 90–110.
Mortland, Carol A. 1987. 'Transforming Refugees in Refugee Camps', *Urban Anthropology and Studies of Cultural Systems and World Economic Development* 16(3–4): 375–404.

Muggah, Robert. 2005. 'Distinguishing Means and Ends: The Counterintuitive Effects of UNHCR's Community Development Approach in Nepal', *Journal of Refugee Studies* 18(2): 151–64.

Office for National Statistics (ONS). 2011. 'Q05b 2011 Census Summary - Ethnic Group'. Retrieved 11 March 2022 from https://www.manchester.gov.uk/downloads/download/6833/2011_census_-_summary_by_topic.

Rapport, Nigel, and Joanna Overing. 2000. *Social and Cultural Anthropology: The Key Concepts*. London: Routledge.

Sales, Rosemary. 2002. 'The Deserving and the Undeserving? Refugees, Asylum Seekers and Welfare in Britain', *Critical Social Policy* 22(3): 456–78.

Scott, James C. 2008. *Weapons of the Weak: Everyday Forms of Peasant Resistance*. New Haven: Yale University Press.

Shaw, Mae. 2006. 'Community Development and the Politics of Community', *Community Development Journal* 43(1): 24–36.

Sigona, Nando, Roger Zetter and David Griffiths. 2004. 'Refugee Community Based Organizations in the UK: A Social Capital Analysis'. Retrieved 11 March 2022 from https://lemosandcrane.co.uk/resources/ESRC%20-%20Refugee%20Community%20Based%20Organisations%20in%20the%20UK.pdf.

Spicer, Neil. 2008. 'Places of Exclusion and Inclusion: Asylum-Seeker and Refugee Experiences of Neighbourhoods in the UK', *Journal of Ethnic and Migration Studies* 34(3): 491–510.

Turner, Victor. 1967. *The Forest of Symbols: Aspects of Ndembu Rituals*. Ithaca, NY: Cornell University Press.

Turton, David. 2002. 'Forced Displacement and the Nation', in Jenny Robinson (ed.), *Development and Displacement*. Oxford: Oxford University Press, pp. 19–75.

UNHCR. 2001. 'Reinforcing a Community Development Approach'. Geneva: UNHCR. UN Docs EC/51/SC/CRP.6. Retrieved 16 February 2022 from https://www.refworld.org/docid/470629c82.html.

Van Hear, Nicholas. 2016. 'Imagining Refugia', University of Oxford: COMPAS. Retrieved 11 March 2019 from https://www.compas.ox.ac.uk/2016/imagining-refugia/.

———. 2018. 'Furthering Refugia: Engaging with Our Critics'. Retrieved 16 February 2022 from https://www.compas.ox.ac.uk/2018/furthering-refugia-engaging-with-our-critics.

Van Hear, Nicholas, and Robin Cohen. 2015. 'Refugia: A New Transnational Polity in the Making', University of Oxford: COMPAS. Retrieved 16 February 2022 from https://www.compas.ox.ac.uk/project/the-refugia-project.

Voicu, Cristina-Georgiana. 2013. 'Cultural Identity and Diaspora', *Philobiblon* XVIII(1): 161–74.

Williams, Lucy. 2006. 'Social Networks of Refugees in the United Kingdom: Tradition, Tactics and New Community Spaces', *Journal of Ethnic and Migration Studies* 32(5): 865–79.

Wright, George, Kim Ward and Esme Peach. 2004. *ICAR Navigation Guide to Key Issues: Resettlement Programmes and the UK*. London: ICAR.

Zetter, Roger. 2007. 'More Labels, Fewer Refugees: Remaking the Refugee Label in an Era of Globalization', *Journal of Refugee Studies* 20(2): 172–92.

Zetter, Roger, and Martyn Pearl. 2000. 'The Minority within the Minority: Refugee Community-Based Organizations in the UK and the Impact of Restrictionism on Asylum Seekers', *Journal of Ethnic and Migration Studies* 26(4): 675–97.

11

Suffering and Vulnerability Reconfigured

Refugee Images of Hungarian Migrants Working in German Refugee Accommodation Institutions

Ildikó Zakariás and Margit Feischmidt

The relationship of European societies with people arriving from Africa and the Middle East constitutes an important aspect of present-day politics. Discourses of deservingness have become central in this relationship, in deploying or denying support towards specific immigrant groups and categories. In this chapter, we aim to investigate a specific aspect of such deservingness discourses by noting the fact that non-European Union (EU) migrants represent only one segment of transnational migration, while intra-EU mobility is also a constitutive element of present-day migratory currents. Against the simplistic idea that discourses of migrant deservingness are produced by the 'host society', understood as essentialized, homogeneous and unitary, we depart from the assumption that encounters and interactions between people and groups from diverse migration backgrounds constitute an important source.

Encounters between various migrant groups will be analysed with a focus on narratives of suffering, vulnerability and victimhood, in the context of refugee accommodation institutions in Germany. As highlighted in the Introduction to this volume, images of legitimate suffering have become a core component in legal, political and media discourses of refugee deservingness in Western societies. After the Second World War, the modern concept of the refugee became closely tied to the institutional-discursive field of humanitarianism, legitimating support of various displaced populations through their suffering, vulnerability and victimhood. While specific forms of suffering became the basis of distributing material, legal and symbolic resources and the attribution of the 'deserving refugee' category itself, other forms of suffering remained unnoticed or became grounds for indifference or outright rejection (such as for deportation) on behalf of Western societies.

These ideas of (un)deservingness are produced and re-created by various institutional actors and domains. Besides the more often foregrounded institutional actors such as legislation, politics or the media, intermediary institutions that contribute to refugees securing a basic livelihood, food, shelter, health, education, social services and employment are also central in reproducing deservingness (Chauvin and Garcés-Mascareñas 2014; Ambrosini 2016). In this chapter, we aim to explore how refugee deservingness frameworks – and concepts of suffering, and 'deserving victimhood' and vulnerability in particular – are re-created in such institutions of refugee accommodation in Germany.

In our case, such institutions are those offering housing and community development for refugees and asylum seekers, or educational organizations providing language or vocational courses. Central for our current project, these are often operated by employees and volunteers (teachers and social workers) who themselves have experiences, life trajectories and identities related to transnational movement. During the last half-century, there have been many waves of immigration to Germany – including Turkish labour immigrants, ethnic Germans from communist and postcommunist Central Eastern European states, and refugees from the Yugoslav wars of the 1990s, the less visible arrival of hundreds of thousands from eastern EU countries since the liberalization of the German labour market, as well as the widely covered arrival of Middle Eastern refugees. All of this implies that a significant proportion of the population of Germany may be considered as being of 'immigrant background' – as confirmed in recent censuses (Statistisches Bundesamt 2022a). Building on Bauder and Jayaraman (2014), we acknowledge the presence of intra-EU migrants and specifically Central Eastern European migrants as workers in refugee accommodation institutions and refugee services in Germany.

We start from the assumption that migrant background, migration experience and migrant biographies might also have their effect on the perceptions of other migrant groups, such as asylum seekers arriving from outside the EU. Restricting our focus at this phase of our research to intra-EU migrant workers, in this case arriving from Hungary, we thus aim to explore how frameworks legitimating support of irregular migrants unfold among Hungarian workers, who carry out paid or unpaid (voluntary) work connected to the reception and integration of refugees into Germany, as education and social work professionals, for example, language teachers, integration trainers and community organizers.[1]

We thus enquire into the narratives of suffering and vulnerability linked to transnational migration and the role these narratives bear in relation to the legitimation of 'deservingness' of refugee and migrant clients and students in Germany. How does the personal migration experience of workers interfere with and relate to their interpretation of the suffering, victimhood and vulnerability of refugee clients and students? How is 'refugee deservingness' based on suffering and vulnerability reproduced (or reshaped) when the institutional discourses of help and support meet with migrant experiences of frontline workers responsible for such support? At first glance, one could assume that the Hungarian migrant workers would conceptualize the 'refugee-ness' defined around the concept of suffering and vulnerability as different from their own personal migration experience as intra-EU migrants who profit from EU citizenship. However, despite these expectations, we found that identification processes related to transnational migration shape the workers' perceptions in a way that the workers do not see themselves as so different from their refugee clients and students, and draw parallels between their experience and those of the refugees.

Exploring the construction of deservingness based on suffering, vulnerability and victimhood provides an analytical tool to understand the distribution of material resources and practical support in the context of (irregular) migration. It also enables us to go further and explore the political stakes of such deservingness frameworks. Images of vulnerability and victimhood, while securing solidarity and responsibility based on universal human insecurities and innocence, may also, by that means, deprive refugees of their agency and may depoliticize related social phenomena in various ways (Malkki 1996; Fassin and Rechtman 2009; Ticktin 2011; Apostolova 2015). Thus, in our chapter we aim to decipher the workings of such frameworks not only from the perspective of solidarity and support versus rejection, but also by extending our concern regarding their consequences for the politicization of refugee migration.

Discourses of Vulnerability in European Refugee Reception Contexts

The political consequences of legitimizing migration by using the vulnerability framework have been criticized – and labelled as depoliticization – from three major vantage points. First, Malkki (1996) and later Ticktin (2011) and others have explored in great detail and in various social contexts how such depoliticization may lead to depriving refugees of their agency and subjectivity. Emphasis on vulnerability leads to refugees' lived experiences being muted and sidelined, and implies perceiving them as powerless and incapable, disembedded from their sociocultural background, often as mere human bodies in need of (physical) help. Second, such deprivation of subjective experience not only implies misrecognition on the individual level, but is also closely interconnected with muting talk about the causes of suffering. Consideration of causes of suffering may have great importance in prompting individual and collective reflection on sociopolitical and socioeconomic processes on various scales: either on the scale of more localized political subject formation and histories or on that of geopolitics, regarding the role and responsibility of larger economic and political processes – for example, responsibilities of the Global North. If reflexivity about the causes weakens, so does reflexivity about the sociohistorical processes behind the movement of people (Sigona 2014). Third, a major critique has been formulated regarding the exclusionary aspects of the vulnerability framework. As widely explored by many (e.g. Apostolova 2015; d'Halluin 2016), the differentiation between economic and political causes of migration (based on the human rights framework legislated in the 1951 Refugee Convention) legitimizes the strict exclusion of a great proportion of migrant groups from regularization. Suffering and vulnerabilities related to 'political' persecution, linked to membership in specific social groups and categories threatened by some form of violence, qualify as legitimate grounds for international protection; at the same time, economic hardship, poverty or unemployment are deemed illegitimate reasons for asking for such protection. Also, according to these critiques, the human rights framework's promotion of distinguishing the domain of 'politics' from that of 'economy' impedes political thinking about human migration in its complexity and disregards the fact that issues of persecution, violence and injustice are also intimately interwoven with economic processes.

In this chapter, we examine the role of suffering and vulnerability in constructing refugee deservingness in the specific institutional context of refugee services in Germany, with a special focus on its depoliticization effects – or the lack thereof. We ask how the migration background of workers, employees or volunteers in these positions plays into such processes of constructing deservingness based on suffering and vulnerability, and how the migration background of helpers affects related processes of depoliticization. Enquiring into the relationship between refugee deservingness and the migration experience of workers in refugee services is not entirely new. Casati (2017) addressed the topic in her research in a small Sicilian town with inhabitants who have a long history of migration and economic hardship. She found that instead of solidarity, the desire of reception workers as well as local inhabitants was to climb higher in the status hierarchy in relation to other marginal groups – in this case, African and Middle Eastern asylum seekers. Thus, a local past experience of emigration provided the basis not for identification, but for redrawing boundaries among performing and deserving Italian former emigrants and present-day asylum seekers arriving in Italy. Schiff and Clavé-Mercier (2019), analysing a resettlement programme offering Syrian refugees relocation to France, also give a rich description of the possible effects of the helpers' migration background and migrant identities on the constructions of refugee deservingness, revealing both care and control mechanisms based on identification with and disciplining of refugee recipients. In a previous work (Zakariás and Feischmidt 2021), we have also shown how images of deservingness of refugee students and clients centred on their valuable performance in education and employment are predominant in the accounts of Hungarian teachers and social workers in Germany, who often constructed such refugee performance by identifying with them and by linking refugees' deservingness to their own experience – struggles, failures and successes – as immigrants in Germany. Furthermore, a disciplining regard built upon educating students and clients on the subject of 'European culture' also unfolded, and these two frameworks of identification and disciplining, linked to the themes of 'employment' and 'culture', point to the specific positioning of these workers as mediators in the governance of refugees in Germany. In this chapter we aim to complement the conceptual map of refugee deservingness, as constructed by Hungarian workers, and take a closer look at narratives of suffering and vulnerability. What is the place of suffering and vulnerability in constructing refugee deservingness in Hungarian workers' accounts? And what consequences do such narratives have for the politicization of the vulnerability framework?

These latter approaches that enquire into the role of individuals' own migration history and experience in support provided to refugees and asylum seekers are in line with recent ethnographic calls for scholars to conceive of reception contexts as conjunctures of heterogeneous actors that not only include refugees and the host society, but also affect various groups and population segments with experiences related to transnational migration who are embedded in transnational networks in diverse ways (Cabot 2018; Çağlar and Glick Schiller 2018; Isin 2018). These descriptions often highlight the nuanced ways in which transnational mobility and connections may influence perceptions and representations and the boundary-making of those involved, and they thus question the simple analytical juxtaposition of the refugee–host society.

Migrant Workers and Volunteers in Institutions of Refugee Accommodation in Germany

Concerning our specific research context – that is, Hungarians involved in refugee support and welfare services in Germany – statistical data also justify such an approach. Although less publicized by politicians, policy-makers and the media compared to the 'refugee crisis' (Eberl et al. 2018), in recent decades Germany has increasingly become a major site of intra-European mobilities and migrations, which has led to a sharp increase in the number of Western, Central and Eastern European EU citizens in Germany (Statistisches Bundesamt 2022b). The liberalization of the labour market towards Central and Eastern European countries resulted, after 2011, in Hungarians also starting to head for Germany (Blaskó and Gödri 2016). At the beginning of 2018, more than 200,000 Hungarian citizens were registered as residents in Germany (Statistisches Bundesamt 2022b).[2]

While intra-EU migration intensified, at the same time the arrival of large numbers of refugees and asylum seekers in Germany created a labour shortage of workers in social welfare institutions, nongovernmental organizations (NGOs) and charities concerned with the reception, accommodation and integration of refugees and migrants (Grote 2018). Bauder and Jayaraman (2014) already revealed that immigrant organizations as well as employees and volunteers with a migration background have a major role in providing such services. According to our findings, some of the arriving Hungarians were also absorbed by this new sector of the labour market, and found paid jobs or volunteered in refugee reception and integration institutions.[3] Such positions offer higher wages as well as higher living standards compared to jobs in the education, social and health sectors in Hungary, and this has been an important factor in attracting Hungarian (and also other Central and Eastern European) migrants to these positions (Feischmidt and Zakariás 2020). The incorporation of migrants as providers of all sorts of refugee support was also embraced by NGO networks in Germany that employed various incentives – many supported by federal-, state (*Länder*)- or municipal-level state funds – to encourage people of 'migrant background' to become volunteers and paid employees of refugee reception institutions, NGOs and charities.[4] Exact data about the migrant backgrounds of individuals working or volunteering in the refugee accommodation institutions in Germany are difficult to obtain. However, besides Bauder and Jayaraman's (2014) qualitative observations, some quantitative analyses also point to a great number of individuals of various migrant backgrounds in these positions.[5]

The methodology of our qualitative enquiry was semi-structured interviews carried out in the summer and autumn of 2017 with sixteen teachers, social workers and community organizers – mostly women – who were active as volunteers or employees in the reception of refugees and asylum seekers in Berlin and Munich.[6]

Members of the oldest cohort of interviewees had arrived in Germany in the 1980s or 1990s, and referred to family migration, work migration and asylum seeking as motives for their movement. At the time of our fieldwork, they had a stable income and social status, and felt well integrated into German society. Rather than paid employees, these were volunteers and were associated either with state institutions or with grassroots initiatives, in two cases even being led and founded by them. Members of the younger generation had arrived in Germany within the last ten years, and pointed to political and economic reasons for leaving Hungary. Arriving with good German- or English-language skills, they typically became teachers at language schools for refugees or started in jobs assisting refugees in social welfare institutions, either in reception centres, *Erstaufnahmeeinrichtungen* (initial reception facilities) or special programmes offered by local governments.

We recruited our interviewees through personal networks and posts advertising our research on social media. Some of the interviewees were connected to the informants from our previous investigation on civic forms of refugee protection in Hungary.[7] The interviews were conducted during two short fieldwork stays in Berlin and Munich (six weeks altogether), which also allowed us to visit some institutions where our acquaintances work with refugees (and in some cases spend their leisure time as well) in a multicultural environment, including various categories of migrants and refugees.

Creating Deservingness through Performance

Our respondents' duties relate to assisting refugees who have arrived since 2015 or, more broadly, migrants and refugees living in Germany. They focus on: teaching-related activities (most often but not exclusively German-language courses that are part of integration programmes subsidized by the German state); organizing bureaucratic procedures and maintaining contact with social welfare or educational institutions; and arranging optional leisure activities for children and adults. As we described in detail in our earlier work (Zakariás and Feischmidt 2021), the figure of the hardworking refugee who is keen to make progress with the reception process and to find education and employment in Germany is deeply embedded in their narratives about refugee reception and support. In almost all of the interviews, respondents noted the willingness of their clients and students to comply with the reception procedures: to adhere to the rules of reception facilities and institutions, to attend to bureaucratic procedures and to participate in the education- and leisure-related programmes that are organized for them. The majority of our respondents also emphasized that their protégés were hardworking and ambitious.

Julia,[8] a woman in her thirties, had initially continued working for her employer in Budapest. However, after a few years, she started to feel the need to find some 'local' employment in Berlin. After futile and frustrating attempts to find jobs in her original profession as a social scientist, she decided to do social work in a refugee reception centre in Berlin. She described one of her clients as follows:

> I know someone ... he's a lawyer, but the problem is, he is still living there [in Germany] without refugee status and until then [i.e. when he receives it] he can't take part in either formal education or employment, only those internships and such ... He was learning German, and I don't know what, he was always translating. He was always called on if there was some need for some professional translation, for 0.8 cents, at the refugee accommodation, because they could give him no other work, but he was happy that he could at least use his brain, and practise his German.

While stating and continuously emphasizing the ambitions and willingness of their clients and students, a great deal of talk is dedicated to describing the problems involved in achieving these desired goals. These vary from a temporary lack of work or education and finding it difficult or failing to keep up with bureaucratic obligations and deadlines, to low levels of attendance in leisure programmes and training organized by the helpers.

When contextualizing such deservingness narratives, it is important to note that producing successfully integrated refugees, by supporting their participation in education and employment and their compliance with the bureaucratic accommodation process in Germany, is at the centre of our respondents' professional tasks. Hence, these interviews provide terrains where respondents not only describe their clients and students from a neutral, external position, but are also deeply implicated as actors responsible for such performance. Besides offering mere descriptions, social workers, language teachers and community workers in this way also implicitly talk about their own deservingness as worthy and competent in professional refugee support.[9] Difficulties with various aspects of the accommodation process of their clients and students threaten with undermining the self-image of these workers as deserving actors, who were competent in 'producing' successful immigrants.

A possible reaction to these challenges could be to present their nonperforming students and clients as unworthy and undeserving in some way, and thus relinking the failure to perform to refugee clients' and students' own – collective or individual – responsibilities. In the following sections, we will show that apart from only a few exceptions, this is not the case. Difficulties in achieving 'performance' are almost never attributed to cultural characteristics or the personal virtues and morality of the recipients of help. Instead, teachers and social workers centre their interpretations around the suffering and vulnerability of their clients before, during and after migration. As already discussed above, concepts of suffering and vulnerability are central in evoking a humanitarian perspective, compassion and a willingness to provide help and support. Moreover, we show that such a focus on suffering and vulnerability is often, though not exclusively, built upon processes of identification: creating similarities and sameness between the migrant experiences and migrant identities of our interviewees, and those of their refugee clients and students.

Exoticizing Suffering in 'Trauma' Narratives

When cooperation between helpers and the recipients becomes narrated as uncertain and problematic, interviewees often resort to the past trauma of their clients and students. Trauma – that is, an experience of past violence, which leaves traces in the body and mind of a victim that hinder everyday life in the present – became part of legal and psychological discourses on forced migration and asylum a long time ago (Fassin and Rechtman 2009: 225–75). Despite varying meanings and usages of the term, such models of trauma have all converged on specific universal perspectives: first, they deny the importance of an essentialized 'culture' in understanding problems and difficulties; second, they assume a nonmoralizing stance towards victims and deny the responsibility of the sufferer; third, they attribute problems and difficulties to extraordinary experiences and events (such as exile or physical violence); and, fourth, trauma concepts promote compassion towards those who suffer and the right of the latter to receive support.

In the context of the psychological and psychiatric care of refugees in Germany, a domain of expertise has been developed that is dedicated to the experience of trauma.[10] However, beyond psychomedical institutions, everyday interpretations of trauma with an emphasis on its normative, moral connotations may also show up in other institutions in the context of (forced) migration (Fassin and Rechtman 2009). In coping with and narrating difficulties – that is, tensions and conflicts faced in their everyday work – our respondents deploy references to trauma stories of war and violence. In the following extract, we see how initial perceptions that point in the direction of a cultural collectivist interpretation become stabilized by social worker Julia in a psychomedicalized narrative of victimhood and trauma:

> We also organize a lot of programmes for women. I had a colleague who had that job … and it's difficult. Sometimes they were a success – usually those [programmes] that included women, and children too, anyways. Often they just didn't come, or very few people came. Of course, this is also cultural [that women rather stay at home], though men also stay away from these programmes. Either because of laziness, or rather it is [due to] depression – evidently, lots of people have depression, not like a mood, but in a medical sense. Losing your housing would already be sufficient [cause to become depressed], but most of them have lost everything.

These brief allusions are often made without precise knowledge of the individual's past; rather, a nonarticulated traumatic past is assumed and imaginatively added to the interpretations. Such trauma references hinder both a critique of the individual client's morals, as well as collectivist, essentializing cultural explanations of their potentially noncompliant behaviour. The often short and abstract allusions to trauma serve as a tool for framing clients and students as deserving despite their noncompliance; maintaining their deservingness and moral integrity in this way contributes to emotionally stabilizing the commitment to helping.

Edith, a volunteer woman in her mid-fifties, who engaged in activities supporting refugees in Munich and with numerous institutions, shared the following experience. It shows how such vague allusions to trauma can become a collective tool in the hands of social workers, trainers or teachers in reacting to cases and behaviours perceived as problematic. Such storytelling, retelling or muting of stories may become part of the reproduction of vulnerability as an auxiliary framework of deservingness in situations when education/employment frames of performance cannot be directly evoked:

> There was this guy from a rich Afghan family who was gay, and his parents sent him [to Germany], to come. I don't know what happened to him; we didn't have much contact afterwards; he just came to boxing [class] – a fantastic, cute kid. He had to be given a separate room even in the first week, [because] he cried and shouted, the [social worker] girl told us. He just followed her, he was always with her; he must have had shocking stories [experiences] which surfaced in the camp.

In this way, refugee service workers, language teachers and social workers prove to be actors who co-constitute the figure of the 'refugee' by translating their behaviour into the psychomedicalized language of trauma. The psychomedical framework also implies a specific temporality for the clients' and students' failure to perform. Trauma can be healed, with professional support, or merely the passing of time may resolve the incapacities and paralysis; thus, trauma always holds the promise of recovery into a 'normal way of life'. Such recovery, formulated from the perspective of our respondents talking about their refugee work, includes adhering to and complying with institutional expectations, that is, searching for and finding employment, educational opportunities and learning German. Thus, evoking the trauma framework – through its temporality of temporariness and the perspective of recovery – while creating passivity and inability to act in the present, also links the figure of the traumatized person with expectations and hopes of performance.

Besides brief and abstract allusions to (imagined) trauma, a different mode of talking about victimhood may be found in the form of personalized stories of past suffering, as formulated by Edith in the following extract. In contrast to frequent and easily accessible media images depicting refugees, often in crowds, as anonymous sufferers and as powerless victims of violence, and also in contrast with abstract references to past suffering, personal stories of war and exploitation during flight are evoked by our respondents as moments of witnessing the power of individuals who survive and struggle despite the terrifying conditions that surround them:

> Those stories have stayed with me so long; one of them, his mother had died, four kids, he was the only boy, their father raised them. He was

a mechanic, and then soldiers came into the village, and asked for their car to be repaired. And the father said they should pay, he has four kids to feed, and then he was shot. This young kid, he was indeed underage, fifteen years old, he went to the capital, hid there, but there was shooting as well, so he left. And he travelled for six months, and he had only terrible experiences.

However, in our interviews, only about half of the respondents focused their interpretations on such references and stories of evoking traumatic pre-migration events; the other half avoided this framing entirely. Such references to and stories of extreme suffering and horror come with various risks, as seen above, and as described by earlier research (Malkki 1996; Fassin and Rechtman 2009; Ticktin 2011). Ágnes, a social worker and community organizer in Berlin in her late twenties, explicitly formulated her reasons for avoiding such framings by critiquing unequal power relations and the potential 'Othering' that may create distance vis-à-vis the recipients of help, and would contribute to undermining clients' and students' agency:

> Then, the helpers, well, I guess Germans, are a bit disappointed, and not because bad people are coming [to volunteer], but because their attitudes are a bit different. So, a lot of volunteers had this idea that, oh my God, everybody is so traumatized, while this is not always so, I have to say; there are a lot of them, but you shouldn't think that they haven't drunk coffee for months ... Of course, there are a lot of traumatized people – children, men as well – but still, it is not so bad that, oh these miserable people, we must hold their hands all the time.

Ágnes creates a distinction between immigrant and German background helpers according to the latter's greater tendency to perceive their clients according to a trauma framework. Such frameworks, it seems, are carefully managed by the helpers we interviewed, who manoeuvre between the intended and unintended consequences of their use and often consciously avoid the image of traumatized recipients, clients or students.

Identification Based on Pre-migration Hardship

Framing their clients' and their students' pasts as traumatic implies 'Othering' and exoticization. However, suffering before and during migration may also be evoked in such a way that similarity and sameness are created between the Hungarian helpers' experiences, position and identities, and the recipients of such support. Such narratives on common suffering, vulnerabilities and persecution create the legitimacy and deservingness of the refugee recipients (clients and students). At the same time, such legitimation differs from exoticizing trauma narratives, in that it assigns a more active self to both helpers and recipients. Instead of perceiving humans as passive victims, as voiceless, as mere biological bodies (potentially) harmed, through processes of identification by the helpers, they are assigned agency and subjectivity.

Some of the interviewees referenced personal memories of exclusion and persecution in their home societies, or during migration, as grounds for identification with and commitment to their clients. Éva, in her mid-forties, was an active volunteer at various civic initiatives and a German teacher in Munich at the time of the interview; she referred to her own experience of flight to Hungary when forced to leave war-torn Yugoslavia in the early 1990s:

> I myself, from my own experience, I knew how tough it is. Especially if you are a girl. So as a woman, I was concerned with this feminist stuff, evidently. And I have focused on the girls, how I could ease their journeys, or help them.

In these narratives, refugees' deservingness is implicitly constructed in line with the conceptual framework of humanitarianism and human rights as laid out by the 1951 Refugee Convention, which legitimizes the refugee position on the basis of political persecution and physical threat or violence.

However, besides vulnerabilities related to the 'political' domain and to human rights concerns, economic causes of intra-EU migration to Germany also evoke identification with their clients or students. More than a third of respondents mentioned some form of previous economic hardship among the causes of their own moving to Germany (Feischmidt and Zakariás 2020). Thus, similarities among motivations often lead to questioning the divide between legitimate mobility within the EU and the illegitimate movement of 'economic migration' from outside the EU, and imply claims of sameness regarding the motives for and causes of migration.[11] For Éva, besides identification based on victimhood and vulnerability quoted above, such identification based on economic hardship also constitutes an important pillar of legitimizing refugee migration:

> Or, for example, they come from a Nigerian minority community, with zero chance of living a normal life, and want to come to Europe, because here life is good. Because the situation is really bad in Nigeria … And I understand all this, like, my husband calls himself an economic refugee.

Because he came from the Netherlands for the prospect of a better job and a better salary ... And indeed, I am here as well – this is not my home country either.

The word 'fleeing' was evoked in the interviews as a term extending beyond the human rights framework. It might imply not only physical or psychological coercion, violence or political persecution, but also all types of suffering related to starting and making a journey under hostile conditions. In particular, references to difficult circumstances related to poverty and lack of economic prospects were commonplace when talking about refugee clients and students. Fleeing may thus refer to the experience of leaving home in extreme circumstances and without personal possessions; also, fleeing may extend to leaving due to material and economic conditions, to the difficulties of living a 'good life' or a 'normal life' in the society of origin – numerous respondents evoked the term 'fleeing poverty'.

Such blurring of boundaries between political and economic causes might result from institutional expectations in these reception and educational facilities of overlooking distinctions between deserving and undeserving migrants. These institutions, in line with their organizational goals, position their workers as facilitators, educators and mentors who introduce their students and clients to the German labour market, administrative state bureaucracy and educational facilities. At the same time, control functions related to exclusions – that is, expulsions, the denial of various permits and documents, and deportations – lie outside their remit.[12] However, such institutional expectations of avoiding distinctions of 'political refugees' and 'economic migrants' also resonate well with personal migration stories of Hungarian migrant workers, who are deeply infused with economic resentment and who easily project 'refugee-ness' and their own stories of past economic hardship in Hungary onto each other.

Identification Based on Struggling with Accommodation in Germany

Narratives of Hungarian workers concerning the suffering and vulnerability of refugees are not confined to their pre-migration. Significant emphasis is also placed upon experiences after arriving in Germany and after becoming refugees or asylum seekers in the German reception system. According to these images, refugees are surrounded by a multitude of expectations on the part of accommodation institutions and the wider public in Germany – expectations they fully engage with and are determined to meet. However, external factors often threaten to stop them meeting these expectations, which puts them under intense physical and psychological pressure.

Denying responsibility for failure to perform, while enhancing the will and moral commitment to do so, allows the reproduction of the figure of the deserving migrant. Such overwhelming dominance of the notion of the deserving refugee who struggles to comply with bureaucratic processes and seeks to gain an education or employment implies sympathy and a willingness and emotional drive to help that was present in the majority of our interviews. Detailed descriptions of the overwhelming circumstances that overburden their clients and students in German accommodation institutions were ubiquitous in the interviews. Kati, a middle-aged woman who had worked in a nonprofit organization in Berlin since its inception in the 1980s, talked extensively about her own struggles with immigration to Germany. She formulated the institutional obstacles to refugees' accommodation in a tone typical of many of our respondents:

> People usually don't know how many obstacles refugees face. They are forbidden to choose where they live, they have no work permit, not all of them are entitled to language courses, etc. Average people are ignorant about all this. This might lead to the general opinion that refugees don't want to work.

Personalized stories of refugees struggling against an extremely hostile environment before or during flight may also be extended from pre-migration vulnerabilities and suffering to the postmigration process of accommodation in the host environment. Thus, these stories might link suffering before migration with ambitions and struggles after arriving in Germany. Eszter, a volunteer and mentor in Berlin to numerous earlier Eastern European labour migrants as well as current refugees and asylum seekers, described one such personalized struggle story as follows:

> And then they [the civic association] sent me Hussain, a Syrian arriving from Aleppo, with a business college degree. And he came via the classic route – what we know from TV – through Turkey, and fleeing here and there. So during his hellish journey ... not through the Hungarian fence, as it wasn't yet erected, but across the sea to Lesbos, his boat sank, so he swam for two hours in the sea, so he lived through the all-too-familiar horror story. Hussain, in my experience, is an exemplary migrant, and if all were like him, Germany should count its lucky stars, because this guy, he is a miracle. When we met, he had been here [in Germany] for half a

year, yet he already was able to make it through the German bureaucratic processes, with help and with talent, or with talent to acquire help, he got out of the refugee home, and obtained access to an apartment for rent; he was awarded refugee status, so he could stay, and what's more, he succeeded in bringing his family as well, his wife and two kids. And, as I learned, he went on to complete various language courses, with limited results to my opinion, yet with an immense willpower, and after all of these he got an internship at a South Berlin accounting company.

Such narratives are often connected to perceived similarities between workers' own migration stories and those of their clients, and they predominantly underline the difficulties encountered while learning the language, searching for jobs, making social contact with locals and acquiring a sense of belonging and feeling at home – just like their clients. Ágnes, a social worker and community organizer in Berlin, referred explicitly to her own past migrant experience – her frustrations – when explaining her professional empathetic attitude towards her clients:

> And then I thought, I'll move to London. [It was] the shittiest decision of my life. I didn't really speak English, and there I was, in total ignorance – and this is why I can terribly [sic] understand these people – because I did the same, that, oh, yeah, I'm going to work in some place, and learn English in the meantime. And of course, nothing worked out like that.

These narratives on the similarities of problems and everyday struggles in settling most often contribute to the reconstruction and maintenance of the concept of performing, and thus of deserving refugees who are 'willing' to overcome obstacles. Moreover, this active, complying (refugee) subject is seen as a parallel to the active and complying self of the speaker. These narratives position helpers as immigrants in German society whose compliance with economic and legal expectations is also expressed. Similarly to identification narratives related to pre-migration suffering and personal motives behind transnational movement described in the previous section, such narratives involve processes of mirroring identification that create performance and deservingness by blurring boundaries between refugees/asylum seekers and other immigrants, among them the Hungarians living in Germany.

Such narratives of identification relate to suffering and hardship during the accommodation process in Germany, and references and interconnections made between one's own and the Other's position lead to technical critiques of the reception institutions, as we saw in remarks quoted above about the missing entitlements to language courses or legal work. However, narratives establishing common positions that could provide grounds for formulating political claims are scarce in our interviewees' accounts. The lack of profound political critique may be explained by various factors. First, the institutional environment and our respondents' frontline-worker positions might have focused attention on the institutional tasks and goals of 'integration'. Second, while talking about their motives for migrating, our respondents emphasized their critique of Hungarian politics, which was deeply hostile and xenophobic towards refugees and asylum seekers. In light of such xenophobic politics, the institutional circumstances and politics of refugee reception and integration in Germany were perceived as open and humane, despite institutional obstacles to achieving 'performance'. Third, Hungarian migrant workers, especially those arriving after 2010, occupy a specific position: wider societal expectations to prove their 'deservingness' as working migrants are answered by employment in these institutions, making them interested in compliance with these institutions rather than in their critique.

All these processes result in the construction of a specific form of agency assigned to refugees and asylum seekers by Hungarian migrant workers. Instead of agency being placed in dichotomous opposition to passivity (in which agency is associated with resistance and subversion), it should be understood as possibly taking multiple forms. Conceptualizing agency as 'modalities', following Shachar and Hustinx (2019), allows us to understand the formulation of refugee agency as adhering to the norms of individualism, meritocracy and employability, and to focus more on individual survival than on historical-political processes, on the potential for social mobilization and on social change.

In this light, narratives of suffering describing refugees' hardship and struggles with institutional and political expectations in Germany, the implied legitimation of 'refugee deservingness' and the parallel deployment of a technical critique of refugee accommodation institutions seem to be severely limited by this individualistic framework of agency. Empathy then occasionally may shift to responsibilization of clients and students, and may become reformulated in a disciplinary tone.[13] Kati, quoted at the beginning of this section, followed her descriptions of the numerous difficulties encountered in Germany by migrants and refugees alike as follows:

> So those who are willing, they have all the opportunities to integrate, and we are the best examples [with a colleague, also from Hungary], of how

if someone is willing, they can achieve a lot in this society. And those who are not really on it, those who only see the obstacles and who are unwilling to act in their own interest, they will not integrate neither in ten nor in twenty years.

Discussion and Conclusion

Based on interviews conducted with sixteen individuals who migrated from Hungary to Germany, working in 2017 either as paid employees or as volunteers in institutions of refugee accommodation, this chapter has explored how frameworks of deservingness legitimating support and helping commitment in these institutions interact with migrant biographies. Specifically, we enquired into deservingness frameworks built upon refugee suffering and vulnerability, as expressed by Hungarian migrant workers. We started from the assumption that although entitlement of refugees and asylum seekers to various services is legally ensured in these institutions, workers' moral concerns as expressed in deservingness narratives may still differentiate their levels of empathy and commitment to help. We also aimed to look beyond these frameworks' immediate consequences of legitimating the redistribution of support and we also kept in focus their potential political implications.

Although the great variation in positions and professions (social workers, teachers, community organizers, volunteers and employees) among our respondents and their implications for deservingness narratives would require further research and empirical data, we nevertheless found general patterns in our respondents' talk. We have shown that narratives of vulnerability and suffering provide frameworks for constructing deservingness of refugees and operate as tools for legitimating support and commitment to help in multiple ways. Classic humanitarian narratives of trauma and victimhood of refugees provide a powerful framework to claim refugee deservingness by building upon imaginings of extreme suffering. Abstract references to or personalized stories of extreme and exoticized suffering and horror have paradoxical consequences for the agency of the recipients of support. Although traumatic victimhood implies passivity and inaction in the present, trauma also carries the potential for recovery and healing, thus promising future agency.

At the same time, suffering is also evoked in a strikingly different manner, building closeness and identification between the helper and the sufferer. Migrant histories and experience play a central role in creating identification, based on similarities and sameness of experience related to transnational movement. With less focus on pre-migration suffering and with more emphasis on difficulties and struggles related to the accommodation process in Germany (understood as 'integration' and more specifically as performance in employment or education), the deservingness of refugees and asylum seekers is reconstructed through and in parallel to the agency of the migrant helpers.

Processes of creating deservingness through identification imply the widening of the forms of suffering that may qualify as proper and legitimate. We have shown that the classic trauma narratives, namely various forms of political persecution and violence, are complemented by needs, suffering and vulnerabilities tied to the 'economic' domain. The boundaries at the core of the humanitarian and human rights distinction between the political and the economic become blurred, when institutions responsible for 'integration' that are disinterested in selection processes employ workers and volunteers migrating out of material and economic resentment.

Moreover, the palette of suffering legitimating deservingness is also complemented with postmigration vulnerabilities. In these narratives, the reception and accommodation institutions in Germany present refugees and asylum seekers with overwhelming difficulties, and their expectations are extremely hard to meet. Migrant workers liken refugee students' and clients' struggle for deservingness to their own experience as migrants aiming for 'integration' in Germany. Despite expectations regarding intra-EU migrants' 'mobility' that is unhindered transnational movement within the EU, in the last decade many researchers have found that socioeconomic, social and psychological effects of migration can also hit intra-EU migrants hard – related to downward mobility, unemployment, precarious labour market positions or de-qualification, as well as social isolation (Favell and Nebe 2009; Glorius et al. 2013). Our respondents, though considering themselves successful in Germany, evoked their respective experiences of struggles and successes, but also their failures regarding specific attempts at finding employment and existential stability. This conceptual move operates by separating the difficult external circumstances of the accommodation process and institutions in Germany from the personal intentions, will and desires of refugees. It thus allows for empathically reconstructing the moral integrity and agency of refugee students and clients, sustaining their deservingness, despite actual or potential dangers of failure.

The shifting of the boundaries of suffering and vulnerability to cover the 'economic' domain, as well as the struggles and difficulties in the process of accommodation, arises not only from the migrant background of employees and volunteers, but such identification processes and empathetic perspectives are also core professional elements in refugee social work in Germany (Kubisch et al. 2017). Furthermore, others have shown how legislative, political and media discourses of vulnerability of refugees and asylum seekers in Germany have shifted in recent years towards an emphasis on deservingness related to employment and education, blurring the boundaries between economic migrants and political refugees, and orienting attention towards the prospects of new arrivals and their benefits to the German society (Schammann 2017, Holzberg et al. 2018). Intermediary organizations of refugee accommodation are designated as major actors responsible for the implementation of these 'meritocratic' policies (Schammann 2017) and for the production of such 'performing' immigrants. These institutional positions coalesce with the ambitions of Hungarian migrant helpers, teachers and social workers to produce their own performance as deserving and performing immigrants in Germany.

These interactions between policy changes, the institutional setting of accommodation institutions and the migrant experience of employees and volunteers have significant consequences for the depoliticization of refugee migration processes and for the agency produced in narratives of migrant workers. We have shown that the focus on refugee suffering and vulnerability is closely linked to the production of the deserving refugee who is willing to comply with the German reception system, find employment or enrol in education. Narratives of deservingness based on suffering and vulnerability, rather than causing tension between the figures of the active performing refugee and the passive victim, in this way become adjusted to the logic of performance. This has specific consequences for constructions of agency. Either suspending agency temporarily (in the case of trauma references) or pre-indicating or claiming performance in the host society (in the case of narratives of identification related to migration), all narratives point in the direction of a specific form of agency: one that is in line with the meritocratic and individualized order of Western capitalist ways of life.

Subordinating suffering-based deservingness to the production of a subjectivity focused on employment, education and compliance with the bureaucratic processes in Germany also implies a narrow perspective on larger societal phenomena. All these divergent forms of identifications and distinctions related to narratives of the suffering and hardship behind migration are not developed into broader reflections on the wider sociopolitical context. Interpretations related to motives and causes remain confined to the Hungarian interviewees' own migratory motivations and, specifically, mainly to the discussion of Hungarian national-level politics (Feischmidt and Zakariás 2020). Apart from a few brief, sometimes ironic, comments, the larger sociopolitical and economic relations and contexts that stand behind current transnational migratory processes within and from outside the EU are almost entirely neglected or out of sight. Causes of poverty, as well as of war and conflicts, remain in the shadows, just like the national order of things (Malkki 1996) that implies the system of (im)mobility responsible for sufferings and vulnerabilities before, during and after the migrant journeys.

Acknowledgements

We would hereby like to thank Humboldt University for supporting our empirical investigation with the Humboldt Talent Travel Award, the Institute for Migration and Integration Research at the same university, which hosted our project, and Magdalena Nowicka, Wolfgang Kaschuba and Sina Arnold, as well as Attila Melegh, Attila Papp Z and Imre Kovách, migration and mobility experts in Budapest. Special thanks to our colleagues from the Centre for Social Sciences, especially to Márton Hunyadi, who conducted the interviews in Munich.

Ildikó Zakariás is Research Fellow at the Centre for Social Sciences, Institute for Minority Studies, Budapest. Her main research areas are civil society and humanitarianism, migration, ethnicity and nationalism. Her dissertation has been published as a monograph (in Hungarian) under the title *Philanthropic Nation: Solidarity and Power in the Support of Ethnic Hungarian Minorities* (Kalligram, 2018). Her recent publications have appeared in the journals *Sociology*, *Voluntas*, *Nations and Nationalism*, and the *Journal of Immigration and Refugee Studies*.

Margit Feischmidt is Senior Researcher at the Centre for Social Sciences, Institute for Minority Studies, Budapest, and teaches at the Institute for Communication and Media Studies, University of Pécs.

She is also editor in chief of *Intersections. East European Journal of Society and Politics*. She has recently published on new forms of nationalism and populism, xenophobia and racism in *Nations and Nationalism, Identities* and *Citizenship Studies*, and on economic migration, refugee support and transnational solidarity in *Sociology* and the *Journal of Immigration and Refugee Studies*. She has also co-edited *Refugee Protection and Civil Society in Europe* (2019, with Ludger Pries and Céline Cantat).

Notes

1. We came to know the specific group of Hungarian immigrants in Germany in our earlier fieldwork, in 2015, which was conducted among Hungarian humanitarian initiatives supporting refugees in Hungary. The current research continues this earlier fieldwork.
2. Individuals of foreign citizenship residing for more than three months in Germany have to register with the Central Registry of Foreigners (AZR) (Statistisches Bundesamt 2022b).
3. Regarding Polish migrants in the refugee reception system, see Nowicka et al. (2017).
4. See the following projects that played a role in inviting migrants of various backgrounds to volunteer for refugee support: www.samofa.de, https://www.damigra.de/damigra/mut-projekt/ueber-das-projekt, https://www.integrationsbeauftragte.de/ib-de/themen/projekte-und-forschung/staerken-was-stark-macht-gewaltpraevention-mit-migrantinnen-fuer-migrantinnen-398756 (retrieved 17 February 2022). We thank Ludger Pries for kindly sharing this information with us.
5. In a quantitative study that analysed solidarity activities and practices towards refugees in Germany in recent years, Kiess et al. (2018) found that a migrant background was strongly related to increased participation in pro-refugee activities. A representative survey carried out in July 2016 among Polish migrants in Germany revealed that 18 per cent of the latter had volunteered or donated to refugees since 2015 (Nowicka et al. 2017).
6. We asked our interviewees about their pre-migration life and motivation for migration, as well as about their experiences in Germany, including those gained through refugee-supporting activities. Most of our interviewees were well educated, with a university degree.
7. See Feischmidt and Zakariás 2019; and Zakariás and Feischmidt 2021.
8. Names have been changed to ensure anonymity.
9. The Hungarian academics conducting the interviews were probably perceived as occupying a position attributed with two main characteristics, which might have influenced our respondents' talk in two ways. First, the interviewers presented themselves as researchers who had previously

studied refugee support initiatives and refugee solidarity in Hungary. Such positions possibly mobilized imagined expectations regarding the interviewees' own solidarity and pro-refugee commitment, as a critical stance towards the heavily xenophobic anti-refugee policies of the Hungarian government. On the other hand, because the interviewers were only visiting researchers on fieldwork in Germany, affiliated with the Hungarian Academy of Sciences, they were possibly perceived by the respondents as representatives of the 'sending' society, towards whom the respondents' own success in migration and 'integration' in Germany had to be created and reinforced.
10. In the institutional sector, see Adorjan et al. (2017); for practical implementation, see Thöle et al. (2017).
11. Besides economic motives, political causes of their own migration were also mentioned by many of our interviewees in Berlin, some of whom are politically active members of the diaspora (Feischmidt and Zakariás 2020).
12. '[Then, do you see a difference if someone is fleeing because of war…?] No, we do not make a distinction; it is strictly forbidden. We do not ask questions. Questions should be posed by those who are keen on the German authorities. We are not the authorities – we are a helping organization. And a helping organization does not question, just helps. We look at the human' (German teacher in an NGO in Munich).
13. For a detailed analysis of disciplining aspects of Hungarian workers' narratives, see Zakariás and Feischmidt (2021).

References

Adorjan, Kristina, et al. 2017. 'Versorgungsmodelle für traumatisierte Flüchtlinge in Deutschland', *Der Nervenarzt* 88: 989–94.

Ambrosini, Maurizio. 2016. 'From "Illegality" to Tolerance and beyond: Irregular Immigration as a Selective and Dynamic Process', *International Migration* 54(2): 144–59.

Apostolova, Raja. 2015. 'The Real Appearance of the Economic/Political Binary: Claiming Asylum in Bulgaria', *Intersections. EEJSP* 2(4): 33–50.

Bauder, Harald, and Sita Jayaraman. 2014. 'Immigrant Workers in the Immigrant Service Sector: Segmentation and Career Mobility in Canada and Germany', *Transnational Social Review* 4(2–3): 176–92.

Blaskó, Zsuzsa, and Irén Gödri. 2016. 'The Social and Demographic Composition of Emigrants from Hungary', in Zsuzsa Blaskó and Károly Fazekas (eds), *The Hungarian Labour Market*. Budapest: Institute of Economics, Centre for Economic and Regional Studies, Hungarian Academy of Sciences, pp. 60–68.

Cabot, Heath. 2018. 'The European Refugee Crisis and Humanitarian Citizenship in Greece', *Ethnos* 84(5): 747–71.

Çağlar, Ayşe, and Nina Glick-Schiller. 2018. *Migrants and City Making: Dispossession, Displacement, and Urban Regeneration*. Durham, NC: Duke University Press.

Casati, Nicola. 2017. 'How Cities Shape Refugee Centres: "Deservingness" and "Good Aid" in a Sicilian Town'*iJournal of Ethnic and Migration Studies* 44(5): 792–808.

Chauvin, Sébastien, and Blanca Garcés-Mascareñas. 2014. '*Becoming Less Illegal*: Deservingness Frames and Undocumented Migrant Incorporation', *Sociology Compass* 8(4): 422–32.

d'Halluin, Estelle. 2016. 'Le nouveau paradigme des "populations vulnérables" dans les politiques européennes d'asile', *Savoir/Agir* 36(2): 21–26.

Eberl, Jakob-Moritz, et al. 2018. 'The European Media Discourse on Immigration and Its Effects: A Literature Review', *Annals of the International Communication Association* 42(3): 207–23.

Fassin, Didier, and Richard Rechtman. 2009. *Empire of Trauma: An Inquiry into the Condition of Victimhood*. Princeton: Princeton University Press.

Favell, Adrian, and Tina Maria Nebe. 2009. 'Internal and External Movers: East–West Migration and the Impact of EU Enlargement', in Ettore Recchi and Adrian Favell (eds), *Pioneers of European Identity: Citizenship and Mobility in the EU*. Cheltenham: Edward Elgar, pp. 205–23.

Feischmidt, Margit, and Ildikó Zakariás. 2019. 'Politics of Care and Compassion: Civic Help for Refugees and Its Political Implications in Hungary – a Mixed-Methods Approach', in Margit Feischmidt, Ludger Pries and Céline Cantat (eds), *Refugee Protection and Civil Society in Europe*. Cham: Palgrave Macmillan, pp. 59–99.

———. 2020. 'Transnational Solidarity in a Differential Migration System: The Actions, Motivations and the Structural Position of Refugee-Solidarian Hungarians in Germany', *Journal of Immigrant and Refugee Studies* 18(4): 481–97.

Glorius, Birgit, Izabela Grabowska-Lusinska and Aimée Kuvik. 2013. *Mobility in Transition: Migration Patterns after EU-Enlargement*. Amsterdam: Amsterdam University Press.

Grote, Janne. 2018. 'The Changing Influx of Asylum Seekers in 2014–2016: Responses in Germany', *Working Paper 79, Federal Office for Migration and Refugees*. Retrieved on 23 March 2022 from https://nbn-resolving.org/urn:nbn:de:0168-ssoar-67637-6

Holzberg, Billy, Kristina Kolbe and Rafal Zaborowski. 2018. 'Figures of Crisis: The Delineation of (Un)Deserving Refugees in the German Media', *Sociology* 52(3): 534–50.

Isin, Engin. 2018. 'Mobile Peoples: Transversal Configurations', *Social Inclusion* 6(1): 115–23.

Kiess, Johannes, Christian Lahusen and Ulrike Zschache. 2018. 'Solidarity Activism in Germany: What Explains Different Types and Levels of Engagement?', in Christian Lahusen and Maria Grasso (eds), *Solidarity* in Europe. *Palgrave Studies in European Political Sociology*. Cham: Palgrave Macmillan, pp. 43–71.

Kubisch, Sonja, et al. 2017. 'Soziale Arbeit und Engagement von Menschen mit und ohne Fluchthintergrund im Kontext von Flucht und Asyl. Abschlussbericht. Technische Hochschule Köln'. Retrieved 17 February 2022 from https://www.th-koeln.de/mam/downloads/deutsch/hochschule/fakultaeten/f01/soziale_arbeit_und_engagement_von_menschen_mit_und_ohne_fluchthintergrund_im_kontext_von_flucht_und_asyl.pdf.

Malkki, Liisa. 1996. 'Speechless Emissaries: Refugees, Humanitarianism, and Dehistoricization', *Cultural Anthropology* 11(3): 377–404.

Nowicka, Magdalena, Lukasz Krzyzowski and Dennis Ohm. 2017. 'Solidarisierung in Europa. Migrant*innen und Osteuropäer*innen und deren Engagement für Geflüchtete', *Solidarität im Wandel? Forschungsbericht*. Berlin: Humboldt-Universität zu Berlin, pp. 10–30. Retrieved 22 March 2022 from https://www.lk-vr.de/media/custom/2297_239_1.PDF?1496213118Shachar, Itamar Y., and Leslie Hustinx. 2019. 'Modalities of Agency in a Corporate Volunteering Program: Cultivating a Resource of Neoliberal Governmentality', *Ethnography* 20(2): 205–26.

Schammann, Hannes. 2017. 'Eine meritokratische Wende? Arbeit und Leistung als neue Strukturprinzipien der deutschen Flüchtlingspolitik', *Sozialer Fortschritt* 66(11): 741–57.

Schiff, Claire, and Alexandra Clavé-Mercier. 2019. 'Becoming, Doing and Letting Go: (Extra)Ordinary Citizens' Engagement with Resettled Syrian Refugee Families in Rural France', in Margit Feischmidt, Ludger Pries and Céline Cantat (eds), *Refugee Protection and Civil Society in Europe*. Cham: Palgrave Macmillan, pp. 161–92.

Sigona, Nando. 2014. 'The *Politics of Refugee Voices*: Representations, Narratives, and Memories', in Elena Fiddian-Qasmiyeh, Gil Loescher, Katy Long and Nando Sigona (eds), *The Oxford Handbook of Refugee and Forced Migration Studies*. Oxford: Oxford University Press, pp. 369–82.

Statistisches Bundesamt (Destatis). 2022a. 'Migration and integration. Population in private households by migrant background in the wider sense and by country of origin, groups of countries'. Retrieved 22 March 2022 from https://www.destatis.de/EN/Themes/Society-Environment/Population/Migration-Integration/Tables/migrant-status-groups-of-countries.html

Statistisches Bundesamt (Destatis). 2022b. 'Migration and integration Foreign population by selected citizenships and years'. Retrieved 22 March from https://www.destatis.de/EN/Themes/Society-Environment/Population/Migration-Integration/Tables/foreigner-citizenship-time-serie.html

Thöle, Anna-Maria, et al. 2017. 'Psychotherapeutische Versorgung von Geflüchteten aus der Sicht niedergelassener Psychotherapeuten in

Deutschland', *Zeitschrift für Psychiatrie, Psychologie und Psychotherapie* 65: 145–54.

Ticktin, Miriam. 2011. *Casualties of Care. Immigration and the Politics of Humanitarianism in France*. Berkeley: University of California Press.

Zakariás, Ildikó, and Margit Feischmidt. 2021. '"We Are That in-Between Nation": Discourses of Deservingness of Hungarian Migrants Working in Institutions of Refugee Accommodation in Germany', *Sociology* 55(2): 400–20. doi:10.1177/0038038520941690.

———. 2020. 'Producing the Nation through Philanthropy: Legitimising Coethnic and Prorefugee Civic Action in Hungary', *Nations and Nationalism*, 26: 1015–32. https://doi.org/10.1111/nana.12607.

Part IV

Debt Relations: The State, Market Actors and Debtors

12

Do Mortgagors in Hardship Deserve Debt Relief?

Legitimizing and Challenging Inequality during the Spanish Home Repossession Crisis

Irene Sabaté Muriel

Deservingness in Times of Crisis

In the wake of the 'neoliberal turn' and more acutely after the recent financial crisis and the subsequent imposition of austerity politics, the contrast between a multitude of people in need and finite public and private resources to be distributed has been highlighted (Watkins-Hayes and Kovalsky 2016). In addition to the considerable social anxieties it produces, this fabricated scarcity (Vaccaro et al. 2020) justifies restrictions in the access to resources. In this way, universal entitlements are eroded, the availability of welfare transfers is questioned and the government's responsibilities become limited accordingly, while market-based solutions to poverty are enhanced. As competition is triggered among applicants for support, suspicion of them being fraudsters is on the rise, which in turn legitimizes increases in the surveillance practised by poverty relief agencies. The provision of resources becomes conditional, as limits are set on the agencies' obligation to support their clients: rather than providing universal relief – for example, on the basis of citizenship or even of common humanity – resources will only be allocated after individual applicants are assessed as meeting certain criteria.

This chapter provides an outline of the process by which, in a crisis context, inequalities become moralized through the lens of deservingness (Streinzer and Tošić, Introduction to this volume), something that happens in at least two senses (Watkins-Hayes and Kovalsky 2016). First, by means of the dynamics of blaming and attributions of responsibility, people are assessed as deserving or undeserving of the social impacts of the crisis. This chapter will focus on one particular impact: the spate of home repossessions that has hit around 700,000 Spanish households in the last ten years.[1] Economic hardship faced in the present is thus attributed to individual dispositions and past behavioural choices: defaulting mortgagors often face recriminations concerning the wasteful lifestyle they allegedly led during the years of economic euphoria, which included irresponsible indebtedness as they intended to live 'beyond their means'. This accusation, in addition to naturalizing or even justifying their current difficulties, is often internalized by debtors themselves, as has also been shown by Matos (Chapter 7 in this volume) for welfare recipients in Portugal during the implementation of austerity measures. This self-blame or 'moral censure' results in a first obstacle – one of an affective or psychological nature (Sanmartín 2019) – in their quest for a way out of the crisis.

But there is also a second sense, related to the first, in which deservingness is also crucially at play: people may be judged as deserving or not deserving of the resources aimed at mitigating the impacts of the crisis. Deservingness may emerge here from the acknowledgement of structural conditions beyond people's control as the main factors of current hardship. Those who are judged as being without fault are thus made into victims and identified as deserving of protection, reparation, justice – and, from a humanitarian viewpoint (Fassin 2005, 2010), compassion – as a precondition for the allocation of poverty relief or, as is my focus here, forms of debt relief such as the cancellation of outstanding debt (sometimes in exchange for the mortgaged property), as well as affordable rent leases as a replacement for the lost home. It is at this stage – necessarily after assessments are made by certain actors in control of resources – that deservingness may have material consequences, channelling debt relief or giving access to alternative housing.

As can be noted, applying the concept of deservingness entails processes of labelling and categorization, of distinction and division, as well as the construction of hierarchies, that often lead to forms of social segregation. In other words, if someone is deserving, it means that others are undeserving, in a historically contingent process of reframing or boundary-making (Chauvin and Garcés-Mascareñas

2014). Of course, these attributions often rely on stereotypes and social prejudices, and result in the construction of an alterity. In general, deservingness tends to be based on proofs of 'social worth', mainly derived from people's role in the realm of production, where some roles and tasks are classified as self-righteous in contrast to others (Cobb 1973), while no attention is paid to what individuals are contributing in other arenas, such as the family (Watkins-Hayes and Kovalsky 2016).

As Gans (1994) points out from a functionalist perspective, the efficacy of this process lies in its contribution to sustaining the whole structure of social inequality, as the mere labelling of the 'undeserving' strengthens existing social privileges and marks 'Otherness'. Those 'undeserving' function as scapegoats and therefore allow the displacement of frustration and fear in times of hardship. Existing inequalities – on the basis of gender, race, legal status, etc. – are reinforced and legitimized by means of deservingness assessments, which add to the construction of an unequal social order based on particular notions of merit.

So, how is deservingness assessed and by whom? As our case study will show and some authors have identified (Watkins-Hayes and Kovalsky 2016), the issue may become the object of public conversation, with society at large trying to establish who the beneficiaries of redistribution should be, often with the intervention of – and the biases introduced by – the mass media. Importantly, those in control of the allocation of resources also resort to the notion of deservingness as a tool. This is how these 'gatekeepers' find themselves not only allocating – or denying – material goods or monetary transfers, but also allocating or denying the legitimacy to receive them.

But the picture becomes even more complex if – as we are intending to do in this chapter – the self-construction as deserving or undeserving by our subjects of study[2] is also taken into account. Attention will be paid to how defaulting mortgagors – enmeshed in their reciprocity networks and sometimes participating in anti-repossession movements – depict themselves as not deserving of how society, creditors and the state are treating them, and as deserving debt relief. They typically state their self-worth (Cobb 1973) – as hardworking people and good faith debtors going through unexpected hardship – in their attempts to be eligible for debt relief, be it in the form of debt cancellation, access to affordable alternative housing after eviction or both. It is thus our intention to address self-definitions of deservingness in addition to heteronomous ones – that is, to assessments made by other actors.

In this aim, it is essential to acknowledge the historicity of deservingness assessments, which are always in the making and often subject to some degree of controversy and struggle, even in the cases where, initially, they seem to be widely shared within society, sometimes even by those seen as undeserving. That was the case at the beginning of the repossession crisis, when thousands of defaulting mortgagors resignedly lost their homes to creditors and did it with shame and guilt, staging no resistance at all. However, the dialectical construction of deservingness, in the sense that it reflects a historical tension between opposing forces, also leaves scope for the questioning of existing inequalities, therefore challenging what can come to be seen as social injustice. By applying an alternative set of deservingness criteria, anti-repossession movements have had considerable success in reframing the public debate about who 'deserves' to be 'rescued' most – or bailed out – from the financial crisis. Should it be 'too big to fail' banks, which were to a great extent responsible for the crisis itself, or should it be the people who found themselves trapped in unpayable mortgage loans and at risk of homelessness?

The following analysis intends to shed some light on the complexities of how deservingness has been used in the framework of the Spanish home repossession crisis.

The Spate of Home Repossessions: The Dynamics of Blame and Emerging Claims for Solutions

As noted in the previous section, in the early years of the current economic crisis in Spain, as the mortgage default rate began to rise, hegemonic discourses depicted defaulting debtors as having lived 'beyond their means', and therefore as culprits of their own situation (Sanmartín 2019). The phenomenon of home repossessions was widely perceived as a marginal one, only affecting borrowers who had overestimated their purchasing power and job stability, or who had failed to resist the temptations of available credit that gave access to conspicuous consumption, as well as to the purchase of overvalued properties during the housing bubble. Their aspiration for material living standards higher than those traditionally attributed to their social condition was then seen as illegitimate. In the rare occasions in which mortgage overindebtedness was the object of public debate, it was framed exclusively in terms of individual guilt, and no further responsibilities were identified. In the words of an economics professor at a prestigious business school, quoted in a 2012 article published on a well-known real-estate webpage, 'homeowners who got mortgage loans beyond their means shouldn't be blithely supported, as those funds will not reach others more in need of them, and who perhaps are not to blame for their own problems' (*Idealista* 2012, translation by the author).

The under-representation of over-indebtedness in the public sphere went on during the last years of the housing bubble. In 2008, repossessions rose to 58,686, more than twice the number in the previous year, and the rate of default amounted to 2.37 per cent, more than three times the rate in 2007.[3] Although bank managers started to be worried, at the beginning they put off really dealing with the problem through a variety of strategies.[4] At that time, virtually no public voices, except for those of some critical scholars (Naredo 2009; López and Rodríguez 2010) and some predecessors of anti-eviction movements (França 2017), questioned the widespread discourses that blamed mortgagors for their own misfortune. Affecting only the most vulnerable and isolated mortgage debtors, those who had accessed home ownership despite their precarious positions in the job market, as was the case for migrant workers (Palomera 2013; Terrones 2013; Suárez 2014; Lundsteen and Sabaté 2017), home repossessions remained out of the public eye and were hardly mentioned in the media.

Nevertheless, as the phenomenon escalated over the course of a few months, serious doubts about its limited reach started to emerge. The initial moral panic and stigma associated with mortgage default would be counteracted by the emergence of an alternative narrative about the mortgage crisis in the subsequent years. Spontaneous expressions of indignation would evolve with the articulation and crystallization of social movements such as the Plataforma de Afectados por la Hipoteca (PAH; Coalition of People Affected by Mortgages), created in 2009 in Barcelona, that would rapidly expand to the rest of the country. The movement gained momentum in the following years, successfully combining direct action against banks, civil disobedience at evictions, mutual counselling and support among mortgagors, and proposals for legal and policy modifications to legislators and public authorities (Colau and Alemany 2012; Sabaté 2014; Suárez 2014; García-Lamarca and Kaika 2016; França 2017; Sanmartín 2019). The movement increased its legitimacy and gained public support after the bailout of financial institutions by the Spanish state, as happened in 2012 when more than €22,000,000 of public money was transferred to the savings bank Bankia, formerly publicly managed but now completely in private hands, in order to prevent its bankruptcy.

This is how home repossessions and evictions started to be perceived as particularly salient and as unprecedented manifestations of the deep economic and financial crisis that has afflicted the country for a decade and a half now. The depiction of defaulting debtors as liable for their inability to repay their loans was thus challenged by a resignification of mortgage default and home repossessions as symptoms of a structural, collective scam that led to a state of popular indignation. Financial institutions started to be accused of greed and predatory practices, and public authorities were perceived as their accomplices, because they would not modify the legal framework – particularly the Mortgage Act – that kept defaulting debtors in a helpless situation even after their eviction, owing not only the outstanding amount, but also late payment fees and trial expenses.[5] They could remain indebted for life. Compliance with the law and with the stipulations of loan contracts, as well as the preservation of property rights and the obligation to repay beyond any other consideration, began to be questioned.

The alternative narrative promoted by social movements highlighted the role of financial and political elites in causing the crisis, thereby attributing them 'responsibility as blame', or liability. But, beyond that, claims concerning 'responsibility as task', or accountability (King 2006: 116), also emerged.[6] Who was to be given the responsibility to mitigate the impacts of the spate of repossessions and evictions? Faced with a social emergency, anti-repossession movements and other critical voices tasked certain social actors – public authorities, policy-makers, judges and creditors themselves[7] – with its remediation, and called for the implementation of several forms of debt relief for households facing repossession and housing provision for those already evicted. Some of the mortgage debtors I spoke to during my fieldwork, like Salvador, an unemployed father of one who had already lost his flat and whose parents-in-law were at risk of losing theirs too as a result of having acted as guarantors of the loan, expressed this attribution of responsibility:

> In fact am I not the only guilty one, so let them [the bank] take their share of the blame. I am already suggesting a solution. Then do it too [you, the bank]. I am yielding in the negotiations: take one of the two flats. My father-in-law or me will lose our property. But don't make it harder for us – we've had enough. I've failed to my family; I haven't been able to cope with everything. That's already hard for me to accept. But don't keep punishing me. I've accepted my share of the blame.

In all, since the end of the housing bubble in 2007, we have witnessed an evolution from the hegemony of discourses blaming defaulting debtors for their fate to the emergence of a counternarrative of the crisis as a collective scam, in which creditors and public authorities were depicted as liable for over-indebtedness and default. The latter has come hand in hand with the claim for tangible, urgent support for the victims of the crisis, in the form of debt relief and/ or alternative accommodation arrangements. Such a claim, in the context of scarce welfare provision and given the reluctant attitudes and legal impunity of creditors, as well as the lack of legal provision for the support of defaulting debtors, opens up what will be the central questions of this chapter: What are the criteria for giving or denying access to debt relief and to an alternative housing solution for defaulting mortgagors? Who deserves to be accorded a way out of indebtedness and homelessness? Who and what defines such deservingness, which entails a judgement based on moral concerns? And, among all actors making such judgements, who has the ability to turn them into imperatives for action?

In the following sections, we will approach the case of home repossessions in Spain through the lens of deservingness assessments. It will be our aim to shed light on the moral, ideological and practical aspects of the production and reproduction of social cleavages in a late capitalist society during a severe economic and social crisis.

Ways out of the Mortgage Crisis: Debt Relief and Alternative Housing

Before addressing the definition of defaulting mortgagors as deserving or undeserving of a solution for their desperate situation, let us describe what such a solution may comprise. Indeed, welfare policies in Spain do not include a comprehensive approach to indebtedness and default as contingencies to be remedied by the state, and the Mortgage Act does not define the creditors' responsibility in this regard; rather, the legislation establishes the right of banks to claim for the whole outstanding debt after three months of arrears. The repossession process can then be initiated, leading to the auction of the property. The financial institution itself can purchase it for 70 per cent of its value, leaving the mortgagor indebted for the rest, plus late payment interest and the legal costs of the process.[8] As a result, most debtors lost their homes and, even after their eviction, a considerable part of their debt remained. In some cases it was even greater than the initial amount, despite the repayments already made for several years.

Before, during and after the repossession process, defaulting debtors may seek an arrangement that allows them to keep their properties, for instance, by adjusting the conditions of repayment in order to make it affordable for them. These forbearance schemes are typically agreed upon when debtors at risk of default approach their bank and ask them for a solution, a frequent situation during the first years of the crisis. However, as anti-repossession activists have argued, such schemes have rarely entailed a real solution for debtors, given the rapid impoverishment of households brought about by long-term unemployment, illness or other adverse circumstances. Hernán, who lost his building company and became trapped in debt, told us his experience in these terms:

> We went to the bank to ask for a reduction in our monthly repayments ... They charged us public notary fees and increased the repayment period to forty-seven years, so my sons would have to pay it off. But, of course, you are desperate and you sign and think, we'll see. Six or seven months later, we could no longer repay and here we are. We were evicted in October 2012, very quickly.

When it becomes evident that the mortgage debt is unsustainable, the quest to have it exonerated begins. This can happen before the repossession process is completed: at that moment, debtors may ask the bank for the cancellation of their loan in exchange for the property. This refers to a legal notion, 'assignment in payment', that was not included in legislation at the beginning of the crisis and that has now been defined in more recent decrees as a mere possibility, a 'good practice' that is advisable in certain cases, but that entirely depends on the goodwill of the creditor.[9] Likewise, after the auction of the property and the eviction of its inhabitants, the latter may try to have their outstanding debt exonerated in order to rebuild their lives. This possibility, too, is completely subject to the bank's final decision, except for a few debtors meeting very strict requirements who, since 2015, can resort to a bankruptcy trial.

In addition, former mortgagors who are about to lose their homes, or who have already lost them, may apply for an alternative accommodation arrangement. In some cases, they have managed to remain in their former properties in exchange for an affordable rent to be paid to the bank that has now acquired the unit. In other instances, debtors may try to access an alternative housing unit, for example, by applying for social housing – a very scarce resource in Spain – or by squatting vacant housing, in some cases with the support of social movements.

All these arrangements, which we have labelled as forms of 'debt relief', may be reached through a variety of strategies, all of them within the framework of the asymmetric relationship between creditor and debtor, of the enduring effects of mortgage loan contracts signed under completely different circumstances and of the financial dynamics that take place beyond ordinary people's control – and often understanding. Some of these strategies involve the intervention of other actors – a public welfare institution, an anti-repossession movement, a third-sector organization, a public defender and a judge who passes sentence. All of these actors, we contend, rather than unconditionally supporting mortgagors in hardship, make their actions dependent on an assessment of mortgagors' deservingness to find their way out of a critical situation.

Assessing Deservingness

According to our data, the categorization of debtors as deserving or not deserving support in the form of debt relief and housing alternatives is a ubiquitous practice. Since the beginning of the crisis, different sets of people, either as individuals or as representatives of institutions, have been assessing the past and present behaviour of defaulting mortgagors with the aim of making such a distinction. Welfare institutions (public agencies or nonprofit organizations), bank employees, members of the anti-repossession movement, the social networks in which debtors are embedded and debtors themselves have engaged in the assessments of deservingness. The scarcity of welfare provision in the form of benefits and social housing has contributed to fostering this practice, and the lack of legal stipulations regarding support for defaulting debtors on a universal basis has introduced a great degree of arbitrariness.

The criteria on which such assessments are founded may either be explicitly defined by law – as in the legal notion of the 'good faith debtor'[10] – or result from more implicit criteria. The latter include a wide range of aspects such as tangible proofs of individual effort and merit, a responsible attitude as heads of their families, compliance with well-established social norms such as showing a docile and modest attitude while applying for assistance, observance of strict bureaucratic rules and protocols, engagement with collective action within social movements, or the accreditation of certain kinds of social disadvantage specified in legislation and welfare policies.[11]

In their quest for debt relief and access to housing, defaulting mortgagors need to meet this set of requirements if they aspire to be judged as deserving. For example, in November 2012, a decree delayed evictions for a two-year period in the case of 'particularly vulnerable households', which were defined as follows:

(a) Large families (with three or more young children).
(b) Single-headed households in charge of two children.
(c) Households including an infant under three.
(d) Households with a member who is disabled, dependent or with an illness that prevents him/her from having a job.
(e) Households where the loan holder is unemployed and has exhausted unemployment benefits.
(f) Households where the housing unit is shared with one or more (up to third-degree) relatives who are disabled, dependent or have a serious illness that prevents them from having a job.
(g) Households including a victim of gender-based violence, if the collateral is their first residence.[12]

As it might be expected, this measure had very limited reach, due to the extremely narrow conditions it set. For this reason, it was criticized not only by debtors themselves and by anti-repossession movements, but also by progressive judges such as Darío Gómez,[13] who told us about an appeal he had made for this reason:

> Of course, together with other colleagues, I have appealed to the International Human Rights Court, regarding their sentences on conventions for the protection of children. So that repossessions involving children over three were cancelled too. I have passed orders to cancel two or three processes with four-, five- or six-year-olds. We need to resort to international law or to international courts in order to reach fairer solutions. It does not seem sensible to me that you cannot repossess when there is a three-year-old, but you can do it to a four-year-old.

In the case of bank employees negotiating with debtors, as long as the legislation did not force them to grant debt relief in the event of default and insolvency, decisions have been rather arbitrary, or subject to a variety of factors that we will not examine here.[14] At certain moments, employees have resorted to the 'good debtor' imaginary in order to persuade debtors not to quit repayments as they encountered hardship, trying to convince them to keep trying to avoid default, or offering them forbearance schemes instead of the assignment in payment, so that they would not go into arrears.

In contrast to that 'good faith', bank employees criticized customers who showed no inclination to accept their financial obligations. Miquel, the former director of a bank's mortgage centre, described these customers as follows:

> I don't know, perhaps I was in the crappiest and most rotten part of the bank's network, but I didn't encounter that profile described by Ada Colau,[15] the poor family who cannot pay and cries and is desperate. I only saw lazy people [*penca*]. Migrants who didn't understand you if they weren't interested ... They didn't give a fuck.

This 'good/bad debtor' dichotomy can also be traced back to the accounts of some mortgagors, who, like Ramon, a former small entrepreneur who lost his firm and his house, insisted on identifying themselves in that way, even after experiencing the empowering effect of activism:

> I am not a professional defaulter, I have become insolvent due to life circumstances, you know? If my firm had gone bankrupt at another time, and I had been able to replace it with a job, I would have been able to keep on repaying, but I simply cannot do it.

Esteban, a former self-employed plumber who had to quit his job due to heart disease, and who was facing repossession and eviction, used a similar argument about his honest intention to face his financial responsibilities if he could afford to do so:

> If we aren't repaying the mortgage, it's because we can't, not because we don't want to. And I'm going to keep repaying other things. But the mortgage, that I can't. Because I can no longer work as I used to.

Salvador's determination to depict himself as an honest worker was notable in his account:

> I want people to know that we are neither outcasts, nor are we in this situation because we want to be. We are workers, ordinary people, who, until yesterday, did not think that this could happen to us, and one day, due to uncontrollable circumstances, you realize that you are in this.

Welfare agents also tended to distinguish their regular clients from this model of a hardworking person with no previous experience of asking for welfare or guidance, who has been caught by surprise in adverse circumstances. In the accounts of agents, a narrative emerged on the crisis becoming chronic and reaching the middle classes, who reluctantly started to visit social services as their last resort. Jordi, a retired bank employee who now volunteers as a counsellor for mortgage defaulters at a charity organization, described this contrast:

> This is not only affecting migrants – our statistics show that most people are nationals. People who had lived well, who had a good wage and would have never imagined they would go to social services or come here asking for help, are coming now. Other better-off layers are being touched. People who do not know the circuits of social services.

At the same time, welfare agents disliked the attitudes of some clients who did not show enough regret, after having acted as risky investors during their years of prosperity. Jordi recalled the following case:

> We met someone who had signed a loan in yen. He had acted like a know-it-all. A small entrepreneur whose properties had been seized. We gave him advice, but he came like [he mimes an arrogant attitude]. His wife was humbler, but he was … Of course, yen were [*sic*] depreciated. He knew; he wasn't ignorant … 'You are all borrowing in euros; I am borrowing in yen.' He was the kind that went to dinner with friends and said, 'look at me'.

According to this, new clients who had never been dependent on welfare provision, who tried hard to find their way through bureaucracy – a task that requires a considerable amount of time and tolerance for frustration (Azis 2016) – and who wanted to regain their autonomy were more likely to arouse the sympathy of welfare agents, who acted as gatekeepers of access to advice and support (Howe 1990; Dubois 2018).

Interestingly, the deserving/undeserving dichotomy not only operated in the field of welfare provision. According to our data, anti-repossession movements also acted to some extent on the basis of deservingness assessments, although they were guided by a different set of criteria. In order to be supported in their battle against banks, participants needed to show commitment and to focus on the interests of the collective rather than on their own. In this way, they fit the model of what Gutiérrez-Garza (2020) has called the 'good activist' and so eventually they acquired enough legitimacy to ask other members, for instance, to help stop their eviction. Otherwise, when people approached the assemblies in a more utilitarian way and especially when it became common knowledge that they were acting simultaneously on several fronts, they were considered disloyal. This became evident in many weekly PAH meetings, when people who attended for the first time were given the opportunity to present their cases, received some specific legal advice from other more experienced participants and then left the room immediately after that, instead of staying until all the cases had been exposed and/or other issues concerning collective action or organization were discussed. In such situations, moderators and other committed participants usually commented on that kind of behaviour as being inappropriate and predicted that those people would reappear one day, shortly before their eviction date, looking for unearned support from the assembly. The PAH refused to work as a provider of debt advice on an individual basis and therefore some commitment was required in order to access the benefits of collective advice and support. Otherwise, people were seen as scroungers of the assembly's knowledge and experience.

As we have seen, assessments about deservingness are not uniform, but are founded on diverging requirements and criteria, as they are applied in different situations and by different sets of people, in a highly personalized, context-dependent manner. Thus, they are shaped by the different social positions of the social actors expressing them and may also vary over time. This contingency, plurality and dependence on context is, in fact, one of the main features of deservingness assessments, as opposed to the more universal logics of entitlements or of humanitarianism. In addition, such assessments may also be mutually conflicting: for instance, a very committed member of an anti-repossession movement may be considered as deserving solidarity from their fellow activists. From a certain viewpoint, they can be seen as responsible parents who fiercely defend their family's livelihood with the decision to go into arrears and to prioritize the purchase of basic products such as food or school equipment. But, at the same time, the reluctance to accept the forbearance scheme offered by the creditor may prevent them from obtaining a favourable sentence from a judge, as not all the available options have been exhausted before defaulting. Finally, the empowering experience of joining the social movement, often including a radical resignification of squatting practices, may prevent the welfare agent who will be filing the debtor's application for social housing from framing them as a 'deserving client'.[16] This is why, in some cases, people find themselves in situations where a certain kind of deservingness – for instance, the productivist one, based on a work ethic – is highlighted, while others – such as those involved in activist empowerment and engagement with social transformation – are frowned upon and therefore it may be strategically preferable to keep them veiled. The outcome of such a complex combination – the transformation of deservingness into actual access to resources (in the form of debt relief or of alternative housing or of support in the battle against creditors) will be our concern in the next section.

The Efficacy of Deservingness and Its Contrast to Unconditional Allocation

As we have seen, during the mortgage crisis in Spain, virtually all social actors have engaged in assessing mortgagors' deservingness to obtain debt relief and/or alternative housing. However, another important aspect should be taken into account: not all of these social actors have the same power to transform their assessments into actual support or resources. In other words, assessments about deservingness are unevenly effective, depending on the relative power of actors in a given setting and how such assessments are related to redistribution mechanisms.

As a rule, judges, welfare agents and bank employees – especially those in managerial positions – as well as politicians and legislators making decisions in this arena are the most likely to have an effect on debtors' financial situations and housing conditions. While acting as professionals, they find themselves either compelled or encouraged to decide on the allocation of resources, and such decisions are made on the basis of assessments that may be morally loaded to different extents.

However, it is not a mere question of access to resources; deservingness assessments have symbolic and political consequences too. Acting as gatekeepers, these dominant actors produce and reproduce ideological representations of deserving and undeserving debtors. Their discourses and practices contribute, for instance, to the legitimation of austerity policies and financial deregulation, as well as – specifically in the Spanish context – to the perpetuation of the lack of accountability of the state regarding housing provision. This runs in parallel to the construction of debtors as neoliberal subjects (Lazaratto 2012) who are expected to prioritize their financial obligations over other concerns, to individually assume the consequences of their failure to honour contracts, and to take care of themselves as they navigate economic hardship.

Yet, we are not suggesting that deservingness assessments made by less powerful actors do not have an effect on debtors' lives. On the contrary, they may also hinder or foster their chances to recover from financial hardship and to keep on satisfying their needs and pursuing their aspirations. Thus, in the everyday practice of anti-repossession movements, assessments of deservingness are also at play, although their criteria are – implicitly – defined in completely different ways. As we have already noted, debtors do not receive the energy, experience and support of the movement in an unconditional manner, but depending on whether they are seen as sufficiently engaged in collective action and mutual help practices (Sanmartín 2019; Gutiérrez-Garza 2020). This is not a condition that every person approaching the movement is ready to comply with, for a variety of reasons – including conflicts with other obligations towards kin, lack of available time (Azis 2016) and, in some cases, an individualistic and utilitarian attitude that matches the neoliberal subject described above.

However, things may be different when we consider members of debtors' informal social networks. Many of our informants described the blaming discourses – as well as the blaming silences – of their kin, which ostensibly contrasted with the actual support that they were receiving from them, for example, in the form of accommodation, material resources, caregiving or financial aid. As they recounted their repossession experiences, they often described how relatives who had initially blamed them for their failure, and who still did so sporadically or in a more implicit manner, were in fact providing them with support, even if this rarely happened free of recriminations. For instance, Mayte relied on the tenacious support of her mother and parents-in-law, even if their own economic situation was also not an easy one, with very humble retirement pensions and with another daughter, Mayte's sister, also facing eviction. The whole family – Mayte, Juan and their three children – were invited for lunch on a daily basis, which allowed them to include meat and fish in their diet, and guaranteed at least a daily meal for the two adults, who did not have dinner at home. Relatives had also provided for private healthcare when one of the children fell ill. However, this support was combined with sporadic recriminations concerning the couple's past decision to sell their old flat and move to a bigger one, perhaps 'beyond their means', as they were misled by the apparent stability of their jobs – particularly Juan's job in the building sector.

These ambiguities emerged in an especially acute manner in those dramatic cases where elderly parents were at risk of losing their already paid-up homes as a result of having acted as guarantors in their children's mortgage loan contracts. Finding himself in such a predicament, Salvador felt he had 'betrayed' his parents-in-law, but still he was dependent on their help in the form of childcare and material support. He worriedly explained that his mother-in-law 'did not understand' the situation and that she was in a permanent state of anxiety that harmed the family's co-existence, but her implicit and explicit reproaches did not lead to a withdrawal of her support. The atmosphere was even more strained in Vanessa's case. She had moved with her two teenage daughters to her parents' house after having her flat repossessed by the bank and now they were all at risk of being evicted. Despite the very tense situation, with daily conflicts and recriminations, her parents were providing shelter and covering her family's basic needs, as well as looking after the children, just as they had been doing before, when Vanessa was a divorced mother working long hours. She described how her father, who considered himself a 'good payer' – for example, never missing the payment of water and energy bills no matter how hard it was to find the money to do so – often embarrassed her in this regard. Vanessa's father never understood her decision to stop mortgage repayments at a certain point, which entailed accepting a home repossession as an inescapable fate. He felt that she should have kept on repaying until she had totally exhausted her means, probably a few months later. This disagreement resulted in a chronic conflict that seriously eroded their relationship.

In the cases described above, even if conflicts and morally loaded recriminations tend to be present to different extents, merit and deservingness seem to have been put on hold for the sake of unconditionality in the form of generalized reciprocity within kin networks. We have also witnessed how family-like ties have emerged among certain members of PAH assemblies, particularly those most deeply and steadily committed to the movement, who often depict themselves as a chosen family (they even use the term *PAHmilia*, merging PAH and *familia*, family). Their experience contrasts with what Desmond (2012) calls 'disposable ties', consisting in intense solidarity relationships that bring together individuals facing evictions, but only ephemerally and dependent on utilitarian criteria. In contrast, decade-long solidarity bonds among some members of the PAH Barcelona, for instance, are experienced as strong, unconditional friendships, and have even led to marriages (Sanmartín 2019). Although this is of course not the case for every participant in the assembly, not even for a majority within it, there is a tightly united core of people who are or used to be *afectados* and who now enjoy their prestige as longstanding activists, courageous fighters and experts on the PAH's struggle.

The deservingness notion seems a useful tool in our attempt to illuminate the moral aspects of welfare provision, of the administration of justice or of the so-called 'corporate social responsibility' of financial elites and institutions. But, in addition, it may also call into question the allegedly universalistic approach of anti-repossession movements (Gutiérrez-Garza 2020). In all these cases, deservingness assessments, based on diverging criteria, are used to classify defaulting debtors into two categories: those deserving and those undeserving of the allocation of resources that are perceived and/or depicted as scarce. Furthermore, such assessments are strongly dependent on moral principles that are subject to variability across social groups and along historical processes, and are not necessarily consistent with institutionalized entitlements or positive rights. However, our ethnography has run into contrasting forms of support, typically those channelled by kin networks and more personalized and permanent social bonds. In the event of a social emergency affecting network members, deservingness assessments seem to be put aside in the name of moral obligation and unconditionality, or, in some cases, do not seem to be perceived as incompatible with enduring support.

Deservingness and the Moralization of Distribution

Our case study has so far illustrated the potential of the concept of deservingness to explain the making or the reproduction of inequalities, social cleavages, and inclusion and exclusion dynamics. Analytically, (un)deservingness is linked to social (in)justice in at least two senses that tend to be intertwined in empirical reality. On the one hand, as a distributive issue, the (un)deservingness of certain resources and material advantages is at stake. On the other hand, at the level of shared social meanings and representations, (un)deservingness is also a key factor in the emergence of grievances and the claims for recognition, legitimacy and social inclusion. As our ethnographic data have shown, the notion illuminates the moral aspects entailed in the provision of welfare (by either public or private institutions), the administration of justice and the social responsibility – or the lack thereof – attributed to financial elites and banking institutions.

Creditors' behaviour has usually been represented as morally neutral and located in merely economistic logics (Gregory 2012). In contrast, defaulting debtors are routinely seen as having incurred a moral failure or a lack of virtue (Watkins-Hayes and Kovalsky 2016), with their past behaviour depicted as an insurmountable mistake after which no second chance will be granted to them. This behaviour is the origin of the construction of their stigma as mortgage defaulters – many of them unemployed or working poor, dependent on welfare transfers and potentially homeless – in a process that shows several similarities to longstanding social categories in the social sciences literature, such as the 'undeserving poor' (Katz 1989), the 'underclass' or the 'lumpen-proletariat' (Ruggiero 2018), all of which lead to the emergence of social antipathies and a politics of disgust on the basis of what Watkins-Hayes and Kovalsky call the 'perversity thesis' (2016).

People need to avoid such labels as a precondition for receiving relief. To do so, they must adhere to behavioural and attitudinal standards involving independence, individual responsibility, entrepreneurship and a work ethic based on sacrifice and restriction in consumption – as opposed to the allegedly sumptuous lifestyle they had previously led. Interestingly, even in contexts where hegemonic ideas are supposed to be challenged, such as activist spaces, a work ethic – together with proofs of belonging and identification – is also a shared social norm, with uncommitted participants being accused of free-riding and sometimes being denied support on that basis. In a broad sense, the notion of deservingness appears as an important aspect of the making of a meritocratic system, where individuals are seen as fully responsible for their actions and their fate. As the home repossession crisis began, no legislation stipulated whether and how mortgagors in hardship were entitled to be granted debt relief. However, as the phenomenon rapidly grew and demands in this sense emerged, it quickly became clear that debt relief procedures needed to be established. But legislators only introduced timid regulations, mainly consisting of 'good practice' recommendations to creditors (Sabaté 2022), and the provision of social housing was not particularly reinforced in the face of the housing emergency. As a result, given the lack of encompassing legislation and policy, cases were addressed individually, through negotiations between debtors and banks. According to the duality of the deservingness notion identified by Watkins-Hayes and Kovalsky (2016), debt relief can be granted through the application of either formal/explicit or informal/implicit criteria, the former consisting of legal stipulations and the latter of moral considerations – either hegemonic in society or at least held by those who make the decisions. The tensions and entanglements between law and morals here are very salient and raise several questions: who is entitled to debt relief? Is it different to 'deserve' a resource (on moral grounds) than to be legally 'entitled' to it? It may be the case, for instance, that subordination in the form of a moral debt to the giver emerges in the former case, as Maussian theory would suggest. However, this is not to say that positive law lacks moral content; rather, what we find are different degrees of institutionalization of moral values and judgements (Vinogradoff 1913; Bourdieu 2000).

The use of deservingness claims and ascriptions can be very restricted in certain cases, when it stems from the identification of a typified behaviour and entails the application of clear-cut criteria. This happens whenever the notion is objectively defined, or at least aspires to be so, in the form of protocols, typologies and positive law. Yet, in most of the cases identified in our ethnography, it has a vaguer sense, leaving some scope for negotiation, conflict and strategic action, but also for uncertainty and arbitrariness. Those eventually assessed as undeserving of debt relief are depicted as having failed to fulfil moral standards in very broad terms and therefore as being legitimately excluded from the group of debt relief beneficiaries. This may not only be translated into access – or the lack thereof – to specific debt relief measures, but may also affect people's position in more general patterns of social stratification and exclusion. Inequality, in the form of exclusion and inclusion from the distribution of resources and recognition, is thus moralized.

However, as was noted at the beginning of this chapter, deservingness assessments are not necessarily formulated only by others in control of resources; debtors themselves, as well as their legal representatives (Vetta, Chapter 13 in this volume) and political supporters, may also resort to them strategically. For example, as they claim for changes in laws that are considered unfair and practise civil disobedience, anti-repossession movements invoke the legitimacy of their actions and often do so with the argument that mortgagors do not deserve the treatment they are receiving and/or that they deserve a home and a second opportunity in the form of debt cancellation. Such narratives often include the establishment of hierarchies of blame and deservingness among the different actors involved in the repossession crisis. Also, in individual negotiations with creditors or while dealing with social services officials, debtors may exert pressure to circumvent legal norms on moral grounds, asking for discretionality, exceptions and personal favours as opposed to the application of bureaucratic, impersonal procedures prescribed in typified situations (Aramburu and Sabaté 2020). As a result of debt relief and social housing being granted case by case, such resources may end up being allocated on the basis of deservingness assessments.

Another aspect that has been illustrated by our ethnographic case is the fact that deservingness often works far beyond its apparent binarism, in a very ambiguous and complex way. For instance, a 'deserving' or a 'good faith' debtor would be a self-disciplined one who makes huge efforts to avoid defaulting and keep a good credit record; however, when defaulting is likely in the near future, such a debtor has less bargaining power with the creditor than someone who is already in default (Sabaté 2018) and therefore may appear – at least temporarily – in the eyes of the creditor as someone not deserving debt cancellation, for instance, on the basis that they are still managing to repay and therefore their situation is not so desperate. Also, the ethnography has shown the co-existence of different perceptions of the situations that have led people to their current circumstances: while some defaulting debtors are seen as having freely chosen default from among several options, therefore being criticized for being 'bad payers' or practising strategic default, others are acknowledged as 'good faith debtors' despite their inability to keep servicing their debt and are considered to have quit repayments only as a last resort in order to survive.

Finally, an analysis of the home repossession crisis through the lens of deservingness also has the potential to reveal the punitive, disciplinary dimension of meritocratic regimes, where people – debtors in this case – are kept under scrutiny and exposed to potential punishment (Watkins-Hayes and Kovalsky 2016) in the form of the denial of any kind of debt relief. This disciplinary dimension seems to prevent or at least to narrow the scope for resistance or contestation in the face of indebtedness (Sabaté 2020). Indeed, deservingness narratives may contribute to fragmenting the interests of debtors as a unitary group and to preventing their aspirations from becoming potential political claims. In this sense, as Vetta (Chapter 13 in this volume) has also contended for the Greek experience, moralization may entail depoliticization. Yet, as the Spanish case illustrates, moral claims may also inspire emancipatory political movements. While not completely discarding the idea of (un)deservingness, but rather using it in the strategic way already described, such movements push for it to be replaced by more unconditional forms of debt relief allocation and social housing provision, in connection with universalist ideas about human dignity, humanitarianism and human rights. In other words, as they advocate for unconditional access to material resources and social recognition, collectively organized debtors are prefiguring a future where the notion of deservingness is no longer in play. Ultimately, the struggle for the emancipation from debt burdens and for the attainment of universal housing rights may be seen as transcending classical struggles for social justice and becomes part of a wider claim for humanitarianism, based on the ontological affirmation of the worth of a person's life – the legitimacy of the simple fact of their living (Fassin 2010) – beyond any distinction or classification.

Acknowledgements

The author would like to thank fellow members of the GER group (*Grup d'Estudis sobre Reciprocitat*) and the CONJUST project (*Concepciones Populares de la Justicia Social ante la Crisis y las Políticas de Austeridad*); as well as editors and reviewers both from the *Etnográfica* journal and Berghahn Books, for the valuable feedback provided and the engaging discussions that emerged. An earlier version of this chapter was included in a special issue on 'Deservingness and the Languages of Injustice' published in 2020 in *Etnográfica* journal, coordinated by the author and Mikel Aramburu (University of Barcelona).

Irene Sabaté Muriel is a social anthropologist and lecturer at the University of Barcelona, where she teaches Economic and Urban Anthropology. Her research interests are political and moral economy, reciprocity and provisioning, work and social reproduction, housing, debt and credit, and financialization. She has published on the moral economy of home repossessions (*History and Anthropology* [2016]), popular understandings of housing financialization (*Critique of Anthropology* [2016]), the delegitimation of mortgage debts during the crisis (*Etnográfica* [2018]), governmentality through debt (*Focaal* [2019]), the deservingness of debt relief (*Etnográfica* [2020]), predatory lending as economic wrongdoing (*Review of Economic Anthropology* [2020]) and resistance to over-indebtedness (*Oxford Research Encyclopedia of Anthropology* [2020]).

Notes

1. Source: Consejo General del Poder Judicial (2020) Datos sobre el efecto de la crisis en los órganos judiciales. Retrieved 16 February 2022 from https://www.poderjudicial.es/cgpj/es/Temas/Estadistica-Judicial/Estudios-e-Informes/Efecto-de-la-Crisis-en-los-organos-judiciales/

2. This chapter is based on ethnographic evidence collected in the metropolitan area of Barcelona between 2012 and 2015. The methodology consisted on participant observation in assemblies and public actions of the anti-repossession movements; on in-depth interviews with mortgage debtors, activists, debt advisors, lawyers, judges, real-estate agents, representatives of public administrations, and other experts and professionals related to my object of inquiry in the metropolitan area of Barcelona; and on the analysis of written documents and secondary data.
3. Source: Consejo Superior del Poder Judicial (see n. 1 above) and *Informe 2008 del Banco de España*. Retrieved March 2022 from https://www.bde.es/f/webbde/SES/Secciones/Publicaciones/PublicacionesAnuales/InformesAnuales/08/inf2008.pdf
4. Such as the concession of grace periods for debtors facing economic difficulties, so that no default could be detected in the bank's accounting books.
5. This is contrary to what happens to firms: for some years into the crisis, bankruptcy law only existed for them, while personal insolvency was not regulated until 2015 (Ley 25/2015, de 28 de julio, de mecanismo de segunda oportunidad, reducción de la carga financiera y otras medidas de orden social).
6. For King (2006: 116), this opposition entails the distinction between two different senses of responsibility. In the first sense, 'being responsible is where one is taken to be the primary cause of a particular situation. One is responsible because the situation would not have arisen but for one's actions or omissions'. In the second sense, 'one is deemed to be the person (or the organisation) who is tasked with dealing with an issue', either by 'initiating or guiding some activity, or in the more negative sense of clearing up some problem that has arisen under one's jurisdiction'.
7. It is interesting to observe that other crucial actors – such as real-estate agencies and other intermediaries who had played a role in the housing bubble – were not highlighted as being responsible to the same extent.
8. The amount has varied over time: it was 50 per cent of its value at the beginning of the crisis, then 60 per cent, and more recently it was set at 70 per cent. This percentage does not refer to the property's value at the moment of purchase, but to an appraisal made before the auction, when the real-estate market has already experienced a devaluation.
9. 'Dation in payment' seems to be another possible translation of the Spanish term *dación en pago*.
10. The prerequisites for being considered a 'good faith debtor' are included in Ley 25/2015, de 28 de julio, de mecanismo de segunda oportunidad, reducción de la carga financiera y otras medidas de orden social.
11. See Dubois (2018) on welfare recipients' docile and modest attitude in the case of France.
12. Real Decreto-ley 27/2012, de 15 de noviembre, de medidas urgentes para reforzar la protección a los deudores hipotecarios (the author's translation and adaptation). In a similar vein, a previous decree enacted in

March 2012 advised banks to grant the assignment in payment to debtors who met the following requirements: (a) no member of the household should be getting a wage or other remuneration; (b) monthly repayments of the mortgage loan should amount to more than 60 per cent of the total income of the household; (c) the members of the household should not have any other properties or goods to cope with the debt; (d) the collateral of the mortgage should be the first residence of the household; (e) there should be no guarantors to the mortgage loan or, if they exist, they should meet all these requirements as well; (f) if there are other joint holders of the loan outside the household, they should also meet requirements (a), (b) and (c).
13. A pseudonym has been used.
14. Including, for example, the evolution of property values, financial operations affecting the bank itself, changes in management strategies over time, as well as the impact of particular campaigns carried out by social movements on the image of banks (Sabaté 2016a, 2016b).
15. Ada Colau, former spokesperson of the PAH and, at the time of writing, Mayor of Barcelona.
16. In Barcelona, until 2015, families who were squatting in a flat as a strategy to avoid homelessness after eviction were excluded from the waiting list of social housing applicants (Sanmartín 2019).

References

Aramburu, Mikel, and Irene Sabaté. 2020. 'Merecimiento y lenguajes de la injusticia', *Etnográfica* 24(1): 157–64. https://doi.org/10.4000/etnografica.8326.

Azis, Georgios. 2016. 'Rising up against the Subordination of Life in Barcelonès: An Ethnography of the Struggle of the "Afectadas" for a Future without Debt Chains', MA dissertation. Uppsala Universitet, Institutionen för Kulturantropologi och Etnologi. Retrieved 16 February 2022 from http://www.diva-portal.org/smash/get/diva2:903456/FULLTEXT01.pdf.

Bourdieu, Pierre. 2000. 'Elementos para una sociología del campo jurídico', in Pierre Bourdieu and Gunther Teubner (eds), *La fuerza del derecho*. Bogotá: Siglo del Hombre, pp. 153–220.

Chauvin, Sébastien, and Blanca Garcés-Mascareñas. 2014. 'Becoming Less Illegal: Deservingness Frames and Undocumented Migrant Incorporation', *Sociology Compass* 8(4): 422–32.

Cobb, Jonathan. 1973. 'Afterword', in Richard Sennett and Jonathan Cobb, *The Hidden Injuries of Class*. New York: Vintage Books, pp. 263–73.

Colau, Ada, and Adrià Alemany. 2012. *Vides Hipotecades. De la bombolla hipotecària al dret a l'habitatge*. Barcelona: Angle.

Desmond, Matthew. 2012. 'Disposable Ties and the Urban Poor', *American Journal of Sociology* 117(5): 1295–335.

Dubois, Vincent. 2018. *El burócrata y el pobre. Relación administrativa y tratamiento de la miseria*. Valencia: Institució Alfons El Magnànim – CVEI.

Fassin, Didier. 2005. 'Compassion and Repression: The Moral Economy of Immigration Policies in France', *Cultural Anthropology* 20(3): 362–87.

———. 2010. 'El irresistible ascenso del derecho a la vida. Razón humanitaria y justicia social', *Revista de Antropología Social* 19: 191–204.

França, João. 2017. *Habitar la trinxera. Històries del moviment pel dret a l'habitatge a Barcelona*. Barcelona: Octaedro/Fundació Periodisme Plural.

Gans, Herbert J. 1994. 'Positive Functions of the Undeserving Poor: Uses of the Underclass in America', *Politics & Society* 22(3): 269–83.

García-Lamarca, Melissa, and Maria Kaika. 2016. '"Mortgaged Lives": The Biopolitics of Debt and Housing Financialization', *Transactions of the Institute of British Geographers* 41: 313–27.

Gregory, Chris A. 2012. 'On Money Debt and Morality: Some Reflections on the Contribution of Economic Anthropology', *Social Anthropology* 20(4): 380–96.

Gutiérrez-Garza, Ana. 2020. '"Te lo tienes que currar": Enacting an Ethics of Care in Times of Austerity', *Ethnos*. DOI: 10.1080/00141844.2019.1687541.

Howe, Leo. 1990. *Being Unemployed in Northern Ireland: An Ethnographic Study*. Cambridge: Cambridge University Press.

Idealista. 2012. 'Iese sobre los desahucios: "no debemos ayudar alegremente a los que abrieron hipotecas por encima de sus posibilidades"', 7 November. Retrieved 16 February 2022 from https://www.idealista.com/news/finanzas/hipotecas/2012/11/07/536357-iese-sobre-los-desahucios-no-debemos-ayudar-alegremente-a-los-que-abrieron.

Katz, Michael B. 1989. *The Undeserving Poor: From the War on Poverty to the War on Welfare*. Oxford: Oxford University Press.

King, Peter. 2006. 'What Do We Mean by Responsibility? The Case of UK Housing Benefit Reform', *Journal of Housing and the Built Environment* 21(2): 111–25.

Lazaratto, Maurizio. 2012. *The Making of the Indebted Man: An Essay on the Neoliberal Condition*. Los Angeles: Semiotext(e).

López, Isidro, and Emmanuel Rodríguez. 2010. *Fin de ciclo. Financiarización, territorio y sociedad de propietarios en la onda larga del capitalismo hispano (1959–2010)*. Madrid: Traficantes de sueños.

Lundsteen, Martin, and Irene Sabaté. 2017. 'The Social Articulation of the Crisis and Political Mobilisation in Spain: Some Reflections on the Shortcomings of the New Social Movements', in Olena Fedyuk and Paul Stewart (eds), *Inclusion and Exclusion in Europe: Migration, Work and Employment Perspectives*. London: Rowman & Littlefield International, pp. 197–221.

Naredo, José Manuel. 2009. 'La cara oculta de la crisis. El fin del boom inmobiliario y sus consecuencias', *Revista de Economía Crítica* 7: 313–40.
Palomera, Jaime. 2013. 'How Did Finance Capital Infiltrate the World of the Urban Poor? Homeownership and Social Fragmentation in a Spanish Neighborhood', *International Journal of Urban and Regional Research* 38(1): 218–35.
Ruggiero, Vincenzo. 2018. *Los crímenes de la economía. Un análisis criminológico del pensamiento económico*. Madrid: Marcial Pons.
Sabaté, Irene. 2014. 'Del país de los propietarios al país de los sobre-endeudados. Reciprocidad, solidaridad y proyectos de transformación sistémica en tiempos de crisis', *Ars & Humanitas* 8(1): 167–87.
———. 2016a. 'The Spanish Mortgage Crisis and the Re-emergence of Moral Economies in Uncertain Times', *History and Anthropology* 27(1): 107–20.
———. 2016b. 'Mortgage Indebtedness and Home Repossessions as Symptoms of the Financialisation of Housing Provisioning in Spain', *Critique of Anthropology* 36(2): 197–211.
———. 2018. 'To Repay or Not to Repay: Financial Vulnerability among Mortgage Debtors in Spain', *Etnográfica* 22(1): 5–26.
———. 2020. 'Overindebtedness and Resistance', in Mark Aldenderfer (ed.), *Oxford Research Encyclopedia of Anthropology*, New York: Oxford University Press. DOI: 10.1093/acrefore/9780190854584.013.228.
———. 2022 Forthcoming. 'State Action and the Movements of Finance during the Spanish Housing Crisis: Alleviating or Amplifying the Social Impacts of Financialization?', *ANUAC. Rivista della Società Italiana di Antropologia Culturale* 11(2), ISSN: 2239-625X.
Sanmartín, Luis 2019. 'Pahwer. Análisis etnográfico de la Plataforma de Afectados por la Hipoteca', Ph.D. dissertation. Barcelona: University of Barcelona.
Suárez, Maka. 2014. 'Movimientos sociales y buen vivir: Ecuatorianos en la lucha por la vivienda en la plataforma de afectados por la hipoteca (PAH)', *Revista de Antropología Experimental* 14: 71–89.
Terrones, Alberto. 2013. 'Segregation, Housing Market Segmentation and the Origin of Over-indebtedness: The Access to Homeownership by Foreign Migrants Based on Over-indebtedness', paper presented at the 25th European Network for Housing Research Conference, Tarragona, Spain.
Vaccaro, Ismael, Eric Hirsch and Irene Sabaté. 2020. 'The Emergence of the Global Debt Society: Governmentality and Profit Extraction through Fabricated Abundance and Imposed Scarcity', *Focaal. Journal of Global and Historical Anthropology* 87: 46–60.
Vinogradoff, Paul. 1913. *Common Sense in Law*. London: Williams & Norgate.
Watkins-Hayes, Celeste M., and Elyse Kovalsky. 2016. 'The Discourse of Deservingness: Morality and the Dilemmas of Poverty Relief in

Debate and Practice', in David Brady and Linda Burton (eds), *The Oxford Handbook of the Social Science of Poverty*. New York: Oxford University Press, pp. 193–220.

13

Households on Trial

Over-indebtedness, the State and
Moral Struggles in Greece

Theodora Vetta

In the spring of 2016, the magistrates court in the mountainous city of Kozani (northwestern Greece) was like a ghost town. Lawyers all over Greece had been on strike in reaction to the new social security and taxation law, which formed part of the austerity reforms. However, every Wednesday and Thursday morning at 11 AM, the court corridors became as loud as a bar and dozens of people packed into the tiny offices of the two local magistrates, or into the two courtrooms, where parallel sessions were performed. Lawyers were there to discuss cases of over-indebted households seeking to renegotiate their debts with their creditors under the 2010 Law for Over-indebted Households, widely known as Katseli's Law. The Law, adopted in the midst of the economic crisis by the socialist party (PASOK), took its name from the former Minister of Economy, Competitiveness and Shipping, Louka Katseli. Its stated goal was to provide a safety net for insolvent households by protecting, under certain criteria, their first residence against foreclosure.

By the time I started my fourteen-month fieldwork in 2015, credit markets were exercising immense power over social reproduction. Household over-indebtedness and despair had become a social phenomenon. Yet, whereas the causes of the onerous public debt and the ways to tackle it have been in the international spotlight since the eruption of the so-called 'Greek crisis' in the late 2000s, little attention has been paid to private indebtedness, the protagonist in other crisis-ridden countries such as Spain, Ireland and Portugal. It is true that Greek private debt started from very low levels (e.g. 35.7 per cent of GDP in 1995), yet its increasing rate between 2001 and 2008 was among the most spectacular in Europe (113 per cent of GDP in 2008).[1] This was an era when booming GDP rates were celebrated as a symbol of 'strong Greece' and 'modernization'. Of course, the dynamics of the credit market were fundamentally global because the declining productivity and the falling rate of profits in the core since the 1970s turned capital to more promising and speculative financial investments (Boyer 2000), particularly targeting certain (semi-)peripheries such as Greece, Spain or Ireland (Lapavitsas 2009; Hadjimichalis 2010, 2018). By 2018, the €106.9 billion of nonperforming loans (NPLs) in Greece (loans with suspended payment), mundanely called 'red loans', represented 45.1 per cent of total loans (the EU average was 5.1 per cent). They laid at the very heart of negotiations with the Troika (European Commission, European Central Bank and International Monetary Fund) for a new possible round of 'meta-memorandum' austerity measures.[2]

This chapter looks into the politics of state intervention in relation to what is loosely understood as financialization – those processes wedded to the capitalist regime of accumulation that manifest a growing dominance of finance capital, financial actors, discourses and practices at various scales (van der Zwan 2014; Aalbers 2015). Indeed, financialization worldwide could only be possible through state intervention (Abdelal 2007; Krippner 2011) and, in the case of Europe, EU integration. Since the late 1980s, state policies of both the socialist and the conservative parties in Greece facilitated capital movement and international trade, deregulated labour markets, and provided liquidity and guarantees to financial actors through numerous legislations and sanctions (Spyrou 1999; Argitis and Michopoulou 2013). The introduction of the euro in 2001 gave a spectacular boost to cheap credit, based on the euro's low interest rates and on the gradual abolition of earlier bank obligations to invest in industry, agriculture or government bonds, 'liberating' capital for newly created financial products targeting household portfolios.

Yet state intervention is not limited to the creation of conditions and regulation for financial expansion and bubbles. In the postbust period, the state's Janus face of discipline and protection continues to partake in processes of rent extraction and class demobilization through its legal mediation between creditors and indebted households.[3] As often happens, social control or democratic deficit stemming from growing juridization (Hirschl 2008; Commaille et al. 2010) goes hand in hand with opportunities for contestation and the quest for justice (Lazarus-Black and Hirsch 1994; Biehl 2013). During the debt disputes in Kozani in which I regularly assisted, these two processes melted into each other: the courts were created as fields of hope for citizens looking for protection and visibility (Jansen 2014). Yet the quest for entitlements entailed deep depoliticization and moral discipline, revealing the ways in which different and differently valued kinds of debts are (re/dis)articulated for various ends.

The analysis of these legal social processes and discursive 'moments' draws from a productive dialogue between economic and legal anthropology. Indeed, economic anthropology has a long tradition of understanding debt as a nexus of moral and social relations unfolding in space and time (Peebles 2010). Debt produces social worth and draws hierarchical lines of inclusion and exclusion (Elyachar 2005; Guérin 2014; James 2014). But what happens when debts transform into legal disputes? What kind of evidence, rationalities but also uncertainties and silences are produced from each side to argue their cases? Legal scholars have approached trials as highly performative events (Merry 1994; Burns 2001), as a 'carefully orchestrated contest through which aggregations of persons, words, stories, and material are legitimately transformed into facts of intention, causality, responsibility, or property' (Silbey 2005: 331). Far from being bounded and restricted social realms, trials can serve as an analytical lens for understanding complex and more diffuse historical societal struggles and tensions, and, most importantly, the way in which these get interpreted and reworked while being subsumed in legal conformities and power relations (Conley and O'Barr 1990; Rubin 2008).

Law is, after all, a semi-autonomous field (Moore 1973) and, indeed, Kozani's courtrooms provided a contested public sphere for debating wider moral and social tensions. Popular understandings and the implementation of the protection law, far from resting on some ironclad bureaucratic criteria, revolved around one question: who deserves to be protected? Deservingness serves as a pertinent analytical tool for understanding debt's moral economy (Palomera and Vetta 2016). Its social mapping, inside and outside the court, provided a powerful mechanism of debt depoliticization, through which unequal social formations were in practice communicated and often justified, notwithstanding their contradictions. The depoliticization of debt was pursued in at least three ways. First, strong moralization and personalization of deservingness inhibited a more structural interpretation of the debt relation: by highlighting over-indebtedness as a consumption choice, as a sign of a certain deceitful character or as economic victimhood demanding humanitarian compassion, both the expropriation aspect of financialization and the ever-deeper inequalities in the production sphere were often left unaddressed. Second, credit markets were dissociated from statecraft. The state's intervention, assumed as a neutral mediator between households and creditors, sidelined state responsibility not only for welfare deficiencies and enforcement of rights, but also for consolidating finance capital and enabling working-class indebtedness while mitigating claims to wealth distribution. Finally, the social hierarchies and fragmentation built around deservingness and the particular expropriative mechanisms of public debt socializing the bailout costs narrowed the horizon of solidarity among the dispossessed.

Over-indebtedness and Katseli's Law

Katseli's Law was adopted in 2010, just a couple of months after the first bailout and austerity memorandum. In a session emotionally charged with humanitarian compassion and a discourse of social justice, the MPs of the social-democratic party PASOK stressed that the extreme deregulation of the financial system and unforeseen factors in the lives of many households (health issues and unemployment) had led to their over-indebtedness and marginalization, demanding the regulatory role of the state (Greek Parliament 2010). The law introduced the possibility of bankruptcy for individuals and granted them the right to protect their primary residence from foreclosure. In order to be eligible for legal protection, certain criteria had to be met, mainly defining a ceiling to households' monthly income and to primary residences' objective value.[4] The Law was adopted with a parliamentary majority, whereas the two parties of the left, Syriza and the Greek Communist Party, voted against it. The latter underlined the 'hypocritical tears' of the protagonists of the postdictatorial bipartisanship system, who were denouncing their responsibilities for the crisis while acting in favour of the financial system. Indeed, the government, on the one hand, had just offered generous cash injections and guarantees/bonds to Greek banks, strengthening their capital adequacy and ensuring that they could borrow cheaply from the European Central Bank while lending to the state at a high rate of interest. On the other hand, with this law, banks would recover parts of unmortgaged red loans that they would otherwise never have been able to recoup; after the final verdict of the court, the debtors would have to satisfy, according to their capacities, a percentage of the total debt to all the creditors, in monthly instalments over four years. They would also have the possibility of repaying in the long run (even over up to twenty years) 80 per cent of the currently deflated commercial value of their first residence. The rest of the debt would be cancelled. In the case of the very vulnerable, the state would subsidize these monthly repayments.

Regardless of the several issues that one might raise about the intentions of this law, it is arguably true that, eight years later and after several amendments, it has provided an important safety net for thousands of debtors that claimed an inability to meet their financial obligations towards private debtors, but also towards public entities such as insurance funds, the Tax Agency, municipalities or public utility companies (electricity, water or heating bills). According to the head of the Bank of Greece, until the first semester of 2018, more than 200,000 household loans (more than €13 billion) have been put under this insolvency regime.[5] Debtors felt the urgency to appeal to the court because, following Troika's pressure on the further liberalization of the credit market, the Law would expire in 2019. Furthermore, banks started selling red loans to more aggressive foreign hedge funds (Swedish Intrum Justitia AB and Aktua Soluciones Financieras). The hedge funds would 'mediate' in order to find a buyer for the mortgaged properties more quickly or they would give the debtors the chance to stay in their mortgage residences by transforming them from homeowners to tenants.

Arguing court cases for indebted households had become the main part of the workload for Kozani's lawyers, who ran modest – often family – practices. In the small rururban district of approximately 150,000 residents, reputation, kinship and social relations of proximity (e.g. those based on common place of origin or common acquaintances) were the main criteria for choosing a lawyer. The banks hired their representatives from this same pool and no big law firms were active in the area. Debtors in almost all the hearings I observed as well as the case research I conducted at one lawyer's firm archive had at least one mortgage and as many as twenty small consumption loans and debts on credit cards. They typically represented low- and medium-income households: civil servants, owners of small family firms (e.g. shops, taverns and construction firms), pensioners and the unemployed, taxi and truck drivers, precarious staff at hospitals and supermarkets, technicians and miners. The latter two were quite numerous because Kozani's economy was heavily dependent on the Public Power Corporation (DEI), the semi-public electricity company, which was undergoing further privatization and whose main power plants and coal mines were in the region. The permanent staff of DEI had arguably been a local target for credit institutions. Indeed, before the crisis, this highly unionized portion of the working class achieved comparably high salaries and benefits as a trade-off for extremely harsh labour conditions, pollution and political votes, but had suffered, together with so many others, big cuts during the austerity decade (Vetta 2020).

Moralities of Deservingness

Act 1: Consumption Mania

BANK'S LAWYER: Your honour, this is a typical case of overconsumption! Eighteen banking products! You can see the irresponsibility of the character of these people, their morals [το ήθος τους]! ... all these years they were living above their means.

DEBTOR'S LAWYER: Your honour, it is not as it seems. The wife took these loans in order to help her father, who was in great difficulties with his shop at the time. The rest she took with her husband when she lost her job [in an insurance company] in order to fulfil their obligations. They had a second child, too.

JUDGE: [Sarcastic laughter] How's this possible? You can't pay your debts and you want a second kid?

BANK'S LAWYER: Exactly. And, your honour, this is not an excuse. She had a good salary. How is it possible that they didn't save any money? In any case, her big salary shows that she did not need all the loans. It is clear that she was living a luxurious life.

DEBTOR'S LAWYER: Your honour, it is impossible to satisfy all the creditors. Their monthly income as you can see today is around 1,000 euros. The dignity for a couple with two kids is defined at 1,700 euros.

BANK'S LAWYER: What? You imply that 600 euros are not enough to live on? [She deducts the monthly payment claimed by creditors.] Others rent and get by with 600 today.

JUDGE: We all face difficulties, but some of us are consistent [συνεπείς] with our obligations [υπο-χρεώσεις]!

(Kozani, June 2016)

Once Katseli cases reached the district court, a so-called provisional trial was set for accepting or rejecting the claims. The magistrate had to decide if the debtors had shown 'a permanent and general incapacity to repay their debts' (Law 3869/2010, Article 1, translation by the author) and, in case of an affirmative answer, assign a final trial date (with a waiting period of as long as seven years) and a usually very small monthly payment to the creditors until the final verdict. For the lawsuits I observed and studied, the quantitative legal requirements on income and property value were met by almost all households. Yet, the argumentation in the courtroom, as the rather typical vignette above shows, was built around other questions that were open to interpretation and moral judgement. It is important to emphasize from the start that in these provisional legal acts, the debtors themselves were absent and only in the final trials were they called as witnesses for examination. Regardless of their absence, the court exercised an impressive intrusion into their private lives, including family planning, and had to debate and monetize 'dignified life' in order to define the temporary payments to the creditors. Private consumption, although a matter irrelevant to the law, was put under public scrutiny, because banks were thoroughly checking their clients' accounts. Extracted fragments of debtors' lives, rearticulated into a new puzzle, were presented as coherent evidence for immoral behaviour. 'Why did he withdraw 2,500 euros within two days, and with such a high interest rate? Was it a case of consumption mania?', creditors' lawyers often concluded.

Such accusations were in line with a general moral shift in crisis-ridden capitalism, from the euphoric moment of 'the happy consumer' and the 'democratization of finance' to the 'sinner debtor' in times of bust (Graeber 2011). This frame served as a powerful denominator in court because it was deeply embedded within a local and historically grounded moral economy according to which a respectful *noikokyris* (lord of the household) had a saving ethos and paying one's debts was ultimately a matter of honour (and masculinity).[6] These cultural values have acquired particular weight during the past decade of crisis, both in mainstream media and in mundane conversations, as 'living above one's means' (both for the state and for its people) was put at the heart of the origins of the crisis (see Mylonas 2014). Creditors' moral sanctioning was powerful precisely because it transcended the domestic sphere, scaling up to the national level: 'This is how we arrived here, your honour', stressed the creditors' defence, alluding to state bankruptcy but also to national shame towards 'Europe'.[7] More than a private matter or a legal dispute between two parties, the accusation of profligacy functioned as a responsibility claim for austerity impacting all – lawyers and judges included.

A certain unease regarding debt was also widespread outside the court, as people did not easily talk in detail about their indebtedness, unless to express their infuriation with how banks' immoral and cunning strategies were 'sucking their blood'. This was part of a more general household secrecy, yet it also carried seeds of self-criticism. Symbols of social status, like branded clothes or expensive/second cars (Knight 2015), most often of others, were now pinpointed as signs of past 'excessiveness' [υπερβολή], of arrogance and showing off.[8] Similarly, many felt guilty for getting into debt and/or losing savings during the spectacular bursting of the stock exchange bubble between 1999 and 2000: 'We lost our minds, thinking we could make money from air [αεριτζίδικα λεφτά] … from paying with eggs in our villages [during childhood], we became investors.' Despite the government's reassurances that investing was safe and the immense peer pressure to gamble, many felt that 'you pay for your greed'. Interestingly, vagueness around private debt went hand in hand with excessive explicitness around current consumption. Without exception, people were constantly putting price tags on all their actions, presenting them as a result of cautious spending and calculation. According to Placas (2018), such discursive practices manifest the production of a certain kind of rational 'austerity consumer', yet I think they rather highlight more an intensified sense of being subjected to public moral evaluation.[9] Consumers did not want their interlocutors to be left with the impression that they did not face economic difficulties or that they were wasteful in times of dearth.

Yet, not all debts were a source of discomfort and shame. Tacit guilt around banking debt was counterbalanced with indignation, indifference or even pride around debt owed to the public sector, as the state in this context represented an imposing outsider and intruder, an extractive machine or even a mafia (Herzfeld 1992). Whereas banking debt was primarily treated as a private matter, debt from unpaid taxes, utility bills or insurance contributions was always connected to a contested citizenship relation and a deeply problematic socioeconomic redistribution: 'What does the state offer me in exchange for financing it?' or 'Let [the government/the state] make the rich pay first, and then I will too'. Debt granting access to homeownership was also considered morally legitimate and, in general, indebtedness related to close-kinship needs did not generally fall into the category of consumption (implying choice) because it originated in particular moral obligations and cultural expectations treated as incommensurable. It was in this latter pool of moral consensus around family 'sacrifices' that debtors' lawyers were looking for defence mechanisms. By doing so, they fell into the same moral trap, replying to creditors' moral accusations with new moral justifications: they argued that credit was not used to buy cars or new furniture, but to help a family member, to create a family, to pay for children's studies or buy them a home, to organize a daughter's wedding or to cover urgent medical family expenses. The creditors could do nothing but sympathetically nod to the judge, who rhetorically asked: 'How can a mother deny her kids education?'

Creditors' lawyers' strategies, on the other hand, also touched on such values, not without conscious contradictions. When related to consumption, credit was treated as someone's individual choice; in contrast, when negotiating debt recovery, social relations and family networks were expected to come to the rescue: 'Why can't her father help her repay? He has a good pension from DEI [the electricity company]'; 'their daughter, now in Switzerland [having migrated], can certainly help'; 'the ex-husband doesn't pay alimony?' Family members were explicitly asked to fulfil their moral obligations to support and in many cases were legally bound to do so, because they so frequently figured as guarantors to the issued loans. Indeed, it was astounding to see the extent to which credit markets were embedded in kinship networks (Kofti 2020). Katseli cases, more often than not, stretched across extended families and three generations, and the kin-guarantors of default loans either had to assume the debt or, if not, to compile a separate law case themselves, this time in order to protect their own primary residence. In any case, the tone of the defence was apologetic. Even if the debtor was officially the plaintiff in these hearings, bringing their cases against their creditors in the court of law, in practice, the roles were reversed: the debtors became de facto the defendants, having to prove their moral innocence and prudent ethos whereas banks were conceived of as natural maximizers – their aggressive strategies of pushing credit cards, of pressuring the debtors to become guarantors to other loans, of illegally bullying clients for delayed payments or of mortgaging new property in order to recapitalize past risky loans were simply part of 'doing their jobs'.

Debt was further depoliticized by the very neutral stance attributed to state mediation. Whereas the state, in its myriad complex facets and effects, was generally very often targeted as being responsible for people's misfortunes, it was completely absent when reflecting upon household debt, both inside and outside the court. Yet, credit markets are a vital means of statecraft and an integral part of the development of the welfare state (Krippner 2011; Streeck 2011). Credit serves as a social lubricant, Krippner perceptively argues, and 'policy makers … rely on debt-financed public spending and private consumption to compensate for lagging social investment and to smooth over distributional conflict in an increasingly unequal society' (2017: 6). Indeed, the credit market was closely linked to the unequal and fragmented transfiguration of the Greek welfare state, outsourcing social costs to the family (Petmesidou 1991; Papadopoulos and Roumpakis 2013). The plethora of loans made available to low- and middle-income households were used to expand homeownership and consumption spending, facilitated by the further deregulation of retail (Bennison and Boutsouki 1995) and an impressive real estate boom that made access to housing impossible on the sole basis of income. Credit was fuelling the promise of the middle-class dream to many previously excluded, yet, vitally, it was also compensating for aggressive labour precarization and informalization of labour markets (Vaiou and Hadjimichalis 1997; Spyridakis 2013), minimal health and education budgets, absent housing policy, and rising unemployment and living costs during the precrisis boom era and after the real currency revaluation of 20 per cent that the introduction of the euro brought with it. As we will see later on, a crucial proportion was also used for covering urgent liquidity needs, accumulated taxes and insurance costs of small family firms, another particular characteristic of the Greek social formation, which manifests the weight of the informal economy, subcontracting and also resistance to proletarianization.

Leaving the state together with the creditors outside the explanatory realm of debt transformed it from a complex and multiscalar social relationship to an individual matter of choice. Depoliticization of debt was further fostered by the very depoliticization of housing within a law that, after all, aimed at protecting debtors' residences. With the legal dispute revolving around moral deservingness, no claims to the right of housing were articulated, despite the constitutional protection of housing after the dictatorship. Since the 1990s, important commodification and financialization processes in the production and disposal of housing have taken place (Mantouvalou and Mpalla 2004), but housing continued to be considered ultimately as a private matter, historically based on a combination of (legal or illegal) self-housing, the barter system of *antiparochi* and family resources (Vaiou et al. 2009).[10] State housing policies were limited to tolerance, tax exemptions, recurrent legalizations and urban rezoning

(Emmanouil 2006), and postwar housing demands were mostly organized around private lobbying of interest groups rather than collective claims (Leontidou 1990; Oikonomou 2012). Not only was social housing almost non-existent (the Workers' Housing Organization – OEK – was abolished by the 2012 austerity memorandum), but, most importantly, it was also generally conceived of in terms of state charity rather than of rights. Such beliefs were reproduced in the court, as the hearings were not so much a quest for legal entitlement, but instead an appeal to the philanthropic face of the state. Legal protection had to pass through the lens of moral forgiveness with debtors' lawyers performing the repentance of their clients rather than arguing for their rights.

Act 2: The Quest for 'Mpatahtsides'

'This law is very generous! Did you see the numbers [of the legal criteria]? Everybody can fit inside [everybody can meet the legal criteria]; there are no filters. It destroyed the banking system – how is the economy to recover? [Pause] Don't be fooled, half of them are *mpatahtsides*; they knew from the start they would never repay.'

Such a belief was a constant feature of the conversations I had with bank lawyers. The pejorative term *mpatahtsis* came to signify the so-called 'strategic bad payers', all those who intentionally avoid paying off their debts. In the past couple of years, it actually colonized the public sphere, with the mainstream media accusing Syriza's government of feeding a culture of default.[11] Inside the courtroom, in almost all the cases I observed, debtors were accused of *dolos* (cheating, deceit) and fraudulent intentions often based on what they called 'lessons of common experience' [διδάγματα καλής πείρας]. *Dolos* was to be found at the moment of payback or at the very moment of borrowing:

BANK'S LAWYERS: Your honour, there is certainly deceit here. The applicant refers to 1,300 euros as the cost of living when he supposedly has an income of 300. How does he live? He obviously has hidden income; . . . electrician and unemployed? Your honour, we all know how electricians work [unregistered]; [pause] here we have undeclared income. Common experience shows us this for ladies that have come from Albania [working as black-market cleaners/caretakers]. [Pause] How did he take out so many loans when he was unemployed? And, back then, how could he pay them back, and now [when he is still unemployed] he cannot?

Allegations of deceit were likewise very frequent when the debtor was accused of being a 'merchant' [εμπορική ιδιότητα]. Katseli's Law was by definition a relief measure for indebted households and individuals. Insolvent firms with debts from business loans instead had to appeal to the bankruptcy law for small and medium-sized enterprises (SMEs). Yet, this was a measure of last resort because, due to restricted amounts of capital, the vast majority of SMEs, the so-called backbone of the Greek economy, were legally registered as General Partnerships or Personal Companies [ομόρρυθμες εταιρείες ή προσωπικές εταιρείες] and not as Sociétés Anonymes (SA or public limited companies). For them, bankruptcy law implied personal property liquidation. This is why the owners of many small firms were instead using Katseli's Law in an attempt to 'save' their homes.

In court, determining whether or not an applicant was a 'merchant' was not an easy task. On the one hand, as elsewhere in Southern Europe (Blim 1990; Narotzky and Smith 2006), the boundaries between family and firm are extremely fluid: much consumption credit was used to finance various business needs, and business loans were issued by mortgaging family assets (Vetta and Palomera 2020). On the other hand, the law opened up a small window of opportunity for so-called little merchants [μικρέμποροι] to sneak in: those with a small turnover or investment capital; and those who did not take big risks or employ workers and whose profit was no more than compensation for personal labour and toil.[12] Once again, categories were interpreted, stretched, negotiated and disputed constantly within a particular field of force. Who deserves to be a 'little merchant' and thus to be entitled to the protection of their housing property? The answer lay in the pre-assumptions behind other questions: how is risk defined? How is deliberate speculative risk distinguished from compulsory decisions? Where does labour compensation stop and where do profits start? What is physical effort and how much is it worth?

Obviously, the above questions were not of a legal order and, regardless of the evidence provided, the banks never accepted the existence of 'little merchants' among their clients. This said, the debtors were neither naïve nor agency-less victims; on the contrary, they were trying to maximize their chances by juggling their strong and weak qualities in order to create an adequate moral and legal profile. As a result, in many debtors' files, there were intentional gaps and vagueness – not necessarily lies, but semi-truths and silences. In many cases, for example, the income of the applicant's spouse, inherited properties in the villages of origin or small agricultural subsidies were not included in the household budgets and assets. Others had previously transferred their firms or extra assets to their children. Family labour was frequently disqualified as not 'real labour' by debtors justifying the existence of unpaid workers' contributions, reproducing well-known inequalities in the production sphere ('we had no workers in the firm; this is just my wife/son'). At other times, couples were presented as separated (not legally divorced) and thus claimed two primary residences, or a two-floor building with two flats was presented as a single vertical residence.

These elements were repeatedly picked up by the banks' lawyers, yet deceit was to be affirmed or denied, once again, only on the side of the plaintiff-debtor. Debtors' lawyers, on the other hand, cleverly manipulated banks' assumed innocence or neutrality in their defence arguments, but not without reaffirming power inequalities in favour of the banks: 'Deceit in taking out loans? No, your honour. At the time they had enough income. Otherwise the bank would not have given them the loans.' In any case, their strategy was not to ask for a total payment suspension, but to suggest to the judge even a tiny monthly payment in order to 'show good face'; to show that debtors' inability to pay back was genuine and not intentional, much less political; and that they were victims of the crisis, honourable but unlucky *noikokyrides*. As a witness lamented, 'your honour, I don't want to stop paying. I just want a job'.

Outside the courtroom, as expected, positionings were more complex and arguments were much more heated. During our individual meetings, debtors' lawyers' adopted a sort of middle ground: on the one hand, they accused the banks of deliberately giving away risky loans, or of taking advantage of some clients' financial illiteracy; on the other hand, they also disapproved of the irresponsibility, indifference [ωχαδερφισμός] or petty/cunning character of some of their clients. Among the debtors, feelings were more mixed, situational and often contradictory, putting up several barriers to the production of a political subject mobilizing collective claims. The category of *hreomenos* (indebted) did not signify a homogeneous group, as debtors too made use of the moral dichotomy of *mpatahtsis* vs. *noikokyris* in order to map different levels of deservingness, legitimacy and responsibility. Naming and labelling was a performance of the self, managing the impressions of others (Goffman 1971) – a conscious or subconscious act of articulating debt discomfort, shame and, as Howe has argued for Irish unemployed, an almost crippling degree of anxiety concerning to which category others assign them (Howe 1998: 536).

In a small place like Kozani, gossip and rumours about undeserving others, as people said, 'travelled with light speed'. Nevertheless, accusations of undeservingness were not just conjectural and abstract. Instead, they reflected deeper inequalities, frustrations and stigma in the production and circulation sphere – tensions that expressed both exploitation and privilege: 'What? A DEItzis [DEI worker] and he can't pay? No way do I feel sorry for him! Mama DEI is gone now, eh? [σιγά μην τον λυπηθώ! Πάει η μαμά-ΔΕΗ, ε]'; 'He has the tractor sitting there and he can't pay now ... so many subsidies they [farmers] take – they just have to learn not to work and to be lazy'; 'they [self-employed] want the state to show mercy now? Why? Did they ever pay their taxes?' Being classified as *mpatahtsis* was thus not only a sign of abstract dishonesty and arrogance; it also articulated wider intraclass antagonisms that, while not new, took on fresh dimensions and significance during the current redistribution regime of austerity (Loperfido and Vetta 2021; Vetta 2020).

In any case, acknowledgement of deceit was always accompanied by the strong conviction that 'everybody cheats! What am I? A fool [not to]?' This often had open connotations of resistance, since it evoked patterns of inequality and pointed to a script of blame distribution: not only were those who 'really cheat' (meaning the political elites and economic oligarchs) more responsible for the crisis, but they were also the ones whose corruption went unaddressed and thus unsanctioned.

Finally, debtors' solidarity was becoming increasingly fragile because of the very expropriative mechanisms of public debt (Davanzati and Patalano 2017). As Marx reminds us, 'the only part of the so-called national wealth that actually enters into the collective possessions of modern peoples is their national debt' (1992 [1867]: 919). Indeed, there was an increasingly widespread discourse among the families I spent time with, regardless of their debt situation. Dimosthenis, a sixty-year-old DEI pensioner, summarizes it well:

> You hear many people saying, to hell with them, let the banks pay too! Yes, OK. But who do you think will pay for the banks now? Their loss is now everybody's loss [η χασούρα τους είναι χασούρα όλων]. And the recapitalizations? Whose money was that? My pension was cut twice [pause]; we are doomed here [είμαστε χαμένοι].

During the past decade, a so-called sanitation of the Greek financial system has taken place, including several aggressive and controversial acquisitions, mergers and liquidations. From 2009 to 2018, Greek banks have been recapitalized four times with dubious results and with the Greek state suffering damage of €36.4 billion (Bank of Greece 2014; Papageorgiou 2015; European Court of Auditors 2017). Such recurrent institutional interventions were accompanied by new rounds of bailouts and austerity measures, and even if they never led to banks' nationalization (as Syriza had promised), they created a strong sense among people of debt socialization and, at times, a very peculiar and uneasy tacit alignment with the creditors' interests. Of course, this is not to say that collective organizing is impossible, as social movements and collectivities against housing auctions are actually growing slowly, mainly in metropolitan Athens and Thessaloniki (Siatitsa 2014). Yet, such properties of public debt, in addition to the constructed scales of victimhood, deservingness and deceit, were, to a certain extent, fragmenting dissent and diverting – rather than taming – social conflict towards intraclass antagonisms.

Conclusions

In recent years, anthropology has shown a remarkable turn towards the analyses of finance-related phenomena, either 'studying up' financiers and financial value (Ho 2009; Ortiz 2013) or focusing on the livelihoods of the dispossessed (Palomera 2014; Pellandini-Simányi et al. 2015; Sabaté 2016). The analysis of the provisional Katseli trials enriches these debates by turning to the much less discussed field of legal regulations (see Riles 2011) and the state as an arena of social struggle in the current regime of accumulation (Jessop 1990). In addition to regulatory policy interventions since the 1980s and entry to the EU, through its porous juridical bodies the state continued to play an active role in rent extraction by creating a realm of intertwined legal refuge and moral discipline: on the one hand, the possibility of residential protection tried to manage the parallel production of an increasing surplus population (Smith 2011) and a predicted and explosive massive wave of evictions and foreclosures; on the other hand, the law urged banks to get rid of a substantial part of their 'red' portfolio, fulfilling the Troika's demands while avoiding a further recapitalization through new public debt. The fact that citizens with accumulated debt only towards the public sector could not apply under this law is more than telling.

The way in which such goals were pursued, enacted and performed via the magistrates' courts is of particular anthropological importance, pointing to a relational and embedded understanding of the state and law (Thelen et al. 2018). As several studies on street-level bureaucrats have shown (Dubois 2010; Bierschenk and de Sardan 2014; Rozakou 2017), laws are usually implemented upon loosely defined criteria and interpretations that, on the one hand, depend on situational interactions and, on the other hand, on the contradictions civil servants are faced with. Indeed, the trials offer insights into what Fassin et al. (2015) call the moral life of the state, as well as into societal moral registers and processes of inclusion/exclusion that might have wider political implications both for the contents of citizenship and for the shape confrontational politics takes (or not). The relational and conditional discourse of deservingness rearticulates and hierarchizes wider moral values and contradictions regarding economic practice, at the same time mapping scalar frames of responsibility and blame. No doubt, such processes are far from new. The trope of deserving/undeserving people in relation to welfare goes as far back as the poor relief structures of early nineteenth-century England and the United States, if not before (Katz 2013; Watkins-Hayes and Kovalsky 2016). Ever since, 'idle paupers', 'scroungers', 'parasites', 'underclass', 'welfare queens' and 'strangers'/'immigrants' were added to the list of undeserving others. The content of 'the unworthy' has been expanding to accommodate new moral debates and socioeconomic realities; yet the deservingness category has been a persistent motif in policy debates and vernacular encounters in different historical and geographical contexts, particularly at times of crisis and social unrest.

Such discourse transformed the court into a social field for producing ethical subjects through a sort of moral catharsis. Debtors were no longer celebrated as modern consumers and investors in 'popular capitalism', and, contrary to creditors, were deprived of the status of rational actors taking risks in a booming economy. Decency and dignity in the aftermath of the financial crisis are to be found in prudent, ascetic lifestyles and moral borrowing. Above all, obsession with private consumption and deceit transformed debt from a complex social and uneven relation to an individual practice of choice, and the only way to subvert this was by appeal to a shared moral hierarchy of monetary valuation (Guyer 2004; Wilkis 2017) and unwritten demands for positive and negative reciprocity (Narotzky and Moreno 2002).

The court, on the other hand, performed the role of neutral state-mediator between financial institutions and indebted households.

The credit market was constructed as a powerful autonomous sphere, dissociated from both state financial policies and welfare, although it is in fact an integral part of them, counterbalancing provisioning deficiencies and managing social conflict. The court embodied the state's altruistic face, offering its left hand of 'protection', but this excessive focus on the sphere of circulation left both the nature of the welfare state and the deep structural inequalities in the sphere of production unaddressed, which were arguably at the root of indebtedness in many observed cases. Debtors' lawyers' apologetic responses and their insistence on their clients' economic victimhood further fostered this uneven regime of negotiations by strategically stimulating humanitarian feelings of compassion. The lack of a structural critique of indebtedness meant that no claims were articulated in terms of economic citizenship, and the opportunity to transform Katseli's Law from charity relief measure to a claim on rights was missed.

Deservingness, Willen and Cook argued, is the flipside of rights: 'Whereas rights claims are expressed in a formal juridical discourse that presumes fundamental equality before the law, deservingness claims are articulated in a vernacular moral register that is situationally specific and context-dependent' (2016: 96). This does not mean that the latter have fewer political implications. Perhaps, as performed in the courtrooms, deservingness was part of what Jamie Peck has identified as the two sides of the 'push' politics of austerity, an attempt to redistribute both costs and responsibility for the crisis: 'the case for austerity must be discursively pushed, since its necessitarian appeal is far from self-evident' (2014: 20). However, deservingness may not be confined to top-down ideology, veiling inequality. As I have shown, my informants were actually very outspoken about inequalities and also had a more abstract understanding of public debt's expropriative mechanisms, which socialize costs via taxation and bank recapitalization. Deservingness rather rearticulates fluid and socially mediated notions of fairness (Smith 2012) with wider material and moral tensions in social reproduction – tensions around inequality and injustice, exploitation and privilege (Narotzky 2016). The political direction of such articulations can go both ways. As the resurgence of dignity movements shows, moral categories can 'enable people – especially those suffering any form of exclusion – to articulate their claims to rights, equality, and social recognition' (Pérez 2018: 518). Yet, as the current rise of the extreme right demonstrates, they can also mark strong processes of scapegoating, narrowing the horizons of nondiscriminatory solidarity.

Acknowledgements

I am deeply grateful to my interlocutors in Kozani, inside and outside the court, for all the time and information they generously shared with me. This chapter owes much to the yearlong discussions with and inspiration provided by many friends and colleagues, first and foremost my colleagues at the European Research Council Advanced Grant Grassroots Economics Project (S. Amarianakis, P. Homs, O. Lafazani, C. Leidereiter, G. Loperfido, P.Matos, J. Palomera, A. Pusceddu, D. Sarkis, and PI S. Narotzky). I would also like to thank Alexandra Bakalaki, the Grup d'Estudis sobre Reciprocitat at the University of Barcelona, Nico Besnier and the anonymous reviewers for their critical comments on earlier versions. Last but not least, Jelena Tošić and Andreas Streinzer for all their effort in putting this volume together.

The research undertaken for and the writing of this chapter have been fully funded by the European Research Council Advanced Grant 'Grassroots Economics: Meaning, Project and practice in the pursuit of livelihood' [GRECO], IDEAS-ERC FP7, Project Number: 323743.

Theodora Vetta is a Juan de la Cierva postdoctoral researcher at the University of Barcelona and co-editor of *Focaal. Journal of Global and Historical Anthropology*. Her current research focuses on austerity regimes, public/private debt and energy transitions in Greece and Serbia. Her recent publications include 'Concrete Stories in Southern Europe: Financialisation and Inequality in the Construction Chain' (*Antipode*, 2020); 'Bondage Unemployment and Intra-class Tensions in Energy Restructuring' (*Grassroots Economics*, 2020); and *Democracy Struggles: NGOs and the Politics of Aid in Serbia* (Berghahn Books 2019).

Notes

1. Retrieved 22 January 2018 from http://ec.europa.eu/eurostat/tgm/table.do?tab=table&plugin=1&language=en&pcode=tipspd20.
2. Retrieved 17 February 2022 from http://www.bankofgreece.gr/Pages/el/Publications/ReportNPE.aspx.
3. The increasing strategies of capital to extract wealth not through expanded reproduction, but through rents (nonproductive forms of

value appropriation) have been highlighted in many works (Andreucci et al. 2017; Harvey 2007 [1982]; Strauss 2009).
4. The main criteria that the indebted had to fulfil in order to be eligible for legal protection were as follows: (a) The residence to be protected should be registered as the primary residence of the debtor and any extra property should be liquidated in order to repay the creditors within four years and according to the debtors' income. The objective value of the primary residence should not exceed €120,000 for the unmarried debtor, increased by €40,000 for the married debtor and €20,000 per child. The objective values of assets are different from commercial values as they are defined by the Greek Ministry of Economy for taxation purposes every ten to fifteen years, according to several indicators such as zone/location, square metres and age. (b) The monthly household income should not exceed the so-called 'Reasonable Subsistence Costs' as determined by the Greek Statistic Agency, running annual Household Budget Surveys, increased by 70 per cent. The Reasonable Subsistence Costs vary depending on the civil state of the applicant: for example, for a single person, they amount to between €537 and €682 per month, for an adult couple to between €906 and €1,160 or for a couple with two children to between €1,347 and €1,720. See https://www.taxheaven.gr/news/news/view/id/18319 (retrieved 17 February 2022).
5. https://www.ethnos.gr/oikonomia/7461_nomos-katseli-stoys-200000-oi-daneioliptes-poy-prostateyontai (retrieved 17 February 2022).
6. In the crisis context, the conservative media widely used the term *noikokyris* to construct the supporters of some kind of 'responsible' political centre, away from the 'political extremes' of the right and left. For the moral or political connotations of this category, see also Karagiannis (2004) and Potamianos (2015).
7. The very inability of the Greek state to repay its international creditors was presented in terms of a loss of honour, with several conservative voices, including MPs and the mainstream media, expressing their agony as to 'what face do we show to Europe?'
8. Consumption was closely linked to social status but, as Karapostolis (1983) has argued for the 1960s and the 1970s, it was also an effort towards social inclusion, bridging inequalities in production.
9. Households were certainly careful about spending money. However, the very prioritization of needs – what constitutes a legitimate expense and what is demoted to waste – was heavily informed by values that might not fit the profile of the 'rational spender'. For example, paying the electricity or heating bills on time was far lower in the priority list than paying for the holiday or rent of an unemployed son in order for him to maintain a healthy relationship with his girlfriend and avoid depression. Also, as Knight (2015) notes, other expenses such as eating out or going out for coffee were linked to both questions of status and escapism, but also resistance.

10. *Antiparochi* is a particular barter system of housing: the landowners, unwilling to sell their land for money, preferred to exchange it for a percentage of the building-to-be-constructed by a private firm, usually in the form of flats (Katsikas 2000).
11. Syriza was blamed for morally alienating people's character by having supported the 'I Refuse to Pay' social movement that mobilized people against highway tolls, property taxes and foreclosures.
12. The most powerful evidence of banks dismissing debtors as 'merchants' was the accumulated debt from unpaid workers' contributions at IKA, the largest social security fund in Greece. This was actually a very contradictory element of Katseli's Law: on the one hand, it was set to protect the weakest; on the other hand, in the case of a debt haircut, it undermined a redistributive insurance mechanism.

References

Aalbers, Manuel B. 2015. 'The Potential for Financialization', *Dialogues in Human Geography* 5(2): 214–19.
Abdelal, Rawi. 2007. *Capital Rules: The Construction of Global Finance*. Cambridge, MA: Harvard University Press.
Andreucci, Diego, Melissa García-Lamarca, Jonah Wedekind and Erik Swyngedouw. 2017. '"Value Grabbing": A Political Ecology of Rent', *Capitalism Nature Socialism* 28(1): 28–47.
Argitis, Georgios, and Stella Michopoulou. 2013. 'Financialization and the Greek Financial System', *Financialisation, Economy, Society & Sustainable Development (FESSUD) Studies*. Retrieved 17 February 2022 from https://econpapers.repec.org/paper/fesfstudy/fstudy04.htm.
Bank of Greece. 2014. *The Chronicle of the Great Crisis: The Bank of Greece 2008–2013: Public Interventions and Institutional Actions to Safeguard Financial Stability and Overcome the Crisis*. Athens: Centre for Culture, Research and Documentation, Bank of Greece.
Bennison, David, and Christina Boutsouki. 1995. 'Greek Retailing in Transition', *International Journal of Retail & Distribution Management* 23(1): 24–31.
Biehl, João. 2013. 'The Judicialization of Biopolitics: Claiming the Right to Pharmaceuticals in Brazilian Courts', *American Ethnologist* 40(3): 419–36.
Bierschenk, Thomas, and Jean-Pierre Olivier de Sardan. 2014. *States at Work: Dynamics of African Bureaucracies*. Leiden: Brill.
Blim, Michael L. 1990. *Made in Italy: Small-Scale Industrialization and Its Consequences*. New York: Praeger.
Boyer, Robert. 2000. 'Is a Finance-Led Growth Regime a Viable Alternative to Fordism? A Preliminary Analysis', *Economy and Society* 29(1): 111–45.

Burns, Robert P. 2001. *A Theory of the Trial*. Princeton: Princeton University Press.
Commaille, Jacques, Laurence Dumoulin and Cécile Robert. 2010. *La juridicisation du politique*. Paris: Lextenso éditions.
Conley, John M., and William M. O'Barr. 1990. *Rules versus Relationships: The Ethnography of Legal Discourse*. Chicago: University of Chicago Press.
Davanzati, Guglielmo F., and Rosario Patalano. 2017. 'Marx on Public Debt: Fiscal Expropriation and Capital Reproduction', *International Journal of Political Economy* 46(1): 50–64.
Dubois, Vincent. 2010. *The Bureaucrat and the Poor: Encounters in French Welfare Offices*. Farnham: Ashgate.
Elyachar, Julia. 2005. *Markets of Dispossession: NGOs, Economic Development, and the State in Cairo*. Durham, NC: Duke University Press.
Emmanouil, Dimitris. 2006. 'Η Κοινωνική Πολιτική Κατοικίας στην Ελλάδα: Οι Διαστάσεις μιας Απουσίας [The Social Housing Policy in Greece: The Dimensions of an Absence]', *Greek Review of Social Research* 120: 3–35.
European Court of Auditors. 2017. *The Commission's Intervention in the Greek Financial Crisis*. Special Report 17. Luxembourg: Publications Office of the European Union. Retrieved 17 February 2022 from https://www.eca.europa.eu/Lists/ECADocuments/SR17_17/SR_GREECE_EN.pdf.
Fassin, Didier, et al. 2015. *At the Heart of the State*. London: Pluto Press.
Goffman, Erving. 1971. *The Presentation of Self in Everyday Life*. Harmondsworth: Penguin.
Graeber, David. 2011. *Debt: The First 5,000 Years*. Brooklyn, NY: Melville House Publishing.
Greek Parliament. 2010. ΙΓ' Περίοδος Προεδρευομενης Δημοκρατίας. Σύνοδος Α' Τμήμα Διακοπής Εργασιών της Βουλής Θέρους 2010. Συνεδρίαση Ζ'. Τρίτη 27 Ιουλίου 2010 [XIII Period of Unitary Republic. First Session I Department of Suspension of Works of Parliament Summer 2010. Meeting XI. Tuesday 27 July 2010]. Retrieved 17 February 2022 from http://www.hellenicparliament.gr/Praktika/Synedriaseis-Olomeleias
Guérin, Isabelle. 2014. 'Juggling with Debt, Social Ties, and Values: The Everyday Use of Microcredit in Rural South India', *Current Anthropology* 55(9): 40–50.
Guyer, Jane I. 2004. *Marginal Gains: Monetary Transactions in Atlantic Africa*. Chicago: University of Chicago Press.
Hadjimichalis, Costis. 2010. 'The Greek Economic Crisis and Its Geography: From R. Kaplan's Geographical Determinism to Uneven Geographical Development', *Human Geography: A New Radical Journal* 3(1): 89–100.
———. 2018. *Crisis Spaces: Structures, Struggles and Solidarity in Southern Europe*. New York: Routledge.
Harvey, David. 2007 [1982]. *The Limits to Capital*. London: Verso.

Herzfeld, Michael. 1992. *The Social Production of Indifference: Exploring the Symbolic Roots of Western Bureaucracy*. Chicago: University of Chicago Press.
Hirschl, Ran. 2008. 'The Judicialization of Mega-politics and the Rise of Political Courts', *Annual Review of Political Science* 11: 93–118.
Ho, Karen. 2009. *Liquidated: An Ethnography of Wall Street*. Durham, NC: Duke University Press.
Howe, Leo. 1998. 'Scrounger, Worker, Beggarman, Cheat: The Dynamics of Unemployment and the Politics of Resistance in Belfast', *Journal of the Royal Anthropological Institute* 4(3): 531–50.
James, Deborah. 2014. *Money from Nothing: Indebtedness and Aspiration in South Africa*. Stanford: Stanford University Press.
Jansen, Stef. 2014. 'Hope for/against the State: Gridding in a Besieged Sarajevo Suburb', *Ethnos* 79(2): 238–60.
Jessop, Bob. 1990. *State Theory: Putting the Capitalist State in Its Place*. Cambridge: Polity Press.
Karagiannis, Giannis. 2004. 'Πολιτικές Συνθηματολογίες και Κομματικός Ανταγωνισμός στην Γ' Ελληνική Δημοκρατία. "Μικρομεσαίοι" και "Νοικοκυραίοι" στον Αγώνα Απόσπασης της Κοινωνικής Συναίνεσης' [Political Slogans and Partisan Antagonism in the Third Hellenic Republic: "Mikromesei" and "Nikokirei" in the Struggle for Social Consensus]', in Christoforos Vernadakis, Ilias Georgantas, Dionisis Gravaris and Dimitris Kotrogiannos (eds), *Τριάντα Χρόνια Δημοκρατία. Το Πολιτικό Σύστημα της Τρίτης Ελληνικής Δημοκρατίας, 1974–2004* [*Thirty Years of Democracy: The Political System of the Third Hellenic Republic, 1974–2004*]. Athens: Political Sciences of University of Crete – Editions Kritiki, pp. 210–50.
Karapostolis, Vasilis. 1983. *Η Καταναλωτική Συμπεριφορά στην Ελληνική Κοινωνία, 1960–1975* [*Consumer Behaviour in Greek Society 1960–1975*]. Athens: E.K.K.E.
Katsikas, Ilias. 2000. 'Το Κοινωνικό Περιεχόμενο της Αντιπαροχής και οι Οικονομικές του Προεκτάσεις [The Social Content of Antiparochi and Its Economic Implications]', *Greek Review of Social Research* 103: 3–26.
Katz, Michael B. 2013. *The Undeserving Poor: America's Enduring Confrontation with Poverty*. Oxford: Oxford University Press.
Knight, Daniel. 2015. *History, Time, and Economic Crisis in Central Greece*. New York: Palgrave Macmillan.
Kofti, Dimitra. 2020. 'Financialized Kinship and Challenges for the Greek Oikos', in Don Kalb and Chris Hann (eds), *Financialization. Relational approaches*. New York: Berghahn Books, pp. 266–85.
Krippner, Greta R. 2011. *Capitalizing on Crisis: The Political Origins of the Rise of Finance*. Cambridge, MA: Harvard University Press.
———. 2017. 'Democracy of Credit: Ownership and the Politics of Credit Access in Late Twentieth-Century America', *American Journal of Sociology* 123(1): 1–47.

Lapavitsas, Costas. 2009. 'Financialised Capitalism: Crisis and Financial Expropriation', *Historical Materialism* 17(2): 114–48.
Lazarus-Black, Mindie, and Susan F. Hirsch (eds). 1994. *Contested States: Law, Hegemony and Resistance*. New York: Routledge.
Leontidou, Lila. 1990. *The Mediterranean City in Transition: Social Change and Urban Development*. Cambridge: Cambridge University Press.
Loperfido, Giacomo, and Theodora Vetta. 2021. 'Handshake Nostalgics and Starter-uppers: Restructuring Governance and Citizenship in Southern Europe', *Antropologia* 8(3): 97–116.
Mantouvalou, Maria, and Evangelia Mpalla. 2004. 'Μεταλλαγές στο Σύστημα Γης και Οικοδομής και Διακυβεύματα του Σχεδιασμού στην Ελλάδα Σήμερα [Changes in the Land and Building System and Challenges of the Planning in Greece Today]', in Dimitris Oikonomou, Georgios Sarigiannis and Konstantinos Serraos (eds), Πόλη και Χώρος από τον 20ο στον 21ο αιώνα [*City and Place: From the 20th to the 21st Centuries*]. Athens: National Technical University of Athens, pp. 316–30.
Marx, Karl. 1992 [1867]. *Capital: A Critique of Political Economy. Volume One*. London: Penguin.
Merry, Sally Engle. 1994. 'Courts as Performances: Domestic Violence Hearings in a Hawai'i Family Court', in Susan Hirsch and Mindie Lazarus-Black (eds), *Contested States: Law, Hegemony, and Resistance*. New York: Routledge, pp. 35–59.
Moore, Sally Falk. 1973. 'Law and Social Change: The Semi-autonomous Social Field as an Appropriate Subject of Study', *Law and Society Review* 7(4): 719–46.
Mylonas, Yiannis. 2014. 'Crisis, Austerity and Opposition in Mainstream Media Discourses of Greece', *Critical Discourse Studies* 11(3): 305–21.
Narotzky, Susana. 2016. 'Between Inequality and Injustice: Dignity as a Motive for Mobilization during the Crisis', *History and Anthropology* 27(1): 74–92.
Narotzky, Susana, and Paz Moreno. 2002. 'Reciprocity's Dark Side: Negative Reciprocity, Morality and Social Reproduction', *Anthropological Theory* 2(3): 281–305.
Narotzky, Susana, and Gavin Smith. 2006. *Immediate Struggles: People, Power, and Place in Rural Spain*. Berkeley: University of California Press.
Oikonomou, Leonidas. 2012. Η Κοινωνική Παραγωγή του Αστικού Χώρου στη Μεταπολεμική Αθήνα. Η Περίπτωση της Βούλας [*The Social Production of Urban Space in Postwar Athens: The Case of Voula*]. Athens: Editions Pataki.
Ortiz, Horacio. 2013. 'Financial Value: Economic, Moral, Political, Global', *HAU Journal of Ethnographic Theory* 3(1): 64–79.
Palomera, Jaime. 2014. 'How Did Finance Capital Infiltrate the World of the Urban Poor? Homeownership and Social Fragmentation in a Spanish Neighborhood', *International Journal of Urban and Regional Research* 38(1): 218–35.

Palomera, Jaime, and Theodora Vetta. 2016. 'Moral Economy: Rethinking a Radical Concept', *Anthropological Theory* 16(4): 413–32.

Papadopoulos, Theodoros, and Antonios Roumpakis. 2013. 'Familistic Welfare Capitalism in Crisis: Social Reproduction and Anti-social Policy in Greece', *Journal of International and Comparative Social Policy* 29(3): 204–24.

Papageorgiou, Giorgos. 2015. 'Η Αλήθεια για την Ανακεφαλαιοποίηση των Τραπεζών με Αριθμούς [The Truth about Bank Recapitalization with Numbers]', *ERT*, 22 November. Retrieved 17 February 2022 from http://www.ert.gr/o-no-featured/i-alithia-gia-tin-anakefaleopiisi-ton-trapezon-me-arithmous

Peck, Jamie. 2014. 'Pushing Austerity: State Failure, Municipal Bankruptcy and the Crises of Fiscal Federalism in the USA', *Cambridge Journal of Regions, Economy and Society* 7(3): 17–44.

Peebles, Gustav. 2010. 'The Anthropology of Credit and Debt', *Annual Review of Anthropology* 39(1): 225–40.

Pellandini-Simányi, Léna, Ferenc Hammer and Zsuzsanna Vargha. 2015. 'The Financialization of Everyday Life or the Domestication of Finance?', *Cultural Studies* 29(5–6): 733–59.

Pérez, Miguel. 2018. 'Toward a Life with Dignity: Housing Struggles and New Political Horizons in Urban Chile', *American Ethnologist* 45(4): 508–20.

Petmesidou, Maria. 1991. 'Statism, Social Policy and the Middle Classes in Greece', *Journal of European Social Policy* 1(1): 31–48.

Placas, Aimee. 2018. 'Disrupted and Disrupting Consumption: Transformations in Buying and Borrowing in Greece', in Doxiadis Evdoxios and Aimee Placas (eds), *Living under Austerity: Greek Society in Crisis*. New York: Berghahn Books, pp. 321–46.

Potamianos, Nikos. 2015. *Οι Νοικοκυραίοι. Μαγαζάτορες και Βιοτέχνες στην Αθήνα 1880–1925* [*The Noikokyraioi: Shopkeepers and Master Artisans in Athens 1880–1925*]. Heraklion: Crete University Press.

Riles, Annelise. 2011. *Collateral Knowledge: Legal Reasoning in the Global Financial Markets*. Chicago: University of Chicago Press.

Rozakou, Katerina. 2017. 'Nonrecording the "European Refugee Crisis" in Greece: Navigating through Irregular Bureaucracy', *FOCAAL. Journal of Global and Historical Anthropology* 77: 36–49.

Rubin, Jonah. 2008. 'Adjudicating the Salvadoran Civil War: Expectations of the Law in Romagoza', *PoLAR: Political and Legal Anthropology Review* 31(2): 264–85.

Sabaté, Irene. 2016. 'The Spanish Mortgage Crisis and the Re-emergence of Moral Economies in Uncertain Times', *History and Anthropology* 27(1): 107–20.

Siatitsa, Dimitra. 2014. 'Αιτήματα για το Δικαίωμα στην Κατοικία στις Πόλεις της Νότιας Ευρώπης: Ο Λόγος και ο Ρόλος των Κοινωνικών Κινημάτων [Claims for the Right to Housing in Cities of Southern Europe: The

Discourse and Role of Social Movements]', Ph.D. dissertation. Athens: National Technical University of Athens.
Silbey, Susan S. 2005. 'After Legal Consciousness', *Annual Review of Law and Social Science* 1: 323–68.
Smith, Gavin. 2011. 'Selective Hegemony and beyond: Populations with "No Productive Function": A Framework for Enquiry', *Identities* 18: 2–38.
Smith, Katherine. 2012. *Fairness, Class and Belonging in Contemporary England*. Basingstoke: Palgrave Macmillan.
Spyridakis, Manos. 2013. *The Liminal Worker: An Ethnography of Work, Unemployment and Precariousness in Contemporary Greece*. Farnham: Ashgate.
Spyrou, Spyros. 1999. 'Financial Liberalization or Financial Repression? The Case of the Greek Equity Market', *Journal of Southern Europe and the Balkans* 1(1): 65–76.
Strauss, Kendra. 2009. 'Accumulation and Dispossession: Lifting the Veil on the Subprime Mortgage Crisis', *Antipode* 41(1): 10–14.
Streeck, Wolfgang. 2011. 'The Crises of Democratic Capitalism', *New Left Review* 71: 5–29.
Swyngedouw, Erik. 2005. 'Dispossessing H_2O: The Contested Terrain of Water Privatization', *Capitalism Nature Socialism* 16(1): 81–98.
Thelen, Tatjana, Larissa Vetters and Keebet von Benda-Beckmann (eds). 2018. *Stategraphy: Toward a Relational Anthropology of the State*. New York: Berghahn Books.
Vaiou, Dina, and Costis Hadjimichalis. 1997. Με τη Ραπτομηχανή στην Κουζίνα και τους Πολωνούς στους Αγρούς. Πόλεις, Περιφέρειες και Άτυπη Εργασία [*With the Sewing Machine in the Kitchen and the Poles in the Fields: Cities, Regions and Informal Work*]. Athens: Exandas.
Vaiou, Dina, Maria Mantouvalou and Maria Mavridou. 2009. Κοινωνικές και Πολιτικές Διαστάσεις της Αστικής Ανάπτυξης στην Ελλάδα. Διαχρονικές Αναγνώσεις [*Social and Political Dimensions of Urban Development in Greece: Readings over Time*].. Athens: National Technical University of Athens.
Van der Zwan, Natascha. 2014. 'Making Sense of Financialization', *Socio-Economic Review* 12(1): 99–129.
Vetta, Theodora. 2020. 'Bondage Unemployment and Intra-Class Tensions in Greek Energy Restructuring', in Susana Narotzky (ed.), *Grassroots Economies: Living with Austerity in Southern Europe*. London: Pluto Press, pp. 25-49.
Vetta, Theodora, and Jaime Palomera. 2020. 'Concrete Stories: Financialization and Inequality in the Construction Chain', *Antipode* 53(3): 888–907.
Watkins-Hayes, Celeste, and Elyse Kovalsky. 2016. 'The Discourse of Deservingness: Morality and the Dilemmas of Poverty Relief in Debate and Practice', in David Brady and Linda Burton (eds), *The Oxford*

Handbook of Poverty and Society. New York: Oxford University Press, pp. 193–220.

Wilkis, Ariel. 2017. *The Moral Power of Money: Morality and Economy in the Life of the Poor*. Stanford: Stanford University Press.

Willen, Sarah S., and Jennifer Cook. 2016. 'Health-Related Deservingness', in Felicity Thomas (ed.), *Handbook of Migration and Health*. Cheltenham: Edward Elgar, pp. 95–118.

14

Victims, Patriots and the Middle Class
The (Un)Deservingness of Debtors in Post-Credit Boom Croatia

Marek Mikuš

As Andreas Streinzer and Jelena Tošić remark in the Introduction to this volume, ideologies of deservingness centre on moral assessments of relations of distribution and inequality – questions such as what various groups in society deserve and what they really get. They tend to be vernacular, contextual, conditional and affect-laden, unlike the more formalized, rule-based and rationalist (human) rights frameworks with which they often intersect (Willen and Cook 2016: 97). Humanitarianism is similar in that it also makes assumptions about kinds of subjects worthy of assistance, namely, passive victims reduced to 'bare life' (Fassin 2012). However, deservingness has a different moral and affective focus – on comparison between groups' entitlements and indignation over real or perceived injustices. Scholarship on deservingness in anthropology and beyond mainly attends to two social domains: welfare, in response to a surge of deservingness politics under neoliberalization (e.g. Howe 1990; Haney 2002; van Oorschot 2006; Katz 2013; Capello, Matos and Lanari, Chapters 6, 7 and 8 in this volume respectively) and the closely related domain of citizenship, as arguments about deservingness figured in the nativist backlash against migration (e.g. Holmes and Castañeda 2016; Jørgensen and Thomsen 2016; Strasser, and Zakariás and Feischmidt, Chapters 9 and 11 in this volume respectively).

This chapter, along with those by Irene Sabaté and Theodora Vetta, develops the focus on deservingness in a field in which scholars largely have yet to take stock of its relevance: that of household finance and debt in particular. This is the case despite the fact that morality is a longstanding, even defining concern in the anthropology of credit/debt (Mattioli 2019). Recent influential contributions in anthropology and sociology traced macrohistories of moral and religious ideas about debt, and their role in the consolidation of debt as a major modern relationship of domination (Graeber 2011; Lazzarato 2012). Others developed a more ethnographic perspective on the interplay between financial obligations of commodified debt and moral obligations stemming from familial and community relationships (e.g. Palomera 2014; James 2015). Particularly relevant contributions pointed to the ways in which moral ideas about mutuality, entitlement and social justice came to frame an emergent politics of household debt in the aftermath of the global financial crisis in 2007 and 2008. Noelle Stout (2019) documented how defaulting Californian debtors expected reciprocity on lenders' part on the basis of their repayment record, while right-wing commentators stigmatized them in moral terms and rejected their entitlement to public assistance. Sabaté (2020) described how Spanish state officials, bank employees, debt activists and debtors differentiated between those who deserved debt relief and those who did not. However, while using the term prominently to interpret these practices, she did not build on her analysis to contribute to the debate about deservingness.

In this chapter, I analyse debates and struggles over household debt in post-credit boom Croatia to untangle multiple ways in which pro-debtor actors and their opponents represented debtors as (un)deserving of public assistance.[1] In addition to demonstrating how Croatian debtors became subject to a politics of deservingness, I draw on this case to make two key contributions to the existing scholarship. First, while most studies examine the deservingness of one or more predefined social categories, such as 'refugees' and '(economic) migrants', in a single field of social life, such as 'welfare' or 'health', my analysis traces connections between discourses of debtor deservingness and other registers of entitlement across social categories and fields. Croatian debtors have been consistently represented as (un)deserving as a result of belonging or conforming to other, more 'established' deserving categories or subjectivities. This exemplifies a mechanism that, drawing on the simple Latin sense of the term, I call 'translation' – that is, 'carrying over' of deservingness attributes of one category/subjectivity to another. By describing this mechanism, I specify one practical way in which deservingness may be relational (Willen and Cook 2016: 97).

Second, I critique, and suggest an alternative to, the somewhat implicit way in which deservingness has tended to be theorized and made to fit within contemporary anthropology at large. Most of this scholarship has focused on social categories defined in terms of state classificatory schemes and/or identity, especially ethnic and racial ones (Willen 2012: 813; Holmes and Castañeda 2016: 21; Willen and Cook 2016: 113). It rarely mentions class as a criterion of deservingness, which dovetails with arguments such as that 'constructions of "undeservingness" ignore structural inequalities' (Willen 2012: 814) and 'shift blame from historical, political-economic structures to the displaced people themselves' (Holmes and Castañeda 2016: 12). It seems that the prototypical idea of studies on deservingness continues to be its negative – *un*deservingness as an evaluative framework and discursive register used by powerful social institutions and forces, such as states, the mainstream media and majoritarian publics, to justify and reinforce the bureaucratic and/or identity-based exclusion of groups such as migrants. The case of Croatian debtors presents a different scenario, in which actors defined by shared grievances and a more implicit, 'economic' form of subordination actively develop a discourse of deservingness to make claims and challenge dominant ideologies and social relations. In terms of theory, this suggests a need to go beyond the view of deservingness as 'moral assessments' in which '[o]ne assesses others' relative deservingness on the basis of two key factors: first, an implicit sense of one's own deservingness, and second, one's sense of actual or presumed social connection to those [being assessed]' (Willen 2012: 814). This reduces deservingness to a metric of individual moral reasoning that social relations enter merely as a subjective 'sense of social connection' and for which history, the economy and politics are just an externalized 'context' (Willen and Cook 2016: 102). Revealingly, Willen (2012: 820) placed the focus on deservingness within the assertive anthropological approach of the past fifteen to twenty years described variously as anthropology of morality/ethics/'the good' or moral anthropology. Its leading figures aspired to a disciplinary paradigm shift centred on issues of ethics treated in terms of moral philosophy rather than social analysis. As critics noted, this entailed a universalization of Western liberal ethics and anti-sociological arguments that privilege individual choice and action while eliding power and politics (Kalb 2018; Kapferer and Gold 2018). While anthropological scholarship on deservingness has not reproduced these tendencies in a purist form, it may have been influenced by its biases.

I suggest a shift in perspective that returns social relations and politics to the centre of the enquiry into deservingness. Accordingly, my analysis works out links between discourses of debtor deservingness and overlapping and competing political projects that sought to maintain or transform aspects of existing social relations. Building on other anthropological engagements with deservingness and my own work (Mikuš 2018), I do so in Gramscian terms. Holmes and Castañeda (2016: 12) discussed German public debates about the deservingness of migrants as part of a 'war of position' – the ongoing struggle over hegemony, which Gramsci famously defined as rule by 'consent' and 'political, intellectual and *moral* leadership' (Gramsci 1971: 12, 55–60, emphasis added). Streinzer and Tošić (Introduction to this volume) argue that 'registers of deservingness' are part of 'common sense' – traditional, taken-for-granted folk worldviews varying between classes and periods (Gramsci 1971: 323–33, 348, 419–25). The common sense of subordinated classes specifically exists in a complex relationship with hegemony: it is inevitably shaped by hegemonic narratives while containing fragments of counterhegemonic ideas ('hidden transcripts') that may be, especially through the work of subaltern 'organic intellectuals', developed into more coherent counternarratives to underpin emergent hegemonic projects (Crehan 2016). In the rest of this chapter, I untangle the ways in which various actors mobilized and elaborated elements of common sense to develop competing narratives and political projects vis-à-vis household debt, and I situate these contestations in wider hegemonic struggles in contemporary Croatia.

The chapter is organized as follows: in the next section, I briefly describe the historical setting of Croatia's debt boom in the 2000s and the subsequent bust. The third section identifies normalization and individualization as two hegemonic narratives about these processes formulated already during the boom. The fourth section focuses on counternarratives about debtors as victims of legal offences, as well as multiple forms of suffering. The fifth section reviews counter-counternarratives that denied the victimhood of debtors in reference to their free will, calculative behaviour or imprudence. The sixth section analyses the ways in which debtors have been represented as members of other deserving groups, namely, veterans and the middle class. Conclusions situate these narratives and politics of debtor deservingness in wider hegemonic struggles in Croatia.

The Croatian Debt Boom and Bust

In the 1990s, after the break-up of Yugoslavia, Croatia went through a period of nationalist politics, wars, hyperinflation and banking crises, during which credit was very expensive and for many inaccessible. This was followed by a major boom in household debt and housing prices in the 2000s. By 2008, Croatia had one of the highest levels of both in Eastern Europe (Égert and Mihaljek 2007: 20; Sugawara and Zalduendo 2011: 3). In the same period, other countries at the eastern, southern and northwestern peripheries of Europe experienced similar processes (Bohle 2018). These debt booms were a crucial part of peripheral forms of financialization, which were based on foreign capital inflows orchestrated by transnational actors to make profits from cross-border interest rate differentials (Becker et al. 2010: 236–41). Like other Eastern European states, Croatia took major steps towards external financial liberalization and sold most of its banking sector to Western European banks by the early 2000s. The latter then imported capital to be lent out to Croatian households and businesses at higher interest rates.

During the boom, Croatia and other Eastern European countries further experienced a 'mainstreaming of predatory lending' (Mikuš 2019: 297) – a targeting of high-risk, high-cost lending practices at prime and subprime borrowers alike, which was de facto endorsed by state regimes of (under-)regulation. This included foreign-exchange (FX) loans, loans with interest rates adjustable by arbitrary decisions of banks, lax credit checks and formalized forms of usury and fraud (Burton 2017; Bohle 2018; Mikuš 2019). In Croatia (and in Hungary, Poland, Romania and other countries), Swiss franc loans, especially mortgages, became particularly problematic as the franc soared against local currencies between 2009 and 2015, inflating outstanding principals and monthly repayments, and trapping debtors in protracted misery (Rodik 2015, 2019; Mikuš 2019: 307–17). In this period, Croatia experienced a comparatively severe and long recession (between 2009 and 2014). Legal reforms between 2010 and 2012 enabled much easier and unrestrained debt enforcement against natural persons, resulting in an astonishing 8 per cent of the total population with 'blocked' bank accounts in 2017 – people whose money was continually confiscated from their accounts towards debt repayment (Mikuš 2020: 242). Arrears on debt repayment and utility bills, nonperforming loans, home repossessions and activities of private debt collection agencies also soared. This proliferation of problems with debts and their politicization by social movements and political parties helped to establish lending and debt enforcement practices as important public issues, while also being key in the rise of several new political actors (Mikuš 2019, 2020).

Hegemonic Narratives about Boom and Bust: Naturalization and Individualization

As the debt boom unfolded, elite actors such as bankers, experts and business, and the general media developed two key ways of narrating that aligned its interpretation with wider hegemonic ideologies, while also tapping into common-sense views about Croatian history and 'national character'. I call these two narrative frameworks 'naturalization' and 'individualization'. First, the debt boom was naturalized as an inevitable part of Croatia's transition from socialism (and postsocialist authoritarianism) to free-market capitalism. The 2000s in particular was a period of liberalization, marketization and rapid development of Western-style mass consumption – shopping malls, new banking and payment infrastructures and, indeed, credit markets. The sociologist Ivan Burić (2010) devoted a whole monograph to an argument that the quick expansion of household debt, despite the moral panic surrounding it, was in fact a normal and benign part of Croatia's transition. Usually, however, this narrative was rendered more implicitly. This can be illustrated by the coverage of household debt issues in *Banka*, the erstwhile flagship magazine of Croatia's banking community. As the boom was peaking, articles with nonchalant (sub)headings such as 'Let Them Spend' elided or denied the notion that the quick growth of debt might be a cause for concern (Martinović 2005; Stojić 2006: 32; Gelenčer 2007). Evan Kraft (2005), director of the Croatian National Bank's (CNB) Research Department, even predicted the boom to happily continue at the same pace for the next ten or fifteen years. In its immediate aftermath, the influential economist and commentator Maruška Vizek (2009) assessed as 'natural' that banks had engaged in risky lending to expand their assets and market shares during the boom and argued that it was 'impossible' for them to conduct adequate credit checks at the pace at which they were approving loans – as if this was something beyond their control.

Also starting early on, the financial industry and the media subjected the debt boom to a culturalist form of individualization with strong moralistic overtones. This narrative attributed the fast growth of debt to a pronounced 'consumer mentality' in Croatia, supposedly manifesting in an obsession with outward signs of prosperity and a tendency to spend more than one can afford (Burić 2010: 11, 15–16, 23–25). A *Banka* article on credit cards noted that 'according to statistical data, every sixth inhabitant of Croatia is poor, but what distinguishes Croatians from a group of similar countries [*sic*] is a penchant for spending and following the rule: "no wage – here comes the card!"' (Gelenčer 2005: 56). Another presented what became the hegemonic ex-post explanation of the debt boom in this key: 'We behaved like drunk billionaires; we constantly lived beyond our means and nourished an illusion that we had more than we [really] had' (Pavičić 2010: 26). This placed the ultimate responsibility for over-indebtedness on individual debtors with their irrational preferences, decisions and actions, even if these were assumed to spring from a 'national psyche'. The narrative thus conforms to the Foucauldian model of neoliberal governmentality that scholars invoked to analyse individualizing biases in much of contemporary governance of personal debt (Payne 2012; Türken et al. 2015). At the same time, this particular individualizing narrative was clearly shaped by the tendency across (South) East Europe to perceive and value oneself in comparison with an inherently superior Western Europe, which can be traced to the narrative of postsocialist transition and older discourses of Orientalism and Balkanism (Todorova 2009).

Notably, the narrative about hyperbolic Croatian consumerism was repeated by many financial professionals as well as ordinary debtors I interviewed. Both mentioned their over-indebted, credit-card juggling acquaintances and criticized them for taking loans for status symbols like skiing vacations in Austria or branded mobile phones for children. Some debtors chastised themselves for unwise purchases of anything from handbags to flats during the boom, while others offered caricature-like vignettes of ostentatious luxury consumption in downtown Zagreb. They were particularly likely to denounce a heavy use of consumer loans and credit cards as irresponsible and irrational.

After the crisis, as elsewhere around the world, 'financial literacy' emerged as another hegemonic narrative about household debt issues, found in 'expert' and policy discourses rather than in general public discourse. Broadly speaking, financial literacy is an individualizing interpretative and discursive framework that makes individuals responsible for their dealings with financial institutions, and sees issues and solutions mainly in terms of their financial knowledge (Guérin 2012; Türken et al. 2015). A Google Scholar search for the

Croatian phrase for 'financial literacy' (*financijska pismenost*) reveals no scholarly articles published in or before 2009, compared to 150+ published between 2010 and 2019. The Croatian government adopted its first financial literacy strategy in 2015 and then a series of annual action plans. *Banka* went from ignoring financial literacy during the boom to publishing recurrent long articles on the subject in the 2010s (e.g. Martinović 2012). Some statements blended financial literacy with the culturalist individualizing narrative by stressing the supposedly low financial literacy of Croatians compared to other nations. Numerical results of international surveys gave a semblance of scientific objectivity to deeply moralistic and auto-Balkanizing statements such as '[Croatians Are] Incapable of the Simplest Money Decisions' (Ralašić 2014).

Counternarratives I: Debtors as Legal Victims

Croatian debtors, activists, sympathetic journalists and others developed several types of counternarratives that challenged the hegemonic narratives about household debt and claimed that (some groups of) debtors deserved public assistance. The first type of counternarrative represents debtors as 'victims' (žrtve, *oštećenici*). Like deservingness, victimhood may be invoked to express moral claims to entitlements, in this case grounded in experiences of abuse and suffering. Two particularly common forms of victimhood are the already-mentioned passive humanitarian victims and martyrs as their active, heroic counterparts (Ronsbo and Jensen 2014: 4). Counternarratives about Croatian debtors as victims mostly do not neatly fit either of these two ideal types, although elements of both are present in some instances. Most importantly, debtors are represented as victims in the sense of having been damaged by legal offences committed by others. It follows on a more moral and ideological plane that the lending boom was not as normal and benign as the hegemonic narrative would have it, and that debtors' hardships were not only due to their individual failures, but also due to others' wrongdoings that should be remedied through public action. Oštećenik (the damaged one in a dispute or proceeding), one of the terms used to describe debtors, expresses this legalistic concept of victimhood better than the more general žrtva (one who suffered) (Hrvatski jezični portal n.d.). It also signals a more knowledgeable and agential victim subject who identifies law as an operational domain in which their victimization is contestable in legitimate and potentially effective ways. This can be seen as a specific kind of translation of deservingness attributes of a legal and political subjectivity (the injured party) rather than a social category (as discussed below). It illustrates that deservingness discourses and more formal legal registers are not necessarily clearly distinct, but may interweave in complex ways.

Activists representing holders of cross-border mortgage loans by Austrian Raiffeisen cooperatives, which resulted in a conspicuously high rate of defaults, repossessions and lawsuits, were particularly likely to label this group of debtors as victims both in public and private (Mikuš 2019: 297, 302, 305). Most obviously, they described them as victims of mass fraud who should be receiving protection and justice through the actions of law enforcement agencies and also, inasmuch as legal reforms or one-off interventions were required, policy-makers. In an interview he gave me, Franjo, an entrepreneur and prominent co-op debtor activist, repeatedly described his own loan as 'pure fraud' and the practices of the co-ops as 'crime' and 'looting and robbery'.[2] Most co-op debtors I interviewed claimed that their gullibility or acute financial need led them to overlook irregular features of this lending (Mikuš 2019: 303–4).

Franjo also made another set of claims common among this group: that 'our state did practically nothing' and that 'they continue to protect crime'. At a public debate about the problems of co-op debtors (Mikuš 2019: 295–96), Franjo mentioned that criminal charges against the co-ops had been filed years ago 'but nothing has happened since, we are a state without a legal order in the service of citizens'. Rather than a banal scam, co-op debtors were victims of a dark conspiracy involving public authorities and malevolent forces pulling strings behind the scenes. One narrative held that the co-op lending was part of a Croatian elites' money laundering scheme routed through Austria. Other narratives subsumed it under a global 'Jewish banker' conspiracy or the continued grip of 'Serbs and Communists' on Croatian courts and prosecution offices (Mikuš 2019: 305–6). In sum, these activists presented debtors as victims of both legal offences and exploitation by ethnic, political and social others, thereby increasing the stakes of their victimhood, lending it an aspect of martyrdom and increasing chances of broader political and social alliances, as discussed below.

While more rarely than co-op debtors, Swiss franc debtors sometimes also described themselves as victims. The Franc Association (FA; Udruga Franak), their main organization, held a series of events called 'Candles for All Victims of Loans' in 2015. Participants employed the imagery of burial by lighting candles in graveyard candle holders in front of the CNB headquarters in Zagreb and bank branches across Croatia. More often, however, FA activists and general franc debtors, including those I interviewed, would describe their position as one of 'debt slavery' to highlight the exploitative and unequal nature of their relationship with the banks. In any case, the FA consistently represented franc debtors as victims in an indirect manner – by stressing the 'illegal' as well as 'dishonest' and 'unfair' nature of franc loans and other lending practices to which they were exposed, such as arbitrarily adjustable interest rates. A banner used at FA protests and displayed in the association's meeting room at the time of my fieldwork summed up the gist of this narrative with the words 'CHF CREDIT / UNCONSTITUTIONAL / IMMORAL / VOID' placed in a 'road closed' traffic sign.[3] Sanja, one of the first cohort of FA activists, told me in an interview that they fought against the tendency to frame franc loans as a 'social issue' (with the pejorative undertones of a 'welfare issue') and instead pushed for its recognition as an issue of 'dishonest market behaviour'. Accordingly, the organization has over the years called on law enforcement agencies, regulators (the CNB) and policy-makers to end contested lending practices, mitigate their impact on debtors and compensate the former financially (by ordering banks to reimburse excess payments) and morally (by sanctioning responsible banks and bankers).

A key field of struggle in which the FA articulated an elaborate legal variant of this counternarrative was its pioneering collective lawsuit against the eight largest Croatian banks, which resulted in its victory and the nullification of clauses on Swiss franc indexation and arbitrarily adjustable interest rates in loan agreements (even if individual litigation remained necessary for effective nullification of those clauses in actual individual agreements).[4] The courts accepted the FA's arguments that the two clauses broke the equality of parties under contract law (by allowing banks to adjust interest rates at will) as well as debtors' consumer rights (by providing inadequate information about the loans and using the franc clause to transfer currency risk to debtors and make illicit profits) (Mikuš 2019: 308–9). Importantly, the FA reproduced simplified versions of these arguments in countless press releases and media statements. Going beyond the responsibility of banks, the association also pointed to a complicity of public authorities in tolerating practices that would have been unthinkable in Western Europe (e.g. FA 2016; Benjak 2017). These arguments likely resonated with the public; some of the debtors I interviewed mentioned the illegal actions of banks, the insufficient state regulation or the apparent second-rate treatment of Croatian borrowers as considerations that gave legitimacy to the struggle of franc debtors.

What the discourses of various groups of debt activists shared was an emphasis on the outward signs of a humanitarian-style victimhood of debtors, especially their dispossession and physical and mental health issues, in extreme cases resulting in death. Political actors focusing on calls for pro-debtor changes to Croatia's debt enforcement system, such as the association Blocked Ones (Blokirani) and the extraparliamentary party Free Croatia (Slobodna Hrvatska), often described people subjected to debt enforcement as impoverished by a greedy and ruthless 'enforcement mafia' (Mikuš 2020). These themes were also prominent in the discourse of Franjo's activist network. Since Raiffeisen co-op loans were all mortgages secured by real estate, debtors often faced repossessions and evictions from homes. This group of activists condemned these practices as 'robbery' and 'throwing out on the street', demanded an end to them and compensation for those already dispossessed, and accused Austrian lenders and Croatian loan mediators of clandestinely buying up the properties in auctions. A range of actors politicized repossessions and evictions from homes in recent years and sought their prevention or retroactive nullification in specific cases as well as systemic reforms. Most prominently, the party Human Shield (HS; Živi zid) has achieved public recognition and support as an activist group organizing physical resistance to evictions, including in Raiffeisen co-op cases. HS politicians frequently evoked the 'right to home' nominally protected by Croatia's Constitution and, after entering Parliament in 2015, proposed a total ban on repossessions of the 'only home' (*jedini dom*), defined as an owner-occupied home that is the debtor's only real estate.

Other parliamentary parties, including the FA's partisan offshoot Force (Snaga), also proposed amendments that would make home repossessions more difficult and provide more protection to homeowners. While these opposition amendments were unsuccessful, government amendments introducing some restrictions on repossessions were adopted in 2017. However, overall, the FA focused especially on the financial dispossession of franc debtors, who typically prioritized continued repayment at all costs precisely in order to avoid repossession. Responding to the media demand for 'human stories', activists mediated between journalists and debtors willing to share their experiences. Their stories, such as those the FA published in a collection entitled *Black Book* (FA 2012), often described how little debtors had left to live on after paying loan instalments and the drastic impact this had on their lives.

The theme of dispossession was closely associated with that of health and death. Aneta, member of a group of Raiffeisen co-op debtors separate from Franjo's activist network, told me in an interview that she knew about at least four people whose deaths could be reasonably attributed to stress caused by their loans. Many other debtors ended up chronically anxious, insomniac and addicted to medication, she claimed. Several people I met at events organized by Franjo's network or Free Croatia blamed the deaths of their relatives on their debt issues, while speakers likened the practices of creditors and debt enforcement agencies to a 'genocide' of the Croatian people. Stories of suicides and other kinds of death due to dispossession were common in articles written by these activists (e.g. Landeka 2016).

The situation was similar with franc debtors. Brankica Ivanković (2014), a medical nurse and FA activist, documented the impact of franc loans on the physical and mental health of debtors in a survey-based thesis. The FA shared the alarming findings with the media, thereby bolstering its narrative about the victimizing effects of franc loans with quantitative data more likely to be perceived as 'hard evidence'. The case of Ivana Mandić (her real name) became particularly well known publicly. Ivana died of a heart attack in her late twenties shortly after a meeting at her bank in which she learned how much her debt had soared due to franc appreciation and how long she would have to continue repaying it.[5] I repeatedly visited her parents, Božica and Drago (their real names), in their home in a small town near Zagreb. Their personal story brought together several of the narratives and frames about debtor deservingness that I have already mentioned or will discuss below. More than five years after their daughter's death, the Mandićs talked about their ongoing mental health issues and a strong sense of despair and anger over a lack of material compensation and punishments for those they held responsible. They presented Ivana and themselves as perhaps gullible but certainly good faith working-class borrowers who 'trusted' the bank and never imagined avoiding repayment, but found themselves unable to keep up repayments due to the bank's deliberate fraud and Ivana's loss of job in the midst of the crisis. They believed that they were further victimized by the police, the prosecution office and judges, who conspired with the bank to obstruct a proper investigation and prosecution of the case, going to such lengths as manipulating the autopsy of Ivana's body. Theirs was thus a rather extreme case of the sense of victimhood and loss of trust in institutions that many Croatian debtors expressed.

Counter-Counternarratives: Denying Debtor Victimhood

As household debt became increasingly politicized, bankers, economic commentators, politicians and other actors responded by developing a set of overlapping counter-counternarratives that denied that debtors were victims of legal and moral offences and therefore, by implication, deserving of aid and compensation through interventions of public institutions. One such kind of narratives reframed the contested lending practices as legally and morally acceptable, thereby elaborating the hegemonic normalizing narrative in response to its questioning. Other counter-counternarratives extended the hegemonic individualizing narrative by characterizing and attributing responsibility to (various groups of) debtors in ways that undermined their pretensions to the status of victims. This included claims that debtors got into debt out of their own free will, that they had engaged in calculation or speculation, and that they were imprudent, irresponsible and financially illiterate.

Most of these arguments make their appearance in the four-part 'Saga of the Swiss Franc', an instructive position piece by Zoran Bohaček, at the time the head of the Croatian Banking Association (CBA; Hrvatska udruga banaka), the interest organization of the banking industry.[6] Parts 1–3 are prefaced as a compilation of main 'facts' and 'theses' from CBA statements on the franc loans affair (Bohaček n.d.: 1). Part 1 starts by normalizing the banks' role in the debt boom as merely servicing a pre-existing demand under a timeless 'logic of capitalism'. This applies to feeding the boom in general and franc lending in particular, which is misrepresented by a banal analogy with 'red apples' that consumers capriciously preferred over 'green apples' (ibid.: 3). It was 'absolutely impossible' for banks to predict the franc appreciation and profit from it through household loans; issues were strictly due to extraordinary external shocks (ibid.: 4–5). Switching to the individualizing narrative, Bohaček (ibid.: 5) refuses that banks 'coaxed' (*navukli*) clients into taking franc loans. In Part 2, he instead emphatically argues that debtors exercised their 'free will', 'decision' and 'choice' (ibid.: 5–6). When they did not make use of 'affordable conversions' that 'some banks' supposedly offered early on, it meant that they '*consciously stayed* in CHF and once again *accepted* continued currency risk' (ibid., emphasis in original). While the 'Saga' mostly employs this dry (neo)liberal rhetoric of freely choosing, responsible subjects, Part 3 ends with a more moralistic assessment that franc debtors were 'less careful and more prone to risk' than those who took kuna loans and hence policies aiding them 'reward [their] carelessness' (ibid.: 14).

Other opponents of pro-debtor policies developed more elaborate counter-counternarratives about franc debtors as calculative and risk-taking participants in ostensibly egalitarian financial markets who had no right to be seen as victims of deception. *Banka* quoted Velimir Šonje, an influential economic commentator, as saying: 'They speculated with the franc, they counted on a lower interest rate than on the euro, and they have to bear the risk the best they can' (Banka. hr 2011). A commentator in the *Slobodna Dalmacija* daily argued that a new line of division emerged in Croatian society between kuna and euro debtors as the 'risk averse' (*ziheraši*) and franc debtors as 'gamblers' (*hazarderi*). The latter were hypocrites who behaved very much like the banks they criticized: earlier they were happy to 'privatize profits' in the form of lower interest payments and now they wanted to 'socialize losses' (Laušić 2015). During an informal conversation at the 2017 Meeting of Governors, the annual conference of the governors of central banks in the Western Balkans, a high-ranking official of a large Croatian bank told me that franc debtors 'knew very well what they were signing' and simply expected things to work out in their favour.

Another kind of counter-counternarratives undermined the victimhood of franc debtors by characterizing them as imprudent, irresponsible and/or financially illiterate, thereby elaborating the hegemonic individualizing narratives. For example, the introduction to the government's financial literacy strategy mentions the crisis of Swiss franc loans as one of the motives for its adoption, thus framing it as an outcome of the financial illiteracy of debtors (Vlada Republike Hrvatske 2015). Several franc debtors I spoke with recalled, with some indignation, Prime Minister Zoran Milanović's comments implying that franc debtors had simply been careless: 'None of us can escape our personal responsibility. It's a business relationship. We must all keep our cool and understand what we're signing' (Milovan 2013).

In a similar fashion to the general individualizing narrative about debtors, a number of my interviewees – finance professionals and debtors alike – evoked this idea of franc debtors as imprudent or even 'greedy' (*pohlepni*), sometimes backed up with examples of acquaintances who were advised not to take such loans, but who nevertheless did so. Several interviewees expressed their displeasure at having to pay for what they saw as somebody else's poor decisions, even though interventions to aid franc debtors did not require any public spending. This suggests that the view of franc debtors as imprudent enjoyed a significant degree of popular support.

The potential significance of these counter-counternarratives for determining the deservingness of individual debtors was illustrated in a court hearing I attended in February 2017. A franc debtor, an elderly lady who told the judge that the loan had 'destroyed' her and her late husband, was suing her bank for excess repayments due to arbitrary increases in interest rates. The bank's lawyer tried to demonstrate the plaintiff's imprudence by posing questions such as whether she knew she had taken out a loan with a variable interest rate, whether she knew what a variable interest rate was or whether she had read the contract. In response to the last question, the debtor reframed her failure to read the contract as a sign that she was a good faith, perhaps gullible debtor: 'I didn't, I mean, one has some trust.' After the questioning, the lawyer announced that she was objecting to the plaintiff's testimony, arguing that it was 'unconvincing' and that it was 'evident that [the plaintiff] did not act responsibly because she did not read the contract ... when the loan is this large, it's not logical that she didn't read the clauses about interest rates'. The same action – such as not reading a loan contract closely, which is widely considered as the norm in Croatia due to a lack of scope for negotiation about terms – was thus attributed markedly different meanings and values in the competing narratives.

Counternarratives II: Debtors as Veterans and the 'Middle Class'

The second type of counternarratives about Croatian debtors carried over their attributes of deservingness from their membership in other valuable and entitled groups to their status of debtors. At the start of this chapter, I argued that much of the scholarship on deservingness is actually modelled on negative, exclusionary discourses of *un*deservingness that typically deny underlying social inequalities. In contrast, this case of positive, affirmative discourses of deservingness shows that such discourses may in fact mobilize particular narratives about inequality as moral grounds for entitlement for those represented as oppressed.

The first social category from which deservingness attributes were translated to (some) Croatian debtors was the veterans of the 1990s Croatian War of Independence (*branitelji*). At first sight, there is no inherent relationship between being a debtor and being a veteran, and their juxtaposition appears arbitrary. However, it becomes almost predictable when one considers the position of veterans in contemporary Croatia. The image of the 1990s war as a just war of self-defence and self-determination constitutes the very core of the hegemonic, state-backed and widely accepted narrative about the building of the independent Croatian state (Jović 2017). Veterans play the lead role in this narrative as patriotic heroes who made enormous sacrifices for the state and the nation, and who deserve compensation in the form of extensive rights and symbolic recognition. Registered veterans – an astonishing 11.7 per cent of the population in 2012 – and their relatives receive higher welfare payments than others as well as a range of special benefits and privileges. Their position as a powerful interest group within a clientelistic political system is reflected in recurrent pre-election expansions of benefits coverage and close connections between the extensive network of veterans' organizations and the hegemonic right-wing party since independence, the Croatian Democratic Union (Stubbs and Zrinščak 2015; Dolenec 2017).

The activists making claims on behalf of Raiffeisen co-op debtors and those facing debt enforcement were particularly likely to mark these debtors as veterans (*branitelji*). In the case of co-op debtors, this corresponded with the already-mentioned nationalist and far-right narratives these activists often evoked, as well as their political and activist alliances (Mikuš 2019: 306). One of the most publicized cases of co-op debtors was that of Mirko Dukić (his real name) whose family's eviction from their repossessed flat in Zagreb in October 2016 became the site of dramatic scenes of despair and resistance. In a series of articles, Nada Landeka, a member of Franjo's activist network, stressed Dukić's background as a veteran and juxtaposed the stories of Dukić and other victimized veterans with claims about privileges enjoyed by Croatian Serbs and their role in Dukić's eviction, thereby narrating the issues of veteran debtors as offences against the Croatian nation and statehood. One headline screamed: 'Are You Ashamed, Politicians? Veterans Fought for Our Freedom and You Throw Them out to the Street' (Landeka 2016). Dukić himself did not hesitate to bring up his veteran status – for example, at the January 2017 public debate, he claimed that the judge in his debt enforcement proceedings told him that his real problem was that he was a veteran, which provoked loud expressions of indignation in the room. These examples show that veterans' victimization by debts lent itself to being portrayed as a particularly severe moral transgression inasmuch as veterans' sacrifices in the war were understood as constituting society's 'debt' to them (Stubbs and Zrinščak 2015: 405).

In comparison, the FA was much more likely to describe franc debtors as dispossessed members of a 'middle class'. While class analysis and class discourse have been generally sidelined in postsocialist Croatia, references to class, often implicit and diffuse, did not entirely disappear from public discourse. Significantly, the FA's references to a middle class appeared against the background of another, more general class narrative in the postcrisis period, versions of which I also heard from my research participants in 2016 and 2017 – namely, that 'the middle class' has been the biggest loser of the recession and was all but eliminated in Croatia (Škokić and Potkonjak 2016). In Serbia, Ivana Spasić (2013: 44–46) noted the seeming paradox of most people identifying as members of 'middle class' – loosely specified at best – and in the same breath claimed that it had all but disappeared. Rather than describing the shrinking of an actual social group, these narratives articulate social critique by generalizing from the experiences of those who had come to identify as middle class, but failed to attain or maintain the material conditions and social status they expected. This narrative thus subsumed franc debtors under 'middle class' as the key aspirational and legitimating class category of the new postsocialist society, broadly in line with what Hadas Weiss (2019) recently argued is an inherently ideological core of the category of middle class.

What distinguished the counternarratives about franc debtors as a dispossessed middle class from many other similar narratives was a more solid grounding in expert knowledge. Petra Rodik, sociologist and member of the first FA's leadership, conducted two surveys of franc debtors in 2012 and 2013–14 that allowed her to observe that these people tended to have above-average incomes and education, and could be therefore described as 'impoverished middle-class households' (Rodik 2019: 172; see also Rodik 2012: 20, 2019: 110; Mikuš 2019: 311). In a public talk in 2013, Rodik described franc debtors as a new, so far unrecognized category of welfare policy: 'members of the middle class who have above-average income but less possibilities of survival than their neighbours on welfare' (Rodik, cited in Petrović 2013). The claim was popularized by other statements by FA activists.

Several franc debtors whom I interviewed reproduced and developed this narrative further. Mladen, a private entrepreneur in his thirties, believed that the franc loans crisis was a 'huge blow for the

Croatian middle layer [*srednji sloj*]' and, by extension, for the whole of Croatia since, as a result, many debtors presumably had fewer or no children and this contributed to the country's demographic crisis. Ines, a nurse in her forties, argued that franc loans impoverished and 'irretrievably damaged' the very 'essence [*srž*] of the society' – highly educated professionals, like economists and lawyers, who 'fell into complete destitution instead of living the life of, let's say, the medium-high layer, of course considering what kind of country this is'.[7] Because these people had above-average incomes, she noted in order to underline the argument about their value to society, the banks' siphoning of their money out of the country also had a major detrimental impact on the national economy.

The opponents of policies to aid franc debtors put forward a class counter-counternarrative that portrayed franc debtors as egoistic rich elites rather than the bread-and-butter middle-class folk they claimed to be. When the government adopted one of the legal reforms to aid franc debtors – the 'fixing' of the exchange rate on franc housing loans in January 2015 – the Croatian Banking Association criticized the policy as 'socially irresponsible' because it failed to differentiate between debtors who were 'socially vulnerable' and those who were not. While an earlier policy to cap interest rates on franc loans was limited to loans below 1 million kuna (ca. €135,000), such a 'justified social component' has now been lost: 'The amendment adopted today … will ultimately be of the most benefit to the one third of franc debtors whose debt, according to CNB calculations, makes up as much as two thirds of the total [franc] debt. In that manner, those who need aid the most will be helped the least' (CBA 2015). Effectively, the CBA inferred that some debtors were too wealthy to deserve aid from the fact that they collectively held most of the outstanding debt, even if one does not follow from the other in any obvious manner. The distribution of franc loans by the initial principal suggests that more than 80 per cent of franc loans were worth less than CHF 100,000 (CNB 2015: 10–11), which would have been enough to buy an apartment of some 40 square metres in Zagreb in 2007.

Still, claims that many franc debtors bought 'luxurious properties or second and third properties in the family' (Banka.hr 2011) and calls for differentiating between such 'elites' and 'welfare cases' (Ivanković 2013) abounded in the opponents' discourse. One of my interviewees, a high-ranking official in a private bank, claimed that franc debtors were wealthier than euro debtors, even though available evidence suggests the exact opposite (Rodik 2019: 110). Another private banker I interviewed talked about people taking loans worth CHF 500,000–800,000, although only 2.5 per cent of franc loans exceeded CHF 200,000 (CNB 2015: 10). A CNB analyst told me that many franc debtors became over-indebted in order to buy a weekend home or a flat of 'a couple of hundred square metres'. Even the European Commission (2015: 61) backed the bankers' narrative by recommending 'targeted relief towards more vulnerable borrowers' and warning against 'one-size-fits-all approaches, which may disproportionately benefit higher-income households and those with properties purchased for investment purposes'. Franc activists and general debtors were familiar with this narrative. Their typical responses were to refuse its truthfulness and to oppose the proposed limiting of assistance to 'welfare cases' by arguing that all franc debtors, rich and poor alike, were victims of legal abuses and regulatory failures, and therefore deserved relief and justice. In such cases, the counternarrative about franc debtors as victims of crime was invoked to resist attempts to differentiate between deserving and undeserving debtors on the basis of (a proxy for) their class.

Conclusions: Deservingness, Debt Politics and Hegemony

On a popular talk show, the HS leader Ivan Vilibor Sinčić refused the host's suggestion that members of his populist party were disciples of Yanis Varoufakis by arguing: 'He is close to Marxism. Our division is not like that – capital and labour. Our division is the creditor – the debtor.' Sinčić explained the focus on this social antagonism by a need to look to the future instead of the past (*Nedjeljom u 2* 2016). In post-credit boom Croatia, debtors have indeed rapidly gained in importance as social and political categories represented by activists, party politicians and others. However, this chapter has shown that this rise of debtors as the new class of the financialized present involved a good deal of mediation ('translation') through more familiar and established categories and subjectivities. As in other debates about migration and welfare, deservingness was a key, if often implicit, moral framework in many of these narratives about debtors. While the literature has so far mainly focused on how negative arguments of *un*deservingness were invoked to extend established bureaucratic exclusions and ethnic hierarchies, here activists employed the affirmative framework of deservingness to justify inclusive claims on public resources in favour of an economically subordinated group. What has been done with deservingness here could not be captured by a moral anthropological abstracting of ethical concepts and reasoning from social dynamics. Neither would it do to theorize deservingness as a stable, monolithic dominant ideology. It is better understood as a part of what Gramsci called 'common sense' – a shared but flexible moral framework that actors mobilized in various ways in their respective projects in the arena of household debt. While plural, the discourses of debtor (un)deservingness were not free-floating and random. They were constrained and shaped by, on the one hand, what Streinzer and Tošić (Introduction to this volume) call the 'moral grammar' of deservingness and, on the other hand, by the stakes of debt politics and the wider public ideologies, social and political antagonisms, and common-sense worldviews in postsocialist Croatia in which this politics was unavoidably embedded. Deservingness was thus also politically flexible – actors invoked it to make 'progressive' claims as well as to deny them and to challenge dominant ideologies and relations of household debt, while aligning debt politics with hegemonic narratives and sociopolitical coalitions.

In this chapter, I identified two general types of translations between debtors and other categories and registers that are, in their specific ways, indicative of the layered social embeddedness of deservingness discourses and politics. Although I separated out types of translations and narratives for the sake of my analytical focus, in the practices of the actors of debt politics, they tended to combine in dynamic discursive and political assemblages, which in turn reflected the shared economic and social backgrounds of the particular groups of debt activists and constituencies they sought to represent. The first type of translations represented debtors as victims in the legal and/or humanitarian register. While scholars have highlighted how vernacular moral idioms of deservingness seep into the interpretation and implementation of legal rules, this illustrates the opposite movement of legal categories to the narratives of deservingness. This played several actual or potential roles. It articulated the experiences and claims of debtors in forms suitable for practices in legal and paralegal domains (individual and collective litigation, advocacy for relevant judicial and legal reforms). It was a way of tapping into the general moral common sense that interprets legal offences, albeit not universally, as simultaneously moral transgressions that give rise to entitlements to justice. And, finally, it aligned debt politics – in various forms and degrees – with the 'rule of law' as a hegemonic ideology with universal declaratory support in the 'Europeanizing', corruption-fighting post-Tuđman Croatia.

The second type of translations associated debtors with other social and political (rather than legal) categories, in particular veterans of the 1990s war and the 'middle class'. This again tapped into aspects of common sense (about the social worth of those categories) and aligned debt politics with pre-existing ideological projects and social blocs vying for hegemony. Elsewhere (Mikuš 2019), I have described in more detail the socioeconomic background and politics of two sets of activists and debtor constituencies for whom associations with these two categories were particularly central: Raiffeisen co-op debtors and activists such as Franjo and his network, and Swiss franc debtors and the FA. The narratives representing co-op debtors as veterans were part of a broader aligning of this particular debt politics with the arguably most successful ideological project in postsocialist Croatia: the right-wing, ethnonationalist and conservative project centred around the Croatian Democratic Union (CDU). This discourse served to identify debtors with veterans as the crucial, symbolically and materially favoured but also politically and economically subordinated component of this social bloc. It also narrated their problems and solutions thereto in terms consistent with this bloc's ideology: as plots of ethnically othered enemies and as compensatory state interventions favouring ethnically belonging and deserving victims. The narratives representing franc debtors as 'middle class' served to associate them with urban white-collar professionals, a key constituent group of the less successful left-liberal social bloc, as well as with a looser idea of the middle class as the foundational class of a postsocialist Croatia striving to become a Western-style capitalist democracy. The Social Democratic Party, the bloc's apex in party policies, governed from 2012 to 2015 and adopted some important measures in favour of franc debtors. The strong legalist tendency in the discourse and practices of the FA and its offshoots in party politics was consistent with the ideology of this bloc, which placed particular emphasis on the rule of law and anti-corruption as its chief (supposed) distinction from the CDU-led bloc. Ultimately, then, the pre-existing social categories did not serve as a passive reservoir of symbols for the constitution of debtors as political subjects. By being implicated in the arena of debt politics, these antagonisms and the wider hegemonic projects in which they were embedded were re-energized through the influx of new agendas and actors. Debtors, in turn, were being constituted as deserving subjects partly in terms of hegemonic ideologies and through alliances with dominant social blocs. The various forms of Croatian debt activism could be therefore described as subhegemonic rather than counterhegemonic inasmuch as they critiqued selected lending practices as deviations from an otherwise legitimate social order and articulated particularistic demands in favour of specific groups of debtors, both of which could be aligned with pre-existing hegemonic projects.

Acknowledgements

Most data used in this chapter were collected during my fieldwork as a member of the 'Financialisation' Research Group at the Max Planck Institute for Social Anthropology (from 2015 to 2018). The writing and revisions took place while starting my own Emmy Noether research group project 'Peripheral Debt: Money, Risk and Politics in Eastern Europe' (2019–), funded by the German Research Foundation and hosted by the Max Planck Institute. Participants in my research in Zagreb, the directors of the 'Financialisation' Research Group Chris Hann and Don Kalb, and fellow group members Tristam Barrett, Charlotte Bruckermann, Natalia Buier, Dimitra Kofti and Hadas Weiss, all shaped and informed the work on this project. I thank my research assistants Marija Vukšić and Anja Grgurinović for their work on interview transcripts, and Andreas Streinzer and Jelena Tošić for their close reading and constructive feedback on earlier drafts of this chapter.

Marek Mikuš is Senior Research Fellow and Head of Research Group at the Max Planck Institute for Social Anthropology in Halle. He is a social anthropologist engaging with work in heterodox economics, geography and sociology. His research has focused on civil society, the state, public policy, social transformation, and private and public finance in Eastern Europe. He currently heads the Emmy Noether Research Group 'Peripheral Debt: Money, Risk and Politics in Eastern Europe', which studies household indebtedness in Croatia, Hungary, Poland and Slovakia.

Notes

1. The discussion here is built on five months of fieldwork in Croatia between 2016 and 2017 and on secondary sources. I conducted participant observation in activist meetings, bank branches, banking events, court hearings, protests, home repossessions and other relevant situations. I

undertook more than ninety in-depth interviews with debtors, bankers, activists, regulators, lawyers, economists and officials of credit bureaus and debt collection agencies, and a survey with thirty-six indebted households covering their demographics, household budgets and balance sheets, etc.
2. Research participants were anonymized unless noted otherwise.
3. Original: CHF KREDIT / NEUSTAVAN / NEMORALAN / NIŠTETAN. CHF is the international code for the Swiss franc.
4. The lawsuit was the first in Croatia to use the provisions of the Law on Consumer Protection that introduced the institution of collective litigation into Croatian law.
5. The story of Ivana Mandić was covered by two documentary films: *U braku sa švicarcem* (*Married to the Swiss Franc*, 2013) and *Ivana (1982–2011)* (2017). The latter film, in the making of which I cooperated, is available on YouTube (in Croatian).
6. The four parts of the *Saga*, numbered 1, 2, 3 and 5 (*sic*), were originally published in 2015 as separate articles on Banka.hr, a now-defunct website of the discontinued *Banka* magazine. I received them in two PDF files, one with Parts 1–3 (Bohaček 2015) and the other with Part 5, in an email from Bohaček himself.
7. The implication is that because Croatia is poor, people who pass as a 'medium-high layer' there probably would not pass as such in a richer country that is assumed to be the benchmark.

References

Banka.hr. 2011. 'Stručnjaci protiv zamrzavanja tečaja švicarca' ['Experts Against the Freezing of the Swiss Franc Exchange Rate']. Retrieved 19 July 2016 from https://webcache.googleusercontent.com/search?q=cache:HbFFIEMFkp0J:www.banka.hr/Default.aspx%3FPrintDetail%3DPrintD%26tabid%3D102%26mid%3D480%26dnnprintmode%3Dtrue%26SkinSrc%3D%255BG%255DSkins/_default/No%2BSkin%26ContainerSrc%3D%255BG%255DContainers/_default/No%2BContainer%26View%3DDetails%26ItemID%3D69582+&cd=15&hl=sk&ct=clnk&gl=it.

Becker, Joachim, et al. 2010. 'Peripheral Financialization and the Vulnerability to Crisis: A Regulationist Perspective', *Competition & Change* 14(3–4): 225–47.

Benjak, Jelena. 2017. 'Zašto pravna država kažnjava aktiviste istodobno štiteći nepoštene banke?' ['Why Does the State of Law Punish Activists While Protecting Dishonest Banks?']. Retrieved 17 February 2022 from https://udrugafranak.hr/zasto-pravna-drzava-kaznjava-aktiviste-istodobno-stiteci-nepostene-banke.

Bohaček, Zoran. n.d. 'Saga o švicarcu' ['Saga of the Swiss Franc']. PDF file, personal email from Zoran Bohaček, 7 April 2017.

Bohle, Dorothee. 2018. 'Mortgaging Europe's Periphery', *Studies in Comparative International Development* 53(2): 196–217.
Burić, Ivan. 2010. *Nacija zaduženih: od komunističkog pakla do potrošačkog kapitalizma* [*A Nation of the Indebted: from Communist Hell to Consumer Capitalism*]. Zagreb: Jesenski i Turk.
Burton, Dawn. 2017. 'Credit Inclusion and the Home Credit Market in Post-communist Member States of the European Union', *Critical Social Policy* 37(3): 444–63.
Crehan, Kate. 2016. *Gramsci's Common Sense: Inequality and Its Narratives*. Durham, NC: Duke University Press.
CBA (Croatian Banking Association). 2015. 'Zakonsko rješenje fiksiranja tečaja švicarskog franka je socijalno neodgovorna mjera' ['The Legal Fixing of the Swiss Franc Exchange Rate is a Socially Irresponsible Measure']. Retrieved 17 February 2022 from https://www.hub.hr/hr/zakonsko-rjesenje-fiksiranja-tecaja-svicarskog-franka-je-socijalno-neodgovorna-mjera.
CNB (Croatian National Bank). 2015. 'Izvješće o problematici zaduženja građana kreditima u švicarskim francima i prijedlozima mjera za olakšavanje pozicije dužnika u švicarskim francima temeljem zaključka Odbora za financije i državni proračun Hrvatskog sabora' ['Report on the Issue of Personal Debt in Swiss Francs and Proposed Measures to Alleviate the Position of Swiss Franc Debtors Based on the Conclusion of the Finance and Central Budget Committee of the Croatian Assembly']. Retrieved 5 March 2022 from https://www.hnb.hr/documents/20182/447389/hp15092015_CHF.pdf.
Dolenec, Danijela. 2017. 'A Soldier's State? Veterans and the Welfare Regime in Croatia', *Anali Hrvatskog politološkog društva* 14: 55–77.
Égert, Balázs, and Dubravko Mihaljek. 2007. 'Determinants of Housing Prices in Central and Eastern Europe', BIS Working Paper 236. Basel: Bank for International Settlements.
European Commission. 2015. 'Country Report Croatia 2015: Including an In-depth Review on the Prevention and Correction of Macroeconomic Imbalances'. Retrieved 17 February 2022 from https://ec.europa.eu/info/sites/info/files/file_import/cr2015_croatia_en_0.pdf.
Fassin, Didier. 2012. *Humanitarian Reason: A Moral History of the Present*. Berkeley: University of California Press.
FA (Franc Association). 2012. *Crna knjiga*. Udruga Franak.
———. 2016. 'Je li gospodin Miro Kovač ministar Unicredita ili Republike Hrvatske?' ['Is Mr Miro Kovač a Minister of UniCredit or the Republic of Croatia?'] Retrieved 22 January 2020 from https://udrugafranak.hr/je-li-gospodin-miro-kovac-ministar-unicredita-ili-republike-hrvatske.
Gelenčer, Gordana. 2005. 'Podgrijavanje potrošnje' ['Reheating Consumption'], *Banka* 14(1): 56–57.
———. 2007. 'Nepodnošljiva lakoća plaćanja' ['The Irresistible Lightness of Paying'], *Banka* 16(1): 51–52.

Graeber, David. 2011. *Debt: The First 5,000 Years*. New York: Melville House.
Gramsci, Antonio. 1971. *Selections from the Prison Notebooks*, ed. and trans. Quintin Hoare and Geoffrey Nowell Smith. New York: International Publishers.
Guérin, Isabelle. 2012. 'Households' Over-indebtedness and the Fallacy of Financial Education: Insights from Economic Anthropology', Microfinance in Crisis Working Paper 1. Paris: Paris 1 Sorbonne University.
Haney, Lynne. 2002. *Inventing the Needy: Gender and the Politics of Welfare in Hungary*. Berkeley: University of California Press.
Holmes, Seth M., and Heide Castañeda. 2016. 'Representing the "European Refugee Crisis" in Germany and beyond: Deservingness and Difference, Life and Death', *American Ethnologist* 43(1): 12–24.
Howe, Leo 1990. *Being Unemployed in Northern Ireland: An Ethnographic Study*. Cambridge: Cambridge University Press.
Hrvatski jezični portal. n.d. Entries for 'oštećenik' and 'žrtva'. Retrieved 22 January 2020 from https://hjp.znanje.hr.
Ivanković, Brankica. 2014. '"Toksični kreditni proizvod" – utjecaj na zdravlje' ['"A Toxic Credit Product" – Impact on Health'], MA thesis. Zagreb: University of Applied Health Sciences.
Ivanković, Željko. 2013. 'Banke na udaru – one su prekomjerno granatirana manjina' ['Banks under Attack – They Are an Overly Shelled Minority']. Retrieved 17 February 2022 from https://www.vecernji.hr/biznis/banke-na-udaru-one-su-prekomjerno-granatirana-manjina-632831.
James, Deborah. 2015. *Money from Nothing: Indebtedness and Aspiration in South Africa*. Stanford: Stanford University Press.
Jović, Dejan. 2017. *Rat i mir: politika identiteta u suvremenoj Hrvatskoj* [*War and Peace: Identity Politics in Contemporary Croatia*]. Zaprešić: Fraktura.
Jørgensen, Martin Bak, and Trine Lund Thomsen. 2016. 'Deservingness in the Danish Context: Welfare Chauvinism in Times of Crisis', *Critical Social Policy* 36(3): 330–51.
Kalb, Don. 2018. 'Why I Will Not Make It as a "Moral Anthropologist"', in Bruce Kapferer and Marina Gold (eds), *Moral Anthropology: A Critique*. New York: Berghahn Books, pp. 65–76.
Kapferer, Bruce, and Marina Gold. 2018. 'Introduction: Reconceptualizing the Discipline', in Bruce Kapferer and Marina Gold (eds), *Moral Anthropology: A Critique*. New York: Berghahn Books, pp. 1–24.
Katz, Michael B. 2013. *The Undeserving Poor: America's Enduring Confrontation with Poverty*, 2nd edn. New York: University of Oxford Press.
Kraft, Evan. 2005. 'Prva liga', *Banka* 14(1): 19–21.
Landeka, Nada. 2016. 'Sramite li se političari? Branitelji su se izborili za našu slobodu a vi ih izbacujete na cestu, ubijaju se zbog vaših loših

zakona…' ['Are You Ashamed, Politicians? Veterans Fought for Our Freedom and You Throw Them out to the Street, They Kill Themselves Because of Your Bad Laws…']. Retrieved 17 February 2022 from https://www.hazud.hr/sramite-li-se-politicari-branitelji-se-izborili-nasu-slobodu-a-vi-ih-izbacujete-cestu-ubijaju-se-zbog-vasih-losih-zakona.

Laušić, Frenki. 2015. '"Švicarska" formula: Neka plate banke, dužnici, pa država' ['The "Swiss" Equation: Let Banks and Debtors Foot the Bill, Then the State']. Retrieved 22 January 2020 from https://slobodnadalmacija.hr/vijesti/hrvatska/svicarska-formula-neka-plate-banke-duznici-pa-drzava-261091.

Lazzarato, Maurizio. 2012. *The Making of the Indebted Man: An Essay on the Neoliberal Condition*. Los Angeles: Semiotext(e).

Martinović, Lidija. 2005. 'Zar je važno tko je kriv' ['Does It Matter Who's to Blame'], *Banka* 14(3): 23–24.

———. 2012. 'U ime povjerenja' ['In the Name of Trust'], *Banka* 21(4): 66–69.

Mattioli, Fabio. 2019. 'Debt, Financialisation and Politics', in James Carrier (ed.), *A Research Agenda for Economic Anthropology*. Cheltenham: Edward Elgar, pp. 56–73.

Mikuš, Marek. 2018. *Frontiers of Civil Society: Government and Hegemony in Serbia*. New York: Berghahn Books.

———. 2019. 'Contesting Household Debt in Croatia: The Double Movement of Financialization and the Fetishism of Money in Eastern European Peripheries', *Dialectical Anthropology* 43(3): 295–315.

———. 2020. 'Making Debt Work: Devising and Debating Debt Collection in Croatia', in Chris Hann and Don Kalb (eds), *Financialization: Relational Approaches*. New York: Berghahn Books, pp. 241–65.

Milovan, Adriano. 2013. '"Nisu nas banke prevarile. Pazite što potpisujete" Milanović o švicarcima' ['"The Banks Did Not Cheat Us. Be Careful What You Sign" Milanović on Swiss Francs']. Retrieved 17 February 2022 from https://www.jutarnji.hr/vijesti/hrvatska/nisu-nas-banke-prevarile-pazite-sto-potpisujete-milanovic-o-svicarcima/1055669.

Nedjeljom u 2. 2016. TV show broadcast by HRT 1 on 22 May.

Palomera, Jaime. 2014. 'Reciprocity, Commodification, and Poverty in the Era of Financialization', *Current Anthropology* 55(9): 105–15.

Pavičić, Tanja. 2010. 'Strah u kostima potrošača' ['Fear in the Bones of Consumers'], *Banka* 19(7): 24–29.

Payne, Christopher. 2012. *The Consumer, Credit and Neoliberalism: Governing the Modern Economy*. Abingdon: Routledge.

Petrović, Sanja. 2013. 'Imaju primanja iznad prosjeka, a žive gore od korisnika socijalne pomoći' ['They Have Above-Average Incomes but Live Worse Than Welfare Recipients']. Retrieved 17 February 2022 from https://net.hr/danas/hrvatska/duznici-u-svicarcima-imaju-primanja-ali-zive-gore-od-korisnika-socijalne-pomoci.

Ralašić, Marina. 2014. 'Nesposobni za najjednostavnije odluke o novcu' ['Incapable of Making the Simplest Money Decisions'], *Banka* 23(8): 62–66.

Rodik, Petra. 2012. 'Istraživački izvještaj: Kreditna zaduženost i pad životnog standarda' ['Research Report: Loan Indebtedness and Decline in Living Standard']. Zagreb: Udruga Franak.

———. 2015. 'The Impact of the Swiss Franc Loans Crisis on Croatian Households', in Serdar M. Değirmencioğlu and Carl Walker (eds), *Social and Psychological Dimensions of Personal Debt and the Debt Industry*. Basingstoke: Palgrave Macmillan, pp. 61–83.

———. 2019. *(Pre)zaduženi: društveni aspekti zaduženosti kućanstava u Hrvatskoj* [*(Over)Indebted: Social Aspects of Household Debt in Croatia*]. Zagreb: Jesenski I Turk.

Ronsbo, Henrik, and Steffen Jensen. 2014. 'Introduction. Histories of Victimhood: Assemblages, Transactions, and Figures', in Steffen Jensen and Henrik Ronsbo (eds), *Histories of Victimhood*. Philadelphia: University of Pennsylvania Press, pp. 1–22.

Sabaté, Irene. 2020. '"Good Faith Debtors" and the Deservingness of Debt Relief during the Spanish Home Repossessions Crisis', *Etnográfica* 24(1): 187–200.

Škokić, Tea, and Sanja Potkonjak. 2016. '"Working Class Gone to Heaven": From Working Class to Middle Class and Back', *Narodna umjetnost* 53(1): 117–32.

Spasić, Ivana. 2013. *Kultura na delu: društvena transformacija Srbije iz burdijeovske perspektive* [*Culture at Work: Serbia's Social Transformation in a Bourdieuan Perspective*]. Belgrade: Fabrika knjiga.

Stojić, Hrvoje. 2006. 'Na rubu bogatstva' ['On the Brink of Wealth'], *Banka* 15(12): 30–32.

Stout, Noelle. 2019. *Dispossessed: How Predatory Bureaucracy Foreclosed on the American Middle Class*. Oakland: University of California Press.

Stubbs, Paul, and Siniša Zrinščak. 2015. 'Citizenship and Social Welfare in Croatia: Clientelism and the Limits of "Europeanisation"', *European Politics and Society* 16(3): 395–410.

Sugawara, Naotaka, and Juan Zalduendo. 2011. 'Stress-Testing Croatian Households with Debt: Implications for Financial Stability', Policy Research Working Paper 5906. Washington DC: World Bank.

Todorova, Maria. 2009. *Imagining the Balkans*, updated edn. Oxford: Oxford University Press.

Türken, Salman, Erik Carlquist and Henry Allen. 2015. 'Chasing Happiness through Personal Debt: An Example of Neoliberal Influence in Norwegian Society', in Serdar M. Değirmencioğlu and Carl Walker (eds), *Social and Psychological Dimensions of Personal Debt and the Debt Industry*. Basingstoke: Palgrave Macmillan, pp. 160–79.

Van Oorschot, Wim. 2006. 'Making the Difference in Social Europe: Deservingness Perceptions among Citizens of European Welfare States', *Journal of European Social Policy* 16(1): 23–42.

Vizek, Maruška. 2009. 'Cijena ekspanzije' ['The Price of Expansion'], *Banka* 18(10): 10.
Vlada Republike Hrvatske. 2015. 'Zaključak Vlade Republike Hrvatske o prihvaćanju Nacionalnog strateškog okvira financijske pismenosti potrošača za razdoblje od 2015. do 2020. godine' ['Conclusion of the Government of the Republic of Croatia on the Adoption of the National Strategic Framework of Consumer Financial Literacy for the 2015–20 Period']. Retrieved 22 January 2020 from https://narodne-novine.nn.hr/clanci/sluzbeni/2015_01_11_224.html.
Weiss, Hadas. 2099. *We Have Never Been Middle Class: How Social Mobility Misleads Us*. London: Verso.
Willen, Sarah S. 2012. 'How Is Health-Related "Deservingness" Reckoned? Perspectives from Unauthorized Im/migrants in Tel Aviv', *Social Science & Medicine* 74: 812–21.
Willen, Sarah S., and Jennifer Cook. 2016. 'Health-Related Deservingness', in Felicity Thomas (ed.), *Handbook of Migration and Health*. Cheltenham: Edward Elgar, pp. 95–118.

Afterword
Differentiating Deservingness

James G. Carrier

In their Introduction to this volume, Andreas Streinzer and Jelena Tošić observe that in many areas of social life, inequality is increasingly talked about in terms of deservingness, a moral assessment, rather than in terms of, say, right, a legal assessment, or qualification, a bureaucratic assessment. As a part of this, they say that it is important to try to figure out 'how people in specific socioeconomic circumstances conceive of inequality and what they think is right or wrong, just or unjust about it'. The inequality that concerns them and that recurs in the chapters in this volume springs from denying individuals or sets of people something that they could reasonably expect or to which they routinely would be entitled, ranging from material resources to the respect and fair treatment normally accorded to people. They want us to consider this talk of deservingness using anthropological approaches that treat people's understandings of who deserves what as neither epiphenomenal expressions of prior socioeconomic forces nor the primary drivers of practices that shape inequality.

The idea of deservingness locates the source of people's social position in the attributes of those people themselves. If that position is disadvantaged, that makes it another instance of the old practice of blaming the victim, which helps protect the prevailing social, economic and political arrangements from criticism. A recent instance of this occurred during the closing days of the US presidential campaign, in an interview with Donald Trump's son-in-law, Jared Kushner. He said that Trump had done a lot to provide opportunities to Blacks in the

United States and that if their position had not markedly improved, it was because they did not really want to get ahead, but instead were busy 'virtue signalling' their support for Black Lives Matter (Karni 2020). Older instances of this are the argument that Blacks have lower IQs than whites and so end up on the bottom rungs of the ladder; the same sort of thing had been said of Irish and Polish immigrants in the decades around the turn of the twentieth century.

As I have cast it, the idea of deservingness involves a number of elements. One is that a person or set of people is different from others, a difference that is seen to inhere in them. Another is that this difference is seen to be important for the situation at issue. A third is that this difference is seen to carry connotations of 'good' and 'bad', which is to say that it has a moral dimension. I illustrate this with what Kushner said of Blacks in the United States. Their desire to signal virtue rather than to better themselves inheres in them, for it is their desire. These attributes are important for their economic success, which itself is virtuous for it is associated with many valued attributes.

The long history of blaming the victim as one who is undeserving suggests that it can serve important purposes, such as justifying inequalities of different sorts and protecting the established order from criticism. This utility makes it attractive as an analytical tool that can help us to explain undesirable social practices and outcomes, and also to challenge them. Because it is attractive, I think that it merits attention in its own right. I attend to it here by trying to situate it in a broader and more general human activity, differentiating among people. In different circumstances that takes different forms, some of which speak of deservingness and some do not. In the process, I shall point to at least one set of anthropological resources that, I think, allows us to address differentiation and deservingness in a way that neither trivializes people's moral evaluations nor treats them as of overwhelming importance.

I do this by considering a range of bases of differentiation, primarily of people, and because space is limited I do so in a somewhat idealized form. This means that often I omit or only allude to some of the corollaries of different sorts of differentiation; they are unexceptionable and likely to come to mind spontaneously. One sort of differentiation is something that we all inevitably do, and I touch on this only briefly; another sort is motivated by pragmatic or utilitarian factors; finally, there is differentiation that reflects and is part of a fundamental ordering of the world that people confront. This last sort differs from the others because, as I shall explain, it inevitably appears to be moral. Also, it is significant because it suggests that if we want to understand it and perhaps influence it, we need to recognize that at least some sorts of differentiation are not reducible to people's practical circumstances or their material or social interest in any simple way.

Differentiation

Whether they use the term or not, when the people described in this volume talk about who does or does not deserve something, they are talking about differentiating among people. There is nothing unusual about this, for we all differentiate among our fellows all the time, frequently without moral evaluation. When I go to my local shops, I differentiate between assistants and customers as surely as I do between bananas and potatoes, without thinking that the assistants and the potatoes are more proper and virtuous than the customers and the bananas. When I walk down the street, I differentiate between the people I pass whom I know and those whom I do not: I nod to the former and not to the latter, again without thinking that one group is better than the other. It appears that all people differentiate all the time, and while this mundane differentiation may be patterned and have important consequences, the reasons for this are contingent rather than arising solely from the process of differentiation.

One thing that can lead to differentiation is recurrent constraints that people face in their lives. The fact that the constraints are recurrent suggests that there may be significant patterns of social causes and consequences of that differentiation, though it does not require the sort of moral evaluation that talk of deservingness entails. I pursue this in terms of what Michael Lipsky (1980) called street-level bureaucrats. These are government officials who deal with the public, either in person or less visibly, and are described in some of the chapters in this volume. Those people are supposed to apply the rules in their work in an even-handed way, one that is fairly 'impersonal, formal and independent of individual assessments of moral character or virtue' (Streinzer and Tošić, Introduction to this volume). Those bureaucrats are likely to face two important, recurrent constraints that reduce the chance that they can apply the rules in an even-handed way, though without necessarily implying assessments of people's virtue.

One constraint is that applying the rules may defeat their purpose, in which case the bureaucrat may be induced to differentiate.

Suppose that a city wants to encourage street trading in certain areas. To ensure that traders are honest and no threat to public health and safety, the city requires that they have a licence, which requires filling in an application form accurately and completely. If the form is at all complex, licensing officials are likely to find that a fair proportion will not be filled out properly, meaning that a licence would not be issued, which would defeat the purpose of encouraging street trading. The more conscientious officials may review the forms and help applicants to ensure that they are completed properly. However, this help is beyond the formal duties of officials and takes time, which is a limited resource. It would be understandable, then, if the officials were more willing to help some applicants rather than others. They might well differentiate between applicants who seem conscientious and those who seem slapdash.

A second constraint is that rules are never perfect. There always will be ambiguous cases, so that the bureaucrat is obliged to exercise judgement in applying them. As an example, traffic police are supposed to intervene when a motorist is driving faster than the speed limit. Suppose an officer sees a car that is exceeding the limit and stops it. In many jurisdictions the officer faces a choice: admonish the driver, issue a formal warning or issue a speeding ticket. So, with only limited guidance from the traffic laws, the officer has to differentiate among speeding that calls for a written ticket, a written warning or only an admonition. Although it is not about street-level bureaucrats, Theodora Vetta's chapter on court hearings in Greece illustrates rules that are not clear. As she describes, it is difficult to apply the ambiguous 'permanent and general incapacity to repay their debts' to concrete cases. The same is true of Sabine Strasser's chapter, which shows the difficulty of applying the vague notion of vulnerability to those seeking the right to asylum in the European Union (EU).

The point of these examples is simple. Practical circumstances are likely to mean that even with thoughtful and conscientious officials, an even-handed application of the rules is impossible, so that those officials have to differentiate among people. Those differentiations may be patterned and have practical consequences, but they do not necessarily reflect a moral ordering. The licensing official who confronts an applicant who appears conscientious may well think that person fairly easy to deal with and may even think that the applicant is more sensible than one who does not. However, these assessments are utilitarian and reflect the relationship between the attributes of the applicant (for instance, the ability to fill out a form) and the practical contingencies of the situation in which the official operates (for instance, a shortage of time and other resources). In a different situation with different practical contingencies, those particular attributes may be insignificant and others important. In the absence of evidence to the contrary, then, there is no reason to assume that the official thinks that one applicant is more moral or virtuous than the other.

What I have said of those officials and their discretion points to the slippery nature of deservingness, which can replace entitlement in common usage with consequences that can be unfortunate. To illustrate: I am a US citizen of voting age, so I am entitled to register to vote. To say that I deserve to register is different. It appears to speak of me, the one who is deserving, but it also speaks of the registration official and our relationship. That is because it implies that the official is making a value judgement rather than a necessary and objective bureaucratic assessment, and that I am a supplicant who needs to persuade that official of my merit, which is different from being able to fill in the voter registration form and produce a birth certificate.

In the idealized form in which I described them, those street-level bureaucrats may be constrained in such a way that they are unable to make objective assessments. However, it is important to recognize what I have noted from time to time, that their differentiations are not necessarily driven by their sense of who is a good or worthy person and who is not, but by their practical desire to do their work in difficult circumstances. Yet, there are circumstances in which a moral evaluation is relatively likely, and I describe some of them below.

The slippage between entitlement and deservingness is illustrated in what Nicole Hoellerer says of Bhutanese refugees in the United Kingdom in this volume. The government agreed to accept Nepali Bhutanese as refugees under its Gateway Protection Programme, which identified what sorts of people were eligible, which is to say entitled. However, because immigration was a political issue in her fieldsites and resources to support the refugees were limited, talk of entitlement came to be displaced by talk of deservingness, of who was really a refugee who deserved support and sympathy, and who was not. In bureaucratic terms, people either fitted the official definition of refugee or did not, and to some degree the talk among refugees of deservingness emerged because of a contingent factor: resources were limited.

However, there are other differentiations that reflect factors that are less mundane or contingent and more systemic than what affects those bureaucrats, and the results can have a clear moral tone. These are the sort of factors that Mary Douglas describes in *Purity and Danger* (1966). There, she considers differentiation in terms of the human need to produce conceptual order, in which people create categories that order the world and 'impose system on an inherently untidy experience' (ibid.: 4). That system of categories identifies things in terms of essential properties that underlie appearances. In my terms, though not in hers, they are an ontology, something that is not likely to be as contingent as what constrains street-level bureaucrats.

The world is not, of course, obliged to conform to the categories contained in people's ontologies, and things that do not conform are anomalous and specially charged, usually negatively but occasionally positively. Douglas describes two sorts of ways that a thing can fail to conform. One way is that the thing can fail to fit easily into a category. So, the pangolin, the positively charged focus of a spirit cult that Douglas (1963) described in her ethnography of the Lele, has scales like a reptile but is warm-blooded and gives birth like a mammal. More outrageous is the duck-billed platypus. It has webbed feet and a bill and lays eggs, which makes it a waterfowl, but it has fur and is warm-blooded, which makes it a mammal. Another way in which a thing can fail to conform is less a matter of attributes and more a matter of context: the thing can be 'out of place' (Douglas 1966: 35), which, she says, makes it dirty. So, for instance, shoes in their proper place, perhaps next to the bed or on the floor of the closet, are fine. However, if they are on the dining table they would be out of place and hence dirty, charged in a negative sense and thus to be avoided and condemned.

Purity and Danger was written to offer a framework for the comparative study of religion, and Douglas says that all religions enjoin people to do some things and not to do others. Those injunctions identify what is proper and improper, clean and unclean, pure and impure, and she says that we can use the injunctions as a means to discern the conceptual order that the religion contains and the categories that it imposes on the world. She illustrates this with her analysis of the abominations of Leviticus – the food taboos in the third book of the Old Testament. She argues that the injunctions in Leviticus reflect a set of underlying assumptions and values, such as that four-legged animals that have cloven hooves also chew the cud, as is the case with sheep. They are the conceptual basis and moral motive for differentiating things in terms of their conformity to that structure, including things like pigs, which have cloven hooves but do not chew the cud and so are unclean.

The same sort of analysis could be done with the lessons offered by the Centro Lavoro Torino that Carlo Capello describes in his chapter in this volume. The content of those lessons is like the abominations of Leviticus, for it identifies what is approved and what is disapproved. From this we could discern a structure of underlying assumptions about what proper human beings are. And just as Leviticus classifies living things in terms of their conformity to its underlying structure, so we could see how the Centro and its practices classify people in terms of their conformity to the underlying structure of those lessons.

I have described two bases and sorts of differentiation that are more obviously social than the mundane differentiation of everyday life. One is the routine, pragmatic differentiation of street-level bureaucrats. This is shaped by the circumstances of their work and the rules that they are supposed to apply, and in the ideal terms in which I have presented it, it is a pragmatic device that makes their work manageable. That pragmatism need not be innocent, of course, for it is likely to reflect the social order that shapes the contingencies that constrain people, and so operate as a taken-for-granted manifestation of that order, thus producing what Pierre Bourdieu (1977) calls misrecognition. However, doing so does not require moral evaluation, any more than structural racism requires that people have racist thoughts. The other sort of differentiation is the ordering that Douglas describes, which she argues rests on humans' need to order their world in some way or another and that is likely to have a clear moral aspect. It differs from pragmatic ordering in two ways.

First, from an analytical perspective, the differentiation carried out by our street-level bureaucrats has to satisfy utilitarian criteria, for it needs to allow those bureaucrats to deal with the ambiguities of the rules that they need to apply and the limited resources that they have to hand. However, Douglas's conceptual ordering does not seem to be required to meet such criteria, at least in any significant way. She is explicit about this in her discussion of attempts to explain the abominations of Leviticus in terms of their possible beneficial effects on health, which is to say in terms of their utility. Ritual washing may help slow the spread of disease and avoiding pigs may reduce the dangers associated with eating pork in hot climates. Nevertheless, she says: 'Even if some of Moses's dietary rules were hygienically beneficial it is a pity to treat him as an enlightened public health administrator, rather than as a spiritual leader' (1966: 29).

The second way in which the two forms of ordering differ follows to some degree from the first. I said that the mundane ordering ultimately is concerned with and rests on practical utility, however socially conditioned that may be. It is adopted to allow people to do their jobs and get through their day, and if it does not, people likely will try some other way of doing things. On the other hand, Douglas's conceptual ordering has a moral force, for it speaks of good and bad, right and wrong. This is the sort of force that lends itself to expressions of the deserving and the undeserving. Because what is important is that it orders the world in a moral way, thinking about it simply in terms of utility would be misdirected, just as Douglas said would be the case if one saw Leviticus simply in terms of public health. Thus, to say that the Hartz IV programme that Stefan Wellgraf describes in his chapter in this volume does not benefit the pupils he studied or help them to get jobs is to miss an important thing that, Douglas would argue, the programme does. That is, it reflects a cultural ordering and evaluates the people in the programme in terms of their conformity to that ordering. Of course, as Wellgraf notes, the programme has utility as well, albeit of a perverse sort: it helps to reproduce the social hierarchy that it expresses.

Variations in Ordering

As I have presented it, Douglas's analysis of the abominations of Leviticus reflects her desire to make sense of their logic, and because she is concerned with the place in human life of order in the abstract, what she says inevitably bestows an air of stability and consensus on those injunctions, and, by extension, on conceptual ordering generally. However, Douglas is not saying that these orderings and their differentiations are stable and free of dissent. I want to describe two forms of variation briefly.

One form concerns what one might call the content of the system of ordering, especially the ways in which it can be changed. In *Natural Symbols*, Douglas (1973: Chapter 9) says that ordering systems regularly are challenged by countermovements that look a lot like what Victor Turner (1969) calls *communitas*. Both she and Turner attend to movements that seek to level all hierarchies and structures in their society and its culture. In other words, they are radically egalitarian challenges to structure per se and to its attendant differentiations. However, because of what Douglas sees as the human need for order and what Turner sees as its practical necessity in social life, the movements are unstable and end up becoming structured. So, order and structure return, but a change of content is possible because the new order and structure need not be the same as the old.

Because she is concerned with what she sees as a basic human need for order, Douglas also does not attend much to the ways in which different ordering systems might exist within a single society. However, the forces and processes that generate and support these systems can operate at levels that are more local than what Douglas describes, though they are more encompassing than the practical contingencies of street-level bureaucrats and so are more clearly collective. Using a model that Douglas developed in *Natural Symbols*, a student of hers, Gerald Mars, presents such a situation in his *Cheats at Work* (1982).

Mars does so in terms of what he calls fiddles. The activities that he describes may technically be wrongs, but they are tolerated, taken for granted and even encouraged by those in different occupational settings that he describes in terms of Douglas's model. These include things like petty pilfering, taking unauthorized time off work, padding expense claims and making private deals within an organization. These are relatively minor infractions of the rules and the law, but they deserve attention because, Mars argues, they are not happenstance or simply opportunistic; rather, they are moral in the sense that they reflect a conception of the proper ordering of the world. The near-collapse of the financial system in 2008 revealed that these sorts of local moral orders had flourished in various parts of the financial sector in the United States and the United Kingdom (Carrier 2018).

I have described one sort of variation in ordering, the way in which the content of the system of meaning, and thus the understanding of the proper state of affairs that it reflects, can change over the course of time or can vary between different groups in society. I now turn to a different sort of variation, not of content but of salience, by which I mean the degree to which members of a group demand conformity to its vision of the proper state of affairs.

Pressure for conformity is prone to be greater when people see themselves as being threatened. There is research that supports this assertion. For instance, Paul Nail and his colleagues (Nail et al. 2009) presented research subjects with threats of different sorts, ranging from reading stories of people who were acquitted of a crime because of a technicality to asking them to contemplate their own deaths. The purpose was to see how this affected subjects' conservatism, which was defined as a need for order and closure, dogmatism and disinclination to openness, which effectively is a desire for conformity. They found that, as they put it in the title of their paper, 'Threat Causes Liberals to Think like Conservatives'.[1]

We should not, of course, be surprised that the perception of threat leads to increasing demand for conformity, for it has long been common sense. In the last third of the nineteenth century, Herbert Spencer, a social evolutionist, argued that the stage that he called 'industrialism' is 'more free' than the preceding stage, militarism. He said that militarism existed in times of regular external threat and societies suppressed internal freedom in order to maintain their unity and strength. With the decline of that threat, societies had less need to suppress that freedom and so became 'more free' (Spencer 1877; see Durkheim 1984 [1893]: 149–51; Carrier 2009: 20–21).

This common sense is manifest in the second half of the twentieth century in the politics of the country that I know best: the United States. Early in the 1950s, Senator Joseph McCarthy and his followers invoked what they saw as a Red Menace to justify repressing criticism of the country and demanding adherence to what was touted as the American moral order. Thirty years later, in 1981, President Ronald Reagan, who was very conservative and popular, addressed a meeting of the International Association of Chiefs of Police (Lescaze 1981). He invoked a different threat to the country when he said that 'we should never forget: the jungle is always there, waiting to take us over'. Fortuitously, if unfortunately, as I write this, the country is going through a wave of protests sparked by what looks like the mindless killing of George Floyd by police in Minneapolis, Minnesota. Reaction to those protests included the President using military force to clear Lafayette Square of peaceful protestors so that he could walk from the White House to St John's Church, hold up a Bible and tell people that he is 'your president of law and order' (Baker et al. 2020).

In all of this, in different ways people invoke what they present as a threat to the group as a whole in order to justify the need to conform to a conceptual and moral order. To say that McCarthy and the rest were successful, self-serving manipulators may be true, but it treats their audiences as gullible and so encourages us to ignore the ways that many Americans saw them as moral leaders, espousing and defending the right way of life and chastising those who violated it.

In different ways, Nail and Spencer are concerned with threats and the ways in which they can lead to demand for conformity to important values. However, their general concerns can only alert us to possibilities; they do not tell us how things work out among particular sets of people and the particular contingencies that they experience. We can only begin to make sense of those particularities if we have the sort of knowledge that Arlie Hochschild acquired in her study of Tea Party supporters in an area of Louisiana in the 2010s. In *Strangers in Their Own Land* (2016), she describes whites in the Bayou country who were poor and lived with extreme environmental degradation caused by nearby chemical works, so extreme that the area is known as Cancer Alley. Perhaps surprisingly, they opposed government welfare programmes that could help address their increasing poverty and the Environmental Protection Agency, the federal body that could help reduce the pollution that they confronted.

Hochschild concluded that those opinions sprang from people's belief that the government, and the country generally, was abandoning the cognitive and moral order that had shaped it. These people held that they had done what was right. They had worked hard all their lives and expected that they would have earned support and security as a result. Instead, they found themselves threatened by a government that, as they saw it, wrongly gave those things to other people, like immigrants and urban Blacks. Their reaction was to support a movement that affirmed the order that, they felt, the government had betrayed.[2] Given the general trends in American attitudes and government practices since the 1950s, which both sprang from and were reactions to the country's past, it is understandable that many of the people Hochschild describes would see a threat in national policies that seemed to benefit urban Blacks and immigrants rather than rural Whites and the native-born, and did so in terms of national regulations rather than local customs and practices. In other circumstances, of course, different contingencies would lead people to see different important threats, values and customs.

From what I have said, it should be clear that the threats that people think that they face are not all alike, and now I want to sketch some of the other ways in which they can differ. For instance, it is possible that a threat affects only a handful of individuals, in which case, it and responses to it may best be approached in terms of individual psychology or very localized factors. Equally, however, threats – whether real or imagined – may affect a large number of people. In that case, a more clearly social approach is appropriate, not least because such threats may well generate social movements in reaction, like those protests in response to the killing of George Floyd. His killing challenged the protestors' cognitive and moral order about how society and its agents ought to operate.

Equally, some threats can be material, which arguably is the case with the Bayou people described by Hochschild. For them, the degradation of their surroundings threatened their livelihoods and their lives. Conversely, some threats are primarily symbolic, such as the challenge to the racial ordering of the American South through the 1950s and the 1960s. Desegregating lunch counters and getting rid of the signs that say that this drinking fountain is only for whites deprives no one of food, shelter or clothing.

Finally, in some cases the threat and reaction to it appear to be best thought of as an overt conflict between orders, while in other cases it is less so. At least as McCarthy presented it, the Red Menace was an example of the former, which also seems to be the case with those Tea Party supporters. The appearance of COVID-19 in early 2020 is an example of the latter. It is true that responses to it tended to become moralized, as people sought to assign blame for it to China, inept government, self-serving public officials and similar wrongdoers. Even so, the responses, both in government policy and public discourse, were cast to a large degree in terms of epidemiology and other sciences that appear morally neutral.

Complex Orders

My examples of threat and response in US politics are of situations in which everyone is admonished to behave in the same, proper way. However, this should not be taken to mean that all ordering systems dictate that same sort of uniformity. That is because a cultural ordering might well identify different types of people, each with an associated rendering of what is proper to them, just as Leviticus identifies different types of living things, each with its proper attributes and behaviours.

Those different types of people may not all be held to be of the same merit or value, in the same way that the different strata in England in the eighteenth century were not all of the same merit. Servants had less merit than their masters, those in trade had less than those who pursued professions, and the gentry had less than the nobility. However, and resembling what Douglas wrote in *Purity and Danger*, it was expected that those in each stratum would be true to their type. This was the point of sumptuary laws, which identified social strata, assigned certain items of consumption to them and forbade those of other strata from having them (Baldwin 1926). In other words, to violate those laws was to behave in ways that were not appropriate to one's place in the social order.

Failing to behave in ways appropriate to one's place in the order may be anomalous, but it does not necessarily bring universal censure.

That is what Elisa Lanari describes in Sandy Springs, Georgia, in her chapter in this volume. The people she attends to are mostly immigrant women from near the bottom of the social scale. However, they did not act in ways that conform to dominant expectations. Instead, they were involved in civic affairs and social-support activities in a way that meshed with the upper middle-class white women who were important in the city's life. In effect, they used this departure from what is appropriate to hold that they had been improperly located. In spite of their skin colour, jobs and education, they were not really from the lower ranks, but were much higher on the scale.

Although Lanari shows that behaving in anomalous ways need not bring censure, often it does so, and it is likely that there was some resentment in Sandy Springs towards the women that she describes. The chance that it brings censure will be greater if a set of people feel threatened because those of a lower set are acting in ways that seem to challenge the distinction between them. So, according to Neil McKendrick, in England in the eighteenth century, after those sumptuary laws had lapsed, the boundaries between the different strata were fairly permeable. This generated common complaint that servants aped their masters, that their masters aped the gentry and that the gentry aped the nobility (McKendrick et al. 1982: Chapter 2).

Fearful that their inferiors would encroach upon their position, many in the higher ranks increased their own consumption in order to maintain their superiority. Also, they stressed things that were less easy to ape, such as gentility and the sort of dispositions that bestow distinction (Bourdieu 1984). A poem by the English writer Arthur Hugh Clough (1972), from around 1850, satirizes the nouveau riche, those with money but no gentility. The poem is 'How Pleasant It Is to Have Money' and the second verse goes:

> I sit at my table en grand seigneur,
> And when I have done, throw a crust to the poor;
> Not only the pleasure, one's self, of good living,
> But also the pleasure of now and then giving.
>   So pleasant it is to have money, heigh ho!
>   So pleasant it is to have money.

The sumptuary laws, then, may have lapsed, but many people seem to have continued to think in terms of the ordering that they expressed.

Things like McCarthyism and sumptuary laws seek to support the moral and conceptual order by suppressing wrong behaviour, holding that those who behave wrongly do not deserve respect or perhaps even freedom. During the McCarthy era, mechanisms were put into place to enforce right behaviour, including mandatory loyalty oaths and increased surveillance, especially of government employees. Even if they were not very effective, sumptuary laws prohibited certain sorts of consumption by certain sorts of people. However, threats to the integrity of the moral order can be dealt with in a different way: by reaffirming its morality. One way in which this can be done is by stressing the immorality and hence unworthiness of those who threaten it.

This is illustrated by what Michael Polson (2018) writes of the Marihuana Tax Act of 1937 in the United States, the first serious federal effort to make its possession a crime. For some time, marijuana had been linked with Blacks and those who associated with them, but it appears not to have been a matter of serious concern. However, in the 1930s, the dominant racial ordering in the United States, which was most pronounced in the South, was coming under threat.

This was visible in the integrationist stance of Eleanor Roosevelt, wife of the President. More dramatically, the trials in Alabama of nine Black youths known as the Scottsboro Boys began in 1932 and, because of appeals, they extended through the decade and after. The trials were important for the publicity that they generated, especially criticism of the all-white juries that were common in the South. This challenge to the existing racial ordering was strengthened by renewed efforts to make lynching a federal offence: the House of Representatives passed such a bill in 1937, though it was defeated in the Senate. It appears, then, that a new racial ordering and its associated moral order were beginning to challenge the old one. Polson argues that these threats to the old ordering were met by efforts to reaffirm it by making the possession of marijuana, associated with Blacks, a federal offence, an argument supported by the 'overtly racist rhetoric' (Polson 2018: 144) of supporters of the bill in their testimony at Congressional hearings.

Conclusion

I said that the idea of deservingness merits consideration in its own right, and I have tried to do this by treating it as one form of a more general thing that people do – differentiate things in the world, especially each other. Treating it in this way encourages us to consider the range of ways in which differentiation appears and the factors that shape it, both in the present and the past, as well as the factors that can encourage talk of deservingness.

I have also done this because the anthropological ideas that I have deployed encourage us to take seriously assertions of deservingness and its absence, as well as those who make such assertions. Over the past fifty years or so, I have seen various efforts to correct what many perceived as social wrongs, and often enough they have had little success. Taking those assertions and the people who make them more seriously can encourage us to try other ways of correcting such wrongs, perhaps with greater success.

James G. Carrier has taught and done research in Papua New Guinea, the United States and the United Kingdom, and has overseen research on environmental conservation in Jamaica. His publications include *Wage, Trade and Exchange in Melanesia* (University of California Press, 1989) and *Gifts and Commodities: Exchange and Western Capitalism since 1700* (Routledge, 1995), and edited volumes, including *Meanings of the Market* (Routledge, 1997) and *Anthropologies of Class* (Cambridge University Press, 2015). He is also interested in economic anthropology as a whole and has recently put together the third edition of *A Handbook of Economic Anthropology* (Edward Elgar, 2022).

Notes

1. For the complexities of this with regard to the threat of COVID-19, see Edsall (2020).
2. Similar thinking is reported in Potts (2020) and, in a different way, in Friedman (2002).

References

Baker, Peter, Maggie Haberman, Katie Rogers, Zolan Kanno-Youngs and Katie Benner. 2020. 'How Trump's Idea for a Photo Op Led to Havoc in a Park', *New York Times*, 2 June.

Baldwin, Frances. 1926. 'Sumptuary Legislation and Personal Regulation in England', *Johns Hopkins University Studies in Historical and Political Sciences* 44(1): 1–282.

Bourdieu, Pierre. 1977. *Outline of a Theory of Practice*. Cambridge: Cambridge University Press.

———. 1984. *Distinction: A Social Critique of the Judgement of Taste*. London: Routledge & Kegan Paul.
Carrier, James G. 2009. 'Simplicity in Economic Anthropology: Persuasion, Form and Substance', in Stephen Gudeman (ed.), *Economic Persuasions*. Oxford: Berghahn Books, pp. 15–30.
———. (ed.). 2018. *Economy, Crime and Wrong in a Neoliberal Era*. Oxford: Berghahn Books.
Clough, Arthur Hugh. 1972. 'How Pleasant It Is to Have Money', in Helen Gardner (ed.), *The New Oxford Book of English Verse*. Oxford: Clarendon Press, pp. 682–84.
Douglas, Mary. 1963. *The Lele of the Kasai*. London: Oxford University Press for the International African Institute.
———. 1966. *Purity and Danger*. London: Routledge & Kegan Paul.
———. 1973. *Natural Symbols*. Harmondsworth: Penguin.
Durkheim, Emile. 1984 [1893]. *The Division of Labour in Society*. London: Macmillan.
Edsall, Thomas B. 2020. 'Why Isn't Trump Riding High?', *New York Times*, 6 May.
Friedman, Jonathan. 2002. 'Champagne Liberals and the New "Dangerous Classes": Reconfigurations of Class, Identity and Cultural Production in the Contemporary Global System', *Social Analysis* 46(2): 33–55.
Hochschild, Arlie Russell. 2016. *Strangers in Their Own Land: Anger and Mourning on the American Right*. New York: New Press.
Karni, Annie. 2020. 'Kushner, Employing Racist Stereotype, Questions if Black Americans "Want to Be Successful"', *New York Times*, 26 October.
Lescaze, Lee. 1981. 'Reagan Blames Crime on "Human Predator"', *Washington Post*, 29 September.
Lipsky, Michael. 1980. *Street-Level Bureaucracy: Dilemmas of the Individual in Public Service*. New York: Russell Sage Foundation.
Mars, Gerald. 1982. *Cheats at Work: An Anthropology of Workplace Crime*. London: George Allen & Unwin.
McKendrick, Neil, John Brewer and J.H. Plumb. 1982. *The Birth of a Consumer Society*. Bloomington: Indiana University Press.
Nail, Paul R., Ian McGregor, April E. Drinkwater, Garrett M. Steele and Anthony W. Thompson. 2009. 'Threat Causes Liberals to Think Like Conservatives', *Journal of Experimental Social Psychology* 45(4): 901–7.
Polson, Michael. 2018. 'Marketing Marijuana: Prohibition, Medicalization and the Commodity', in James G. Carrier (ed.), *Economy, Crime and Wrong in a Neoliberal Era*. Oxford: Berghahn Books, pp. 140–71.
Potts, Monica. 2020. 'Covid-19 and the Rural Fear of "Taking Advantage"', *New York Times*, 31 May.
Spencer, Herbert. 1877. *Principles of Sociology*, vol. I. London: Williams and Norgate.
Turner, Victor W. 1969. *The Ritual Process: Structure and Anti-structure*. Chicago: Aldine.

Index

abominations of Leviticus, 418–420
accumulation, 51, 103, 231, 360, 373
   capital accumulation, 18, 32, 36, 54, 103, 231, 360
   "primitive" accumulation, 54
accusation, 7, 16, 150, 159, 162, 163, 164, 170, 200, 269, 334, 365–367, 372
activation, 7, 18, 148, 152, 172, 182–184, 188,
   active job search, 174, 176, 179, 181–185, 187
Aegean, 251, 254, 256,
affect/affective, 9, 13, 21, 41, 52, 72, 148, 149, 155, 233, 239, 240, 334, 385
   affective registers, 147, 148, 149, 169
Africa, 87, 90, 102, 126, 130, 289, 304
ageism, 32
agency, 82, 216, 235, 287, 306, 307, 315, 316, 320
ambivalence, 190, 216 252–277
antagonism, 103, 117, 296, 298, 372, 373, 403, 404, 405
anthropotechniques, 182
anxiety, 156, 157, 256, 348, 371
Armed Love (Miriam Ticktin), 257
asylum seekers, 6, 11, 79, 88, 90, 252, 282, 283, 293, 294, 305, 306, 308, 309, 317, 318, 319, 320, 321, 322, 323
Atlanta, 222, 223, 223, 226, 227, 228, 229, 242
austerity, 17, 21, 32, 33, 39, 42, 47, 50, 71, 73, 104, 108, 200, 201–205, 212, 213–216, 346, 359, 360, 362, 364, 366, 369, 372, 373, 375
Austria, 1, 8, 11, 104, 108, 158, 164, 251, 265–266, 270, 272n8, 273n25, 393, 395,
Austrian Freedom Party (FPÖ), 8, 266
Austrian People's Party (ÖVP), 11, 266, 269

balkan route, 101, 254, 266
belonging, 116, 137, 202, 229, 242n7, 319, 351, 387, 405
   moral categories of, 22
   to the city, 226, 239
   unequal distributions of, 280
benevolence, 216
Berlin, 21, 147, 148, 154, 158, 159, 166, 179, 311, 315, 318, 319,
Bhutan, 280, 281, 282, 283, 284, 285
   Bhutanese refugees, 282–283, 285, 290–298
biographies, 114, 155, 164, 291–294, 305, 321
blame, 22, 75, 83, 147, 169, 170, 334, 336–339, 351, 372, 374, 387, 424
   blame game, 150, 159–164
   blaming the victim, 7, 176
Bodrum, 254–256, 265
body, 85, 92, 155, 157, 159, 290, 313, 396
borders, 101, 111, 158, 251, 257, 263, 269
   border regime, 252, 253, 254, 256, 257, 261, 267, 268

borderlands, 253
boundaries, 6, 11, 49, 114, 117, 130, 131, 136, 138–141, 238, 280, 283, 291, 293, 297, 298, 299n7, 308, 317, 319, 322, 323, 370, 425
Brexit, 20, 104, 109, 111, 114,
bureaucracy, 39, 232, 317, 344
   administration of justice, 349
   categorizations, 284, 285, 289
   labels, 267, 284, 286, 287, 288, 289, 350
   protocols, 43, 45, 59n32, 127, 341, 351
   socio–legal/moral registers, 7, 18, 374, 393
   typologies, 202, 208, 209, 210, 213, 214, 351
   See also street–level bureaucrats

calculation, 32, 33, 41, 44, 46–48, 53, 128, 366, 397, 403
capital, 18, 31, 32, 36, 40, 41, 44, 49, 51, 52, 54, 102, 103, 105, 106, 111, 113–115, 117, 203, 360, 362, 370, 376n3, 389, 403
capitalism, 3, 14, 16, 18, 31, 32, 35, 54, 107, 115, 117, 119n14, 148, 231, 365, 374, 390, 397
care / carer, 3, 20, 32, 33, 35, 36–39, 41, 42, 44, 45, 51, 52, 74, 76, 77, 78, 83, 88, 149, 158, 163, 169, 227, 238, 257, 262, 308
   care labour, 52
   health care, 32, 84
   psychiatric, 313
categorization, 2, 17, 50, 259, 272n17, 283, 284, 285, 289, 334
charities/charity, 9, 21, 84, 85, 184, 199, 201, 206, 206–213, 215, 216, 226, 230, 231, 234, 310, 344, 369, 375
Cheats at Work (by G. Mars), 421
China, 103, 281, 424
Central and Eastern Europe, 20, 309, 310
Central European University (CEU), 112, 118n10, 131

citizenship, 3, 11, 13, 21, 69, 80, 85, 90, 181, 203, 214, 215, 226, 229, 232, 234, 238, 240, 242n7, 256, 265, 396, 366, 374, 375, 385
claims, 3, 6, 7, 12, 41, 71, 81, 111, 115, 116, 128, 130, 133, 139, 170, 200, 201, 212, 226, 238, 239, 253, 269, 280, 289, 316, 320, 336, 338, 349, 352, 362, 369, 375, 392, 400, 404
   belonging of, 226, 240
   deservingness to, 3, 5, 9, 10, 13, 17, 71, 103, 117, 118n2, 351, 387, 403,
class, 2–3, 17, 103–104, 106–107, 109–110, 111, 113–117, 147, 162, 169, 203, 223, 224, 234, 360, 387, 388, 401, 403
   anthropological class, 103, 106
   classness, 106, 113
   class 'positions', 18, 114
   'class without class', 107, 114, 115
   middle class, 40, 108, 113, 114, 157, 158, 205, 210, 222, 225, 226, 228, 230, 231, 233, 234, 235, 236, 238, 240, 256, 263, 343, 368, 388, 399, 401, 405, 425
   relational class, 103
   working class, 34, 38, 40, 107, 110, 113, 114, 115, 119n11, 151, 157, 168, 174, 178, 179, 180, 228, 235, 362, 364, 398
classification, 285
   bureaucratic labels, 287
Clough, Arthur Hugh, 425
Cold War, 102, 103, 128, 130, 134
colonial history, 259
common sense, 3, 4, 5–6, 10, 17, 20, 70, 71, 72, 75, 78, 89, 91, 162, 170, 181, 388, 390, 404, 405, 422
communitas, 278, 296, 420
community, 6, 8, 77, 80, 103, 136, 177, 180, 206, 224, 229, 229–232, 236, 238, 240, 278, 279, 279, 283, 284, 286, 290, 291–292–297, 305, 310, 312, 316, 386, 390
   development, 279, 290, 294, 297, 306,

Index ◆ 431

divisions, 280, 294, 295
imagined community of taxpayers
    and insurance members, 6
comparison, 20, 80, 126, 127, 128,
    130–135, 141, 143nn3–4
compassion, 9, 115, 184, 212, 222, 233,
    254, 257, 312, 334, 362, 362, 375
compassionate repression, 257
conceptual order, 418, 419, 420, 425
    differentiation within, 2, 70, 158,
        279, 280, 289, 290, 296, 297,
    salience of, 72
    threats to, 426
    uniformity in, 424
    variation in, 420, 421
conformity, 136, 137, 141, 418, 419,
    421, 422
    pressure to conform, 234
    threat, 78, 82, 84, 90, 101, 104,
        105, 107, 149, 150, 159, 165,
        166, 258, 263, 268, 316, 416,
        421–424
conjunctures, 1, 108, 309
consumption, 22, 35, 210, 212, 236,
    350, 362, 363, 364, 365, 366, 368,
    377n8, 390, 391, 424, 425, 426
contestation, 3, 4, 280
    debtor's movements, 352, 361, 388
    protest, 31, 45, 55n2, 116, 127, 263,
        266, 394, 422, 423
    social struggle, 2, 3, 13, 373
corporations, 18, 226, 232, 242n7
courts, 78, 361, 373, 393, 394
credit, 205, 336, 252, 359, 360, 362,
    363, 367–368, 375, 386, 389, 390,
    394. *See also* debt, mortgages
crisis, 20, 41, 44, 49, 51, 71, 73,
    119n11, 141, 150, 154, 169, 174,
    176, 191, 193, 200, 201, 203, 256,
    270, 272n12, 333, 336, 337, 339,
    340, 343, 346, 350, 351, 352, 360,
    365, 372, 375, 398, 401
    "refugee crisis", 8, 10, 11, 12, 22,
        251, 253, 257–258, 269, 278,
        288, 309
    See also financial crisis
Croatia, 389, 391, 395

cruelty, 134, 136, 137, 138, 139, 140
cultural, 14, 16, 33, 40, 82, 84, 89
    identity, 286, 292, 299n13
    hegemony, 5, 91
culture of poverty debates, 16

debt, 3, 14, 23, 35, 40, 56n4, 110, 151,
    153, 203, 217n7, 218n8, 218n10,
    334, 345, 351, 359, 361, 366, 367,
    368, 372, 373, 378n12, 386, 389,
    390, 394, 396, 400, 402,
    advice / counseling, 345
    cancellation / exoneration, 352
    debt arrears, 339, 342, 345, 389
    debt relief, 22, 333, 335, 338–340,
        346, 350, 352
    household debt, 367, 386, 388, 389,
        391, 392, 397, 404
    instalments, 211, 363, 395
    over–indebtedness, over indebted,
        337, 339, 359, 362, 391
    politics of, 403–406
    predatory lending, 338, 389
    reverse mortgage, 39, 40, 41, 51,
        56n3, 56n5, 57nn16–17
debtors, 334, 336, 338, 339, 340, 341,
    342, 346, 347, 349, 350, 352, 363,
    365, 367, 369, 371, 386, 388, 391,
    397, 398, 399, 400, 403, 404, 405
    Austrian Raiffeisen cooperatives,
        393
    bad debtors / bad payers, 343, 352,
        369
    contestation / politization /
        emancipation, 353, 361, 388
    good debtors / good faith debtors
        / good payers / debtors with
        good credit records, 335, 341,
        342, 343, 348, 352, 355n10, 399,
    group as a, 371
    legal victims as, 392–396
    movements, 335, 336, 337, 338, 341,
        342, 344, 347, 349, 351, 354n2,
        390
    neoliberal subjects as, 346
    Swiss franc, 393, 397, 398, 405,
        407n5

See also mortgages, credit
deindustrialization, 33, 174, 177, 178, 179, 195n2
dependency, 16, 37, 38, 39, 41, 42, 48, 52, 200, 201, 214, 215, 232, 267
deservingness
  assessments of, 7, 10, 12, 13, 73, 78, 166, 223, 235, 292, 297, 341, 347
  claims to, 103
  condition as, 4, 5, 81, 293
  condition to access resources as a, 2, 4, 15, 17, 48, 202, 212–213, 216, 305, 340, 350, 374
  context dependency of, 16
  compliance with social norms / fulfilment of moral standards as, 168, 268, 319, 341
  criteria of, 7, 13, 15, 37, 43, 46, 70, 73, 74, 78, 91, 204, 212, 261, 287, 336, 339, 341, 344, 345, 348, 349, 351, 359, 361, 377n4, 419
  engagement with collective action as, 341, 347
  entitlement versus, 4, 6, 8, 10, 127, 139, 200, 210
  form of differentiation as, 1, 2, 5, 12, 287, 289, 298, 414, 415–420
  hierarchies of, 11, 148, 351
  historicity of, 336
  human rights versus, 7, 75, 280, 307, 316, 317, 321, 352, 385
  moral assessment as, 2, 6, 7, 12, 18, 76, 159, 165, 174, 180, 187, 235
  moral grammars of, 15, 70, 170, 224, 226, 227, 229,
  processes of distribution, 2, 14, 256, 279
  processional and relational notion as, 4, 293
  role in large-scale reconfiguration of political–economic systems, 15
  role of gatekeepers, 335, 344, 376
  self-construction as deserving / undeserving, 335
  social worth / legitimacy / (individual) merit as, 42, 49, 103, 148, 149, 335, 361
  stakeholders, 13, 70, 71, 74, 75, 76–77, 79, 80, 81, 82, 86, 89, 91
  tool for resource allocation / denial as a, 18, 175, 188, 253, 297, 331, 335, 348, 361
  versus generalized reciprocity, 348
  versus undeservingness, 8, 17, 73, 81, 117, 147, 148, 152, 163, 168, 187, 285, 372, 387, 387, 399, 403
  See also figures of

dialogues, 159, 164
differentiation, 1, 2, 5, 12, 18, 54, 278, 287, 289, 297, 298, 308, 414–420
  mundane, 415, 417, 418
  ontological, 149
  utilitarian, 419
dignity, 17, 31, 33, 44, 106, 214, 215, 352, 374, 375
discourse, 31, 34, 50, 54, 71, 72, 75, 105, 127, 137, 169, 175, 179, 191, 192, 193, 195, 201, 206, 213, 224, 226, 238, 254, 257, 258, 268, 279, 280, 281, 284, 285, 288, 292, 293, 296, 297, 304, 307–309, 312, 323, 336, 346, 347,
  neo–orientalist, 253
discrimination, 21, 43, 47, 48, 91, 147, 155, 226, 236, 237, 241, 253, 264, 281
dispossession, 20, 34, 54, 107, 200, 215, 240, 395, 396
distribution, 2, 4, 5, 6, 8, 9, 14, 22, 72, 103, 127, 148, 200, 201, 202–206, 212, 213, 253, 256, 263, 278, 280, 306, 349–353, 362, 368, 385, 402,
diversity, 39, 82, 131, 140, 201, 224, 229, 259, 264
double devaluation, 105, 106, 107, 114, 117
double polarization, 105, 106, 113
Douglas, Mary, 418–421

Eastern EU countries, 305

elderly, 11, 20, 32, 33, 35, 37, 39, 41, 42, 45–46, 50, 51–53, 55
embodiment, 149, 155–159
entitlement, 5–8, 13, 15, 17–18, 31, 39, 74, 127, 139, 200, 203, 210, 213, 214, 215, 216, 223, 363, 319, 321, 333, 345, 348, 361, 369, 385, 386, 392, 399, 404, 416, 417
ethnicity, 82, 147, 291, 299n7
ethnography, 4, 5, 126, 127, 128, 129, 130, 131, 133, 138, 142n1, 142nn5–6, 224, 279, 292, 349, 351
  theory and, 4
European Union, 101, 251, 304, 416
  border regime, 252, 257, 261, 267–268
EU–Turkey
  borderlands/border regime, 22, 253, 256
  deal, 258, 260, 261, 262, 272n16
  statement, 251, 253, 254, 261, 267, 268, 271n4, 272n18, 273n27
European Research Council (ERC), 131, 217n5
exclusion, 12, 20, 58n26, 91, 92, 127, 135, 138, 139, 154, 155, 157, 161, 165, 237, 239, 257, 262, 267, 268, 269, 279, 293, 299n3, 307, 316, 317, 349, 351, 361, 374, 375, 387, 399, 403
explaining, 31, 101, 127, 128, 141, 285, 319
expulsive dynamics, 178
extraction, 22, 44, 51, 203, 360, 373

Fassin, Didier, 183
fear, 148, 149, 150, 151, 152, 153, 154, 155, 157, 164–168, 265, 289, 335,
figures of deservingness
  banker, 14, 390, 393, 394, 397
  debtor, 41, 334, 335, 336, 338, 341, 342, 343, 346, 349, 351, 352, 355n12, 365, 369, 371, 375, 377n4, 386, 388, 392, 393, 396, 397–399, 402, 403, 404, 405
  dependent, 15, 36, 37, 39, 151, 187–188, 210, 342, 350

fraudster, 19, 333
migrant, 19, 70, 75, 78–82, 85, 118n2, 226, 238, 254, 257, 271n6, 284, 285, 304, 317, 318, 322, 374, 388
refugee, 8, 12, 19, 22, 71, 101, 153, 252, 253, 254, 255, 257, 260–261, 263, 265, 267, 269, 270, 271nn6–7, 278–282, 284, 285 (*see also* 'fake refugee')
single mother, 16, 210, 212
taxpayer, 1, 6
victim, 7, 8, 9, 79, 175, 194, 241–242n4, 258, 259, 263, 287, 288, 305, 323, 334, 392, 393, 397, 404, 405, 414
welfare Cadillacs, 16
welfare queen, 16, 150, 374
welfare scrounger, 15
finance
  literacy, 233, 371, 391–392, 398
  lobbying, 15
financial crisis, 14, 17, 19, 31, 36, 50, 126, 188, 215, 333, 336, 338, 386
  austerity politics and, 21, 333
  anti–repossession / anti–debt movements / activists, 335, 336, 338, 340, 341, 342, 344, 345, 347, 349, 351, 354n2,
  economic and social crisis, 339
  evictions, 337, 338, 339, 342, 348, 373, 395,
  fabricated scarcity, 333
  housing bubble (burst of), 49, 51, 336, 337, 338, 354n7, 360
  Plataforma de Afectados por la Hipoteca, 337
  scam (collective), 338, 339, 393
financialization
  miss–selling financial products, 41
  securitization, 40, 56n5
France, 9, 85, 87, 104, 115, 183, 189, 193, 354n11,
Fraser, Nancy, 16, 119n14, 202, 235
Freud, Sigmund, 149, 152, 155
Friedman, Jonathan, 105–106, 113, 118n5, 427n2

gender, 16, 81, 139, 148, 232, 235, 241N3, 253–254, 257–258, 268, 295, 352
genealogies, 16, 18, 298
Germany, 147, 148, 150, 154, 158, 163, 169, 170, 182, 258, 304, 305, 306, 308, 309–311, 316, 317–323
global, 17, 102, 105, 108, 118n5, 128, 130, 133, 254, 260, 262, 297, 360,
  crisis, 126, 174, 176, 188, 387
  systems, 113
government, 2, 11, 14, 43, 46, 87, 89, 105, 169, 179, 183, 201, 203, 204, 215, 226, 230, 232, 235, 239, 240, 252, 266, 270, 284, 286, 287, 295, 310, 333, 360, 366, 369, 392, 395, 398, 415, 423, 424, 426
  local government, 223, 232, 243n2
  privatization, 42, 43, 74, 167, 217n4, 224, 229, 240, 364
governmentality, 148, 214
  dispositives, 182
  neoliberal, 175, 182, 391
  new modes of, 148
gratitude, 52, 212, 267,
Greece, 14–15, 22, 252–261, 359ff (376), 416
group membership, 3, 76, 78, 89, 231, 238, 264, 279, 280, 290–296, 307, 341, 396, 401

Hall, Stewart, 5, 108, 111, 279, 292–293
Hartz IV, 147–170
Hauptschule, 147–170
Hauptschüler*innen, 147–170
health, 8, 11, 32, 35, 37, 42, 43–49, 69–93, 101, 126, 157, 203, 225–226, 254–256, 266, 305, 347, 367–368, 395–396, 419–420
hegemony, 5, 91, 102, 109, 182, 338, 388, 403–405
  hegemonic narratives, 91, 388, 390–392, 404
  hegemonic projects, 405–406
  and social blocs, 405–406
heteronormativity, 257

Hochschild, Arlie, 423
homogeneity, 229, 281
homo–nationalism, 9, 253, 259, 268–269
household, 22, 38, 80, 114, 199–200, 207, 211, 216, 228, 334, 338, 340–342, 355, 359–375, 380, 388, 390, 404–405
housing, 35, 44, 50–51, 211, 227–229, 238, 282, 334, 337–342, 346, 351–353, 368–370, 373, 378n10
humanitarianism, 6, 8–10, 75, 134, 253–254, 256, 305, 316, 345, 353
  See also deservingness versus
Hungary, 104, 111–112, 306, 309–311, 316–317, 321, 389

identification, 81, 109, 138, 140, 150, 156, 268, 287, 308, 312, 315–324, 350–351
identity, 34, 78, 155, 183, 192, 259, 266–267, 286–287, 291–292, 299n7–n13, 387
ideology, 4, 13, 21, 182, 192, 404–405
  anti–poverty ideology, 21, 148, 187, 191, 224, 375,
  dimensions of inequality, 193, 375,
  ideological apparatuses, 181–182, 187, 192–194,
  neoliberal ideology, 148, 182, 183, 214, 231,
  See also moral vocabularies
imagined communities, 1, 4, 6, 280, 286, 297
immigration, 11, 15, 75, 81–87, 118n8, 226, 236, 238, 242n5, 285, 305.
  See also migration
inequality, 1–6, 9–10, 19, 31, 136, 140, 206, 222–225, 333– 336, 400, 413–415
  affective dimensions of, 147–148, 170
  capitalism and, 31, 73, 102, 116, 153, 180, 204, 206, 242n9, 335–336, 362, 371, 387
  global, 72–73, 102, 106, 110, 280
  moralization of, 11, 14, 19, 148, 153,

175, 334, 351, 375, 385, 413
  questioning / delegitimation of, 19, 140, 225, 372, 400
  legitimation of, 9, 53, 175, 254, 335, 351, 371, 414
  (de)politization of, 18, 168, 170, 188, 225, 241, 375
  social cleavages, 12, 22, 36, 140, 203, 349, 400
  integration, 272n11, 282, 289–290, 294, 306, 309, 320, 322
Israel, 88–90

job centre, 151–153, 164, 173–194, 211, 419

Keynesianism, 102, 177–178, 188
kinship, 17, 41, 53, 258, 363, 366–367
Kushner, Jared, 413–414
Kurz, Sebastian, 11, 269, 272n8

labour, 3
  devaluation of, 20, 35–36, 102, 106, 228, 231, 305, 309, 360, 368
  productivist ideal of, 16, 80, 118, 148, 157, 239
  labour market, 15, 38, 44, 50–53, 115, 158, 163–164, 168, 175, 182, 187, 191, 256, 294, 306, 309, 317, 360
  labour struggles, 33–34, 49, 103, 112, 148, 368, 403
  income and, 15, 35, 50, 200, 231, 235, 370, 371
  See also care, 231, 234
Latinxs, 77, 84, 223, 226–231, 235–240, 241n3
Lazarus, Emma, 68–69, 91
law, 5–6, 36, 38–41, 52, 71, 74, 77–78, 90, 127, 148, 162, 243n10, 256, 259–262, 281, 285, 338, 341, 350–351, 354n5, 359, 361–372, 374, 392–394, 404, 421, 424–426
  legitimacy, 9, 134, 140, 201–202, 212,-213, 316, 335, 337, 349, 353, 394
LGBTIQ+, 253, 259, 263, 265, 268–269

Malkki, Lisa, 8, 280, 287–288, 306–307, 315, 324
Marx, Karl, 54, 372
Marxism, 2, 101, 106, 114, 231
  marxist anthropology, 2, 106–107, 231
  'cultural marxism', 101, 110
  'sexo–Marxism', 110
McCarthy, Joseph (US Senator), 422, 424–425
Mediterranean, 11, 101, 251, 269, 298n1
merit, 104–107, 113, 116–117, 148, 154, 191, 294, 320, 323, 335, 341, 348, 352, 417, 424
middle class, 40, 107, 113–114, 157–158, 205, 225, 343, 385, 388, 399–401, 405
Middle East, 70, 101, 126, 304–305, 308
migration, 7, 13–14, 16–18, 68–71, 83–84, 109, 113–115, 130, 150, 226, 251, 257, 265–266, 292, 316, 374, 414, 421, 426
  irregular, 74, 226, 306–308
  othering, 20, 286–288, 294, 385
  perspectives of migrants, 78–80, 89, 279, 292, 310, 316, 319
  regimes of, 20, 68, 81, 84, 134, 226, 238, 257–266, 283
  See also immigration, anti–immigrant discourse
mobility, 93n3, 178, 181, 256, 304, 316, 322
  existential, 180, 256, 322
  social, 147, 203, 228
morality, 4, 7, 10, 81, 126–127, 134–135, 213, 222, 312, 426
mortgage, 34, 39–41, 207, 334–350, 354n12, 363, 389–391, 395
Muehlebach, Andrea, 18, 163, 177, 179, 213, 218n10, 233
Muslim people, 22, 82, 253, 258–270

narratives, 22, 91, 231, 240, 283, 306, 312–316, 319, 323, 388, 392–405
neoliberalism, 113, 148, 179, 184, 213

neonationalism, 103, 107–113
Nepali Bhutanese, 278–298
Netherlands, 13, 104, 115–116, 317
NGOs, 90, 101, 127, 217n4, 242n7
normalization, 3, 235, 388

obligation, 5, 47, 50, 77, 80, 163, 203, 210–214, 231, 311, 333, 347, 363–367, 386
Orban, Victor, 101, 110
othering, 6, 279–280, 293–295, 315

pandemic / COVID-19, 2, 19, 31–55, 70–74, 101, 252, 271n4
pension / pensioner, 1, 33–42, 48–52, 161, 209, 367
Poland, 104, 108, 389
polarization, 91, 105–106, 113, 157, 203, 298
police murders, 7, 422
populism, 105–113, 179, 325, 403
Post–Socialism, 17, 112, 116, 390–393, 405
poverty, 12, 149, 158, 225
  administration of, 17, 201, 206, 333
  (de)politicization of, 21, 163, 202, 224, 240, 317
  legitimization of, 3, 15–17
  poverty risk, 36, 79, 205, 225, 228, 317
precarity, 9, 17, 31–34, 52, 102, 113, 149, 154, 157–159, 163, 167, 226, 322, 363
privilege, 35, 50–51, 74, 212–214, 226–228, 287, 372, 400
protection, 21, 29, 44, 107, 112, 206, 214, 252–254, 259–264, 268, 285, 310, 342, 362, 393

queer, 259, 274n23

race/racism, 2, 11, 48, 72, 82, 91, 162, 224, 228, 235, 253, 259, 335, 419, 426
Reagan, Ronald, 105, 163, 422
redistribution, 2, 7, 14–18, 50, 104, 115, 127, 134–135, 141, 204, 224, 335, 366, 372
reflexivity, 127–142, 307
refugees, 71, 80, 101, 153, 251–278, 278–304, 304–332
  anti–refugeeism, 8, 10, 386
  crisis, 8, 12, 101
  deservingness of, 8, 12, 21, 417
  responsibility, 148, 159, 169, 175, 188, 200, 212–215, 256–269, 306, 312, 336, 339, 349, 361–363, 375, 398
  resettlement, 252–254, 259–269, 279–285, 290–295
Rorty, Richard, 126–143

sacrifice, 211, 350, 367, 400–401
self–sufficiency, 16, 223, 232–234, 141n4
senses/ sensing, 5, 10, 116, 147–155, 290
sexuality, 2, 81, 254, 258–259, 266
social justice / injustice, 5, 9, 11, 43, 47, 75–76, 128, 141, 307, 334, 336, 349, 353, 362, 375, 385–387
social reproduction, 2, 103, 106–107, 200, 203, 359
  crisis of, 203
  labour of, 231, 234–235
social struggle, 2, 4, 7, 13, 33–34, 49–53, 155, 202, 215, 296, 353, 361, 388, 394
solidarity, 50, 115, 128, 135–140, 162, 263, 288–289, 308, 362
  arrangements, 102, 115
  kin solidarity, 50, 53
  loss of, 162, 169, 292
  networks, 17, 292, 308, 345, 348, 372
Spain, 32–48, 336–340, 346, 360
state, 12–13, 16, 48, 55, 71, 89, 104–105, 109–110, 114, 128–130, 134, 151–153, 167, 194, 200, 214, 224, 232, 238, 259, 267, 283, 290, 305, 309, 335, 346, 360, 362, 374, 387, 390, 400
  in neoliberal capitalism, 3, 35, 39, 55, 102, 175, 202, 208
stigma, 81, 154–155, 181, 188, 234,

337, 350, 372, 386
street–level bureaucrats, 76, 374, 415–419, 421
structural adjustment, 32, 203–205
subjectivity and subjectivation, 16, 20, 186, 192–195, 316, 386–387, 403
subsidy / subsidies, 37–39, 52, 161, 187, 311, 363
suffering, 9, 81, 86, 134, 138, 190, 209, 304–308, 312–315, 321–323, 364, 375, 392
Switzerland, 208, 218, 367, 393
Syria, 8, 22, 102, 253–255, 258, 260–262, 288, 318

tax / taxation, 1, 6, 18, 47, 139, 204, 224, 359, 367, 375, 377n4, 426
Thatcher, Margaret, 47, 105, 163
Thompson, E. P., 3, 107, 116
Ticktin, Miriam, 9, 86–87, 134, 253, 257, 307, 315
triage, 31–55
Turin, 173–194
Trump, Donald, 68, 91, 108–110, 114, 226, 239, 413
Turkey, 102, 251–266, 318

United Kingdom, 22, 85–87, 109, 114, 163, 182, 279–298, 421
uncanny, 102, 149–155, 255
underclass, 16, 148, 151, 374
undeservingness, *See under* deservingness
unemployment, 11, 15–17, 21, 36, 151, 163, 173–176, 180, 340, 350
  activation and, 7, 175, 184, 350
  benefits, 17, 147–149, 180
  crisis, 34, 180, 193, 200, 217n3, 284, 368
  fear of, 150–151, 159, 168–169, 193
  policies, 147–150, 174, 176
UNHCR, 253, 260–263, 266–268, 282

unions, 33, 112, 132, 364
United States, 7, 13, 16–18, 21, 68–73, 83–85, 109, 113–115, 130, 150, 163, 223–224, 231, 265–266, 283, 374, 414, 421–424

valorization, 19, 31–33, 44–46, 48–55, 103, 106, 116, 148, 186–187, 192
valuation, 20, 31–34, 37, 44, 48–51, 73, 79, 103, 105–107, 134, 169, 187, 201, 212–216, 366, 374, 414–415
veterans, 388–405
victimhood, 286–288, 305–307, 313–316, 321, 362, 373, 388, 392–395
volunteerism, 18, 213, 231–236, 240–241
vulnerability, 20, 45–46, 74, 81–82, 251–253, 261–263, 267–269, 304–318, 416

Weiss, Hadas, 2, 4, 114, 401
welfare
  arrangements of, 1, 13, 15, 17–19, 35, 89, 102, 134, 162, 178, 188, 200–201, 215, 310, 344, 368, 385, 423
  dependency, 80, 200
  deservingness and, 1, 11, 14–15, 72–74, 139, 163, 182, 215, 282, 311, 341, 403
  policies, 13, 72–73, 167, 200, 202–203, 206, 214, 226, 339, 362, 400
  welfare state retrenchment, 3, 11, 14–16, 101, 148, 163, 167, 175, 200, 204, 224, 230, 400
  welfare queens/ Cadillacs, 16, 150, 374
workfare, 17, 181

youth, 13, 83–84, 149, 158, 229, 426

www.ingramcontent.com/pod-product-compliance
Lightning Source LLC
Chambersburg PA
CBHW051522020426
42333CB00016B/1740